WORLD TRADE ORGANIZATION

Dispute Settlement Reports

1999
Volume I

Pages 1-517

CAMBRIDGE
UNIVERSITY PRESS

PUBLISHED BY THE PRESS SYNDICATE OF THE UNIVERSITY OF CAMBRIDGE
The Pitt Building, Trumpington Street, Cambridge, United Kingdom

CAMBRIDGE UNIVERSITY PRESS
The Edinburgh Building, Cambridge CB2 2RU, UK
40 West 20th Street, New York, NY 10011–4211, USA
477 Williamstown Road, Port Melbourne, VIC 3207, Australia
Ruiz de Alarcón 13, 28014 Madrid, Spain
Dock House, The Waterfront, Cape Town 8001, South Africa

http://www.cambridge.org

Printed in the United Kingdom at the University Press, Cambridge

French edition and Spanish edition paperbacks of this title are both available directly from WTO Publications, World Trade Organization, Centre William Rappard, 154 rue de Lausanne, CH-1211 Geneva 21, Switzerland   http://www.wto.org

ISBN 0 521 80320 9 hardback
ISBN 0 521 00562 0 paperback

THE WTO DISPUTE SETTLEMENT REPORTS

The *Dispute Settlement Reports* of the World Trade Organization (the "WTO") include panel and Appellate Body reports, as well as arbitration awards, in disputes concerning the rights and obligations of WTO Members under the provisions of the *Marrakesh Agreement Establishing the World Trade Organization*. The *Dispute Settlement Reports* are available in English, French and Spanish. Starting with 1999, the first volume of each year contains a cumulative index of published disputes.

This volume may be cited as DSR 1999:I

TABLE OF CONTENTS

KOREA - TAXES ON ALCOHOLIC BEVERAGES

Report of the Appellate Body
WT/DS75/AB/R, WT/DS84/AB/R

*Adopted by the Dispute Settlement Body
on 17 February 1999*

<table>
<tr><td>

Korea, *Appellant*

European Communities, *Appellee*

United States, *Appellee*

Mexico, *Third Participant*

</td><td>

Present:

Matsushita, Presiding Member

Ehlermann, Member

Feliciano, Member

</td></tr>
</table>

TABLE OF CONTENTS

Page

I. INTRODUCTION

1.   This is an appeal by Korea from certain issues of law and legal interpretation developed in the Panel Report, *Korea - Taxes on Alcoholic Beverages.*[1] That Panel was established[2] by the Dispute Settlement Body (the "DSB") to examine the consistency of two Korean tax laws: the Korean Liquor Tax Law of 1949 and the Korean Education Tax Law of 1982, both as amended (the "measures"), with Article III:2 of the GATT 1994. The Liquor Tax Law imposes an *ad valorem* tax on all distilled spirits. The rate of that tax depends on which of the eleven fiscal categories a particular alcoholic beverage falls within. The Education Tax Law imposes a surtax on the sale of most distilled spirits, the rate of the surtax being a percentage of the liquor tax rate applied to the spirit in question. A detailed description of the operation of these two taxes is to be found at paragraphs 2.1 to 2.23 of the Panel Report.

2.   The Panel considered claims made by the European Communities and the United States that the contested measures are inconsistent with Article III:2 of the GATT 1994 because they accord preferential tax treatment to soju, a traditional Korean alcoholic beverage, as compared with certain imported "western-style" alco-

---

[1]   WT/DS75/R, WT/DS84/R, 17 September 1998.

[2]   The Panel was established 16 October 1997 with standard terms of reference (see WT/DS75/7, WT/DS84/5, 10 December 1997) that were based on requests for the establishment of a panel made by the European Communities (WT/DS75/6, 15 September 1997) and the United States (WT/DS84/4, 15 September 1997).

holic beverages. The Panel Report was circulated to the Members of the World Trade Organization (the "WTO") on 17 September 1998. The Panel "reached the conclusion that soju (diluted and distilled), whiskies, brandies, cognac, rum, gin, tequila, liqueurs and admixtures are directly competitive or substitutable products."[3] The Panel also concluded that "Korea has taxed the imported products in a dissimilar manner and the tax differential is more than *de minimis*" and that "the dissimilar taxation is applied in a manner so as to afford protection to domestic production."[4] The Panel made the following recommendation:

> We recommend that the Dispute Settlement Body request Korea to bring the Liquor Tax Law and the Education Tax Law into conformity with its obligations under the General Agreement on Tariffs and Trade 1994.[5]

3.   On 20 October 1998, Korea notified the DSB of its intention to appeal certain issues of law covered in the Panel Report and legal interpretations developed by the Panel, pursuant to paragraph 4 of Article 16 of the *Understanding on Rules and Procedures Governing the Settlement of Disputes* (the "DSU"), and filed a Notice of Appeal with the Appellate Body, pursuant to Rule 20 of the *Working Procedures for Appellate Review* (the "*Working Procedures*"). On 30 October 1998, Korea filed its appellant's submission.[6] On 16 November 1998, the European Communities and the United States filed their respective appellees' submissions[7] and Mexico filed a third participant's submission.[8] The oral hearing, provided for in Rule 27 of the *Working Procedures*, was held on 24 November 1998. At the oral hearing, the participants and the third participant presented their arguments and answered questions from the Division of the Appellate Body hearing the appeal.

II.   ARGUMENTS OF THE PARTICIPANTS AND THE THIRD PARTICIPANT

A.   *Korea - Appellant*

1.   *"Directly Competitive or Substitutable Products"*

4.   Korea contends that the Panel misinterpreted and misapplied the term "directly competitive or substitutable product", especially the word "directly" which, in Korea's view, is at the heart of the term at issue. At some level all products are competitive, in that they compete for the consumer's limited budget, and it is therefore "directly" which gives meaning to the legal text and prevents Article III:2 from becoming an "unbridled instrument of tax harmonization and deregulation".

---

[3]   Panel Report, para. 11.1.

[4]   *Ibid.*

[5]   Panel Report, para. 11.2.

[6]   Pursuant to Rule 21(1) of the *Working Procedures*.

[7]   Pursuant to Rule 22 of the *Working Procedures*.

[8]   Pursuant to Rule 24 of the *Working Procedures*.

(a)   Potential Competition

5.   Korea claims that the alleged evidence of "potential" competition was essential to the Panel's finding of a directly competitive or substitutable relationship between the products at issue.[9] However, Article III:2 does not speak of "potential" competition. Accordingly, it is at least ambiguous whether "potential" competition is embraced by the second sentence of Article III:2 of the GATT 1994. Given that ambiguity, Article 19.2 of the DSU and the principles of predictability and *in dubio mitius* should have been respected by the Panel.

6.   In Korea's view, the term "directly competitive or substitutable" is not meant to exclude products that do not compete directly or are not substitutable because of the contested measure itself. The absence of a competitive relationship on the market concerned should be taken as a powerful counter-indication that the products involved are not "directly competitive or substitutable". The Panel, however, has read Article III:2 as covering both products that "are either directly competitive now or *can reasonably be expected to become* directly competitive in the *near future.*"[10] (emphasis added) In so doing, the Panel relieved the complainants of the need to prove that the lack of actual competition is caused by the contested measure, and opened the door to speculation about how the market could evolve in the future, irrespective of the measure in question. Korea warns against speculation about what consumers might (or might not) do, as opposed to looking at what they actually do. The Panel repeatedly excused the complainants' failure to produce evidence about actual competition by saying that preferences in the Korean market might have been *frozen* by government measures.[11] However, Korea points out that, at the time this case was argued, its market had been open for eight years.

7.   Korea contends that the "potential" standard is impermissibly broad and speculative, and the wording and the purpose of Article III:2 do not permit this interpretation. There is nothing wrong with requiring complainants to wait until, if ever, their case becomes "ripe" and products actually compete directly. What if a Member has been forced to change its tax law because products might compete and then, in fact, they do not? Should that Member return to the panel to request permission to restore its tax system?

(b)   Expectations, the "Trade Effects" Test and the
"Nature" of Competition

8.   Korea notes the considerable emphasis the Panel placed on "expectations" of an "equal competitive relationship" between imported and domestic products.[12] However, Korea argues that these "expectations" exist only for those products which are "like" or "directly competitive or substitutable". If products are not currently directly competitive or substitutable, there can be no relevant expectations with respect to them.

---

[9]   Panel Report, para. 10.97.

[10]   Panel Report, para. 10.48. Korea also refers to paras. 10.40 and 10.73 of the Panel Report.

[11]   See, for example, Panel Report, para. 10.94.

[12]   Panel Report, para. 10.48.

9.   The Panel erroneously considered that to "focus on the quantitative extent of competition instead of the nature of it, could result in a type of trade effects test being written into Article III cases."[13] This is a misunderstanding of the "trade effects" test. While past cases held that a lack of "trade effects" is not a defence to an Article III:2 violation, in those cases the products involved had *already been shown* to be "like" or "directly competitive or substitutable".

10.   Korea observes that the Panel referred to the "nature" of competition many times in its findings, making statements such as: "the question is not of the degree of competitive overlap, but its nature."[14] By examining the *nature* of competition, the Panel added a vague and subjective criterion which is not present in Article III:2, and dispensed with the complainants' obligation to show *direct* competitiveness or substitutability and also with the need to look at actual markets.

(c)   Evidence from Other Markets

11.   The Panel stated that it could "look at other markets and make a judgement as to whether the same patterns could prevail in the case at hand."[15] In Korea's view, this amounts to little more than guesswork and constitutes an impermissible broadening of the scope of Article III:2. The Panel also disregarded the fact that consumer responsiveness to different products "may vary from country to country".[16] Moreover, there was no basis for the Panel to assume that the Korean and Japanese markets were, or were becoming, the same. Korea further contends that, even if evidence from other markets were relevant, the Panel should not have limited itself to looking at only one other country's market. To ensure a balanced view, evidence from more than one other market ought to have been reviewed.

12.   Korea submits that all of the above misinterpretations of Article III:2 constitute a violation of provisions of the DSU and general principles of law, namely, the principle that neither panels nor the Appellate Body can add to or diminish the rights and obligations provided in the covered agreements (Article 19.2 of the DSU), the principle of predictability, and the principle of *in dubio mitius*.

(d)   Grouping of the Products

13.   Korea stresses the importance of the methodology used to compare domestic and imported products under Article III:2. It considers that the Panel committed a major legal error in wrongly defining the comparison it had to undertake. The Panel grouped together products that are not physically identical; are produced in different ways by different manufacturers using different raw materials; taste differently; are used differently; are marketed and sold differently at considerably different prices and are subject to different tax rates in Korea. The Panel also failed to carry out a

---

[13]   Panel Report, para. 10.42.

[14]   Panel Report, para. 10.44. Korea also refers to Panel Report, paras. 10.42, 10.44 and 10.66 in this respect.

[15]   Panel Report, para. 10.46.

[16]   Panel Report, *Japan - Taxes on Alcoholic Beverages* ("*Japan - Alcoholic Beverages*"), WT/DS8/R, WT/DS10/R, WT/DS11/R, adopted 1 November 1996, para. 6.28.

separate analysis for diluted and distilled soju.[17] Korea urges that the Panel erred in conducting its analysis on the basis of an agglomeration of the characteristics of two such different products. To extend conclusions that are primarily based on diluted soju to distilled soju is unacceptable logic. Further, by treating diluted soju and distilled soju together, the Panel overlooked the relevance of the considerable price differential between diluted soju and whisky.

14.   Korea points out that the Panel decided to treat all the imported distilled spirits as one group.[18] In Korea's view, the Panel's decision to group all these beverages together was, in effect, a decision (or at least a presumption) that they are directly competitive or substitutable everywhere, without considering whether that was true in the Korean market. By grouping all the imported beverages together, the Panel made it impossible to appreciate the differences between the imported products. The Panel could not, for example, conclude that in Korea diluted soju was directly competitive or substitutable for vodka, but not whisky.

15.   Korea acknowledges that when the Panel considered the product characteristics, it examined the products in the group one by one. But the Panel dismissed as insignificant, differences between the products regarding such characteristics as colour, taste and price. In so doing, the Panel "trivialized" actual consumer perceptions which are at the heart of the "directly competitive or substitutable" standard. The erroneous approach adopted by the Panel makes it impossible to determine what the outcome of the case would have been if the Panel had not erred at the outset.

2.   *"So as to Afford Protection"*

16.   According to Korea, the Panel erred in finding that the Korean taxes had a protective effect mainly on the basis of an analysis of the structure of the law itself. The Panel ignored Korea's explanation for the structure of the law.[19] The Panel also made too much of the fact that there is virtually no imported soju, overlooking the fact that there has simply been a lack of interest abroad in the manufacture of these typically Korean products. More importantly, the Panel did not follow the Appellate Body's ruling in *Japan - Alcoholic Beverages*, to the effect that, even though the tax differential may, in some cases, show that the tax is applied "so as to afford protection", "in other cases, there may be other factors that will be *just as relevant or more relevant* to demonstrating that the dissimilar taxation was applied 'so as to afford protection'."[20] (emphasis added)

17.   Korea reiterates the argument it made before the Panel that, in view of the large, intrinsic pre-tax price-differences between diluted soju and the imported products at issue, the tax differential cannot be said to have the effect of "afford[ing] protection" to diluted soju. Where the price-difference between two products is so

---

[17]   Panel Report, para. 10.54.

[18]   Panel Report, para. 10.60.

[19]   Korea's explanation of the structure of its tax regime is set out at paras. 5.172 to 5.181 of the Panel Report. In its arguments before the Appellate Body, Korea placed particular emphasis on the arguments summarized at para. 5.176 of the Panel Report.

[20]   Adopted 1 November 1996, WT/DS8/AB/R, WT/DS10/AB/R, WT/DS11/AB/R, DSR 1996:I, 97, at 122.

significant, the additional difference created by the variation in tax can have no protective effect. Korea also maintains that demand for distilled soju is specific and static, and that it would not be affected a great deal by altering the price, especially not to the degree at issue in this case. Korea, therefore, claims that the tax differential does not "afford protection" to distilled soju, contrary to the conclusion reached by the Panel.

3. *Application of Article III:2 of the GATT 1994*

18.   Korea submits that the Panel erred in several ways when assessing the evidence. While Korea recognizes that appellate review is limited to questions of law, it considers that, in reviewing a panel's interpretation and application of Article III:2, second sentence, the Appellate Body cannot avoid considering the factual underpinnings of the panel's assessment. In this case, the Panel drew conclusions which the evidence before it did not support. Errors of this type were decisive in the adjudication of the dispute in favour of the complainants, and thus constitute reversible legal errors.

19.   The Panel also erred in applying different standards of proof to the evidence. The Panel was far more exacting when looking at evidence submitted by Korea than when considering evidence brought by the complainants. The Panel, in effect, applied a "double standard of proof ".[21] The Panel also misapplied the requirements on the burden of proof which follow from the Appellate Body Report in *United States - Measure Affecting Imports of Woven Wool Shirts and Blouses from India* (*"United States - Shirts & Blouses"*).[22]

20.   Despite evidence to the contrary provided by Korea, the Panel relied upon the notion that consumer preferences in the Korean market might have been frozen by the measures at issue. By so doing, the Panel unfairly put Korea in the position of having to prove a negative - that the lack of competition was not due to the contested measures - rather than requiring the complainants to prove positively that consumer preferences in Korea had been frozen.

(a)   Product Characteristics

21.   Korea notes that the Panel found that "[a]ll the products ... have the essential feature of being distilled alcoholic beverages."[23] In essence, the Panel considered this sufficient to raise a presumption that all distilled alcoholic beverages are "directly competitive or substitutable". Korea disagrees that such a generic statement could give rise to a presumption of this type. The Panel erred in dismissing the importance of flavour in a case concerning beverages. The flavour of products is one of the consumer's primary considerations when choosing a beverage and distinctions between flavours are, therefore, not "minor"[24] from the consumer's perspective.

---

[21]   Korea's appellant's submission, para. 85.

[22]   Adopted 23 May 1997, WT/DS33/AB/R, WT/DS33/R, DSR 1997:I, 323, at 333-338.

[23]   Panel Report, para. 10.67.

[24]   *Ibid.*

22.   The Panel's focus on the fact that all the alcoholic beverages at issue are produced by distillation means that certain industrial products (e.g., paint thinner) or medicinal products (e.g., rubbing alcohol) would also be in a directly competitive or substitutable relationship with the beverages in question. Similarity in raw materials and the methods of production are, therefore, meaningless in defining a directly competitive or substitutable relationship between products.

23.   That the Panel applied a "double standard of proof" is shown by its rejection, on the one hand, of Korea's example of bottled and tap water, which Korea believes demonstrated that close physical similarity is not always probative evidence of a directly competitive or substitutable relationship. On the other hand, the Panel relied on the United States' example of branded and generic aspirin to show that physical similarity was highly significant. Moreover, the Panel dismissed Korea's bottled and tap water example, in part, because it referred to "different products in different countries".[25] Yet, in another part of its Report, the Panel said that evidence from "other countries" was relevant.[26]

(b)   End-Uses

24.   Before the Panel, Korea showed that, in Korea, the overwhelming end-use of diluted soju is consumption during meals whereas western-style drinks are hardly ever consumed with meals. The Panel, however, found that this distinction did not suffice to prevent the products from being considered as directly competitive or substitutable.[27] Korea believes the Panel erred, both as to the application of Article III:2 and as to requirements of the burden of proof, in accepting that all the beverages at issue were drunk for the same purposes, *inter alia*, socialization and relaxation. In reaching this finding, the Panel drew upon three sources: (a) trends and anecdotal evidence; (b) marketing strategies; and, (c) the presence of admixtures.

25.   The Panel placed emphasis on "trends and changes in consumption patterns"[28] which it said were demonstrated in the Nielsen Study and the Dodwell Study. However, neither of these studies nor the Trendscope Study contains evidence of trends. They show, instead, a "snapshot" of the market at a particular moment in time; they do not show changes over time. The Panel erred in considering that these studies contained evidence of trends, and the Panel's statements amount to mischaracterization of the evidence presented. Moreover, the Panel erred in speculating that those trends were "likely to continue",[29] without pointing to any supporting evidence.

26.   Korea argues that the Nielsen Study was used "selectively" by the Panel. For example, even if it showed some overlap in beverages available in Japanese and western-style restaurants, it also showed that in the large majority of outlets there was no overlap. Thus, the overlap shown in the Nielsen Study is very limited and, in light of contrary evidence, cannot be considered as conclusive proof of the similarity

---

[25]   Panel Report, para. 9.23.
[26]   Panel Report, para. 10.45.
[27]   Panel Report, para. 10.76.
[28]   Panel Report, para. 10.48.
[29]   Panel Report, para. 10.76.

of end-uses between the drinks at issue. In other words, the overall consumption pattern sufficiently rebuts any presumption of common end-uses raised by the minor overlap indicated by the Nielsen Study. The same is true of the figures given in the Nielsen Study for home-consumption of alcoholic beverages with meals. Even if 5.8 per cent of respondents stated that they drink whisky with their meals, that still leaves 94.2 per cent who do not. This evidence supports Korea's argument regarding the "meal" end-use of particular alcoholic beverages. Instead, it was turned around to become evidence of "overlap" in end-use. The speculation engaged in by the Panel was made worse by the Panel's consideration of trends on the Japanese market.

27.   The Panel's treatment of Korean companies' marketing strategies discloses again a "double standard of proof ". Where the Panel considered that marketing strategies supported a finding that the products were "like" or "directly competitive or substitutable", they became important evidence [30], whereas the Panel dismissed evidence from marketing strategies that it considered did not support such a finding.[31]

28.   The Panel also erred when assessing the evidence submitted concerning admixtures. Korea argued that diluted soju and distilled soju are consumed "straight" in Korea (unlike some of the imported beverages at issue in this case), a fact borne out in its market study.[32] That soju cocktails are different from diluted soju and distilled soju is reflected in Korea's tax law. Korea maintains that the presence of diluted soju in admixtures cannot support a finding of similarity with other drinks which are drunk in a mixed form, just as the existence of Bailey's[33] is not proof that whisky is often drunk mixed. Like Bailey's and whisky, diluted soju, distilled soju and admixtures are different drinks and are treated as such under the Liquor Tax Law. The Panel wrongfully rejected Korea's point which rebutted the evidence on admixtures.

(c)   Channels of Distribution

29.   While recognizing that channels of distribution are revealing for a market structure, the Panel wrongly dismissed Korea's distinctions regarding on-premise consumption, and thereby erred in its assessment of the evidence.

30.   The essence of Korea's argument was that most of the volume of diluted soju and of western-style drinks was sold and consumed in different types of outlets. This was borne out by the Nielsen Study which clearly shows that, except in the case of Japanese restaurants and café/western-style restaurants, there was no overlap for on-premise consumption. Before the Panel, the United States responded to this by noting that that their embassy personnel knew of nine "traditional Korean-style restaurants" in Seoul serving both whisky and soju. Korea argues that the Panel should not have dismissed Korea's evidence about differences in places of consumption on the

---

[30]   Panel Report, para. 10.79.
[31]   Panel Report, paras. 10.65 and 10.66.
[32]   See in particular Panel Report, paras. 5.268 and 5.273.
[33]   Panel Report, para. 7.11. Bailey's Irish Cream is an alcoholic beverage which is a mixture of whisky and cream.

basis of evidence concerning nine restaurants, provided by the United States' embassy personnel.

31.   The Panel also applied "double standards" to the evidence Korea and the complainants supplied on this issue. While Korea presented a market survey covering 320 restaurants that showed that there are different channels of distribution for the drinks in dispute, the Panel accepted the anecdotal evidence produced by the United States about only nine Korean restaurants.

(d)   Prices

32.   Korea considers that the large, undisputed price differences between diluted soju and the imported beverages are key elements of evidence, and that the larger the price difference between two products, the less influence a change in the price of one will have on the demand for the other. In the present case, there is no price overlap between diluted soju, including its premium version, and any of the western-style drinks.

33.   Korea believes that the only evidence on consumer responsiveness to changes in prices which was submitted by the complainants was the Dodwell Study. But Korea raised "fundamental objections" about the Dodwell Study before the Panel, and the Study is so flawed that it should have been rejected. The Panel erred in failing to recognize the weaknesses in the Study. Korea notes that the Panel considered the Dodwell Study "helpful evidence"[34] sufficient to raise a presumption of a directly competitive or substitutable relationship, and rejected the "hard evidence" Korea had submitted in rebuttal. The Panel, therefore, wrongly allocated the burden of proof and also applied a "double standard" since it was lenient with the complainants' evidence, but strict with Korea's rebuttal evidence.

34.   Korea contends that the evidence of the large price differences between diluted soju and most of the imported beverages is sufficient to rebut the complainants' claims about the existence of a directly competitive or substitutable relationship between the imported and domestic beverages. However, the Panel essentially disregarded the evidence and did not address Korea's argument that the absolute price differences were so great that behavioural changes were unlikely.

35.   When stating that premium diluted soju was a "fast growing category"[35], the Panel neglected Korea's evidence. Korea had emphasized during the second meeting with the Panel that premium soju production was declining, apparently as a result of Korean consumers' unwillingness to pay more for an up-market version of diluted soju.

36.   According to the Panel, cognac is a directly competitive or substitutable product for standard diluted soju even though, before any tax is applied, the products differ in price by a factor of 20.[36] Admittedly, for some of the western-style beverages, the price differential from soju is smaller, and even negative (e.g. distilled soju as compared to standard whisky). However, the Panel did not distinguish

---

[34]   Panel Report, para. 10.92.

[35]   Panel Report, para. 10.94.

[36]   This factor is based on the prices of the Dodwell Study. However, the Panel mentions an even higher price difference: a factor of 24 (Panel Report, footnote 408).

between types of product and concluded broadly that "the price differences [were] not so large as to refute the other evidence".[37] Korea believes that in the case of consumer products, to say that an actual price difference of a factor of 10 or 20 is insufficient to refute hypothetical evidence on competition, such as the Dodwell Study, flies in the face of common sense and shows that the Panel wrongly applied Article III:2.

(e)   Treatment of Tequila

37.   Korea observes that, although virtually no evidence on tequila was submitted by either the complainants or the third party, the Panel found that Korea had violated Article III:2 with respect to this beverage. The United States identified tequila as one of the products covered by the measures at issue, and tequila was included in the Dodwell Study presented by the European Communities. Mexico also made certain descriptive comments concerning the physical characteristics, tariff classification and patterns of consumption of tequila and mescal. The Panel included tequila in its examination because evidence was presented with respect to it[38], although it excluded mescal which "was mentioned without positive evidence" being provided.[39] The only additional elements concerning tequila were statements made by the complainants that tequila is drunk with spicy food in Mexico, that tequila is becoming popular in Japan[40] and that tequila was included in the Dodwell Study. Korea considers the evidence on tequila to be insufficient to give rise to a presumption of a directly competitive or substitutable relationship with soju.

38.   The Panel made no attempt to analyze what the Dodwell Study actually said. The Dodwell Study shows that consumers responded inconsistently to a possible price change for tequila. In fact, it even appears from the Dodwell Study that demand for tequila may not change if its price were lowered. The Panel, nonetheless, concluded that there was evidence that consumers were sensitive to relative price changes of soju and tequila.

4.   *Article 11 of the DSU*

39.   Korea submits that, contrary to Article 11 of the DSU, the Panel failed to apply the standard of review appropriate to an Article III:2 dispute. Korea maintains that, in this case, the Panel simply did not have sufficient evidence to enable it to conduct an "objective assessment" and, instead, relied on speculation. The Panel also failed to accord due deference to Korea's description of its own market. Korea believes that, when faced with conflicting descriptions of a foreign market, a panel should be very careful in making assertions about what this market is like and should certainly not engage in speculation about its possible future development. Where there was disagreement between the parties about the Korean market, the

---

[37]   Panel Report, para. 10.94.
[38]   Panel Report, para. 10.58.
[39]   *Ibid.*
[40]   Panel Report, paras. 5.72 and 6.182.

Panel should have accepted Korea's description, unless the complainants brought compelling evidence to the contrary.

40. Despite its "strong misgivings" about the Panel Report, Korea states that it does not assert that the Panel acted in bad faith. However, Korea believes that the matters it has raised under Article 11 of the DSU are, nonetheless, serious enough to merit reversal of the Panel's conclusions.

5. *Article 12.7 of the DSU*

41. Finally, Korea claims that the Panel failed to fulfil its obligation under Article 12.7 of the DSU. Korea considers much of the Panel's reasoning to be obscure, making it very difficult to determine the evidence the Panel relied upon in reaching its conclusions and the weight it gave to different evidence and arguments. In addition, the Panel Report is also "unacceptably vague". The Panel relies upon open-ended concepts, such as "potential" competition in the "near term", "potential" end-uses and the "nature" of competition, to support its conclusions which can be stretched to cover any outcome. Furthermore, certain evidence, such as the Sofres Study, was simply ignored without the Panel giving reasons therefor. The inadequate reasoning, in Korea's view, also prevented the Panel from making an objective assessment under Article 11 of the DSU.

B. *European Communities - Appellee*

1. *"Directly Competitive or Substitutable Products"*

42. The European Communities submits that Korea's appeal is grounded on the erroneous premise that the term "directly competitive or substitutable" must be interpreted "strictly". That proposition finds no support in the GATT, in its drafting history or in previous panel reports. As noted by the Panel, the drafting history of Article III:2 suggests that the drafters had in mind a rather broad notion of "directly competitive or substitutable" products, that could include apples and oranges.[41] Furthermore, the Korean argument that Article III:2, second sentence, must be interpreted "strictly" is equally applicable to virtually any GATT provision.

(a) Potential Competition

43. The European Communities believes that the Panel's finding that there is "present direct competition" between the imported beverages and soju[42] would be sufficient to conclude that those products are "directly competitive or substitutable". The additional finding of "a strong potentially direct competitive relationship" provides further support for that conclusion but is not indispensable.

44. In any event, the Panel's analysis of the evidence of "potential" competition is consistent with the wording of Article III:2, its object and purpose, as well as previous Appellate Body and panel reports. Korea relies on the fact that neither Article III:2 nor the *Ad* Article mention "potential" competition. But nor do they men-

---

[41] See Panel Report, para. 10.38.
[42] Panel Report, para. 10.98.

tion "actual" competition. In the European Communities' view, potential competition *is* "competition", both in the ordinary economic sense and within the meaning of the *Ad* Article. The use in the *Ad* Article of the words "competitive" (rather than "competing") and "substitutable" (instead of "substitute") is a further indication that the drafters envisaged the application of Article III:2 in the case of both "actual" and "potential" competition. The French and Spanish texts also support this view.

45.   To the European Communities, the relevance of potential competition flows directly from the fact that Article III does not protect export volumes but expectations of an equal competitive relationship. The prohibition against protective taxation applies even if there are *no* imports of "directly competitive and substitutable" products. Korea's insistence on the existence of actual competition is, therefore, inconsistent with the proper interpretation of Article III:2. Korea's "but for" test is an admission that potential competition is relevant in some circumstances, but that test is too restrictive and finds no support in Article III:2, second sentence.

(b)   Evidence from Other Markets

46.   A determination of whether two products are "directly competitive or substitutable" must be made on a case-by-case basis and in respect of the market of the Member applying the contested tax measures. Nevertheless, other markets may provide a strong indication of the nature of the competitive relationship between the products in the market at issue. This may be particularly true in cases where there is either very little or no actual competition on the market at issue. In the present case, the Panel made very limited use of evidence drawn from third country markets. The Panel looked at evidence from the Japanese market to corroborate findings made concerning the Korean market. Although the Panel could have looked at other markets in addition to the Japanese market, that was not necessary.

47.   The European Communities contends that Korea's interpretation of Article III:2 diminishes the rights of Members. Furthermore, the principle *in dubio mitius* is a supplementary method of interpretation that applies only where there is a genuine ambiguity. That is not the case here. Finally, the Panel's interpretation promotes "predictability".

(c)   Grouping of the Products

48.   The European Communities views the Panel's decision on how to group the products as a methodological one made for analytical purposes only. It does not involve any interpretation of Article III:2 and does not, therefore, raise any "question of law" which could form the subject of an appeal, unless the Panel failed to make an "objective assessment" of the facts.

49.   Contrary to Korea's assertions, the Panel did not find that distilled soju and diluted soju were directly substitutable and competitive products. The Panel held that if diluted soju were found to be directly competitive or substitutable with imported spirits, it would follow necessarily that distilled soju, which is more similar

to imported spirits, would also be directly competitive or substitutable with those spirits.[43] Korea has not challenged the premise underlying the Panel's reasoning.

50.   The European Communities contends that, in deciding to consider together all imported beverages, the Panel did not anticipate the outcome of the case nor did it find that the imported products were directly competitive or substitutable *inter se*. Korea has not shown that applying a different analytical approach would have led to a different result. There is no significant difference between Korea's strict product-by-product approach and the Panel's method. In practice, the Panel switched to a product-by-product approach whenever there were differences between the imported spirits in respect of a particular criterion.

2.   *"So as to Afford Protection"*

51.   According to the European Communities, the Panel's finding that Korea's measures are applied "so as to afford protection to domestic production", is based on three factors: the sheer magnitude of the tax differential, the lack of rationality of the product categorization, and the fact that there were virtually no imports.[44] There is no indication in the Panel Report that the Panel considered the second of these three factors to be particularly important.

52.   Korea has not explained why it was necessary to add a series of exceptions to the definition of soju which resulted in the most important categories of imported spirits being placed in a much higher tax bracket than soju. The reasons why there are no imports of soju are irrelevant. What matters is that, in practice, imports of soju are and always have been negligible.

53.   The European Communities considers the Korean argument that the measures do not appreciably change the competitive opportunities of the imported products to be factually wrong. In any event, comparing pre-tax price-differences is not sufficient to take account of all possible price distortions caused by the measures.[45] Furthermore, prices may be affected by extraneous factors, such as fluctuations in exchange rates.[46]

54.   The European Communities argues that the "so as to afford protection" requirement is concerned exclusively with *whether* the contested measures protect domestic production and not with *how much* protection is afforded. If two products are directly competitive or substitutable, then any tax differential which is more than *de minimis* may affect the competitive relationship between the products and, as a result, "protect" the less taxed product. The only remaining issue is whether protecting the less taxed product favours "domestic production".

3.   *Application of Article III:2 of the GATT 1994*

55.   The European Communities asserts that Korea's claims under this heading do not raise any "question of law", but only factual issues which, in principle, are not

---

[43] Panel Report, para. 10.54.

[44] Panel Report, paras. 10.101 and 10.102.

[45] See Panel Report, para. 10.94 and footnote 410.

[46] *Ibid.*

subject to appellate review. These claims can only be considered by the Appellate Body under Article 11 of the DSU. However, an appellant invoking this ground of appeal must show that the Panel abused its discretion in a manner which attains a "certain level of gravity".[47] The European Communities contends that the Panel did not make the errors Korea alleges. However, even if Korea could demonstrate that the Panel committed those errors, they would not come close to constituting "egregious errors that call into question the good faith of the Panel".[48]

(a) Product Characteristics

56.   According to the European Communities, Korea's argument that flavour is one of the consumer's primary considerations when choosing a beverage is flawed. If two products are nearly identical, the consumer's choice between them will necessarily turn on very minor differences. For instance, the only reason for choosing a green necktie instead of a red necktie is the colour. Yet, colour remains a relatively minor feature of neckties and differences in colour do not prevent neckties from being "directly competitive and substitutable".

57.   Korea also considers that the Panel erred in relying on the "commonality of raw materials" and the similarity of manufacturing processes as a decisive criterion. In the European Communities' view, Korea improperly characterizes the Panel's reasoning. The Panel stated in unequivocal terms that "commonality of raw materials" is a relevant factor, but not a dispositive one. Nor did the Panel consider that the similarity of manufacturing processes is, in and of itself, decisive.

58.   The European Communities does not accept that Korea's tap and bottled water example is comparable with that of generic and branded aspirin. Generic aspirin and branded aspirin are identical or nearly identical products, even if they are marketed differently. Tap water and bottled water have the same appearance, but it may be highly questionable whether they have close physical characteristics.

(b) End-Uses

59.   The European Communities argues that the Nielsen Study refutes Korea's assertions on consumption patterns of soju and western-style spirits. It showed that some consumers drank whisky with their meals and that soju is not always drunk with meals. The Trendscope survey confirmed that western-style spirits are sometimes consumed with meals. The Panel did not base its conclusion that soju and western-style spirits have similar end-uses on the Nielsen Study's finding that 6 per cent of consumers drank whisky with their meals. Rather, the Panel rejected the relevance of the narrow distinction between consumption with meals and without meals, and also between consumption with "snacks" or with "meals".[49]

---

[47]   European Communities' appellee's submission, para. 68, citing Appellate Body Reports in *European Communities - Measures Affecting the Importation of Certain Poultry Products* ("*European Communities - Poultry*"), WT/DS69/AB/R, adopted 23 July 1998 and *EC Measures Concerning Meat and Meat Products (Hormones)* ("*European Communities - Hormones*"), WT/DS26/AB/R, WT/DS48/AB/R, adopted 13 February 1998.

[48]   *European Communities - Hormones, supra*, footnote 47.

[49]   Panel Report, para. 10.76.

60.   The European Communities disagrees with Korea that there is a contradiction in the Panel's treatment of marketing strategies. Although the Panel stated that marketing strategies can be used to create primarily perceptual distinctions between products, it also stated that marketing strategies can be useful tools for analysis if they highlight fundamental product distinctions or similarities.[50] The Panel thereafter relied on marketing strategies that highlight underlying product similarities.[51]

61.   The European Communities recalls that the complainants adduced evidence before the Panel that certain pre-mixed drinks contained soju, thereby refuting Korea's claim that soju is always drunk straight. Whether pre-mixes are considered as soju or as liqueurs for tax purposes is altogether irrelevant. Pre-mixed "gin and tonic", "whisky and cola" or "piña colada" would not be classified as whisky, gin or rum. Yet, their very existence constitutes irrefutable evidence that some consumers like to drink those spirits mixed with non-alcoholic beverages.

(c)   Channels of Distribution

62.   The Panel relied on the "anecdotal" evidence provided by the United States embassy staff to show that Korea was drawing distinctions which were too fine. The Panel's reasoning, in the European Communities' view, was that the only relevant distinction was between off-premise consumption (i.e. consumption at home or at friends' places) and on-premise consumption (i.e. consumption at public places such as restaurants and bars).[52] Korea does not challenge the Panel's finding that both soju and western-style spirits are currently sold in a similar manner for off-premise consumption. Nor has Korea disputed that off-premise consumption represents a substantial share of total consumption. Further, if western-style spirits were taxed similarly to soju, more people would drink them in inexpensive public places than at present.

(d)   Prices

63.   The European Communities notes that Korea does not challenge the Panel's view that consumer responsiveness to changes in relative prices is, in principle, more relevant than a comparison of absolute prices when assessing whether products are directly competitive or substitutable. Korea argues that premium soju "only represents 5 per cent of the market". To put things in perspective, the European Communities recalls that the total sales volume of premium diluted soju exceeds the combined sales volume of all imported spirits.

64.   Korea also claims that the Panel "wilfully neglected"[53] Korea's evidence when it observed that premium diluted soju was a "fast growing category"[54] of product. The Panel, however, responded to Korea's arguments during the interim review, stating that, although sales had slowed, that was true for all higher priced

---

[50]   Panel Report, para. 10.65.
[51]   Panel Report, para. 10.79.
[52]   Panel Report, para. 10.86.
[53]   Korea's appellant's submission, para. 155.
[54]   Panel Report, para. 10.94.

products and was a consequence of the financial crisis. In any event, Korea did not submit evidence to show that sales of premium diluted soju had decreased.

65.   Korea's arguments concerning the Dodwell Study seek, purely and simply, a *de novo* examination by the Appellate Body of facts already determined by the Panel. Korea's critique of the Dodwell Study's methodology was refuted point-by-point by the European Communities in its submissions to the Panel, and the European Communities does not consider it necessary to repeat those arguments on appeal.

66.   The European Communities underlines that the authors of the Sofres Report, who also prepared the Dodwell Study, assumed that all spirits were part of the same market. Although overlooked by Korea, this Report also states that imported beverages are increasingly preferred by Koreans. The passages Korea relies on have been quoted out of context.

(e)   Treatment of Tequila

67.   The Panel's finding that tequila and soju are "directly competitive or substitutable" products was based on the similarity of their physical characteristics and end-uses.[55] In addition, the Panel relied upon the Dodwell study.

4.   *Article 11 of the DSU*

68.   In respect of Korea's assertion that the Panel failed to accord due deference to Korea's description of the Korean market, the European Communities states that the "deferential" standard of review advocated by Korea finds no support in either the DSU or the GATT 1994. As stated by the Appellate Body[56], the appropriate standard of review for the application of the GATT 1994 and of all other covered agreements (with the sole exception of the *Agreement on the Implementation of Article VI of GATT 1994*) is contained in Article 11 of the DSU. A different standard of review would alter a "finely drawn balance".[57]

5.   *Article 12.7 of the DSU*

69.   This ground of appeal does not raise any issue that has not been addressed already.

C.   *United States - Appellee*

1.   *"Directly Competitive or Substitutable Products"*

70.   The United States observes that many of Korea's complaints in this case relate to questions of fact. Each allegation must be examined to determine whether it concerns a legal question that may be the subject of appellate review.

---

[55]   Panel Report, para. 10.58.
[56]   *European Communities - Hormones, supra,* footnote 47, para. 114.
[57]   *European Communities - Hormones, supra,* footnote 47, para. 115.

(a)   Potential Competition

71.   According to the United States, the Panel followed the Appellate Body's guidance in *Japan - Alcoholic Beverages* that the breadth of the category of "directly competitive or substitutable" products "is a matter for the panel to determine based on all the relevant facts", and that product comparisons "involve an unavoidable element of individual, discretionary judgment." [58]

72.   The United States considers that the concepts of "potential" and "actual" competition are redundancies. Competition may be shown by many means, including through a demonstration that current substitution is occurring or through the inherent degree of substitutability evidenced by the products' similar physical characteristics and basic end-uses.

73.   Contrary to Korea's claims, the United States observes that the Panel did not rely exclusively, or even mostly, on evidence of potential competition. The Panel's reference to "significant potential competition" [59] does not detract from the fact that it concluded that there was evidence of "present direct competition". [60]

74.   In any event, the Panel was correct to consider evidence of potential competition in concluding that the imported products and the domestic products were "directly competitive or substitutable". Korea's argument to the contrary finds no support in the ordinary meaning of the relevant GATT 1994 provisions, taken in their context and read in light of their object and purpose, nor is it consistent with past panel and Appellate Body reports.

75.   According to the United States, the purpose of the provisions at issue is to prohibit protective taxation. The word "substitutable" clearly shows that Article III:2, second sentence, applies in the case of "potential substitution" (i.e. where products are *able* to be substituted). The French and Spanish texts of the provision support this reading. Likewise, the ordinary economic sense of the word "competition" is not limited to actual instances of observed substitution. The phrase "competition was involved"[61] must be read as referring to situations where competition - both current and potential - is present.

76.   Article III:2 protects "expectations" and Members' "potentialities" as exporters. The Panel was, therefore, correct to reject Korea's argument for a quantification of current substitution. A complete absence of imports is not a defence in the case of a violation of Article III and a particular degree of current market penetration of imports should not, therefore, be required.

77.   The Panel was also correct, the United States believes, to consider that evidence from other markets could be "relevant, albeit of less relative evidentiary weight" than evidence from the market actually at issue.[62] Indeed, evidence from another market may be highly probative, whereas evidence from the market at issue

---

[58]   Appellate Body Report, *Japan - Alcoholic Beverages, supra*, footnote 20, pp. 25 and 21.

[59]   Panel Report, para. 10.97.

[60]   Panel Report, para. 10.98. The United States also refers to Panel Report, paras. 10.71 - 10.73, 10.79, 10.82, 10.83, 10.86 and 10.95, all of which refer to aspects of current competition between the products.

[61]   *Ad* Article III:2, second sentence.

[62]   Panel Report, para. 10.78.

may be unreliable because of protection. Although the Panel could have considered more than one other market, it may have felt it most relevant and useful to consider the Japanese market, given its history of restrictions and the structure of its tax laws which appear similar to those of the Korean market. The United States also notes that the Panel's decision to consider other markets is consistent with broader GATT practice.[63]

78.   The United States views Korea's arguments concerning Article 19.2 of the DSU, the principle of *in dubio mitius* and the so-called principle of "predictability" as aids to the interpretation of Article III rather than as independent claims. In any event, the United States argues that it is Korea's interpretation which would violate Article 19.2 of the DSU and the principle of predictability. Furthermore, the principle *in dubio mitius* only applies in case of ambiguity, and there is none here.

(b)   Grouping of the Products

79.   The United States contends that the Panel properly examined extensive evidence concerning the categorization of products, including physical characteristics, end-uses, channels of distribution and points of sale, and prices. The Panel's determinations with regard to the "grouping" of products was an analytical methodology that was not used to "prejudge the substantive discussion". Moreover, the Panel also analyzed the competitive relationship between individual categories of imported and domestic products. Thus, the use of the "analytical tool" had no practical repercussions on the outcome of the case.

80.   Korea's objections to the Panel's decision to "combine" diluted and distilled soju for the purposes of the comparison with imported spirits amount to a disagreement with the Panel's finding that the two types of soju are similar. Pursuant to Article 17.6 of the DSU, such issues cannot, however, form the subject of an appeal.

2.   *"So as to Afford Protection"*

81.   The Panel analyzed the protectionist character of the measures in a manner consistent with the guidance given by the Appellate Body in *Japan - Alcoholic Beverages*. The three factors relied upon by the Panel were: the size of the tax differentials, the structure of the Liquor Tax Law and its application. The United States observes that Korea's explanation of the structure of the tax provides no objective reason to tax the domestic and imported products at issue so differently, given the very minor physical differences between them. The fact that detailed product definitions, corresponding to the western beverages, were introduced over time shows a specific intent to apply different fiscal treatment to soju and imports as the imports entered the Korean market. The fact that there was no imported soju shows only that the design of the law can be safely equated with protection of domestic production.

82.   To the United States, Korea's argument that the large price differences between diluted soju and the imported products prevented the tax measures from af-

---

[63]   The United States refers, in particular, to *Panel on Poultry*, GATT Doc. L/2088, unadopted report issued 21 November 1963, para. 10, and *Japan - Restrictions on Imports of Certain Agricultural Products*, BISD 35S/163, adopted 22 March 1988, para. 5.1.3.7.

fording protection is specious. First, the magnitude of the tax differentials itself can be sufficient to conclude that there is a protective effect. Second, the Panel had already made a factual finding that, despite the large price differentials, the products were directly competitive or substitutable. Third, since the tax differentials exceeded *de minimis* levels, there is no factual or legal basis to argue that the measures are *incapable* of affording protection.

3.   Application of Article III:2 of the GATT 1994

83.   According to the United States, Korea's request to have the Appellate Body review the "misapplication of the facts" and Korea's arguments under various articles of the DSU and international law principles amount, in essence, to an attempt to relitigate the facts. To the extent that Korea has raised any legal claims, for instance, specific violations of Article 11 and 12.7 of the DSU, these are without basis and would, if accepted, undermine Article 17.6 of the DSU.

84.   Korea alleges that the Panel refused to recognize that the complainants did not satisfy the burden of proof requirements. According to the United States, these arguments amount to an objection to the Panel's weighing of the evidence.

4.   Article 11 of the DSU

85.   In short, to establish that the Panel has failed to discharge its duties under Article 11 of the DSU, Korea must show that the Panel committed an error so egregious that it calls into question the "good faith" of the Panel. This is a high standard and appropriately so. As Korea concedes, its allegations concerning the facts do not call into question the Panel's good faith. Therefore, none of Korea's allegations meet the requisite standard for a violation of Article 11 of the DSU.

86.   Nevertheless, Korea asks the Appellate Body to look beyond instances of bad faith. In particular, Korea asks the Appellate Body to lower the present standard by introducing new criteria for the term "objective assessment". The Appellate Body should reject these proposals as they would require it to undertake a *de novo* factual review, thereby contradicting Article 17.6 of the DSU.

87.   Korea's criticisms of the Dodwell Study and the Sofres Report basically find fault with the credibility and weight given to a piece of evidence, which the Appellate Body has confirmed is "part and parcel of the fact finding process".[64] Although the Panel does not explicitly mention the Sofres Report in its findings, the Panel is clearly aware of that Report. It is mentioned in the Panel Report and is quoted extensively in Korea's oral arguments.[65]

88.   Korea's allegations concerning the application of a "double standard" of proof relate largely to the Panel's appreciation of the evidence before it. Korea's argument that the Panel did not have enough evidence to enable it to conduct an objective assessment is, essentially, an objection to the sufficiency of the evidence before the Panel. This is, again, a criticism of the weight and credibility of the facts.

---

[64]   *European Communities - Hormones, supra,* footnote 47, para. 132.
[65]   See, for example, Panel Report, paras. 6.121 and 6.125.

89.   While the United States agrees that a country's description of its own market and culture should be respected, there is no basis in the DSU for Korea's claim that, in the event of a disagreement about the Korean market, the Panel should accept Korea's descriptions unless the complainants submit compelling evidence to the contrary. Moreover, this is a standard never before contemplated in any panel or Appellate Body report.

5.   *Article 12.7 of the DSU*

90.   The term "basic rationale" is not defined in the DSU. Under Article 31(1) of the *Vienna Convention on the Law of Treaties*[66], the text of a provision is to be given its "ordinary meaning". Dictionary definitions emphasize the minimal nature of the explanation required by Article 12.7 of the DSU.[67]

91.   Given the ordinary meaning of these terms, the United States sees no basis for Korea's allegation that the Panel failed to provide a sufficient explanation of its findings. A panel need not give a detailed and exhaustive statement of its reasons for every factual determination it makes. It need only provide the fundamental reasoning behind each factual and legal finding or recommendation, thereby making it possible for the Appellate Body to exercise its review and ensuring that Members understand the manner in which the panel applied the provision in question. The Panel has more than satisfied this threshold, examining each legal element in great detail and listing the factual elements it considered important.

D.   *Arguments of the Third Participant - Mexico*

1.   *"Directly Competitive or Substitutable Products"*

(a)   Potential Competition

92.   Mexico contends that Korea overlooks that the Panel made an express ruling concerning "direct competition"[68] and applied all of the criteria established by the panel, and endorsed by the Appellate Body, in *Japan - Alcoholic Beverages*. These criteria are: physical characteristics, common end-uses, tariff classifications and the market-place.

93.   Mexico also considers that Korea's assertions regarding the "potential competition" criterion are contradictory. Korea sometimes accepts, through the "but for" test, that potential competition may be a necessary element in analysis under Article III:2, while at other times it objects to that criterion.

---

[66]   Done at Vienna, 23 May 1969, 1155 U.N.T.S. 331; (1969), 8 International Legal Materials, 679.

[67]   Webster's Dictionary defines the word "basic" as "of, relating to, or forming the base or essence; fundamental; constituting or serving as the basis or starting-point", and "rationale" as "an explanation of controlling principles of opinion, belief, practice, or phenomena; an underlying reason; basis". The Concise Oxford Dictionary defines "basic" as "forming or serving as a base; fundamental; simplest or lowest in level," and "rationale" as "the fundamental reason or logical basis of anything; a reasoned exposition; a statement of reason".

[68]   Panel Report, paras. 10.95, 10.97 and 10.98.

94.   In Mexico's view, Korea places considerable emphasis on the irrelevancy and danger of speculating on the possible future evolution of a market. It is difficult to believe that Korea really thinks that the complainants and the third party in this dispute have any interest in such speculation or that they would invest considerable resources merely to obtain a hypothetical, advisory opinion. Mexico seeks only to be able to export tequila to Korea without having to face a discriminatory tax regime.

(b)   Evidence from Other Markets

95.   According to Mexico, the Panel analyzed evidence from the Japanese market because the Korean market "still has substantial tax differentials"[69], and, in those circumstances, the Japanese market was relevant. The Panel did not evade its obligation to examine the Korean market since that market was also analyzed.

(c)   Grouping of the Products

96.   Mexico is of the view that Korea has misunderstood the Panel's intention in proceeding primarily with an examination of the relationship between diluted soju and the imported beverages. The Panel simply based its examination on diluted soju and, when it detected a relevant difference between the two types of soju, highlighted that difference.

97.   The Panel did not improperly group the imported beverages nor did it ignore differences between them. The Panel based its comparison on the characteristics common to all of them and, in any event, also noted relevant distinctions between the beverages where appropriate.

2.   *"So as to Afford Protection"*

98.   Mexico contends that Korea's arguments under this heading are wrong because the Panel mentioned not only the difference in tax burden between the domestic beverages and the imported beverages, but also noted that the structure of the Liquor Tax Law itself was discriminatory.

3.   *Application of Article III:2 of the GATT 1994*

99.   Mexico considers that, since this is a dispute concerning alleged failure to comply with obligations in the GATT 1994, Korea's measures are presumed to nullify or impair benefits accruing under that Agreement and, consequently, under Article 3.8 of the DSU, the burden of refuting the allegations is incumbent upon Korea and not on the appellees or the third party. Contrary to Korea's assertions, the complaining parties and Mexico submitted several pieces of evidence, including: evidence on the physical similarities of the spirits; evidence on the tariff classification of tequila and soju; and evidence from the market-place, in the form of the Dodwell Study, which also covered the relationship between tequila and soju.

100.   Mexico agrees with the Panel's rejection of Korea's arguments that the appropriate end-use to be considered in this case was consumption of the beverages

---

[69]   Panel Report, para. 10.45.

with or without meals. As regards admixtures, Mexico considers that the existence of soju cocktails is evidence that soju is not only drunk straight, but is also drunk mixed.

101.   Korea argues that it has greater authority than the Panel to analyze its own market. In Mexico's view, this claim is not only difficult to defend, but is also contradictory. If the Koreans have a special authority not possessed by others, why did Korea entrust analysis of the Korean market to non-Korean companies, such as A.C. Nielsen?

III.   ISSUES RAISED IN THIS APPEAL

102.   This appeal raises the following issues:

(a)   whether the Panel erred in its interpretation and application of the term "directly competitive or substitutable product" which appears in the *Ad* Article to Article III:2, second sentence, of the GATT 1994;

(b)   whether the Panel erred in its interpretation and application of the term "so as to afford protection", which is incorporated into Article III:2, second sentence, by specific reference to the "principles set forth in paragraph 1" of Article III of the GATT 1994;

(c)   whether the Panel erred in its application of the rules on the allocation of the burden of proof;

(d)   whether the Panel failed to make an objective assessment of the matter as required by Article 11 of the DSU; and

(e)   whether the Panel failed to set out the basic rationale behind its findings and recommendations as required by Article 12.7 of the DSU.

IV.   INTERPRETATION AND APPLICATION OF ARTICLE III:2, SECOND SENTENCE, OF THE GATT 1994

103.   The first issue that we have to address is whether the Panel erred in interpreting Article III:2, second sentence, of the GATT 1994.

104.   Article III:2 provides:

> The products of the territory of any contracting party imported into the territory of any other contracting party shall not be subject, directly or indirectly, to internal taxes or other internal charges of any kind in excess of those applied, directly or indirectly, to like domestic products. Moreover, no contracting party shall otherwise apply internal taxes or other internal charges to imported or domestic products in a manner contrary to the principles set forth in paragraph 1.[70]

---

[70]   The provisions of Article III:2, second sentence, of the GATT 1994 include paragraph 2 of *Ad* Article III and, by specific incorporation, the term "so as to afford protection" which appears in paragraph 1 of Article III.

105.   The meaning of the second sentence of Article III:2 is clarified by paragraph 2 of *Ad* Article III, which reads:

> A tax conforming to the requirements of the first sentence of paragraph 2 would be considered to be inconsistent with the provisions of the second sentence only in cases where competition was involved between, on the one hand, the taxed product and, on the other hand, a directly competitive or substitutable product which was not similarly taxed.

106.   Article III:1 provides:

> The contracting parties recognize that internal taxes and other internal charges, and laws, regulations and requirements affecting the internal sale, offering for sale, purchase, transportation, distribution or use of products, and internal quantitative regulations requiring the mixture, processing or use of products in specified amounts or proportions, should not be applied to imported or domestic products so as to afford protection to domestic production.

107.   In our Report in *Japan - Alcoholic Beverages*, we stated that three separate issues must be addressed when assessing the consistency of an internal tax measure with Article III:2, second sentence, of the GATT 1994. These three issues are whether:

> (1)   the imported products and the domestic products *are "directly competitive or substitutable products" which are in competition with each other*;
>
> (2)   the directly competitive or substitutable imported and domestic products *are "not similarly taxed"*; and
>
> (3)   the dissimilar taxation of the directly competitive or substitutable imported and domestic products *is "applied ... so as to afford protection to domestic production"*.[71]

A.   *"Directly Competitive or Substitutable Products"*

108.   The Panel concluded its examination of the first issue arising under Article III:2, second sentence, as follows:

> We are of the view that there is sufficient unrebutted evidence in this case to show present direct competition between the products. Furthermore, we are of the view that the complainants also have shown a strong potentially direct competitive relationship. Thus, on balance, we find that the evidence concerning physical characteristics, end-uses, channels of distri-

---

[71]   Appellate Body Report, *Japan - Alcoholic Beverages, supra*, footnote 20, at 116.

> bution and pricing, leads us to conclude that the imported and
> domestic products are directly competitive or substitutable. [72]

109.   According to the Panel, the "key question" with respect to the first issue arising under Article III:2, second sentence, "is whether the products are **directly competitive or substitutable.**" [73] (emphasis in the original) The Panel stated that "an assessment of whether there is a direct competitive relationship between two products or groups of products requires evidence that consumers consider or could consider the two products or groups of products as alternative ways of satisfying a particular need or taste." [74] The determination of whether domestic and imported products are directly competitive or substitutable "requires evidence of the direct competitive relationship between the products, including, in this case, comparisons of their physical characteristics, end-uses, channels of distribution and prices." [75] The Panel reasoned, furthermore, that the "focus should not be exclusively on the quantitative extent of the competitive overlap, but on the methodological basis on which a panel should assess the competitive relationship." [76] "[Q]uantitative analyses, while helpful, should not be considered necessary." [77] Similarly, "quantitative studies of cross-price elasticity are relevant, but not exclusive or even decisive in nature." [78] A determination of the precise extent of the competitive overlap can be complicated by the fact that protectionist government policies can distort the competitive relationship between products, causing the quantitative extent of the competitive relationship to be understated. [79] The Panel cautioned that "a focus on the quantitative extent of competition instead of the nature of it, could result in a type of trade effects test being written into Article III cases." [80]

110.   The Panel noted that assessment of competition has a temporal dimension. [81] It considered that panels should look at "evidence of trends and changes in consumption patterns and make an assessment as to whether such trends and patterns lead to the conclusion that the products in question are either directly competitive now or can reasonably be expected to become directly competitive in the near future." [82] The Panel stated:

> ... We will not attempt to speculate on what could happen in
> the distant future, but we will consider evidence pertaining to
> what could reasonably be expected to occur in the near term
> based on the evidence presented. How much weight to be ac-
> corded such evidence must be decided on a case-by-case basis

---

[72]   The "products" referred to by the Panel are diluted soju, distilled soju, whiskies, brandies, cognac, rum, gin, vodka, tequila, liqueurs and admixtures. Panel Report, para. 10.98.
[73]   Panel Report, para. 10.39.
[74]   Panel Report, para. 10.40.
[75]   Panel Report, para. 10.43.
[76]   Panel Report, para. 10.39.
[77]   Panel Report, para. 10.42.
[78]   Panel Report, para. 10.44.
[79]   Panel Report, para. 10.42.
[80]   *Ibid.*
[81]   Panel Report, para. 10.47.
[82]   Panel Report, para. 10.48.

> in light of the market structure and other factors including the quality of the evidence and the extent of the inference required. ... Obviously, evidence as to what would happen now is more probative in nature than what would happen in the future, but most evidence cannot be so conveniently parsed. If one is dealing with products that are experience based consumer items, then trends are particularly important and it would be unrealistic and, indeed, analytically unhelpful to attempt to separate every piece of evidence and disregard that which discusses implications for market structure in the near future.[83]

111. According to Korea, the Panel misinterpreted the term "directly competitive or substitutable product" by, *inter alia*, "relying on 'potential' competition, comparing the Korean market to the Japanese market and undertaking the wrong product comparisons."[84]

1. *Potential Competition*

112. Korea argues that the Panel took an unacceptably broad and speculative approach to the role of potential competition, which is not permitted by the wording, context and object and purpose of Article III:2, second sentence.[85] Korea agrees that this provision is not intended to exclude products that are not directly competitive or substitutable because of the contested measure itself. However, the Panel's overly broad approach has opened the door to speculation about how the market could evolve in the future, irrespective of the tax measure in question.[86]

113. Contrary to Korea's assertions, the Panel has not relied on potential competition in order to overcome the absence today of a "directly competitive or substitutable" relationship between the domestic and imported products on the basis that such a relationship might develop in the future. The Panel concluded that "there is sufficient unrebutted evidence in this case to show *present* direct competition between the products".[87] (emphasis added) This legal finding is not a speculative one concerning the future, but is based firmly in the present. The reference to "a strong potentially direct competitive relationship" does no more than buttress the Panel's finding of "present direct competition".[88]

114. The term "directly competitive or substitutable" describes a particular type of relationship between two products, one imported and the other domestic. It is evident from the wording of the term that the essence of that relationship is that the products are in competition. This much is clear both from the word "competitive"

---

[83] Panel Report, para. 10.50.

[84] Korea's appellant's submission, para. 22.

[85] Korea's appellant's submission, paras. 26 and 31.

[86] Korea's appellant's submission, para. 28.

[87] Panel Report, para. 10.98. Likewise, the Panel also stated that "the evidence overall supports a finding that the imported and domestic products at issue *are* directly competitive or substitutable" (para. 10.95). (emphasis added)

[88] Panel Report, para. 10.98.

which means "characterized by competition" [89], and from the word "substitutable" which means "able to be substituted". [90] The context of the competitive relationship is necessarily the marketplace since this is the forum where consumers choose between different products. Competition in the market place is a dynamic, evolving process. Accordingly, the wording of the term "directly competitive or substitutable" implies that the competitive relationship between products is *not* to be analyzed *exclusively* by reference to *current* consumer preferences. In our view, the word "substitutable" indicates that the requisite relationship *may* exist between products that are not, at a given moment, considered by consumers to be substitutes but which are, nonetheless, *capable* of being substituted for one another.

115.   Thus, according to the ordinary meaning of the term, products are competitive or substitutable when they are interchangeable [91] or if they offer, as the Panel noted, "alternative ways of satisfying a particular need or taste". [92] Particularly in a market where there are regulatory barriers to trade or to competition, there may well be latent demand.

116.   The words "competitive or substitutable" are qualified in the *Ad* Article by the term "directly". In the context of Article III:2, second sentence, the word "directly" suggests a degree of proximity in the competitive relationship between the domestic and the imported products. The word "directly" does not, however, prevent a panel from considering both latent and extant demand.

117.   Our reading of the ordinary meaning of the term "directly competitive or substitutable" is supported by its context as well as its object and purpose. As part of the context, we note that the *Ad* Article provides that the second sentence of Article III:2 is applicable "only in cases where competition *was* involved". (emphasis added) According to Korea, the use of the past indicative "was" prevents a panel taking account of "potential" competition. However, in our view, the use of the word "was" does not have any necessary significance in defining the temporal scope of the analysis to be carried out. The *Ad* Article describes the circumstances in which a hypothetical tax "*would* be considered to be inconsistent with the provisions of the second sentence". (emphasis added) The first part of the clause is cast in the conditional mood ("would") and the use of the past indicative simply follows from the use of the word "would". It does not place any limitations on the temporal dimension of the word "competition".

118.   The first sentence of Article III:2 also forms part of the context of the term. "Like" products are a subset of directly competitive or substitutable products: all like products are, by definition, directly competitive or substitutable products, whereas not all "directly competitive or substitutable" products are "like". [93] The notion of

---

[89]   Lesley Brown (ed.), *The New Shorter Oxford English Dictionary*, Vol. I, p. 459 (Clarendon Press, 1993).

[90]   Lesley Brown (ed.), *op. cit.*, Vol. II, p. 3125.

[91]   Appellate Body Report, *Canada - Certain Measures Concerning Periodicals* ("*Canada - Periodicals*"), WT/DS31/AB/R, adopted 30 July 1997.

[92]   Panel Report, para. 10.40.

[93]   Panel Report, *Japan - Alcoholic Beverages, supra*, footnote 16, para. 6.22, approved by the Appellate Body, DSR 1996:I, 97, at 117.

like products must be construed narrowly[94] but the category of directly competitive or substitutable products is broader.[95] While perfectly substitutable products fall within Article III:2, first sentence, imperfectly substitutable products can be assessed under Article III:2, second sentence.[96]

119.   The context of Article III:2, second sentence, also includes Article III:1 of the GATT 1994. As we stated in our Report in *Japan - Alcoholic Beverages*, Article III:1 informs Article III:2 through specific reference.[97] Article III:1 sets forth the principle "that internal taxes ... should not be applied to imported or domestic products so as to afford protection to domestic production." It is in the light of this principle, which embodies the object and purpose of the whole of Article III, that the term "directly competitive and substitutable" must be read. As we said in *Japan - Alcoholic Beverages*:

> The broad and fundamental purpose of Article III is to *avoid protectionism* in the application of internal tax and regulatory measures. ... Toward this end, Article III obliges Members of the WTO to *provide equality of competitive conditions* for imported products in relation to domestic products. ... Moreover, it is irrelevant that the "trade effects" of the tax differential between imported and domestic products, as reflected in the volumes of imports, are insignificant or even non-existent; Article III *protects expectations* not of any particular trade volume but rather of the *equal competitive relationship* between imported and domestic products.[98] (emphasis added).

120.   In view of the objectives of avoiding protectionism, requiring equality of competitive conditions and protecting expectations of equal competitive relationships, we decline to take a static view of the term "directly competitive or substitutable." The object and purpose of Article III confirms that the scope of the term "directly competitive or substitutable" cannot be limited to situations where consumers *already* regard products as alternatives. If reliance could be placed only on current instances of substitution, the object and purpose of Article III:2 could be defeated by the protective taxation that the provision aims to prohibit. Past panels have, in fact, acknowledged that consumer behaviour might be influenced, in particular, by protectionist internal taxation. Citing the panel in *Japan - Customs Duties, Taxes and Labelling Practices on Imported Wines and Alcoholic Beverages* ("*1987 Japan - Alcohol*")[99], the panel in *Japan - Alcoholic Beverages* observed that "a tax system

---

[94]   Appellate Body Report, *Japan - Alcoholic Beverages*, *supra*, footnote 20, at 112, and *Canada - Periodicals*, *supra*, footnote 91, at 466.

[95]   Appellate Body Report, *Japan - Alcoholic Beverages*, *supra*, footnote 20, at 117.

[96]   *Canada - Periodicals*, *supra*, footnote 91, at 473.

[97]   Appellate Body Report, *Japan - Alcoholic Beverages*, *supra*, footnote 20, at 116.

[98]   Appellate Body Report, *Japan - Alcoholic Beverages*, DSR 1996:I, 97, at 109-110, with references to earlier Panel Reports.

[99]   *Japan - Customs Duties, Taxes and Labelling Practices on Imported Wines and Alcoholic Beverages*, adopted 10 November 1987, BISD 34S/83. The panel in *Japan - Alcoholic Beverages*, *supra*, footnote 16, cited para. 5.9 of this panel report.

that discriminates against imports has the consequence of creating and even freezing preferences for domestic goods."[100] The panel in *Japan - Alcoholic Beverages* also stated that "consumer surveys in a country with ... a [protective] tax system would likely understate the degree of *potential* competitiveness between substitutable products".[101] (emphasis added) Accordingly, in some cases, it may be highly relevant to examine latent demand.

121.   We observe that studies of cross-price elasticity, which in our Report in *Japan - Alcoholic Beverages* were regarded as one means of examining a market[102], involve an assessment of latent demand. Such studies attempt to predict the change in demand that would result from a change in the price of a product following, *inter alia*, from a change in the relative tax burdens on domestic and imported products.

122.   Korea itself recognizes that potential demand may be taken into account in determining whether products are "directly competitive or substitutable". Before the Panel, Korea acknowledged that this term is not intended to exclude products that are not directly competitive or substitutable because of ("but for") the contested measure itself. At the oral hearing before us, Korea accepted that this "but for" test would permit account to be taken "not only [of] the direct price increasing effect of a tax differential but also [of] other elements that could show an impairment of competitive opportunities because of the tax differential, that distribution costs had been higher, etc." [103]

123.   We note, however, that actual consumer demand may be influenced by measures other than internal taxation. Thus, demand may be influenced by, *inter alia*, earlier protectionist taxation, previous import prohibitions or quantitative restrictions. Latent demand can be a particular problem in the case of "experience goods", such as food and beverages, which consumers tend to purchase because they are familiar with them and with which consumers experiment only reluctantly.[104]

124.   We, therefore, conclude that the term "directly competitive or substitutable" does not prevent a panel from taking account of evidence of latent consumer demand as one of a range of factors to be considered when assessing the competitive relationship between imported and domestic products under Article III:2, second sentence, of the GATT 1994. In this case, the Panel committed no error of law in buttressing its finding of "present direct competition" by referring to a "strong potentially direct competitive relationship".[105]

2.   *Expectations*

125.   In the course of its reasoning on potential competition, the Panel referred to the "settled law that competitive expectations and opportunities are protected"[106]

---

[100]   Panel Report, *Japan - Alcoholic Beverages*, *supra*, footnote 16, para. 6.28. This passage was expressly approved by the Appellate Body in its Report in this case pp. 120-121, DSR 1996:I.
[101]   *Ibid*.
[102]   Appellate Body Report, *Japan - Alcoholic Beverages*, *supra*, footnote 20, at 117.
[103]   Response by Korea to questions at the oral hearing.
[104]   Panel Report, paras. 10.44, 10.50 and 10.73.
[105]   Panel Report, para. 10.98.
[106]   Panel Report, para. 10.48.

and noted our statement in *Japan - Alcoholic Beverages* that "Article III protects expectations not of any particular trade volume but rather of the equal competitive relationship between imported and domestic products".[107]

126.   Korea takes the view that "expectations" exist only for products which are already "like" or "directly competitive or substitutable" and that it was improper for the Panel to consider that there could be expectations regarding products that are not currently "directly competitive or substitutable", but which might become so in the near future.[108]

127.   As we have said, the object and purpose of Article III is the maintenance of equality of competitive conditions for imported and domestic products.[109] It is, therefore, not only legitimate, but even necessary, to take account of this purpose in interpreting the term "directly competitive or substitutable product".[110]

3.   *"Trade Effects" Test*

128.   The Panel expressed concern that "a focus on the quantitative extent of competition instead of the nature of it, could result in a type of trade effects test being written into Article III cases." [111]

129.   Korea complains that this is a misunderstanding of the "trade effects" test.[112] In our view, when the Panel referred to a "type of trade effects test", it was simply expressing its scepticism about the consequences of placing undue emphasis on quantitative analyses of the competitive relationship between products. This is clear from the sentence immediately following the sentence containing the reference to a "type of trade effects test":

> That is, if a certain *degree* of competition must be shown, it is
> similar to showing that a certain *amount* of damage was done
> to that competitive relationship by the tax policies in ques-
> tion.[113] (emphasis in the original)

130.   Thus, the Panel stated that if a particular degree of competition had to be shown in quantitative terms,· that would be similar to requiring proof that a tax measure has a particular impact on trade. It considered such an approach akin to a "type of trade effects test".

131.   We do not consider the Panel's reasoning on this point to be flawed. [114]

---

[107]   *Supra*, footnote 20, at 110, with references to earlier panel reports.

[108]   Korea's appellant's submission, para. 33, citing, in part, the Panel Report, para. 10.48.

[109]   *Supra*, para. 119.

[110]   Moreover, as we noted earlier, the Panel concluded that there was evidence of "*present* direct competition" between the imported and domestic products. (Panel Report, para. 10.98, emphasis added).

[111]   Panel Report, para. 10.42.

[112]   *Supra*, para. 9.

[113]   Panel Report, para. 10.42.

[114]   We note, moreover, that the Panel cites correctly the "trade effects" test in para. 10.42 of the Report, the very paragraph in which it refers to a "type of trade effects test".

4.   *Nature of Competition*

132.   The Panel makes numerous references to the "nature of competition".[115] Korea considers that, through the use of the term "nature of competition", the Panel has inserted a "vague and subjective element" which is not found in Article III:2, second sentence.[116] Korea argues that this reference to the "nature of competition", therefore, amounts to another failure properly to interpret the term "directly competitive or substitutable".

133.   We believe that the Panel uses the term "*nature* of competition" as a synonym for *quality* of competition, as opposed to *quantity* of competition. The Panel considered that in analyzing whether products are "directly competitive or substitutable", the focus should be on the *nature* of competition and not on its *quantity*:

> ... the question is not of the degree of competitive overlap, but its *nature. Is there a competitive relationship and is it direct?* ...[117] (emphasis added)

134.   In taking issue with the use of the term "nature of competition", Korea, in effect, objects to the Panel's sceptical attitude to quantification of the competitive relationship between imported and domestic products. For the reasons set above, we share the Panel's reluctance to rely unduly on quantitative analyses of the competitive relationship.[118] In our view, an approach that focused solely on the quantitative overlap of competition would, in essence, make cross-price elasticity *the* decisive criterion in determining whether products are "directly competitive or substitutable". We do not, therefore, consider that the Panel's use of the term "nature of competition" is questionable.

5.   *Evidence from the Japanese Market*

135.   The Panel considered that, in assessing whether products are directly competitive or substitutable, it was appropriate to look at "the nature of competition in other countries".[119] It stated:

> [A]s we are looking at the nature of competition in a market that previously was relatively closed and still has substantial tax differentials, such evidence of competitive relationships in other markets is relevant. ... We do not need, in this case, to give substantial weight to conditions in markets outside Korea, but such factors are relevant... . To completely ignore such evidence from other markets would require complete reliance on current market information which may be unreliable, due to its tendency to understate the competitive relationship, because of the very actions being challenged. Indeed, the result could be that the most restrictive and dis-

---

[115]   See Panel Report, paras. 10.42, 10.45, 10.66, 10.76, 10.78 and 10.92.
[116]   Korea's appellant's submission, paras. 37 and 38.
[117]   Panel Report, para. 10.44.
[118]   *Supra*, para. 120.
[119]   Panel Report, para. 10.45.

> criminatory government policies would be safe from chal-
> lenge under Article III due to the lack of domestic market
> data.[120]

136.   According to Korea, the Panel's approach constitutes an impermissible broadening of the scope of Article III:2, second sentence. Moreover, Korea believes that if evidence from other markets were to be admitted, more than one other market ought to be reviewed. In this case, as there was "considerable evidence available as to what is taking place within the Korean market" [121], Korea considers that there was no reason to rely on evidence drawn from another market when making conclusions about the Korean market.

137.   It is, of course, true that the "directly competitive or substitutable" relationship must be present in the market at issue[122], in this case, the Korean market. It is also true that consumer responsiveness to products may vary from country to country.[123] This does not, however, preclude consideration of consumer behaviour in a country other than the one at issue. It seems to us that evidence from other markets may be pertinent to the examination of the market at issue, particularly when demand on that market has been influenced by regulatory barriers to trade or to competition. Clearly, not every other market will be relevant to the market at issue. But if another market displays characteristics similar to the market at issue, then evidence of consumer demand in that other market may have some relevance to the market at issue. This, however, can only be determined on a case-by-case basis, taking account of all relevant facts.

138.   In the present case, the Panel did not err in referring to the Japanese market in its reasoning.

6.   *Grouping of the Products*

139.   Before embarking on its assessment of whether the imported and domestic products at issue are directly competitive or substitutable, the Panel considered how it would carry out that assessment. It stated:

> ... With respect to the domestic product, soju, there are two
> primary categories identified. There is distilled soju and di-
> luted soju.
>
> ...
>
> ... If we find that diluted soju is directly competitive with and
> substitutable for the imported products, it will follow that this
> is also the case for distilled soju because distilled soju is in-

---

[120]   Panel Report, paras. 10.45 and 10.46.

[121]   Panel Report, para. 10.46.

[122]   Appellate Body Report, *Japan - Alcoholic Beverages, supra*, footnote 20, at 117, and *Canada - Periodicals, supra*, footnote 91, at 470-471.

[123]   Panel Report, *Japan - Alcoholic Beverages, supra*, footnote 16, para. 6.28, with reference to Working Party Report on "Border Tax Adjustments", L/3464, adopted 2 December 1970, BISD 18S/97, p. 102, para. 18, approved by the Appellate Body Report, *Japan - Alcoholic Beverages, supra*, footnote 20, at 117.

termediary between the imported products and diluted soju. Indeed, distilled soju is, on the one hand, more similar to the imported products than diluted soju and is, on the other hand, more similar to diluted soju than are the imported products. [124]

With respect to the imported products, the Panel said:

> ... We ... do not accept the Korean argument that we are required to make an item by item comparison between each imported product and both types of soju. Relying on product categories is appropriate in many cases. ... The question becomes where to draw the boundaries between categories, rather than whether it is appropriate to utilize categories for *analytical* purposes. ... [W]e find that, on balance, all of the imported products specifically identified by the complainants have sufficient common characteristics, end-uses and channels of distribution and prices to be considered together.[*] (emphasis added)[125]

---

[*]This decision does not prejudge the substantive discussion; rather we are merely identifying an *analytical* tool. It is possible that during the course of a dispute, evidence will show that an *analytical* approach should be revised. ... (emphasis added)

140.   Korea argues that the Panel erred in failing to examine distilled soju and diluted soju separately and also in examining all of the imported products together. Korea's argument is based, in large part, on allegedly significant differences between the products that the Panel grouped together. Korea is concerned that by considering the products together, the Panel overlooked important differences between them. Korea believes that, in so doing, the Panel was able to conclude that all the products at issue were directly competitive or substitutable, whereas had the imported products been examined individually, this result would not have been possible.

141.   We consider that Korea's argument raises two distinct questions. The first question is whether the Panel erred in its "analytical approach". The second is whether, on the facts of this case, the Panel was entitled to group the products in the manner that it did. Since the second question involves a review of the way in which the Panel assessed the evidence, we address it in our analysis of procedural issues.

142.   The Panel describes "grouping" as an "analytical tool". It appears to us, however, that whatever else the Panel may have seen in this "analytical tool", it used this "tool" as a practical device to minimize repetition when examining the competitive relationship between a large number of differing products. Some grouping is almost always necessary in cases arising under Article III:2, second sentence, since generic categories commonly include products with *some* variation in composition, quality,

---

[124]   Panel Report, paras. 10.51 and 10.54.
[125]   Panel Report, paras 10.59 and 10.60.

function and price, and thus commonly give rise to sub-categories.[126] From a slightly different perspective, we note that "grouping" of products involves at least a preliminary characterization by the treaty interpreter that certain products are sufficiently similar as to, for instance, composition, quality, function and price, to warrant treating them as a group for convenience in analysis. But, the use of such "analytical tools" does not relieve a panel of its duty to make an objective assessment of whether the components of a group of imported products are directly competitive or substitutable with the domestic products. We share Korea's concern that, in certain circumstances, such "grouping" of products *might* result in individual product characteristics being ignored, and that, in turn, *might* affect the outcome of a case. However, as we will see below, the Panel avoided that pitfall in this case.

143.   Whether, and to what extent, products can be grouped is a matter to be decided on a case-by-case basis. In this case, the Panel decided to group the imported products at issue on the basis that:

> ... on balance, all of the imported products specifically identified by the complainants have sufficient common characteristics, end-uses and channels of distribution and prices... .[127]

144.   As the Panel explained in the footnote attached to this passage[128], the Panel's subsequent analysis of the physical characteristics, end-uses, channels of distribution and prices of the imported products confirmed the correctness of its decision to group the products for analytical purposes. Furthermore, where appropriate, the Panel did take account of individual product characteristics.[129] It, therefore, seems to us that the Panel's grouping of imported products, complemented where appropriate by individual product examination, produced the same outcome that individual examination of each imported product would have produced.[130] We, therefore, conclude that the Panel did not err in considering the imported beverages together.

145.   With respect to diluted soju and distilled soju, the Panel did not "group" these products as such. Rather, it concentrated on diluted soju in assessing the competitive relationship between the domestic and imported beverages. The Panel considered that distilled soju was an "intermediary" product, with respect to physical characteristics, end-uses and prices, between diluted soju and the imported products. On that assumption, it reasoned, *a fortiori*, taking the view that if diluted soju was shown to be competitive with the imported products, the intermediate product, distilled soju, would also necessarily be "directly competitive or substitutable" with them.[131] We do not consider the Panel's reasoning on this point to be objectionable.

---

[126]   The Panel mentions the product category of "whiskies" which include several subcategories of types of whisky such as Scotch (premium and standard), Irish, Bourbon, Rye, Canadian, etc., all of which differ. Panel Report, para. 10.59.

[127]   Panel Report, para. 10.60.

[128]   Panel Report, footnote 375. See also Panel Report, footnotes 382 and 399.

[129]   See Panel Report, paras. 10.67, 10.71, 10.72, 10.85 and 10.94 and footnotes 385, 386, 387 and 408.

[130]   We note that the panels in *1987 Japan - Alcohol* and in *Japan - Alcoholic Beverage*, followed the same approach. This approach was implicitly approved in our Report on *Japan - Alcoholic Beverages*.

[131]   Panel Report, 10.54.

B.   *"So as to Afford Protection"*

146.   We now address whether the Panel erred in its application of the term "so as to afford protection", which is incorporated into Article III:2, second sentence, by specific reference to paragraph 1 of Article III.

147.   With regard to this third element of Article III:2, second sentence, the Panel stated:

> The Appellate Body in the *Japan Alcoholic Beverages* case stated that the focus of this portion of the inquiry should be on the objective factors underlying the tax measure in question including its design, architecture and the revealing structure. In that case, the Panel and the Appellate Body found that the very magnitude of the dissimilar taxation supported a finding that it was applied so as to afford protection. In the present case, the Korean tax law also has very large differences in levels of taxation, large enough, in our view, also to support such a finding.
>
> In addition to the very large levels of tax differentials, we also note that the structures of the Liquor Tax Law and the Education Tax Law are consistent with this finding. The structure of the Liquor Tax Law itself is discriminatory. It is based on a very broad generic definition which is defined as soju and then there are specific exceptions corresponding very closely to one or more characteristics of imported beverages that are used to identify products which receive higher tax rates. There is virtually no imported soju so the beneficiaries of this structure are almost exclusively domestic producers.[*] Thus, in our view, the design, architecture and structure of the Korean alcoholic beverages tax laws (including the Education Tax as it is applied in a differential manner to imported and domestic products) afford protection to domestic production.[132]
> …
>
> ---
> [*]The only domestic product which falls into a higher category that corresponds to one type of imported beverage is distilled soju which represents less than one percent of Korean production.

148.   According to Korea, the Panel committed several errors in applying the third element of Article III:2, second sentence. It ignored Korea's explanations for the structure of the tax. It made "much" of the virtual absence of imported soju. It did not observe the Appellate Body's guidance in *Japan - Alcoholic Beverages*, that, even though the tax differential may prove that a tax is applied "so as to afford protection", "in other cases, there may be other factors that will be just as relevant or

---

[132]   Panel Report, paras. 10.101 and 10.102.

more relevant to demonstrating that the dissimilar taxation at issue was applied 'so as to afford protection'." [133]

149.   In our Report in *Japan - Alcoholic Beverages*, we said that examination of whether a tax regime affords protection to domestic production "is an issue of how the measure in question is *applied*", and that such an examination "requires a comprehensive and objective analysis" [134]:

> ... it is possible to examine objectively the underlying criteria used in a particular tax measure, its structure, and its overall application to ascertain whether it is applied in a way that affords protection to domestic products.
>
> Although it is true that the aim of a measure may not be easily ascertained, nevertheless its protective application can most often be discerned from the design, the architecture, and the revealing structure of a measure. The very magnitude of the dissimilar taxation in a particular case may be evidence of such protective application ... . Most often, there will be other factors to be considered as well. [135]

150.   The Panel followed this approach. In finding that the Korean measures afford protection to domestic production, the Panel relied, first, on the fact that "the Korean tax law ... has very large differences in levels of taxation." [136] Although it considered that the magnitude of the tax differences was sufficiently large to support a finding that the contested measures afforded protection to domestic production, the Panel also considered the structure and design of the measures. [137] In addition, the Panel found that, in practice, "[t]here is virtually no imported soju so the beneficiaries of this structure are almost exclusively domestic producers". [138] In other words, the tax operates in such a way that the lower tax brackets cover almost exclusively domestic production, whereas the higher tax brackets embrace almost exclusively imported products. In such circumstances, the reasons given by Korea as to *why* the tax is structured in a particular way do not call into question the conclusion that the measures are applied "so as to afford protection to domestic production". Likewise, the reason why there is very little imported soju in Korea does not change the pattern of application of the contested measures.

151.   Korea claims that the Panel erred in failing to find that the "intrinsic" pre-tax price difference between diluted soju and the imported alcoholic beverages was so large that "the additional difference created by the variation in tax can have no

---

[133]   *Supra*, footnote 20, at 122.

[134]   *Supra*, footnote 20, at 119-120.

[135]   *Supra*, footnote 20, at 120.

[136]   Panel Report, para. 10.101. In para. 10.100, the Panel set out the tax differentials: "the total tax on diluted soju is 38.5 percent; on distilled soju and liqueurs it is 55 percent; on vodka, gin, rum, tequila and admixtures it is 104 percent; on whisky, brandy and cognac it is 130 percent".

[137]   Panel Report, para. 10.101.

[138]   Panel Report, para. 10.102. We note that we considered a similar finding by the panel in *Japan - Alcoholic Beverages*, *supra*, footnote 16, at 122, to be relevant for the establishment of the third element of Article III:2, second sentence.

[protective] effect".[139] According to Korea, the Panel "should have inquired whether the tax is capable of affecting reasonable expectations about the competitive relationship between the products."[140] Korea also argued that "the demand for a product like distilled soju is specific and static and that it would be difficult to affect it a great deal in either direction by altering the price."[141]

152.   In making these arguments, Korea seems to be revisiting the question whether the products can be treated as directly competitive or substitutable. As regards diluted soju, Korea seems to be saying, in effect, that the large pre-tax price difference is such that consumers do not treat the products as substitutable, and that consumers' decisions whether to buy the imported products will not, therefore, be affected by the higher tax burden imposed on these imports. Similarly, as regards distilled soju, Korea is arguing that there is no cross-elasticity of demand between distilled soju and the imported beverages. However, Korea overlooks the fact that the two products have already been found to be directly competitive or substitutable.[142] Its arguments are, therefore, misplaced at this stage of the analysis and do not cast doubt on the Panel's finding that the contested measures afford protection to domestic production.

153.   Korea also seems to be insisting that a finding that a measure affords protection must be supported by proof that the tax difference has some identifiable trade effect. But, as we have said above, Article III is not concerned with trade volumes.[143] It is, therefore, not incumbent on a complaining party to prove that tax measures are capable of producing any particular trade effect.

154.   We believe, and so hold, that the Panel did not err in its application of the term "so as to afford protection", which is incorporated into Article III:2, second sentence, by specific reference to paragraph 1 of Article III.

C.   Allocation of the Burden of Proof

155.   Korea argues that the Panel misapplied the burden of proof and that it applied a "double standard" when assessing the evidence. We note that although the Panel did not actually articulate the rules on allocation of the burden of proof, it made specific reference to passages of our Report in *United States - Shirts and Blouses* where we enunciated these rules.[144]

156.   It is clear from paragraphs 10.57, 10.58 and 10.82 of the Panel Report that the Panel properly understood and applied the rules on allocation of the burden of proof.[145] First, the Panel insisted that it could make findings under Article III:2, sec-

---

[139]   Korea's appellant's submission, para. 75.

[140]   Korea's appellant's submission, para. 76.

[141]   Korea's appellant's submission, para. 79.

[142]   The significant price differential between the products was taken into account in determining whether the products are, in fact, directly competitive or substitutable (Panel Report, para. 10.94).

[143]   *Supra*, para. 119.

[144]   Panel Report, footnote 374.

[145]   In paragraphs 10.57 and 10.58 of its Report, the Panel considered whether it was entitled to make findings with respect to products, including tequila, mescal and certain other alcoholic bever-

ond sentence, only with respect to products for which a *prima facie* case had been made out on the basis of evidence presented.[146] Second, it declined to establish a presumption concerning all alcoholic beverages within HS 2208.[147] Such a presumption would be inconsistent with the rules on the burden of proof because it would prematurely shift the burden of proof to the defending party. The Panel, therefore, did not consider alleged violations of Article III:2, second sentence, concerning products for which evidence was not presented.[148] Thus, the Panel examined tequila because evidence was presented for it, but did not examine mescal and certain other alcoholic beverages included in HS 2208 for which no evidence was presented. Third, contrary to Korea's assertions, the Panel did consider the evidence presented by Korea in rebuttal[149], but concluded that there was "sufficient *unrebutted* evidence" for it to make findings of inconsistency.[150] (emphasis added)

157.   It is, therefore, clear that the Panel did not err in its application of the rules on allocation of the burden of proof.

158.   We note, finally, that many of Korea's arguments concerning the burden of proof are, in reality, arguments about whether the Panel made an objective assessment of the matter before it. This is considered in the next section.

D.   Article 11 of the DSU

159.   Korea claims that the Panel failed to make an objective assessment of the matter before it and failed to apply the appropriate standard of review under Article 11 of the DSU. Korea contends that the Panel did not have sufficient evidence before it to enable it to conduct an objective assessment of the matter, and that, as regards the evidence that was, in fact, before it, the Panel made a series of "manifest and/or egregious errors of assessment".[151]

160.   In *European Communities - Hormones*, we stated:

> Under Article 17.6 of the DSU, appellate review is limited to appeals on questions of law covered in a panel report and legal interpretations developed by the panel. ... Determination of the credibility and weight properly to be ascribed to (that is, the appreciation of) a given piece of evidence is part and parcel of the fact finding process and is, in principle, left to the discretion of a panel as the trier of facts. The consistency or inconsistency of a given fact or set of facts with the require-

---

ages, for which "virtually no evidence" had been provided. In para. 10.82, the Panel assessed whether the complainants had satisfied the burden of proof with respect to end-uses.

[146]   Panel Report, para. 10.57. See also Panel Report, para. 10.82, where the Panel considered that, with respect to end-uses, "the complainants submitted adequate evidence ... to establish this portion of their case".

[147]   Panel Report, para. 10.57. HS 2208 is the category in Section IV, Chapter 22 of the Harmonised System of Customs Classification that applies to "Undenatured ethyl alcohol of an alcoholic strength by volume of less than 80% vol; spirits, liqueurs and other spiritous beverages".

[148]   Panel Report, paras. 10.57 and 10.58.

[149]   See, for example, Panel Report, paras. 10.71, 10.82 and 10.85.

[150]   Panel Report, para. 10.98.

[151]   Korea's appellant's submission, para. 84.

> ments of a given treaty provision is, however, a legal characterization issue. It is a legal question. Whether or not a panel has made an objective assessment of the facts before it, as required by Article 11 of the DSU, is also a legal question which, if properly raised on appeal, would fall within the scope of appellate review.[152]

161.   The Panel's examination and weighing of the evidence submitted fall, in principle, within the scope of the Panel's discretion as the trier of facts and, accordingly, outside the scope of appellate review. This is true, for instance, with respect to the Panel's treatment of the Dodwell Study, the Sofres Report and the Nielsen Study. We cannot second-guess the Panel in appreciating either the evidentiary value of such studies or the consequences, if any, of alleged defects in those studies. Similarly, it is not for us to review the relative weight ascribed to evidence on such matters as marketing studies, methods of production, taste, colour, places of consumption, consumption with "meals" or with "snacks", and prices.

162.   A panel's discretion as trier of facts is not, of course, unlimited. That discretion is always subject to, and is circumscribed by, among other things, the panel's duty to render an objective assessment of the matter before it. In *European Communities - Hormones*, we dealt with allegations that the panel had "disregarded", "distorted" and "misrepresented" the evidence before it. We held that these allegations amounted to charges that the panel had violated its duty under Article 11 of the DSU, allegations which, at the end of the day, we found to be unsubstantiated:

> ... Clearly, not every error in the appreciation of the evidence (although it may give rise to a question of law) may be characterized as a failure to make an objective assessment of the facts. ... The duty to make an objective assessment of the facts is, among other things, an obligation to consider the evidence presented to a panel and to make factual findings on the basis of that evidence. The deliberate disregard of, or refusal to consider, the evidence submitted to a panel is incompatible with a panel's duty to make an objective assessment of the facts. The wilful distortion or misrepresentation of the evidence put before a panel is similarly inconsistent with an objective assessment of the facts. "Disregard" and "distortion" and "misrepresentation" of the evidence, in their ordinary signification in judicial and quasi-judicial processes, imply not simply an error of judgment in the appreciation of evidence but rather an egregious error that calls into question the good faith of a panel. A claim that a panel disregarded or distorted the evidence submitted to it is, in effect, a claim that the panel, to a greater or lesser degree, denied the party submit-

---

[152]   *Supra*, footnote 47, para. 132.

> ting the evidence fundamental fairness, or what in many juris-
> dictions is known as due process of law or natural justice.[153]

163.   We have scrutinized with great care Korea's allegations that the Panel acted in breach of its duty under Article 11 of the DSU, especially Korea's contentions that the Panel applied a "double standard" in assessing the evidence before it: one standard, relaxed and permissive, for the complainants, and another, very strict and demanding, for the defending party, Korea. In our view, notwithstanding Korea's express disclaimer that it is not challenging the good faith of the Panel, an allegation of a "double standard" of proof in relation to the facts is equivalent to an allegation of failure to render an "objective assessment of the matter" under Article 11 of the DSU. In *European Communities - Poultry*, we observed:

> An allegation that a panel has failed to conduct the "objective
> assessment of the matter before it" required by Article 11 of
> the DSU is a *very serious allegation. Such an allegation goes
> to the very core of the integrity of the WTO dispute settlement
> process itself. ...* [154] (emphasis added)

164.   We are bound to conclude that Korea has not succeeded in showing that the Panel has committed any egregious errors that can be characterized as a failure to make an objective assessment of the matter before it. Korea's arguments, when read together with the Panel Report and the record of the Panel proceedings, do not disclose that the Panel has distorted, misrepresented or disregarded evidence, or has applied a "double standard" of proof in this case. It is not an error, let alone an egregious error, for the Panel to fail to accord the weight to the evidence that one of the parties believes should be accorded to it.

165.   In light of the above, we do not believe that the Panel has failed to make an objective assessment of the matter before it within the meaning of Article 11 of the DSU.

E.   Article 12.7 of the DSU

166.   Korea claims that the Panel has failed to fulfil its obligation under Article 12.7 of the DSU to set out the basic rationale behind its findings and recommendations. Korea maintains that "much" of the Panel Report contains contradictions and that it is vague.[155]

167.   Article 12.7 of the DSU reads, in relevant part:

> Where the parties to the dispute have failed to develop a mu-
> tually satisfactory solution, the panel shall submit its findings
> in the form of a written report to the DSB. *In such cases, the
> report of a panel shall set out the findings of fact, the appli-
> cability of relevant provisions and the basic rationale behind*

---

[153]   *Supra*, footnote 47, para. 133.

[154]   *Supra*, footnote 47, para. 133. This passage was cited in our Report in *Australia - Measures Affecting Importation of Salmon*, adopted 6 November 1998, WT/DS18/AB/R, para. 265.

[155]   Korea's appellant's submission, para. 172.

> *any findings and recommendations that it makes.* ... (empha-
> sis added)

168.   In this case, we do not consider it either necessary, or desirable, to attempt to define the scope of the obligation provided for in Article 12.7 of the DSU. It suffices to state that the Panel has set out a detailed and thorough rationale for its findings and recommendations in this case. The Panel went to some length to take account of competing considerations and to explain why, nonetheless, it made the findings and recommendations it did. The rationale set out by the Panel may not be one that Korea agrees with, but it is certainly more than adequate, on any view, to satisfy the requirements of Article 12.7 of the DSU. We, therefore, conclude that the Panel did not fail to set out the basic rationale for its findings and recommendations as required by Article 12.7 of the DSU.

V.   FINDINGS AND CONCLUSIONS

169.   For the reasons set out in this Report, the Appellate Body:

(a)   upholds the Panel's interpretation and application of the term "directly competitive or substitutable product" which appears in the *Ad* Article to Article III:2, second sentence, of the GATT 1994;

(b)   upholds the Panel's interpretation and application of the term "so as to afford protection", which is incorporated into Article III:2, second sentence, by specific reference to the "principles set forth in paragraph 1" of Article III of the GATT 1994;

(c)   upholds the Panel's application of the rules on the allocation of the burden of proof;

(d)   concludes that the Panel did not fail to make an objective assessment of the matter as required by Article 11 of the DSU; and

(e)   concludes that the Panel did not fail to set out the basic rationale behind its findings and recommendations as required by Article 12.7 of the DSU.

170.   The Appellate Body *recommends* that the Dispute Settlement Body request Korea to bring the Liquor Tax Law and the Education Tax Law into conformity with its obligations under the General Agreement on Tariffs and Trade 1994.

KOREA - TAXES ON ALCOHOLIC BEVERAGES

Report of the Panel
WT/DS75/R, WT/DS84/R

*Adopted by the Dispute Settlement Body on 17 February 1999
as upheld by the Appellate Body Report*

TABLE OF CONTENTS

I.   PROCEDURAL BACKGROUND

1.1.   This proceeding has been initiated by two complaining parties, the European Communities and the United States.

1.2.   On 2 April 1997, the European Communities requested consultations with Korea under Article XXII:1 of GATT and Article 4 of the Understanding on Rules and Procedures Governing the Settlement of Disputes ("DSU") (WT/DS75/1). The United States (WT/DS 75/2) and Canada 6(WT/DS75/3) requested to be joined in those consultations, pursuant to Article 4.11 of the DSU on 17 and 21 April 1997, respectively. Korea agreed to those requests (WT/DS75/4 and WT/DS75/5). Consultations between the European Communities and Korea were held in Geneva on 29 May 1997, in which the United States and Canada participated.

1.3.   On 23 May 1997, the United States requested consultations with Korea under Article XXII:1 of GATT and Article 4 of the DSU with respect to the same matter (WT/DS84/1). Canada (WT/DS84/2) and the European Communities (WT/DS84/3) requested to be joined in those consultations, pursuant to Article 4.11 of the DSU, on 29 May and 5 June 1997, respectively.

1.4.   Consultations were held in Geneva on 24 June 1997, between the United States and Korea, and the European Communities and Canada participated as third-parties. Another set of consultations were held on 8 August 1997, to address US requests for further clarifications, but the parties were unable to settle the dispute.

1.5.   On 10 September 1997, the European Communities (WT/DS75/6), and the United States (WT/DS84/4), each requested the establishment of a panel pursuant to Article 6.1 of the DSU.

1.6.   In its panel request, the European Communities claims that:

> Korea, by according a preferential tax treatment, through the Liquor Tax Law and the Education Tax Law, to soju vis-a-vis certain alcoholic beverages falling within HS heading 2208, has acted inconsistently with Article III:2 of GATT 1994, therefore nullifying or impairing the benefits accruing to the European Communities under the GATT 1994.

1.7.   In its panel request the United States claims that:

> Korea, under its general Liquor Tax Law, imposes a lower tax on the traditional Korean distilled spirit soju than the high taxes it applies to other distilled spirits such as whisky, brandy, vodka, rum, gin and "ad-mixtures". This difference in tax burden is made even more dramatic by the application of an Education Tax.

1.8.   The Dispute Settlement Body (DSB) agreed to these two requests for a panel at its meeting of 16 October 1997, establishing a single panel pursuant to Article 9.1 of the DSU with the following standard terms of reference:

> "To examine, in light of the relevant provisions of the covered agreements cited by the European Communities in document WT/DS75/6 and the United States in document WT/DS84/4, the matter referred to the DSB by the European Communities and the United States in those documents and to make such findings as will assist the DSB in making the recommendations or in giving the rulings provided for in those agreements".

1.9.   Canada and Mexico reserved their rights to participate in the Panel proceedings as third-parties.

1.10.   On 26 November 1997, the United States and the European Communities jointly requested the Director-General to determine the composition of the panel, pursuant to paragraph 7 of Article 8 of the DSU. On 5 December 1997, the Director-General composed the Panel as follows:

> Chairman: Mr. Åke Lindén
>
> Panelists: Professor Frédéric Jenny
>
> Mr. Carlos da Rocha Paranhos

1.11.   The Panel had substantive meetings with the parties on 5 and 6 March 1998, and on 21 and 22 April 1998.

II.   MEASURES IN ISSUE

2.1.   Korea maintains a multi-tiered taxation regime on the sale of alcoholic beverages. Under the Liquor Tax Law of 1949, as amended, Korea creates various categories of distilled spirits, on which it imposes different ad *valorem* taxes. Under the Education Tax Law of 1982, as amended, Korea assesses a surtax on certain of these sales, determined as a percentage of the established liquor tax.

2.2.   Both the liquor tax and the education tax on alcoholic beverages are imposed at the wholesale level. The tax is payable by the manufacturer of the beverages or, in the case of imports, by the importer. Tax liability accrues at the time of shipment from the factory (in the case of alcoholic beverages made in Korea) or of withdrawal from the bonded warehouse (in the case of imported alcoholic beverages).

A.   *The Liquor Tax Law*

2.3.   The Liquor Tax Law lays down a system of excise taxes applicable to all alcoholic beverages (whether manufactured in Korea or imported) intended for consumption in Korea. The taxes applied to the categories in dispute are in the form of *ad valorem* taxes.

2.4.   For the purposes of assessing the tax, the value of imported alcoholic beverages includes transport and insurance costs as well as the import duty imposed. In other words, the tax base for imports is the price noted on the import declaration when the goods are withdrawn from the bonded warehouse (i.e., the CIF import value plus duty).[1]

2.5.   Domestic alcoholic beverages are taxed on the value of production costs, sales costs (including advertising), extraordinary costs, and profits, i.e., the tax base is the price of the goods when they are shipped from the production site.[2] The categories of distilled spirits established by the Liquor Tax Law, and the applicable tax rates, are described below.

1.   *Categories*

2.6.   Liquor Tax Law divides alcoholic beverages into eleven categories, some of which are further divided into sub-categories, and assigns to each of them a different tax rate. These categories include "soju," "whisky," "brandy," "general distilled liquors" (which covers beverages such as vodka, gin, rum and tequila), "liqueurs," and "other liquors" (to the extent that liquors falling within this category may contain distilled spirits or liqueurs falling within any of the preceding categories). Article 3 of the Liquor Tax Law sets forth definitions of these categories.[3]

---

[1]   Article 19.2 of the Liquor Tax Law.

[2]   Presidential Decree, Article 26.

[3]   A translation of the relevant provisions of Article 3 is provided as US Exhibit A.

(a)   Soju

2.7.   Article 3.6 has four sub-categories of soju. Sub-categories A and B apparently refer to "distilled soju," while sub-categories C and D apparently refer to "diluted soju."

2.8.   Article 3.6.A and 3.6.B states the legal definition of soju as:

    (a)   Soju may be produced from discontinuous distillation of a fermented mash developed from the basic constituents of a starch source, yeast and water.

    (b)   Soju may be produced from discontinuous distillation as in Paragraph A above, but during the fermentation and production process other ingredients may be added as determined by Presidential decree.

2.9.   Thus paragraphs (A) and (B) describe two "types" of soju: (i) soju created by fermentation and discontinuous distillation, but without additives; and (ii) soju created by fermentation and discontinuous distillation and containing additives.

2.10.   According to Article 3.6.A, distilled soju cannot

    (a)   be produced from sprouted grain;

    (b)   be filtered through charcoal of white birch; or

    (c)   be produced in a process whereby water is mixed with grain and the mash sealed for fermentation and subsequent distillations.

2.11.   The chapeau of Article 3.6 specifies that soju must have an extract content of 2% or less.

2.12.   The legal definition of diluted soju in Article 3.6.C and 3.6.D is as follows soju:

    (a)   Soju may be produced by diluting neutral spirits with water or by adding thereto those ingredients as determined by Presidential Decree;

    (b)   Soju may be produced by adding to the products produced in accord with paragraphs A through C immediately above the product of paragraph A, when determined by Presidential Decree, or other grain spirits as determined by Presidential Decree.

2.13.   The definition of diluted soju in 3.6.C and D relies on "neutral spirits," which is defined by Article 3.1 of the Liquor Tax Law as follows:

    (a)   Neutral spirits may be produced from the distillation of a fermented mash developed from the basic constituents of a starch source and a sugar source that results in a product that is 85 percent or more alcohol;

    (b)   Neutral spirits may be produced from the distillation of ingredients containing alcohol, resulting in a product that is 85 percent or more alcohol.

(b)   Whisky, brandy, and "general distilled liquors"

2.14.   Whisky, brandy and "general distilled liquors" are defined in Articles 3.7, 3.8 and 3.9, respectively. The definitions include a 2% extract limitation that distinguishes them from liqueurs. All three include fermentation and distillation as the manufacturing process. However, unlike the definition for soju, they generally specify starch sources.

2.15.   Article 3.7 of the Liquor Tax Law, the "whisky" category, includes all types of whisky made totally or partly from sprouted grain and aged in wooden casks, as well as, under certain conditions, admixtures of whisky and other spirits or ingredients.[4]

2.16.   Article 3.8, the "brandy" category, includes all liquors distilled from a fermented mash of fruit or fruit wine and aged in wooden casks. Subject to certain conditions, it includes also ad-mixtures of those liquors with other spirits or ingredients.[5]

2.17.   The category of "General Distilled Liquors" is a miscellaneous category comprising several kinds of distilled spirits. It consists of six paragraphs.

- Paragraph (A) specifies kaoliang-ju lees as a starch source, and the manufacturing process includes sealing prior to fermenting and distilling; it is designed to address *kaoliang-ju*, which can be imported from China.

- Paragraph (B) specifies sugar cane, sugar beet, sugar, and/or molasses as a starch source; it addresses *rum*.

- Paragraph (C) specifies "fruits of juniper tree" as an ingredient; it addresses *gin*.

- Paragraph (D) specifies filtering of the alcohol; it addresses *vodka*.

- Paragraph (E) merely concerns "materials mainly containing starch or sugar produced by fermentation and distillation." It covers *tequila* and any distilled spirit. Its wording is the same as that used in the first part of the definition of "neutral spirits".[6]

- Paragraph (F) addresses *mixed distilled drinks* (e.g., gin and rum mixed drinks).

(c)   Liqueurs

2.18.   Article 3.10, the "liqueurs" category, covers liquors with more than 2% extract content produced by distillation of a starch or sugar source to which ginseng juice, fruits or fruits extracts are added.[7]

2.19.   Article 3.11 sets forth the category of "other liquors," a residual category including all liquors (whether fermented or distilled) not falling within any of the

---

[4]   See Article 3.7 of the Liquor Tax Law. The whisky definition includes three subparagraphs. Paragraph (A) specifies only sprouted grains and thus addresses malt whisky. Paragraph (B) appears to broaden the starch source to normal grain as well as sprouted and thus addresses ordinary grain whisky. Both (A) and (B) provide for aging in wooden barrels and thus address premium brands of whisky. Paragraph (C) addresses premium blended whisky and/or whisky with sugars, acids, seasonings, fragrances, colouring, or carbon dioxide added.

[5]   See Article 3.8 of the Liquor Tax Law.

[6]   See Article 3.1 of the Liquor Tax Law.

[7]   See Article 3.10 of the Liquor Tax Law.

other categories defined by the Liquor Tax Law.[8] It includes *inter alia* admixtures of whisky and brandy.

2. *Tax Rates*

2.20. The Korean law imposes different *ad valorem* tax rates on the various categories and sub-categories of distilled spirits. Pursuant to the definitions, soju is given a tax rate of 35 to 50 percent, while other distilled alcoholic beverages are taxed at 80 to 100 percent. The applicable liquor tax rates are:[9]

Item	Ad Valorem Tax Rate (%)
Diluted soju	35
Distilled soju	50
Whisky	100
Brandy	100
General distilled liquors (vodka, gin, rum)	80
General distilled liquors containing whisky or brandy	100
Liqueur	50
Other liquors:	
- With 25% or more alcohol	80
- With less than 25% alcohol	70
- Which contain 20% or more whisky or brandy	100

B. *The Education Tax Law*

2.21. The Education Tax Law of 1990 is assessed as a surtax on the sale of a variety of items, including most alcoholic beverages. For alcoholic beverages, the applicable rate is determined by reference to another tax - the applied liquor tax rate.[10] For those assessed a liquor tax rate of 80% or greater, the law imposes an education surtax calculated as 30% of the liquor tax imposed.[11] For alcoholic beverages assessed a liquor tax rate of less than 80%, the law imposes an education surtax calculated as 10% of the liquor tax imposed.

2.22. This tax structure results in a 30% surtax for imported distilled alcoholic beverages, including whisky, brandy and general distilled liquors (vodka, rum, gin, tequila, shochu, etc.) except for imports of Japanese shochu, which are classified for tax purposes and taxed at 10%. Of all distilled alcoholic beverages, only soju and liqueurs are subject to the lesser 10% surtax. Prior to 1995, soju was exempted from

---

[8] See Article 3.11 of the Liquor Tax Law.

[9] The applicable tax rates are set forth in Article 19.2, and Korean Taxation: 1997, § 3(b) p. 188 (Korean Ministry of Finance and Economy).

[10] In addition to the liquor tax, other taxes upon which the Education Tax is levied include the Special Excise Tax, the Per Capita Inhabitant Tax, the Registration Tax, the Horse Race Tax, the Property Tax, the Aggregate Land Tax, the Tobacco Consumption Tax, the Automobile Tax and the Transportation Tax.

[11] Education Tax Law, Art. 5.

the Education Tax. However, after negotiations between Korea and the European Communities that Korea agreed to subject soju to the Education Tax at a rate of 10%.

2.23. The applicable rates on the categories concerned by this dispute, expressed as a percentage of the amount payable pursuant to the Liquor Tax, is as follows:

Tax rates applied pursuant to the Education Tax Law	
Product	As % Liquor Tax
Diluted soju	10
Distilled soju	10
Whisky	30
Brandy	30
General distilled liquors	30
General distilled liquors containing whisky or brandy	30
Liqueurs	10
Other Liquors:	
- more than 25% alcohol content	30
- less than 25% alcohol content	10
- containing whisky or brandy	30

III. FACTUAL ARGUMENTS

A. *European Communities*

3.1. The European Communities proceeds from the premise that in response to its reiterated requests, Korea has reluctantly acceded to make a number of changes to its liquor tax system which have reduced (but by no means eliminated) the difference between the internal taxes applied to soju and those applied to other categories of distilled liquors.

3.2. The European Communities states that as of 1 January 1991, Korea abolished the Customs Defence Tax, which until then had been applied only to imported liquors. It further states that on the same date, Korea also abolished the Liquor Defence Tax, which had been levied at a lower rate on soju than on other distilled spirits and liqueurs. Further, the European Communities states that Korea eliminated an uplift ratio of 1.0:1.1 (the so-called "times 1.1 multiplier") which had been applied in order to inflate artificially the import duty paid value on which the Liquor Tax is assessed in the case of imported beverages.

3.3. The European Communities adds that these amendments were followed by a reduction of the Liquor Tax rates on the category of "whisky" from 200% to 150%, and on the category of "general distilled liquors" from 100% to 80%, both effective from 1 July 1991. According to the European Communities, this decrease, however, was partially nullified by a simultaneous increase in the Education Tax rates, which were raised to 30% for most distilled liquors other than "soju". At the same time, the category of "soju" was divided into the sub-categories of "distilled soju" and "diluted soju" and the rate on "distilled soju" raised from 35% to 50%.

3.4. According to the European Communities, in June 1993, it reached an agreement with Korea (the "1993 Agreement") whereby Korea undertook to reduce progressively over a period of two years the liquor tax rate applicable to the "whisky" and "brandy" categories from 150% to 100%. The European Communities asserts that Korea further agreed to levy the Education Tax on both sub-categories of soju (which had until then been exempt from such tax) at a rate of 10% as from 1 January 1994[12] and to increase the tax on admixtures containing whisky or brandy (which are mainly bottled in Korea) from 80% to 100%.

3.5.   The European Communities further asserts that the 1993 Agreement envisaged that a new round of consultations would take place in 1996 in order to discuss further reductions of the remaining tax differences. According to the European Communities, as compensation for the continued application in the meantime of much lower taxes to soju, Korea agreed to further reduce the effectively applied import duties on whisky, brandy other than wine brandy (which already benefited from a 15% applied rate), rum, gin, vodka and liqueurs (but not on soju) from 30% to 20%.

3.6.   The European Communities allege that the consultations provided for by the 1993 Agreement eventually took place in January 1997. Nevertheless, according to the European Communities, Korea did not meet the EC's request to eliminate the remaining tax differentials so as to bring its liquor tax system in conformity with the GATT.

The Korean market for distilled liquors

3.7.   The European Communities states that the Korean market for distilled spirits and liqueurs was virtually closed to imports until the late eighties. According to the EC's argument, until 1 January 1989, imports of distilled spirits in bulk were subject to quotas, whereas imports of distilled spirits in bottles were prohibited until 1 July 1989, and thereafter subject to quantitative restrictions until 1 January 1990.

3.8.   The European Communities further argues that, Korea applied prohibitively high import duties: 150% until 1984; 100% until 1988; and 50 % until 1991. According to the European Communities, until March 1990 Korea applied an import deposit requirement. The EC's position is that, currently the applied import duty rate is 20% for all distilled spirits and liqueurs, except brandy (which is subject to a 15% import duty) and soju (which is subject to a 30% import duty).[13]

3.9.   The European Communities further argues that, following the elimination of the import quotas and a substantial reduction of import duties and internal taxes, imports of distilled spirits and liqueurs have grown steadily but still represent only around 3.5% of the market. According to the European Communities, this share is unusually low. The European Communities is of the view that in most other OECD countries the share of imported sprits is between 30% and 40% of the market for distilled liquor. By comparison, the European Communities states that in Japan the share of imported spirits was 8% in 1995, despite the fact that at that time Japan applied a system of discriminatory internal taxes similar to the one in dispute.

3.10.   According to the European Communities, the Korean spirits market is overwhelmingly dominated by soju. In 1996 sales of soju amounted to 90 million 9L

---

[12]   The EC claims that Korea did not implement this commitment until 1 January 1995.

[13]   A table summarising the recent evolution of the tariff treatment of the products concerned by this dispute is included in EC Annex 4.

cases (810 million litres), which represents as much as 94% of the distilled spirits market.[14] Soju's position, however, is allegedly being eroded by growing sales of imported spirits and liqueurs, and in particular of whisky. Over the past few years, sales of soju have allegedly increased at a lower pace than the total spirits market (between 1993 and 1994 sales of soju even decreased in absolute terms). As a result, the market share of soju fell from 96.37 % in 1992 to 94.39 % in 1996.[15]

3.11.   The European Communities states that imports of soju are insignificant. In 1997, Korea allegedly imported just 1,625 litres.[16] In contrast, argues the European Communities, Korea exports large quantities of soju. The European Communities further asserts that during the first eleven months of 1996, exports of soju totalled 43 million litres of soju, which represents about 5% of the Korean soju production. According to the European Communities, the main export market is Japan, where soju is considered for customs and tax purposes as being the same product as local "shochu".

3.12.   The European Communities further asserts that almost all soju sold in Korea is diluted soju. Distilled soju is estimated to account for just over 1% of the total sales of soju. While diluted soju is generally an inexpensive liquor, distilled soju may fetch very high prices, similar to those paid for imported premium brands of whisky.

3.13.   The European Communities argues that, confronted with growing sales of western-style liquors, the manufacturers of diluted soju have been forced to address what are generally perceived by Korean consumers as negative attributes of that liquor as compared with the "western style" distilled liquors: inferior quality, harsh taste, hangover effects.

3.14.   According to the European Communities, this has led to the emergence of new so-called "premium soju" brands, whose distinctive characteristics are a milder taste, the use of flavouring (e.g. with honey) and/or ageing processes, and more so-phisticated packaging. The European Communities asserts that the prices for pre-mium soju brands are between two and three times higher than those for standard diluted soju. According to the European Communities, in spite of that, sales of pre-mium soju are growing very rapidly. By EC estimates, in 1996 they represented 6% of soju sales and reached 10% in 1997.

3.15.   The European Communities points out that whisky is the largest category of distilled spirits after soju. Sales of whisky allegedly increased from 11 million litres in 1992 to 27 millions in 1996, i.e. by almost 140%. As a result, the European Communities argues that the share of whisky rose from 1.53% in 1992 to 3.14% in 1996. According to the European Communities, one of the main reasons for this increase is the progressive reduction in the applicable liquor tax rate from 200% in 1990 to 100% in 1996. The European Communities further argues that Scotch whisky imported from the European Communities, whether in bottles or in bulk, accounts for virtually all of the sales within this tax category.

---

[14]   EC Annex 5.

[15]   EC Annex 6.

[16]   EC Annex 7.

3.16.   The European Communities further argues that the category of brandy is still very small but growing rapidly. The increase has allegedly been particularly remarkable in the case of cognac, which went up from just 13,000 litres in 1992 to 193,000 litres in 1996. As in the case of whisky, the argument goes, this increase is in part due to the progressive reduction of the Liquor Tax rate from 150% in 1990 to 100% in 1996. Almost all brandy sold in Korea is imported, whether in bottles or in bulk.

3.17.   According to the European Communities, the category of "General Distilled Liquors" is also very small. In the EC view, unlike sales of whisky and brandy, sales of liquors falling within this category have stagnated and in some cases even declined. One of the reasons for this, according to the European Communities is that, unlike whisky and brandy, this category has benefited only from a marginal reduction of taxes. The European Communities alleges that. Although the liquor tax rate on this category was lowered from 100% to 80% as from 1 July 1991, this reduction was almost totally offset by a simultaneous increase of the applicable Education tax rate from 10% to 30%.[17] A significant proportion of sales within this category is imported. According to estimates of the EC industry, imports would represent approximately 20% of the sales of gin, 50% of the sales of rum and 70% of the sales of vodka.

3.18.   The European Communities further alleges that pre-mixes of distilled liquors and non-alcoholic beverages account for a major portion of sales (95% according to the estimates of the EC industry) within the category of "liqueurs". According to this argument, soju-based cocktails (e.g. lemon flavoured soju, cherry flavoured soju) account for the vast majority of the sales of pre-mixes. The EC view is that soju cocktails are a relatively new product targeted at the young generation and enjoy considerable success. According to the European Communities, during 1995 alone, sales of soju cocktails increased by 1250%. There are no imports of soju cocktails.

3.19.   In contrast, the European Communities argues that it may be estimated that as much as 90% of the sales of "authentic" or "single item" liqueurs are imported. Sales of this type of "liqueurs" have been growing off a small base at 15-20% every year and are currently estimated to represent 300,000 litres out of total market for liqueurs of 13.5 million litres.

3.20.   The European Communities further argues that although no official sales figures have been made available by the Korean Government, the EC industry estimates that while sales of whisky and other imported liquors declined during 1997, sales of soju would have increased. As a result, the European Communities argues, soju may have regained its lost share of the market. This new development is the result of extraordinary circumstances.

3.21.   According to the European Communities, in the first place, the depreciation of the Korean won, which has made imported liquors more expensive[18]. To this, states the European Communities, it must be added the effects of the boycotts against imported products orchestrated by civic groups and by business associations such as the Central Council of Korean Night-spots' Operators during the first

---

[17]   EC Annex 2.

[18]   The average monthly exchange rate between the Korean Won and the ECU fell from 1028.35 Wons to an ECU in January 1997 to 1616.28 wons in December 1997, i.e. by almost 60 %.

months of 1997. Finally, according to the European Communities, the financial crisis which broke in October of last year, and the ensuing slow down in the Korean economy has made consumers much more price conscious and further depressed the sales of imported liquors to the benefit of the less taxed and less expensive soju.

3.22.   The European Communities argues that western-style liquors used to be perceived by Korean consumers as "luxury" items. According to the European Communities, at present the prices for western-style liquors remain much higher than the prices for diluted soju. Nevertheless, according to the European Communities, following the lifting of the import quotas and the lowering of import duties and liquor taxes, there has been a clear trend towards lower consumer prices, broader availability in all sales channels and consumption patterns which are more similar to those of soju.

3.23.   The European Communities concludes that the remaining tax differentials stand as an obstacle to that trend and hinder further competition between soju and imported western-style distilled spirits and liqueurs.

B.   United States

3.24.   From the US perspective, the products concerned by this dispute are soju, a locally produced distilled liquor, on the one hand, and imported distilled spirits classified under the Harmonized System (HS) heading 2208, on the other hand,[19] including spirits such as vodka, whisky, gin, rum, brandy and liqueurs. Exports in 1996 of U.S. distilled spirits to Korea were allegedly only $1.8 million compared to an average export level in recent years of $90 million to Japan.

3.25.   The United States alleges that the current tax system and the state of the Korean market grows out of many years of protecting soju. It claims that although Korea has dismantled some of its trade barriers to imports over the last ten years (an effort that has produced inroads for imported spirits in the Korean market), Korea retains two tax laws that categorizes liquor products arbitrarily, and imposes corresponding discriminatory tax rates.

3.26.   The United States further alleges that Korea's current tariff and tax regime governing the sale of alcoholic beverages has grown out of a historically restrictive market for alcoholic beverages that has shaped the Korean market as it stands today.

3.27.   The United States asserts that after 1949, high tariffs, quotas and other measures were used by the Korean government to discourage the importation of distilled alcoholic beverages and conserve the country's foreign exchange reserves. It cites, for example, that in the 1970's Korea assessed a duty of 150% C.I.F. on whisky imports. Until January 1989, Korea maintained quota restrictions on bulk imports of whisky, and it prohibited the importation of bottled whisky until July 1989. Importers were required to pay a deposit on the value of their imports, and the government permitted only twelve licensed importers until 1989.

---

[19]   Undenatured ethyl alcohol of an alcoholic strength by volume of less than 80 percent vol.; spirits, liqueurs and other spirituous beverages; compound alcoholic preparations of a kind used for the manufacture of beverages.

3.28.   The United States further alleges that in the 1980's, Korea began to liberalize these barriers to distilled spirits imports by reducing applied rates on whisky. In 1982, the government reduced the rate of duty imposed on whisky from 150% to 100% for products certified for use in tourist hotels. In 1984, the government extended this rate reduction to all whisky imports regardless of destination. In 1988 the customs duty was further cut to 50%, where it remained until a reduction to 40% in 1991, followed by 30% in 1993. In 1996, Korea applied a tariff rate of 20% on whisky. Korea's WTO bound rate, as a result of negotiations during the Uruguay Round, descends from a base of 100% in 1995 to a final rate of 30% in 2004 in equal annual instalments.

3.29.   The United States also alleges that, following pressure from the European Communities, Korea has also recently dismantled a number of its non-tariff barriers against distilled alcoholic beverages. In 1988, Korea eliminated the import deposit requirements for small and medium sized importers. In 1989, it reduced this deposit for large importers from 10% to 5%; increased the number of licensed importers from 12 to 25; lifted quota restrictions on the import of bulk whisky; and permitted the import of whisky bottled abroad for the first time, albeit subject to a quota. In 1990, the government removed this quota, abolished the import deposit requirement for large importers, and removed government limitations on the number of licensed importers. In 1991, Korea allowed foreign investment in the importation and distribution of spirits.

3.30.   The thrust of the US case is that concurrent with these tariff and non-tariff measures, Korea maintained a discriminatory system of internal taxes weighted against imported alcoholic beverages. According to the United States, after World War II, taxes on whisky and beer provided the government with a steady and easily collected form of revenue. However, in the face of increasing pressure, especially from the EC, Korea enacted a series of tax reductions on some imported distilled alcoholic beverages. Korea allegedly decreased the liquor tax rate on whisky and brandy from 200% to 150% in July 1991, 120% in January 1994, and 100% in January 1996.

The current Korean market for distilled liquors

3.31.   The United States submits that the Korean market for distilled alcoholic beverages, valued at approximately 2 trillion won in 1989, has been one of the largest in Northeast Asia. However, the United States adds that the Korean market for distilled spirits and liqueurs was virtually closed to imports until the late eighties. Until 1 January 1989, imports of distilled spirits in bulk were subject to quotas, and imports of distilled spirits in bottles were prohibited and thereafter subject to quantitative restrictions until 1 January 1990. Applied tariffs were prohibitive until 1991. Currently, the applicable import duty is 20% for all distilled spirits and liqueurs, except brandy (which is subject to a 15% import duty) and soju (which is subject to a 30% import duty).

3.32.   The United States argues that in light of this background, the Korean market for alcoholic beverages has been dominated by traditional beverages, such as soju, with a relatively low alcohol content (25%) and bottled for mass consumption. In 1996 sales of soju amounted to 89.825 million nine-litre cases (i.e., 808 million litres), which represents as much as 94% of the distilled spirits market.

3.33.   The United States further argues that imports of soju into Korea are insignificant. Last year Korea allegedly imported less than 2000 (1,625) litres. However, Korea exports large quantities of soju. During the first eleven months of 1996, exports of soju totalled 43 million litres, which represents about 5% of Korean soju production. The main export market is alleged to be Japan.

3.34.   According to the United States, almost all soju sold in Korea is diluted soju. Distilled soju is estimated to account for less than 1% of the total sales of soju. The United States claims that although diluted soju is generally inexpensive, distilled soju can fetch very high prices, similar to those paid for imported premium brands of whisky.

3.35.   The United States asserts that in the last ten years, the Korean government's relaxation of several import barriers has increased the competitiveness of the domestic market for alcoholic beverages, even though the retail prices for Western-style liquors remain much higher than the prices for diluted soju.

3.36.   The United States argues that manufacturers of soju have addressed what are generally perceived by Korean consumers as its negative attributes compared with the imported liquors: poor quality, bad flavour, hangover effects, etc. This has led to the emergence of a new segment of so-called "premium soju" brands, whose distinctive characteristics are a milder taste, the use of flavouring (e.g., with honey), and/or ageing processes and more sophisticated bottle designs. The prices for premium diluted soju brands are between two and three times higher than those for standard diluted soju. It is estimated that sales of premium soju represented 6% of soju sales in 1996 and probably reached 10% in 1997.

3.37.   The United States further argues that in addition to developing new types of soju for consumption in Korea, soju makers have also begun to exploit the export market for soju. Exports have risen dramatically in the last few years.

3.38.   According to the United States, Korean consumption of whisky has increased by about 30% annually since 1994. Between 1992 and 1996, the Korean market for whisky increased from 315 million won to 880 million won. Moreover, whisky bottled abroad makes up an increasing share of this market, growing from 1.7% of this market in 1992 to 46.7% of the market in 1996.

3.39.   However, the United States adds that although imports of distilled spirits have grown steadily, they still represent only around 3.5% of the Korean market. In most other OECD countries, the share of imported spirits is allegedly between 30% and 40%.

C.   Korea

3.40.   According to Korea, the complainants spend considerable time arguing that Korea has a history of protecting its soju industry. Korea states that no case has been brought against it for these alleged violations. In Korea's view, therefore, these allegations are irrelevant to the case at hand, and they should be disregarded.

3.41.   Korea also notes that in the same way that the complainants wish to gloss over the differences between the Korean and Japanese markets, they also wish to gloss over the characteristics of the Korean market and products that do not fit their line of argument. Korea notes for example, that the complainants treat 'soju' as one product. According to Korea, however, Korean distilled soju is very different from what the complainants refer to as 'diluted' soju. In Korea's view, the latter is certainly not a 'dilution' of the former.

3.42.   Korea further argues that no Korean producer or consumer would consider distilled and diluted soju to be substitutes. Korea further states that although the complainants mention the existence of important differences between a 'diluted' soju and 'distilled' soju, the complainants dismiss these differences by saying that distilled soju occupies less than 1% of the soju market.

3.43.   Korea argues that, having so dismissed distilled soju, the complainants proceed to use examples drawn from the exceptions in order to support general statements about all soju.

3.44.   According to Korea, this dispute is about 'diluted' soju, ('standard' soju),[20] which represents more than 99% of all 'soju' sold in Korea. Further, according to Korea, the question in this case is whether Korea's system of taxing distilled beverages discriminates against imported distilled alcoholic beverages, to the advantage of standard soju. Of those western-type liquors, Korea argues that the Panel must be cognisant that whisky is by far the most important, representing the greatest proportion of all the imported distilled beverages.

3.45.   Korea seeks to show that its system for the taxation of alcoholic beverages is not discriminatory, because the products at issue in this case are simply not in competition. According to Korea, the United States and the European Communities try to establish that competitive relationship by making generalizations such as "all are drunk with the same purposes: thirst-quenching, socialization", that they are made from the oxymoronic "same large variety of raw materials", by drawing specific examples from clearly exceptional cases, or - their last resort- by arguing that the products are in 'potential' competition with each other.

3.46.   Korea gives a general background about alcoholic drinks. Korea states that if one travels around the world, one will encounter a seemingly infinite variety of alcoholic beverages, many having a long and interesting history. Korea further argues that throughout the ages, virtually every culture in the world discovered that the natural process of decomposition of certain raw materials, typically fruits and vegetables, led to sometimes tasty results. Over time, through trial and error, the process of creating certain alcoholic beverages has become increasingly refined.

1.   Features of Distilled Alcoholic Beverages

3.47.   Korea states that within the broad category of alcoholic beverages, one can distinguish distilled beverages. According to Korea, to make a distilled alcohol, one first starts with fermented raw material. That fermented matter is put through a proc-

---

[20]   There is a disagreement between the complainants and Korea on whether to use the term diluted soju or standard soju. For purposes of clarity, we adopt the term diluted soju. Within the category of diluted soju are two sub-categories of premium diluted soju and standard diluted soju. No substantive determination is implied by this decision regarding terminology. We also note that this appears to be the terminology used by the Korean Fair Trade Commission in the decision submitted by Korea (Attachment 1 to Korea's first submission).

ess of refinement and concentration, called distillation.[21] Beverages that have been distilled are generally referred to as 'spirits', and spirits are the products at issue in this case.

3.48.   Korea further states that distilled liquors can be derived from materials as varied as grain, corn, rice, fruit, sugar cane or beets, potatoes, or tapioca. Korea asserts that the selection of raw materials for the manufacture of distilled alcoholic beverages may be traced to different geographical, cultural and consumer requirements and can play an important role in determining the ultimate qualities of the finished product.

3.49.   Korea notes that another distinction is sometimes drawn between 'brown' and 'white' spirits. According to Korea, this distinction refers to the production process and appearance of the beverages: brown spirits are brown (e.g., whisky or cognac); white spirits are clear (e.g., Korean soju or gin). Korea further states that brown spirits are generally matured in wooden casks and derive their flavour mainly from this process and from the original distilled ingredients. White spirits are not aged before bottling and instead rely on the addition of ingredients during the distillation process, or afterwards, to provide their distinctive flavour. These ingredients differ from one drink to another (e.g., gin derives its special flavour from the juniper berry).

2.   *Consumer Behaviour*

3.50.   Korea argues that consumer preferences for alcoholic beverages vary from country to country. Certain countries have their own national drink. For instance, argues Korea, in France, wine is the national drink, in Germany it is beer, and in Japan it is sake. Korea adds that some national drinks are virtually unknown in other countries. According to Korea, this is the case for Korean soju, which is hardly known outside Northeast Asia and Korean communities abroad.

3.51.   Korea further argues that these national drinks reflect the different cultures and traditions of the various countries. In addition, argues Korea, the climate, food and history of a country also determine the customs of its people and the way they drink alcoholic beverages. Thus, according to Korea, in hot countries one drinks certain alcoholic beverages to quench one's thirst, while in cold countries one drinks certain alcoholic beverages to keep warm. In other countries people drink particular alcoholic beverages for mere entertainment purposes, i.e., in bars, night clubs or posh hotels. In other countries one drinks particular alcoholic beverages as an accompaniment to a meal.

3.52.   Korea further asserts that in France, for instance, it is common to drink wine over a meal. In Korea's view, this is because the nuanced flavour of wine complements the food French people eat. However, with spicy food one is unlikely to order a beverage such as wine, because such food would overwhelm wine's subtle flavours. In Korea, the argument goes, Koreans drink soju with their spicy food. Soju

---

[21]   Distillation is defined in Webster's dictionary as 'a process that consists of driving gas or vapour from liquids or solids by heating and condensing to liquid products. . .'

goes well with Korean barbecue and other Korean meals, because the drink's harshness cuts the spiciness of the food.

3.53.   Korea further argues that people can also drink alcoholic beverages either mixed, on the rocks or straight, cold or hot or a combination of both. According to Korea, soju is never drunk mixed, whereas whisky, vodka and Japanese shochu are drinks which commonly are drunk both straight and mixed.

3.   Price

3.54.   Korea further argues that alcoholic beverages can vary widely in price. Korea gives as an example, a bottle of bordeaux which has allegedly been known to fetch thousands of dollars at auction, while a bottle of potato-based alcohol can be very cheap. In Korea's view, one of the factors affecting the price of an alcoholic beverage is the type of raw materials used to produce it. Additional manufacturing processes, such as ageing, increase the value and price of a product, partly because only a selected portion of the product is suitable for ageing. Prices will also be affected by distribution costs and margins, product image, consumer demand, etc.

4.   *Korean Soju*

3.55.   Korea notes that despite their similarity in names, a sharp distinction must be drawn between 'diluted' or 'standard' soju on the one hand, and distilled soju on the other hand. Standard soju is *not* a diluted form of distilled soju.[22]

3.56.   According to Korea, standard soju is a very common beverage, and millions of litres are sold each year.[23] Korea asserts that it is made from cheap raw materials: joojung (ethyl alcohol), which is drawn from fermented sweet potatoes, tapioca or corn and distilled so as to obtain as pure an alcohol as possible. To make standard soju, that alcohol (joojung) is not further distilled, but is diluted with water, and six to seven additives are added.[24] Korea adds no further ageing or colouring is permitted by law. Korea asserts that this drink has a relatively low alcoholic strength for a spirit: 25%.

3.57.   Korea further argues that another unusual characteristic of standard soju is that, unlike other spirits, it is commonly consumed with meals. This is also recognized outside Korea, in areas with important Korean communities. Korea cites as an

---

[22]   Korea asserts that the word 'soju' is a term which has become generic.

[23]   The exact figure for standard soju taxed volume in 1996 is 787 195 kl. (Sources: National Tax Administration, Statistical Yearbook of National Tax 1996 (1997); Customs Administration & Korean Traders Association, *Statistical Yearbook of Trade 1996* (1997)). The exact figure for standard soju taxed volume in 1997 is 814 159 kl. (Source: National Tax Administration, not yet published.)

[24]   Sugar, citric acid, amino acid, solbitol, mineral salt, stevioside, and aspartame. These additives all serve a particular purpose to enhance the taste of soju , i.e., sugar, to make it sweet; citric acid, to give soju a sour taste; amino acid, to enhance its flavour and act as a sweetener, adding a seaweed-like taste; solbitol, a form of sweetener which has a thick sweet taste; mineral salt, which acts as a catalyst to bring a change of taste to all the additives; stevioside, which has strong light sweet taste 150 to 300 times sweeter than sugar; and aspartame (nutrasweet), which is a chemical flavour enhancement 200 times sweeter than sugar.

example Santa Clara, California, where Korean restaurants that only have a license to sell low alcohol drinks are permitted a special exemption to sell standard soju as well. According to Korea, this is a recognition of the fact that it is customary for Koreans to drink a distilled beverage (of 25% alcohol content) with their meals.[25]

3.58.   Korea argues that distilled soju, on the other hand, is an artisanal product,[26] sold in tiny quantities (0.2% of the volume of standard soju).[27] According to Korea, distilled soju is usually made from grain or rice.[28] Korea states that the production process is quite sophisticated, no additives are added. By law, argues Korea, distilled soju can be aged for up to two years prior to sale. Korea also asserts that the alcoholic strength of distilled soju is 40% to 45%, which is considerably stronger than standard soju. Korea also argues that moreover, distilled soju has a distinct taste, which is smoother than standard soju. Distilled soju is 10 to 20 times more expensive than standard soju, pre-tax, and is packaged in special ceramic bottles, and is often offered as a gift.

3.59.   Korea states that it should be noted that the Korean liquor tax law classifies standard soju and distilled soju separately and attaches a different tax rate to each, 35% and 50% respectively. Korea also notes that while the United States acknowledges that standard soju and distilled soju have the same rate of Education Tax (10%), it fails to mention that the liquor tax on distilled soju is 50%, while the liquor tax on standard soju is 35%. Korea also notes that another mistaken attempt at trivializing the distinctions between distilled and standard soju is the EC assertion that the distinction in the tax law was introduced only in 1991, and that this was in response to pressure from the European Communities. According to Korea, the distinction was made as early as 1962.

3.60.   Korea notes that in recent years certain "up-market" varieties of standard soju have been introduced, which are commonly referred to as 'premium' soju. The composition of "premium" is slightly different from standard soju, giving the drink a somewhat milder taste.[29] The producers charge a higher price for this variety, up to twice the price for standard soju before tax. According to Korea, to justify this higher price, they sometimes make exaggerated claims.

---

[25]   According to Korea, 'Today, soju and a platter of barbecued meat are as inseparable in South Korea as beer and hot dogs or margheritas and chips in the United States', San Jose Mercury News, http://infi.net/global/cgi-bin/sj/slwebcli_post.pl.

[26]   The artisans who make distilled soju are recognised as 'Human Treasures' by Korean Governmental Decree. Their skill is recognised as an 'Intangible Cultural Asset'. One such example (Moon Bae-Sool) is shown in US Exhibit D.

[27]   The exact figure for distilled soju consumption in 1996 is 1325 kl. Source: National Tax Administration, Statistical Yearbook of National Tax 1996 (1997).

[28]   The complainants state that distilled soju is made of potato or grain. Korea claims that in reality potatoes are not used. The leading brands of distilled soju (Moon Bae-Sool and Andong Soju) are made from grain or rice.

[29]   For instance, in the leading brand of 'premium' soju, Kimsatgat, honey replaces stevioside as one of the seven additives.

3.61.   Korea also argues that the complainants focus on these claims to draw infer-ences for the entire soju market,[30] or even to question the credibility of information Korea gave during the consultations which took place prior to this Panel proceeding, implying that Korea drew a false distinction between distilled and standard soju.[31] In Korea's view, the reality is, however, that premium soju is no more than an upgraded commodity. It is classified as standard soju in the liquor tax law. Premium soju only represented 4.46% of standard soju sales in 1996 and 5.39% in 1997.[32]

5.   Changes since 1990

3.62.   Korea asserts that there is a strong undertone in the complainants' submis-sions that there has always been something wrong with Korea's liquor and education taxes, and under pressure from the EC and the US, Korea finally came to recognize this. Korea further states that the complainants suggest that the changes Korea intro-duced since 1990 came too slowly, and ultimately did not remove the illegal nature of the taxes.

3.63.   According to Korea, the European Communities and the United States have indeed gone to great lengths to influence Korea's domestic policies in the recent past. Korea submits that in the interest of avoiding friction with important trading partners and allies, Korea has tried to accommodate US and EC demands by fore-going tax revenue. In Korea's view, this was not an admission of fault.

3.64.   Korea notes that the European Communities alleges that decreases in Ko-rea's liquor tax were 'almost totally offset by a simultaneous increase of the applica-ble education tax rate'.[33] According to Korea, the European Communities should have also mentioned that at the time that the education tax was increased from 10% to 30%, the defence tax (30%) was repealed. Thus, in Korea's view, there was an overall reduction in the applicable tax rate.

3.65.   Korea presents the following table that purports to show the reduced tax burden on whisky since 1991:

(in %)	Whisky liquor tax	Education tax	Defence tax	Combined surtax burden	Combined tax burden

---

[30]   To illustrate, the 15 pages of advertisements included in the EC first submission only include two advertisements for standard soju (about 95% of the soju market), all the rest being advertise-ments for premium soju (4 to 5% of the soju market).

[31]   According to Korea, the EC, in support of this suggestion, cited advertisements for a standard soju brand which claimed that this soju was aged. However, the Korean Fair Trade Commission, in a decision of 30 November 1996, found that this claim constituted false advertising. The decision is reproduced in Attachment 1.

[32]   According to Korea, in 1996, total taxed volume of premium soju was 35 108 kl (including the leading brands 'Chamnamoo' produced by Jinro, 'Kimsatgat' produced by Bohae and 'Chungsanri' produced by Kyoungwoul). In 1997, total taxed volume was 43 873 kl (including the same brands). (Source: National Tax Administration). The EC and US estimate, unsubstantiated, that premium soju sales represented 6% of total soju sales in 1996 and increased to 10% in 1997 is therefore incorrect. (See EC first submission at para. 54 and US first submission at para. 41.) Note that the total taxed volume of standard soju was 787 195 kl in 1996 and 814 159 kl in 1997.

[33]   EC first submission, para. 57.

Before 1991	200	10	30	80	280
Before 1994	150	30	-	45	195
Before 1996	120	30	-	36	156
Since 1996	100	30	-	30	130

IV.   CLAIMS OF THE PARTIES

4.1.   The European Communities claims that:

(i)   Korea is in breach of its obligations under GATT Article III:2, first sentence, by applying internal taxes on imported vodka pursuant to the Liquor Tax Law and the Education Tax which are in excess of those applied on soju; and

(ii)   Korea is in breach of its obligations under Article III:2, second sentence, by applying higher internal taxes pursuant to the Liquor Tax Law and the Education Tax Law on imported liquors falling within the categories of 'whisky', 'brandy', 'general distilled liquors, 'liqueurs', and 'other liquors' (to the extent that they contain other distilled spirits or liqueurs) than on soju, so as to afford protection to its domestic production of soju.

4.2.   The United States claims that the Korean laws outlined above differentiate among distilled spirits on the basis of arbitrary characteristics, resulting in great disparities in the treatment of soju and imported distilled spirits. According to the United States, at the very minimum:

(i)   Korea's application of internal taxes on vodka that exceed taxes applied to soju is inconsistent with the first sentence of GATT Article III:2; and

(ii)   Korea's application of higher internal taxes to imported distilled spirits classified under HS heading 2208 falling within its legal categories of "whisky," "brandy," "general distilled liquors," "liqueurs" and "other liquors" (to the extent that they contain other distilled spirits) afford protection to its domestic production of soju, inconsistent with the second sentence of Article III:2.

V.   LEGAL ARGUMENTS

A.   *Preliminary Issues*

1.   *General*

5.1.   The complainants argue that Korea's request for preliminary rulings was not properly formulated and it was unclear what provisions of the WTO Agreement, if any, Korea considers to have been violated by the complainants, and that it was also unclear what precisely is the issue being addressed by Korea to the Panel.

5.2.   According to the European Communities, it is unclear whether Korea is asking the Panel to find that the European Communities has violated certain procedural provisions of the DSU, or whether it is asking the Panel to dismiss the complaint because certain procedural pre-requisites were not fulfilled, or whether it is asking the Panel to discharge itself.

5.3.   The United States was of the view was that given the scarce information provided by Korea in Korea's oral statement (which formed the basis of its request for preliminary rulings) it considers that any preliminary ruling by the Panel would not be warranted. The United States adds that to the extent the request for a preliminary ruling warrants any attention, it may be addressed in the Final Panel report.

2.   *Specificity of the Panel Requests*

5.4.   Korea takes issue with the specificity of the requests for a panel made by both the European Communities and the Unites States.

5.5.   Korea notes that the European Communities, in its request for a panel, has referred to a preferential tax rate on 'soju' vis-a-vis 'certain' alcoholic beverages falling within HS heading 2208. Korea states that the European Communities has not clarified its position even in its written submission. Korea further notes that the European Communities claim that 'all other distilled spirits and liqueurs' other than 'soju' falling within HS 2208 are within the purview of this dispute.

5.6.   Korea states that the US' request for a panel lacks specificity as well. Korea notes that the United States, in its request for a panel, refers to higher tax rates on 'other distilled spirits', while specifically mentioning 'whisky, brandy, vodka, rum, gin, and ad mixtures'. Korea further notes that the United States, in its first submission, seeks to broaden the dispute to all distilled spirits, other than soju, that are classified under HS 2208.

5.7.   Korea argues that such vaguely worded complaints violate its rights of defence. According to Korea, HS 2208 is a very broad tariff classification, which covers a wide variety of alcoholic beverages, including non-western liquors such as koryangu, Korean soju, Insam ju, Ogapiju, and Japanese shochu. Korea notes that it is surprising that both complainants refer to 'western-style liquors', yet HS 2208 also includes non-'western-style liquors'.

5.8.   Korea argues that this lack of specificity of the complainants' claims is improper for two reasons -

    (i)   it frustrates Korea's right of defense, which is a general principle of due process implicit in the DSU; and

    (ii)   it violates a clear obligation of the DSU, which is that such a request should 'identify' the specific measures at issue, and 'present the problem clearly', as stipulated in Article 6.

5.9.   Korea, therefore, requests the panel to issue a preliminary ruling, limiting the products at issue in this dispute. Korea submits that the only imported liquors whose tax rates are to be compared with the tax rate on the domestic soju products are: whisky, brandy, vodka, gin, and rum. According to Korea, these are the liquors identified specifically by the United States in its request for a panel In Korea's view, parties to a dispute cannot unilaterally alter the terms of reference by expanding, in their first submission, on issues not previously raised.

5.10.   Korea also submits that it is unable to identify which items the United States is referring to by its reference to 'ad mixtures' in its request for a panel.

5.11.   Korea also claims that the complainants have not clearly distinguished the domestic liquors that are supposed to be more favourably taxed in Korea. Korea states, in particular, that the complainants have not distinguished between Korea's distilled soju, an artisanal product sold at very high prices in tiny quantities, and subject to a 50% tax rate, on the one hand, and, on the other hand, diluted or standard soju, which is a large volume, inexpensive drink, consumed with meals and taxed at a rate of 35%.

5.12.   Korea argues that both complainants, in their requests for a panel, have referred to one 'soju' product, without acknowledging that there are, in reality, two different products, with two different tax rates. Korea also states that the complainants have not recognized that one group of western-style spirits ('liqueurs'), which they have mentioned in passing, is taxed at the same rate as distilled soju (50%).

5.13.   The European Communities argues that its panel request is more than sufficiently specific to meet the minimum requirements of Article 6.2 of the DSU. According to the European Communities, the mere fact that HS 22.08 covers many different types of liquors is no basis to consider that it lacks specificity.

5.14.   The European Communities also rejects Korea's assertion that it has, through its first submission, broadened the scope of its complaint as contained in the request for a panel. According to the European Communities, its request for a panel refers to '.. certain alcoholic beverages falling within HS 22.08'. In the EC's view, that HS position does not cover only 'spirits' but also 'undentured ethyl alcohol of an alcoholic strength by volume of less than 80% 'liqueurs' and 'other spirituos beverages' not falling within any other position of chapter 22 of the HS.

5.15.   The European Communities notes that its first submission refers to 'soju and all other distilled spirits and liqueurs falling within HS 22.08. In the EC's view, therefore, its first submission if anything narrows rather than broadens the scope of its complaint.

5.16.   The United States argues that Article 6.2 of the DSU requires, inter alia, that the request for a panel "identify the specific measures at issue and provide a brief summary of the legal basis of the complaint sufficient to present the problem clearly." According to the United States, its panel request satisfied both these requirements, and it also clearly includes all distilled spirits within HS heading 2208, as maintained in the first US submission.

5.17.   The United States argues that in accordance with Article 6.2 of the DSU, its request for the establishment of a panel defined the Korean measures at issue: the general liquor tax law and the Education Tax; and provided a brief summary of the legal basis of the complaint. The United States refers to *Bananas III*, where the Appellate Body allegedly noted that this provision concerning the legal basis requires that the request for a panel must be sufficiently specific with respect to the claims being advanced, but need not lay out all the arguments[34] that will subsequently be made in the party's submission. The United States argues that with respect to its request in this dispute, the legal claim is clear: that Korea's taxes are higher on imported distilled spirits than on its domestic product "soju," in violation of Article III:2 of the GATT.

5.18.   The United States argues that Korea's request that the Panel limit the proceeding to five specific products - whisky, brandy, vodka, rum, and gin, is equally

---

[34]   Appellate Body Report on *European Communities - Regime for the Importation, Sale and Distribution of Bananas (Bananas III)*, adopted on 25 September 1997, WT/DS27/AB/R, para. 141.

without basis. According to the United States, the panel request, which defines the terms of reference of the panel, refers to taxation of "other distilled spirits" - *i.e.*, distilled spirits other than soju. By using the term "such as," it sets forth the five products and "ad mixtures"[35] as examples, and not as an exclusive list. According to the United States, the extent to which the United States and European Communities establish to the Panel that all such products are "like" or "directly competitive or substitutable" is a matter to be determined through the course of these proceedings, beginning with the first submission. The United States notes that, under Article 7 of the DSU, the Panel may not decline to address products that are clearly within its terms of reference, but must base its findings on the entirety of the proceeding.[36]

5.19.   As regards the challenge of defining which soju is referred to, the European Communities states that it regards all the varieties of soju as one product, with the necessary result that 'liqueurs' are more heavily taxed than some soju. According to the European Communities, the question of whether soju is or is not a single product is a substantive issue which cannot be decided by the panel in a preliminary ruling.

5.20.   The United States also argues that with respect to the use of the word "soju," its panel request made it clear that the tax preference for all soju was covered, giving Korea ample objective notice that the entire category was to be challenged. According to the United States, given the major emphasis in Korea's first submission concerning the differences between diluted and distilled soju, it is evident that Korea in fact did have ample notice - sufficient to structure its entire first submission on the basis of alleged differences in the two kinds of soju.

3.   *Adequacy of Consultations*

5.21.   Korea also submits that explicit obligations of the DSU - namely 3.3, 3.7 and 4.5 - have been violated. Korea in effect alleges that the complainants did not engage in consultations in good faith with a view to reaching a mutual solution as envisaged by the DSU.

5.22.   Korea alleges that there was no meaningful exchange of facts because the complainants treated the consultations as a one-sided question and answer session, and therefore, frustrated any reasonable chance for a settlement.

5.23.   Korea considers this non-observance of specific provisions of the DSU as a "violation of the tenets of the WTO dispute settlement system" and requests the Panel for a ruling (no indication is made as to what relief Korea is seeking on this point).

---

[35]   According to the United States, ad-mixtures are generally low grade distilled spirits composed of a percentage of high grade spirits combined with neutral spirits and water. They are taxed as "other liquors" under Article 3.11 of the Korean Liquor Law, and are thus well within the terms of reference. For instance, in Korea, there are many brands of ad mixes, such as Black Joker malt whisky. The alcohol in Black Joker contains 19.9% whisky, with the other 80.1% coming from neutral spirits. The product then looks and tastes like whisky, but is considerably cheaper. This is due to the fact that neutral spirits do not undergo any post distillation processing, unlike whisky which must be aged in wooden barrels for two years, or more.

[36]   Appellate Body Report on *Japan - Taxes on Alcoholic Beverages* adopted on 1 November 1996, WT/DS8/AB/R, WT/DS1O/AB/R, WT/DS11/AB/R at 117; Appellate Body Report, *Bananas III*, paras. 145-147.

5.24.   Both complainants assert that Korea's claim would appear to be that they have infringed Articles 3.3, 3.7 and 4.5 of the DSU because they did not attempt to reach a mutually acceptable solution to the dispute in the course of the consultations that preceded the establishment of this Panel. They note that at the first meeting with the Panel, Korea asserted that the United States and the European Communities have "ignored":

(i)   Article 3.3 of the DSU, which provides that the "prompt settlement of disputes is essential to the effective functioning of the WTO";

(ii)   Article 3.7 of the DSU, to the extent it calls for a "mutually acceptable" and "positive" solution; and

(iii)   Article 4.5 of the DSU, which states that in the course of consultations, Members should attempt to "obtain satisfactory adjustment" of the matter.

5.25.   The complainants refer to the panel decision in Bananas III in which it was stated

[....] Consultations are, however, a matter reserved for the parties. The DSB is not involved; no panel is involved; and the consultations are held in the absence of the Secretariat. In these circumstances, we are not in a position to evaluate the consultation process in order to determine if it functioned in a particular way. While a mutually agreed solution is to be preferred, in some cases it is not possible for the parties to agree upon one. In those cases, it is our view that the function of the panel is only to ascertain that consultations, if required, were in fact held or, at least, requested.

As to the EC argument that consultations must lead to an adequate explanation of the complainants' case, we cannot agree. Consultations are the first step in the dispute settlement process. While one function of the consultations may be to clarify what the case is about, there is nothing in the DSU that provides that a complainant cannot request a panel unless its case is adequately explained in the consultations. The fulfilment of such a requirement would be difficult, if not impossible for the complainant to demonstrate if a respondent chose to claim a lack of understanding of the case, a result which would undermine the automatic nature of the panel establishment under the DSU. The only per-requisite for requesting a panel is that consultations have 'failed to settle a dispute within 60 days of receipt of the request for consultations... Ultimately, the function of providing notice to a respondent of a complainant's claims and arguments is served by the request for the establishment of a panel and by the complainants' submissions to that panel.[37]

The complainants point out that Korea cannot dispute the fact that consultations were in fact held on three separate occasions between itself and both the United States and the European Communities.

---

[37]   Panel Report on *Bananas III*, WT/DS27/R, paras. 7.18-7.19.

5.26.   The complainants state that, in any event it is not true that they refused to engage in a 'meaningful exchange of facts' during the GATT Article XXII consultations. They allege that it was Korea's attitude during the consultations which prevented such exchange from taking place.

5.27.   The United States further argues that Korea's complaints about the alleged inadequacy of the complainants' attempts to settle the dispute or engage in good faith consultations have no bearing on the authority of the Panel or the progress of this proceeding.

5.28.   The United States asserts that Korea's assertion that the United States and the European Communities failed to engage in good faith consultations is belied by the record. According to the United States, the three parties to this dispute (Korea, the United States and the European Communities) held consultations on three separate occasions over a six-week period, in which numerous factual and legal issues were discussed, including the fact that the Korean Liquor Law applies to all types of distilled spirits covered by HS 2208. The United States asserts that it presented detailed factual questions to Korea and requested that the answers be provided in writing. According to the United States, Korea refused to reply in writing but did agree to provide oral answers. The United States also states that Korea acknowledged that it was in possession of a market study commissioned by Korean producers of distilled spirits, but declined to provide a copy.

5.29.   The United States asserts that with the European Communities, it requested Korean data for 1990-1996 on all distilled spirits under HS heading 2208, by both volume and value, Korea initially stated at the 24 June consultation that it would try to provide this information. According to the United States, however, during the consultations held on 8 August 1997, the Korean delegation refused to provide copies of this information, stating that it was only for the use of its private lawyers for defensive purposes in the event a panel proceeding was initiated.

5.30.   The United States, therefore, believes that these events make all the more baffling Korea's request for a procedural ruling, given that the United States failed to obtain sufficient factual information from Korea.

4.   *Confidentiality*

5.31.   Korea alleges that both complainants breach the confidentiality requirement of Article 4.6 of the DSU by making reference, in their submissions, to information supplied by Korea during consultations.

5.32.   The European Communities argues that Korea's interpretation of Article 4.6 of the DSU is wrong. According to the European Communities, the confidentiality requirement of Article 4.6 of the DSU concerns parties not involved in the dispute and the public in general. The European Communities stresses that the requirement cannot in any way be read as referring to the panel itself. In the EC view, Article 4.6 cannot be interpreted as a limitation on the rights of parties at the panel stage.

5.33.   It is also the EC view that, if the interpretation by Korea of Article 4.6 were correct, it is Korea which has violated Article 4.6 of the DSU by making extensive reference to the consultations in support of its claim under Article 3.3, 3.7, and 4.5 of the DSU.

5.34.   The European Communities concludes that it is not the purpose of Article 4.6 of the DSU to limit the possibilities available to a panel to be apprised of information on the dispute before it. In the EC's view, there can be no 'artificial wall' between the consultation and the panel proceeding through which the transfer of information is blocked.

5.35.   The United States considers that Korea's claim concerning a breach of confidentiality in the U.S. and EC submission is unclear concerning the relief it requests. to the extent it alleges a violation of the DSU, such a claim is not within the panel's terms of reference. Moreover, according to the Untied States, the citation in a footnote in the first U.S. submission cited by Korea attempted to highlight a factual issue concerning which there was confusion in the Korean law, a point that was rectified by the first submission and is of no consequence as a factual or legal matter.

B.   Panel and Appellate Body Reports on *Japan - Taxes on Alcoholic Beverages*

1.   Complainants

5.36.   According to the European Communities, the Korean liquor tax system at issue in this dispute is very similar to the system in place in Japan until very recently. The European Communities argues that, like Korea in the instant situation, Japan applied a much lower rate to shochu (a local distilled liquor which, the European Communities consider is "like" Korean soju) than to "western-style" distilled spirits and liqueurs which are "like" or "directly competitive or substitutable" with shochu.

5.37.   The European Communities notes that the Japanese liquor tax system was found to violate Article III:2 of GATT by the 1987 Panel Report on *Japan - Customs Duties, Taxes and Labelling Practices on Imported Wines and Alcoholic Beverages*[38] (*Japan - Taxes on Alcoholic Beverages I*) and again by the 1996 Panel and Appellate Body Reports on *Japan - Taxes on Alcoholic Beverages*[39] (*Japan - Taxes on Alcoholic Beverages II*).

5.38.   The European Communities concedes that, in accordance with the Panels' terms of reference, that finding was limited to the Japanese market. In the EC view, however, this does not mean that it is irrelevant to the present dispute. The EC view is that although there may still subsist superficial differences between the Japanese and the Korean market, the underlying dynamics of both markets are very similar. According to the European Communities, there is no good reason why the findings made by prior Panels with respect to the Japanese market should not be considered as pertinent in the present dispute.

5.39.   The United States argues that the Korean liquor tax system at issue in this dispute is very similar to the system in place in Japan until very recently.   The United States further argues that like Korea, Japan has long protected shochu, a local distilled liquor which, in its pure form, is identical to Korean soju. According to

---

[38]   Panel Report on *Japan - Customs Duties, Taxes and Labelling Practices on Imported Wines and Alcoholic Beverages, (Japan - Taxes on Alcoholic Beverages I)* adopted on 10 November 1987, BISD 34S/83.

[39]   Panel Report on *Japan - Taxes on Alcoholic Beverages II*, WT/DS8/R, WT/DS10/R, WT/DS11/R, as modified by the Appellate Body Report, *supra*.

the United States, until recently, Japan applied a much lower tax rate to shochu than to other categories of Western distilled spirits that -are "like" or "directly competitive or substitutable with" shochu. The United States alleges that the structure of its law is remarkably similar to the Korea tax law, including a broad definition for shochu from which beverages such as those using a birch filter (i.e., vodka) are arbitrarily excepted.

5.40.   According to the complainants, the main difference between the Korean liquor tax system and the Japanese system is that in the Korean system the taxes take the form of an *ad valorem* duty whereas Japan applied specific taxes. In the complainants view, for the purposes of this dispute, however, this has the consequence only of rendering even more transparent the protective effects of the Korean system as compared to those of the Japanese system. According to the complainants, in *Japan - Taxes on Alcoholic Beverages II*,[40] Japan's main line of defence was that while the rates on shochu were lower, the "tax/price ratios" (i.e. the tax burden expressed as a percentage of the retail price) for all categories were "roughly the same". In the complainants view, in the present case, since the taxes are *ad valorem*, Japan's attempted defence is not available to Korea.

5.41.   The European Communities states that during the consultations Korea claimed, although without providing any supporting evidence, that current consumption patterns in Korea differ from consumption patterns in Japan. According to the European Communities, even if the alleged differences were proved to be significant, they would merely reflect the fact that western-style liquors became a mass product in Japan earlier than in Korea, to a large extent as a result of an earlier liberalization of imports.

5.42.   The European Communities further argues that the Korean market has no inherent or permanent characteristic which makes it so different from the Japanese market as to warrant the conclusion that the very same liquors which were found to be "substitutable and competitive" on the Japanese market in 1987 and 1996 cannot be regarded as such in Korea. To the contrary, the EC argument goes, the current Korean market for distilled sprits and liqueurs is in many ways reminiscent of the Japanese market in the early eighties.

5.43.   The European Communities argues that, as in Japan one decade before, since the early nineties an increase in the levels of disposable income, coupled with the lifting of import quotas and a reduction in the applicable tariffs and internal taxes, have led to a spectacular increase in sales of western-style liquors on the Korean market, and in particular of whisky.

5.44.   According to the European Communities, Korean consumers, like their Japanese neighbours, at first perceived western-style liquors as "luxury" items to be offered as gifts or to be consumed only on special occasions and at special places. Over time, however, the argument goes, there has been, both in Japan and in Korea, a clear trend towards lower prices, greater availability in all sales channels, and consumption patterns which are more similar to those of the "traditional" local liquor.

---

[40] Panel Report on *Japan - Taxes on Alcoholic Beverages II*, WT/DS8/R, WT/DS10/R, WT/DS11/R, as modified by the Appellate Body Report, *supra* paras 4.154-4.166.

5.45.   The European Communities further states that there has also been a trend towards the "internationalization" of the local liquors, which in Korea is illustrated by the recent emergence of the premium soju segment and in Japan by the proliferation of whisky-like and vodka-like shochus. The result of these two converging trends is an ever increasing degree of competition between shochu/soju and western-style liquors.

5.46.   The European Communities concludes, that given the close resemblance between the Korean liquor tax system and the Japanese measures at issue in *Japan - Taxes on Alcoholic Beverages I and II*, the Panel and Appellate Body reports adopted in those disputes are particularly relevant and should provide decisive guidance to this Panel. It is submitted by the European Communities, in particular, that the findings of those two Panels and of the Appellate Body to the effect that vodka and shochu/soju are "like" products and that shochu/soju and all other distilled spirits and liqueurs are "substitutable" and "competitive" products, are equally relevant for this dispute.

5.47.   The United States also takes the position that the development of the distilled spirits markets in Japan and Korea are very similar. According to the United States, since the early 1990's an increase in the levels of disposable income, coupled with the lifting of the import restrictions and a reduction in the applicable tariffs and internal taxes, have led to a spectacular increase in sales of Western-style spirits on the Korean market, in particular whisky.

5.48.   The United States further asserts that, like their Japanese neighbours, Korean consumers at first perceived Western-style liquors as "luxury" items to be offered as gifts or to be consumed only on special occasions and at special places. Over time, however, there has been, both in Japan and in Korea, a clear trend towards consumption of all types of distilled spirits on more and varied occasions, and in different methods of consumption, i.e. in mixed drinks, warm, cold, etc. According to the United States, the expanding methods and venues of consumption have also been aided by greater availability of all types of spirits in all sales channels.

5.49.   According to the United States, the result of expanded purposes for spirits, and the burgeoning styles of soju is an ever increasing degree of competition between soju and Western-style liquors. Those trends are converging in Korea, as in Japan.

5.50.   The United States also concludes that the close similarity between the Korean liquor tax system and the Japanese measures at issue in the recent WTO/GATT disputes make the Panel and Appellate Body findings in that case very pertinent to this Panel's examination of Korean tax measures. In particular, the United States argues that the findings of those two panels and of the Appellate Body to the effect that vodka and shochu/soju are "like" products and that shochu/soju and all other distilled spirits are directly competitive or substitutable products are especially relevant for this dispute.

2.   *Korea*

5.51.   Korea notes that both the United States and the European Communities demonstrate the desire simply to superimpose the results of the 1996 *Japan - Taxes on Alcoholic Beverages* Panel on this case. In Korea's view, the complainants attempt to equate Japan and Korea, their markets, and the products at issue. According to Korea, they do so by asserting that soju and shochu are 'identical', and that the 'underlying dynamics of both [the Japanese and Korean] markets are very similar', save some 'superficial differences'. Korea argues that this approach is not compatible with Article III:2 GATT.

5.52.   Korea argues that Korean soju is not identical to Japanese shochu, irrespective of statements made in the context of the Japan case, to which Korea was not a party. Korea cites the example from the complainants to say that Korean companies are exporting soju to Japan. According to Korea, when Korean soju is exported to Japan, it is destined for the Korean community in Japan,[41] and sold in Korean stores and restaurants. However, argues Korea, Korean producers exporting to Japan are primarily aiming to capture Japanese consumers. For this purpose, they export a different product, a sort of 'Korean shochu'. These two products are taxed differently under the Japanese liquor tax law. Korea adds that 'Korean shochu' is not sold in Korea.

5.53.   Korea further argues that despite the complainants' contentions, the Korean case is not a 'mirror image' of the Japanese case, and Korea will not entertain arguments in that vein. Korea argues that it need only point to the *Japan - Taxes on Alcoholic Beverages II* Panel report itself, which repeatedly stresses that an Article III examination must be carried out on a 'case-by-case basis',[42] noting in particular that 'consumers' tastes and habits . . . change from country to country'.[43]

5.54.   Korea acknowledges that the *Japan - Taxes on Alcoholic Beverages II* case sets forth the legal framework for the application and interpretation of Article III of GATT. Korea accepts that it will follow that framework in its analysis, but adds that when these legal rules are applied to the facts of this case, the result is completely different than under the dissimilar set of facts of the Japanese case.

Korea and Japan: differences between their products and markets

5.55.   According to Korea, the first noticeable difference between soju and shochu is taste. Korea argues that Japanese shochu has a neutral taste compared to Korean soju, which is sweeter.[44] Consumers easily recognize that taste difference; Koreans prefer soju and will not accept shochu as a substitute; the Japanese feel the same way about shochu.

5.56.   Secondly, according to Korea, soju is allegedly only drunk straight at a cold temperature. In Japan, on the other hand, different consumption patterns exist for the

---

[41]   Korean residents in Japan numbered 699 847 persons as of June 1997.

[42]   Panel Report, paras. 6.21, 6.22, and 6.28 of the 1996.

[43]   Panel Report, paras. 6.21.

[44]   Korea argues that soju contains six to seven additives whereas shochu only has up to two (citric acid and sugar). Korea notes that this distinction is not recognised in the 'test report' by the Scotch Whisky Research Institute, appended as EC Annex 8. Korea further notes that according to this 'test report', Korean standard soju and Japanese standard shochu are 'like' products (see para. 5). Thus, Korea concludes the report is not relevant because it does not distinguish the different additives.

consumption of shochu: one can drink it straight or mixed with warm or cold water.[45]

5.57.   Korea argues that these differences are so important that Korean companies attempting to sell Korean soju in Japan have had to make a special product to appeal to the Japanese consumer. As an example Korea refers to the Korean company Jinro, which sells two products on the Japanese market, Jinro Gold and Jinro Export. According to Korea, the first product is exported to Japan in very small quantities (32 kl in 1997) with the primary purpose of targeting the Korean residents in Japan. This brand is only distributed to Korean restaurants and Korean supermarkets in Japan. The second brand, Jinro Export, targets Japanese consumers and represents the bulk of Jinro's exports to Japan (27 182 kl in 1997).[46] Korea argues that it is made to suit the Japanese taste,[47] sold in differently shaped bottles,[48] at much higher prices,[49] and is not available on the Korean market.

5.58.   Korea also alludes to the EC contention that in Japan, soju is considered for tax purposes as being the same product as local 'shochu', which Korea argues is incorrect. According to Korea, when Korean standard soju (such as Jinro Gold) is exported to Japan, it is treated as a 'spirit' for tax purposes. Only the specially-produced 'Korean shochu', such as Jinro Export, is treated like Japanese shochu by the Japanese tax authorities. The tax rate for Korean standard soju exports is higher than for 'Korean shochu' exports.[50]

5.59.   Korea also argues that there are notable differences in the way shochu is marketed in Japan and the way that standard soju and distilled soju are marketed in Korea. Shochu is marketed more like western-type liquors that can be drunk as cocktails.

5.60.   Korea further argues that Japanese shochu producers even make a shochu A (the standard version) that is aged and is brown in colour, and they make an effort to convince consumers that there are a plethora of similarities between brown shochu and whisky. Korea states for example, that the leading brand of brown shochu A in Japan, Takara Legend, closely resembles whisky in colour and packaging. Korea also asserts that in Korea, it is legally prohibited to add colour to standard soju.[51]

5.61.   Korea contends that another important difference is the pricing structure of the Japanese market. Shochu B (the distilled version) and shochu A are similarly priced, and are selling in comparable volumes. This contrasts to the Korean soju

---

[45]   Korea argues that this difference is further illustrated by US Exhibit I, which shows advertisements for Japanese shochu for Japanese consumers, in which several types of uses are proposed for shochu which do not exist for soju in Korea, i.e., shochu can be drunk warm, mixed with chilled soda or on the rocks.

[46]   Source: manufacturer's information. The total amount of Korean soju and 'shochu' exports to Japan in 1997, covering other manufacturers as well, was 36 478 kl (source: National Tax Administration).

[47]   Unlike Jinro Gold, Jinro Export contains only two additives: sugar and citric acid.

[48]   As is shown by US Exhibit H.

[49]   According to Korea, by at least a factor of 5, before Japanese taxes and charges are applied.

[50]   The current tax rate on standard soju and general spirits in Japan amounts to 367 188 yen/kl. The current rate for Japanese shochu is 201 900 yen/kl.

[51]   Standard soju by law must have a coloration level of less than 0.1 degree. (Whisky has a higher coloration level.)

market in which distilled soju is selling in much smaller volumes and at much higher prices than standard soju. According to Korea, in the Japanese shochu market, shochu A and shochu B have comparable market shares, whereas in the Korean market distilled soju takes up 0.2% of the soju market and standard soju takes up 99.8% of the market.

5.62.   Korea notes that as the European Communities argued in the *Japan - Taxes on Alcoholic Beverages II* case, the prices of imported liquors and Japanese shochu were within a relatively short range, with the tax removed.[52] Korea further notes that in contrast, as the EC experts have recognized in this case, the pre-tax prices for imported liquors in Korea are much higher than the prices for standard soju.[53]

5.63.   In its rebuttal submissions, the European Communities argues that Korea is understandably anxious to escape the clear implications for this dispute of the Panel Report on *Japan - Taxes on Alcoholic Beverages I,*[54] and the Panel and Appellate Body Reports on *Japan - Taxes on Alcoholic Beverages II.*[55] The EC view is that Korea unjustly accuses it of trying to apply mechanically the conclusions of those reports to the present case. According to the European Communities, that is an obvious misrepresentation of its position.

5.64.   According to the European Communities, the present dispute must be determined on its own merits. The EC view, however, is that this Panel must take into account any adopted Panel and Appellate Body reports which are relevant to this dispute. The European Communities refers to the Appellate Body decision in *Japan - Taxes on Alcoholic Beverages II*, wherein it was stated:

> Adopted Panel reports are an important part of the GATT acquis. They are often considered by subsequent Panels. They create legitimate expectations among members, and, therefore should be taken into account where they are relevant to any dispute.[56]

5.65.   The EC position is that it has demonstrated that the two Panel reports and the Appellate Body report on *Japan - Taxes on Alcoholic Beverages II* are particularly relevant for the present dispute because:

(a)   the tax measures are very similar;

(b)   the products concerned are the same; and

(c)   there is no fundamental difference between the Japanese market and the Korean market.

The European Communities argues that Korea fails to refute any of those similarities.

5.66.   In its rebuttal submission, the United States recalls that its first submission cited the reports of the WTO panel and Appellate Body in the *Japan - Alcoholic Beverages II* case as setting forth the applicable legal standards and factual findings concerning a market, tax measures and products that are identical or analogous to

---

[52]   Panel Report, para. 4.82.

[53]   EC Annex 13, p. 20.

[54]   Panel Report on *Japan - Taxes on Alcoholic Beverages I, supra.*

[55]   Panel Report on *Japan - Taxes on Alcoholic Beverages II, supra.*

[56]   Appellate Body Report, p. 14.

those presented in this dispute. The United States argues that it has not called for a "mechanical" application of the analysis of the Japanese market to the Korean market, as suggested by Korea.[57]

5.67.   According to the United States, it is well established that the issue of what is a "like" or "directly competitive or substitutable" product for purposes of Article III:2 must be determined on a case-by-case basis on its own merits. However, in the US view, given the similarities of the tax measures and products involved in the Japanese and Korean markets, this Panel should consider that the conclusions of the panel concerning the products, measures, and extent of competition in the Japanese market can also be reasonably drawn with respect to the facts presented here.

5.68.   The United States notes that Korea has contested any similarities between soju and shochu, and between the Korean and Japanese markets and disputes the US point that soju and shochu are "identical." According to the United States, while Korea understandably is entitled to dispute the point, the source for the point made by the United States was the government of Japan, which in *Japan - Taxes on Alcoholic Beverages II* stated that, "Essentially shochu and soju are identical products."[58] With respect to the fundamental similar qualities of the product, Japan noted that:

> These [shochu/soju] products have the following common three features: First, they use grains or potatoes as the base material, which is readily available at low cost in this part of the world. Second, they have a relatively low alcoholic strength. . . . Third, they are consumed directly after distillation. They do not normally undergo further post-distillation processing.[59]

5.69.   According to the United States, as the largest importer of Korean soju (Korean imports account for 8 percent of Japan's shochu A market), Japan would appear to be reasonably authoritative regarding the objective characteristics of the products.

5.70.   The United States further argues that, even using the marketplace approach, the similarities between the present Korean market and the Japanese market make the Japan panel's findings analogous for purposes of this proceeding. In the US view, in both markets, Western distilled spirits are more expensive and considered premium types of spirits compared to local shochu/soju, and in both markets Western spirits are used for gift-giving more frequently than the local product, although in this dispute, Korea has characterized distilled soju as uniquely suited to gift-giving. The marketplace reacted similarly in Japan and Korea, as consumption of

---

[57]   See Appellate Body Report, *Japan - Alcoholic Beverages II, supra,* at 20; see also *Canada - Certain Measures Concerning Periodicals,* adopted on 30 July 1997, WT/DS31/AB/R, at 21; *The Australian Subsidy on Ammonium Sulphate,* adopted on April 3, 1950, BISD II/188; *EEC - Measures on Animal Feed Proteins,* adopted on March 14, 1978, BISD 25S/49; *Spain - Tariff Treatment of Unroasted Coffee,* adopted on June 11, 1981, BISD 28S/102; *Japan - Alcoholic Beverages I, supra*; *U.S. - Taxes on Petroleum and Certain Imported Substances,* adopted on June 17, 1987, BISD 34S/136.

[58]   Panel Report, para. 4.178. Japan also stated that "the tax legislation of the Republic of Korea defines soju into two sub-categories of diluted soju, which is equivalent to shochu A, and 'distilled soju, which is equivalent to shochu B, in a manner similar to Japan's definition.'" *Ibid.*

[59]   Panel Report, para. 4.175.

Western spirits increased with the lifting of trade barriers and the narrowing of tax disparities. The United States notes for instance, that US exports of Bourbon to Japan have increased from 6.3 million litres in 1987 to 12.2 million litres in 1997 due to 1989 reforms in the Japanese liquor tax, and US exports of distilled spirits to Korea increased from 170,000 litres in 1990 to 644,000 litres in 1996 following the removal of quota restrictions on bottled imported spirits.

5.71.   The United States also notes that the evolution of the marketplace in Korea and Japan also bears great similarity. Only a decade ago, Japanese "izakayas" (the Japanese equivalent of traditional Korean restaurants) used to serve only shochu, sake and beer, whereas western style "snack bars" would serve western distilled spirits, but not shochu. Today, shochu and western distilled spirits are usually available at both the "izakayas" and "snack bars." Korea is beginning to resemble the Japanese market of today, with increasing availability of western spirits in traditional, casual Korean restaurants and bars. According to the United States, Korea's greater constraint of choice of distilled spirits availability in various bar and restaurant venues bears a closer resemblance to Japan before its last round of market liberalization in 1989.

5.72.   The United states notes that the marketplace does reveal some differences between Korea and Japan. The market for Western spirits in Korea is predominantly served by one type of imported spirit (whisky), while Japan has matured into a market for many types of imported spirits, with the most recent spirit to become popular being tequila. According to the United States, Korean consumption patterns are much more fixed in traditional, family-type restaurants than in Japan, where a wider range of distilled spirits is consumed. However, most of these differences between shochu/soju consumption in Korea and Japan are a function of market maturity and evolution of drinking tastes and styles.

5.73.   The United States further states that Korea has conceded that it classifies both soju and shochu in the same HS classification at the eight-digit level - item 2208.90.40. The fact that Korean manufacturers may export two kinds of soju to Japan (namely, Jinro Gold and Jinro Export) does not make these products any less similar. It is common for companies to modestly differentiate their products in order to meet the needs of different sets of consumers - one version for expatriates and another, seasoned differently, to meet local tastes and customs. Korean manufacturers do the same when they market two versions of soju in Japan. In fact the differences in the two kinds of soju exports probably reflect Japanese laws and cost considerations more than anything else. Most of the additives in Korean soju are sweeteners with varying thickening qualities (fructose, oligosaccharide and stevioside) - functions served by sugar in the version for Japanese consumers. Most importantly though, these are clearly additives, as opposed to ingredients. Liquor laws around the world, including Korea's, recognize the distinction by placing a limit on the percentage of sugar that may be added to a distilled spirit (on the order of 2 percent), after which it becomes yet another competitive product, a *liqueur*. At the same time, there is no requirement in Korean law to use any sweetener at all in soju, thus making it possible for soju to contain no additives at all. Korea also classifies soju and shochu identically for both tax and tariff purposes.

5.74.   Furthermore, according to the United States, Korea's reliance on differences in the additives between shochu and soju as establishing that they are fundamentally different is contradicted by its description of premium soju. Even though premium soju differs from standard soju by its additives, such as honey, Korea states that premium soju is "only an upgraded version of standard soju." Why are differences in additives critical in the context of vodka and shochu, but irrelevant with respect to premium and standard soju? Clearly, Korea's conclusion concerning premium soju is the legally correct one: such additives should not be decisive in examining these products under Article III.

C.   The Burden of Proof

1.   Korea

5.75.   Korea proceeds from the premise that to prove a violation of the first sentence of Article III:2, the Appellate Body in the Japanese Liquor Taxes case clearly stated that there are two limbs that must be proved by the complainant. First the complainants must prove that the products concerned are in fact 'like'. Secondly, the complainants must prove that the imported product was taxed in excess of the domestic 'like' product.

5.76.   According to Korea, regarding Article III:2 second sentence, the complainants must prove three things: first, that the imported and domestic products are directly competitive and substitutable products, second, that foreign products are subject to tax differentials that are more than 'de minimis', and third that tax was applied 'so as to afford protection' to domestic production.

5.77.   Korea further argues that under both the first sentence and second sentence, the obligation rests on the complainant to prove all the requirements of the respective sentences. In Korea's view, this burden cannot be discharged by making inadmissible analogies to another case and another set of facts. Korea emphasizes that the burden must be discharged with regard to the facts of the case at hand.

5.78.   According to Korea, the Panel can make no ruling about the tax rates of all products falling under HS 2208 in the abstract. Therefore, the complainants must prove, on a product-by-product basis, that the products at issue are directly competitive or substitutable, or even 'like', products.

5.79.   Korea points out that the complainants have only submitted evidence regarding a limited number of imported alcoholic drinks falling under HS 2208: whisky, brandy, vodka, gin, and rum. They have also mentioned by name a few other, though by no means all, alcoholic beverages (liqueurs, tequila, ad mixtures, koryangju, Japanese shochu) covered by HS 2208, without providing an intelligible argument or evidence in their regard.[60] In Korea's view, the complainants have not met their burden of proving that these are 'like', or directly competitive or substitutable products with the Korean sojus.

---

[60]   Korea argues that these products are granted only the most perfunctory mentions by the EC and the US. They do not even figure on the comparative charts that the US and EC have provided (see, for example, EC Annex 9, which only shows standard soju, distilled soju, whisky, brandy, gin, and rum, and the US first submission, table at page 20, which only shows whisky, brandy, gin, rum, vodka, soju and shochu).

5.80.   Korea submits that the complainants' principal and theoretical argument that all distilled spirits necessarily compete everywhere in the world, because of some similarities in physical characteristics and end use, runs counter to the controlling precedent. This precedent, *Japan - Taxes on Alcoholic Beverages II*, clearly requires a concrete market analysis. Furthermore, to the extent the complainants have analyzed the Korean market, this analysis is demonstrably poor. Accordingly, the complainants have not met their burden of proof; and they cannot meet their burden by quibbling with Korea's positions.

5.81.   Korea submits that it is not up to Korea to prove that the western-style liquors are not DCSP or 'like' any of the Korean sojus. It is up to the complainants to show that they are. Korea does not need to prove that there is no cross-elasticity of demand. In Korea's view, the complainants brought this case; they ought to carry their burden of proving that such cross-elasticities exist. All Korea has to do is rebut the proof brought by the complainants.[61]

5.82.   Korea further argues that there is not much evidence in the complainants' documents. According to Korea, the complainants make many assertions without any attempt at evidence. Korea further argues that, absent an intelligible argument and supporting evidence, Korea has had no way to defend itself so that this part of the complaint also infringes a fundamental principle of due process.[62]

5.83.   Korea therefore submits that the Panel should reject any such broad-ranging complaints out of hand.

2.   *Complainants*

5.84.   The European communities notes that Korea alleges that it has only submitted evidence regarding a limited number of imported alcoholic beverages (namely whisky, brandy, vodka, gin and rum) and claims that the Panel should reject the EC complaint as far as other distilled spirits falling within HS 2280 are concerned.

5.85.   According to the European Communities, Korea's claim is factually wrong. In the EC view, Korea appears to have derived its list of products from Annex 9 of the EC submission, yet that Annex is by no means the only piece of evidence submitted by the EC in this case. Other pieces of evidence submitted by the European Communities allegedly do cover specifically other types of distilled spirits.

5.86.   In particular, the European Communities takes issue with the proposition that, in order to meet its burden of proof in this case, it is required to provide specific evidence with respect to each and every single type of distilled liquor falling within HS 2208.

5.87.   The European Communities refers to Korea's assertion that, "if one travels around the world, one will encounter a seemingly infinite variety of alcoholic beverages." In the EC view, even a much shorter trip within the borders of the EC would

---

[61]   According to the European Communities, this case is not like *US - Measure Affecting Imports of Woven Wool Shirts and Blouses from India*, adopted on 23 May 1997, *WT/DS33/AB/R. & WT/DS33/R*. There the defendant bore the burden of proof in invoking an *exception* to the GATT.

[62]   See *India-Patent Protection for Pharmaceutical and Agricultural Chemical Products*, adopted on 16 January 1998, WT/DS50/AB/R, at para. 94 (Korea states that due process is a principle implicit in the WTO Dispute Settlement Understanding).

suffice to convince the Panel of the large variety of distilled spirits produced in the EC.

5.88.   According to the European Communities, had the EC submitted specific evidence with regard to each and every known type of distilled spirit manufactured in the European Communities, the Panel would have been unnecessarily overburdened. Further, the EC view is also that in some cases it would have been materially impossible to gather such evidence. The European Communities refers to one of the criticisms levelled by Korea against the Dodwell study, that the respondents may have been confused by an allegedly too complex set of questions. What, asks the European Communities, if the respondents had been asked to look at the prices of forty or fifty different types of western distilled spirits instead of just seven?

5.89.   The European Communities reiterates that all distilled spirits are produced according to the same method and, as a result, share the same basic physical characteristics. The European Communities states that the distilled spirits for which it has submitted specific evidence are those traded in largest volumes, both between the European Communities and Korea, and globally. They are allegedly representative of the full spectrum of distilled spirits. According to the European Communities, there is virtually no distilled spirit whose production process and physical characteristics do not resemble closely those of at least one of the spirits for which the EC has provided specific evidence.

5.90.   The European Communities concludes, therefore, that if the Panel found, as it should, that those spirits for which specific evidence has been submitted are "directly competitive and substitutable" with soju, it should infer that all other distilled spirits falling within HS 2208 also are "directly competitive and substitutable" with soju.

5.91.   According to the European Communities, this approach has been endorsed by the Appellate Body in *Japan - Taxes on Alcoholic Beverages II*. In that case, the complainants claimed that shochu was "directly competitive or substitutable" with all other distilled spirits falling within HS 2208. Nevertheless, like the complainants in this case, they submitted specific evidence only with respect to a limited number of representative spirits. The Panel concluded that only certain spirits falling within HS 2208 were "directly competitive or substitutable" with shochu.[63] According to the European Communities, on appeal, this finding was reversed by the Appellate Body which ruled that the Panel's failure to incorporate in its conclusions all the liquors falling within its terms of reference (i.e. all distilled spirits falling within 2208) was an error of law.[64]

5.92.   The United States noted Korea's claim that product-specific evidence must be submitted for every conceivable type of distilled spirit classified under Heading 2208. The United States clarified that the Dodwell study covered the full spectrum of distilled spirits in this dispute and those currently being exported by the United States. While there may be other products of importance, such as pre-mixed cocktails and admixtures, these are only variations of the products employed in the Dod-

---

[63]   Panel Report, para. 7.1.

[64]   Appellate Body Report, at 118.

well study. There is no distilled spirit produced in the United States that is not akin to those employed in the Dodwell study.

5.93.   More importantly, argues the United States, given the fundamental similarities between all distilled spirits, it is not necessary to provide specific evidence, even less a market study, for every conceivable product that might fall within HS heading 2208. The products are all fairly highly concentrated forms of distilled alcohol consumed for socialization and relaxation, and all markets recognize them as being in competition. The Korean measures themselves group these products together in the same law, mostly as exceptions to soju. In the Korean tax law, to the extent the Western spirits are not designated in specific categories such as whiskey and brandy, most are lumped in the general category of "general distilled spirits,"[65] with the same tax rate. Given Korea's own recognition of the similarities of the products, and the other evidence presented in this dispute that the products in the Dodwell study are directly competitive or substitutable with soju, it is reasonable to conclude that all imported distilled spirits are equally so. The Appellate Body in the *Japan* case took precisely this approach. In the *Japan* case, the panel had not included all products within HS heading 2208 in its findings under Article III:2, second sentence, having specified only whisky, brandy, rum, gin and liqueurs.[66] The Appellate Body found the limited finding was in error and modified it to include all distilled spirits in HS 2208.[67]

D.   Article III Arguments

1.   Complainants

5.94.   In this sub-section, the arguments of the European Communities and the United states are combined as the arguments of the "complainants".

(a)   GATT Article III:2, first sentence

i)   General

5.95.   The complainants draw the attention of the Panel to GATT Article III:2, first sentence, which provides *that*:

> "The products of the territory of any contracting party imported into the territory of any other contracting party shall not be subject, directly or indirectly, to internal taxes or other internal charges of any kind in excess of those applied, directly or indirectly to like domestic products"

5.96.   The complainants state that as confirmed by the Appellate Body in *Japan - Taxes on Alcoholic Beverages II*,[68] in order to establish whether an internal tax is applied in violation of Article III:2, first sentence, it is necessary to make two determinations:

---

[65]   Korean Liquor Tax Law, Article 3.9.

[66]   Panel Report in *Japan - Taxes on Alcoholic Beverages II*, *supra*, at para. 7.1.

[67]   Appellate Body Report in *Japan -Taxes on Alcoholic Beverages II*, *supra*, at 118, 123.

[68]   Appellate Body Report in *Japan -Taxes on Alcoholic Beverages II*, DSR 1996:I, 97 at 112. See also Appellate Body Report on *Canada - Certain Measures Concerning Periodicals*, *supra*.

(i)   whether the taxed imported and domestic products are "like"; and

(ii)   whether the taxes applied to the imported products are "in excess of" those applied to the like domestic products.

5.97.   According to the complainants, before making those two determinations, it must be ascertained whether the taxes in question constitute an "internal tax".

5.98.   The complainants refer to the decision by the Appellate Body in *Japan - Taxes on Alcoholic Beverages II*, wherein the Appellate Body stated that the general principle contained in Article III:1 informs also the first sentence of Article III:2. Nevertheless, in order to establish a violation of Article III:2, first sentence, it is not necessary to show that the measure at issue is applied "so as to afford protection to domestic production" separately from the above requirements.[69]

ii)   The Liquor Tax and the Education Tax are "internal taxes"

5.99.   The complainants state that the Liquor Tax and the Education Tax are levied on all distilled spirits and liqueurs intended for consumption in Korea, whether locally manufactured or imported, and not just "on" or "in connection" with the importation of distilled spirits and liqueurs. Accordingly, in the EC view, they constitute "internal taxes" in terms of GATT Article III:2, and not "import charges" within the purview of GATT Articles II and VIII.

iii)   Vodka is "like" soju

5.100. The complainants state that GATT does not define the notion of "like product". According to the complainants, the approach followed by previous Panels has been to examine whether products are "like" on a case-by-case basis in light of factors such as the physical characteristics of the products concerned, their end uses and their customs classification. This approach was endorsed expressly by the Appellate Body in *Japan - Taxes on Alcoholic Beverages II*[70] and in *Canada - Certain Measures Concerning Periodicals.*[71]

5.101. The complainants note that in the same reports the Appellate Body held that the terms "like products" should be construed "narrowly" for the purposes of Article III:2, first sentence[72]. The complainants further notes that "like" products need not be identical in all respects[73]. Thus, it has been established by a previous Panel that in the case of alcoholic beverages:

---

[69]   Appellate Body Report on *Japan - Taxes on Alcoholic Beverages II, supra,* at 112. See also Appellate Body Report on *European Communities - Bananas III, supra,* para. 216.

[70]   Appellate Body Report on *Japan - Taxes on Alcoholic Beverages II, supra,* at 113.

[71]   Appellate Body Report on *Canada - Certain Measures Concerning Periodicals, supra,* at 466.

[72]   Appellate Body Report on *Japan - Taxes on Alcoholic Beverages II, supra,* at 112; See also Appellate Body Report on *Canada - Certain Measures Concerning Periodicals, supra,* at 466.

[73]   See Panel report on *Japan - Taxes on Alcoholic Beverages II, supra,* para. 6.21. See also the Panel Report on *Japan - Taxes on Alcoholic Beverages I, supra,* para 5.5, referring to the Panel Report on *United States - Taxes on Petroleum and Certain Imported Substances, supra,* para 5.11, where the Panel found that some of the imported and domestic products, albeit not identical, were like products since they served substantially the same uses.

[m]inor differences in taste, colour and other properties (including different alcohol contents) do not prevent products from qualifying as like products.[74]

5.102. The complainants take the position that in this instance, vodka and soju are "like" products because they have the same physical characteristics and, consequently, are objectively apt to serve identical end uses. Furthermore, according to the complainants, Korean soju is the same liquor as Japanese shochu, which has already been found by the two Panels on *Japan - Taxes on Alcoholic Beverages* to be "like" vodka.

> (a)   Soju and vodka have virtually the same physical characteristics and, therefore, serve for the same end uses

5.103. According to the complainants, the essential characteristics of vodka and soju can be summarized as follows:

Table 3

	Vodka	**Distilled soju**	**Diluted soju**
Raw materials	Potatoes, grains Neutral spirits	Potatoes, grains	Neutral spirits
Process Distillation	Continuous distillation	Pot Still distillation	Continuous Charcoal filtration excluded
Usual bottling strength	37.5-40% ABV	40-45% ABV	20-30% ABV
Appearance	Clear	Clear	Clear

5.104. According to the complainants, from the above table, it emerges that the main differences between soju and vodka are confined to the following:

(i)   diluted soju is usually bottled at an alcoholic strength of 25 % ABV whereas vodka is sold at 37.5%-40% ABV

(ii)   unlike vodka, distilled soju is obtained by non-continuous distillation and cannot be filtered through white birch charcoal, although it can be filtered through any other materials.

5.105. At the request of the EC industry, the Scotch Whisky Research Institute has conducted a series of analyses on a sample of well known brands of soju and vodka, which prove that the manufacturing processes and the physical characteristics of the two liquors are nearly identical[75] According to the European Communities the analyses indicate that:

(i)   all the sampled brands had been fermented from similar carbohydrate sources;

(ii)   all of them had been distilled to concentrate alcohols;

(iii)   none had been matured in wood post-distillation;

---

[74]   Panel Report on *Japan - Taxes on Alcoholic Beverages I, supra*, para 5.9.

[75]   See EC Annex 8.

<table>
<tr><td>(iv)</td><td>none contained significant levels of residue;</td></tr>
<tr><td>(v)</td><td>none had significant levels of obscuration;</td></tr>
<tr><td>(vi)</td><td>the major volatile congeners were at similar levels in vodka and diluted soju. They are only marginally higher in distilled soju; and</td></tr>
<tr><td>(vii)</td><td>all contained similar levels of methanol.</td></tr>
</table>

(b)   The differences between vodka and soju are the same as between vodka and Japanese shochu

5.106. According to the complainants, the differences between vodka and soju are clearly minor and do not prevent soju and vodka from being "like" products. In the EC view, the existence of the very same differences between vodka and Japanese shochu did not prevent the two Panels on *Japan - Taxes on Alcoholic Beverages* from reaching the conclusion that those two liquors were "like" in the sense of Article III:2, first sentence.

5.107. The complainants state that the average alcoholic strength of shochu A is, as that of Korean diluted soju, around 25%. In spite of that, notes the complainants, the two Panel Reports on *Japan - Taxes on Alcoholic Beverages* concluded that shochu A was like vodka. The Panel Report on *Japan - Taxes on Alcoholic Beverages II* noted in this regard that:

> "... a difference in the physical characteristics of alcoholic strength of two products did not preclude a finding of likeness especially since alcoholic beverages are often drunk in the diluted form..."[76]

5.108. The complainants further note that like distilled soju, both shochu B and shochu A may not, by law, be filtered through white birch charcoal. In addition, the complainants note that the Japanese Liquor Tax Law requires that shochu B must be obtained through discontinuous distillation. In the EC view, however, these differences were not an obstacle for the Panel Report on *Japan - Taxes on Alcoholic Beverages II* to conclude that both types of shochu were like vodka.

(c)   Korean soju is treated as shochu in Japan

5.109. As mentioned above, Korean soju is exported in large quantities to Japan, where it is treated for all purposes as being the same product as shochu. Diluted soju corresponds to Japanese shochu A, whereas distilled soju is the equivalent to Japanese shochu B.

5.110. The complainants note that in *Japan - Taxes on Alcoholic Beverages II*, the Japanese Government stated that:

> "... the largest producer of shochu is either the Republic of Korea or the People's Republic of China ... the liquor tax legislation of the Republic of Korea defines soju in two sub-categories of 'diluted soju', which is equivalent to shochu A, and 'distilled soju', which is equivalent to shochu B, in a manner

---

[76] Panel Report on *Japan - Taxes on Alcoholic Beverages II, supra*, para. 6.22.

similar to Japan's definition. Essentially, shochu and soju are identical products[77]."

5.111. The complainants further note that in response to these claims, the Panel "accepted the evidence submitted by Japan according to which a shochu-like product is produced in various countries outside Japan, including the Republic of Korea..."[78] In the US view, the similarities in the way Japanese shochu and Korean soju are advertised further confirm the "equivalence" of these products.

5.112. The complainants conclude that the "likeness" of soju and shochu is further confirmed by the results of the analytical tests conducted by the Scotch Whisky Research Institute.[79]

iv) Imported vodka is taxed "in excess of" soju

5.113. The complainants argue that the prohibition of discriminatory taxes in Article III:2, first sentence, is not conditional on a trade effects test nor is it qualified by a *de minimis* standard[80]. The complainants refer to the Appellate Body in *Japan - Taxes on Alcoholic Beverages II*, which stated that "even the smallest amount of 'excess' is too much"[81].

5.114. The Table below is presented by the complainants purportedly to summarize the differences in taxation between vodka and soju. It purportedly indicates that both the Liquor Tax and the Education Tax are applied to vodka at a much higher rate than to diluted soju and distilled soju. In all, the combined tax rate applied on vodka is 1.9 times higher than the combined rate on distilled soju and 2.7 times higher than the combined tax rate on diluted soju.

Table 4
Comparison of the tax rates on soju and vodka

	Liquor Tax	*Education Tax* (as % of Liquor Tax Base)	*Combined Tax Rate*	*Discrimination Index*
Diluted soju	35%	3.5%	38.5%	1.00
Distilled soju	50%	5%	55%	1.43/1.00
Vodka	80%	24%	104%	2.70/1.89

5.115. The complainants conclude that it is indisputable that the taxes applied to imported vodka pursuant to both the Liquor Tax Law and the Education Tax Law are "in excess of" those applied to soju.

---

[77] Panel Report on *Japan - Taxes on Alcoholic Beverages II, supra*, para. 4.178.

[78] *Ibid.*, para. 6.35.

[79] See EC Annex 8.

[80] Appellate Body Report on *Japan - Taxes on Alcoholic Beverages II, supra*, at 115.

[81] *Ibid.*

> (b)   GATT Article III:2, second sentence

> i)   General

5.116. The complainants note that GATT Article III:2, second sentence, reads as follows:

> [M]oreover, no contracting party shall otherwise apply internal taxes or other internal charges to imported or domestic products in a manner contrary to the principles set forth in paragraph I.

5.117. The complainants further note that GATT Article III:1 provides in relevant part that:

> The contracting parties recognize that internal taxes .... should not be applied to imported or domestic products so as to afford protection to domestic production.

5.118. The complainants further note that the Interpretative Note to Article III:2 states that:

> A tax conforming to the requirements of the first sentence of paragraph 2 would be considered to be inconsistent with the provisions of the second sentence only in cases where competition was involved between, on the one hand, the taxed product and, on the other hand, a directly competitive or substitutable product which was not similarly taxed.

5.119. According to the complainants, in *Japan - Taxes on Alcoholic Beverages II*,[82] the Appellate Body confirmed that in order to determine whether an internal tax measure is inconsistent with Article III:2, second sentence it is necessary to address the following three issues:

> (i)   whether the imported products and the domestic products are "directly competitive or substitutable products" which are in competition with each other;

> (ii)   whether the directly competitive or substitutable imported and domestic products are "not similarly taxed"; and

> (iii)   whether the dissimilar taxation of the directly competitive or substitutable imported products is "applied ... so as to afford protection to domestic production".

5.120. The European Communities in particular note that, in addition, it must be determined whether the measures at issue are "internal taxes". As already discussed above in connection with the application of Article III:2, first sentence, both the Liquor Tax and the Education Tax are internal taxes within the meaning of Article III:2, rather than import charges within the purview of GATT Articles II and VIII. That conclusion, in the complainants' view, is equally valid for the purposes of applying Article III:2, second sentence.

---

[82]   Appellate Body Report on *Japan - Taxes on Alcoholic Beverages II, supra*, at 116; See also Appellate Body Report on *Canada - Certain Measures Concerning Periodicals, supra*, at 470.

> ii)   Soju and all other distilled spirits and liqueurs are competitive and substitutable products

5.121. According to the complainants, in *Japan - Taxes on Alcoholic Beverages II*, the Appellate Body stated that a determination whether two products are "competitive or substitutable" must be made on a case-by-case basis and in light of "all the relevant facts in that case".[83]

5.122. The complainants further argue that in the same report, the Appellate Body found that in deciding whether two products are directly competitive or substitutable, it may be appropriate to look not only at such matters as physical characteristics, end uses and customs classification but also "at competition in the relevant markets".[84] In doing so, it is appropriate, according to the Appellate Body, to examine the "elasticity of substitution".[85]

5.123. The complainants argue that it is important to note that Article III:2, second sentence is concerned not only with differences in taxation between products which are actually competitive on a given relevant market but also with differences in taxation between products which are potentially competitive. Indeed, according to the complainants, whereas consumer tastes and habits may differ from one market to another, tax measures should not be used to "freeze" consumers' preference for a domestic product. For that reason, the complainants argue, evidence that two products are not competing actually in a market at a given point in time is not a defense if the absence of actual competition is due, at least in part, to the tax measures in dispute.[86]

> (a)   Soju and all other distilled spirits and liqueurs have the same basic physical characteristics and are apt for the same end uses

5.124. The complainants argue that the notion of "directly competitive and substitutable" products is broader in scope than that of "like" products. According to the complainants, two products which are too "different" in terms of physical properties or of end uses to qualify as "like" for the purposes of Article III:2, first sentence, may still be "competitive or substitutable" in the sense of Article III:2, second sentence. The complainants note that as recently recalled by the Appellate Body in *Canada - Certain Measures Concerning Periodicals*[87], a case of "perfect substitutability" would no longer fall within the second sentence of Article III:2, but within the first sentence.

5.125. The complainants further note that the Panel Report on *Japan - Taxes on Alcoholic Beverages I* indicated that:

---

[83]   Appellate Body Report on *Japan - Taxes on Alcoholic Beverages II, supra*, at 117.

[84]   Appellate Body Report on *Japan - Taxes on Alcoholic Beverages II, supra*, at 117.

[85]   *Ibid.*

[86]   Panel Report on *Japan - Taxes on Alcoholic Beverages II, supra*, para. 6.28. See also Appellate Body Report on *Canada - Certain Measures Concerning Periodicals, supra*, at 473.

[87]   Appellate Body Report on *Canada - Certain Measures Concerning Periodicals, supra*, at 473.

> [t]he flexibility in the use of alcoholic drinks and their common characteristics often offered an alternative choice for consumers leading to a competitive relationship. In the view of the Panel there existed - even if not necessarily in respect of all the economic uses to which the product may be put - direct competition or substitutability among the various distilled liquors.[88]

5.126. According to the complainants, the basic physical properties of soju and the other categories of liquors concerned in this dispute are essentially the same. All distilled spirits are concentrated forms of alcohol produced by the process of distillation. In the complainants' view, at the point of distillation, all spirits are nearly identical, which means that raw materials and method of distillation have almost no impact on the final product. Post-distillation processes such as ageing, dilution with water or addition of flavourings, do not change the basic fact that the product sold is still a concentrated form of alcohol.

5.127. The complainants present a table below which compares the key characteristics of soju and the main types of distilled sprits at issue in this dispute. This table purports to show that all of them have essentially the same physical characteristics. For instance, according to the complainants, the main differences between soju and whisky, the largest category after soju, are limited to the following:

(i) whisky must be made, at least in part, from sprouted grain;

(ii) whisky has an average alcoholic strength of 37-40% ABV, whereas diluted soju is generally sold at 25% ABV (in contrast, the alcoholic strength of distilled soju is similar to that of whisky); and

(iii) whisky must be aged in wooden casks.

DISTILLED SPIRITS - COMPARISON OF PHYSICAL CHARACTERISTICS AND MANUFACTURING PROCESSES

	WHISKY	BRANDY	GIN	RUM	VODKA	SOJU	SHOCHU
Raw Material	Grain	Grapes	Grain; neutral spirits[*]	Sugar Cane; Molasses	Grain; Potatoes; neutral spirits[*]	Grain; Potatoes; neutral spirits*	Grain; Potatoes; neutral spirits[*]
% of Alcohol at Distillation	†Less than 95%	†Less than 95%	†At or above 95%	†Less than 95%	At or above 95%	Not less than 85%	Not less than 85%
% of Alcohol at Bottling	†Not less than 40%	†Not less than 40%	†Not less than 40%	†Not less than 40%	Not less than 40%	Not less than 20%	Not less than 20%
Method of Distillation	Continuous or Pot Still	Continuous or Pot Still	Continuous	Continuous	Continuous	Continuous or Pot Still	Continuous or Pot Still
Aged in Wooden Casks	Yes	Yes	Yes/no	Yes/no	No	Yes/no	Yes/no
Color	Amber	Amber, Clear[1]	Clear to Amber	Clear to Amber	Clear[2]	Clear	Clear to Amber
% of Alcohol	37-50	36-50	37-50	37-50	37-50	20-45	20-45

---

[88] Panel Report on *Japan - Taxes on Alcoholic Beverages I, supra*, para. 5.7.

	WHISKY	BRANDY	GIN	RUM	VODKA	SOJU	SHOCHU
Added Flavorings	Variety[3]	Peach, Blackberry, Cherry, Apricot, Coffee	Spice, Lemon	Spice, Lemon	Currant, Lemon, Orange	Lemon, Honey	Lemon, Variety of Fruit Flavors
Body/Taste Intensity	Medium	Medium	Light to Medium	Light to Medium	Light	Light to medium	Light to Medium

[1]   Examples of clear brandies include grappa, pisco

[2]   Addition of flavoring adds color, e.g. red/purple

[3]   US and Canadian regulations permit the addition of flavorings; EU regulations do not

*   Vodka, gin, soju and shochu may be produced from neutral spirits, which is an alcoholic spirit distilled at not less than 95% alcohol by volume from *any material* of agricultural origin.

†   Based on U.S. standards of identity (Title 27 Code of Federal Regulations, part 5); EU and other countries allow bottling of brandy at 36% and vodka, gin and rum at 37.5%, Australia allows whisky to be bottled at 37 per cent. Japan maintains no minimum alcohol requirements for these products.

5.128. The complainants argue that in practice, the above differences are even less important than they might appear at first sight:

(i)   soju can be made and is often made from the same type of cereal grains as whisky, even if they are not sprouted;

(ii)   whisky is often served on the rocks or mixed with water or other non-alcoholic beverages and is therefore consumed at a similar strength as diluted soju;

(iii)   distilled soju can and is sometimes aged for up to two years in wooden casks. Some brands of diluted premium soju claim to be aged in oak barrels.

5.129. The complainants argue that the above differences are clearly not sufficient to prevent soju and whisky from being directly "substitutable" or "competitive" products in the sense of Article III:2, second sentence. According to the complainants, the existence of similar differences between whisky and Japanese shochu did not preclude the 1987 and 1996 Panels on *Japan - Taxes on Alcoholic Beverages* from finding that those liquors were in competition on the Japanese market.[89]

5.130. The complainants further argue that having essentially the same basic physical properties, soju and all the other distilled spirits and liqueurs are objectively apt to serve the same end-uses:

(i)   all of them are drunk with the same purposes: thirst quenching, socialization, relaxation, etc.

(ii)   all of them may be drunk in similar ways: "straight", diluted with water or other non-alcoholic beverages or mixed with other alcoholic beverages;

(iii)   all of them may be consumed before, after or during meals; and

---

[89]   See Panel Reports on *Japan - Taxes on Alcoholic Beverages I, supra*, para. 5.7; and on *Japan - Taxes on Alcoholic Beverages II, supra*, paras. 6.28-6.32.

(iv)   all of them may be consumed at home or in public places such as restaurants, bars, etc.

5.131. In the complainants' view, the above reasons alone are more than sufficient to conclude that soju and all other distilled spirits and liqueurs are objectively "substitutable" and potentially "competitive" in the Korean market. In addition, the complainants argue that there is conclusive evidence that, despite the distortions introduced by the Korean liquor tax system, competition between soju and other distilled liquors on the Korean market is not just potential but, to a significant degree, also actual.

(b)   Soju and the other distilled spirits and liqueurs are sold in the same sales channels and are promoted and advertised in a similar way

5.132. The complainants assert that the consumption of western-style liquors used to be confined to upmarket restaurants and entertainment establishments. However, the argument goes, over the past few years western-style liquors have gained considerable distribution penetration. According to the complainants, with the main exception of traditional Korean-style restaurants, where soju and other traditional local liquors continue to predominate, western-style liquors are now widely available alongside soju in most sales channels, both for on-premise and off-premise consumption.

5.133. As evidence of the increasing availability of western-style liquors, the complainants point to a recent survey completed by Hankook Research in May 1997 and covering more than 700 sales outlets, which allegedly found that the leading brands of whisky were sold in a majority of outlets within each relevant category. More specifically, the survey established that 'Imperial', 'Passport' and 'Dimple', the "three big" brands of whisky, were sold in 76%, 81% and 61%, respectively, of the surveyed on-premise outlets and in 64%, 98 % and 85%, respectively, of the surveyed off-premise outlets.[90]

5.134. The complainants further purport to show by the photographs included in their exhibits[91] that off-premise outlets often display soju and other distilled sprits and liqueurs side-by-side on the same shelves, thus providing evidence in their view, that both the retailers and the public regard them as being in competition.

5.135. According to the complainants, the advertising of soju, and especially of premium soju, is very similar to the advertising of western-style liquors and tends to emphasize precisely those characteristics which are generally attributed by Korean consumers to western-style liquors, such as pureness, mild taste, maturity, no-hangover effects, etc.[92]

5.136. The complainants assert that likewise, the packaging of soju, and in particular of premium soju, is similar to the packaging of western-style spirits and liqueurs.

---

[90]   See EC Annex 10.

[91]   See EC Annex 11 and US Exhibit G.

[92]   See the advertising materials included in EC Annex 12 and US Exhibit G.

5.137. The complainants state that, like their Japanese neighbours, Korean consumers at first perceived Western-style liquors as "luxury" items to be offered as gifts or to be consumed only on special occasions and at special places. Over time, however, there has been, both in Japan and in Korea, a clear trend towards consumption of all types of distilled spirits on more and varied occasions, and in different methods of consumption, i.e. in mixed drinks, warm, cold, etc. According to the United States, the expanding methods and venues of consumption have also been aided by greater availability of all types of spirits in all sales channels.

5.138. The complainants further state that, to capitalize on Korean consumer's expanded awareness, the soju market has been creating new categories and brands of soju at a fast pace. Most of the activity has been in the recently established premium soju segment. For example, in Korea, Bohae Brewery first successfully used the strategy of incorporating flavoured additives such as honey to soju in its Kim Sat Gat brand soju. Kim Sat Gat was quickly followed by other premium sojus that also contained honey, or were flavoured by aging in wood.

(c)   Consumers' demand for soju has been responsive to the changes in the price of whisky

5.139. The complainants argue that there is statistical evidence indicating that, despite the competitive distortions created by Korea's liquor tax system, demand for soju has been responsive in the past to changes in the prices of the other categories of distilled liquors, and in particular to changes in the price of whisky.

5.140. The complainants further argue that the applicable liquor tax rate on whisky has been progressively lowered from 200% in 1990 to 100% in 1996. According to the complainants, during the same period, the applicable import customs duties were lowered from 70% to 20%. These tax and tariff changes were followed by a reduction of the prices for whisky and a spectacular increase in sales from 11 million litres in 1992 to 27 million litres in 1996.

5.141. The complainants argue that, the increase in sales of whisky took place, to a significant extent, at the expense of soju. According to the complainants, until last year sales of soju have grown at a lower pace than overall demand for distilled spirits and liqueurs. As a result, the complainants argue, soju lost market share, mainly to the benefit of whisky. Thus, the argument goes, whereas the market share of soju fell from 96.37% in 1992 to 94.39% in 1996, during the same period the share of whisky increased by a similar percentage from 1.53% to 3.14%. The complainants conclude that this transfer of market share from soju to whisky shows that the two liquors are in competition with each other on the Korean market.

5.142. The complainants further explain that this trend may have reversed itself during 1997 as a result of the depreciation of the Korean won, the campaign of boycotts against imported products and the financial crisis of last autumn. According to the complainants, this reversal of market trends constitutes an additional proof of the substitutability between soju and imported western-style liquors.

> (d) The Dodwell study shows that there is a significant
> degree of cross-price elasticity between soju and all
> other distilled spirits and liqueurs

5.143. The complainants presented a document,[93] which purports to contain a copy of a study completed on 17 July 1997 for the Confederation of European Producers Spirits by Dodwell Marketing Consultants Ltd. in co-operation with Frank Small and Associates, Korea ("the Dodwell study").

5.144. The complainants argue that the purpose of the Dodwell study was to test the hypothesis that a reduction in the prices of western-style spirits and liqueurs and/or an increase in the prices of soju following a change in the applicable liquor tax rates will lead to a relative increase in the consumption of western-style liquors at the expense of soju.

5.145. According to the complainants, the research method used in the Dodwell study is the same as that followed in the ASI study, which was cited by the Panel on *Japan - Taxes on Alcoholic Beverages II* as one of the reasons for its conclusion that shochu and all other spirits and liqueurs were competitive in the Japanese market.[94]

5.146. The complainants further state that the Dodwell study is based on the responses to questions from a representative sample of 500 Korean spirits drinkers. The complainants also state that the survey-takers showed to each respondent pictures of representative brands of soju, premium soju and three brown spirits (standard scotch, premium scotch and cognac) and a list of prices for each, and asked which type of beverage the respondent would most like to buy given the prices specified.

5.147. The complainants argue that initially, both the proposed price for standard soju and the proposed prices for the other beverages were based on current representative prices on the Korean market ("Level 1" prices). The prices for soju were then successively increased to "Level 2" and to "Level 3". At each of the three price levels for soju, the prices for the other beverages were reduced in two steps ("Level 2" and "Level 3"). Thus, the complainants argue that the respondents were confronted with nine different price combinations. All the prices proposed to the respondents were within the range of the price levels which could reasonably result from the elimination of the existing differences in tax rates. The same research was carried out also with respect to the main types of white spirits (gin, vodka, rum and tequila) and liqueurs.

5.148. The complainants argue that the Dodwell study confirms that there is a significant degree of cross-price elasticity between soju and brown spirits, as allegedly evidenced by the following findings:

> (i) even very small price movements gave raise to significant changes in
> the preferences of the respondents. For example, if the current repre-
> sentative price of standard soju was increased by just 100 won (10%
> of the Level 1 price) and the prices for brown liquors remained the

---

[93] See EC Annex 13.

[94] See Panel Report on *Japan - Taxes on Alcoholic Beverages II*, *supra*, paras 6.29 and 6.32.

same, the share of respondents who would buy brown liquors instead of soju would increase by 8% from 15.2% to 16.4%;

(ii)   the respondents were even more sensitive to an equivalent decrease in the price of the brown sprits. For instance, if the price for a bottle of standard Scotch whisky fell from 11,500 won (Level 1) to 10,150 won (Level 2) and the price of standard soju remained unchanged, the share of standard Scotch whisky would increase from 7.4% to 10% (i.e. by 35%);

(iii)   the switch is most marked when the price for soju increases and, si-multaneously, the prices for brown liquors decline. At current repre-sentative prices (Level 1), the share of consumers who prefer brown spirits to soju (including premium soju) is 15.2%. If the price of standard soju was increased by 200 won to Level 3 and, at the same time, the prices for brown liquors fell to Level 3, the share of brown spirits would increase to 28.4%, i.e. by as much as 87%.

5.149. The complainants also argue that the Dodwell study shows that cross-price elasticity between soju and white sprits and liqueurs is also significant. Thus, it is alleged that according to the study, if the price of soju was increased by 200 won to Level 3 and, simultaneously, the price for white sprits and liqueurs was reduced to Level 3, the share of consumers who would prefer white spirits and liqueurs to soju (including premium soju) would increase from 13.8% to 23.8% (i.e. by 72 %).

iii)   Soju and other distilled spirits and liqueurs are "not similarly taxed"

5.150. The complainants note that, as confirmed by the Appellate Body in *Japan - Taxes on Alcoholic Beverages*, for two competitive or substitutable products to be deemed as "not similarly taxed", the difference in taxation must be more than *de minimis* [95]. The complainants further notes that in the same report, the Appellate Body held that whether any particular tax differential is or is not *de minimis* must be determined on a case-by-case basis[96].

5.151. The complainants presented the following table which purports to show the differences in taxation between each of the sub-categories of soju and the other categories concerned in this dispute. According to the complainants, the table evidences that diluted soju is taxed at the lowest combined rate, whereas distilled soju is taxed at a lower combined rate than any other category with the only exception of "liqueurs".

---

[95]   Appellate Body Report on *Japan - Taxes on Alcoholic Beverages, supra*, at 119.

[96]   *Ibid.*

Table 5

**Comparison of the tax rates applied to soju
and other distilled spirits and liqueurs**

	Liquor Tax rate (%)	*Education Tax rate (% Liquor Tax Base)*	*Combined Tax rate (%)*	*Discrimination Index*
Diluted soju	35	3.5	38.5	1.00
Distilled soju	50	5	55	1.43/1.00
Whisky	100	30	130	3.38/2.36
Brandy	100	30	130	3.38/2.36
General distilled spirits	80	24	104	2.70/1.89
- (containing whisky or brandy)	100	30	130	3.38/2.36
Liqueurs	50	5	55	1.43/1.00
Other Liquors				
- more than 25% alcohol content	80	24	104	2.70/2.36
- less than 25% alcohol content	70	7	77	2.00/1.40
- containing whisky or brandy	100	30	130	3.38/2.36

5.152. The complainants conclude that table 5 provides evidence that the differences in taxation are in all cases far from being "de minimis" and, therefore, that soju is not "similarly taxed". According to the complainants, the combined tax rate on whisky and brandy, for instance, is 2.36 times higher than the rate on distilled soju and 3.38 times higher than the rate on diluted soju.

> iv)   The differences in taxation are applied so as to afford protection to the domestic production of soju

5.153. The complainants note that in *Japan - Taxes on Alcoholic Beverages II*, the Appellate Body laid down the following approach for establishing whether dissimilar taxation of directly competitive or substitutable products is applied "so as to afford protection to domestic production":

> we believe that an examination in any case of whether dissimilar taxation has been applied so as to afford protection requires a comprehensive and objective analysis of the structure and application of the measure in question on domestic as compared to imported products. We believe it is possible to examine objectively the underlying criteria used in a particular measure, its structure, and its overall application to ascertain whether it is applied in a way that affords protection to domestic products.
>
> Although it is true that the aim of a measure may not be easily ascertained, nevertheless its protective application can most often be discerned from the design, architecture and revealing structure of a measure. The very magnitude of the dissimilar taxation in a particular case may be evidence of such

protective application, ... Most often, there will other factors to be considered as well. In conducting this inquiry, panels should give full consideration to all the relevant facts and all the circumstances in any given case.[97]

5.154. The complainants argue that in the present case, the following facts and circumstances regarding the *"structure of the measures"* as well as its *"overall application on domestic as compared to imported products"* constitute irrefutable evidence that the Liquor Tax Law and the Education Tax Law are applied "so as to afford protection" to Korea's domestic production of soju. For this proposition, the complainants gives the following factors:

(i)   the very magnitude of the tax differentials;

(ii)   the lack of rationality of the product categorization;

(iii)   the fact that there are virtually no imports of soju;

(iv)   the fact that soju accounts for the vast majority of the Korean production of distilled spirits and liqueurs;

(v)   the fact that almost all whisky and brandy, as well as a significant proportion of the liquors falling within the categories of General Distilled Liquors and Liqueurs are imported; and

(vi)   the existence of a long history of tax discrimination and protectionism.

(a)   The magnitude of the tax differentials

5.155. The complainants argue that in *Japan - Taxes on Alcoholic Beverages II*, the Appellate Body found that the very magnitude of the difference in taxation between shochu and other distilled spirits and liqueurs was sufficient evidence to conclude that the Japanese Liquor Tax Law was applied so as to afford protection to the domestic production of shochu.[98]

5.156. According to the complainants, the situation is similar in the present dispute. It argues that the tax differentials between soju and other distilled spirits and liqueurs are so large that they constitute sufficient evidence in themselves that the Liquor Tax Law and the Education Tax Law are applied so as to afford protection to the domestic production of soju.

5.157. The complainants state that the tax differentials at issue in this dispute appear to be even bigger than those taken into consideration by the Panel and the Appellate Body in *Japan - Taxes on Alcoholic Beverages II*.[99] They add that, it must be recalled that the tax differentials between soju and other distilled spirits and liqueurs

---

[97]   Appellate Body Report on *Japan - Taxes on Alcoholic Beverages II, supra*, at 120.

[98]   Appellate Body Report on *Japan - Taxes on Alcoholic Beverages II, supra*, at 122.

[99]   In *Japan - Taxes on Alcoholic Beverages II*, the taxes in dispute were specific taxes per litre of beverage instead of *ad valorem* taxes. This makes it extremely difficult to compare the tax differentials at issue in the two cases. Nevertheless, it is worth noting that, according to the complainants, in *Japan - Taxes on Alcoholic Beverages II* the differences in specific taxes translated into a difference in tax/price ratios between shochu and whisky of between 10 % and 32 % of their retail sales price (See Panel Report on *Japan - Taxes on Alcoholic Beverages II, supra,* at para. 4.159). In comparison, in the present case, the tax differential between soju and whisky may represent as much as 91.5 % of the CIF import value of whisky.

would be much larger but for the successive changes introduced by Korea since 1990 in response to pressure from the Community.

(b)   The product categorization is arbitrary

5.158. The complainants are of the view that the Liquor Tax Law defines soju almost exclusively in negative terms, by excluding from a very broad, catch-all formula any type of distilled spirits which happen to be imported in significant quantities. According to the complainants, the lack of specificity of the legal definition of soju is further attested by the overlap between that definition and the legal definitions of other residual categories (e.g. the sub-category defined in Article 3.9 E of the Liquor Tax Law). In the complainants' view, this clearly shows that the application of a lower rate of tax to soju does not correspond to any distinguishing characteristic of soju, but is merely aimed to afford protection to Korea's domestic production of distilled spirits.

5.159. For instance, the complainants argue that according to their respective legal definitions, the only difference between diluted soju and gin is that the latter has juniper berries and plant flavourings added before distillation[100]. However, according to the complainants, this obviously minor difference entails a tax differential equivalent to more than 90% of the import CIF value of a bottle of imported gin. In the complainants' view, this huge tax differential is clearly disproportionate and can only be explained as being aimed at affording protection to the domestic production of soju.

(c)   Domestic soju is "isolated" from imports of soju

5.160. The complainants further note that in *Japan - Taxes on Alcoholic Beverages II*, both the Panel and the Appellate Body noted that:

> "... the combination of customs duties and internal taxation in Japan has the following impact: on the one hand, it makes it difficult for foreign-produced shochu to penetrate the Japanese market and, on the other, it does not guarantee equality of competitive conditions between shochu and the rest of 'white' and 'brown' spirits. Thus, through a combination of high import duties and differentiated internal taxes, Japan manages to 'isolate' domestically produced shochu from foreign competition, be it foreign produced shochu or any other of the mentioned white and brown spirits".[101]

5.161. According to the complainants, the situation is similar in the present case. The complainants argue that Korean soju is effectively "isolated" from competition from foreign soju. It is alleged that imports of soju into Korea have always been negligible. It is argued that in 1997 for instance, the imported volume of soju was just 1,625 litres, which allegedly represents barely 0.0002% of the total soju sales in

---

[100] See the legal definitions of diluted soju and gin at Articles 3.1 and 3.9 C of the Liquor Tax Law, respectively.

[101] Panel Report on *Japan - Taxes on Alcoholic Beverages II, supra*, para. 6.35, cited by the Appellate Body Report on the same case, *supra*, at 122.

Korea. According to the complainants, therefore, it is indisputable that by favouring soju vis-a-vis other liquors, Korea protects a "domestic production".

5.162. The complainants further argue that Korean soju is even more "isolated" from imports of foreign soju than Japanese shochu was from foreign shochu in *Japan - Taxes on Alcoholic Beverages*. It is argued that in that case, Japan could point to the existence of a significant, even if small in relative terms, flow of shochu imports (between 1-2%). In contrast, it is argued that imports of soju into Korea are virtually non-existent.

5.163. The complainants assert that as in the case of shochu in *Japan - Taxes on Alcoholic Beverages II*, one of the reasons why Korean soju is "isolated" from imports of foreign soju is the high level of the import duties on that product. It is argued that currently, the bound rate on soju is 79% and the applied rate 30%. In comparison, it is alleged that in *Japan - Taxes on Alcoholic Beverages II*, the bound and applied rates on shochu were 26.7% and 17.9%, respectively. It is further argued that the applied import duty rate on soju (30%) is higher than the applied rate on any other category of distilled spirits and liqueurs (15%-20%).

> (d) Soju accounts for the vast majority of the Korean production of distilled spirits and liqueurs

5.164. According to the complainants, it may be estimated that soju accounts for more than 95 % of the Korean production of distilled spirits and liqueurs. Thus, by applying a lower tax rate to soju, Korea is affording protection not just to its domestic production of soju but more generally to its entire domestic industry of distilled spirits and liqueurs.

> (e) Almost all whisky and brandy sold in Korea is imported

5.165. The complainants argue that whereas imports of soju are almost non-existent, virtually all the sales of whisky and brandy, as well as a significant proportion of the sales of white spirits and liqueurs are imported. In the complainants' view, this makes the Korean liquor tax system even more protective in effect than the tax measures at issue in *Japan - Taxes on Alcoholic Beverages I and II*, where a majority of sales within the more taxed category of "whisky/brandy" was domestically produced.

> (f) There is a long history of tax discrimination and protectionism

5.166. The complainants further argue that the Korean soju industry has traditionally benefited from a very high degree of protection against imports. According to this view, until 1989 the Korean market for distilled spirits and liqueurs was almost closed to imports through the combined application of quantitative restrictions and dissuasive import duties. Since then, the argument continues, Korea has been forced to lift the import quotas and to negotiate with the complainants a reduction of the applied customs duties as part of the 1993 Agreement. The complainants assert that in light of Korea's past record of protectionism in this sector, it becomes evident that the measures at issue are but a last ditch attempt by Korea to continue to afford protection to its domestic soju industry against imports of western-style liquors.

5.167. The complainants respectfully request the Panel to find that:

    (i)   Korea is in breach of its obligations under GATT Article III:2, first sentence, by applying internal taxes on imported vodka pursuant to the Liquor Tax Law and the Education Tax Law which are in excess of those applied on soju; and

    (ii)   Korea is in breach of its obligations under GATT Article III:2, second sentence, by applying higher internal taxes pursuant to the Liquor Tax Law and the Education Tax Law on imported liquors, classified under HS heading 2208, currently falling within the categories of "whisky", "brandy", "general distilled liquors", "liqueurs" and "other liquors" (to the extent that they contain distilled spirits or liqueurs) than on soju, so as to afford protection to its domestic production of soju.

2.   *Korea*

(a)   General

5.168. Korea notes that in bringing this case before the Panel, the United States and the European Communities have called into question the validity of the Korean tax regime on alcoholic beverages, claiming that this regime discriminates against some imported spirits, to the benefit of a Korean distilled alcoholic beverage called 'soju', and in violation of Article III:2 of the GATT. Korea concedes, as the complainants point out, that it imposes a different rate of tax on soju than it imposes on certain imported alcoholic beverages. However, in Korea's view, not every difference in rates of tax amounts to a violation of Article III:2.

5.169. Korea asserts that Article III:2 is perhaps the provision of the GATT that treads most heavily upon national sovereignty. In Korea's view, a nation's taxation system is the product of a long and intricate domestic political process. Korea argues that taxes are built up over years, and reflect different and evolving policy goals. No country imposes a single rate of tax on all products. Korea also notes that the GATT contains no requirement that countries harmonize their tax systems. Korea asserts that the fundamental purpose of Art. III:2 is to avoid protectionism.

5.170. Korea further argues that the prohibitions of Art. III:2, while honouring their anti-protectionist purpose, must be strictly interpreted. In Korea's view, before the tax rates of imported and domestic products can be compared, the competitive relationship between these two products must be strong, if not very strong indeed.

5.171. Korea's position is that according to Article III:2, imported products ought not be taxed less favourably than competing domestic products. Korea further argues that where products are perfect substitutes, or 'like', no difference in tax treatment can be tolerated. Where products are not 'like', but are still 'directly competitive or substitutable', the argument continues, there is more room for tax differences, as long as they do not have a protectionist effect.

(b)   The Korean Tax System

5.172. Korea proceeds to give an explanation of its internal tax system. It states that it has 32 different types of taxes, which are largely divided into national and local taxes. Korea further states that like other countries, it distinguishes between direct taxes and taxes on goods and services. Unlike some other countries in Korea the share in total tax receipts of indirect taxes is much higher than direct taxes.[102]

5.173. Korea notes that all alcoholic beverages are subject to several taxes, such as value added tax, liquor tax and education tax. The latter two taxes, as applied to certain imported alcoholic beverages, are disputed in this case.

i)   The Liquor Tax

5.174. Korea notes that the Liquor Tax Law was enacted in 1949, and has been amended more than twenty times since. An important step in the development of the Liquor Tax Law was the change from a specific tax system to an *ad valorem* tax system in 1968.[103] According to Korea, the reason for this alteration was mainly that the Korean legislature wanted to raise taxes in proportion to the prices of products. It is of some significance, notes Korea, in view of the allegations that Korea's taxes are protectionist, that at the time of enactment of the Liquor Tax Law, and at the time of the change to an *ad valorem* system, Korea had very little imports of liquor.

5.175. Korea notes that the parts of its Liquor Tax Law that are relevant to this case are contained in the general provisions and in the chapter dealing with imposition. In the general provisions, a description is given for each drink in such way that it sets the requirements as to the content of each of the liquors in order to fit into the classification of the Liquor Tax. The section of the law dealing with imposition fixes the rates which apply to each particular group of liquors. The descriptions in the law determine the different applicable rates, thus, Korea concedes imposing a different tax rate on standard soju and whisky.

5.176. However, Korea argues that the complainants attempt to create the mistaken impression that the law's very structure reveals a protectionist intent.[104] According to Korea, the reality is different. For a long time, soju was the only spirit subject to liquor taxes. Korea notes that though the law's definition was broad, it covered only what was known. Over time, other spirits were marketed, and as they appeared, new tax categories were created.

5.177. Korea notes that the Liquor Tax relates to spirits and beverages containing at least 1% of alcohol. The persons falling under the Liquor Tax are either manufacturers of alcoholic beverages supplying from their factory, or importers. These persons pay taxes on the basis of the price at the time of delivery, when the beverages are delivered from a factory, or, when the liquors are imported, on the basis of the CIF plus duty price.

---

[102] In 1994, for instance, according to OECD methodology, the share of indirect taxes amounted to 43.4% of total tax revenue in Korea, whereas the comparable figure for the United States was 17.9%. The Korean figure for 1996 (predicted) is 43.7%.

[103] In this respect, the Korean liquor taxes differ from the liquor taxes at issue *in Japan - Taxes on Alcoholic Beverages II*, which were specific.

[104] See EC first submission, at para. 24; US first submission, at para. 24.

5.178. Korea further notes that the applicable tax rates on the alcoholic beverages are described in the Liquor Tax Law.[105] The tax system and the applicable rates have evolved over time. The applicable rate does not depend on the origin of the liquor. Korea presents the following rates that purportedly apply to the distilled beverages in dispute:

Drinks	Ad valorem %
Soju: a)　standard (or 'diluted') soju b)　distilled soju	 35% 50%
Liqueurs[106]	50%
General distilled spirits[107]	80%
Whiskies, brandies	100%

5.179. Korea states that being a high-volume, common drink that Koreans usually consume with meals, standard soju is in a class of its own, and so is distilled soju, being an artisanal drink, that is unique to Korea.

5.180. Korea notes that there is also a substantial domestic production of liqueurs, general distilled spirits and, particularly, of whisky, that fall under the higher tax rates.

5.181. According to Korea, the liquor taxes are an important tool for the government of Korea to raise revenue. According to the most recently available figures, liquor taxes amounted to 3.52% of national tax revenues.[108] Their share in indirect taxes represented 9.08%. The largest contributor to the liquor taxes traditionally has been beer, which is mostly domestically produced, which accounts for 69% of the Liquor Tax revenues in 1996.

ii)　　The Education Tax

5.182. Korea states that in addition to the Liquor Tax, an education tax is levied. According to Korea, Education Tax is an earmarked tax, meaning that the revenues collected through the Education Tax can only be used for the specific purpose of improving the educational system. The Liquor Tax regime is not the only regime that has an Education Tax. Korea asserts that there are ten other regimes to which the Education Tax is attached, such as tobacco consumption tax, property tax and transportation tax. Likewise, taxpayers liable for the payment of liquor taxes are also subject to the education tax. In Korea's calculation, the revenues generated by liquors in the education tax proceeds amount to 12.5%.

---

[105]　Article 19(2).

[106]　Examples of 'liqueurs' are Insam (ginseng) ju, Ogapiju, Bailey's, Grand Marnier, and Kahlua.

[107]　Examples of 'general distilled alcoholic spirits' are koryangju, rum, gin, and vodka.

[108]　This percentage is based on figures from 1996. In the two preceding years the revenue collected from the liquor tax was 3.54% and 3.53%.

5.183. Korea states that the tax basis for the Education Tax, as levied on payers of the liquor tax, is the Liquor Tax corresponding to each kind of drink. The Education Tax applies as follows: alcoholic beverages whose *ad valorem* tax rate is higher than 80% are subject to 30% education tax on the amount of the Liquor Tax, and alcoholic beverages with an *ad valorem* tax below 80% are subject to 10% Education Tax.

5.184. Korea notes that the Education Tax is levied irrespective of the origin of the products. The proceeds of the Education Tax are allocated exclusively to the improvement of Korea's educational system, notably at the mandatory education level from primary to middle school.

(c)   Legal Analysis

5.185. Korea notes that the complainants argue that because Korea imposes a different rate of tax on 'soju' than the rate which is imposed upon a number of alcoholic beverages, its tax system unfairly burdens imported spirits, to the benefit of the domestic spirit 'soju'.

> i)   The purpose of Article III of the GATT is to prevent protectionism, not to harmonize taxes

5.186. According to Korea, Article III, perhaps more than any other provision of the GATT, steps into a realm which is traditionally the province of national sovereignty - the domestic tax system.

5.187. Korea notes that as each Member joins the WTO, it brings with it its individual tax system, an intricate web of rules built up over many years reflecting a mixture of government objectives (ranging from social policies to the need to raise revenues).

5.188. Korea further states that no Member of the WTO has the same rate of internal taxation for all products, and the tax differences that have built up throughout the years may not always seem completely coherent. However, the argument continues, it is not the role of the GATT to attempt to render each tax system internally coherent, and nor is it the province of GATT to harmonize the tax systems of its many Members.

5.189. Korea takes note of the 1992 Panel report in *United States - Measures Affecting Alcoholic and Malt Beverages* in which it was stated:

> The purpose of Article III is not to harmonize the internal taxes and regulations of contracting parties, which differ from country to country.[109]

In Korea's view, tax harmonization is a sensitive matter even between countries that have achieved a high level of integration, such as the member states of the European Communities.

---

[109] Panel Report on *United States - Measures Affecting Alcoholic and Malt Beverages*, adopted on 19 June 1992, DS23/R, BISD 39S/206, 276, at paras. 5.71 - 5.72.

5.190. Korea further argues that it should be noted that Article III is not intended to encroach upon the powers of WTO Members to pursue their legitimate objectives through their tax systems. In this regard Korea draws attention to a statement by the Appellate Body put in *Japan -Taxes on Alcoholic Beverages*, in which it said:

> Members of the WTO are free to pursue their own domestic goals through internal taxation or regulation so long as they do not do so in a way that violates Article III or any of the other commitments they have made in the WTO Agreement.[110]

5.191. Korea, therefore asserts that Article III of the GATT is only meant to step into this sensitive realm of taxation in certain narrowly circumscribed circumstances, in order to pursue a specific objective. According to Korea, the fundamental purpose of Article III is to avoid protectionism and to oblige the WTO members to provide for equality of competitive conditions for imported products in relation to domestic products. As the Appellate Body put it in *Japan - Taxes on Alcoholic Beverages II*:

> The broad and fundamental purpose of Article III is to avoid protectionism in the application of internal tax and regulatory measures. Toward this end, Article III obliges Members of the WTO to provide equality of competitive conditions for imported products in relation to domestic products.[111]

ii)   The analysis required under Article III:2

5.192. Korea states that reconciling the anti-protectionist purpose of Article III:2 with the need to recognize each WTO Member's discretion to maintain and develop its own tax policy has not been an easy exercise.

5.193. Korea further states that the *Malt Beverages* panel construed the so-called 'aims and effects' test. Under that test, as long as the tax system introduced product distinctions for policy purposes that were unrelated to the protection of domestic production, the resulting tax differences could not violate Article III:2.[112] According to Korea, this approach did not find favour with the Appellate Body in *Japan - Taxes on Alcoholic Beverages II*. In Korea's view, the Appellate Body (as well as the Panel in the first instance) ruled that the aims and effects test strayed too far from the text of Article III:2, ignoring the distinction made between the two prohibitions contained, respectively, in the first and the second sentence of this provision. The first sentence tolerates no differentiation whatsoever between tax rates that apply to 'like' products. The second sentence imposes constraints on tax differentials that apply to 'directly competitive and substitutable products'.

5.194. Korea further argues that according to the Appellate Body, the wording of the first sentence leaves no room to inquire whether a tax rate differential, which applies to 'like' products, was really introduced with protectionist 'aims and effects'. By this argument, differential tax rates applying to 'like' products violate Article III:2.

---

[110] See Appellate Body Report on *Japan - Taxes on Alcoholic Beverages II, supra*, at 110.

[111] Appellate Body Report, *supra*, at 110.

[112] Panel Report on *United States - Measures Affecting Alcoholic and Malt Beverages, supra*, para. 5.25.

5.195. Korea argues, however, that this does not mean that the Appellate Body was insensitive to the concerns of the WTO membership about preserving discretion to develop individual tax policies. Korea notes that in its report, the Appellate Body took great pains to underline 'how narrow the range of "like" products is meant to be'.[113] Korea further notes that the Appellate Body, affirming the Panel,[114] also clarified that 'like' products are a subset of directly competitive and substitutable. In Korea's view, this indicates that Article III:2 only comes into play when the products at issue are in a particularly close relationship (they should be at least "directly competitive or substitutable"). Where there is no relationship, or an insufficiently close relationship between two products, argues Korea, the WTO Members retain the sovereignty to impose taxes according to their own discretion.

5.196. Korea argues that the determination of whether two products are 'like' or directly competitive and substitutable products is based upon an overall appreciation, on a case-by-case basis, of their qualities and their relationship. Korea refers to one general remark regarding both the determination of 'like' products and of directly competitive and substitutable products which was made in *Japan - Taxes on Alcoholic Beverages II*, which allegedly emphasized that a particularly appropriate test to define whether two products are 'like' or 'directly competitive or substitutable products' is the 'marketplace'.[115] Korea notes that while noting that there might be other means to identify the broader category of directly competitive and substitutable products, the Appellate Body upheld this reasoning, stating that the: 'GATT 1994 is a commercial agreement, and the WTO is concerned, after all, with markets.'[116]

5.197. Korea also states that it is useful to make some preliminary comments about the threshold condition of Article III:2: i.e. how does one analyze whether there is a sufficiently close competitive relationship between the Korean sojus and the remaining imported liquors? Korea poses the question, when are products sufficiently competitive for the purposes of comparing their tax rates under Article III.2?

5.198. Korea argues that to answer this threshold question, it is useful to recall first the factors that are relevant to establish a competitive relationship between two products and then analyze the degree of competition that will trigger the application of Article III.2, first and second sentences.

iii)   Relevant factors

5.199. According to Korea, first, one must determine whether the products at issue are at least roughly comparable. Where potable liquids are concerned, it makes little sense to compare soft drinks with alcoholic beverages for example. Consumers who want a soft drink will not consider alcohol a suitable alternative.

---

[113] Appellate Body Report on *Japan - Taxes on Alcoholic Beverages II, supra*, at 112-113.

[114] Panel Report on *Japan - Taxes on Alcoholic Beverages II, supra*, para. 6.22.

[115] Panel Report on *Japan - Taxes on Alcoholic Beverages II, supra*, para. 6.22.

[116] See *Japan - Taxes on Alcoholic Beverages II*, Appellate Body Report, *supra*, at 117. The Appellate Body reiterated this reasoning in its more recent report in *Canada - Certain Measures Concerning Periodicals, supra*, at 470.

5.200. Korea further states that within the broad category of alcoholic beverages, a further distinction can be made according to product characteristics, such as:

-    *Raw materials* - Are products rice-based, grain-based, potato-based, tapioca-based, etc? Which additives are used? In Korea's view, these elements may influence the taste of the beverage, and the consumer's perception in general.

-    *Production process* - Are the alcoholic drinks based on fermentation only, or on distillation? Are they aged, and if so how, before being sold? According to Korea, these are factors that may influence the final appearance and taste of the drink, but also its image in the marketplace. Ageing in wooden casks, for instance, gives a drink an 'artisanal' image, that may make quite a difference to consumers, even though objectively it is debatable whether more industrial production processes (e.g., mere storage in metal containers) result in inferior products.

-    *Physical characteristics* - of the finished products. Are the products similar in terms of their appearance, the degree of alcoholic strength?

Other notable factors determining whether two products compete revolve around price and end use.

-    *Price* - Are the products at issue in the same price range? According to Korea, if prices differ greatly, two seemingly similar products cannot be considered directly competitive. Korea notes that in *Japan - Taxes on Alcoholic Beverages II*, the complainants argued that Japanese shochu and the imported liquors were in the same price range before tax.[117] Korea further notes that Japan does not appear to have contested this. Korea asserts that the price differences in Korea between standard soju and the disputed imported liquors are very considerable.

-    *End uses* - Do consumers use these products in the same way? Do they drink a particular drink straight or mixed; with meals, or on other occasions? Korea states that these elements were highlighted in *Japan - Taxes on Alcoholic Beverages I*.[118] Korea argues for instance, that depending on the food they usually eat, consumers will show a preference for different alcoholic drinks during meals. In countries with a spicy food tradition, consumers may favour strong alcohol that cleans the palate, when eating meals. In countries where spicy food is not a tradition, consumers will by definition have a different preference for an alcoholic drink that goes best with their national cuisine.

5.201. Korea argues that the existence, or absence, of a competitive relationship can also be gleaned from other factors, such as the places of sale and consumption. According to Korea, one relevant question in this connection is whether the disputed liquors are sold through the same outlets, so that consumers are actually offered a choice between them. If not, this is an indication that they are not, in fact, competing.

---

[117]   See Panel Report in *Japan - Taxes on Alcoholic Beverages II, supra*, at para. 4.82. See also the more recent *Canada - Certain Measures Concerning Periodicals*, Appellate Body report, at 472, where the Appellate Body, in finding a directly competitive and substitutable relationship between certain imported and domestic periodicals, approvingly cited evidence of 'considerable price competition' between the two.

[118]   See Panel Report on *Japan - Taxes on Alcoholic Beverages I, supra*, para. 5.7.

iv)   The degree of competition or substitutability

5.202. Korea poses the question, how strong must competition between two products be, before one can speak of a directly competitive and substitutable, or even a 'like' product relationship within the meaning of Article III:2?

5.203. Korea argues that it is good policy to give a strict reading to the terms of Article III:2. In Korea's view, given that the WTO is an organization which brings together a large number of diverse countries, and that it has no mandate to harmonize tax policies, the threshold to review taxes under Article III:2 GATT (i.e., the competitive relationship between differently taxed products) is both important and substantial.

5.204. According to Korea, for 'like' products, the competitive relationship must be very strong indeed. Korea cites the Appellate Body report on *Canada - Certain Measures Concerning Periodicals*, in which it was stated that 'like' products are 'perfect substitutes'.[119]

5.205. Korea argues that in relation to the examination of the legal obligation under Article III:2 second sentence, the existence of competitive relationship is also an essential requirement for the determination of whether products can be determined to be directly competitive and substitutable. In Korea's view, unlike 'like' products, substitution does not have to be perfect between the products. Korea asserts that the texts of Article III:2 second sentence and its Interpretative Note require that the competitive relationship must still be strong before the products can be considered directly competitive and substitutable. This is why the text refers to "*directly* competing or substitutable products".

5.206. In Korea's view, the complainants have not shown that there is any close relationship between the imported products and soju. Korea therefore, is of the view that they have been unable to show actual competition on the market between the products and are now trying to introduce the argument that the absence of actual competition was due, at least in part, to the tax measures.

5.207. According to Korea, such a loose interpretation of Article III.2 runs counter to the text of the Interpretative Note to Article III.2. This Note adds that 'only where competition was involved' between two 'directly competitive or substitutable' products could a tax differential conceivably amount to a violation of the second sentence of Article III:2. In Korea's view, this language strongly suggests that there must be actual competition between the directly competitive or substitutable products before their tax rates are to be compared.

5.208. Korea further argues that it is clear that in the present case the complainants have neither shown that imported liquors actually compete with the Korean sojus, nor have they shown that these liquors would directly compete with each other in the absence of the tax differential. Korea refers to the argument by the complainants that there is a substantial measure of price elasticity between the Korean sojus and imported liquors. According to Korea, the complainants seek to argue that various product combinations are in competition with each other, on the grounds that relatively small changes in the price of soju will persuade Korean consumers to switch

---

[119] Appellate Body Report on *Canada - Certain Measures Concerning Periodicals, supra*, at 473.

to imported liquors such as whisky. Korea notes that in support of this argument the European Communities submitted a market survey,[120] which has been endorsed by the United States.

5.209. Korea points out that given the considerable price differences (even pre-tax) and different end uses between these liquors, the complainants' conclusion flies in the face of common sense. Korea adds that another study funded by the European Communities, and conducted by the same organization but not for legal proceedings, found that "soju in particular remains unaffecetd by imported drinks".[121]

5.210. Korea submits that this particular study (the 'Dodwell' study) constitutes poor evidence. Korea puts forward the following reasons for its assertion that the Dodwell study cannot be relied upon as constituting evidence of product substitutability:

v)   Problems in the Dodwell Report

Internally inconsistent results

5.211. Korea expounds upon the peculiarity and problems, namely flaws in design or oddities in the reported results. Korea mentions as an example that in chart 2, the percentage choosing soju rises when price of soju increases from 1,100 to 1,200 won, even though all other prices are held constant. Korea argues that this seems to imply a positively-sloped demand curve, which is, as the United States noted before the *Japan - Taxes on Alcoholic Beverage II* case, "contrary to one of the fundamental tenets of micro-economic theory.[122] Moreover, Korea observes, the percentage choosing premium and standard scotch rises as the price of soju rises from 1,000 to 1,100 won but falls as the price of soju rises from 1,100 to 1,200 won. Korea notes that such odd findings are frequent: indeed, they appear in every chart.[123]

5.212. Korea argues that there is no theoretical reason why the quantity demanded of one good should not fall as the price of a related good rises, although the implication that soju and whisky, for example, are complements in consumption, so that a fall in the price of whisky would increase consumption of soju, might seem to many economists implausible. Korea notes that the difficulty with the Dodwell report is that it sometimes shows the quantity of scotch demanded rising as the price of soju rises, and sometimes falling. Korea finds the facts reported, though curious, are less troubling than their lack of internal consistency.

---

[120] See EC Annex 13.

[121] EC Commission, Your Guide to Exporting Food Products to Korea, Alcoholic Beverages 1997 (Sofres Report), p.22.

[122] Panel Report in *Japan - Taxes on Alcoholic Beverages II, supra*, at para. 4.86.

[123] In chart 1, the percentage choosing premium scotch falls as the price of soju rises from 1,100 to 1,200 won even through all other prices-including that of premium scotch-are held constant; in chart 3, the percentage choosing premium soju falls as the price of standard soju rises from 1,100 won to 1,200 won; in chart 4, the percentages choosing gin and tequila both fall as the price of soju rises from 1,000 won to 1,100 won; in chart 5, the percentage choosing tequila falls as the price of soju rises from 1,000 to 1,100 won, and the percentages choosing vodka, gin and premium soju all fall as the price of soju rises from 1,100 to1,200 won; and in chart 6, the percentages choosing liqueur and premium soju both fall as the price of soju rises from 1,000 to 1,100 won, and the percentages choosing vodka and gin both fall as the price of soju rises from 1,100 to 1,200 won.

5.213. Korea suggests that consumers in actual markets are unlikely to be so random in their responses to price changes. Korea concludes that the members of the Dodwell sample may have treated the Dodwell question with less gravity than the report's authors might like to believe.

Standard and premium soju

5.214. Korea points to another peculiarity in the treatment of standard and premium soju. Korea observes that in the Dodwell report, the premium soju is offered as a choice side-by-side with western-style spirits in the pairwise choice between white spirits and standard soju and in the pairwise choice between brown spirits and standard soju. Thus, Korea notes, in the Dodwell "brown spirits" test, respondents are offered a choice between scotch, cognac and premium soju on the one hand, and standard soju on the other; and in the white spirits test they are offered a choice between vodka, gin, rum, tequila, liqueur, and premium soju on the one hand, and standard soju on the other.

5.215. Korea argues that grouping soju with western-type spirits rather than with standard soju is eccentric, and suggests a lack of familiarity with these two soju products. According to Korea, standard and premium soju are regarded as close substitutes in Korea. Korea states that premium soju is more expensive than standard soju-the "current price" of premium soju in the Dodwell report is 2,400 won as compared to 1,000 won for standard soju. Korea notes, however, that is hardly a compelling case for putting premium soju in the same group as 20,000 won scotch or 32,000won cognac.[124]

Problems

5.216. Korea states that studies of the Dodwell type must be carefully designed if they are not to fall foul of bias. Korea points out that the Dodwell report clearly has not managed this. Korea discusses two sources of bias and claims that either is sufficient to eliminate the credibility of the Dodwell Report.

---

[124] According to Korea, taxation of premium soju is identical to that of standard soju, and the natural division between soju on the one hand, and western-style spirits on the other would on its face have given clearer results. Rejection of the natural division seems to be a major flaw is the design of the Dodwell study, and it would be interesting to know how it came about and why it was maintained.

Korea claims that, as it is, the outcome of the study is blurred by interactions between standard and premium soju, which account for much of the change reported. The first Dodwell results, for example, are based on holding at current levels the price of brown and white spirits(and premium soju) while the price of standard soju is hypothetically raised from 1000 to 1200 won. The reported result is that standard soju loses 5.2 percentage points to "brown spirits." Three of these points, however, are gained by premium soju. Against white spirits, standard soju loses 5 percentage points, but 4 are gained by premium soju.

According to Korea, if these results are treated seriously, as presumably they were by the authors of the report, they strongly suggest that standard and premium soju are close substitutes in consumption. That finding might have been expected to lead the authors of the Dodwell report to use the natural division. It is curious that it apparently did not have that effect.

Choice of respondents

5.217. Korea points out that no reason is given for the exclusion of males above the age of 49 or of the rural population when the Dodwell report states "It was decided to select as respondents for the research 500 Korean men in 3 Korean cities aged between 20 and 49 who have purchased soju in the last month."[125]

5.218. Korea states that no information is provided on how and where the same was selected, or on how its members were induced to spend their time answering the survey questions. Korea notes that no information is given on the drinking habits of respondents-for example, where they typically purchase alcohol, or how much they consume(although questions 5-13 deal with these matters). Korea further notes that no information is provided on the actual characteristics of the sample-for example, average age, occupation, income-that would permit a check on whether the sample is even representative of "Korean males aged between 20 and 49 who have purchased soju in the last month."

5.219. Korea argues that the restriction and exclusion of the rural population are not the only ones placed on the sample. Korea indicates that p. 3 of the report announces that "additional criteria for the respondents were whisky purchase in the last 3 months." Korea notes that no reason is given for rejecting persons who have not purchased whisky in the last three months. Korea conjectures that, possibly, the results of the study in the absence of this condition were disappointing. Korea notes that it is certainly true that a good way to obtain a strong response to a fall in the price of whisky and a rise in the price of soju is to select a sample of persons that drink both soju and whisky(and, of course, a whisky purchase in the last three months and a soju purchase in the last month is consistent with a purchase of both in the last week, day or hour).

5.220. Korea states that the effects of selection bias are evident, regardless of the motivation for the additional restriction,. Korea points out that in the Dodwell sample, at current prices, 72 per cent of respondents select soju when asked to choose between brown spirits and soju; and 72 per cent select soju when asked to choose between white spirits and soju (Korea refers to the Dodwell study, p. 6). Korea notes, however, that the actual share of soju in consumption of distilled spirits in Korea, however, is about 95 per cent.

5.221. Korea asserts that the discrepancy between those who prefer soju at current prices in the Dodwell study and the true figure is very large[126] Korea nevertheless

---

[125] The Dodwell Report at p. 2.

[126] The figure of 72 per cent is used by the authors of the Dodwell report (p. 6). According to Korea, an alternative would have been to take the percentage of the sample choosing either standard or premium soju at current prices: 84.8 per cent then choose soju and 15.2 per cent brown spirits proper when offered that pair, and 86.2 per cent choose soju and 13.8 per cent western-type white spirits of that pair. This reduces one discrepancy between the Dodwell sample and actual market shares-the Dodwell percentage choosing brown spirits proper fall to only five times actual market share. But it also highlights other discrepancies. In the Dodwell sample 14.85 per cent of those choosing soju opt for premium soju: in fact, premium soju takes about 4 to 5 per cent of total soju sales. In the Dodwell sample, 13.8 per cent choose western-type white spirits, which have an actual market share of 1.8 per cent.

states that the difference between 72 per cent of the sample and 95 per cent that choose soju in reality is likely to seriously understate how unrepresentative the sample is. Korea attributes the discrepancy to the fact that respondents were given a pairwise choice between soju and brown spirits, and then a pairwise choice between soju and white spirits. They were not offered a three-way choice between soju or brown spirits or white spirits.

5.222. Korea acknowledges that some respondents may choose brown spirits rather than soju from that pair, but soju rather than white spirits when offered that pair; while others might select white spirits rather than soju in that pairwise offering, but soju rather than brown spirits. Offered a three-way choice, all of those who reject soju in the pairwise choice will continue to reject soju. Korea, however, emphasizes that those who chose white spirits when offered a choice between soju and white spirits need not be the same as those who choice brown spirits when offered a choice between soju and brown spirits. Korea states that it follows that the figure of 72 per cent choosing soju rather than brown spirits in the Dodwell sample, and the similar percentage selecting soju rather than white spirits, gives the highest possible percentage of those in the sample who would have chosen soju had they been offered a three-way choice.

5.223. Korea points out that the actual percentage choosing soju in a three-way choice would be 72 per cent only if all those who prefer white spirits to soju also prefer brown spirits to soju and vice versa. Korea notes that at the opposite extreme, though, if all of those choosing whisky over soju prefer soju to white spirits; and if all of those choosing white spirits rather than soju prefer brown spirits, the percentage opting for soju in a three-way choice would be 44 per cent-28 per cent would reject soju in favour of brown spirits, and 28 per cent would reject soju for white spirits. Korea states that only 72 per cent of Dodwell respondents choose soju at current prices indicates the unrepresentative nature of the Dodwell sample: that a lower figure is avoided only by the failure to offer a three-way choice; and that in such a choice, the number choosing soju might fall as low as 44 per cent, puts the Dodwell report into a world entirely different from that of Korean reality.

5.224. Korea argues that the Dodwell study is based upon a sample of persons who are strongly biased towards western-type spirits, relative to the Korean population as a whole. Korea asserts that the Dodwell sample is not a credible sample. Korea states that, even leaving aside other grounds for doubt, the response to hypothetical

---

According to Korea, these discrepancies strongly suggest sample bias. The Dodwell report, though, does not provide enough information to translate percentages of Dodwell respondents into a figure directly comparable with actual market shares, so that it does not allow calculation of whether the comparisons above understate or overstate the degree of bias. One problem is that Dodwell respondents are asked to choose a single bottle: in fact, drinkers are likely to consume different drinks at different times. Another problem is that those choosing soju in the Dodwell sample, for example, might on average consume more soju than those choosing whisky consume whisky. The implied market share of soju would then be more than 72 per cent. To approach actual market shares, Dodwell soju choosers, if they drank nothing but soju, would have to consume a volume of soju about 13 times greater than Dodwell whisky drinkers, if they drank nothing but whisky.

price changes of a group so unrepresentative cannot be taken to reflect anything of the responses of the Korean population as a whole to real price changes.

The single choice drink

5.225. Korea indicates that the Dodwell study respondents are confronted with an either-or choice. Korea notes that according to the Dodwell script, interviewers say: "As you can see, there are five types of spirits and photos of typical brands of these types. Which spirit would you choose at these prices?"

5.226. Korea states that reliable information about how different prices might change drinking habits-that is, whether a person who is a regular soju drinker might switch to becoming a regular whisky drinker were the price of soju higher and the price of whisky lower-might be relevant in this case. However, Korea argues, that is not what the Dodwell interviewers ask about. Korea notes that they ask which bottle a respondent would choose at the different prices. Korea points out in the Lexecon/Hindley Report that respondents might perfectly naturally interpret the Dodwell questions asking: "If you saw these prices the next time you bought a bottle of spirits, which bottle would you choose?" Korea notes that such questions opens the possibility that some respondents interpreted the hypothetical prices as a one-time offer: "If you saw these prices the next time you bought a bottle of spirits, but knew that usual prices would be back in force the time after that, which bottle would you buy? " Korea emphasizes that some Dodwell respondents may simply be saying that they would try a bottle of high-price cognac were it temporarily on offer at such a low price.

5.227. Korea argues that respondents interpreting the question as asking "would you try a bottle of cognac if it was offered at this price?" are almost certainly more likely to answer affirmatively than those interpreting the question as asking "would these prices cause you to change your drinking habits?". Accordingly, Korea concludes, the ambiguity in the question almost certainly increases the number saying they would buy a bottle of brown or white spirits at a lower price.

5.228. Korea emphasizes that there is absolutely no reason to suppose that respondents are speaking about a change in their drinking habits-that their answers imply that if soju rose in price from 1,000 won to 1,200 won, they would switch their regular drink, during meals for instance, from soju to cognac at 32,000 won or scotch at 20,000 won.

5.229. Korea argues that market surveys, carried out specifically for the purposes of legal proceedings at the request of an interested party, are, of course, to be treated with caution. The analysis must be rigorous, and bias must be avoided at all cost. According to Korea, the Dodwell study does not meet these standards. Korea sums up what it perceives to be the most glaring defects of this study:

 (i) It is not at all clear whether the sample of Korean consumers used for the analysis was representative.

 (ii) The questions posed were, in Korea's view, ambiguous. Korea argues that the question 'which spirit would you choose at this different price?' for example, might have been interpreted by respondents as asking whether they would change their habit of drinking soju with meals and switch instead to a western-type spirit; *or* as the different

> question of whether, at the hypothetical lower price, they would buy
> an experimental bottle of a western-type drink.

(iii)   Korea argues that the conclusions drawn from this study by the complainants are fanciful. According to Korea, it does not rebut the common sense presumption that, given the enormous price differences (even before tax) between standard soju and western-type liquors and their different end uses, no appreciable number of Korean consumers consider them to be substitutes.[127]

5.230. Korea further argues that in contrast, more credence can be given to a study, which was not prepared specifically for regulatory purposes, but which tries to explain in objective terms to exporters the situation on the Korean market. Korea refers to a recent report initiated by the European Commission recently, which stated:

> Soju is consumed widely, from the young to the old, and is the most popular traditional drink in Korea. Soju in particular remains unaffected by imported alcoholic drinks. Furthermore Soju, is insulated from economic downturns and maintains a loyal following of steady consumers.[128]

5.231. Korea asserts that the constant and independent demand for soju is not the result of any protective government policies. Korea refers to the same EC study which notes that:

> "The Korean alcohol market is no longer a market protected by the government with market shares contested by local producers. In fact, it is becoming a truly global market where multinational companies convene to compete with one another for the lucrative and promising Korean market".[129]

(d)   Product-by Product Analysis

5.232. Korea submits that as competitive relationships differ from product to product and from market to market, the United States and the European Communities bear the burden of proving for each individual product combination that a 'like' or 'directly competitive and substitutable' relationship exists in the Korean market before they can put the applicable tax rates into question.

5.233. Korea states that, without assuming the complainants' burden of proof, it will demonstrate the failure of the complainants to discharge this burden in the following way:

(i)   that the complainants have confused various products that are called soju.

(ii)   Korean soju is a different product from Japanese shochu.

(iii)   Korean standard soju is unlike distilled soju. Korea argues that these are different products in terms of *inter alia* their raw materials, production process, taste, price, place of consumption, end use, and their

---

[127]   See Attachment 2 of Korea, which is a critique by Lexecon Ltd and Dr. Brian Hindley (London School of Economics) of the Dodwell Study.

[128]   Sofres Report, p. 22.

[129]   *Ibid.*, p. 12.

marketing. Korea also submits that they are subject to different tax rates: 35% for standard soju and 50% for distilled soju.

5.234. Korea, therefore argues that both diluted soju and distilled soju must be compared individually to each of the imported liquors in question. Further, it states that although premium soju is a variation of diluted soju, Premium's price is somewhat higher, though still far below the price of the imported liquors. Premium soju represents only a small volume of diluted soju sales (currently, around 5%). In the discussion below of diluted soju due account is taken, where necessary, of any of premium's special features.[130]

5.235. Korea notes that the only products that the United States and the European Communities have alleged are 'like' are standard soju and distilled soju and vodka. Korea states that it will therefore only make representations about the lack of a 'like product' relationship as far as vodka is concerned. In its view, it goes without saying that Korea does not accept that any 'like product' relationships exist in this case.[131]

5.236. Korea also seeks to point out the very considerable price differences that exist between the imported liquors and diluted soju. According to Korea, the complainants recognize these differences at actual market prices.[132] However, Korea argues that these price differences remain considerable, even when the disputed taxes are eliminated. Korea points out that this is shown by the complainants' own expert study, the Dodwell Study.[133] Korea's position is that although it contests the results of the Dodwell Study, the raw price data provided in that study appear to be generally correct. Korea feels that these data are so compelling that it has not felt it necessary to go beyond the data set forth by the complainants. In its view, the one exception is whisky, where, given its importance to this case, Korea has supplemented the Dodwell data with its own figures.

5.237. In short, Korea is seeking to show that an inexpensive local meal drink such as diluted soju is not in direct competition with expensive western-type liquors. In the alternative, Korea is seeking to show why the complainants have not shown that Korea's tax system meets the other criteria of Article III:2, assuming that the Panel would still find a competitive relationship between some products,

5.238. Korea states that contrary to what the complainants are alleging, the so-called soju based cocktails are not soju. According to Korea, these are sweetened mixtures, with a low alcohol percentage (10-15%), that were introduced in 1994. They are not comparable to either standard or distilled soju. Korea adds that to make the distinction, manufacturers never use the word 'soju' in the brand names for these products. They are classified differently, like liqueurs, according to the liquor tax

---

[130] For instance, in giving average prices of standard soju, the higher price of premium is taken into account.

[131] Korea is mindful of the fact that in the most recent Japanese liquor taxes case, a 'like' product relationship was found to exist between one product pair: Japanese shochu and vodka. However, given the differences between Japanese shochu and the Korean sojus, as well as the differences between the Korean and the Japanese markets, this holding is inapplicable to the case at hand, according to Korea.

[132] Sofres Report, at p. 53 (1997), reproduced in Attachment 3.

[133] Pre-tax prices are provided in the Dodwell Study on page 20, in the column marked 'NET'. See Attachment 4.

law. Korea points out this classification also covers such imported liqueurs as Bailey's, Grand Marnier, Kahlua, etc. Liqueurs are subject to a tax rate of 50%. It is unclear to Korea what, if any, complaint the European Communities and the United States are formulating in this respect.

5.239. Korea also argues that contrary to EC assertions, sales of soju-based cocktails did not increase by 1250% in 1995. According to Korea, the taxed volume of soju-based cocktails increased by 419% in 1995, from 1,583 kl (1994) to 8,218 kl (1995), and that in 1996 sales decreased by 8% (to 7,562); in 1997 by 22% (to 5,893) kl).[134]

i)   Diluted soju

Diluted soju and Whisky

5.240. Korea argues that diluted soju and whisky are entirely different products, regardless of the perspective from which one looks at them. Korea points out that, firstly, the physical difference between these two products is immediately obvious to the eye and to the palate. Even more striking, according to Korea, are the market differences between the way that diluted soju and whisky are sold and consumed in Korea. Korea states that the primary differences boil down to this: in Korea, diluted soju is the drink one finds on the dinner table, the drink that is consumed with meals. As such, it is an inexpensive beverage. According to Korea, diluted soju is not drunk in bars or clubs. Whisky, by contrast, is an expensive drink that is primarily consumed in high-class bars and clubs - hardly ever with meals.

5.241. According to Korea, these factors show that there is no actual competitive relationship between diluted soju and whisky, and a removal of the tax differential would not create direct competition between those two drinks either.

5.242. Korea argues that at first glance, one can see that diluted soju is a 'white' spirit, transparent and colourless, while whisky is a 'brown' spirit, of a translucent golden-brown colour (an element much prized by consumers). Korea adds that, diluted soju has an alcoholic strength of 25% by volume, while the alcoholic strength of whisky is at least 40% by volume.

5.243. As to their organoleptic qualities, Korea states that the most important types of whisky - Scotch, Irish, Bourbon and Canadian - have in common a very typical flavour and smell. It states that the elements that are often mentioned in connection with whisky are that it has a warm, smooth and smoky flavour. According to Korea, one of the objectives in the production process is, as with wine, to develop the taste and aroma imparted to the beverage as a result of the raw materials used for its production (maize, barley, rye or malt) and its ageing in wooden casks.

5.244. Korea further argues that, on the other hand, diluted soju has quite a 'rough' flavour and tends to leave a stinging sensation in the mouth and throat. Korea submits that this is a function of the raw materials of which standard soju is made and its production process. In Korea's view, the emphasis in the production process of diluted soju is on making the product as cheaply as possible, not, as with whisky, on ageing and adding value and subtle flavours. That is why, according to Korea, stan-

---

[134] Source: National Tax Administration.

dard soju tends to have a 'cold' mouth feel that makes the drink suitable for consumption with the typically spicy Korean cuisine for which whisky is not suited. Hence, Korea concludes, as a matter of taste, Korean consumers do not consider whisky and diluted soju as substitutes for each other.

5.245. Korea further states that diluted soju is the alcoholic beverage that Koreans prefer with their meals. It is an effective foil for the hot and spicy food Koreans prefer, and Koreans consider that it is important to have some food when consuming diluted soju, in order to protect the stomach from the drink's harshness.

5.246. Korea concedes that it may seem unusual that Koreans prefer a distilled alcoholic beverage with their meals. Korea points out that in many cultures, particularly western ones, the alcoholic beverage found at the table is usually a fermented beverage with a lower alcohol content, such as wine or beer. It is in fact a western notion that distilled alcoholic beverages are not drunk with meals, but as straight drinks or cocktails. However, Korea points out that not all cultures share this trait, and gives as an example the Chinese, who allegedly also enjoy distilled alcoholic beverages with their meals. Finally, Korea notes that as in most countries, whisky is not consumed with meals in Korea.

5.247. Korea argues that these differences have follow-on effects. In conjunction with meals, standard soju is often consumed at home, while whisky is not. Whisky is instead consumed primarily in high-class hotel bars, night clubs, room saloons, and karaoke bars. Diluted soju not only not consumed in those places, it is not even on offer. Korea adds that when diluted soju is drunk away from home, it is mainly in Korean restaurants (including barbecue houses), mobile street vendors and inexpensive Chinese restaurants, where whisky is not normally available.

5.248. Korea therefore states that the Hankook Study introduced by the European Communities[135] begs the question. It allegedly shows that whisky is available in shops, hotels, danlanjujum (karaoke bars), Japanese restaurants, cafés, bars, nightclubs and discos. According to Korea, however, it does not show that soju is available in all of these outlets. Furthermore, argues Korea, it omits to mention the outlets in which diluted soju is drunk, but whisky is not available, such as the outlets where Koreans typically eat (Korean restaurants, including barbecue houses, mobile street vendors and inexpensive Chinese restaurants).

5.249. Korea states that in addition to the fact that diluted soju is a 'meal drink' while whisky is not, another element which shows in a most definitive way that diluted soju and whisky are not directly competitive and substitutable is their large difference in price. According to Korea, whisky is not nearly in the same price range as standard soju.

5.250. Korea asserts that in order to exclude any possible distortive effect from the disputed taxes, it will only compare pre-tax prices.[136] At this level, in Korea's analysis, striking price differences emerge from the Dodwell Study. According to Korea, Premium Scotch whisky is 12 times the price of diluted soju. North American whiskies are 10.8 times the price of diluted soju, and standard Scotch whisky is 7.2 times

---

[135] EC Annex 10.

[136] Pre-tax prices are provided in the Dodwell Study on page 20, in the column marked 'NET'. See Attachment 4 Korea.

the price of diluted soju. Even the cheapest whisky, bottled in Korea, is cited as 6.3 times the price of standard soju.[137] In Korea's view, these figures show that diluted soju and whisky are far from being in the same price range.

5.251. To further support that point already made through the Dodwell data, Korea provides in the following table, average pre-tax prices for the past three years using its own figures. Korea explains that because these figures are calculated by dividing the total taxed value by the total taxed volume, they show the weighted average (pre-tax) prices of whisky and diluted soju (including premium soju) in Korea. In Korea's view, the results[138] show more pronounced price differences:

(in Korean won, pre-tax)	1995	1996	1997
Standard soju (360 ml)	289.94	305.11	322.46
Whisky (360 ml)	3401.27	3582.09	4111.50
Factor of:	11.73	11.74	12.75

5.252. Korea submits that these price differences are maintained even if taxes are harmonized, either down to the diluted soju level, or up to the whisky level. According to Korea, this is a compelling indication that whisky and diluted soju would not be in direct competition, even if the tax differential were eliminated.

5.253. Korea points out that this is not to say that whisky sales would not rise if the tax on whisky were reduced. It concedes that this might well be the case, just as in the past tax rate reductions on whisky have led to increased whisky sales. Korea points out, however, that whisky would still not be in direct competition with diluted soju. According to Korea, their price and other differences would remain too important and diluted soju sales would continue to develop largely independently.[139]

5.254. Korea states that this observation was also made by the recent European Commission study already cited:

> Soju in particular remains unaffected by imported alcoholic drinks. Furthermore Soju, is insulated from economic downturns and maintains a loyal following of steady consumers.[140]

---

[137] According to Korea, it is to be noted that this is not a representative price for domestic whisky. For some reason, the Dodwell Study has split up the domestic brands (BIK stands for 'bottled in Korea') and has listed some of them among Premium Scotch Whisky as well. An example is the leading domestic brand (Imperial Classic), which is an expensive brand.

[138] The underlying data are set out in Attachment 5 of Korea.

[139] Korea states that the complainants' allegation that in recent years diluted soju sales have been eroded by growing sales of imported liquors is improbable. See EC first submission, at para. 51. The only thing they show is a slight (2%) reduction in the market share of diluted soju on the total spirits market from 1992 to 1996 (EC first submission, at Annex 6). In absolute terms, however, diluted soju sales rose by almost 13% (EC first submission, at Annex 5). During those five years, the spirits market increased in size (more than 15%); and diluted soju sales grew somewhat more slowly than sales of imported liquors. Increased income, the relative maturity of the market for diluted soju, etc., are more likely explanations to explain the difference in growth rate than any competition between whisky and diluted soju.

[140] Sofres Report, at p. 22 (1997). See Attachment 3 of Korea.

5.255. Korea also notes that the complainants have also not taken into account external factors such as currency fluctuations that also have an impact on sales of imported whisky.

5.256. Accordingly, Korea concludes that it is not under any legal obligation, by virtue of Article III.2 GATT, to reduce taxes on whisky to diluted soju levels (or, for that matter, to increase taxes on standard soju to whisky levels). In Korea's view, these two products are simply not sufficiently related on the Korean market for a tax differential to raise GATT concerns.

5.257. Korea submits that there are also other factors that contribute to the conclusion that diluted soju and whisky are not directly competitive and substitutable. Korea cites for instance, the marketing strategies for both drinks follow from the distinct consumption patterns and the price aspects described above. According to Korea, the target consumer is clearly different for both drinks and the producers and importers market the drinks accordingly. According to Korea, diluted soju is marketed as an everyday drink, consumed during meals, barbecues - not in luxurious surroundings. It is contended that these advertisements typically show Korean citizens in day-to-day clothes having diluted soju while eating. In contrast, according to Korea, whisky is positioned as a high class luxury drink that is meant for special occasions. The advertising is allegedly meant to appeal to consumers who are prepared to pay a considerable price for this privilege.[141]

5.258. Korea also argues that each product has its own branding strategy. Korea contends that no trademark for whisky is used for sales of diluted soju, neither is a soju trademark used for sales of whisky. Korea states for example, that the Jinro company sells its domestic whisky under the 'Imperial Classic' brand, whereas its diluted soju is sold as 'Jinro Gold'. In Korea's view, this is yet another indication demonstrating that both products do not compete, and are not substitutable on the Korean market.

Diluted soju and Brandy/Cognac

5.259. Korea argues that there are a myriad of differences between diluted soju and brandy/cognac. Some of these differences are apparent at first glance. Korea contends that in their packaging, brandies/cognacs are presented in an elegant fashion in keeping with their distinguished character. This makes these drinks very suitable for gifts. The same cannot be said about diluted soju, bottled in common plastic or glass bottles and geared toward frequent consumption, rather than to occasional consumption.

5.260. Korea further argues that another striking difference is in the appearance of the alcohol itself: brandy/cognac is generally a deep golden brown colour and has substantial body, while standard soju is a white clear spirit, with little body. Bran-

---

[141] See Attachment 6 of Korea for typical Korean advertisements for diluted soju and whisky. According to Korea, the advertisements submitted by the complainants are misleading in this regard. Many of them are directed not to the Korean market but to foreigners (see US, Exhibit D, which is a 'Sky Shop' duty free advertisement offered to international airline passengers; Exhibit F, which is an advertisement in English published in an international industry journal; or Exhibits H and I, which are advertisements in the Japanese language for the Japanese market).

dies/cognacs have an alcohol content of at least 40%, as opposed to diluted soju's 25%. Further, the flavour and aroma of brandy has been much celebrated, and described as 'velvety' and full-bodied, with a powerful and pleasant bouquet. Part of the typical flavour of brandies/cognacs can be attributed to the fact that they are derived from fermented fruit. Korea also points out that in addition, brandies/cognacs undergo an important ageing process in oak casks (e.g., in order to bear the name 'cognac', this special brandy must be aged for at least 6 years in wooden casks). It is contended that diluted soju on the other hand is most often made of tapioca, and has a much more industrial production process with no ageing. Suffice it to say that the resulting diluted soju has none of the refined characteristics of brandies/cognacs.

5.261. Korea further states that the price of brandy/cognac compared to diluted soju clearly spells out that competition between these products is improbable: pre-tax, brandy is 19.2 times as expensive as diluted soju.[142] In Korea's view, this is certainly not 'within a relatively short range' of prices.

5.262. Korea submits that consumers perceive brandies/cognac and diluted soju as completely different products and use them in completely different ways. According to Korea, brandies are very expensive luxury drinks, and are consumed in places in keeping with their stature: room saloons, clubs, hotel bars, and other luxurious premises where standard soju is not on offer. Korea adds that brandy/cognac would not be consumed with a meal while diluted soju is the traditional cheap Korean drink essentially drunk during meals. It is contended that it is drunk (often in rather large quantities) by ordinary folks in less illustrious settings than brandy, such as with a meal at home or in a family restaurant. Korea states that a request for a glass of cognac such as Rémy Martin in these settings would likely be met with incredulity.

5.263. According to Korea, these differences are further reflected in the fact that the marketing strategies of diluted soju and brandies are essentially different. Korea states that of all the drinks concerned by this dispute, brandy probably has the most luxurious image, and is marketed as such, in its packaging, advertising, the target consumer class, and of course, its price range. The marketing of diluted soju, is, as stated before, concentrated on meal consumption and is the 'common' man's drink.

Diluted Soju and Vodka

5.264. Korea states that vodka is the only product for which the United States and the European Communities have claimed a 'like' relationship with diluted soju. Korea raises doubts as to the evidence brought by the complainants for alleging 'likeness' of diluted soju and vodka. According to Korea, out of six physical characteristics of vodka and diluted soju which the United States compared, only two corroborate their point of view. Korea notes that the Panel in the *Japan - Taxes on Alcoholic Beverages II* stated that "'like products' need not be identical in all respects". However, Korea further notes that this statement was immediately followed by an insistence that "the term 'like product' should be construed narrowly...."[143]

---

[142] According to the Dodwell Study submitted by the complainants, page 20.

[143] Panel Report on *Japan - Taxes on Alcoholic Beverages II, supra,* para. 6.21.

5.265. Korea states that as far as the alleged 'likeness' is concerned, it should be noted that vodka and diluted soju do not fall under the same tariff classification. Vodka is allegedly classified under HS Classification 2208.60.00, while diluted soju falls under HS Classification 2208.90.40. Korea also mentions that there are other differences that suggest that there is no direct competitive relationship between these two products. Korea states that even though the difference between standard soju and vodka is not as striking as the differences between diluted soju and whisky, brandy, and cognac, described above, diluted soju and vodka are not like. However, Korea points out that both diluted soju and vodka also resemble tap water and paint thinner- a sign, according to Korea, that appearances can be deceptive.

5.266. Firstly, Korea states that consumers are unlikely to treat vodka and diluted soju as substitutes for each other in light of the price differences between them. Even the comparison of the pre-tax prices of diluted soju and vodka shows that vodka is 5.7 times the price of diluted soju.[144] According to Korea, if these products were truly as 'like', in competition, or substitutable for each other, it would be diffi- cult to understand how such a vast price discrepancy could exist.

5.267. Korea further argues that vodka and diluted soju are not consumed in the same ways or in the same places. In Korea's view, this follows, not only from the price difference, but also from the difference in alcohol percentage (vodka: 40%; standard soju: 25%). Korea contends that vodka is primarily a 'mixing' drink, and that there are even recipe books dedicated to cocktails one can make with vodka. According to Korea vodka is mostly consumed, though at considerably lower vol- umes than whisky, in room saloons, hotel bars, night clubs, karaoke bars, in short, places where meals, and standard soju, are not offered.

5.268. Korea also states that diluted soju is drunk straight in a typical small glass and is decidedly not a mixer. Korea contends that the outlets for diluted soju are generally eating establishments, and they are more 'ordinary' than those at which vodka is offered. It is contended that one can buy soju in places like barbecue houses, restaurants, mobile street vendors and Chinese restaurants, while one cannot generally buy vodka there.

5.269. Korea further states that diluted soju is a volume drink, which vodka is not. According to Korea, the small volumes of vodka sold in Korea are not attributable to the tax differential. Whisky, with a higher tax than vodka, sells at considerably larger volumes in Korea. In Korea's view, the more likely explanation for vodka's small sales volume is simply that Korean consumers have no particular taste for it.

5.270. According to Korea, in light of all these differences, vodka and diluted soju are certainly not 'like' products, and they are also not directly competitive and sub- stitutable.

Diluted Soju and Gin

5.271. Korea states that even though diluted soju and gin look alike, there is more to these products than meets the eye. Firstly, Korea states that gin is usually 40% alco- hol while diluted soju is only 25% alcohol. Secondly, gin is derived from maize and

---

[144]   According to the Dodwell Study, at p.20.

flavoured with certain aromatics and spices, in particular juniper berries, which impart to gin a unique flavour and aroma, reminiscent of spices - a taste which is not comparable to any other liquor. By contrast, diluted soju is made with tapioca or potatoes, and has a more harsh and neutral flavour. Korea argues that, accordingly, a consumer desiring the specific taste of gin will not settle for soju. Conversely, a Korean consumer interested in soju will not turn to gin with its typical, even overbearing, taste.

5.272. Korea further states that another reason why consumers would not substitute gin for diluted soju is the fact that gin is a product which is significantly more expensive than diluted soju. According to Korea, even without taking into account the disputed taxes levied on both drinks, the price differential between the average price of diluted soju and gin amounts to a factor of five.[145] Korea maintains that at harmonized tax rates this large price difference would remain.

5.273. Korea argues that the fact that consumers do not consider gin and diluted soju to be substitutable for each other is borne out in the patterns of consumption and places of sale. According to Korea, the vast majority of diluted soju is drunk straight, with meals. Gin on the other hand is served as a long drink, not straight, and is not drunk during meals. Korea contends that gin is an 'occasional' drink in Korea, only rarely purchased on the Korean market even compared to whisky. Compared to diluted soju consumption volumes, gin is a mere drop in the bucket, showing that in terms of demand, gin is not a substitute for diluted soju.

Diluted Soju and Rum

5.274. Korea states that rum comes in two varieties, light and dark, and while light rum looks like diluted soju, dark rum does not. However, Korea states that both varieties of rum are very different from standard soju. Firstly, Korea argues that diluted soju has an alcoholic strength of 25% by volume, while rum is at least 38% alcohol by volume. Secondly, Korea argues that rum is distilled at less than 96% by volume from the juice of cane sugar or molasses, specifically so that the distillate retains the specific organoleptic characteristics imparted to it from those raw materials. Thirdly, rum is aged. According to Korea, the result is a sweetness and a caramel flavour and smell that is smooth and appealing. Korea notes that, on the other hand, diluted soju is made from more neutral raw materials (tapioca, potatoes, corn), and is not aged. It has a 'rough' flavour and tends to leave a burning sensation in the mouth and throat. According to Korea, therefore, due to this difference in taste, a consumer would not be willing to accept rum when he wants diluted soju, or vice versa.

5.275. Korea further argues that like with the other liquors, consumers are even less likely to consider these two products as substitutes for each other in light of the difference in price between them. Korea states that pre-tax, rum is already 6.2 times more expensive than diluted soju.[146]

---

[145] According to the Dodwell Study submitted by the complainants, p. 20 (see Attachment 4 of Korea).

[146] According to the Dodwell Study submitted by the complainants, p. 20 (see Attachment 4 of Korea).

5.276. Korea states that in addition to, and likely because of, the physical and price differences, diluted soju and rum are consumed in very different fashions. Rum is allegedly usually mixed as a cocktail and sold at bars and night clubs, where diluted soju is not even available while diluted soju is almost exclusively drunk neat and is normally served as an accompaniment to food.

5.277. Korea argues that these differences are borne out in the marketing of both products: rum is presented as a special and exotic beverage, intended for consumption in elegant establishments such as those mentioned above. Diluted soju on the other hand, is the commoner's drink, and is marketed as such.

5.278. Korea therefore concludes that, as with gin, the disparity in the volumes of rum sold and the volumes of diluted soju sold should be kept in mind. In other words, diluted soju is a commodity, while rum is a special, 'niche' drink.

5.279. Korea submits that it has presented a product-by-product analysis of the relationship of diluted soju and the imported liquors at issue. Korea considers that the conclusion of this analysis is that none of these products is in a directly competitive and substitutable relationship with any other (and, of course, that vodka, and for that matter, none, of the imported beverages is 'like' diluted soju).

5.280. Korea further submits that even if the Panel considers that any one of the imported products is directly competitive and substitutable for standard soju, there is still no violation of Article III. That is because the complainants have failed to prove, as is required under Article III:1, that the tax differential at issue in this case is 'so as to afford protection to domestic production.'

5.281. Korea argues that, firstly, it should be recalled that in *Japan - Taxes on Alcoholic Beverages II*, a protectionist effect was found in the combination of customs duties and the tax differentials, which 'isolated' Japanese shochu from competition. Korea contends that this combination does not exist in Korea. Korea submits that although it levies a (GATT-compatible) customs duty, its market for soju is not 'isolated' at all. Korea recalls once more the recent report published by the European Commission:

> The Korean alcohol market is no longer a market protected by the government with market shares contested by local producers. In fact, it is becoming a truly global market where multinational companies convene to compete with one another for the lucrative and promising Korean market.[147]

5.282. Korea further argues that making diluted soju basically involves mixing joojung with water, and in Korea the vast majority (approximately 70%) of the joojung used to make diluted soju is imported in a semi-finished state. Korea adds that when joojung is locally produced it is primarily made from imported ingredients (notably tapioca). According to Korea, therefore, even if the Panel concludes that standard soju is 'protected' by the difference in tax, one could only say that Korea protects one imported product at the expense of another.

5.283. Korea argues that on the other hand, if Korea's diluted soju production is nevertheless considered substantial enough to amount to domestic production, then it must also be considered that Korea has a domestic whisky industry as well. According to Korea, the production of whisky in Korea is in fact similar to the produc-

---

[147] See Attachment 3 of Korea.

tion of diluted soju, in that concentrated whisky is imported, then mixed with water and caramel, and then bottled. Korea states that this process, though it can be described in these simple terms, does add a substantial amount in value.[148] From this perspective, therefore, by imposing a higher tax on whisky, Korea has in fact been penalizing its own domestic whisky industry.

5.284. Korea also argues that the fact that there are few imports of soju (e.g., from Japan) can be explained by commercial realities, rather than regulation: Japanese shochu sells at prices that are much closer to western-type liquors in Japan.

ii)   Distilled Soju

5.285. Korea argues that if one could speak of a 'soju market', diluted soju would represent more than 99.8% of that market, and distilled soju, 0.2%.

5.286. Korea points out that the small volume of sales of distilled soju is indicative of the fact that distilled soju is a special artisanal product. Korea states that it is in fact difficult to compare a product that is mass-marketed around the world such as the imported liquors at issue in this case to such a tiny niche product, sold only in Korea. According to Korea, distilled soju is not in the same league as these worldwide players.

5.287. Korea further states that because distilled soju is prepared with great care and in small quantities, it is an expensive product in the price range of top-range whiskies and brandy/cognac. This is in contrast to diluted soju which is far less expensive than the imported products, and falls completely on the other end of the scale.

5.288. Korea also states that distilled soju comes in an expensive ceramic bottle and is most often offered as a gift to friends or colleagues, to be taken home and consumed there. It is marketed as such.

Distilled Soju and Whisky

5.289. Korea argues that the differences in the appearance of distilled soju and whisky are obvious. Distilled soju is a 'white' spirit, while whisky is a brown spirit. As regards taste, whisky has a typical flavour, described as smooth, smoky and warm. Korea adds that one can detect the taste and aroma imparted to the beverage as a result of its raw materials (maize, barley, rye) and its mandatory ageing in wooden casks for at least 3 years. Distilled soju has a full-bodied liquor with a clean aftertaste. This flavour is achieved by using mainly rice or grain as a raw material. Korea states that distilled soju can be, but need not be, aged (for a maximum of 2 years) in order to refine its flavour.

5.290. Korea also argues that distilled soju and whisky are used for very different consumer needs. Korea states that the most common way to drink whisky in Korea is as a cocktail, on the rocks, diluted with water or another mixer while distilled soju is almost exclusively drunk neat, that is, not diluted or mixed.

---

[148]   Korea understands that the cost of raw materials as a proportion of pre-tax prices can be comparable for standard soju and domestic whisky production.

5.291. Korea states that most whisky is sold in Korea through channels as bars, hotels, room saloons, night clubs, karaoke bars and restaurants while distilled soju is a typical artisanal 'gift' item and as such is mostly sold through retail shops (and, recall, in very small quantities). Korea further states that distilled soju offered as a gift is then consumed at home, rather than in trendy bars like whisky.

5.292. Korea argues that consistent with these different patterns of consumption is a different type of marketing: whisky, a chic drink to be sipped in swanky venues; distilled soju, a traditional product to be offered as a gift.

Distilled Soju and Brandy/Cognac

5.293. Korea argues that as with whisky, the differences between distilled soju and brandy/cognac are apparent at first glance. Brandies/cognacs are brown spirits, contrary to distilled soju which is a clear white spirit. In addition, Korea states that brandies have more body as they are aged for a longer period than distilled soju. As to their taste, brandies/cognacs have a warm and fruity taste, while the taste of distilled soju is full-bodied with a clean aftertaste.

5.294. According to Korea, the difference in raw materials and production processes is the origin of this difference in taste and appearance. Brandies/cognacs are derived from fermented grapes, then aged in wooden casks, generally from 3 to 12 years. Distilled soju is usually made with rice and grain, and can only be aged for 2 years.

5.295. Korea argues that brandy/cognac is usually consumed neat in a high-brow restaurant as a digestif. Distilled soju, as mentioned above, is generally received as a gift, and therefore is consumed at home. Further, the marketing of distilled soju is specifically geared at offering the product as a gift, whereas brandy/cognac is more often consumed by the glass in restaurants or high class drinking establishments.

Distilled Soju and Vodka

5.296. Korea states that there are similarities between distilled soju and vodka. They are both white spirits, and they have similar degrees of alcoholic strength. However, Korea argues that, in light of other, more important differences in price, places of sale and consumption, end uses and marketing, distilled soju and vodka cannot be considered as 'like products' or as directly competitive or substitutable products.

5.297. Korea argues that distilled soju is a very special product that has a different flavour from vodka. Vodka approaches 'flavourlessness', while the taste of distilled soju is linked to its raw material. Vodka and distilled soju are also not consumed in the same fashion or in the same places. Due to its absence of flavour, vodka is particularly suitable for use in mixed drinks and is most often consumed as long drink in Korea. In so far as vodka is consumed in Korea, it is mostly sold through bars, discos, and room saloons. By contrast, distilled soju is only consumed straight. In general, distilled soju is sold through shops as it is a typical artisanal gift item. When received as a gift, distilled soju is subsequently consumed by the recipient at his home.

5.298. According to Korea, the above differences are reflected in the marketing of these products. Distilled soju is marketed as a traditional beverage and an appropriate gift, while vodka is marketed as a drink suitable for cocktails to be consumed while out on the town in the evening.

Distilled Soju and Gin

5.299. Korea states that one of the most important differences between distilled soju and gin is their tastes. Gin allegedly has an immediately recognizable flavour, which is unique and distinct, due in particular to one of its raw materials: juniper berries. Distilled soju is usually made of rice or grain and is not produced with such distinctive added flavours.

5.300. Korea also states that consumers do not consume gin and distilled soju in the same way or in the same places. The special flavour of gin is generally only appreciated as a long drink, not straight, and is most often consumed in up-scale locations, such as bars, room saloons and comparable places. Distilled soju, on the other hand, is always consumed straight and never mixed. Korea states that distilled soju is a typical gift, and subsequent to receipt is usually consumed at home, rather than out in bars and clubs.

5.301. Korea also states that distilled soju is marketed as a traditional Korean gift. Gin, on the other hand, is marketed as a drink suitable for cocktails to be drunk out on the town.

Distilled Soju and Rum

5.302. Korea states that rum and distilled soju differ in price, physical characteristics, organoleptic qualities, and are used by consumers to fill different needs. For these and other reasons distilled soju and rum are not directly competitive and substitutable.

5.303. Korea states that rum comes in both light and dark varieties. The light rum is a clear white spirit, and therefore could be said to resemble distilled soju. Dark rum however is a brown spirit, and does not resemble distilled soju.

5.304. Korea states that both types of rum have a very different flavour from distilled soju. Rum is distilled from the juice of cane sugar or molasses in such a way that the distillate has discernible organoleptic characteristics deriving from those raw materials; the result is a mildness and a caramel flavour that is smooth and appealing. Unlike rum, distilled soju is usually made of rice and is a dry alcohol which does not have the same mild caramel flavour.

5.305. According to Korea, as a result of these differences, distilled soju and rum are consumed in very different fashions. First of all, in so far as rum is consumed in Korea, the most common way to drink rum is as a cocktail in places such as bars, hotels, and room saloons. By contrast, distilled soju is almost exclusively drunk neat, that is, not diluted or mixed with other liquids. Korea also argues that distilled soju is most often presented as a gift, which is bought by the giver in a shop, and consequently drunk by the recipient at home.

Analysis of the "so as to afford protection" requirement

5.306. According to Korea, the marketing strategies of rum and standard soju reflect the different geographical origins of the drinks. Rum is marketed as an exotic drink, which is ideally used as a cocktail during night-time occasions. The marketing of distilled soju, on the other hand, reflects the traditional Korean life-style (illustrated by its presentation in special Korean ceramic bottles, often as a set with ceramic cups).

5.307. Korea states that, as with diluted soju, Korea has presented an explanation, product-by-product, of why distilled soju is not 'like' vodka or directly competitive and substitutable for any of the imported liquors involved in this case.

5.308. Korea states that even if the Panel disagrees with Korea's point of view, the complainants have still failed to make out a violation of Article III. In Korea's view, in order to prove a violation, the complainants must show that the tax differential at issue is 'so as to afford protection to domestic production.'

5.309. Korea states that distilled soju is a traditional, artisanal product. It is not a mass-marketed, international product such as the imported beverages concerned. In other words, the demand for a product like distilled soju is specific and static - it would be difficult to affect it a great deal in either direction by altering the price, especially not to the degree at issue in this case. Indeed, despite the lower tax applied to distilled soju, its sales are still minuscule.

5.310. Korea wants the Panel to imagine, *quod non,* that it found that whisky and distilled soju were directly competitive and substitutable products, and that the other conditions of Article III were met. Korea would then be forced to harmonize the tax rates on these two products. Korea submits that it could not lower the tax rate on whisky for distilled soju, as the impact on its revenues would be too great. Instead, it would have to raise the tax rate on distilled soju, crippling a tiny artisanal product which is part of its heritage, with no benefit to the imported beverages.[149]

5.311. According to Korea, the result of this analysis is that even if the Panel disagrees with Korea's arguments that distilled soju is not directly competitive and substitutable to any of the imported beverages concerned, the requirement of Article III:1 has still not been met: the complainants have not proved that the different tax applies 'so as to afford protection' to distilled soju.

VI.   REBUTTAL ARGUMENTS

A.   *European Communities*

1.   *Shochu and Soju*

6.1.   The European Communities notes that according to Korea, the only difference between shochu and soju is that shochu contains two additives only (sugar and citric acid) whereas soju contains four to five more additives. However, according to the European Communities, it is still unclear whether there is a legal requirement to use any of those additional four to five additives or whether it is simply a characteristic of certain brands.

6.2.   The European Communities argues that all the extra additives except one (mineral salt) supposedly found in soju but not in shochu are sweeteners. Thus, the EC view is that the alleged difference between soju and shochu appears to be nothing other than the fact that soju is somewhat "sweeter" than shochu. The European Communities adds that Korea does not specify how much "sweeter" soju must be. According to the European Communities, there appears to be no legal requirement

---

[149]   According to Korea, in this regard, it could even be said that the special position of distilled soju for Korea merits an exception under Article XX(f) of the GATT.

in Korea regarding the minimum sugar content of soju. The analytical tests conducted by the Scotch Whisky Research Institute have allegedly revealed no trace of this supposed difference in "sweetness" alleged by Korea.[150]

6.3.   The European Communities further argues that at any rate, the difference alleged by Korea is a very minor one. The European Communities asserts that Coca Cola, for example, also is slightly sweeter in some countries than in others, so as to match different local tastes. Significantly, Korea does not even allude to this supposed characteristic of soju when it attempts to distinguish it from vodka and other distilled spirits.

6.4.   The EC view is also that Korea also implies that, unlike soju, the majority of shochu A is frequently aged and brown coloured. According to the European Communities, over 99% of shochu is white[151] and non aged.[152]

6.5.   The European Communities also notes Korea's contention that, unlike soju expressly manufactured for the Japanese market, "true" soju consumed by the Korean minority in Japan is not treated as shochu by the Japanese authorities for customs and tax purposes. According to the European Communities, this claim seems to be at odds with the statements made by Japan before the 1996 Panel on *Japan - Taxes on Alcoholic Beverages II*.[153] The EC view is that even if Korea' claims were correct, they would only go to show that Japan applied its Liquor Tax Law so as to afford protection to its domestic production of shochu not only vis-à-vis imports of western spirits but also vis-à-vis imports of soju.

2.   *The Japanese Market and the Korean Market*

6.6.   The European Communities argues that according to Korea, the main difference between the Korean market and the Japanese market would be that in Japan the prices of shochu and of imported liquors are "within a relatively short range", whereas in Korea soju is much less expensive than imported liquors.

6.7.   According to the European Communities, Korea does not provide any evidence to support its allegations regarding the Japanese market, but instead makes a misleading reference to an argument made by the European Communities in the *Japan - Taxes on Alcoholic Beverages II* case.

6.8.   The European Communities argues that the prices of shochu on the Japanese market vary considerably. At one extreme, there is inexpensive standard shochu sold in bulky plastic bottles of 1.8 to 4 litres or even in paper packages. At the other extreme, there are premium brands sold in 0.7 litre bottles which are generally three to four times more expensive than standard shochu.[154] According to the European Communities, standard shochu still accounts for the majority of sales, like in Korea, even though sales of premium shochu are growing rapidly. The price range for west-

---

[150]   See EC Annex 8. The EC states that although Korea attempts to discredit that research by describing it as a "partisan report", it offers no evidence to dispute the findings of that report.

[151]   The optical density of shochu, measured by the light of 430 nana-meter wavelength is, at the maximum, 0.08. The usual optical density of Scotch whisky is between 0.45 and 0.70.

[152]   See Panel Report on, *Japan - Taxes on Alcoholic Beverages II, supra*, para. 4.54.

[153]   *Ibid.*, para. 6.35.

[154]   See EC Annex 1.

ern-style spirits is allegedly even wider than that of shochu, especially in the case of whisky and brandy.

6.9.   The European Communities explains that when it argued that in Japan the pre-tax prices for shochu and western spirits were within a relatively close range, it based itself on a comparison of the prices for premium shochu brands, on the one hand, and standard brands of western spirits, on the other hand[155]. According to the European Communities, even on that basis, the pre-tax prices for standard imported whisky were sometimes as much as twice the price for shochu. It was never disputed by the EC that the prices of premium whisky or premium brandy in the Japanese market could be many times higher than the prices of standard shochu.

6.10.   The European Communities notes that like Korea in this dispute, Japan submitted to the Panel a comparison of pre-tax weighted average prices. According to that comparison, the pre-tax price for brandy and whisky were 13 times and 5 times higher, respectively, than the pre-tax price for shochu A.[156]

6.11.   The European Communities also notes Korea's claim that another important difference is that in Japan shochu A and shochu B are sold in comparable volumes and at similar prices. The EC view is that this is correct but irrelevant. The European Communities fails to see how this difference can be conducive to stronger competition between shochu and western spirits, as compared to soju.

6.12.   Finally, the European Communities notes that Korea invokes differences in drinking styles. According to Korea, soju is always drunk "straight", whereas shochu is drunk in other styles in addition to "straight", such as diluted with warm water and mixed in cocktails. According to the European Communities, this is inaccurate as far as soju is concerned. The EC view is that soju is not always drunk straight, and in particular, it is also drunk as cocktail, as attested by the growing sales of pre-mixes. As to the fact that shochu is drunk with warm water (i.e. in a style which is not characteristic of any western spirit) the European Communities fails to see how this may have had the paradoxical result of making shochu more competitive with western spirits than soju.

3.   All Types of Soju are one and the Same Product

(a)   Distilled and diluted soju

6.13.   The European Communities notes that Korea attempts to create an artificial distinction between the two basic types of soju: distilled soju and diluted soju[157], with an obvious strategy: many of the alleged differences which, according to Korea, make soju "unlike" or "not directly competitive or substitutable" with western-style liquors (including in particular the differences in pricing) cannot be substantiated when those liquors are compared to distilled soju.

---

[155]   See EC Annex 2.

[156]   See EC Annex 3.

[157]   The EC argues that "diluted soju" is a term used in the Liquor Tax Law and other official Korean sources and not one created by the complainants, as Korea seems to imply. See, for example, the decision of the Fair Trade Commission in Attachment 1 to Korea's First Submission and the 1997 Korean Taxation Guide published by the Ministry of Finance in Annex 4 to this submission.

6.14.   According to the European Communities, Korea seems to be ready to "sacrifice" distilled soju in order to spare diluted soju. In the EC view, that sacrifice would be more apparent than real, in view of Korea's statement that under certain conditions the producers of distilled soju may be designated as possessors of an "intangible cultural asset". The European Communities retorts that Korea carefully omits to say that this may entail an exemption from the Liquor Tax and the Education Tax.[158]

6.15.   According to the European Communities, the reality, however, is that distilled soju and diluted soju are but two varieties of the same product, as it should be obvious already from the fact that the two bear the same name. The European Communities notes that many other spirits are also produced in different types or varieties. In the case of whisky, for instance, it is possible to distinguish between malt Scotch, grain Scotch, blended Scotch, Canadian, Irish, Bourbon, Rye, etc. According to the European Communities, in relative terms distilled soju is no more different from diluted soju than, for example, malt Scotch from grain Scotch.

6.16.   The European Communities argues that the distinction between distilled soju and diluted soju was not introduced in the Liquor Tax Law until 1991.[159] In the EC view, it was a distinction created exclusively for tax purposes as no similar distinction is found in Korea's tariff schedule, where all soju is classified within a single heading with the description "soju".[160]

6.17.   The European Communities notes that until the 1960s, most soju sold in Korea was produced according to the method described in the legal definition of "distilled soju". The origins of what the Liquor Tax Law calls "diluted soju" go back to 1962, when, in order to cope with a severe shortage of grains, the Korean Government adopted a series of measures to encourage the use of ethyl alcohol. By the mid seventies, the European Communities further argues, distilled soju had given way to diluted soju. According to the European Communities, such swift transition was possible only because, in the eyes of Korean consumers, the two varieties of soju are the same product.

6.18.   The European Communities asserts that the differences between distilled soju and diluted soju are aptly described by a decision of Korea's Fair Trade Commission.[161] According to the first "Established Fact" of that Decision,

> "Distilled soju is made from a mix of additives and water blended into an alcohol solution extracted by a method of 'single-step' distillation. On the other hand, 'diluted' soju refers to soju made from a mix of additives, water and grain solution (or distilled soju solution - the Liquor Tax act classifies soju as being diluted soju where the ratio of the grain solution or the distilled soju solution amounts to 20 % or less of the total volume of alcohol) blended into an alcohol solution extracted by a method of 'continuous 'distillation'.

---

[158]   See the 1997 Korean Taxation Guide published by Korea's Ministry of Finance in EC Annex 4.
[159]   The distinction was introduced in response to pressure from the EC to eliminate the tax differentials between soju and the other distilled spirits. The creation of the category of distilled soju was but a fig leaf, which allowed Korea to claim that "expensive" soju was no less taxed than "some" imported liquors (namely the category of "liqueurs").
[160]   See EC Annex 5.
[161]   See Attachment 1 to First Submission of Korea.

Thus, the basic difference between those two types of soju lies in whether the alcohol was extracted by means of single-step distillation or continuous distillation."

6.19.   The European Communities notes that other spirits such as whisky and brandy can also be obtained either by single-step distillation (also referred to as "pot still" or "discontinuous") or by continuous distillation. It further notes for instance, that malt Scotch whisky is produced by pot-still distillation, while grain Scotch whisky is obtained by continuous distillation.

6.20.   The European Communities argues that the close similarity of the two types of soju is attested by the fact that distilled soju and diluted soju can be and are often blended with each other. When distilled soju represents more than 20% of the total alcohol content, the admixture is taxed as distilled soju and not as diluted soju. Again, a parallelism can be drawn to whisky. The most common type of Scotch whisky is blended whisky, which is produced by mixing malt Scotch and grain Scotch.

6.21.   The European Communities further argues that the other differences between diluted soju and distilled soju alleged by Korea are either exaggerated or irrelevant because:

(a)   there is no legal requirement to use only rice or grains for making distilled soju. In accordance with the legal definition of distilled soju, other raw materials containing starch can be used as well. On the other hand, diluted soju can also be produced from grains;[162]

(b)   although diluted soju cannot be aged by law, it is perfectly legal to blend previously aged distilled soju and neutral spirits in order to make diluted soju;

(c)   as stressed by Korea at another point of its submission where it seeks to distinguish distilled soju from whisky, "distilled soju can be, but need not be, aged";

(d)   the price difference between distilled soju and diluted soju are no larger than, for example, the prices differences between certain types of whisky;

(e)   there are also appreciable differences in taste between Premium diluted soju and Standard diluted soju or, for example, between Scotch Whisky and Bourbon;

(f)   many other spirits are produced both artisanally and industrially;

(g)   there is no legal requirement regarding the minimum alcohol content of either distilled or diluted soju.

(b)   Premium and standard diluted soju

6.22.   The European Communities reiterates that, a new segment of so-called "premium soju" brands is emerging rapidly within the category of diluted soju. Pre-

---

[162]   For instance, according to the Sofres Report, the Premium Soju brand Kim Sat Gat uses rice or barley. See the Sofres Report, p. 23.

mium soju is characterized by a milder taste, the use of flavourings and/or ageing and more sophisticated packaging.[163] All this makes premium diluted soju even more similar to western-style spirits than standard diluted soju.

6.23.   The European Communities argues that Korea cannot deny that premium diluted soju is the same product as standard diluted soju, since this is not a distinction which is reflected in Korea's regulations. Instead, Korea allegedly attempts to minimize the importance of premium soju by presenting it as an exception of minor importance and then ignores it in the remainder of its submission.

6.24.   The European Communities notes, however, that this "exception" accounts for a volume of sales which exceeds the combined sales volume of all imported spirits. The EC claimed that premium diluted soju may have accounted for as much as 10 percent of soju sales in 1997.[164]

4.   Soju and Vodka are Like Products

The standard for the interpretation of "like products"

6.25.   The European Communities argues that Korea seems to consider that it is sufficient to point to the existence of any difference, however minor, between two liquors, such as for instance a vaguely defined difference in taste, in order to exclude a finding of "likeness" for the purposes of GATT Article III:2, first sentence.

6.26.   According to the European Communities, as clarified by the Appellate Body in *Japan - Taxes on Alcoholic Beverages II*, in Article III:2, first sentence, the notion of "like" product must be construed "narrowly".[165] Nevertheless, the EC view is that it is also a well established principle that in order to be "like" two products need not be "equal" or "identical" in all respects.[166] The European Communities notes that according to *Japan - Taxes on Alcoholic Beverages I*:

> [m]inor differences in taste, colour and other properties (including differences in alcohol contents) do not prevent products from qualifying as like products.[167]

---

[163]   See the Sofres Report, at pp. 23-24.

[164]   According to footnote No 30 of Korea's First Submission, in 1996 the total taxed volume of premium soju was 35,108 kl. In comparison, the total volume of imports of whisky, cognac, rum, gin and vodka during the first eleven months of 1996 was 22,286 kl (see EC's First Submission, Annex 7).

Also according to footnote No 30 of Korea's First Submission, in 1997 total taxed volume of premium soju was 43.878 kl. During the same year, the total taxed volume of "whisky" was 24.530 kl (see Attachment 5 to Korea's First Submission,).

There is no legal definition of "premium soju". The discrepancy between the market share of premium soju estimated by the EC in its First Submission (at para. 54) and the share mentioned by Korea may be explained by the fact that Korea uses a narrower definition of premium soju.

[165]   Appellate Body Report on *Japan - Taxes on Alcoholic Beverages II, supra*, at 112-113.

[166]   See Panel Report on *Japan - Taxes on Alcoholic Beverages II, supra*, para. 6.21. See also the Panel Report on *Japan - Taxes on Alcoholic Beverages I, supra*, at par. 5.5, referring to the Panel Report on *United States - Taxes on Petroleum and certain Imported Substances, supra*, at para. 5.1.1, where the Panel found that some of the imported and domestic products, albeit not identical, were like products since they served substantially the same uses.

[167]   *Ibid.*, para. 5.9.

6.27.   According to the European Communities, Korea's position appears to be based on the mistaken notion that in order to be "like" two products must be "perfectly substitutable". The European Communities argues that contrary to Korea's allegations, the Appellate Body has never taken such an extreme view, and that Korea's reasoning is a classical *non sequitur*. The European Communities further argues that in *Canada - Certain Measures Concerning Periodicals*,[168] the Panel noted that a case of perfect substitutability would fall within Article III:2, first sentence, in order to reject an argument by the defendant to the effect that between the products concerned there was "imperfect substitutability" only. According to the European Communities, the Appellate Body, however, did not thereby imply that two products must always be "perfectly substitutable" in order to be "like". Indeed, such an interpretation would make Article III:2, first sentence, inapplicable except in cases of overt origin based discrimination between identical products.

6.28.   The European Communities asserts that, in order to escape the implications of the two Panel reports on *Japan - Taxes on Alcoholic Beverages* , Korea over-emphasizes the importance of the "consumers' tastes and habits" as one of the relevant criteria for a "like" product determination. According to the European Communities, that criterion was indeed mentioned by the Working Party on *Border Tax Adjustments*,[169] which has been cited with approval by the Appellate Body in *Japan - Taxes on Alcoholic Beverages*[170] and *Canada - Certain Measures concerning Periodicals*.[171]

6.29.   The European Communities argues however, that in practice, past panels have given little weight to "consumers' tastes and habits" when making "like product" determinations. Instead, they have focused on objective factors such as the physical characteristics of the products and their end uses. According to the European Communities, the reason for that approach is that "consumers' tastes and habits", unlike the physical characteristics of products and their objective end uses, are influenced by prices and, consequently, also by taxes. Alleged differences in "consumers' tastes and habits" may have been created, or at least "fossilized", through discriminatory internal taxes and cannot, therefore, constitute a valid justification for continuing to apply those discriminatory taxes.

6.30.   According to the European Communities, an example of this approach is provided by the Panel report in *Japan - Taxes on Alcoholic Beverages II*:

> [E]ven though the Panel was of the view that the "likeness" of products must be examined taking into account not only objective criteria (such as composition and use by consumers) the Panel agreed with arguments submitted to it [...] that Japanese shochu (Group A) and vodka could be considered as like products in terms of Article III:2 because they were both white/clean spirits, made of similar raw materials, and their end uses were virtually identical [...] Since consumer habits are variable in time and space and the aim of Article III:2 of ensuring neutrality of internal taxation as regards competition be-

---

[168]   Appellate Body Report on *Canada - Certain Measures Concerning Periodicals, supra*, at 473.
[169]   Report of the Working Party on *Border Tax Adjustments*, BISD 18S/97, para. 18.
[170]   Appellate Body Report on *Japan - Taxes on Alcoholic Beverages II, , supra*, at 113.
[171]   Appellate Body Report on *Canada - Certain Measures Concerning Periodicals, supra*, at 466.

tween imported and domestic like products could not be achieved if differential taxes could be used to crystallize consumer preferences for traditional domestic products, the Panel found that the traditional Japanese habits with regard to shochu provided no reason for not considering vodka to be a "like" product.[172]

6.31.   The European Communities asserts that Korea invokes the fact that vodka is allegedly more expensive than soju as one of the reasons that make those two spirits "unlike". According to the European Communities, the differences in prices between diluted soju and vodka have been grossly overstated by Korea, whereas distilled soju may, in fact, be more expensive than vodka.

6.32.   The EC view is also that prices are not relevant for a "like" product determination. According to the European Communities, prices are not one of the criteria mentioned in the Working Party on *Border Tax* Adjustments. Nor are they mentioned as a relevant criterion by the Appellate Body in *Japan -Taxes on Alcoholic Beverages* or *Canada - Certain Measures affecting Periodicals*. The EC view is that it is not aware of any single case in which prices have been taken into account for a "like" product determination, whether for the purposes of Article III:2, or of any of the other GATT provisions incorporating that notion.

6.33.   In fact, notes the European Communities, in *Japan - Taxes on Alcoholic Beverages II*, the Panel rejected in categorical terms an argument by Japan to the effect that local spirits were not "like" imported ones because they were less expensive:

> [T]he Panel was of the view that "like" products do not become "unlike" merely because of differences in prices, which were often influenced by external government measures (e.g. customs duties) and market conditions (e.g. supply and demand, sales margins). The Panel was convinced that such an interpretation would run counter to the objective of Article III:2 to avoid that discriminatory or protective internal taxation of imported products would distort price competition with domestic like or directly competitive products, for instance by creating price and consumer categories and hardening consumer preferences for traditional home products.[173]

6.34.   The European Communities also argues that there are two additional reasons for disregarding prices when making a "like" product determination. The first reason is that Article III:2, first sentence, purports to establish a hard-and-fast rule. Once it is determined that two products are sufficiently similar to be "like", it is irrefutably presumed that any difference in taxation between them will afford protection to the domestic production and, therefore, must be condemned. The European Communities continues that implicit in this presumption, there is also the assumption that products which are sufficiently similar to be "like" must of necessity be "directly competitive or substitutable". According to the EC view, Korea's interpretation would undermine that assumption and require complainants to prove that products which are sufficiently similar to be "like" are also "directly competitive and substi-

---

[172]   Panel Report on *Japan - Taxes on Alcoholic Beverages II, supra*, para. 5.7.
[173]   Panel Report on *Japan - Taxes on Alcoholic Beverages II, supra*, para. 5.9 (b).

tutable" in terms of price. The European Communities argues that if a such view was upheld, the presumption established in the first sentence of Article III:2 would lose much of its effectiveness and the clear textual distinction between the first and the second sentences of Article III:2 would become blurred.

6.35.   The European Communities argues that the second reason is that Korea's reliance upon price differences for justifying a different tax treatment is fraught with dangerous implications for the world trade system. According to the European Communities, the present dispute is concerned with a situation where imported products tend to be more expensive than the local products. Yet, if prices were deemed relevant for a "like" product determination, it would be open for developed country Members to claim that cheap imports from low cost developing country Members are too inexpensive to be on the same market with identical local products and to impose higher taxes on those imports. In the EC view, the mere possibility for a developing country Member to demonstrate before a Panel, in respect of each single category of products, that its exports do compete in terms of price with identical products of the importing country is likely to be an ineffective deterrent against this kind of abuses.

(a)   Vodka and diluted soju

6.36.   The European Communities also argues that Korea is able to identify only one single difference between vodka and diluted soju, namely that vodka has a higher alcohol content than diluted soju. According to the European Communities, whereas diluted soju is usually bottled at an alcoholic strength of 25%, vodka has between 37% and 40% alcohol content by volume[174].

6.37.   The European Communities further notes that the two Panel Reports on *Japan - Taxes on Alcoholic Beverages* have established that differences in alcoholic content do not suffice to make two liquors "unlike". In particular, *Japan - Taxes on Alcoholic Beverages II* concluded in unequivocal terms that:

> [A] difference in the physical characteristic of alcoholic strength of two products did not preclude a finding of likeness, especially since alcoholic beverages are often drunk in diluted form.[175]

6.38.   According to the European Communities, this conclusion was not based on the observation of the specific "tastes and habits" of the Japanese consumers but purported to have a general validity on all markets.

6.39.   The European Communities also notes that Korea, while admitting implicitly that vodka and diluted soju are virtually identical, denies that they are "like" by pointing to differences in customs classification, end-uses and pricing.

6.40.   In the EC view, the alleged differences regarding end uses are the same as those invoked by Korea with respect to other spirits. They are allegedly either overstated or irrelevant.

6.41.   The European Communities argues that the difference in customs classification is totally irrelevant. The European Communities notes that Korea's tariff is

---

[174]   This difference is not reflected in the Liquor Tax Law, which sets no minimum alcohol content for either diluted soju or vodka.

[175]   Panel Report on *Japan - Taxes on Alcoholic Beverages II, supra*, para. 6.23.

based on the 1996 version of the Harmonized System (HS). Under the previous version of the HS, vodka was allegedly classified into the same basket heading as soju (HS 2208.90, "other"). In the 1996 HS classification, it was allegedly decided to create a separate position for vodka (HS 2208.60) simply because that spirit had become one of the most internationally traded spirits and not because in the meantime it had developed new physical characteristics or end uses which made it "unlike" soju and all the other liquors falling within HS 2208.90.

6.42.   According to the European Communities, for these reasons, the alleged differences in prices are also irrelevant. The EC view is that in any event, Korea grossly overstates the actual differences. The pre-tax prices for soju shown in the Dodwell Study, on which Korea bases its comparison, are prices for standard diluted soju. The pre-tax prices for premium diluted soju are between two and three times higher.[176] If an adjustment is made to take into account differences in alcohol content, the pre-tax price for a bottle of imported vodka is two to three times higher than the pre-tax price for a bottle of premium soju.[177] In the EC view, in relative terms the difference in prices between premium diluted soju and vodka is the same as the difference between standard and premium diluted soju and much less than the difference between either premium or standard diluted soju and distilled soju.

(b)   Vodka and distilled soju

6.43.   The European Communities asserts that it has identified two differences between distilled soju and vodka:

> (a)   unlike vodka, distilled soju cannot be filtered through white birch charcoal, although it can be filtered through any other materials; and

> (b)   distilled soju must be obtained through non-continuous distillation.

6.44.   The European Communities asserts that Korea does not even mention these two differences in its argument. The EC view is that this confirms that, as claimed by the EC, those differences in manufacturing process have little impact on the final characteristics of the products and do not prevent vodka and distilled soju from being "like" products.

6.45.   The European Communities notes that in Korea's submission, the main difference between distilled soju and vodka would be a difference in taste: "Vodka approaches 'flavourlessness', while the taste of distilled soju is linked to its raw material".

6.46.   According to the European Communities, this difference, however, is clearly minor and cannot preclude a finding of "likeness". Once again, it is necessary to recall that according to *Japan - Taxes on Alcoholic Beverages I* : "[M]inor differences in taste, colour and other properties (including differences in alcohol contents) do not prevent products from qualifying as like products."[178]

---

[176]   See EC Annex 6.

[177]   See EC Annex 7.

[178]   Panel Report on *Japan - Taxes on Alcoholic Beverages I, supra*, para. 5.9.

6.47.   The European Communities argues that in terms of flavour, distilled soju is no more different from vodka than, for example, Japanese shochu B, which is also obtained by non-continuous distillation of, *inter alia*, grains.

6.48.   The European Communities further argues that in order to compensate for the absence of any significant difference in physical characteristics between distilled soju and vodka, Korea invokes differences in end uses and marketing.

> 5.   *Soju and the other Distilled Spirits are Directly Competitive and Substitutable Products*
>
> (a)   Standard for the interpretation of "directly competitive and substitutable"

6.49.   The European Communities notes that at several points of its submission, Korea argues that the notion of "directly competitive and substitutable products" must be applied "strictly".

6.50.   According to the European Communities, the restrictive interpretation of the terms "directly competitive or substitutable" advocated by Korea finds no support in the text of Article III, and that it is refuted by the drafting history of GATT 1947 as well as by prior panel reports.

6.51.   According to the European Communities, during the discussions within the Geneva Preparatory Committee and subsequently at the Havana Conference, the delegates discussed a number of examples of "directly competitive or substitutable products" which indicate clearly that the drafters had in mind a rather broad interpretation of those terms. Those examples included apples and oranges;[179] linseed oil and tung oil;[180] synthetic rubber and natural rubber;[181] coal and fuel oil;[182] and tramways and buses.[183]

6.52.   The European Communities argues that past panels which have interpreted the notion of "directly competitive or substitutable products" have also refrained from taking the narrow approach advocated by Korea. The European Communities also argues that the two Panel reports on *Japan - Taxes on Alcoholic Beverages* reached the conclusion that all distilled spirits were directly competitive or substitutable products. Another example, according to the European Communities, is provided by the Panel report on *EEC - Measures on Animal Feed Proteins*, which concluded that vegetable proteins and skimmed milk powder were "directly competitive or substitutable" products for the purposes of applying the second sentence of Article III:5.[184]

6.53.   The European Communities also notes that Korea, in order to justify its restrictive interpretation of "directly competitive or substitutable", argues that the purpose of Article III:2 is not to harmonize tax policies but to avoid protectionism.

---

[179]   EPCT/A/PV.9, at 7.
[180]   E/CONF.2/C.3/SR.11 p. 1 and Corr.2.
[181]   *Ibid.*, p. 3.
[182]   E/CONF.2/C.3/SR40, at 2.
[183]   *Ibid.*
[184]   Panel Report on *EEC - Measures on Animal Feed Proteins, supra*, para. 4.3.

6.54.   The EC view is that it would agree that the purpose of Article III:2 is to avoid protectionism, but nevertheless takes issue with Korea's contention that this purpose commands a "strict" reading of the notion of "directly competitive and substitutable" product.

6.55.   The European Communities notes that in *Japan - Taxes on Alcoholic Beverages II*, first the Panel and then the Appellate Body concluded that the notion of "like product" must be construed "narrowly" in the first sentence of Article III:2. According to the European Communities, this interpretation was deemed necessary in view of the fact that, as put by one of the complainants in that dispute, Article III:2, first sentence, is like a "guillotine": once it has been established that two products are like, any tax differential between them is deemed prohibited, without it being necessary to ascertain whether the tax differential is applied "so as to afford protection".[185]

6.56.   The European Communities notes further that in contrast, there is no indication in *Japan - Taxes on Alcoholic Beverages II* that the notion of "directly competitive or substitutable" product must also be construed "narrowly" or "strictly". According to the European Communities, this reflects the different wording and structure of the second sentence of Article III:2. Unlike the first sentence of Article III:2, the second sentence makes express reference to the first paragraph of Article III. This means, in the EC view, that in order to establish a violation of Article III:2, second sentence, it must be determined first, as one of three separate requirements, that the tax differential is "applied .... so as to afford protection to domestic production". According to the European Communities, therefore, a "strict" or "narrow" reading of the terms "directly competitive or substitutable" is not warranted in order to ensure that only protectionist measures are condemned.

6.57.   The European Communities notes that in the same vein, Korea also argues that Article III:2 second sentence applies only where there is "actual" competition, as opposed to "potential" competition. According to Korea, this interpretation is "strongly suggested" by the Interpretative Note to Article III:2 and, in particular, by the terms ".... where competition was involved". According to the European Communities, those terms, however, refer to "competition" only, without requiring that it must be "actual" competition. "Potential" competition is already "competition" within the meaning of the Note.

6.58.   According to the European Communities, the use in the Interpretative Note of the terms "competitive" (and not "competing") and substitutable (instead of "substitute") is a further indication that the GATT drafters envisaged the application of Article III:2 not just in instances of "actual" competition but also where there is "potential" competition. This is allegedly even clearer in the equally authentic French and Spanish versions which refer to ".... *un produit directement concurrent ou un produit qui peut lui être directement substitué.. .*" and "*... un producto directamente competidor o que puede substituirlo directamente...*", respectively.

---

[185]   The European Communities states that giving a narrow meaning to "like products" is also justified by the inescapability of violation in case of taxation of foreign products in excess of domestic products.

6.59.   The European Communities argues that Korea's interpretation is also refuted by prior Appellate Body and Panel reports which have recognized the relevance of "potential" competition for the purposes of Article III:2.

6.60.   The European Communities recalls that *Japan - Taxes on Alcoholic Beverages I* stressed that internal tax measures should not be used to "crystallize" consumer preferences for domestic products.[186]

6.61.   The same view was reiterated in Japan - Taxes on Alcoholic Beverages II:

> [t]he responsiveness of consumers to the various products offered in the market] .... may vary from country to country, but should not be influenced or determined by internal taxation. The Panel noted the conclusions in the 1987 Panel Report that a tax system that discriminates against imports has the consequence of creating and even freezing preferences for domestic goods. In the Panel's view this meant that consumer surveys in a country with such a tax system would likely understate the degree of potential competitiveness between substitutable products.[187]

6.62.   The European Communities also notes that the relevance of potential competition has also been recognized by the Appellate Body in *Canada - Certain Measures Affecting Periodicals*:

> [W]e are not impressed either by Canada's argument that the market share of imported and domestic magazines has remained remarkably constant over the last 30-plus years, and that one would have expected some variation if competitive forces had been in play to the degree necessary to meet the standard of "directly competitive" goods. This argument would have weight only if Canada had not protected the domestic production of Canadian periodicals through, among other measures, the import prohibition of Tariff Code 9958 and the excise tax of Part V.1 of the Excise Act.[188]

6.63.   According to the European Communities, the relevance of potential competition for the application of Article III:2, second sentence, flows from the well established principle that Article III does not protect export volumes but expectations on the competitive relationship between imported and domestic products.[189] Those expectations may exist even if there is no "actual" competition yet between imported and domestic products due to protective tax measures.

6.64.   The European Communities further argues that, Korea's position would have the absurd result of actually rewarding those Members who apply the most protec-

---

[186]   Panel Report on *Japan - Taxes on Alcoholic Beverages I*, para. 5.7. At the same paragraph, the Panel added that:

> "The increasing imports of "western-style" alcoholic beverages into Japan bore witness to this lasting competitive relationship and to the potential products substitution through trade among various alcoholic beverages."

[187]   Panel Report on *Japan - Taxes on Alcoholic Beverages*, para. 6.28.

[188]   Appellate Body Report on *Canada - Certain Measures Concerning Periodicals, supra*, at 473.

[189]   See e.g. Working Party on *"Brazilian Internal Taxes"*, adopted 30 June 1949, II/181, 185, at para. 16; Panel Reports on *United States - Taxes on Petroleum and Certain Imported Substances, supra*, para. 5.1.9; *United States - Measures Affecting Alcoholic and Malt Beverages, supra*, 271; and *United States - Measures affecting the Importation, Sale and use of Tobacco*, adopted on 4 October 1994, DS44/R, paras. 99-100.

tionist tax measures. If a Member applies a tax in such a way as to completely exclude imports of a competitive product, it would never be possible for other Members to show that there is "actual" competition between that product and the protected domestic product and, therefore, that such measures violate Article III:2. Meanwhile, a Member applying a less protectionist tax measure which restricts but does not pre-empt "actual" competition between domestic and imported goods would be found to violate Article III:2

6.65.   The European Communities notes that Korea, in support of its peculiar interpretation of Article III:2, emphasizes that this provision is perhaps the GATT provision "that treads most heavily upon national sovereignty." Korea implies that since taxation is at the core of the Members' sovereignty, Panels should adopt a deferential standard whenever taxes are concerned.

6.66.   According to the European Communities, this argument is totally misguided. In the EC view, it is instructive to compare the wording of Articles III:2 and III:4 of GATT. Article III:4, the general national treatment provision, is concerned only with discrimination between "like products". In contrast, Article III:2 is concerned with discriminatory taxation not only between "like products" but also between the larger category of "directly competitive and substitutable" products. In the EC view, this shows that the GATT drafters were well aware that discriminatory taxation may be one of the most pernicious forms of protectionism and, for that reason, aimed to provide stricter rules with respect to internal tax measures than with respect to other internal regulations, rather than the opposite.

(b)   Physical characteristics

6.67.   The European Communities notes that Korea's submission lingers upon the differences in physical characteristics between soju and other spirits. Korea implies that those differences are sufficient to conclude that soju and other spirits are not "directly competitive or substitutable" with each other.

6.68.   The European Communities states that it is necessary to recall that two products do not have to be similar in terms of physical characteristics in order to be "directly substitutable and competitive". As noted in *Japan - Taxes on Alcoholic Beverages II*,

> "competition can and does exist among the products that do not necessarily share the same physical characteristics. In the Panel's view, the decisive criterion is whether they have common end uses..."[190]

6.69.   The European Communities argues that it is obvious that if two products have similar physical characteristics, this constitutes a strong indication that they are "directly competitive or substitutable". According to the European Communities, in the present case, the similarity between soju and the other distilled spirits is such that it is a sufficient reason for the Panel to conclude that all of them are "directly competitive or substitutable".

6.70.   The European Communities does not deny the existence of differences in physical characteristics between soju and other spirits. According to the EC view, if

---

[190]   Panel report on *Japan - Taxes on Alcoholic Beverages II, supra*, para. 6.22.

there were no such differences, it would have claimed that soju and the other distilled spirits are "like" and not simply "competitive or substitutable".

6.71.   According to the European Communities, the differences invoked by Korea are, in essence, the same shown in EC Annex 9. In the EC view therefore, there seems to be no disagreement with Korea as to the nature of the differences, only as to their significance.

6.72.   In the EC view, those differences are relatively minor and do not prevent soju from being "directly competitive or substitutable" with other distilled spirits. Indeed, according to the European Communities, many of the differences invoked by Korea, such as differences in alcohol content, colour or flavour, would not be sufficient even to exclude a finding of "likeness".[191]

6.73.   The EC claims its position is supported by the two Panels on *Japan - Taxes on Alcoholic Beverages*, which allegedly concluded that all distilled spirits were "directly competitive or substitutable" on the Japanese market, notwithstanding their different physical characteristics. Even if, as claimed by Korea, Japanese shochu was not "like" Korean soju, it remains that the differences between Korean soju and the other types of distilled spirits alleged by Korea are the same as the differences between Japanese shochu and those spirits.

(c)   End uses

6.74.   The European Communities notes Korea's argument that soju and the other spirits are not used in the same way by Korean consumers and, for that reason, are not "directly competitive or substitutable." Korea also points to differences in drinking style, drinking occasion and place of consumption.

6.75.   According to the European Communities, firstly, Korea seems to rely on the mistaken premise that in order to be "directly competitive or substitutable" two products must compete or substitute each other in respect of all possible economic uses. According to the European Communities, that narrow view has been rejected by the Appellate Body in *Canada - Certain Measures Concerning Periodicals*.[192] In that case, Canada argued that US magazines were not "directly competitive or substitutable" with Canadian magazines because, while they provided a reasonable substitute as an advertising medium, they were poor substitutes as an entertainment and communication medium. Thus, according to Canada, US and Canadian magazines were only "imperfect substitutes". The Appellate Body dismissed this argument by pointing that a case of "perfect substitutability" would fall within Article III:2, first sentence and ruled that all the magazines concerned were directly competitive or substitutable.

6.76.   The European Communities further argues that similarly, in *Japan - Taxes on Alcoholic Beverages I*, the Panel based its conclusion that Japan's Liquor Tax Law violated Article III:2, second sentence, on the finding that there existed direct competition or substitutability among the liquors concerned, "even if not necessarily in respect of all the economic uses to which the product may be put"[193]

---

[191]   Panel report on *Japan - Taxes on Alcoholic Beverages II, supra*, para. 5.9.

[192]   Appellate Body Report on *Canada - Certain Measures Concerning Periodicals, supra*, at 473.

[193]   Panel Report on Japan - *Taxes on Alcoholic Beverages I, supra*, para. 5.7.

6.77.   According to the European Communities, these two reports make it very clear that in order to establish that two products are "directly competitive or substitutable", it may be sufficient to show that they are "directly competitive or substitutable" in respect of certain uses.

6.78.   Secondly, according to the European Communities, the consumption patterns of soju and the other spirits concerned in this dispute are much more diverse and flexible than Korea's simplistic presentation would suggest. According to the European Communities, Korea would have the Panel believe that soju is always drunk straight and with meals and only at certain types of outlets, whereas western spirits are always drunk in styles other than straight, before or after meals and at different types of outlets. In the EC view, the reality is much more complex than this black-and-white picture. According to the European Communities, although the consumption patterns of soju and western spirits are not identical, there is a substantial degree of overlapping and, therefore, competition between the two categories.

6.79.   The European Communities further argues that Korea's submission focuses exclusively on the most traditional consumption patterns and disregards the rapid emergence of a new drinking culture which is increasingly comparable to that of other developed countries, especially among young consumers.[194]

6.80.   Thirdly, in the EC view, consumption patterns are affected by prices, which in turn are affected by tax differentials. It is certainly not a coincidence if in the present case the less taxed product is consumed more often with meals[195] or if the more taxed products are more often found at expensive outlets than at less expensive ones. According to the European Communities, it is necessary to discern those differences which may reflect the genuine "tastes and habits" of the Korean consumers from those which have been created or, at least, "fossilized" by discriminatory taxation.

6.81.   Finally, the EC view is that Korea's sweeping and categorical statements regarding the end uses of the different types of spirits are not supported by any evidence whatsoever, even though Korea is in possession of the necessary market surveys. According to the European Communities, the Panel should draw appropriate inferences from Korea's refusal to disclose those surveys.

---

[194]   See the Sofres Study, pp 3-7. According to the Sofres Report (at p. 4), the main changes in the Korean drinking culture are:
-   Consumers prefer premium drinks for their taste and aroma,
-   Consumers (young generation) prefer western style atmosphere
-   A drinking culture where 3 to 4 people, instead of a large group, gather to drink in moderate amounts,
-   A drinking culture where people drink lightly at home with family members.

[195]   The EC claims that Korea defies economic logic when it states that "In Korea, standard soju is the drink one finds on the dinner table, the drink that is consumed with meals. As such it is an inexpensive beverage" (Korea's First Submission, para. 130).

According to the European Communities, it seems more logical that soju has acquired the status of "every-day meal drink" because it is inexpensive, rather than the opposite. If soju had been subjected to import quotas and then to dissuasive import duties and very high discriminatory internal taxes, it could have never achieved that status.

(d)   Drinking styles

6.82.   The first difference alleged by Korea is that soju is always drunk straight. The EC view is that this is simply not true. The most frequent style for drinking soju is straight. But soju is also consumed in other styles, including mixed with other non-alcoholic beverages, especially by young consumers. This is attested by the growing sales in recent years of soju-based pre-mixes, of which some samples have been provided to the Panel. For tax purposes, soju-based pre-mixes are not considered as soju but as liqueurs. Nonetheless, the success of those pre-mixes proves that Korean consumers enjoy drinking soju mixed with other beverages.[196]

6.83.   Furthermore, western-style spirits also are consumed straight. In particular, straight is the most frequent drinking style of brandy. Similarly, whisky is most often consumed alone, diluted with water or on the rocks, all of which are effectively "straight".

(e)   Drinking occasion

6.84.   The European Communities notes that, according to Korea, soju is consumed always with meals. In the EC view, this is an over-simplification. Soju is often, but not always, consumed with meals. For instance, according to the European Communities, *sojubangs* are one of the most typical places for drinking soju. Yet *sojubangs* are bars and not restaurants. In addition, it is the EC view that soju-based cocktails are rarely consumed with meals. On the other hand, other spirits can be and sometimes are drunk with meals, even if admittedly less frequently than soju.

6.85.   The European Communities further notes that according to Korea, the reason why Korean consumers drink soju and no other spirit with their meals is because soju has a unique "harsh" (or "rough") flavour that goes well with Korean hot and spicy food.

6.86.   According to the European Communities, this "culinary exception" argument, however, is far from convincing. In the EC view, the traditional tastes and habits of Korean consumers alone are not sufficient to explain why soju is consumed more often with meals. Koreans do not eat hot and spicy food all the time. Nor does all soju respond to the "harsh/rough" description, as allegedly evidenced by the advertisement for the soju brand Jinro Bisun which praises itself on being "mild".[197] In the EC view, there are other spirits which may go just as well with hot and spicy food, such as vodka or, as pointed out by Mexico in its oral intervention before the Panel, tequila. Finally, the European Communities states that the peculiarities of Korean cuisine would not explain why, according to Korea, soju predominates in "inexpensive Chinese restaurants" but not in the rather more expensive Japanese restaurants.

---

[196]   The Sofres Report describes this development in the following terms, at p.24:
> "Also the sale of other liquors in the form of soju cocktail (lemon flavoured soju, cherry flavoured soju, etc.) have been introduced since 1994, targeting the young generation. The sale of soju cocktails have exploded and in July 1995, sales were up 12.5 times compared to the same period of the previous year. This is proof of the changing consumption patterns of Korean consumers."

[197]   Attachment 6 to Korea's First Submission.

6.87.   According to the European Communities, one of the main reasons why soju is more often consumed with every-day meals than western-style spirits is simply because western-style spirits are more expensive, to a large extent as a result of protective taxation. In the EC view, if western-style spirits were taxed as soju, they would be less expensive and Korean consumers could afford to drink them with meals more often.

6.88.   The European Communities also notes that Korea does not claim that distilled soju is consumed with meals, yet until the 1960s most soju was distilled soju. The European Communities asks whether this means that Koreans' allegedly traditional habit of drinking soju with meals did not start until the 1960s? or rather, as it seems more plausible, that most Koreans cannot afford to drink their every-day meals with the now rather expensive distilled soju and instead tend to keep it for special occasions and drink it in smaller doses than required to accompany a meal, just like they do with western-style spirits?

(f)   Place of consumption

6.89.   The European Communities refers to Korea's claim that soju is typically drunk in places where western-style spirits are not available yet, such as "Korean restaurants, mobile street vendors and inexpensive Chinese restaurants".

6.90.   The EC view is that it is true that western-style spirits still have little presence in certain types of outlets, but that cannot be explained, as Korea pretends, simply as the result of "consumers' tastes and habits." In the EC view, it is surely not coincidental that those outlets where the penetration of western spirits remains the lowest are also the least expensive.

6.91.   According to the European Communities, Korea's submission totally disregards the existence of a clear trend towards wider availability of western-style spirits. The EC position is that only a few years ago, western-style spirits could be found only in upmarket restaurants and entertainment establishments. Since then, as shown by the Hankook survey included in the EC First Submission, western style-spirits have gained considerable distribution penetration and are now available at a wide range of outlets. According to the European Communities, the continued application by Korea of protective internal taxes stands as an obstacle to that trend.

6.92.   The European Communities states that in this regard, it is instructive to compare the Korean and Japanese markets. According to the European Communities, only a decade ago, Japanese *izakayas* (the equivalent of traditional Korean restaurants) used to serve only shochu, sake and beer, whereas western-style *snack bars* would serve western drinks but not shochu. Today, shochu and western style spirits are allegedly usually available at both *izakayas* and *snack bars*.

6.93.   The European Communities further argues that it is important to note that a considerable and growing proportion of both soju and western-style spirits is purchased for consumption at home. In the EC view, this is totally ignored in Korea's submission. Specifically, the EC industry estimates that between 30 % and 35 % of western spirits and more than 20 % of soju are consumed at home.

6.94.   According to the European Communities, as evidenced by the Hankook survey, western-style spirits are sold for home consumption through the full range of retail channels, where they compete head-on with soju.[198] The European Communities further claims that as shown by the photographs attached to its First Submission, retail establishments of different types often display soju and other distilled spirits side-by-side on the same shelves.

(g)   Gift giving

6.95.   The European Communities notes that in the case of distilled soju, Korea advances the additional argument that its main use is for gift giving. The EC view is that although this may be so, western-style spirits, and in particular whisky and brandy, are also often offered as a gift. The advertisements for Robbie Dhu and Johnny Walker Gift Set includes two advertisements promoting specifically the purchase of whisky for gift-giving.[199] According to the European Communities, Korea incurs in an even more embarrassing contradiction when, in comparing diluted soju and cognac, it states that the latter is "very suitable for gifts."

(h)   Pricing

6.96.   The European Communities also notes that Korea contends that the pre-tax prices of soju are much lower than the pre-tax prices of western style spirits. Korea alleges that, because of that price difference, there cannot be competition between soju and western-style spirits.

6.97.   The European Communities takes issue with Korea's contention that it is sufficient to compare pre-tax prices in order to exclude "any possible distortive effect from the disputed taxes."

6.98.   The European Communities states for example, that tax differentials may affect the relative importance of the different price segments within each tax category. The European Communities refers to the Panel Report in *Japan - Taxes on Alcoholic Beverages II*, in which it was stated that one of the consequences of a protective system of internal taxes may be to make it more difficult for the cheaper brands of the more heavily taxed products to enter the market.[200] The EC view is that in Korea, this effect is attested by the fact that premium brands account for a disproportionate share of imports,[201] whereas the cheapest brands of western spirits are virtually absent. On the other hand, lower taxes have given to soju producers an advantage to target in particular the low end of the market.

6.99.   The European Communities also argues that protective taxes limit the sales growth of the more heavily taxed imported categories and, as a result, keep their unit costs at an artificially high level, as compared with less taxed domestic products which are sold in much greater volumes.

6.100. In any event, according to the European Communities, absolute price differences are not of themselves determinative of whether two products are "directly

---

[198]   Attachment 6 to Korea's First Submission.

[199]   *Ibid.*

[200]   Panel Report on *Japan - Taxes on Alcoholic Beverages II, supra*, para. 6.33 (d).

[201]   See the Sofres Report, at p. 26.

competitive or substitutable." In the EC view, what really matters is the consumers' response to changes in relative prices. The Dodwell study allegedly provides evidence of that type of response. The European Communities notes that Korea has criticized the supposed methodological flaws of the Dodwell study, but it has not put forward any contrary evidence showing that there is no significant degree of cross-price elasticity between soju and western spirits.

6.101. According to the European Communities, in the present case, absolute price differences are even less determinative in view of the nature of the products concerned. The European Communities adds that spirits are not like cars, which are purchased by most consumers in developed countries only once every four or five years. Spirits are consumable products, which can be purchased many times over a relatively short period of time. According to the European Communities, Korea's argument assumes that each Korean consumer drinks always the same type of spirit. In practice, however, most consumers, even if they prefer a certain type of spirit, may drink also other spirits depending not only on the occasion but also on the prevailing prices for each of them.

6.102. In the EC view, the above reasons explain why the two Panels on *Japan - Taxes on Alcoholic Beverages* did not take into account absolute prices differences, even though such differences were also substantial in the Japanese market.[202]

6.103. The European Communities further argues that at any rate, the comparisons made by Korea grossly overstate the actual price differences. The pre-tax prices for diluted soju shown in the Dodwell study, on which Korea has based its price comparisons, are prices for standard diluted soju. The pre-tax price for premium soju is between two and three times higher.[203] In the EC view, if an adjustment is made to take into account the differences in alcohol content, the pre-tax price for a bottle of standard whisky is about two to three times higher than the pre-tax price for a bottle of premium soju[204].

6.104. The European Communities also argues that the differences between the pre-tax prices for distilled soju and standard diluted soju are even larger than the differences between the pre-tax prices for standard whisky and standard diluted soju.[205]

6.105. The European Communities notes that as additional evidence, Korea submits a comparison of the "weighted average prices" for whisky and soju. According to the European Communities, that comparison, however, is meaningless. The prices for whisky vary enormously. Even if one considers only mainstream brands, the prices for standard blended whisky may be as much as ten times less than the prices for de luxe and single malt whiskies. The EC view is that although to a lesser extent,

---

[202] According to the European Communities, in *Japan - Taxes on Alcoholic Beverages I, supra*, the Panel ruled that price differences were irrelevant for a like product determination. Prices are not mentioned in the Panel's analysis under the second sentence of Article III:2. In *Japan - Taxes on Alcoholic Beverages II, supra*, differences in prices were examined by the Panel only in connection with Japan's argument that, because tax/price ratios were "roughly the same", the products were not taxed "similarly" (paras. 6.33-6.34) but not for the purposes of determining whether the products were "directly competitive or substitutable" (paras. 6.28-6.32).

[203] See EC Annex 6.

[204] See EC Annex 7.

[205] See EC Annex 6.

the prices for soju also vary. The pre-tax prices of premium diluted soju may be two to three times higher than the prices for standard diluted soju. According to Korea, premium soju accounts for 5 % of the total sales of diluted soju. According to the European Communities, therefore, as a result, the weighted average price for all diluted soju calculated by Korea is virtually the same as the average price for standard diluted soju.

i)   Other alleged differences

6.106. The European Communities refers to Korea's claim that the advertising for soju is targeted at the "common man" whereas the advertising for western-style spirits targets the up-market consumer. In the EC view, the soju advertisements included in Attachment 6 to Korea's submission fail to support those allegations. They do not show farmers or labourers but rather business men in shirts and ties. According to the European Communities, Korea has carefully omitted to include in Attachment 6 to its submission any example of recent soju advertising for premium brands, which is even more clearly targeted to the up-market Korean consumer.[206]

6.107. The European Communities contends that Korea's allegations regarding the differences in advertising imply that while soju is the poor man's drink, whisky and other imported spirits are a luxury drink for the most affluent classes. In the EC view, this is totally misleading, as both soju and whisky are now widely consumed across social boundaries.[207]

6.108. The European Communities also notes that Korea makes the argument that the fact that some Korean companies which sell both whisky and soju do so under different trademarks is an indication that the two products do not compete in the same market, yet some of those companies use also different brands for premium diluted soju and standard diluted soju.

6.109. According to the European Communities, even less convincing is Korea's argument that diluted soju does not compete with vodka, gin and rum because the latter are sold in small volumes whereas soju is a mass volume product. In the EC view this is because only a few pages later Korea reverses this argument without any apparent embarrassment in order to claim that distilled soju is a "tiny niche product."

---

[206] EC Annex 12.

[207] The Sofres Report describes as follows the profile of the whisky drinkers (at p. 25):

> Whisky, an expensive drink perceived as the drink of the upper class, was used mainly for gift purposes and sold in upmarket restaurants and entertainment establishments. However, whisky is widely becoming more of a drink of choice among various age groups. With market liberalisation and overseas travel liberalisation, many Koreans have ready access to whisky and it is becoming well accepted by the general public. In reflection to this trend, whisky consumption is increasing at a rapid pace".

According also to the Sofres Report (at p.23), in the Korean alcohol market, Soju is a very popular product drunk by all classes.

6.   *The Dodwell Study*

6.110. According to the European Communities, until the early 1990s, western spirits were virtually excluded from the Korean market by a combination of trade barriers. In the EC view, too few sales figures are available to allow an econometric analysis of the substitution relationship between soju and Western style spirits. This leaves a survey such as the Dodwell study as the only method. In the EC view, Korea does not appear to question the rationale for the survey. However, as Korea has presented a number of criticisms to the Dodwell report, the European Communities responds to those criticism as follows-

(a)   Alleged "inconsistency" of results

6.111. The European Communities notes that Korea points to the fact that there are a number of anomalies in the study. Notably, on a few charts there appears anomalous behaviour in terms of slightly higher soju purchases when prices for the soju increase. According to the European Communities, these anomalies are far less troublesome than Korea is suggesting:

(a)   Despite some unexpected sign reversals the results show very clearly and consistently that:

    (i)   more people choose western spirits when the price of soju increases; and

    (ii)   less people choose soju when the price of other spirits decreases.

(b)   Anomalies are in practice limited to switching between western spirits. The moving away from soju when its price increases is very robust.

(c)   The anomalies affect only some 15 percent of the observed changes in quantities. Moreover, if one were to compare only the selection at the 1000 Won price level with the selection at the 1200 Won price level only 5 (small) anomalies arise out of 48 possibilities.

In the EC view, this is far from being a bad result for a survey because, as Korea pointed out, it has to be kept in mind that the survey deals with fallible human beings. A perfectly consistent result from interviewing five hundred people cannot be expected, and would actually be highly suspicious. The anomalies also run counter to the implicit insinuation that the survey results are biased by the patron of the study.

(b)   Standard vs. premium soju

6.112. The European Communities notes that the inclusion of premium diluted soju as an object of choice biases the results upwards. According to the European Communities, this is not the case because:

(a)   Premium diluted soju is a close substitute for standard diluted soju, as Korea has acknowledged. Therefore, the inclusion of premium soju in the sample provides an extremely useful benchmark with which it can be compared the price reaction of the other spirits. The survey clearly establishes that the pattern of consumer choices of premium soju and other spirits is the same. In both cases higher prices for standard soju lead to higher consumption of alternative drinks (whether premium soju or others), even if the changes for western spirits are less pronounced. Therefore, the inclusion of premium soju in the sample allows to demonstrate strongly that the other liquors in the sample are soju substitutes.

(b)   The study shows quite clearly the choices made by the surveyed persons. The fact that many people move to premium soju does not distract from the fact that many also switch to western-style drinks.

(c)   Lower prices for western drinks increase their consumption, even if the price for premium soju is lowered at the same time.

(d)   The elimination of premium soju from the choices would probably make more people pick any of the other spirits.

(c)   Choice of respondents

6.113. According to the European Communities, the criticisms made by Korea with respect to the choice of respondents are also unfounded because:

(a)   The survey does not intend to estimate a cross-price elasticity. It is much less ambitious. Its purpose is solely to establish that soju and other liquors are in competition.

(b)   There is no direct link between the percentage of soju volume consumed by the Korean population and the number of people that prefer soju as a drink. It is very conceivable that the average soju drinker consumes larger quantities of soju than the average whisky drinker consumes whisky. Therefore the differences in percentage figures should not be over-dramatized.

(c)   Even if the percentage figures for western style drinks were too high, Korea claims nowhere that this would change the direction of change in consumer behaviour. In fact, the criticism of the "inconsistencies" of the study implicitly acknowledges that consumers should move away from soju as soju becomes relatively more expensive. This relationship is exactly what the survey attempts to show, and Korea's acceptance of this basic tenet should be welcome.

(d)   The survey cannot show that in all markets and under all conditions people react to prices. However, it does show that at least in the (important!) market of male Korean city dwellers between 20 and 49, the issue of price differences is important. It is a simple question of survey economy to concentrate on those interviewees that are most likely to give an informed answer. Furthermore, it is unquestionable that the surveyed population group is an important market segment for spirits. It is reasonable to assume that the established relationship also holds in other market segments.

(d)   Pair-wise choices

6.114. The European Communities reiterates that the fact that the survey sample might have a higher preference for drinking western beverages than the Korean sales volume figures suggest is of no consequence to the validity of the results. In the EC view, what matters is that a cross-price relationship is established.

6.115. The European Communities also states that it should be mentioned in this context that the separate paring of brown and white liquors actually biases the reaction to price increases downwards rather than upwards. The European Communities refers to Korea's explanation that a preference for white liquor does not imply a preference for brown liquor over soju. A person with a preference for brown liquor might therefore not be impressed by the rising soju prices to drink white liquor, and vice versa. In the EC view, this means the price reaction of the survey will be underestimated.

(e)   Single drink choice

6.116. The European Communities notes that Korea claims that the phrasing of the survey question may be ambiguous. In particular, Korea presumes that the question could be interpreted as a unique and non-repeated sales offer.

6.117. In the EC view, it is difficult to see why this should be the case, in particular since the phrasing of the question belongs to the standard repertoire of market surveys. However, even if it were interpreted thus, it is quite clear that people react to price changes and choose more imported liquors, at the expense of soju. This means clearly that the consumer interprets the liquors for choice as substitutes.

6.118. According to the European Communities, Korea would have preferred a phrasing "would these prices cause you to change your drinking habits?" In the EC view, this question would produce lower figures (which is actually why it is proposed). The reason for this is simply that people are less able to make a statement about permanent behavioural change. The European Communities add that the proposal of Korea also sits oddly with a remark earlier on the internal consistency of the results.

6.119. In the EC view, the conclusions of the survey are quite clear: consumers are sensitive to the relative prices of soju and other drinks and change their behaviour accordingly. This indicates very strongly that the consumers view Western liquors and soju as substitutes. According to the European Communities, Korea's critique does not affect these conclusions.

(f)   Overall

6.120. The European Communities also argued that the spirits markets have two defining characteristics. First, spirits consumption is habitual behaviour in that people tend to order the same drink they ordered on a previous given occasion. Thus, behaviour changes only gradually. Second, spirits are experience goods in that they must be purchased and consumed to be evaluated by consumers. Descriptions do not suffice. Market penetration increases slowly as it is necessary to get consumers actually to try the products first. Market surveys such as the Dodwell study must be evaluated in light of these factors.

7.   *The Sofres Report*

6.121. The European Communities notes that Korea, while disparaging the Dodwell study, places considerable reliance on another document commissioned   by   the

European Communities and prepared by the same market research organization as the Dodwell study: the document entitled "Your Guide to Exporting Food Products to Korea - Alcoholic Beverages" (the "Sofres Report").

6.122. In the EC view, although it is obvious that Korea has perused the Sofres Report for "quotable" passages, the results of that search are rather meagre: just two short passages of two sentences each.

6.123. According to the European Communities, the Sofres report is a generic report intended to provide a description of the current market situation, which may serve as a guide to the EC exporters. The Sofres report did not even attempt to address the question tackled by the Dodwell study, namely whether a connection can be established between the price of western-style spirits and the sales of soju and vice-versa.

6.124. The European Communities further argues that the Sofres Report relies on the assumption that, not just soju and western-style spirits, but all alcoholic beverages are part of the same market. For instance, market shares are calculated with respect to the entire alcoholic beverages market, which would have been meaningless if the authors of the report had considered that soju and other spirits do not compete on the same market.

6.125. The European Communities also argues that when the Sofres report states that "soju remains virtually unaffected by imported alcoholic drinks" it means simply that, despite the considerable increase in imports of whisky and other western-style liquors, soju continues to account for the vast majority of sales of spirits. At the same time, the use of the term "virtually" before "unaffected" shows that the authors considered that there was actual, even if limited in terms of the volumes concerned, competition between soju and other western-style spirits. In the EC view, the term "remains" clearly indicates that the authors of the report did not regard the current predominance of soju as a fixed and permanent feature of the Korean market but as a temporary situation which could change in the future as a result of increased sales of western-style spirits.

8.   *The Trendscope Survey*

6.126. The Trendscope survey addresses two questions, the first of which was - "in which of the following places have you drunk whisky/soju during the last six months."

6.127. According to the European Communities, the response to this question confirms that although soju is still consumed more often at traditional Korean venues and whisky at western-style or entertainment outlets, there is no rigid segregation between the two.

6.128. The European Communities further argues, that the survey shows that, contrary to Korea's allegations, there is already a significant degree of overlap. Firstly, the European Communities alleges that soju is also consumed in places where whisky has already established a presence. The EC view is that 8% of respondents declared to have drunk soju at Karaoke bars, which are still the main places for drinking whisky. Furthermore, the European Communities states that the Trendscope survey shows that whisky is also drunk in places where soju has traditionally been the predominant spirit, such as Korean restaurants and bars.

6.129. The European Communities also argues that the survey confirms that home consumption at home is one of the main end-uses for both whisky and soju. According to the European Communities, as much as 34% of respondents declared to have drunk whisky at home whereas the percentage of respondents who had drunk soju at home was 43%.

6.130. The second question asked to the respondents was whether they had the habit of drinking whisky/soju with meals or without meals. According to the European Communities, the response to this question confirms that whisky is also drunk with meals, even if less often than soju. The European Communities claims that 7% of the respondents answered that they had the habit of drinking whisky with meals.

6.131. The European Communities further argues the survey also shows that, contrary to the claims repeatedly made by Korea, soju is by no means always consumed with meals. It is the EC view that the respondents who declared to have the habit of drinking soju with meals was just 36%.

6.132. As a complement to the second question, the respondents were also asked whether they had the habit of drinking whisky/soju with or without food. According to the European Communities, the response to this question was very similar in both cases: whereas the percentage of respondents who declared to have consumed whisky with food was 86%, the percentage of respondent who declared to have drunk soju with food was 97%.

6.133. The European Communities concludes that both the Nielsen study and Trendscope survey show that despite the fact that western spirits have been virtually excluded from the Korean market until very recently, and that western spirits remain subject to much higher taxes than soju, there is already a significant degree of overlap as regards their end-uses. In the EC view, the extent of that overlap could only increase if the tax differentials between soju and western spirits were eliminated.

9.   *The Measures are Applied "so as to Afford Protection to Domestic Production"*

6.134. The European Communities argues that Korea has not presented any meaningful argument in order to refute the claim that the measures at issue afford protection to its domestic production.

6.135. According to the European Communities, Korea's main defence is that whisky bottled in Korea from imported concentrated whisky should be considered as a domestic production. In the alternative, Korea claims that soju produced in Korea from imported neutral spirits should be considered as imported.

6.136. In the EC view, there is an obvious difference between those two situations. Concentrated whisky has already all the essential characteristics of whisky and can be used only to bottle whisky. It is imported under the same tariff heading as bottled whisky (HS 2208.30) and is subject to the same import duties.

6.137. The European Communities further argues that in contrast, neutral spirits are a raw material which can be used to produce a variety of alcoholic beverages, including for example vodka and gin, as well as other products, such as heating fuel or pharmaceutical products. Neutral spirits are imported under a different tariff heading and are subject to much lower import duty than soju. In the EC view, if Korea takes the view that soju is the same product as neutral spirits, it should explain why it does not apply the same taxes to all liquors made from neutral spirits.

6.138. The European Communities further argues that at any rate, even if Scotch whisky bottled in Korea had to be considered as a domestic product, soju would still account for almost all of Korea's domestic production of spirits. It is thus beyond question that by protecting soju, Korea protects its domestic production of sprits.

6.139. The European Communities asserts that in this regard, it is worth recalling that the existence of a substantial production of genuine domestic whisky in Japan did not prevent the two Panels on *Japan - Taxes on Alcoholic Beverages* from concluding that Japan's Liquor Tax Law infringed Article III:2, second sentence. [208] Further, according to the European Communities, it is also worth noting that almost all Japanese shochu A is made from imported neutral spirits. Yet, the two Panels on *Japan - Taxes on Alcoholic Beverages* had no hesitation to consider shochu A as a domestic production.

6.140. The European Communities argues, therefore, that Korea's allegation that soju is isolated from imports by "commercial realities", rather than regulatory action has not been substantiated and is in any event totally irrelevant. What matters is that imports of soju are and have always been negligible and, therefore, that by favouring soju the Korean Government can be assured that it protects a domestic production, and a domestic production alone.

6.141. According to the European Communities, Korea's argument that the tax differentials cannot be protective because the pre-tax price differentials are too large is logically flawed. If the Panel found that the products concerned are "directly competitive or substitutable" despite the pre-tax price differentials, it would follow necessarily that those price differentials are not large enough to exclude, of themselves, the possibility that the tax differentials may afford protection to domestic production.

6.142. The European Communities also notes that Korea denies emphatically that the Liquor Tax Law's very structure and design reveals a protectionist purpose, but fails to offer a minimally reasonable explanation for the Liquor Tax Law's many apparent inconsistencies.

6.143. The European Communities states for instance, that Korea attempts to explain the Liquor Tax Law's product categorization by saying that, originally, soju was the only product subject to the Liquor Tax Law and new tax categories were created only as other spirits appeared on the market. In the EC view, this does not explain why it was considered necessary to add to the definition of soju a series of exceptions, so as to exclude the most important categories of imported spirits, nor does it explain why it was necessary to apply much higher rates on the newly created categories.

6.144. According to the European Communities, the closest that Korea comes to giving a coherent explanation for the Liquor Tax Law's apparent lack of rationality

---

[208] According to the European Communities, in *Japan - Taxes on Alcoholic Beverage I, supra,* Japan argued that the Liquor Tax Law did not afford protection to domestic production because imports of special grade whisky accounted for merely 14.6 % of total sales of that product. This argument was disregarded by the Panel which only took into account the fact that the less taxed product (Shochu) was produced almost exclusively in Japan. Panel Report on *Japan - Taxes on Alcoholic Beverages I, supra,* paras. 3.10 (f) and 5.11.

is when it states that "as tax rules are developed, they must accommodate varying levels of taxpayer resistance" and that "in sum, taxes are a delicate balancing act for any government." In the EC view, this means that if soju is subject to lower taxes it is simply because soju producers have more political weight than importers of whisky.

6.145. With respect to distilled soju, the European Communities notes that Korea advances the argument that equalizing the taxes for distilled soju and whisky would "cripple" the distilled soju industry with no benefit to the imported beverages industry. According to the European Communities, this argument, is totally irrelevant in order to determine whether the current system "affords protection to domestic production." It is also allegedly at odds with Korea's previous allegation that demand for distilled soju is "specific and static" and that, for that reason, "it would be difficult to affect it a great deal in either direction by altering its price".

B.   United States

1.   General: Violation of Article III:2

6.146. The United States notes that in its first submission, it showed that Korea's application of preferential tax rates to soju discriminates against vodka, a "like" product and against all other distilled spirits, which are directly competitive or substitutable, in violation of Article III:2. According to the United States, in response, Korea has principally argued that soju is a unique product in a unique market, and that a violation of Article III cannot be alleged in light of the differences it cites between soju and other distilled spirits.

6.147. The United States notes that Korea, in an attempt to assist its attempt to distinguish western distilled spirits from soju, characterizes distilled soju as a product distinct from diluted soju in an apparent willingness to sacrifice the tax preference for this "special" artisanal product that makes up 0.2% of its total soju sales. The United States argues that the effort is to downplay the characteristics of distilled soju that are identical to those of western distilled spirits, such as its alcohol content and use of aging. According to the United States, however, the different types of soju, however, are the same or "like" product for all practical purposes.[209]

6.148. The United States asserts that in the first instance, the two varieties have the same name. Both standard and distilled are clear in appearance and filtered similarly, and unlike vodka, which is taxed at 30 percent, the Education Tax rate of distilled and standard soju is 10 percent. The United States adds that although distilled soju is made from discontinuous (pot still) distillation, the distinction has minimal tangible effect on the product. Products such as whisky and brandy can be manufactured by either continuous distillation or pot still (discontinuous) distillation. The United States further argues that both types of soju are derived from the same raw materials, and Korean law apparently does not require the use of any particular

---

[209] The United States argues that it is not necessary, for purposes of Article III:2, to determine whether a product is the same product or simply "like." The drafters obviously avoided limiting the application of the national treatment disciplines to the "same" products for fear of definitional disagreements on the basis of minor variations in products.

starch source such as rice; any starch source can be used. Finally, the United States notes that, as to their packaging, whether a product is marketed as "artisanal" or not is a reflection of the manufacturer's marketing savvy, rather than a fundamental departure from the nature of the product.

6.149. The United States argues that a better perspective on Korea's emphasis on differences between standard and distilled soju (namely price, taste, and marketing) may be seen by comparing with another category of alcoholic beverage such as wine. According to the United States, wines cover a broad range of prices and qualities, yet it would be difficult to argue that a $10 table wine and a $100 bottle of Bordeaux wine are not "like." The price difference between inexpensive and expensive wine can vary by a factor of ten or more. The United States continues that, similar to distilled soju, expensive wines are marketed in small volumes with distinctive advertising and packaging in order to emphasize uniqueness, and might, in the opinion of some, possess more complex bouquet and aroma than inexpensive wines.

6.150. According to the United States, therefore, variations in price, taste and marketing of products with similar end uses simply offer consumers alternative choices and do not mean they are not the same or "like" products.

2.   *Violation of Article III:2, First Sentence*

6.151. The United States considers that vodka is "like" soju and that, under Article III:2 first sentence, Korea must eliminate any tax on vodka that exceeds the tax on soju. The US view is that Korea wrongly suggests that the absence of "perfect substitutability," the presence of minor differences in physical characteristics and production processes, differences in price, and differences in the end-uses in a particular market prevent two products from being "like."

6.152. The United States argues that Korea's argument that "like" products include only those that are "perfectly substitutable," has no basis in the text of Article III:2 or in Appellate Body reports, because if products were perfectly substitutable, they would likely be identical. The United States notes that in *Canada - Certain Measures Concerning Periodicals*, the Appellate Body noted that perfectly substitutable products would "fall within" the scope of "like" products,[210] but that does not mean that only perfectly substitutable products can be considered "like" products. According to the United States, the text of Article III:2 that refers to "like" products (in French, *produits similaires*) avoids the obvious tax discrimination that could result between similar products that do not share every single characteristic and accordingly are not "perfectly substitutable."

6.153. The United States further argues that, although the Appellate Body has clarified that the term "like" in Article III:2 must be narrowly construed, it is well established in GATT practice that products do not have to be identical to be considered "like" products.[211] Korea's insistence that minor differences such as alcohol content

---

[210] Appellate Body Report, p. 28.

[211] *Japan - Taxes on Alcoholic Beverages I*, *supra*, para. 5.6 ("minor differences do not prevent products [from] qualifying as "like"); *U.S. - Taxes on Petroleum and Certain Imported Substances,*

and additives prevent two distilled spirits from being "like," runs directly counter to findings such as that in *United States - Measures Affecting Alcoholic and Malt Beverages,* in which the panel considered a low-quality style of Mississippi wine made from a special "scuppernong" kind of grape to be "like" all other kinds of wine.[212] The United States further notes that in *Japan - Taxes on Alcoholic Beverages I,* taxes on alcoholic beverages, vodka and shochu were considered "like" products even though vodka was filtered differently. The US view is that Korea's argument that in a few instances vodka might be made of different raw materials than soju is not relevant if it does not affect aspects of the product identifiable to the consumer. According to the United States, whatever the original starch source, it is ethyl alcohol from various sources that is used in the production of US vodka, Korean soju and Japanese shochu. The production process allegedly varies only by filtration methods and level of dilution with water, resulting in minimal differences in the products produced.

6.154. The United States also argues that Korea's attempts to distinguish vodka from soju exaggerate the importance of the attribute. With respect to diluted soju, Korea has identified alcohol content as an important physical difference. According to the United States, the alcohol content of diluted soju is bottled at about 25%, while vodka is bottled at about 40%. But the United States notes that the WTO Japan panel conclusively rejected the notion that a difference in alcoholic strength of two products precluded a finding of likeness, on the basis of the simple observation that "alcoholic beverages are often drunk in diluted form."[213]

6.155. According to the United States, such a difference in alcohol content does not even exist with respect to distilled soju. The United States notes that Korea, with respect to distilled soju, emphasizes the taste. In the US view, any such difference in flavour is probably linked to the distillation process rather than raw material, since vodka and soju are often derived from the same raw materials. In this regard, soju is no more different from vodka than Japanese shochu B, which is also obtained through a non-continuous (pot-still) distillation process.

6.156. The United States also argues that the fact that vodka has now been placed in its own tariff heading in Korea's schedules (2208.60) is also irrelevant. According to the United States, it was previously in the same basket category as soju (2208.90), but was broken into a separate heading to correspond to changes in the 1996 Harmonized System, which created a separate category to reflect the vast international trade in the product.

6.157. The United States further argues that Korea's emphasis on consumer tastes and habits as a dispositive factor in determining whether two products are "like" is also misplaced. According to the United States, the original identification of this factor derives from the Report of the Working Party on *Border Tax Adjustments.*[214] However, the United States notes that the report emphasized that the interpretation

---

supra, (liquid hydrocarbon products although not identical were "like" crude oil and natural gas because they served substantially same end uses).

[212] BISD 39S/206, 276-77.

[213] Panel Report on *Japan - Taxes Alcoholic Beverages II, supra,* para. 6.23.

[214] BISD 18S/97, 102.

of "like" or "similar" products "should be examined on a case-by-case basis," which "would allow a fair assessment in each case of the different elements that constitute a 'similar' product."

6.158. According to the United States, *Japan - Alcoholic Beverages I* and *II* did not consider consumer tastes and habits to be significant in determining likeness where the market was previously restricted. The United States further argues that although the 1987 GATT panel agreed that in theory both objective factors and "the more subjective consumers' viewpoint" should be considered, it chose to disregard the "subjective" factor of "traditional Japanese habits" on the following basis:

> Since consumer habits are variable in time and space and the aim of Article III:2 of ensuring neutrality of internal taxation as regards competition between imported and domestic like products could not be achieved if differential taxes could be used to crystallize consumer preferences for traditional domestic products, the Panel found that the traditional Japanese consumer habits with regard to shochu provided no reason for not considering vodka to be a "like" product.[215]

6.159. The United States asserts that for the same reasons, the same panel also disregarded Japan's argument that differences in prices between local shochu and imported distilled spirits could prevent a finding of "like." According to the United States, the panel "was of the view that 'like' products do not become 'unlike' merely because of differences . . . in their prices, which were often influenced by external government measures (*e.g.* customs duties) and market conditions (*e.g.* supply and demand, sales margins)." Further, according to the United States, under the circumstances presented in the Japan dispute (a long history of protection, as in Korea), the panel considered that giving any weight to factors such as consumer traditions in a country or differences in price would run counter to the objective of Article III:2, by "creating different prices and consumer categories and hardening consumer preferences for traditional home products."[216] In the US view, such reasoning is equally compelling in this dispute.

6.160. With respect to vodka, the United States argues that Korea's attempt to draw a stark distinction between vodka and soju does not correspond to the very similar physical attributes and manufacturing processes of these products. Vodka is often made from the same grain-based neutral spirits as soju. Although a little costlier, white birch charcoal filtration produces virtually the same results as using other types of charcoal filtration - and accordingly this difference did not prevent the *Japan - Taxes on Alcoholic Beverages II* panel from finding that vodka and shochu are "like" products. The United States also claimed that it is also wrong to emphasize alcoholic strength as a dispositive factor in selecting a distilled spirit. Once they are prepared, many mixed drinks, such as vodka cocktails have a lower alcohol content than straight soju. As determined by the panel in the *Japan* case, a difference in the alcoholic strength of two products "did not preclude a finding of likeness, especially since alcoholic beverages are often drunk in diluted form.

---

[215] *Japan - Taxes on Alcoholic Beverages I, supra*, para. 5.7.
[216] *Ibid.*, at para. 5.9.

6.161. The United States argues that, with respect to the taste and sensation of the products, it is not the raw materials that are responsible for the so-called "stinging sensation" supposedly imparted by soju. If this were true, then all spirits could and can claim a "stinging sensation in the mouth and throat", since the raw materials are similar in many other spirits. For example, Archer Daniels Midland Company's grain neutral spirits are used for both soju and Smirnoff vodka (produced in the United States). The claimed unique "cold" mouth feel may come from the fact that soju, like vodka, is usually refrigerated before consumption. Moreover, although Korea cites to "harshness" as a unique desirable characteristic of standard soju compared to the smoothness or mildness of Western-style spirits, as the representative from the European Community pointed out, the advertisement in its submission for Jinro Bisun, produced by Korea's largest producer of soju (Attachment 6), boasts how it is a "mild" one, the same way Western-style spirits are marketed.

6.162. The United States also argued that as a factual matter, the characterization of Korean soju as unique is also at odds with the view of even the top Korean soju producer Jinro. On its Internet home page, Jinro sets out the following question: "What is Soju?" It provides the following response: "Jinro Soju, a sort of *vodka-like spirits* which began life in the 13th century, is the traditional Korean liquor. . ."(US Exhibit Q.) Similarly, an Internet search reveals the description of soju by an apparently French Canadian food critic as "la vodka coreene" (Korean vodka). (US Exhibit R.)

3. Violation of Article III:2, Second Sentence

6.163. The United States reiterates that Korea's taxes on imported distilled spirits in addition to vodka are applied so as to afford protection to domestic production of soju, in violation of Article III:2, second sentence. The United States notes that as set out by the Appellate Body in the Japan case, a violation of the second sentence requires three elements to be shown. First, the products must be directly competitive or substitutable; second, the products must be taxed in a way that is not "similar"; and third, the measure must be applied so as to afford protection to domestic production. According to the united States, Korea's attempted defence has focused accordingly on the first element, substitutability, and the vast majority of the Panel's questions also pertain to this element.

(a) The Text

6.164. The United States argues that Korea, in attempting to show that soju does not compete with imported distilled spirits, mainly relies on the argument that in order for products to be considered "directly competitive or substitutable," the complaining parties must show that "actual competition" between soju and all distilled spirits is occurring on the Korean market for all end uses. In the US view, although the complaining parties have shown actual competition and common end uses for most of the products in question, it is also potential competition with imported distilled spirits that is at issue in this dispute. The United States adds that Korea's legal interpretation is belied by an examination of the ordinary meaning of the relevant provisions, taken in their context, and in light of their object and purpose, as required under principles of international treaty interpretation.[217]

6.165. The United States argues that the overriding purpose in Article III:2, second sentence is the incorporation as an obligation of the objective stated in Article III:1, that taxes should not be applied so as to afford protection to domestic production. The interpretive note to the second sentence, that it applies only "where competition was involved, between, on the one hand, the taxed product, and on the other hand, a directly competitive or substitutable product which was not similarly taxed" must be read in light of this overall purpose.

6.166. According to the United States, Korea's argument that competition must be actual runs counter to the text of the interpretive note and the purpose of the central obligation. The phrase "competition was involved" is more likely to mean the situation where competition is presented, rather than where competition is "currently occurring for every use," as suggested by Korea. Further, in the US view, this interpretation is more consistent with other terms in Article III:2, because in addition to proscribing protective taxation between directly competitive products, the interpretive note applies to "directly substitutable" products.[218] The United States further argues that the word "substitutable" is one that clearly shows the application of the second sentence to potential substitution - i.e. it means able to be substituted; it does not require a test of whether and how many products are currently being substituted. The French text, in the US view, underscores the application of the obligation to potentially competitive products even more clearly: "un produit qui peut lui être directement substitué" (a product that can be directly substituted for the taxed product).

6.167. The United States further argues that the scope of the obligation to include potential competition is also consistent with the obligation in Article III:4, which requires national treatment for "like" domestic and imported products. According to the United States, the Article III:4 obligation has long been understood to apply to regulations that "might adversely modify the conditions of competition" between imported and domestic products, regardless of current trade.[219]

6.168. The United States refers to the *United States - Section 337 of the Tariff Act of 1930* case, wherein it was noted that the Article III:4 obligation "calls for effective equality of opportunities" for imported products, rather than particular export volumes.[220] The United States further notes that the 1949 Working Party Report on *Brazilian Internal Taxes* takes the view that Article III:2, first sentence applies, "whether imports from other contracting parties were substantial, small, or non-existent," and stresses their "potentialities as exporters."[221] Similarly, concerning Article III:2 second sentence, unless "directly competitive or substitutable" is inter-

---

[217] See Article 31 of the Vienna Convention on the Law of Treaties.

[218] According to the United States, although the English text of the interpretative note is ambiguous on the point, the French translation appears to suggest that the word "directly" also applies to the word "substitutable." Either way, it does not have implications for this dispute.

[219] *Italian Discrimination Against Imported Agricultural Machinery*, adopted on 23 October, 1958, BISD 7S/60, 64.

[220] BISD 36S/345, 386-87.

[221] GATT/CP.3/42, adopted 30 June, 1949, II/181, 185.

preted as applying to potential competition, its scope will be much narrower and permit the perpetuation of unfair competitive conditions that result from protected markets.[222]

6.169. The United States argues further that the application of Article III:2 to potential competition is also confirmed by GATT and WTO cases that have emphasized the distorting effect of past restrictions in the market. *Japan - Taxes on Alcoholic Beverages I* disregarded traditional Japanese habits in determining that vodka and shochu were "like," emphasizing that they resulted from past protection.[223] *Japan - Taxes on Alcoholic Beverages II* similarly noted that "consumer surveys in a country with . . . a [discriminatory] tax system would likely understate the degree of potential competitiveness between substitutable products."[224] The United States also notes that the Appellate Body in *Canada - Certain Measures Concerning Periodicals* had a similar response to Canada's arguments that static market shares over 30 years showed a lack of "direct competition." It noted, "this argument would have weight only if Canada had not protected the domestic production of Canadian periodicals through, among other measures, the import prohibition of Tariff Code 9958 and the excise tax of Part V.1 of the Excise Act."[225]

6.170. The United States argues that Korea is also wrong to insist that in order to be substitutable, products must be substitutable for all economic uses, such as consumption in restaurants or as an accompaniment with Korean food. According to the United States, although the GATT and WTO panels and the Appellate Body in the Japan case praised the concept of examining uses in a given market, as a practical matter they did not provide much weight to consumer tastes and habits. In the US view, the GATT Japan panel specifically noted that there was direct competition and substitutability as between all the liquors in dispute "even if not necessarily in respect of all the economic uses to which the products may be put."[226] More recently, in *Canada - Measures Concerning Periodicals*, the Appellate Body specifically found that the products in question were directly competitive or substitutable even if they were poor substitutes for certain purposes.[227] According to the United States, such an approach is consistent with other GATT panel findings, such as the application of Article III:2 in *EEC - Measures on Animal Feed Proteins* to products that were substitutable only "under certain conditions."[228] In the US view, the products involved - skim-milk powder on the one hand, and oilseeds, cakes and meals, dehydrated fodder and corn gluten feed, on the other - confirm the appropriate broad scope of the term "directly competitive or substitutable."

---

[222] The United States believes that this interpretation is all the more compelling because the second sentence is meant to compensate for the narrow interpretation required of the term "like" in Article III:2, first sentence, as acknowledged by the panel and Appellate Body in the *Japan - Alcoholic Beverages* case.

[223] *Japan - Taxes Alcoholic Beverages I, supra*, para. 5.7.

[224] Panel. Report on *Japan - Taxes on Alcoholic Beverages II, supra*, para. 6.28.

[225] Appellate Body Report on *Canada - Certain Measures Concerning Periodicals, supra*, at 473.

[226] *Japan - Taxes on Alcoholic Beverages I, supra*, para. 5.7.

[227] Appellate Body Report on *Canada - Certain Measures Concerning Periodicals, supra*, at 473.

[228] BISD 25S/49, 63-64, adopted on 14 March, 1978.

(b)   Drafting History

6.171. The United States argues that the drafting history of the GATT 1947 supports the broad textual interpretation of the scope of "directly competitive or substitutable." According to the United States, prior to the Geneva drafting session, the text of what became the second sentence of Article III:2 was not in the nature of an obligation and referred only to competitive products. At the Geneva session, according to the United States, delegates discussed the scope of the language that eventually provided the basis for the present obligation. Concerning which products would be compared, some country delegates cited examples of domestic and imported products that could be "competitive" and trigger the application of the legal obligation. These included quite broad categories of products, such as domestic apples and imported oranges;[229] domestic linseed oil and imported tung oil;[230] and domestic synthetic rubber and imported natural rubber.[231]

6.172. The United States further notes that the record discloses that no disagreement was expressed by delegates with the breadth of these specific examples of "competitive" products, including the reference to apples and oranges. In Havana, when the text of the legal obligation on national treatment was approved, the Chairman of the Sub-committee reported "only one important change in substance" from the Geneva text. Provisions for a negotiated elimination of discriminatory internal taxes in the previous draft evolved into to their outright elimination.[232]

6.173. According to the United States, at that point, the term "directly competitive or substitutable" was added in the text. After adoption of the present text and interpretive note, one additional question was raised concerning examples of what might be considered "directly competitive or substitutable products" for purposes of the interpretive note to Paragraph 2. One delegate allegedly asked if "coal vs. fuel oil" and "tramways vs. busses" could be considered directly competitive or substitutable. Another delegate allegedly noted the need for actual cases in order to interpret the provision, but opined that such products were not substitutable. A third delegate, however, allegedly stated that decisions could not be made except in relation to a particular factual situation, but that a tax on coal in a particular case might be designed to protect the fuel oil industry.[233] In the US view, this comports with the Appellate Body's finding in *Japan-Taxes on Alcoholic Beverages II* that determinations are to be made on the basis of "all relevant facts," when examining each of the "number of means" for identifying the "broader category of products that might be described as 'directly competitive or substitutable.'"[234]

6.174. The United States concludes that the examples discussed in the drafting history show that the comparison of internal taxes on domestically produced soju, on the one hand, and imported distilled spirits, on the other, is well within the scope contemplated by the drafters. The emphasis was obviously not on particular attrib-

---

[229] E/PC/T/A/PV/9, p. 7.

[230] E/CONF.2/C.3/SR.11, p. 1 and Corr.2.

[231] E/CONF.2/C.3/SR.11, p. 3.

[232] E/Conf.2/C.3/SR.40, p.1.

[233] E/Conf.2/C.3/SR.40, p. 2.

[234] Appellate Body Report on *Japan - Taxes on Alcoholic Beverages II, supra,* at 117.

utes of the products such as physical characteristics, production processes, or quality, but on the ability of the products to be used in the same manner, and the extent to which a government acted to protect a domestic product to prevent such substitution in its market.

(c)   Directly competitive or substitutable

Physical characteristics

6.175. According to the United States, Korea's submissions argue that some differences in production processes and physical characteristics prove that soju and imported distilled spirits are not in fact "like," "substitutable" or "competitive" products. The United States argues that from a basic economic perspective, however, differences in production or physical characteristics are not *a priori* determinative of whether two products are substitutable or directly competitive. For example, cane sugar and artificial sweeteners are totally different in terms of production process and chemical composition, yet they clearly compete directly in coffee houses and restaurants. In order to determine substitutability, the Panel should consider whether the products in question compete for consumer spending on a category of goods. In this case, all spirits should be considered as in competition because they compete for consumers' spending on various products within the category of alcoholic spirits. Similar production processes, physical characteristics, and end uses are indicative of "like" products, but some differences in these factors do not establish that two products are not substitutable. Another factor in determining substitutability is the extent to which consumers respond to relative price increases in one product by increasing purchases of another. These products are likely to be substitutes. Thus, Korea's reliance on minor differences in the production and physical characteristics as dispositive evidence of non-substitutability is misplaced. Furthermore, Korea greatly exaggerates the differences between soju and imported spirits.

6.176. The United States argues that it is unlikely that two identical products would not, to some degree, be substitutable, though they may not be perfectly substitutable. Even physically identical products might be packaged differently, marketed differently, or ultimately targeted at different consumer groups, but they would nonetheless remain "able" to be substituted. For example, two identical bottles of aspirin (with the same contents, price and packaging) are perfectly substitutable, whereas two bottles of aspirin with a different package size, branding, or price, but containing aspirin of the same chemical composition are not *perfectly* substitutable but remain substitutable, with demand for one being influenced by the price of the other.

6.177. According to the United States, with respect to other Western distilled spirits, the Korean submission stresses difference in color as between whisky and soju as a factor that rules out competition between these products. However, the United States argues that color may not only differ as between types of spirits, but also within spirit categories. For instance rum, tequila and shochu all have clear and amber versions, yet they do not become different non-competing products because of it.

6.178. According to the United States, it is also wrong to emphasize alcoholic strength as a dispositive factor in selecting a distilled spirit. Once they are prepared, many mixed drinks, such as vodka cocktails have a lower alcohol content than straight soju. As determined by the panel in *Japan - Taxes on Alcoholic Beverages*

II, a difference in the alcoholic strength of two products "did not preclude a finding of likeness, especially since alcoholic beverages are often drunk in diluted form."

6.179. The United States agrees that flavour and aroma are important factors in selecting a distilled spirit, but again argues that a different flavor hardly precludes substitutability between classes of distilled spirits such as whisky, soju, vodka and rum. Indeed, the range of flavours and aromas *within* a class of spirit have as much of an impact on consumer choice as does the range of flavours and aromas *between* classes of spirits. In fact, soju itself is available in different flavorings, such as honey and wood. Under Korea's theory, different flavours of soft drinks such as Coke and Fanta do not compete, but it is doubtful that anyone familiar with the market would agree.

6.180. The United States further argued that Korea's invocation of so-called distinguishing physical characteristics for other Western distilled spirits is entirely arbitrary. The United States argues that Korea's citation of physical characteristics to distinguish soju from other Western distilled spirits are the same characteristics that happen to distinguish various kinds of Korean soju from each other. For example, Jinro's promotional material for its premium soju brands on its Internet home page cites factors such as a "rich smooth taste" and oak flavoring, the same factors Korea relied on in its first submission to distinguish soju from whiskey.[235] According to the United States, Jinro's descriptions in fact confirm the competitive relationship between soju and Western spirits.

6.181. The United States further argues that, with respect to the taste and sensation of the products, it is not the raw materials that are responsible for the so-called "stinging sensation" supposedly imparted by soju. If this were true, then all spirits could and can claim a "stinging sensation in the mouth and throat", since the raw materials are similar in many other spirits. For example, Archer Daniels Midland Company's grain neutral spirits are used for both soju and Smirnoff vodka (produced in the United States). The claimed unique "cold" mouth feel may come from the fact that soju, like vodka, is usually refrigerated before consumption. Moreover, although Korea cites to "harshness" as a unique desirable characteristic of standard soju compared to the smoothness or mildness of Western-style spirits, as the representative from the European Community pointed out, the advertisement in its submission for Jinro Bisun, produced by Korea's largest producer of soju, boasts how it is a "mild" one, the same way Western-style spirits are marketed.

6.182. The United States also challenges the Korean claim that soju is uniquely suited to spicy food and unlike Western spirits, is consumed exclusively during meals in Korean restaurants or at home. According to the United States, that does not mean that Western-style spirits are not equally suitable for such use. Other countries also have hot and spicy food, and consume distilled spirits other than soju. For instance, in the United States, when consuming hot and spicy Mexican food, it is common to consume tequila in the form of a Margarita. In Poland, vodka is drunk with herring. Consumers' habits are not fixed, and can change with the introduction of alternative products. Indeed, in Korea a considerable proportion of imported Western-style distilled spirits is not consumed in bars and posh hotels, but at home,

---

[235] US Exhibit Q.

similar to soju. The United States says it understands that after dinner at home, both soju and Western- style spirits are an option.

6.183. The United States argues that, as the GATT drafting history demonstrates, in order to be directly competitive or substitutable, products need not share a majority of physical characteristics, and a basic commonality of physical properties is sufficient. The basic physical properties of soju and Western distilled spirit categories are essentially the same: all are concentrated forms of alcohol that are produced through distillation and used for human consumption. Their variations - distillation method, appearance, taste, alcoholic content, and raw material inputs - do not create any particular product not substitutable for the other. The 1987 *Japan* liquor panel did not consider the minor variations in distilled spirits important, instead stressing the flexibility of use: "Alcoholic drinks might be drunk straight, with water, or as mixes. . . . [T]he flexibility in the use of alcoholic drinks and their common characteristics often offered an alternative choice for consumers leading to a competitive relationship."[236] According to the United States, this approach, consistent with the consideration by the drafters that oranges and apples are competitive, confirms that it is most appropriate to consider a broad commonality of physical characteristics.

End Uses

6.184. According to the United States, in examining the current uses of distilled spirits in the Korean market, it should be recalled that already both soju and Western-style distilled spirits are sold and advertised side by side. In the Korean Air duty free magazine[237] (US Exhibit D), presumably catering to both Korean and foreign travellers, Johnnie Walker Blue Label, Johnnie Walker Gold Label and Moon Bae-Sool soju are advertised on the same page. Moreover, as shown in the pictures in U.S. Exhibit G, soju and Western-style spirits are sold together in a range of retail establishments. In the first picture, Cherry 15 is next to Seagram Extra Dry Gin, and Alexander vodka is next to Korean premium soju (aged in oak) in a convenience store. In the fourth picture, Something Special Scotch whisky is next to Kim Sat Gat premium soju in a Seoul supermarket. The fact that these products are sold through the same retail channels is important evidence of direct competition in the market place.

6.185. The United States argues that Korea has implied that soju, because it is less expensive, is marketed to an entirely different group of consumers than Western spirits and therefore is not directly competitive with Western spirits. The United States disagrees with that implication. In fact, according to the United States, given the greater degree of availability of Western spirits, it is more likely that many Koreans will consume both soju and Western spirits, differentiating the timing, degree and occasion of their consumption mix based on personal preferences and the relative prices of the two products. Moreover, The United States agrees with the representative of the European Communities that, as shown in Attachment 6 of the Korean submission, soju is also aimed at businessmen in shirts and ties, and not farm-

---

[236] See panel Report on *Japan - Taxes on Alcoholic Beverages I, supra*, at para. 5.7.
[237] US Exhibit D.

ers or factory workers. This is exactly the same group of people Western spirits companies are targeting - Korea's middle and upper class professionals.

6.186. The United States also claims that Korea's narrow approach to end uses looks at whether a distilled spirit is consumed before, during or after a meal; as a mixed drink, with ice, or straight; and what type of food is served at a restaurant. In fact, Korea attempts to draw strict categories where none exists in the Korean market or any place else US manufacturers are familiar with. Before addressing the issue of mealtime consumption, the United States recalls recall that Korea says little regarding other sub-categories of usage in which even Korea admits Western distilled spirits compete, such as consumption in bars, after meals, and in the home, or providing as a gift. Korea, does, however, concede in its answer to U.S. question 3, that some standard soju will also be consumed at home without a meal, as are western spirits.

6.187. According to the United States, Korea's narrow approach to end use is also undermined by the GATT drafting history citing to apples and oranges as directly competitive products. As stated by Korea, "A member of a group of products that are related in consumption need not be a substitute for all other members of the group - just for *some* other members of the group." In its second submission Korea refers to the U.S. citation of differing end uses for apples and oranges as evidence that such products may not be competitive or substitutable. Although it is unlikely that oranges would be substituted as filling for apple pies, this does not preclude their substitutability for several other end uses, such as fruit juices, fruit jellies and jams, and overall fresh fruit consumption. Differences in product end uses may vary, but they do not erect a wall preventing substitution between differing types products within the same category.

6.188. The United States also argues that Korea's focus on differences in consumption within the on-premise and off-premise market segments is not appropriate for purposes of Article III:2. On-premise consumption covers a broad range of establishments that must be considered together for purposes of substitutability, particularly since the availability of Western spirits has continually expanded. In addition, in the on-premise consumption segment, serving particular distilled spirits is up to the discretion of the owner of the particular establishment. In general, establishments such as inexpensive Korean restaurants that appeal to low-income patrons are less likely to serve expensive high-end distilled spirits, and vice versa. However, with all of the variability in types of restaurants, bars and night clubs in Korea, it is not realistic to assume distinct rigid categories with respect to marketing and distribution of distilled spirits, and Korea has shown no support for such allegations.

6.189. The United States further argues that in the off-premise sector, making generalizations about particular kinds of stores would be equally incorrect. In Korea's retail sector, virtually all types of spirits are available in all types of establishments, yet in different proportions. For instance, a small family-owned shop will have cases of soju available and a few bottles of premium Scotch whisky on the shelves. Conversely, upscale department stores, such as Lotte and Shinsegae in downtown Seoul, will carry a preponderance of imported spirits, and may only have a small display for domestically-produced soju. The wide range of availability of imported spirits is clearly established in the Hankook study submitted by the EC as well as photographs of a range of retail establishments in which soju and Western spirits share the same store shelves submitted by the United States. Korea's argument that such placement is unimportant because in one photograph submitted by the United States, Gillette shaving foam is also apparent, overlooks the fact that the shaving foam is on a neighbouring set of shelves, not in the same group with the distilled spirits.

6.190. The United States notes that Korea's market for imported distilled spirits has been open for less than a decade, and is not a mature market with respect to consumer's awareness of, and receptivity toward, different types of spirits, their uses and places of consumption. Even though there are some differences in the methods of consumption compared to other countries, such as consumption of soju with Korean meals, it is wrong to assume, that end use must be identical for all uses under Article III:2. Given the fact that the spirits industry has been barred from the Korean market until recently, the industry has not had the opportunity to address and capitalize on every possible usage of its products in Korea. However, since all distilled spirits are fundamentally interchangeable, as Western spirit products become more familiar to Korean consumers, it is expected that methods of consumption will continue to expand.

6.191. The United States claims that with respect to on-premise consumption, Korea has also implausibly maintained that there is no overlap between the types of restaurants or bars that serve soju, and those that serve imported spirits. In fact, in its answers to U.S. question 4, Korea has already conceded at least some potential overlap between distilled soju and Western spirits when it recognizes that soju is offered in so-called "very expensive and traditional Korean and Japanese restaurants." Given its earlier statement that Western spirits are sold in Japanese restaurants, Korea minimally acknowledges substitutability in such restaurants.

Price

6.192. With respect to Korea's arguments on the different prices of the various products, the United States claims that although Korea glosses over the concept of substitutability, it does not go so far as to claim that the existence of large pre-tax price differentials precludes two products from being substitutable. In fact, Korea acknowledges such substitutability when it states that standard soju and premium soju, two products with a typical price differential of more than 100%, are considered "close substitutes" in Korea.

6.193. The United States notes that the substitutability of alcoholic beverages in a wide price range is not uncommon. Moreover, a range of prices exists within several product types. For example, whisky prices can range from ten to a hundred dollars for a bottle. The Korean submission frequently cites whisky as 11 times higher in price than soju, ignoring the price ranges within the whisky product category. For example, pre-tax imported whisky prices (for 375 ml bottles) range from over 5,000 won for premium scotch whisky to over 3,000 won for standard scotch whisky. Thus, at the extremes, imported scotch whisky pre-tax prices are 7.2 to 12 times higher than standard soju, not including domestic bottled whisky which is 6.3 times higher. Notably, imported standard scotch whisky pre-tax prices are only 3.6 times higher than premium soju.

6.194. The United States further argues that price differences are not of themselves evidence of a lack of actual or potential competition. Changes in consumer purchase behaviour are dependent on relative price changes, not absolute prices between competing products. Constructing a price demarcation where products with relative prices exceeding a specific threshold are considered not directly competitive or substitutable ignores the reality that these products are arrayed along a price continuum available to consumers in the marketplace. The availability of products across a spectrum of prices in the Korean market attests to a commensurate range of differing consumer tastes and preferences for distilled spirits, as well as the desire of individual consumers to vary their individual consumption choice on the basis of occasion, place of consumption and other factors. Moreover, purchases of distilled spirits, unlike purchases of items such as automobiles or homes, occur on numerous occasions over a relatively short time frame. Consequently, at the margin, changes in relative prices between spirits, such as soju and Western spirits, may alter *some* individual consumption decisions, but not *all*.

6.195. Furthermore, the United States notes that Korea's price analysis devotes substantial attention to comparisons of standard soju and the more upscale whisky products, giving limited attention to the variability of prices within spirit categories such as whisky and soju. For example, the pre-tax price of premium soju is two to three times higher than standard soju, and in some instances distilled soju pre-tax prices exceed those of Western spirits. In comparing soju and whisky weighted average prices, the United States claims that Korea's analysis failed to account for the variation of prices among differing whisky products. Furthermore, when adjustments are made for alcoholic content, pre-tax price differences between standard soju and Western spirits range from 3 to 6 times higher and for premium soju, 2 to 3 times higher.

Broader substitutability of distilled spirits

6.196. The United States argues that there is evidence that Korean Consumers are not substantially different from other consumers around the world in the ways that they form tastes for alcoholic beverages. According to the United States, the US, EC and Korean submissions show that the advertising for the products is similar and aimed at similar audiences. In fact, the advertisements would not be out of place in Western magazines except for the Korean print. In addition, in Korea, as in the rest of the world, distilled spirits are sold in stores, bars and restaurants, among other locations. In Korea, soju and Western spirits are purchased from the same shelves in different retail outlets. Thus, there is m market evidence supporting the US statements that all spirits should be considered as in competition because they compete for consumers' spending on various products within the category of alcoholic spirits.

6.197. The United States argues that Korea's implication that all distilled spirits are not a recognized category of competing goods is contradicted by both international and Korean practices. There is a reason that the international convention on the Harmonized System, to which Korea is a party, has grouped all distilled spirits, including soju, under the same customs heading. This classification reflects the fact that on the international scene, distilled spirits are considered a distinct product group that includes soju. One need only look at a recent issue of an industry trade journal, *Drinks International*[238] which puts out a list of the top spirits brands in the world each year, to see that soju is considered a competitor to all other distilled spirits in HS heading 2208. On page 35 of the March 1998 edition, one sees that Jinro Soju is ranked the number one spirits brand in the world.

6.198. The United States notes that Korean government itself groups imports of soju with other distilled spirits in its implementation of the Harmonized System, and groups all alcoholic beverages together - soju, beer, vodka, whiskey, sake etc. - in a single liquor tax law. In its responses to our questions, Korea admits that sake and beer compete with soju. It is self-serving to insist that the other products in its liquor law (such as imported distilled spirits) do not compete, despite their being grouped together in Korea's own laws.

6.199. According to the United States, several other factors support what should be the obvious conclusion that Korean consumers can be presumed to recognize the similarity of soju and imported spirits. Western spirits and Korean soju are sold alongside each other in retail outlets, and their advertisements are aimed at a similar clientele with similar sales pitches. The development, by Korea's own soju producers, of bottling operations for imported whiskey is also significant. These producers have obviously recognized that the products compete and are taking advantage of the distribution channels already developed for traditional soju brands.

6.200. The United States argues further that Korean manufacturers have advertised soju in the same international media as Western distilled spirits and seek to take advantage of characteristics of soju that are similar to those of Western distilled spirits. The United States refers again to a recent edition of *Drinks International*. Page 14 of the March 1998 issue contains an advertisement for Jinro Soju, which asks potential purchasers to "experience its unique smooth taste" and boasts of its "incomparable versatility for cocktails." It even shows soju in a glass "on the rocks" with a lemon slice and a maraschino cherry. Obviously, Korea's top soju producer, Jinro, considers soju substitutable for Western distilled spirits and eminently suitable for a variety of their uses - like Western spirits, not only drunk straight in a shot glass, but also "on the rocks" or mixed with other products to make cocktails.

6.201. The United States argues that Jinro's recognition of soju's substitutability with other spirits in its international export markets is not reconcilable with the position of the Korean government in these proceedings that soju is not "like" or "directly competitive or substitutable" with any Western distilled spirit. Overseas, Korean soju competes on a level playing field with all other distilled spirits, but at home Korea rejects any notion that the products are in competition, and insists on a reading of Article III that would protect soju through burdensome taxes on imports. The United States considers that this position finds no support in the letter or spirit of Article III:2.

6.202. The United States considers that there is also some empirical evidence supporting the general notion that consumers budget for alcoholic beverages separately than other goods.[239] This study of consumers (Alley *et al.*) reveals that the con-

---

[238] US Exhibit P.
[239] The United States cites A.G. Alley, D.G. Ferguson, K.G. Stuart, *An Almost Ideal Demand System for Alcoholic Beverages in British Columbia*, 17 Empirical Economics 416 (1992).

sumption of alcoholic beverages is separate from their consumption of other goods. Hence, "after compensating for income changes, consumption of other goods is unaffected by price changes" of alcoholic beverages.[240] Furthermore, in Alley and in two additional studies[241] there is evidence of substitutability between domestic and imported spirits in Canada and Finland, respectively. Accordingly, there is further support for the conclusion that all imported spirits compete with soju in the distilled spirits market in Korea.

Korean market developments

6.203. The United States argues that the development of the premium soju market is a most important indicator of the fact that Western spirits directly compete and are substitutable for soju. Soju sales increased significantly with the introduction of premium soju, whose sales volumes have surpassed the combined sales of all imported spirits. This development demonstrates that Korean consumers are receptive to trying and buying newly introduced types of spirits, including those with a higher prices. Furthermore, development of premium soju is clearly intended to move soju up market by borrowing the cachet from imported spirits, which contradicts Korea's contention that soju is only the cheap drink of "commoners" or "ordinary folks".

6.204. The United States argues that another development in the Korean market further dispels Korea's notion that soju is in a market of its own: the production of flavoured soju and juice cocktails starting in 1995. Although it may well be that much of soju is consumed as described in Korea's submission, these market developments show that new forms, venues and usage of various distilled spirits will continue to develop in Korea.

6.205. The United States considers that market developments and present conditions in Korea directly undermine Korea's reliance on pre-tax price differentials as precluding substitutability between soju and Western spirits. Despite competitive distortions created by Korea's liquor tax system, demand for Western spirits, particularly whisky, has increased as the relative prices of whisky and soju declined (there were 100% and 250% reductions in the applicable liquor tax rate and import custom duties, respectively. During this period, sales of whisky in Korea increased over 136 percent as compared to a 13 percent increase in soju sales. These differing rates of growth in sales of whisky and soju amidst tax and duty reductions on imports demonstrates that the products are in competition.

6.206. The United States claims that without precise data regarding Korean consumer purchasing activity, it is virtually impossible to determine with complete certainty that product demand, in this case whisky, is driven by factors unrelated to the demand and price of the other product in question, i.e. soju. However, the United

---

[240] The United States cites A.G. Alley, D.G. Ferguson, K.G. Stuart, *An Almost Ideal Demand System for Alcoholic Beverages in British Columbia*, 17 Empirical Economics 414 (1992).

[241] The United States cites Andrikopoulos, et al., The Demand for Domestic and Imported Alcoholic Beverages in Ontario, Canada: A Dynamic Simultaneous Equations Approach, 29 Applied Economics 945-953 (1997); Holm, Alcohol Content and Demand for Alcoholic Beverages: A System Approach, 20 Empirical Economics 75-92 (1995).

States considers that several market developments suggest that changes in market share between soju and whisky are not unrelated:

1) A noticeable slow-down in soju sales occurred in the early 1990's as the import duties in Korea were lowered on whisky and import restrictions were eliminated, propelling increased sales of whisky and other Western spirits.

2) It was not until 1996, when a new soju product was introduced (premium soju), that soju sales rebounded. Between 1995 and 1996, sales of soju increased by 5 percent, exceeding the growth rate for the previous three years combined.

3) In 1997, in the midst of a sharp currency depreciation and economic difficulties, sales of Western spirits, particularly whisky, declined, while soju sales actually increased.

Thus, according to the United States, the two concurrent trends of Korean consumers trading up to Western spirits while trading up to premium domestic soju are a strong indication of the substitutability between Western spirits and soju.

4. *The Dodwell Study*

6.207. The United States argues that the results of the Dodwell study provide ample evidence that Korean consumers treat soju and imported Western spirits as substitute products. The United States notes first that a cross- price elasticity study might be a helpful addition to the Article III:2 analysis, but it is not a necessary one. The emphasis on case-by-case analysis in the drafting history of Article III, and the practice among GATT and WTO panels, make it clear that it would not be appropriate to establish a general rule concerning the percentage shift in consumer preferences. The complaining parties have not put forward any precise estimate, but some empirical results of studies conducted in various national markets indicate that there is a statistically significant trade-off between types of spirits.

6.208. First, the United States notes that the Dodwell study was patterned after the ASI study utilized in the *Japan-Taxes on Alcoholic Beverages II,*[242] in which the panel stated "contained persuasive evidence that there is significant elasticity of substitution among the products in dispute."[243]

6.209. According to the United States, the small anomalies in the Dodwell study should not lead the panel to a conclusion that the Dodwell study reflects "independent movements of independent variables." In the US view, drawing such a conclusion on the results of the Dodwell study is tantamount to concluding that relative prices of soju, premium soju and imported spirits have no impact on consumption decisions. In fact, the overall trends in the Dodwell study should lead the Panel to the opposite conclusion: consumer preferences in the Korean market for distilled spirits are significantly related to relative prices of soju and imported distilled spirits.

---

[242] Panel Report on *Japan - Taxes on Alcoholic Beverages II, supra*, para. 6.29.

[243] *Ibid.*, para. 6.32.

6.210. According to the United States, the anomalies pointed out by Korea are merely deviations from what is usual, normal or expected.[244] The US argument is that a study that relies on sampling to draw inferences about an overall population may yield results that contain some random variation, and therefore will be susceptible to occasional anomalous results.[245] In the US view, what is important in the Dodwell study is that the overall trend displayed in the sample responses suggests that relative prices are a factor in consumption of distilled spirits, and that consumers normally will substitute imported spirits for soju as the relative price of soju rises.

6.211. According to the United States, the analysis of the Dodwell survey results as described in the first US submission detailed the percentage changes in those choosing Western spirits (excluding premium soju) as the relative price of standard soju rises. Therefore, the aggregate effects of nearly all of the scenarios demonstrate that respondents increasingly choose Western spirits when faced with higher relative prices for standard soju.

6.212. The United States notes that Korea's critique of the Dodwell study alleges flawed results and methodological weaknesses. Yet, despite these assertions, the study establishes a connection between changes in relative prices of soju and western spirits and purchasing behaviour. The Dodwell survey followed the methodology of the ASI study, attempting to determine whether the typical Korean spirits customer varies consumption preferences between soju and Western spirits as relative prices of spirits change. In the US view, the study did not attempt to determine the actual shares or shifts in market shares between spirits products, an objective that would not be relevant to this proceeding. Rather it sought to establish whether Korean spirits consumers view the products as substitutable. The fact that the observed percentages of survey responses do not perfectly correlate with actual soju market shares does not undermine the study's conclusions, and focusing on it overlooks the study's objective.

6.213. The United States notes that Korea further asserts that the Dodwell study reflects a sample bias and posed ambiguous questions. According to the United

---

[244] In the US view, Korea's critique of the Dodwell study focuses on random anomalies to the exclusion of the underlying findings that Korean consumers view standard soju and imported spirits as substitute products. For example, Korea's critique highlights that in chart 1 of the Dodwell study, the percentage of respondents choosing premium scotch falls as the price of standard soju rises from 1,100 to 1,200 won. The critique ignores that in the same scenario a rising percentage of respondents chose standard whisky and cognac as soju prices rose. In aggregate, the percentage choosing Western spirits in this scenario actually rose, indicating respondents' responsiveness to changes in the relative prices of Western brown spirits and soju. Moreover, the aggregate trends in nearly all the scenarios indicate increasing percentages of respondents choosing Western spirits amidst the relative rise of standard soju prices. In focusing narrowly on selective inconsistencies Korea has obfuscated the underlying study results evidencing that respondents frequently choose to substitute imported spirits for standard soju as the relative price of these products narrowed. See First Korea Sub., Attachment 2, at pp. 4-5.

[245] In the US view, in only one of the price scenarios (medium brown spirit price levels) in the Dodwell study did the aggregate results run counter to theory. However, it should be noted that in terms of respondents, a net of 3 respondents choose non-Western spirits as the relative price of standard soju reached its highest level.

States, with respect to the survey questions, it is unreasonable to impute confusion to the entire survey population. With respect to the sample, inclusion of survey respondents having recently purchased soju and whisky suggests that, at least for brown spirits, respondents' familiarity with these products runs contrary to the assertion that the survey questions implied a one-time or experimental purchase. Finally, the separation of brown and white distilled spirits does not affect the fundamental movement of respondents from standard soju to Western spirits as standard soju's relative price increased.

6.214. The United States also notes that Korea questioned, as did the Panel, the grouping of premium soju with other Western distilled spirits in the Dodwell study. According to the United States, as with whisky (standard and premium), it was considered appropriate to establish more than one price point for diluted soju given that diluted soju products differed in price. Setting a price benchmark for the soju category based on the actual prices for the higher price premium soju to the exclusion of standard soju would have ignored the majority of the overall diluted soju market. Standard soju, due to its market share significance, was chosen as the benchmark for comparison. The fact that premium soju was selected as an alternative product, alongside Western spirits, to standard soju, and that some respondents switched to premium soju, does not undermine the validity of the study's conclusion.

5.   *The Measures are Applied "so as to Afford Protection to Domestic Production"*

6.215. The United States does not address this issue in its rebuttal submission, but in its oral statements argues that, with respect to this element of the case, the Appellate Body stated in *Japan - Taxes on Alcoholic Beverages II*, the protective application of a tax can most often be discerned from "the design, the architecture and the revealing structure of the measure," which includes the very magnitude of the dissimilar taxation.

6.216. The United States further argues that Korea has largely ignored this element of the analysis. However, the Korean measures at issue do present a structure applied so as to afford protection to domestic production. According to the United States, the very large differentiation in tax rates between imported and domestic products, on the basis of a law that consists mainly of arbitrary exclusions from the definition of Korea's domestic product, soju, can only be considered protective. Moreover, in contrast to the facts presented in the *Japan* case, the protection of soju in Korea can be equated even more directly with the protection of a domestic industry. In Japan, there were significant imports of soju from Korea (which the panel in *Japan - Taxes on Alcoholic Beverages II* found were the same product as shochu), but in Korea, there have been only negligible imports of soju - or shochu - from any other country.

6.217. The United States further notes that Korea makes the claim that soju cannot be considered "domestic" production at all, because its raw material is often imported. According to the United States, this assertion ignores Korea's own legal structures, however. It is true that the main ingredient for soju is ethyl alcohol, 70% of which is imported. But, unlike whisky, ethyl alcohol is a raw material that can be used for a variety of end products. Ethyl alcohol is classified separately under HS heading 2207, and the process of manufacturing soju results in a substantial transformation of that raw material, while any imported soju is classified under HS heading 2208. Whisky, whether bottled or in bulk, is classified under HS heading 2208. Thus, it is plain that soju is a domestic product, while whisky is exclusively imported.

6.218. Finally, according to the United States, Korea's invocation of progressive social policies as a pretext for this discrimination is unrelated to the structure of its law, which is drawn on the basis of arbitrary physical characteristics and not on price of the product. While Korea may have a social policy objective of imposing lower internal taxes on inexpensive products purchased by lower income consumers, Article III does not permit Members to draw artificial product categories for tax purposes so as to discriminate against imports and protect domestic production. According to the United States, the same or similar arguments by Japan have been rejected in two panel proceedings.

C.   Korea

1.   The Nielsen Study

6.219. Korea states at the outset that in order to rebut assertions of the complainants in the Dodwell Study and elsewhere in their submissions, it has commissioned another study, carried out by the company A.C. Nielsen (Nielsen study).[246]

6.220. Korea states that the Nielsen study concluded that while all Korean restaurants, Chinese restaurants and mobile street vendors sell standard soju, most cafés/western style restaurants and bars sell whisky. The study also found that 29.3% of the respondents consumed alcoholic beverages at home with their meals, while 81% were found to have consumed such beverages with meals at restaurants. The study claims that diluted soju was the alcoholic beverage predominantly consumed with meals. Drinking diluted soju with meals was most popular at Korean restaurants (73%), followed by Japanese restaurants (18%). According to the study, of the seven beverages offered to the respondents, none were consumed with meals at cafés/western style restaurants, bars and hotel bars. Finally, the survey found that soju is predominantly consumed straight (98.6%), while whisky is usually consumed "on the rocks" (with ice) (63.8%).

6.221. In Korea's view, therefore, the Nielsen study substantiates its argument that there is no demand substitutability between soju and the western-type drinks at hand in the Korean market.

2.   General Comments

6.222. Korea argued in its first submission and continues to maintain that a violation of Article III:2 cannot be made in the abstract. According to Korea, in order to begin to prove the existence of a violation, the complainants must show that there is a 'like' or directly competitive or substitutable relationship between specific prod-

---

[246] Korea claims that unlike the Dodwell Study, the Nielsen Study has focused on factual evidence rather than speculation. Rather than asking respondents 'what would you do?', it has asked them 'what do you do?'

ucts in a specific market. The decision as to whether two products have such a relationship is based upon an overall appreciation of many factors, such as their physical similarities, their end uses, price, and consumers' tastes and habits. Two products may be similar to some degree in some ways, and different to some degree in other ways.

6.223. Korea claims that the complainants have preferred to discuss each relevant criterion in the abstract and for all the products at once. Taking each criteria separately allowed them to make generalizations about all the products without addressing the specific arguments that Korea raised for each individual product. In Korea's view, as a result of that approach, the complainants do not provide a total view of the relationship between any particular product pair.

6.224. According to Korea, the effect of this approach is three-fold. First, it allows the complainants to gloss over or ignore differences between products. Second, it allows them to highlight and exaggerate the importance of exceptional cases. Third, through this approach they make it more difficult for the Panel to have a clear overall view of any one product pair.

6.225. Korea also asserts that what the complainants lack in evidence and argument, they try to make up for by allusions to Korea's past, its alleged protective measures, its lack of imports etc. According to Korea, its past as a developing country is not at issue in this case. What is at issue is Korea's market today. Korea refers to a neutral study funded by the EC Commission which observed that:

> The Korea market is no longer a market protected by the Government with market shares contested by local producers. In fact, it is becoming a truly global market, where multinational companies convene to compete with one another for the lucrative and promising Korean market.[247]

3. Generalizations about the Korean Products

6.226. Korea notes that consistent with their contention that all distilled spirits are the same, the complainants also refuse to recognize differences in the Korean spirits at issue in this case, claiming that 'soju', whether it be standard or distilled, is one product.

6.227. Korea has insisted from the beginning that standard soju and distilled soju are too different for these two products to be lumped together. Korea seeks to show that in trying to rebut this fact, the complainants first draw support from the fact that standard soju and distilled soju share, in part, the same name. According to Korea, the similarity in the names of standard soju and distilled soju is meaningless (for example, one would not consider 'beer' and 'root beer' to be 'like' or directly competitive or substitutable on the basis of their names).

6.228. Korea further notes that the complainants then go on to argue that the physical differences between standard soju and distilled soju are insignificant. However, those physical differences are obviously enough to affect consumer behaviour, as standard soju and distilled soju do not compete, indeed do not have the same end uses, and are sold at vastly different prices. The complainants have not been able to

---

[247] See Sofres Report, Introduction.

counter those arguments. In addition, it should be noted that the distinction between standard soju and distilled soju existed prior to this case, that these two products fall into different tax brackets,[248] and that despite the EC's statements to the contrary, distilled soju is not exempt from tax.

6.229. Korea states that another point made by the complainants is that the difference between distilled and standard soju is really not important because, "*they can be, and are, often blended with each other.*"[249] The complainants then point out that whisky is often blended too. Korea points out that the complainants again offer no proof whatsoever for their allegation that distilled and standard soju are often blended. Accordingly, this example of the reference to whisky is irrelevant to a comparison between standard and distilled soju.

6.230. Korea refers to what it calls another astonishing, assertion of the complainants that, *'swift transition'* occurred in the mid 1970s from distilled to standard soju, which and *'was possible only because, in the eyes of Korean consumers, the two varieties of soju are the same product'*[250] Korea recalls that standard soju was introduced in 1962 because, due to food shortages, distilled soju made of rice could no longer be produced. Production of distilled soju only started again in 1991. If a swift transition from one product to another following food shortages is an indication of a close relationship between them, Korea recalls that Parisians also made a *'swift transition'* from eating beef meat to eating rat meat during the Fall of Paris in the 1870s, due to a food shortage.[251] According to Korea, peoples' behaviour in times of food shortage says very little about which products consumers would consider substitutes in normal circumstances.

6.231. Korea states that the complainants argue that the only reason Korea wants to distinguish between standard soju and distilled soju is because it wants to 'sacrifice' distilled soju, which makes up 0.2% of the 'soju market' in order to 'spare' standard soju. According to Korea, it has no intention of sacrificing distilled soju. While distilled soju differs from the imported beverages in different ways than standard soju, it still differs from them too greatly to be 'like' or directly competitive or substitutable for those products.

6.232. Korea further argues that this allegation that Korea is willing to 'sacrifice' distilled soju to 'spare' standard soju is characteristic of another facet of the complainants' approach to this case. In Korea's words, where it suits them, the complainants trade their inverted telescope for a microscope, 'zooming in' on exceptional cases that seem to support their argument. In the same way that looking at the situation from a great distance obscures the reality, zooming in too closely also means that your view is distorted.

---

[248]   According to Korea, while the US notes that standard soju and distilled soju have the same rate of Education Tax (10%), they fail to mention that the liquor tax on distilled soju is 50%, while the liquor tax on standard soju is 35%. Another mistaken attempt at trivialising the distinctions between distilled and standard soju is the EC's assertion that the distinction in the tax law was introduced only in 1991 (see EC written rebuttal, at para. 34), supposedly in response to pressure from the EC. In fact, the distinction was already made in 1962.

[249]   See EC written rebuttal, at para. 38.

[250]   See EC written rebuttal, at para. 35.

[251]   See Horne, Alistar, The Fall of Paris: The Siege and the Commune 1870-71, London 1965.

6.233. Korea notes that the complainants allege that Korea is willing to 'sacrifice' distilled soju because it only represents 0.2% of the 'soju market'. What this highlights is the fact that the complainants are asking the Panel to do the opposite: they would like to use examples drawn from this 0.2% in order to prove a point about the other 99.8% of 'soju' sold in Korea, which is standard soju. For example, the complainants want the Panel to ignore the substantial price differences between standard soju and the western-style liquors at issue in this case, on the basis of the high prices of that 0.2%.

4.   Actual (or potential) Competition

6.234. Looking carefully at the evidence and arguments that the complainant have presented, Korea submits that the arguments are misleading, flawed, or insufficient to meet the complainants' burden of proof. According to Korea, therefore, the complainants have not established that there is a direct competitive or substitutable relationship, actual or potential, between soju and the imported distilled spirits that are within the scope of this dispute.

(a)   Physical differences

6.235. Korea points out that there are important physical differences between the products at issue. These differences have an impact on consumer preferences and hence on the competitive relationship between the products. According to Korea, the complainants have attempted to trivialize those differences by looking at the products from a great distance, such that they can say that all the products have 'essentially the same characteristics'. In Korea's view, however, even a slight physical difference might be enough to render two products not competitive. For example, if a consumer does not like the taste of one particular additive, its addition to a product will eliminate that consumer as a potential buyer - even if that additive does little to change the appearance or chemical composition of the product.

6.236. Korea also points out that the complainants display ignorance of the very real possibility that two products that are ostensibly similar might not compete. For example, Korea cites the US argument that 'under Korea's theory, different flavours of soft drinks such as Coca-Cola and Fanta do not compete, but it is doubtful that anyone familiar with the market would agree.' Korea disagrees with this. According to Korea, the directorate of the European Commission responsible for competition law matters has more than once drawn a distinction between cola-flavoured carbonated soft drinks and other types of soft drinks, deciding in the recent *Coca-Cola/Amalgamated Beverages* merger that the relevant market was the market for cola-flavoured carbonated soft drinks, explicitly excluding other flavours of carbonated soft drinks.[252] National competition authorities have come to the same conclusion.[253]

6.237. Korea argues that, the European Communities, in its discussion of physical differences, tries to take consideration back to the moment of distillation, at which point, it argues, 'all spirits are nearly identical' because 'all of them are concentrated forms of alcohol.' Korea argues that firstly, the principal test for whether products compete is the marketplace. Spirits are not sold at the point of distillation. Moreover, the difference in physical characteristics, starting with a difference in raw materials, is not negated by distillation. In addition, there are important post-distillation processes that also have an impact on the physical characteristics of products. Brown spirits, for instance, are generally matured in wooden casks and derive their flavour from this process, and from the original distilled ingredients.

6.238. According to Korea, the analysis at the point of distillation is meaningless as the subsequent addition of additives or ingredients can, and in the liquors discussed here, does, make a crucial difference for consumers when they choose a particular liquor in a particular market, such as the Korean market. Korea concludes, therefore, that although all spirits may be 'nearly identical' at the point of distillation, the most casual observation clearly shows that does not mean that drinkers are indifferent between them.

6.239. According to Korea, if physical characteristics at the point of distillation were meaningful, that would lead to the conclusion that products as disparate as fuel or pharmaceutical products are also directly competitive and substitutable with, for example, vodka.[254]

6.240. Korea also asserts that the complainants try to use evidence about production process to make up for the essential evidence about markets that is missing from their presentations. According to Korea, no evidence offered by the complainants shows that 'distilled spirits' is a group that is relevant to consumer choice in the Korean market. Korea asks: Why is 'distilled spirits' such a group rather than 'brown distilled spirits' or, 'white distilled spirits'? Why not 'alcoholic beverages' - spirits, wine and beer? Why not 'cold drinks', alcoholic or not?

6.241. In Korea's view, any one of these might be a grouping relevant to consumption - or might not be. Whether it is or not depends on the tastes and preferences of consumers. According to Korea, the effects of a failure to adequately research relations between products in consumption cannot be escaped by reference to modes of production. In particular, it cannot be demonstrated that distilled spirits is a relevant grouping for consumers on the basis that 'having essentially the same characteristics, soju and other distilled spirits and liqueurs are objectively apt to serve the same end uses'.

---

[252] Korea cites Commission Decision of 22 January 1997 declaring a concentration to be compatible with the common market and the functioning of the EEA Agreement, Case No IV/M.794 *Coca-Cola/Amalgamated Beverages*, 1997 OJ L 218, p. 15.

[253] Korea cites for example Decision no 96-D-67 of the French Conseil de la Concurrence (Competition Council) of 29 October 1996, *Coca Cola Beverages*.

[254] Korea alleges that the EC stated during its oral statement (p.12) that: neutral spirits are a raw material which can be used to produce a variety of alcoholic beverages, including for example vodka and gin, as well as other products, such as fuel or pharmaceutical products.

6.242. According to Korea, a member of a group of products that are related in consumption need not be a substitute for all other members of the group - just for some other members of the group. Korea states that a high-end Ferrari and a low-end Renault Clio are both motor cars, and could be seen by a person of sufficiently limited imagination as 'having essentially the same characteristics' (four wheels, one engine, steering wheel) and to be 'objectively apt to serve the same end uses'. The fact that both are motor cars, though, is not enough to allow deduction of elasticity of substitution between them. Indeed, in the case of Ferraris and Clios, it seems very likely that the elasticity in substitution between the two products is nil: that if the price of Clios changes by 1 per cent (or 10 percent or 100 per cent), the effect on demand for Ferraris will be zero.

6.243. Likewise, according to Korea, given the notable differences between standard soju and the western-style liquors there is no reason to assume that there would be elasticity of substitution between them. The complainants need to show this, but have failed to do so.

6.244. Korea also claims refers to the EC claim that 'according to Korea, the main difference between soju and gin is that gin is flavoured with juniper berries.' According to Korea it is true that Korea argued that juniper imparts a very particular flavour to gin that some consumers do not like. However, this was one of many differences, not least differences in price and end use, that Korea pointed out with respect of gin.

6.245. Korea notes, furthermore, that in interpreting the term 'substitutable', the United States, rather than proving that for Korean consumers a western-style liquor like whisky is directly[255] substitutable for standard soju, despite the very considerable price difference, cites the example of bottled water and tap water, two products that ostensibly have similar physical characteristics and similar end-uses.

6.246. According to Korea, products that conceivably can be substituted for each other yield a very broad field. Korea states for example, that one could say that woollen sweaters and coal can be substituted for each other. If you are cold, you could either put on a sweater or throw another lump of coal on the fire. Washing machines and socks could be substitutable. The easier and cheaper the availability of laundry facilities, the fewer socks a person needs in order to have a constant clean supply. With this view of substitutability, baby carriages and wheelbarrows could be substitutable!

(b)   Price

6.247. According to Korea, on the basis of the facts provided in the complainants' Dodwell Study, it is apparent that there is a huge discrepancy in the pre-tax prices of the products at issue. Korea states that taking whisky and standard soju as an example, the Dodwell Study data shows that the ratio of their prices varies from 6.3 to 12 times, with no overlap in price at all. Furthermore, according to Korea, the weighted average figures that Korea provided in its first submission showed that whisky is on

---

[255] Korea maintains that the United States, the European Communities and Korea are in agreement that the word 'directly' applies to both 'competitive' as well as to 'substitutable.

average 11 times more expensive than standard soju.[256] Large pre-tax price differences are shown for all the imported liquors at issue. This casts serious doubts on the existence of a directly competitive and substitutable relationship between these products, and highlights an important difference between this case and *Japan - Taxes on Alcoholic Beverages II* .

6.248. Korea points out that there are enormous pre-tax price differences. Based on the figures provided by the Dodwell study, Korea found the following pre-tax price differences:

Standard soju v.	whisky(premium)	ratio of 1 to 12
	whisky(North American)	ratio of 1 to 10.8
	whisky(standard scotch)	ratio of 1 to 7.2
	whisky(bottled in Korea)	ratio of 1 to 6.3
	brandy/cognac	ratio of 1 to 19.2
	vodka	ratio of 1 to 5.7
	gin	ratio of 1 to 5
	rum	ratio of 1 to 6.2

6.249. Korea indicates that the Dodwell study data shows that the ratio of price difference varies from 6.3 to 12 times with no overlap in price at all. Furthermore, according to Korea, the weighted average prices showed that whisky is 11 times more expensive than standard soju. In response to the European Communities' claim that weighted average prices are "meaningless," Korea states that a weighted average price is an accepted means of getting a typical price for a product. Large pre-tax price differences are shown for all the imported liquors at issue. This casts serious doubts on the existence of a directly competitive and substitutable relationship between these products, and highlights an important difference between this case and *Japan-Taxes on Alcoholic Beverages II.*

6.250. Korea considers that pre-tax price differences of this magnitude must be taken into account in discussing whether it can reasonably be argued that any of these products are "like" or directly competitive or substitutable. Korea argues that these price differences refute any argument that it was taxes that have "frozen" consumer preferences. Furthermore, argues Korea, as to directly competitive or substitutable products, it must be addressed whether, in the face of these price differences prior to the application of tax, the tax differentials at issue in this case can be said to "afford protection" to domestic production.

6.251. Korea argues that the complainants have been unable to provide a response to the proposition that large pre-tax price differential leads to the absence of a directly competitive or substitutable relationship. Rather than addressing the price discrepancy between standard soju and the imported liquors head on, the complainants attempt to divert the Panel's attention to premium diluted soju, which is the

---

[256] Korea refers to Attachment 5 to Korea's first submission.

somewhat more expensive variety, representing some 5% of total diluted soju volume.

6.252. Korea refers to the EC argument that using pre-tax prices for the purposes of comparison does not remove the "distortive effect from the disputed taxes", because the tax has kept low-priced imports from entering the market. Korea reminds the parties that, unlike Japan, it has *ad valorem* taxes. In Korea's view, while it might be argued that a high specific tax would keep low-cost products out of the market, an *ad valorem* tax is just that - it is linked to the price of the product, and therefore, the lower the price, the lower the tax amount.

6.253. Korea states that in determining whether two products are directly competitive or substitutable products, price cannot be excluded. In Korea's view, it is obvious that when one product is many times more expensive than another, it is difficult to argue that those two products are in competition. Korea notes that the US and EC competition authorities consider price as one of the most relevant factors.[257] Korea also recalls that during the Panel meetings, the EC representative stated that competition law analysis was relevant to an analysis of Article III:2.

6.254. Korea draws attention to the importance of the reasoning in *Japan - Taxes on Alcoholic Beverages II*, wherein it was stated that:

> the extent to which two products are competitive in economics is measured by the responsiveness of the demand for one product to the change in the demand for the other product (cross-price elasticity of demand). The more sensitive demand for one product is to changes in the price of the other product, all other things being equal, the more directly competitive they are.[258]

6.255. Korea argues that common sense tells us that the larger the price differences between two products, the less influence a change in the price of one will have on the demand for the other. In Korea's view, the complainants have not been able to overcome this common sense presumption.

6.256. According to Korea, the price difference between premium diluted soju and standard diluted soju is far less important than the price difference between standard diluted soju and western-style spirits. Korea claims that premium diluted soju is, on average, less than 80% more expensive than standard diluted soju,[259] and the difference in price reflects the other very small differences between premium and standard diluted soju.

---

[257] Korea notes that in its written rebuttal the EC states that only consumers' responses to changes in relative prices are relevant and not absolute price differences). In competition law, price is one of the assessed criteria to determine whether there is competition between products. In such an analysis, prices are assessed both in nominal and relative terms (see Commission Decision of 22 July 1992, Case No. IV/M 190 Nestle Perrier, OJ L 356, p.1). In Korea's view, the difference in nominal terms is of such a degree that it renders improbable any change in the consumers' responses resulting from relative price changes.

[258] Panel report, para. 6.31.

[259] As appears from Korea's answer to question 5 of the second set of questions from the Panel, the weighted average price of standard diluted soju (excluding premium soju) is 306.58 won, while the weighted average price of premium diluted soju alone is 539.70 won.

6.257. Korea also refers to an assertion by the European Communities, which in Korea's view is unfounded: 'western-style spirits are more expensive, to a large extent as a result of discriminatory taxation. If western-style spirits were taxed as soju, they would be less expensive and Korean consumers could afford to drink them with meals more often.' Korea's argument is that western-style spirits are indeed more expensive, but the rest of this statement does not follow.

6.258. Korea points out that using the Dodwell data provided by the EC, the pre-tax price differences between these beverages is great. These price differences would thus be maintained if tax rates were harmonized, and they are too great for it to follow that consumers would suddenly find imported alcoholic beverages an affordable alternative to diluted soju for meal-use, even disregarding the matter of taste. According to Korea, even the European Communities cannot think that its evidence shows that the addition of a few hundred won to the price of a bottle of diluted soju will have any substantial effect on demand for, for example, whisky.

6.259. Korea also states that another unfounded allegation appeared in the EC oral statement, where it stated that:

> "Tax and tariff changes were followed by a substantial reduction of prices and a considerable increase in the sales of whisky. This increase took place at the expense of soju. Whereas the market share of soju fell from 96 per cent in 1992 to 94 per cent in 1996, during the same period, whisky increased by a similar percentage from 1.5 per cent to 3 per cent. Soju's declining market share in an expending market evidences that soju and whisky are in direct competition".[260]

6.260. Korea states that it is probably true that if the price of whisky falls, the volume of whisky purchased will increase. According to Korea, that the quantity of whisky purchased is responsive to the price of whisky, does not, however, further the EC and US case. According to Korea, they need to show that this increase was at the expense of soju - that the demand for soju is responsive to the price of whisky.

6.261. Korea argues that if whisky sales increase at a greater percentage rate than soju sales, the share of whisky in the hypothetical 'soju-whisky market' will rise, and that of soju will fall. In Korea's view, that is entirely consistent with sales of soju rising at the same rate both before and after the increase in the share of whisky. The increase in whisky market share and the fall in soju market share says nothing about whether whisky grew at the expense of soju.

6.262. According to Korea, the point can be underlined by taking two goods that most people will accept to be unrelated - say whisky and floor polish - and aggregating them into an artificial market. In that 'market', the share of whisky might rise: whisky sales might grow at a higher percentage rate than sales of floor polish. But this does not prove or even suggest that whisky sales have grown at the expense of floor polish sales. Indeed, since the two products are, *ex hypothesi*, unrelated, it is clear that they have not.

6.263. In Korea's view, this 'proof' that whisky has grown at the expense of floor polish is in no way different from the 'proof' offered by the European Communities and the United States that whisky has grown at the expense of soju in the 'whisky-

---

[260] See EC oral statement, p. 6.

soju market'. Whisky's gain of market share in the 'whisky-soju market' shows that sales of whisky have grown at a faster percentage rate than soju: it shows no more and no less.

6.264. According to Korea, the arguments of the European Communities and the United States that market evolution in Korea supports their claim that whisky and soju are substitutes deserve no weight. In Korea's view, sales in whisky have certainly increased in Korea as its price fell, which is to be expected. Korea argues that in itself that fact has no bearing on the case. What the European Communities and the United States need to show is that the increase in sales of whisky was at the expense of sales of soju, which in Korea's view, they have not done.

6.265. Korea argues that the complainants display an interesting approach to the alcoholic strength of products. According to Korea, the complainants argue that a difference in alcoholic strength should not be taken into account in certain instances (such as, it should not affect the determination of whether products meet the strict 'like' product criteria). In Korea's view, the complainants only analyze price in this way in a last-ditch attempt to deal with evidence that is very damaging to their case. Korea further argues that the EC cannot bring itself to compare alcohol-adjusted prices of an average standard soju price - instead, it compares an atypical bottle of standard whisky to a bottle of premium soju, and still comes out with a 2 to 3 times price difference.

6.266. Korea argues that the EC is focusing on exceptions in describing the Korean market. When it comes to the price of premium soju in this case, they take the most expensive premium soju brand (Kimsatgat) as representative. The sales volume of such high-priced premium soju is minimal. Korea further argues that he European Communities takes inexpensive whisky as an example, which is atypical as well.

6.267. Korea also argues that the calculations of the European Communities are misleading. When taking the price per degree of alcohol based on weighted averages, so as to obtain a representative price, whisky is still 7.96 times the price of standard soju per degree of alcohol. Looking at premium soju alone, whisky is 4.71 times the price of premium soju per degree of alcohol.[261] Again, these are pre-tax prices.

6.268. Korea asserts that contrary to its contention in *Japan - Taxes on Alcoholic Beverages II*, that pre-tax prices were within a relatively short range, the European Communities now claims that there were actually significant price differences in Japan, and submits figures that are supposed to show this. According to Korea, the European Communities even goes so far as to suggest that the Japan - Taxes on Alcoholic Beverages consciously disregarded substantial price differences.[262]

6.269. Korea observes that prices of western-style liquors and the Japanese shochus, once the tax is removed, appear to be rather close, with a number of overlaps.[263] Furthermore, Korea notes that Japan chose not to dispute the EC's contentions about prices and price competition. However, rather than speculating about the evidence,

---

[261] Calculations based on data from the National Tax Administration.

[262] EC written rebuttal, at para. 130.

[263] See Annex 2 to EC written rebuttal.

and the arguments presented to the panel in *Japan - Taxes on Alcoholic Beverages*, Korea submits it is safer to recall the explicit finding by that panel:

> (T)he Community argued that the retail prices of shochu and of the other distilled spirits and liqueurs are within a relatively short range once the liquor taxes and the ad valorem taxes are deducted. This, in the Community's view, confirms that all of them are, at least potentially, competitive in terms of price.[264]

6.270. Korea also notes that the Panel repeated the Community's argument:

> [t]hat, but for the discriminatory taxes imposed pursuant to the Liquor Tax Law, many western-style liquors would be less expensive than shochu in real terms.[265]

6.271. According to Korea, one can only conclude that the European Communities was describing the facts in one way before the Japanese liquor taxes Panel, and is now changing its story before this Panel. In Korea's view, these two versions simply do not match. Korea asks how the European Communities was able to say that pre-tax, prices of many western-style liquors would be less expensive than Japanese shochu, and now say that pre-tax prices of western style liquors in Japan were actually significantly higher than shochu?

6.272. Korea further argues that neither the Panel nor the Appellate Body in their legal findings reflected on any significant price differences in *Japan - Taxes on Alcoholic Beverages II*. According to Korea, it is clear from the evidence presented to this panel that in Korea, after the removal of the liquor taxes, none of the western-style liquors would become cheaper than Korean soju. On the contrary, very substantial price differences would remain.

6.273. Korea maintains that, together with the other distinguishing factors such as end use (whisky is not a meal drink, etc.) these price differences demonstrate that there is no directly competitive or substitutable relationship between the western-style drinks in dispute and standard soju.

(c) End use

6.274. Korea states that it has also shown in its submission that the end uses for diluted soju differ greatly from those of the imported liquors at issue in this case. In particular, Korea states that it has pointed out that the overwhelming use of diluted soju is as an accompaniment to meals - a use for which the imported liquors are considered unsuitable and too expensive.

6.275. According to Korea, the complainants have not been able to provide an answer to this argument. While the European Communities allegedly acknowledges that standard soju is 'often consumed with meals', it argues that there are exceptions, such as sojubangs. However, meals are served as well at sojubangs. In Korea's view, to the extent that Koreans sometimes drink soju without a meal, these are the exceptions that confirm the rule.

---

[264] Panel Report on *Japan - Taxes on Alcoholic Beverages*, para. 4.82.
[265] *Ibid.*

6.276. Korea notes that neither of the complainants has been able to demonstrate concretely that any of the five western-style liquors in dispute are consumed with meals in Korea.[266]

6.277. According to Korea, the European Communities closes its eyes to the existing differences in end use, simply asserting that, in the case of vodka: 'Vodka and soju are like products because they have virtually the same physical characteristics and, therefore, serve for the same end uses.' [267] In Korea's view, even if the EC assertions about physical characteristics were true, the one does not necessarily follow from the other, and the actual behaviour of customers belies the EC assertion.

6.278. Korea further argues that according to the United States, bottled water and tap water must be directly substitutable within the meaning of Art. III.2 GATT, despite their large difference in price, because they serve similar end uses. According to Korea, if one accepts that, one could start to argue that price differences alone need not justify tax differences. That argument might seem to go against Korea's case, although it must be recalled that Korea's case not only relies on price differences, but also on differences in physical characteristics (and taste), as well as differences in end use (meal drink versus non-meal drinks).

6.279. According to Korea, consumers are not silly. If they are consistently willing to pay a much higher price for one product, compared to a seemingly similar product, then small differences are probably very important to them, and thus for the market performance of these products. According to Korea, the United States and the European Communities obviously have difficulties accepting that, as a difference in market performance would block the application of Art. III.2.

6.280. Korea further argues that in some developing countries bottled water is safe, and tap water may not be safe for tourists. For tourists, that makes quite a difference, and they will probably be willing to pay a higher price for bottled water. Again, the US's argument is flawed by its refusal to look at market-specific situations. Korea asks whether Article III:2 GATT would prohibit developing countries from charging a higher tax rate on bottled water than on their tap water?

6.281. Korea further argues that in developed countries as well, bottled water may in fact target an entirely different group of consumers or have different end uses than tap water. Korea gives the example that in Brussels parents are advised not to use tap water to prepare baby formula, as tap water contains too many additives and residues. Parents therefore use much more expensive and purer bottled water. Further, according to Korea, in the United States restaurants commonly serve pitchers of tap water with meals. Nevertheless, quite a number of customers order bottled water, for reasons such as health or taste. According to Korea, despite their ostensible physical similarities and capability for the same end use, these products are not substitutes at all in many countries and markets. Korea asserts that it has been able

---

[266] According to Korea, the EC has merely asserted that *other spirits can be and sometimes are drunk with meals*, without providing examples and their relative importance (EC oral statement, p. 8).

[267] See EC oral statement, p. 3.

to ascertain that tap water and bottled water are taxed differently, at least in the EC.[268]

6.282. Korea also notes the US argument that 'end use can differ between substitute or competing products. For example, one would not use oranges in an apple pie . . . but these products do compete for consumer spending on fruit purchases.' [269] Korea notes the alleged US commitment to the idea that consumers have a fixed budget for classes of expenditure, for example, for fruit purchases and distilled spirit purchases, and wonders, if this proposition is to be central to the US case, whether it is going to provide any evidence in support of it.

6.283. According to Korea, even if that view of the world could be substantiated, the United States in effect concedes, in the quotation above, that apples belong to two distinct budgetary items - consumer spending on fresh fruit and consumer spending on pie fillings. It also allegedly concedes that oranges do not compete in the pie filling segment. In a country where the principal use for fruit is making pies, therefore, substantial changes in the price of apples may have little or no impact on the demand for oranges. In Korea's view, this would be powerful evidence that in that particular country apples and oranges are not directly competitive or substitutable.

6.284. In the present case, according to Korea, the end use for diluted soju with which imported liquors do not compete, is far and away the most important use to which diluted soju is put: it is typically consumed with meals, and the imported beverages are not.[270] In Korea's view, that major difference in end use means that the products at issue in this case are neither 'like' nor directly competitive or substitutable.

6.285. Korea adds that, rather than addressing Korea's specific arguments about end uses, the United States tries to divert the discussion back into generalities, saying 'distilled spirits around the world are used for socialization, relaxation and celebration.' The standard that the US sets for itself is much too low. There are innumerable types of foods and drinks that could be said to serve these general purposes. However, that does not mean that all of those things are 'like' or directly competitive or substitutable.

6.286. Korea notes that both complainants attribute the argument to Korea that in order to be directly competitive or substitutable, products would have to share 'all' possible economic uses. According to Korea, that is not what Korea has been saying, but it has been referring to the most important end use of each liquor. In Korea's view, it has observed that the most important end use of standard soju is different from the most important end use of western-style liquors.

6.287. Korea reiterates that standard soju is typically a 'meal' drink, while the western-style liquors at issue in this case are not drunk with meals, but rather in room salons and other high-class bars where standard soju is not even on offer.

---

[268] Korea states that in Belgium tap water is subject to a VAT of 6% while bottled water is subject to a VAT of 21%.

[269] See US oral statement, para. 8.

[270] According to Korea, this is shown by the Nielsen study.

6.288. Korea notes that the European Communities admits that 'soju is more often consumed with every-day meals than western-style spirits', but it argues that this is so 'simply because western-style spirits are more expensive'.[271] According to Korea, the European Communities would like this Panel to believe that if taxes were harmonized, Koreans would start drinking western-style spirits with their meals, in spite of the fact that, whisky, for example, would still be on average 11 times more expensive than standard soju. Korea disagrees, especially in light of the fact that regardless of price, Koreans do not consider whisky to be appropriate to drink while eating.

6.289. Korea argues that, those facts being uncontested, the European Communities has then tried to say that Korea has been exaggerating, and alleges that Korea has claimed that soju is 'always' drunk with meals. Korea denies claiming that, but has stated that the bulk of standard soju is drunk with meals, which is its most important end use. Korea further alleges that the European Communities claims that sojubangs are one of the most typical places for drinking soju, and supposedly a place where meals are not served. In fact, according to Korea, sojubangs are an exceptional outlet and they do serve meals. This contrasts with the end use of western-style liquors which are hardly, if ever, drunk with meals. According to Korea, the Nielsen study which Korea attached to its written rebuttal bears this out.

6.290. According to Korea, the complainants have not provided any evidence to dispel this important difference in end use. One point they have made much of is that some respondents to Nielsen said that they drank whisky with their meals. That was a very small percentage indeed, and could also be a human error. The complainants are focusing on exceptions again. The ordinary fact of life is that very few, if any, Koreans would buy whisky to drink with their meals at home. They receive whisky as a gift, and enjoy this on a special occasion that is usually not a meal.

6.291. Korea states that soju is not suited to penetrate the establishments where western-style liquors are sold. The main characteristic of soju is that it is an inexpensive meal drink. Barring exceptions, you would not expect to find such a drink in bars. This was borne out by the Nielsen study, which Korea submitted. In Korea's view, the complainants have submitted no evidence to contradict this. The Hankook study, which they submitted earlier on the distribution patterns of liquors only refers to whisky, and ignores soju.[272]

6.292. Korea further argues that western-style liquors are not, or very rarely, found in Korean restaurants, mobile street vendors and Chinese restaurants. These establishments always serve standard soju. Western style liquors are found more often, though not always, in Japanese restaurants (presumably as a before or after meal drink, as customers reported that they do not drink whisky with Japanese meals). Japanese restaurants always serve soju. Again, there is a notable difference in distribution.[273] Korea notes that the EC Hankook Study does not even mention restaurants.

---

[271] EC written rebuttal, at para. 115.

[272] See EC Annex 10.

[273] According to Korea, these are the findings of the AC Nielsen study.

6.293. Korea notes the recent visits of US Embassy personnel to Korean restaurants. According to Korea, they are nine of the most expensive restaurants in Seoul. The fact that Embassy officials visit these restaurants explains, Korea suspects, why they had whisky in stock. It really says very little about the drinking behaviour of the vast mass of the Korean population.

(d)   Places of sale and consumption

6.294. One of Korea's arguments that standard and distilled soju do not compete with imported liquors has been that diluted soju and distilled soju are not even available in many of the outlets in which imported liquors are consumed, notably, in room salons and other high class bars. In order to provide the Panel with support for that proposition, Korea commissioned the Nielsen study. This study surveyed room salons, night clubs and danlanjujums, asking which alcoholic beverages they offered. According to Korea, in this survey, 96.7% responded that they sell whisky, while 0% responded that they offered diluted soju.

6.295. Korea argues that, contrary to what the European Communities seems to suggest, Korea has not argued that whisky has not 'gained considerable distribution penetration'. Korea's point is rather that diluted soju and the western-spirits are not available in the same outlets, an important indicator of a difference in end use and lack of competition. According to Korea, its emphasis has been in particular on the fact that standard soju does not penetrate the establishments where the western-style liquors are available.

6.296. Korea also states that it does not find persuasive the US exhibit showing, for example, Seagram Extra Dry Gin and Alexander vodka next to Korean premium soju in a convenience store.[274] According to Korea, the same photograph shows that Gillette shaving foam is also displayed next to these alcoholic beverages. Korea's argument is that convenience stores are pressed for shelf space. The fact that two items are displayed next to each other would hardly be compelling evidence of a competitive relationship in any context, but in the context of a small Korean convenience store, is truly devoid of meaning.

(e)   Consumer spending "categories"

6.297. Korea also claims that instead of the classic more detailed analysis outlined above, the United States suggests that the Panel only needs to "consider whether the products in question compete for consumer spending on a category of goods." Korea further claims that the United States asserts that "consumers in Korea, like anywhere else, budget their spending on alcoholic beverages, and subsequently spend that budget according to taste, prices and social occasions." Korea believes that the United States is confusing a model of reality with reality. According to Korea, academic researchers may find it interesting to hypothesize that consumers act as if they first decide how much to spend on a category of goods, and then on how that amount will be divided between the goods within the category. That academic re-

---

[274] US Exhibit G.

searchers may find it interesting to hypothesize, however, is very far from saying that this is how consumers have been shown to behave 'in Korea, as elsewhere'.

6.298. According to Korea, the more important point is that the notion of a category of goods begs the central question in this proceeding. Korea asks how the United States knows what categories are relevant for actual consumers - in particular, for Korean consumers? In Korea's view, it presents no evidence to underpin its conjectures. Korea adds that the United States itself seems unsure of what the relevant category is. Korea notes that sometimes the United States says that it is 'alcoholic beverages', but at other points it is 'alcoholic spirits.' According to Korea, `alcoholic beverages', which includes wine and beer, is very different, especially in Korea, from 'alcoholic spirits'.

(f)   Future competition

6.299. Korea also states that the complainants suggest that the market is developing so that the imported beverages and standard soju and distilled soju might compete in the future.[275] Korea considers this assertion to be speculative, at best. If the pre-tax price differences remain the same, there is no reason to assume that future consumers will consider them to be direct substitutes.

6.300. Korea notes the US argument that, Korea's population is changing and becoming more 'internationally-oriented' and it may be that in the future the market for imported beverages will grow. In Korea's view, however, the idea that Koreans may wish to drink more whisky does not mean that they will abandon standard soju as the drink to accompany their meals. The growth, for example, of the whisky market could be completely independent of the standard soju market.

6.301. Korea claims that this was observed by the EC Guide on exports of alcoholic beverages to Korea:

> "Soju in particular remains virtually unaffected by imported alcoholic drinks. Furthermore, soju is insulated from economic downturns and maintains a loyal following of steady consumers".[276]

6.302. Korea argues that if in the future, the market does develop such that standard and distilled soju and the imported liquors compete, then the complainants are free to resort again to WTO proceedings. However, at the present time, the products are not competing, and that lack of competition has not been shown to be tax-related.

5.   *Broad or Narrow Interpretation of Products in Dispute*

6.303. Korea notes the EC argument that the GATT drafters aimed to provide stricter rules with respect to internal tax measures (Article III:2) than with respect to other internal regulations (Article III:4), rather than the opposite which is supposedly argued by Korea.

6.304. Korea further notes the EC argument that by including directly competitive or substitutable in Article III:2, the drafters intended to create stricter rules for tax discrimination than for internal regulation. If not, they would have limited them-

---

[275] See for example, the EC oral statement at p. 5 and the US oral statement at para. 19 et. seq.

[276] Korea cites the Sofres report, p. 22.

selves to 'like products' just as in Article III:4. Korea submits that this is as yet undecided.

6.305. Korea points out that firstly, in *Japan - Taxes on Alcoholic Beverages*, the Panel said that the coverage of Article III:2 might or might not be identical to that of Article III:4.[277] In Korea's view, therefore, it is not clear, as the European Communities claims, that the GATT drafters aimed to provide stricter rules with respect to internal tax measures than with respect to other internal regulations.

6.306. According to Korea, however that may be, it does not alter the fact that Article III:2 treads heavily upon national sovereignty. Korea refers to the Appellate Body's statement in *Japan - Taxes on Alcoholic Beverages*, that 'the members of the WTO have made a bargain'.[278] In Korea's view, that bargain implies limitations on the sovereignty of the Member in exchange for benefits which they expect to derive as a Member of the WTO.

6.307. Korea argues that in this context, WTO Members agreed that Article III:2 prohibits tax discrimination on 'like products' and on directly competitive or substitutable products. Thus, the language of Article III:2 expresses the concessions that the WTO members were ready to make in this regard. In Korea's view, every concession represents a limitation of the sovereignty of the members. A broad interpretation of the expressed restriction could threaten the carefully negotiated balance between the restriction and the benefit which the members expected from this restriction.

6. *"So as to Afford Protection"*

6.308. Korea notes the EC statement that Korea has dealt with the 'so as to afford protection' matter in a 'perfunctory' manner.[279] According to Korea, while it is true that Korea does not spend a great deal of time on the 'so as to afford protection' facet of this case, this is mainly because Korea is so convinced that there are no 'like' or directly competitive or substitutable relationships in this case, such that the 'so as' part of this case will never be reached.

6.309. However, Korea has also argues that taxes in this case are not 'so as to afford protection' - that the price differences in this case are too great for the tax to have afforded any protection to domestic production, in particular the production of standard soju. Korea notes that according to the European Communities, it is illogical to mention these price differences here: if the products concerned are found to be directly competitive or substitutable 'despite the pre-tax price differentials',[280] then these price differentials are not really meaningful. In Korea's view this is not a very compelling point, coming from party which has been arguing that price differences are not relevant to a directly competitive or substitutable finding, and that it is sufficient for the Panel to look at physical characteristics only. Thus, according to Korea, if this Panel, despite the force of precedent, followed the EC view on directly com-

---

[277] Panel Report on *Japan - Taxes on Alcoholic Beverages II*, *supra*, para. 6.20. The Appellate Body did not take a position on this issue.

[278] Appellate Body Report on *Japan - Taxes on Alcoholic Beverages II, supra*, at 108.

[279] EC written rebuttal, at para. 1.

[280] EC written rebuttal, at para. 166.

petitive or substitutable, the absolute differences in pre-tax prices would be an entirely separate issue to be addressed in connection with the 'so as to afford protection' requirement.

6.310. Because the differences in price are so large, Korea contends that the additional price difference that can be attributed to the tax would not have any effect on consumer behaviour, and therefore could not afford protection to a domestic industry. Korea states that apart from its dubious appeal to logic, the European Communities does not show how the liquor taxes can afford protection, to standard soju in particular, given the considerable differences in pre-tax prices with western-style liquors.

6.311. Korea notes that, in contrast, the United States has recognized the pertinence of the price differences to this third leg of Article III:2. While it also contests the relevance of Korea's price-based arguments to the determination of 'like' or directly competitive or substitutable relationships, it argues that 'differences in prices . . .[are] more appropriately considered in the third element of analysis under Article III:2: whether the taxes are applied so as to afford protection to domestic production.'[281] However, Korea notes that the US has not addressed the price differences cited by Korea in connection with the 'so as to afford protection' requirement.

6.312. Accordingly to Korea, it is clear that the complainants have not carried their burden of proof regarding this third requirement of Article III:2 either. They would have had to show that, despite the much higher pre-tax prices of western-style liquors, the tax differential had protected domestic production of standard soju.

6.313. In respect of distilled soju Korea's defence has been different, as the pre-tax prices of distilled soju are even higher than or in about the same range as western-style liquors. However, according to Korea, the sales of this traditional, artisanal product are minimal. The complainants have not shown how the continued presence of this product, taxed at the current rate, would hurt them.

7.   *Comments of Korea to the EC Trendscope Survey*

6.314. Korea notes that at the second substantive meeting of the Panel, the European Communities submitted a new consumer survey which Korea had not seen before.

6.315. Korea submits that interpretation of this survey is not easy, and that the European Communities, by presenting the survey so late in the proceedings, has deprived Korea of the possibility of exploring these problems by questioning specific aspects of it before the Panel.

6.316. Korea claims that some of the "Key Findings of the Consumer survey"[282] strongly support points made by Korea by showing, for example, the considerable degree of specialization of Korean outlets for these products. According to Korea, the Trendscope Survey shows that soju is almost never consumed in hotel bars, western restaurants, cafés, room salons and night clubs, but is the drink of choice in

---

[281]   US written rebuttal, at para. 70.

[282]   Trendscope survey, Charts entitled "Key Findings of Consumer Survey".

Korean restaurants. The survey also allegedly backs up Korea's assertions that whisky is almost never consumed in Korean, Japanese or Chinese restaurants.

6.317. Korea states that the survey also contains results that are inconsistent with Korea's understanding of Korean drinking habits, and is puzzled that 66% of Trendscope respondents claim to drink soju "without a meal" (though only 3% "without food"); and that 86% claim to drink whisky "with food" (though only 7% "with a meal").

6.318. Korea also notes that only 34% of those surveyed by Trendscope responded that they drank soju with their meal. According to Korea, the respondents might have been thinking about meals consumed at home, where according to the Nielsen study, 29.3% of the respondents consumed diluted soju with their meal.

6.319. Korea argues that the Trendscope result is inconsistent with Korea's understanding of the market as far as "on-premise" consumption is concerned. Korea refers to the Nielsen study, wherein it was found that 73% of consumers drank diluted soju with their meals in Korean restaurants.

6.320. Korea further argues that, to interpret the Trendscope results properly, it is necessary to know how respondents distinguished between "meal" and "food". According to Korea, the distinction between "food" and "meal" is vague and dependent on context in Korean and English. Korea recalls that in referring to the main end use of soju as meals, it has excluded snacks.

6.321. Korea maintains that western-style liquors like whisky are not normally drunk with meals (i.e. lunch or dinner) whereas most soju is consumed with meals.

6.322. Korea also argues that another ambiguity arises from the Trendscope Survey's use of the term "umsik" for "food". According to Korea, the usual meaning of "umsik" in Korean is "food and drink", and as such "umsik" can be interpreted broadly to include drinks as well as snacks. In Korea's view, this ambiguity would mean that respondents who, for example, eat peanuts with their whisky may well have answered that they drink whisky "with food".

6.323. Korea asserts that there is also an ambiguity in the definition of "with meals". Korea poses the question whether "with meals" was necessarily interpreted by their respondents as eating contemporaneously with drinking, or whether it was interpreted more liberally to include "before dinner" and "after dinner" meals.

6.324. Korea points out that there is also an ambiguity in the sense that it is unclear whether the respondents, being faced with questions about food and meals at the same time, would have considered the questions as mutually exclusive. In Korea's view, some respondents might have thought that the questions about "food" were intended not to include "meals", while others might have assumed that because meals are food, then soju which is usually consumed with meals is as of necessity consumed with food too.

6.325. Korea submits that since the complainants have submitted this survey too late, it did not have the opportunity to pursue the ambiguities with questions through the Panel. Korea adds that this late submission of this survey also means that there is insufficient time to evaluate its evidentiary value, and therefore, the panel should disregard it.

D.   EC and US Comments on the Nielsen Study

6.326. The complainants responded to this survey, which was commissioned at the instance of Korea, by pointing out that there were several categories of overlapping end-uses. They state for example, that all Japanese restaurants served soju and 40% of them served whisky; a further 6.7% served brandy or cognac. According to the complainants, of the responding Western-style restaurants and cafés, 90% served whisky and a lesser number served other types of western-style beverages, and 21.7% served soju.

6.327. The complainants also note that while only 1.7% of the individual respondents drank whisky at home with meals, only 29.3% of all respondents consumed any alcoholic beverages at home with meals. In the complainants view, the proper comparison was that between the 1.7% and the 29.3%, thus leaving 5.8% of all respondents who consumed alcoholic beverages at home as drinkers of whisky with their meals.

6.328. The complainants have also questioned some of the findings of the Nielsen study, arguing that these results are actually indications of overlapping end-uses. The complainants note that there were almost no western-style beverages in Korea until the last five years following changes in the duty rates on imported distilled beverages.

6.329. The complainants argue that alcoholic beverages, like many foods and beverages, are habit based products. In their view, people tend to purchase what they are used to and change their tastes only over a period of time. They must become familiar with the taste of new products and will only make minor substitutions for the familiar product at first and more significant changes will tend to occur over a period of time until a fairly stable rate is achieved.

6.330. According to the complainants, the trends shown in the Nielsen study, as well as the substitutability shown in the EC market survey (the Dodwell study), show unmistakable evidence of the beginnings of substitutability and common end-use by imports.

6.331. The United States claims that the Nielsen study also contradicts Korea's emphasis that soju is only drunk straight in alleged contrast to Western spirits. According to the United States, survey respondents reported that in addition to being drunk straight, standard soju is consumed mixed with cola, cider, juice or some other manner. The results confirm that even if standard soju were predominantly consumed straight by survey respondents, it was not consumed *only* straight. Moreover, survey respondents were asked how they "normally" like to drink standard soju and whisky, and they were limited to a single response, suggesting that the reporting of multiple styles of consumption were avoided by the design of the question.

6.332. The United States further notes that the results of the Nielsen study also run counter to the supposedly rigid styles of whiskey consumption Korea paints in its submissions and first oral statement. For example, one-third of the survey respondents reported preferring consuming whisky straight and a smaller percentage indicated, similar to standard soju, a preference for whisky mixed with cola, cider, and juice. According to the United States, with a third of respondents preferring their whisky straight, just as Korea claims standard soju is largely consumed, it is clear that whisky and soju consumption styles overlap significantly.

6.333. The United States further claims that the Nielsen study also directly undermines Korea's assertion that soju is "never drunk mixed." Korea says this assertion was based on "common knowledge,"[283] but apparently such common knowledge may not be a reliable source of information. Korea has insisted that the burden is for the complaining parties to show its factual assertions to be untrue. In our view, the Nielsen study's direct contradiction of Korea's so-called common knowledge places doubt on all similar unsubstantiated assertions by Korea concerning consumption in its market.

6.334. The United States asserts that, in response to the Korean Nielsen study, the U.S. Embassy in Korea identified nine large traditional Korean restaurants in Seoul that serve traditional Korean food based on the common knowledge among Embassy staff. U.S. embassy employees then asked whether the establishments served whiskey and whether they served soju. It turned out that every single one of these nine restaurants serves both soju and whisky.[284] The United States does not claim to have taken a representative market survey, but such a survey is not necessary for the point at hand. We are simply saying that Korea's depiction of stratified end uses in different restaurants in Korea is contradicted by a simple tour of its capital city. These observations based on simple anecdotal evidence stand in stark contrast to the Nielsen finding that no surveyed Korean style restaurants served whisky and soju, whether in Seoul or elsewhere. This tends to confirm that the Nielsen study selectively sampled the restaurants known to limit the variety of spirits, representing an additional bias in the sampling. Moreover, the Trendscope survey, which the EC has described in detail earlier, further contradicts the Nielsen results by also showing that whisky is consumed at venues such as Korean restaurants where soju is the main item. Additionally, the Trendscope study shows that soju, similar to whisky, is most often enjoyed without meals.

6.335. According to the United States, even if the Panel were to accept these contradictions and biases, the Nielsen survey, highlighted by the EC, survey in fact lends credible support to the U.S. position in this case by indicating significant overlaps in usage between soju and Western spirits. Again, given the recent removal of barriers to entry, it is not expected that Western spirits will be consumed in every venue and in equal proportions to the traditional Korean spirit of soju. Nevertheless, the survey indicates whisky is consumed with meals, whisky is served in three out of six types of restaurants surveyed (four out of seven if you include hotel bars), and whisky and soju are both consumed straight, or mixed with cola, cider or juice.

VII.   ANSWERS TO QUESTIONS

A.   *European Communities*

7.1.   In response to a question concerning levels of cross-price elasticity, the European Communities states that:

---

[283]   Korean response to a U.S. Question.
[284]   US Exhibit S.

(a)   As noted by the Appellate Body in *Japan - Taxes on Alcoholic Beverages II*, how much broader the category of "directly competitive or substitutable products" may be in a given case is a matter for the panel to determine based on all the relevant factors in that case.[285] Accordingly, it would be inappropriate to try and define a standard of general application, and in particular a quantitative one.

(b)   There is no support for Korea's contention that the notion of "directly competitive or substitutable products" must be interpreted "strictly". On the contrary, as demonstrated by the complainants, an examination of the drafting history of GATT and of previous Panel and Appellate Body reports (including the two cases on *Japan - Taxes on Alcoholic Beverages II*) shows that in practice the "directly" has been given a rather broad interpretation.

(c)   In *Japan - Taxes on Alcoholic Beverages II*, the Appellate Body made it clear that cross-price elasticity is not "*the* decisive criterion"[286] for establishing whether two products are directly competitive or substitutable. According to the Appellate Body, cross-price elasticity is but one of the means of examining a relevant market. In turn looking at competition in the relevant markets is just "one among a number of means"[287] of identifying the products that are directly competitive or substitutable in a particular case. The other means mentioned by the Appellate Body are the physical characteristics, the end uses and the customs classification of the products.

(d)   Furthermore, the relevance of a particular level of cross-price elasticity may vary according to the circumstances of each case. For instance, if two products have been sold for a long time and under similar conditions on the same geographical market, a "very low rate of cross-price elasticity" could be an indication that they re not "directly competitive or substitutable".

(e)   On the other hand, in a situation where one of the products concerned has dominated a geographical market for a long time and the other product is a new entrant in that market (e.g. because until then it has been excluded therefrom by import and/or tax barriers), it would be unwarranted to conclude from the mere fact that the initial cross-price elasticity is relatively low that the two products are not "directly competitive or substitutable". The more so in the case of products such as spirits, where market penetration is slow and short-term reactions to price changes tend to be relatively low.

(f)   Korea's position in this case appears to be that Article III:2, second sentence, would apply only if and when imported products succeed in establishing themselves in a market. Foreign products would have to

---

[285] Appellate Body Report, *supra*, at 470.
[286] Appellate Body Report, *supra*, p. 25.
[287] *Ibid.*

achieve first a level of market penetration such that it is possible to prove statistically a high rate of cross-price elasticity. This approach, however, disregards the obvious fact that protective taxes may be a factor that delays or prevents imported products from ever reaching that level of market penetration. Clearly, such an approach is at odds with the well-established principle that Article III protects "competitive opportunities". There is no reason to limit such "opportunities" to those that are available to a product in the very short term. Article III protects any competitive opportunities that a given product may have by reason of its inherent characteristics.

(g)   In connection with this question, the European Communities further argued that the Dodwell study does not purport to provide a precise measurement of cross-price elasticity. In order to do that, it would have been necessary to carry out an econometric analysis based on historic sales and price data. In the present case, however, that type of analysis was precluded by the fact that western spirits have been virtually excluded from the Korean market until only a few years ago. This means that the available sales and price data are too few to allow a statistically valid analysis.

(h)   The Dodwell study has a more modest purpose. It aims at testing by means of a consumer survey the hypothesis that a reduction in the prices of western spirits and/or increase in the prices of soju resulting from the elimination of the existing tax differentials will lead to an increase in the consumption of western-style spirits at the expense of soju. The results of the Dodwell study clearly validate that hypothesis.

(i)   Additionally, the study indicates that the extent of potential substitution could be significant. For example, in one of the possible after-tax harmonization price scenarios the percentage of respondents who would choose whisky instead of standard soju would increase from 14.2% to 23.8%. While, for the reasons explained elsewhere, it was appropriate to distinguish in the survey between premium and standard soju, this has the consequence that the survey only measures the shift of respondents from standard soju to western spirits, and not the additional shift from premium soju to western spirits. Furthermore, since the prices of premium soju are not increased in parallel with the prices of standard soju (so as to reflect the fact that taxes would be increased on all diluted soju), but rather decreased, the survey overestimates the shift from standard to premium soju at the expense of the shift from standard soju to western spirits. In comparison, in the same scenario, the percentage of respondents choosing premium soju would increase from 12.6% to 19.8%. Thus, the Dodwell study suggests that the elasticity of substitution between standard soju and whisky could be higher than the elasticity of substitution between standard soju and premium soju, two products which have been described by Korea as being close "substitutes".

(j)   Moreover, it should be borne in mind that a consumer survey like the Dodwell study necessarily underestimates the degree of potential competition between soju and western spirits.

(k)   In the first place, the Dodwell survey can show only the immediate reaction of consumers to price changes. Yet, spirits consumption is to a large extent based on habits, which only change gradually. This means that, over a certain period of time, the price changes resulting from the elimination of tax differentials will lead to a more substantial shift from soju to western spirits than the one shown in the Dodwell study.

(l)   Secondly, it must be recalled that western spirits are new entrants in the Korean market and still hold only a small share of that market. This has two implications. The first one is that the respondents are generally less familiar with western spirits than with soju. This leads to a lower response in the survey than in the case of two products which were both well known to the respondents. The second implication is that western spirits still have considerable potential to increase their share of the market through marketing efforts (in advertising, distribution, etc.). The impact of those efforts would be considerably boosted by the price changes envisaged in the Dodwell study. On the other hand, the continued application of protective taxation would discourage such efforts. The interaction of these two factors, however, is not and cannot be addressed by a survey like the Dodwell study.

(m)   Finally, the Dodwell study considers only the price changes that could result directly from the elimination of the existing tax differentials. It does not take into account that the elimination of tax differentials could lead as well to a decrease of the pre-tax prices of western spirits and, consequently, to further substitution.

7.2.   In response to a question as to whether there is a *de minimis* standard in assessing the question of "so as to afford protection", the European Communities states that:

(a)   In *Japan - Taxes on Alcoholic Beverages II*, the complainants expressed different views with respect to the interpretation of the third element of Article III:2, second sentence. The European Communities argued that the measures at issue afforded protection to domestic production because a majority of the sales of the less taxed product (shochu) were domestically produced in Japan. In turn, the United States argued that the measures afforded protection to domestic production because their structure and design evidenced that they were not aimed at achieving any legitimate policy objective but only at providing an advantage to Japanese shochu. The approach established by the Appellate Body in *Japan - Taxes on Alcoholic Beverages II* appears to combine both positions. While putting the emphasis on the objective aim of the measures, as revealed by their structure and de-sign,[288] the Appellate Body also noted the fact that Japanese shochu was "isolated" from imports of shochu[289]. Thus, the Appellate Body seems to have considered that the demonstrated actual protective effects of a measure may be taken into account as an indication that a measure is aimed at protecting domestic production.[290]

(b)   On the other hand, there is no suggestion in *Japan - Taxes on Alcoholic Beverages II* that in order to meet the third element of Article III:2, the tax measures must afford a minimum "degree" of protection to the less taxed product. The Appellate Body agreed with the Panel that the reasoning required under Article III:2, second sentence, is the following:

> If directly competitive or substitutable products are not "similarly taxed", and if it were found that the tax favours domestic products, then protection would be afforded to such products, and Article III:2 second sentence is violated.[291]

(c)   Thus, the third element of Article III:2, second sentence, is concerned only and exclusively with the question whether, by taxing one product less than another directly competitive or substitutable product, the measures "favour" domestic production over imports, not with the extent of the "protection" afforded to the less taxed[292] product. In other words, the third element of Article III:2, second sentence, is not about how much protection is afforded, but rather about who is protected.

(d)   The view that in order to establish a violation of Article III:2 it is necessary for the complainants to show that the measures actually afford a certain "degree" of protection by effectively reducing sales of imports above a *de minimis* level would be in contradiction with the well established principle that GATT Article III is concerned with the protection of competitive opportunities and not of actual trade flows. More specifically, according to the Appellate Body:

> [i]t is irrelevant that the "trade effects" of the tax differentials between imported and domestic products, as reflected in the volumes of imports, are insignificant or even non-existent: Article III protects expectations not of any particular trade volume but rather of the

---

[288] Appellate Body Report, *supra*, at 120.

[289] *Ibid.*, at 122.

[290] See also the Appellate Body Report on *Canada - Certain Measures Concerning Periodicals*, *supra*, at 474-476.

[291] See also the Appellate Body Report, *supra*, at 121.

[292] In contrast, under Article III:2, first sentence, it is not necessary to demonstrate that a difference in taxation between two types of "like" products leads to discrimination between imports and "domestic production". Like products must always be taxes equally.

> equal competitive relationship between imported and domestic products.[293]

(e)   In sum, the European Communities is of the view that the third element of Article III:2, second sentence, does not introduce another *de minimis* threshold, in addition to those which result from the application of the first and the second element. If two products are "directly" competitive or substitutable, any tax differential above the *de minimis* level must be deemed to affect that competitive relationship and, as result, to "protect" the less taxes product. The only remaining issue is then whether the "protection" given to the less taxed product favours a "domestic production".

7.3.   In response to a question concerning the price mix of exports to Korea compared to other markets, the European Communities states that:

(a)   The pre-tax prices of western spirits are not higher than the pre-tax prices of soju only because of Korea's Liquor Tax system. The differences in prices reflect also differences in production and transportation costs as well as the impact of tariffs. Nevertheless, the pre-tax prices of western spirits are higher than they would be under a neutral tax system.

(b)   As already explained in the EC submissions, one of the effects of Korea's tax regime is that higher priced premium brands account for a disproportionate share of the sales of western spirits. For example, as shown by Annex 1, premium brands account for as much as 70 per cent of all sales of Scotch whisky in Korea. The same Annex shows that in a number of representative export markets with a neutral system of taxation the proportion of premium brands is much lower: 3 per cent in Australia; 6 per cent in New Zealand and 14 per cent in Venezuela. The preponderance of premium brands in the Korean market as compared to other export markets is further confirmed by the fact that whereas in 1997 the average unit price of all exports of Scotch whisky (for 70 cubic litre bottles at 40% volume) was £2.79, the average unit price of the exports of Scotch whisky to Korea was £4.42.

7.4.   In response to a question concerning comparison of legal standards under competition law with standards under Article III, the European Communities states that:

(a)   The basic criteria applied in order to define the relevant product market for the purposes of EC Competition law are the same as those applied in order to establish whether products are directly competitive

---

[293]   In contrast, under Article III:2, first sentence, it is not necessary to demonstrate that a difference in taxation between two types of "like" products leads to discrimination between imports and "domestic production". Like products must always be taxes equally.

or substitutable for the purposes of GATT Article III:2, second sentence".[294]

(b)   There is, nevertheless, an essential difference. When applying GATT Article III:2, first sentence, Panels must take into account the "potential" competition which would materialize between the products concerned in the absence of the tax differential in dispute and not the "actual" competition existing under current taxation conditions. In contrast, competition authorities tend to consider tax differentials as a permanent barrier to competition and disregard any additional competition which may arise from removing that barrier.[295] As a result, the scope of the "relevant product" markets defined for competition purposes will generally be narrower than the scope of "directly competitive products" defined for the purposes of Article III:2, second sentence.

(c)   It must also be borne in mind that the notions of "competition" and of "substitutability" are relative ones. From an economic perspective, two products are not either "competitive" or "non competitive". Rather, products are "more or less" competitive. For that reason, as important as the criteria for defining a relevant market or for defining the notion of "directly competitive or substitutable products" is the degree of competition which is deemed relevant in each case. That degree will determine the standard by which the criteria are to be interpreted. That standard may vary depending on the purpose of the legal provision to be applied. It may vary also from one jurisdiction to another.

(d)   This link is expressly recognized in an EC Commission Notice on the definition of relevant markets for Competition law purposes, which states that "the concept of relevant market is closely related to the objectives pursued under Community competition policy".[296] Further,

---

[294]   The applicable EC competition regulations define the notion of "relevant product market" for the purposes of EC Competition law as follows:

> A relevant product market comprises all those products and/or services which are regarded as interchangeable or substitutable by the consumer, by reason of the products' characteristics, their prices and their intended use.

See the Commission Notice on the definition of relevant market for the purposes of Community competition law (published in OJ of 9.1.97, C 372/5, hereafter "the Notice"), para 7.

[295]   See the Commission Notice on the definition of relevant market for the purposes of Community competition law (published in OJ of 9.1.97, C 372/5, hereafter "the Notice"), at para. 42. The decision in the *Case No IV/M 938 - Guinness/Grand Metropolitan* mentioned by Korea in one of its questions to the EC provides an excellent illustration of this difference. The parties to the merger had provided to the Commission consumer surveys which suggested that all spirits were within the same relevant market. The Commission, however, disregarded those surveys because:

> where those surveys (most of which were originally aimed at addressing taxation issues) employed price-change data, the overall levels of change (which mainly reflected changes in taxation) were much higher than those normally used by competition authorities as an aid to market definition (para. 10).

[296]   Notice, para. 10.

that Notice acknowledges that the definition of the relevant market may vary depending "on the nature of the competition issue being examined."[297]

(e)   In this regard, it is clear that the objective of competition law is very different from the objective pursued by GATT Article III:2, and more generally by the WTO Agreement. The general objective of competition law is to preserve a certain degree of competition against action by the market participants. If the competition authorities of a certain country aim at maintaining a high degree of effective competition, they will apply the relevant criteria strictly, thereby arriving at a narrow definition of the relevant market.

(f)   On the other hand, the purpose of GATT Article III:2, second sentence is to prevent Members from applying internal taxation so as to afford protection to domestic production. Unlike the objective of competition law, the objective of Article III:2, second sentence, is furthered by a broad interpretation of the relevant criteria, rather than a strict one.

(g)   For the above reasons, the EC is of the view that the decisions taken by its competition authorities with regard to the definition of relevant product markets are devoid of relevance for the purposes of applying the notion of "directly competitive or substitutable products" in this dispute.

(h)   In this regard, a parallelism can be drawn to the notion of "like product". The criteria for applying the notion of "like products" are the same in all the GATT provisions where that notion is found. Yet, in *Japan - Taxes on Alcoholic Beverages II*, the Appellate Body confirmed that the notion of "like products" is a relative one which may have a different scope in each GATT provision concerned.[298] In Article III:2, first sentence, it must be construed narrowly. In other GATT provisions, it may be construed more broadly. *A fortiori*, the notion of "directly competitive or substitutable" may also have a different scope in Article III:2 of GATT and in the competition laws of Members, which pursue an altogether different objective.

(i)   More relevant for the interpretation of GATT Article III:2 is the case law of the European Court of Justice (ECJ) regarding the application of Article 95 of the EC Treaty,[299] whose wording is almost identical to that of GATT Article III:2 and therefore, unlike EC Competition

---

[297]   Notice, para. 12.

[298]   Appellate Body Report on *Japan - Taxes on Alcoholic Beverages II, supra*, at 113.

[299]   Article 95 of the EC Treaty reads as follows in the pertinent part:

No Member State shall impose, directly or indirectly, on the products of other member States any internal taxation of any kind in excess of that imposed directly or indirectly on similar domestic products.

Furthermore, no member State shall impose on the products of other Member States any internal taxation of such nature as to afford indirect protection to other products.

Law, shares a similar purpose. In a long line of cases, the ECJ has concluded that all distilled spirits are either "similar" (the equivalent concept of "like") or "directly competitive or substitutable".[300]

7.5.   In response to a question concerning the relevance of production processes to assessing whether products are like or directly competitive or substitutable, the European Communities states that:

(a)   Similarities or differences in production processes may be relevant only to the extent that they affect the characteristics of the products. This principle flows clearly from the Panel Report on *US - Standards for Reformulated and Conventional Gasoline*.[301] Although that Panel report is concerned with GATT Article III:4, the European Communities is of the view that the same principle applies also with respect to Article III:2.

(b)   In the present case, it is relevant that all distilled spirits are obtained by the same manufacturing process (distillation) because it has the consequence that all of them share the same basic physical characteristics. On the other hand, differences regarding the method of distillation (continuous or pot-still), the method of filtration (through white birch or other methods) or the production volume (artisanal v. industrial) are irrelevant because they have either no impact at all or only a minor impact on the physical characteristics and end uses of the products.

B.   United States

7.6.   In response to a question whether if two products have a very low cross-price elasticity that is sufficient to consider them directly competitive or substitutable products, the United States asserts that:

(a)   The standard that should be used to establish that two products are "directly competitive or substitutable" within the meaning of Article III:2 is a case-by-case examination that may consider a number of factors. There is no one standard that can operate across all cases.

---

[300]   The standard reasoning followed by the ECJ in those cases is the following:
"There is, in the case of spirits considered as a whole, an indeterminate number of beverages which must be classified as "similar products" within the meaning of the first paragraph of Article 95, although it may be difficult to decide this in specific cases, in view of the nature of the factors implied by distinguishing criteria such as flavour and consumer habits. Secondly, even in cases in which it is possible to recognise a sufficient degree of similarity between the products concerned, there are nevertheless, in the case of all spirits, common characteristics which are sufficiently pronounced to accept that in all cases there is at least partial or potential competition. It follows that the application of the second paragraph of Article 95 may come into consideration in cases in which the relationship of similarity between the specific varieties of spirits remains doubtful or contested" (Judgement of the ECJ of 27 February 1980, *Commission of the European Communities v Kingdom of Denmark*, Case 171/78, ECR 1980, 447, at para. 12).

[301]   Panel Report on *US - Standards for Reformulated and Conventional Gasoline*, adopted on 20 May 1996, WT/DS2/R, paras. 6.11-6.12.

Cross-price elasticity is but one factor that may be helpful in conducting an analysis of whether products are directly competitive or substitutable. It is unlikely that a very low cross-price elasticity in and of itself will be sufficient to make a determination in any particular case.

(b)   The quotation from the second US submission expresses the economic point that any shift away from one product to another in response to a relative rise in the first product's price is a sign of cross-price elasticity and therefore substitutability. However, the US response did not purport to establish what degree of substitutability was "direct" within the meaning of Article III:2. Clearly the word "directly" in the Note *Ad* Article III:2 places some limits on the scope of Article III:2. However, this case does not present a situation where it is necessary to test those limits. In this case, the products are physically similar, and several other factors support the fact that the products are directly competitive or substitutable.

(c)   The Panel should be in a position to determine substitutability largely on the basis of common physical characteristics, which are reflected in a common HS heading,[302] and the Dodwell study presents evidence of a supplementary nature. The Appellate Body in *Japan - Taxes on Alcoholic Beverages II* did not, as Korea has claimed incorrectly, require a market analysis or prescribe the use of a cross-price elasticity study as the sole means of establishing whether products are directly competitive or substitutable. To the contrary, the issue only arose because some parties argued it was inappropriate to place undue emphasis on the market place generally or such studies specifically. The Appellate Body first determined that it "did not seem appropriate" to look at the actual market in addition to physical characteristics, common end uses and tariff classification. In approving the Panel's use of the ASI cross-price elasticity study (which the Dodwell study emulated) the Appellate Body underscored that cross-price elasticity of demand was not the "decisive criterion" for its determination that the products were directly competitive or substitutable. The Appellate body Report finds no support for the suggestion that a failure to show a positive cross-price elasticity in general or a particular cross-price elasticity can be the basis for concluding that products are not directly competitive or substitutable under GATT Article III:2.

7.7.   In response to a question about whether there is a *de minimis* standard in assessing the question of "so as to afford protection", the United States argues that:

---

[302] According to the United States, contrary to Korea's allegation, the Appellate Body in *Japan - Taxes on Alcoholic Beverages II* did not reject the existence of a single tariff heading as significant guidance in examining substitutability. The Appellate Body distinguished between tariff nomenclature and tariff bindings, which it said could include a wide range of products and therefore must be viewed with caution in examining the term "like". Appellate Body Report, *supra*, at 114-115.

<table>
<tr><td>(a)</td><td>the criterion for meeting the third element of the analysis under the second sentence of Article III:2 is set out by the Appellate Body in Japan - Taxes on Alcoholic Beverages II:</td></tr>
</table>

> "[P]rotective application can most often be discerned from the design, the architecture, and the revealing structure of the measure. The very magnitude of the dissimilar taxation in a particular case may be evidence of such a protective application, as the Panel rightly concluded in this case. Most often, there will be other factors to be considered as well. In concluding this inquiry, panels should give full consideration to all the relevant facts and all the relevant circumstances in any given case".[303]

(b)   In concluding that the panel had not erred in determining that the tax was protective solely on the basis of the large differentials between tax rates applied to shochu and Western spirits, the Appellate Body appears to have reasoned that the large differences between such physically similar products could not be otherwise explained. The United States considers that the magnitude of the differences in tax rates between such similar products in this case compel the same inference. On the other hand, however, the Appellate Body did not determine that panels must find a large differential in rates in order to find protective application; the differentials in rates is addressed by the second element of the Article III:2 analysis, whether the products are not "similarly taxed".

(c)   It would not be appropriate to determine that a measure does not have a protective application simply on the basis of significantly different pre-tax prices. A number of factors can affect pre-tax prices, such as exchange rates, and recent experience has shown how quickly those factors can change. It would not be appropriate to base determination of protective effect on a "snapshot" of pre-tax prices. Instead, the Appellate Body Report makes it clear that the panel must examine all the facts and circumstances concerning the structure of the law. In this instance, the structure of Korea's Liquor Tax Law distinguishes between products on the basis of arbitrary physical characteristics in a way that can only be explained by an intention to identify and define products that happen to be imported. Combined with Korea's long history of protecting soju from imports of western spirits, the differential tax rates then further support the conclusion that the law is structured to protect imports.

(d)   There is no de minimis interpretation of the concept "so as to afford protection to domestic production." The prohibition is absolute - any measure applied so as to afford protection of a directly competitive or

---

[303]   Appellate Body Report, supra, at 120.

substitutable import that is not "similarly" taxed is providing too much protection.

(e)   In light of the Appellate Body's emphasis on the structure of the measure, it would not be appropriate to limit the inquiry to the tax differentials and require a complaining party to determine the extent to which in the current market, with respect to current products at current prices, the taxes are effective in reducing sales of imports. Such an approach would, at a minimum, be at odds with the basic principles of the WTO Agreement. As Korea's law applies obviously punitive taxes on Western spirits not on the basis of price differences, but on the basis of arbitrarily physical criteria, the higher rates adversely affect all products within the criteria - including products in a wide range of prices available in the United States.

7.8.   In response to a question concerning the price mix of exports to Korea compared to other markets, the United States argues that:

(a)   The pre-tax prices of imports reflect costs such as transportation and tariffs (20% ad valorem in Korea), costs that are not reflected in prices of domestic products. The punitive taxes on Western spirits likely contribute to higher pre-tax prices than would otherwise exist under a neutral tax structure".

(b)   The majority of imports of distilled spirits into Korea are from the European Community, and accordingly, the United States is not in a position to draw any general conclusions about marketing of obvious brands in the Korean market at this time. Aside from some bulk shipments, the overwhelming majority of US exports are of Jack Daniels and Jim Beam Whisky, brands which enjoy particular international name recognition. Such name recognition is of particular value in developing a presence in new markets due to the high costs of exporting.

(c)   The US Government does not have access to the pre-tax prices charged by distilled spirits around the world by particular brand, which, according to industry representatives, is considered confidential information by the respective companies.

7.9.   In response to Panel questions and arguments raised by Korea with respect to competition issues, the United States notes that it did not consider it would be appropriate to borrow market analysis under national competition laws in analyzing what products are "directly competitive or substitutable" for purposes of Article III:2. The United States considers it important to bear in mind the different objectives of antitrust law, on the one hand, and of GATT Article III:2 on the other. Article 3.2 of the DSU makes clear that the provisions of the GATT 1994 and other WTO agreements are to be construed "in accordance with customary rules of interpretation of public international law." As the Appellate Body has noted on several occasions, Articles 31 and 32 of the Vienna Convention of the Law of Treaties embody the customary international law of interpretation. Article 31 sets forth the basic principle that treaties are to be interpreted "in good faith in accordance with the ordinary meaning to be given to the terms of the treaty in their context and in the light of its object and purpose."

7.10.   According to the United States, consistent with this principle, GATT Article III:2 should be interpreted in the light of the overall purpose of Article III, which is "to avoid protectionism in the application of internal tax and regulatory measures."[304] Article III is an anti-discrimination provision aimed at ensuring that government measures do not skew competitive conditions in favor of domestic products. Competition laws, by contrast, address privately-created threats to market competition, regardless of whether the competing producers or products are domestic or foreign. Because the object and purpose of the two sets of rules are quite different, it would not be appropriate to borrow and apply a competition analysis in deciding whether a tax measure is consistent with GATT Article III:2.

C.   Korea

7.11.   In response to a question concerning the ingredients and comparability of pre-mixes, Korea states that:

(a)   Pre-mixes first became available in May 1994 with a view to attracting women consumers and consumers in their twenties who preferred low alcoholic beverages.[305] Pre-mixes have 10 per cent to 15 per cent alcoholic content.

(b)   Standard soju has 25 per cent alcoholic content. The salient features which distinguish premixes from standard soju are that the former contains scent, coloration and more than 2 per cent extract. To be precise, pre-mixes do not contain standard soju. The mixture is a combination of various ingredients and joojung (ethyl Alcohol) which is the raw material from which standard soju is produced.

(c)   To make the pre-mixes appeal to women, the producers first eliminated the pungent odour and taste of joojung by adding fruit scents (such as lemon and cherry). Thus, the producers add lemon/cherry juice concentrate, acerola juice concentrate, and lemon/cherry spices which cannot be added to standard soju pursuant to the law. Sweeteners such as stevioside, sugar and fructose are added in higher dosage than standard soju to give the pre-mixes a sweeter taste.

Pre-mixes	*Standard soju*
(Lemon/cherry remixes)	(Green, Chungsaek soju)
Sugar	Sugar

---

[304]   Appellate Body Report on *Japan - Taxes on Alcoholic Beverages II, supra*, at 109.

[305]   See the Sofres report: "In the past Korean women had negative sentiments towards alcohol. However, the current generation of women is drinking more frequently each year. The Korean distillers and producers reflect this trend by offering low alcoholic content drinks like ... "Lemon Soju". Please note that Korean producers do not use the term "soju" in the brand name for these premixes. Some examples of names are "Lemon 15", "Cherry 15", "Lemon Remix" and "Cherry Remix".

Citric Acid	Stevioside
Co2 Gas	Citric Acid
Lemon/Cherry concentrate	Mineral Salt
Acerola juice concentrate	Amino acid
Lemon/cherry spices	Solbitol
Food colours	
Fructose	
Stevioside	

(d)   Korea further stated that standard soju is served in a typical small glass, and is rarely if ever drunk mixed. Standard soju is served "straight", and commonly drunk with meals.

(e)   Pre-mixes, otherwise known as soju-based cocktails, have quite a different, much sweeter taste than standard soju (they are also classified as liqueurs in the liquor tax law). They have a lower alcohol content as well. Their composition is different, as indicated above. Soju-based cocktails are not suited for consumption with meals.

(f)   It is inappropriate to associate pre-mixes with standard soju, in the same way that it would be inappropriate to associate Bailey's (a blend of, *inter alia*, fresh cream and whisky) with whisky. Bailey's and soju-based cocktails are classified under the same heading, with other liqueurs, in the Korean liquor tax law.

(g)   Finally, it is easy to overestimate the popularity of soju-based cocktails, as the European Communities has done. As their novelty has worn off, the increases in sales of them have tapered off.

7.12.   In response to a question concerning whether Article III:2 covers potential or future competition, Korea states that:

(a)   If "potential competition" refers to competition that would exist "but for" an allegedly discriminatory tax, Korea could imagine that potential competition falls within the scope of Article III:2. Korea's discussion of "pre-tax" prices addressed this argument and shows that even if the effect of the tax were eliminated, the products at issue would not be in direct competition. The pre-tax prices of the products at issue, according to the complainants' own figures, range from 400 per cent more expensive than soju before tax to more than 1 800 per cent more expensive.

(b)   If by "future competition", the panel means competition that would appear at some point in the future if, for example, consumers changed their habits, or if the pre-tax price of whisky fell to the level of soju, then Korea considers that "future competition" is not covered by Article III:2. Complainants cannot base Article III:2 allegations on speculations about future changes in the market. Rather, complainants must wait to bring a WTO case if and when relevant changes appear.

7.13.   In response to a question about the possible explanations of apparent inconsistencies in the Dodwell study, Korea states that:

(a)   Choice subject to large random elements

(i)   If one were seeking an explanation of ostensible inconsistencies of choice in real life, the idea that choice is subject to a large random element would be an obvious first hypothesis. It leads to a view of buyers choosing good X one day or hour and good Y the next, depending on mood or a host of other circumstances. The relative price of X and Y might affect the frequency with which each is chosen. In a short enough period of observation, however, the random element might dominate, so that some consumers will appear to respond to a rise in the price of X by buying less Y.

(ii)   As an explanation of inconsistencies in answers to a questionnaire based upon hypothetical prices, however, this hypothesis is problematic. An interview will normally be short, so that mood or other factors that might drive the purchase of one good rather than another might reasonably be assumed to be constant throughout the interview. If that assumption is correct, however, random elements affecting demand cannot be called upon to explain inconsistencies in results.

(iii)   Of course, the assumption that mood is constant through the interview may be false. If it is false, however, interpretation of the results of the survey faces a different problem. In the present context, for example, the purpose of the Dodwell survey is to isolate the effects of changes in prices from other factors that might affect demand. But if mood or other factors change within the interview, or if respondents are allowed to imagine themselves making one choice in one mood, and another choice in another mood, the interview has failed to isolate changes in prices from other factors affecting demand. Its results will give a false picture of the effect of prices on demand.

(b)   Mistakes in reporting responses

A simple explanation of the inconsistencies is that respondents are being consistent, but that interviewers are mis-reporting their responses. This hypothesis is included for completeness only.

(c)   Possible explanation of unexpected responses

Were the responses in unexpected directions, but consistent, the facts to be explained would be different. We offer below two hypotheses that might in principle explain unexpected results, and also comment on why these seem incapable of explaining inconsistencies in result.

(d)   Gifts and prices

(i)   Respondents who think they are being asked about a single bottle purchase, may answer questions with the purchase of a bottle of spirits as a gift in mind. In that case, however, they might respond to price changes in ways that appear perverse. A reduction in price might make a spirit less desirable as a gift, and an increase might make it more desirable. The position would be further complicated if respondents answered some questions thinking in terms of gifts, and some questions thinking in terms of personal consumption.

(ii)   But while the gift motive might in principle explain ostensibly perverse reactions to changes in price, it lacks explanatory power in the present case. That is because, first, it is inconsistent rather than perverse reactions that are primarily at issue here. Second, the inconsistent reactions in chart 2 are responses to changes in the price of soju, not whisky, and standard soju is not usually given as a gift: it is too cheap to play that role.

(e)   Whisky and soju are complements in consumption

(i)   There is no great difficulty in imagining circumstances in which two alcoholic beverages are complements, at least for some drinkers. In some communities, for example, whisky is typically drunk with a beer "chaser". Alternatively, drinkers might follow a ritual of drinking two rounds of whisky and then two rounds of beer. In either case, beer and whisky might behave as complements rather than substitutes - rather than a rise in the price of whisky increasing the quantity consumed of beer, which is what would happen if beer and whisky were substitutes, the rise in the price of whisky might reduce the quantity consumed of beer.

(ii)   Drinkers may act as if whisky and a beer chaser, for example, is a single drink. Thus, an increase in the price of either beer or whisky will reduce the number of drinks taken. It will therefore reduce the quantity consumed of the drink whose price has remained constant.

(iii)   The problem, though, is that in Dodwell Chart 2, whisky and soju act like substitutes when the price of soju rises from 1 000 to 1 100 won, but like complements when the price of soju rises from 1 100 to 1 200. It is not the latter fact that is hard to explain (at least in principle!) - it is the inconsistency between the two.

(iv)   One might think in terms of a population made up of some drinkers who regard scotch and soju as substitutes, and some who regard them as complements. For some price changes the first group dominates, while for others the second group determines the direction of the net change.

(v)   Before pressing along that theoretical path, however, it is well to recall what is driving the problem. At issue is the effect of a 100-won change in the price of a bottle of soju[306]. But for soju and scotch to be complements, they must be drunk in a tight combination with one another. What then counts is the price of the combination. But with the price of scotch so many multiples of the price of soju, a 10 per cent change in the price of soju will have only a very small effect on the price of a soju-whisky *combination*. For a 100-won rise in the price of soju to cause the number selecting premium whisky to fall from 41 to 36, and the number selecting standard scotch to fall from 56 to 49 requires a sensitivity to price that is nether plausible nor suggested by anything else in the Dodwell findings.

(f)   Korea concludes by noting that in its first submission, it described the inconsistencies as "troubling", but commented that the Dodwell Study "has much more serious problems".[307] Korea sees no reason to change that assessment.

(g)   Korea also continues to believe that the attention of respondents might have wandered during their progress though the 16 sets of hypothetical prices offered them by Dodwell interviews (to say nothing of that of the interviewers themselves). That hypothesis is the one that seems to best fit the facts.

7.14.   In response to a question concerning the water content of distilled and diluted soju, Korea states that:

(a)   For the benefit of the Panel Korea hereby provides an answer related to the water content of both standard and distilled soju and also explains briefly the manufacturing process to better understand the differences.

(b)   In case of standard soju, water is added before and after distillation. Prior to distillation, one steams tapioca and/or sweet potatoes so that they are in a mashed form. Second, water is added. Third, enzymes and yeast are added so that the mashed tapioca and/or sweet potatoes will ferment. This fermentation process will lead to a 10-11 per cent alcoholic content liquid which is in a sludge form. The ingredients constitute 20 per cent, water 79.9 per cent and yeast 0.1 per cent.

(c)   Then the material undergoes continuous distillation until one obtains as pure an alcohol as possible (95 per cent ethyl alcohol). After distillation, water is added and then six to seven additives are inserted. Ethyl alcohol (joojung) constitutes 26.4 per cent and water constitutes 73.6 per cent at this stage.

---

[306]   At the current exchange rate, 100 won equals US$ 0.0691 and ECU 0.0637 (as of 23 March 1998).

[307]   See Attachment 2 of Korea, p. 6.

(d)   Contrary to the notion that standard soju is simply a diluted form of distilled soju, the latter uses different base materials, primarily rice and sometimes other grains. Water is added only prior to distillation. No water is added after distillation. Producing a 45 per cent distilled soju through single distillation is a know-how developed by Korean producers over several hundred years.

(e)   In case of distilled soju, one takes white rice and steams it. Afterwards, one adds water and yeast which acts as a catalyst to commence the fermentation process. The ingredients take up 40 per cent, water 59 per cent and yeast 1 per cent. After the material ferments, one has a product which has a low alcoholic content. Then the fermented product undergoes a single distillation so that the final product has 45 per cent alcoholic content. No water is added after distillation.

The percentage of water added is illustrated in the following chart:

	Before distillation	*After distillation*
Standard soju	79.9%	73.6%
Distilled soju	59.0%	0%

7.15.   In response to a question about the physical differences between exports of soju and shochu to Japan, Korea states that:

(a)   The three leading brands of standard soju exported to Japan are Jinro, Doosan's Green and Bohae. Jinro and Doosan only use sugar and citric acid in their products exported to Japan. Bohae's standard soju exported to Japan uses no additives. On the other hand, Korean standard soju can use seven additives.

(b)   The difference in additives can be illustrated by the difference in additives by the two products Jinro exports to Japan.

	Jinro Gold	**Jinro Export**
Alcohol content	25%	25%
Citric acid	x	x
Sugar (natural)		x
Fructose	x	
Oligosaccharide	x	
Stevioside	x	
Refined salt	x	
Amino acid	x	

(c)   The difference in the number of ingredients leads to different consumption patterns. In Japan, shochu A is almost always consumed with water, either warm or cold, other beverages and on the rocks. In Korea, standard soju is almost always consumed straight.

(d)   The source of this information is enterprises such as Jinro that are engaged in marketing these products on the Japanese market, and who have found it necessary to export soju to satisfy Korean expatriates living in Japan, and to produce a different product to meet the needs of Japanese consumers.

(e)   This can be easily verified by the Panel by looking at the bottles of Jinro Gold (the Korean soju, which targets the Korean residents in Japan) and Jinro export (targeting Japanese consumers) provided by Korea. The labels of Jinro Gold contain Korean characters, whereas those of Jinro Export contain no Korean characters.

(f)   The labels of these bottles also give an indication regarding their tax treatment in Japan. The label on the back of Jinro Gold refers to "spirits", whereas the label on the back of Jinro Export refers to "shochu A".

7.16.   In response to a question concerning a hypothetical comparison of an expensive bottle of wine and a cheaper table wine, Korea states that:

(a)   For the purposes of Article III:2, in order to find that two products are "like", one must show to begin with, that the two products are "directly competitive or substitutable". According to the panel in the recent *Japan - Taxes on Alcoholic Beverages II*:

> "Like" products should be viewed as a subset of directly competitive or substitutable products.[308]

Accordingly, a finding of "likeness" in Article III:2 presupposes an even stronger competitive relationship between two products than a finding of directly competitive or substitutable products.

(b)   Price has an impact upon the competitive relationship between products. Where prices vary greatly, this can mean that two products do not compete. In the example given by the Panel of cheap wine and a rare Bordeaux, it might be that in a particular market the large difference in price means that the two products do not compete, and are therefore neither "like" nor directly competitive or substitutable products. This is so because most consumers will not consider a $1 000 bottle of wine to be a substitute for a $5 bottle of wine, notwithstanding apparent similarities concerning physical characteristics between the two products (colour, packaging, alcoholic content).

(c)   That conclusion is likely to be supported by other divergences. Indeed, the fact that a person chooses to pay more for a rare bordeaux when he or she has the option of buying a cheap table wine is a measure of the differences between the two products. Between a cheap wine and a vintage bordeaux, for example, important differences might be the age of the wines, the type, year, and provenance of the grapes used, the blending, the way the wine was cared for and stored, all of which have an impact on the organoleptic qualities of the wine. The rare bordeaux might come from a famous vineyard or

---

[308]   See Panel Report on *Japan - Taxes on Alcoholic Beverages II, supra*, at para. 6.22.

chateau, and the purchaser might not be interested in drinking the wine at all, or at least not with a regular meal. He might see it as an investment or as a wine for very special occasions These types of differences would also support the conclusion that these products are not "like" or directly competitive or substitutable products.

(d)   In the case at hand, Korea has shown that price is an important factor in the directly competitive or substitutable products, and therefore, "like" product analysis. The complainants' own evidence (notably, the Dodwell Study) indicated that there are no overlaps in the prices of standard and premium soju on the one hand, and western-style spirits on the other hand. Thus, the most expensive form of standard soju (i.e., premium) is still much less expensive than the cheapest western-style spirits. In contrast, prices of wine might cover a whole range of prices.

(e)   Moreover, the products in this case also differ in a number of other ways, in particular in their physical characteristics and end uses. Korea maintains that an overall assessment of the products at issue in this case must lead to the conclusion that these products are neither "like" nor directly competitive or substitutable products.

7.17.   In response to a question about the likeness or competitiveness of physically similar products, Korea states that:

(a)   When two products are physically identical in the sense that no known test or procedure can distinguish between them, it seem to Korea that the products must be like. Physical identity in this strict sense, however, seems to imply either that the market prices of the products are the same, or that only one of them is sold, *or* that consumers are ignorant of their likeness. If two products both appear in a market, selling at different prices, but chemists, physicists, or other experts maintain that they cannot distinguish between them, there is therefore a problem. In effect, there is a conflict of evidence experts say they cannot detect any differences but consumers of the products act as if they can.

(b)   In that event, Korea does not believe that the expert evidence alone is enough to declare the products either "like" or "directly competitive or substitutable products". To take that step, it is necessary to refute the hypotheses that the expert tests are incapable of detecting differences that are significant to consumers; or that the experts have not properly designed or targeted their tests to detect them; or that they are misinterpreting their results.

(c)   With respect to "physically identical or nearly so", it seems to Korea that the addition of "or nearly so" to "physically identical" raises difficulties. One problem is circularity; defining "nearly so" so that any change in the product that has only a small effect on consumer demand is judged to leave a "nearly identical" product, whereas any change that has a substantial effect on demand is judged to lead to a different product. Such a definition of "nearly identical" would render this question meaningless - if such a definition is used, products that fall under it are likely to be directly competitive or substitutable products.

(d)   Korea believes, however, that many changes that are "small" in a technical sense will lead to products that are very different by the test of market performance. To take one example, the addition to a food or drink product of small amounts of an unpleasant substance, or a substance perceived to be unpleasant, may, if known to consumers, cause demand for the product to fall to zero, even though the substance does not alter taste or threaten health and its presence cannot be detected by consumers. The "small" addition may convert a sought-after product into one that is no longer saleable at any price. Moreover, the elasticity of substitution between the original product and the "nearly identical" product may be zero or insignificant. Korea is far from convinced that "nearly identical products" with different market demands and prices and a low or zero cross-price elasticity of demand should be considered directly competitive or substitutable products.

(e)   Korea believes that products may be physically identical or nearly so but not directly competitive or substitutable products. Korea believes that differences that are small in a technical sense may be important to buyers, and that performance in the market place is the ultimate test of directly competitive or substitutable. Alternatively stated, Korea does not believe that there is any technical short-cut that can determine direct competitiveness or substitutability without reference to market performance.

(f)   The relevant physical distinctions are those that are important to customers. The WTO is concerned with markets, and markets are ultimately dependent on consumer tastes and habits. In the present case, regarding spirits, Korea has pointed to the following distinguishing physical characteristics:

　　　　　(i)   raw materials, additives

　　　　　(ii)   production process

　　　　　(iii)   alcohol percentage

　　　　　(iv)   flavour, smell and colour

(g)   Together with the difference in end-use and price, the distinctions indicate the lack of a directly competitive and substitutable relationship between Korean sojus on the one hand, and the western-style liquors at issue on the other hand.

(h)   When looking at physical characteristics, the appropriate measure of relevance is the importance to consumers. In the present case, Korea has argued that the differences in physical characteristics, together with other market-related factors (such as price and end use), indicate that none of the western-style liquors competes directly with any of the two Korean sojus on the Korean market.

7.18.   In response to a question about comparing premium diluted soju to standard diluted soju, Korea states that:

(a)   Korea included premium diluted soju in its comparison of diluted soju with other liquors because the differences between premium and standard diluted soju, as compared to the differences between diluted soju (including premium soju) and imported liquors, are of minor importance. Premium diluted soju is only an "upgraded" version of standard soju. Thus, premium diluted soju could be compared to a Renault's compact car "Clio" with leather seats which, although it is a luxury version, is still a compact car. To proceed with this analogy: imported liquors are Mercedeses, Jaguars and Rolls Royces compared to diluted soju. The price of a Renault Clio, even equipped with leather seats, is substantially lower than the cheapest Mercedes, let alone a Jaguar or Rolls Royce.

(b)   By taking the same criteria by which one distinguishes products in a like-or directly competitive or substitutable products-analysis, the differences resulting from a premium and standard comparison are small. For example, the price difference between standard diluted soju and premium diluted soju amounts to a factor of 1.76, as opposed to a factor of 5 for the cheapest imported liquor (gin), and more than 19 for the most expensive imported liquor (cognac/brandy).

(c)   For one of the leading premium diluted soju brands, Kimsatgat, the primary difference has been that one of the seven possible additives (stevioside) is replaced by honey. In contrast, for the imported liquors at issue (whisky, vodka, gin, brandy, rum) there are differences in taste, physical characteristics, and end-use. The taste of gin, for instance, is quite different from the taste of diluted (including premium) soju, due to the different physical composition. Gin is not drunk with Korean meals, whereas diluted (including premium) soju is, and so on.

(d)   This analysis led Korea to the conclusion that standard diluted soju and premium diluted soju are sufficiently similar and sufficiently competitive that they should be grouped together in the analysis required by this case. To be sure, Korea has treated distilled soju separately from diluted soju, as between these two products the differences are significant (price, use, marketing, raw material, tax classification).

7.19.   In response to a question about competition between types of whiskies, Korea states that:

(a)   There is no reason to assume that imported whiskies are not directly competing with or unlike domestic whiskies because of the price differences cited. The prices cited concern individual brands. Both domestic and imported whiskies cover the whole gamut of prices (for instance, cheap whiskies are bottled in Korea, but also expensive ones). Taking into account all sales, domestic whisky is on average somewhat more expensive than imported whisky.[309]

(b)   There are no other differences (such as physical characteristics or end use) to suggest that imported and domestic whisky are positioned differently on the Korean market. Next to the small difference in price, this is relevant as well. As Korea has emphasized before, the decision of whether products are "like" or directly competitive or substitutable products is a matter of an overall appreciation of their relationship, weighing all the relevant factors. Of course, no distinction is made in Korea's liquor and education tax rates between imported and domestic whisky.

7.20.   In response to a question about the negotiating history of Article III and *Ad* Article III, Korea states that:

(a)   These examples show that physically different products may be in a sufficiently close competitive relationship for Article III:2 to apply. Whether that is, in fact, the case, depends on a case-by-case analysis, according to the Appellate Body in *Japan - Taxes in Alcoholic Beverages II*.

(b)   It may well be that apples and oranges are directly competitive or substitutable products in certain markets. Then again, one can conceive of a number of reasons why such fruits are not directly competitive or substitutable (e.g., with breakfast it is more common to have orange rather than apple juice; most consumers can make orange juice themselves, but not apple juice; apple pie is more common in many countries than orange pie; in countries where oranges are not grown they are more expensive than apples; etc.). In fact, certain fresh fruits, such as bananas, have been found to be in a market of their own, at least in the EC market.[310] Such determinations, also in respect of the other products cited, cannot be made in the abstract.

(c)   These examples then are relevant to the present case, in that they illustrate that products with different physical characteristics may be directly competitive or substitutable products. This was also shown in the *Japan - Taxes on Alcoholic Beverages II*, where whisky and certain other spirits were found to be in a directly competitive or substitutable product-relationship with Japanese shochu. That case also shows, however, that such findings depend on a factual analysis of individual markets.

7.21.   In response to a question concerning legal requirements for sweetness in soju, Korea states that there is no legal requirement regarding the minimum sugar

---

[309] See Korea's Attachment 5.

[310] Judgement of the Court of Justice of the European Communities of 14 February 1978, Case 27/76, *United Brands Company and United Brands Continental BV v. Commission of the European Communities*, 1978 ECR 207.

content for soju in Korea. The sweeter taste of Korean soju can be explained by the use of such additives as stevioside and/or aspartam, which are 150-300 times sweeter than sugar.

7.22.   In response to a question about consumption of soju with food, Korea states that the bulk of standard soju is consumed with meals. Other than this, a small proportion is consumed in some other on-premise locations. Some standard soju will also be consumed at home without a meal (finishing a bottle after the meal is over, for instance).

7.23.   In response to a question about uses of distilled soju as a gift, Korea states that, as has been emphasized in Korea's first submission, distilled soju is an artisanal product that occupies a "niche" in the Korean market, and is mainly given as a gift. When distilled soju is received as a gift, it is usually consumed with meals on traditional occasions such as New Year's Day and Korean "Thanksgiving" (August 15). Other instances in which distilled soju is consumed are rare. In some very expensive and traditional Korean restaurants and Japanese restaurants, distilled soju is offered, at very high prices.

7.24.   In response to a question whether the questions and methodology in the Dodwell study are similar to those used in the ASI study in *Japan- Taxes on Alcoholic Beverages II*, and whether Korea disagrees with that Panel's use of the ASI study in reaching its conclusions, Korea states that it is confident that the Panel in *Japan - Taxes on Alcoholic Beverages II* examined the ASI study with appropriate care. Korea, however, has not studied the detail of the ASI report, which was submitted to a different panel in a different case, and is concerned with a market in a different country. It is therefore unable to comment on the merits of the ASI study. Moreover, Korea doubts the value of a post-mortem on either the ASI study itself, or the use of it by the Panel in *Japan - Taxes on Alcoholic Beverages II*. If the ASI study is free of the flaws of the Dodwell study, its use by the Panel was proper, but that fact cannot provide a sound argument for reliance on the flawed Dodwell study in this proceeding. If the ASI study is as defective as the Dodwell Study, the fact that the Panel relied on it cannot make a sound case for repeating the same mistake.

7.25.   In response to a question concerning cross-price elasticity, Korea stated:

(a)   Korea agrees with the implied observation that the position of the US on this issue is inconsistent with that of the EC.

(b)   To discuss the comments of either party, however, a context is needed. One important element of such a context is the kind of world to which the comments are intended to apply - is it a theoretical world in which information is fully and freely available, or the real world in which accurate information is difficult to get?

(c)   The US suggestion that +*any* shift ... should be interpreted as a sign of positive cross-elasticity and therefore substitution" seems to Korea to cast the Article III:2 net too widely if it is intended to apply to a full-information world, and therefore to be a statement of principle. That criterion would make spirits, beer and wine DSSP, spirits and soft drinks quite possibly DCSP, and beer and soft drinks almost certainly DCSP. It seems unlikely that any WTO member thought that membership entailed an obligation to apply the same rate of tax to such a wide range of products - and few, if any, do.

(d)   If the US criterion is intended for application to the real world, however, imperfections of information provide additional reasons to reject it. In the real world, there are problems of error in the construction and organization of samples and problems of statistical error - to say nothing of the blundering of those "fallible human beings" that have become a feature of recent EC argument in this case. Even if the US criterion were accepted in principle, the existence of such sources of mistakes in estimation would require a substantial margin to allow for errors in estimation - a margin that the US position denies.

7.26.   In response to a question about a *de minimis* standard for the question of "so as to afford protection", Korea stated:

(a)   If products that are only very weakly substitutable can be DCSP, a tax on a domestic product that is lower than the tax on a DCSP foreign product may have only a very small effect on the quantity demanded of the foreign product in the country applying the tax. Korea considers that such a small effect should not be sufficient to meet the "so as to afford protection" requirement of the second sentence Article III:2.

(b)   Indeed, Korea submits that *de minimis* protective effects do not trigger the application of the second sentence. This is based on the text and structure of this provision, which is unlike the hard-and-fast prohibitions incorporated in the first sentence of Art. III:2, or such other GATT provisions as Art. I or XI.

(c)   To begin with, where DCSP are concerned, not just any tax differential is problematic. Only tax differentials that are more than *de minimis* can become a problem. WTO members are thus left with some flexibility in designing their tax systems.

(d)   Similarly, the insertion of the "so as to afford protection "requirement in the second sentence of Article III:2 must also have been meant to allow governments a measure o flexibility. Article III:2 only interferes in a Member's tax system where an (appreciable) tax discrepancy raises real concerns about protectionism.

(e)   Therefore, Korea considers that where the tax differential can only be said to have a minimal protective effect, it should not be considered to have met the "so as to afford protection" threshold.

7.27.   In response to a question concerning the product mix of imports, Korea stated:

(a)   Under a system of specific taxes, all bottles of scotch, for example, have the same tax whatever their price, so the specific tax raises the price of high-price brands by a smaller percentage than the price of low-price brands. Alternatively stated, the specific tax lowers the price of high-priced scotch relative to low-priced scotch, and therefore provides an incentive to the purchase of high-price brands.

(b)   Korean taxes on sprits, however, are *ad valorem* - they have no effect on the price of one spirit in a particular class (for example, whisky, brandy) relative to another member of that class. Korea therefore sees no basis for the proposition of the EC that the Korean tax system favours the purchase of high-price rather than low-price brands of scotch.

(c)   Korea does not know whether its residents import a higher proportion of high-priced scotch than those of similar countries. If it is a fact, however, Korea believes that an explanation for it must be sought elsewhere than in its tax system.

VIII. THIRD-PARTY ARGUMENTS

A.   *Canada*

8.1.   Canada's submission is limited to the issue of the criteria to be taken into account in assessing whether a difference in tax rates is applied so as to afford protection to domestic production.

8.2.   Canada asserts that it welcomed the outcome of the *Japan - Taxes on Alcoholic Beverages II* case and was pleased with the principles for the interpretation and application of Article III of GATT 1994, set out by the Appellate Body in its report. Canada notes that the issues which arise in the context of the Korean liquor tax regime bear strong resemblance to matters which were under dispute in *Japan - Taxes on Alcoholic Beverages II* and accordingly, the Panel's disposition of the present dispute should be guided by the principles established in the reports of the Panel and Appellate Body in that case.

8.3.   Canada notes that all of the participants appear to have embraced the principles of the Appellate Body report in approaching this case and in particular with respect to the interpretation of the second sentence of Article III:2 of GATT 1994. In Canada's view, all participants appear to agree that the phrase "so as to afford protection" in Article III:1, as it applied to the second sentence of Article III:2, should be interpreted only with respect to objective effects and that no subjective element of intent should be taken into consideration. Canada urges the Panel to base its decision in the present case on these principles.

8.4.   In that context, having examined the submissions and evidence presented thus far, Canada agrees with the European Communities and the United States that the assessment of whether the measures are applied so as to afford protection to domestic production involves an objective analysis. Canada further agrees that the facts and circumstances regarding the "structure of the measures" as well as their "overall application on domestic as compared to imported products" demonstrate that the Korean measures at issue are applied so as to afford protection to the domestic production of soju in Korea.

8.5.   Canada stresses that in examining the "design, architecture and revealing structure" of a measure, only objective factors should be taken into account. For example, as noted by the Appellate Body in *Japan - Taxes on Alcoholic Beverages II*, the magnitude of dissimilar taxation (which is an objective factor that can be discerned from the structure of a measure) in and of itself can be evidence of protective application.[311] In fact, in Canada's view, given the magnitude of the tax differentials in the dispute at hand, it is unnecessary to examine any other factors.[312]

8.6.   Thus, in Canada's view, assessing whether a measure is applied so as to afford protection to domestic production is an analysis to be based on objective criteria, and in this case, the amount of the tax differential is sufficient to make a finding that the measures at issue are applied in a manner that protects domestic production.

B.   Mexico

1.   Background

8.7.   Mexico claims that since 1949, the Government of Korea has used various measures to protect its domestic production of soju such as quotas and exceedingly high tariffs. Until 1989, Korea maintained quotas on bulk imports of whisky, and until July of that year, it prohibited the import of bottled whisky.

8.8.   Mexico further claims that it was not until the end of the 1980s that Korea began to liberalize these barriers to the import of distilled spirits, and subsequently, in the wake of the Uruguay Round, it committed itself to reduce its tariffs of 100 per cent *ad valorem* to 30 per cent *ad valorem* in ten annual periods. Its current bound tariff is 79 per cent *ad valorem* for almost all spirits of heading 22.08 of the Harmonized Commodity Description and Coding System (HS).

8.9.   Mexico asserts that at the beginning of the 1990s Korea reduced some of its internal taxes. In the case of the liquor tax, as of 1 July 1991 Korea reduced the rate applicable to whisky and brandy from 200 per cent to 150 per cent; in January 1994 to 120 per cent; and in January 1996 to 100 per cent. The category "other liquors" benefited from a single reduction from 100 per cent to 80 per cent in July 1991. A tax of 35 per cent was levied on soju[313] until 1991, when soju was divided into two subcategories, "diluted soju" and "distilled soju", taxed at 35 per cent and 50 per cent respectively.

8.10.   Mexico further asserts that in 1990 the Korean Government began to apply the Education Tax Law to certain spirits, thus offsetting to a certain extent the reduction in the Liquor Tax. The Education Tax is a surtax applied to the sale of certain products pursuant to the application of the other taxes. In this case it is levied upon the Liquor Tax.

8.11.   The application of the Liquor Tax Law in conjunction with the Education Tax Law favours the marketing of soju to the detriment of other spirits, thus affecting the marketing of the latter.

---

[311]   Appellate Body Report, *supra*, at 122.

[312]   Canada notes that according to the EC and the US, the magnitude of the tax differentials at issue in this dispute appear to be larger than those found to be sufficient evidence of protective application in *Japan - Taxes on Alcoholic Beverages II*. In Canada's view however, even if the Panel were to find it necessary to take into account additional evidence, the other factors presented by the EC and the US are more than sufficient to establish protective application.

[313]   According to Section I-A of Korea's Schedule, soju belongs to tariff heading 2208.90.4000.

2.   *Legal Aspects*

(a)   General

8.12.   Mexico claims that:

(a)   The differential between the internal taxes applied to soju and other imported spirits is a *prima facie* violation of Korea's obligations under Article III.2 of the GATT 1994 and, ultimately, constitutes a case of nullification or impairment of the benefits accruing to Mexico under the said Agreement;

(b)   because it is a *prima facie* violation of Korea's obligations under the GATT 1994, it is up to Korea to rebut the charge.

(b)   Article III.2, first sentence

8.13.   Mexico notes that the first sentence of Article III. 2 of the GATT 1994 stipulates that:

"the products of the territory of any contracting party imported into the territory of any other contracting party shall not be subject, directly or indirectly, to internal taxes or other internal charges of any kind in excess of those applied, directly or indirectly, to like domestic products".

8.14.   Mexico argues that according to the Appellate Body in *Japan - Taxes on Alcoholic Beverages II*, for a tax measure to be in conformity with the first sentence of Article III.2 of the GATT 1994, it is necessary to determine, "first, whether the taxed imported and domestic products are 'like' and second, whether the taxes applied to the imported products are 'in excess of' those applied to the like domestic products".[314]

8.15.   Mexico considers that Korea has contravened the first sentence of Article III.2 of the GATT 1994 for the following reasons:

(a)   Soju is a like product to the spirits of HS heading 22.08.[315]

(i)   The notion of "like products" varies according to the provision of the GATT 1994 to which it applies. Thus, in practice, likeness of products is established on a case-by-case basis. With respect to Article III.2, the practice of various panels[316] in the past suggests the application of the criteria of final use of the product in a given market, consumer taste and habits, and the properties, nature and quality of the products.

(ii)   Spirits of HS heading 22.08, including tequila and mescal, have the same final use as soju in that they are drunk on their

---

[314]   Appellate Body Report, *supra*, para. 1 of Section H, pages 18-19.

[315]   This heading includes tequila and mescal, which are Mexican products.

[316]   See *Border Tax Adjustments* (L/3464, 18S/97); *The Australian Subsidy on Ammonium Sulphate (BISD II/188); EEC - Measures on Animal Feed Proteins*, adopted on 14 March 1978, (BISD 25S/49); *Spain - Tariff Treatment of Unroasted Coffee*, adopted on 11 June 1981 (BISD 28S/102); *Japan - Taxes on Alcoholic Beverages I, supra;* and *United States - Taxes on Petroleum and certain Imported Substances, supra.*

own, with spicy food "because the drink's harshness cuts the spiciness of the food." They also correspond to the tastes and habits of consumers of spirits and are equivalent in terms of their properties, their nature and their quality. Mexico states that it should be noted that soju like tequila and mescal, is divided into two categories: white tequila and mescal correspond to diluted soju, while matured tequila and mescal correspond to distilled soju. In both cases, the beverages are normally drunk on their own in small glasses. In Mexico's view, like diluted soju, both tequila and white mescal are clear very common and sold in great quantities, while matured tequila and mescal are more expensive drinks whose production process is more sophisticated and which, in many cases, are packaged in special bottles and offered as gifts.

(b)   Even if the tariff classification does not suffice in itself to determine whether the products are "like products", it should be noted that both tequila and mescal are in the same tariff subheading (six-digit classification) as soju, i.e. HS subheading 2208.90.[317] It should be recalled that the six-digit classification is the maximum level of precision in the HS. Moreover, the Appellate Body in *Japan - Taxes on Alcoholic Beverages II* stipulates that "if sufficiently detailed tariff classification can be a helpful sign of product similarity". [318]

8.16.   Mexico asserts that the taxes levied on soju are higher than those levied on tequila. To illustrate this point, Mexico submits to the Panel the following comparative table demonstrating that the taxes levied on tequila and mescal, for example, are much "higher than those levied on soju":

	Distilled *soju*	Tequila and mescal	Margin of discrimination against tequila and mescal
Liquor Tax	50%	80%	160%
Education Tax	10%	30%	300%
Education Tax (applied)	5%	24%	480%
Total taxes	55%	104%	189.1%

---

[317] Mexico states that it is particularly interesting to note that in arguing that diluted *soju* and vodka are not "like products" or "directly competitive or substitutable for each other", Korea points out that they are classified under different HS subheadings. This would imply that Korea somehow recognizes the importance of the classification of products, and that more specifically, tequila and mescal are like products and directly competitive or substitutable for each other.

[318] Report of the Appellate Body on *Japan - Taxes on Alcoholic Beverages II, supra,* Section H, para. 1(a). See also: *EEC - Measures on Animal Feed Proteins, supra; Japan - Taxes on Alcoholic Beverages I, supra;* and *United States - Standards for Reformulated and Conventional Gasoline, supra.*

	Diluted *soju*	Tequila and mescal	Margin of discrimination against tequila and mescal
Liquor Tax	35%	80%	228.6%
Education Tax	10%	30%	300%
Education Tax (applied)	3.5%	24%	685.7%
Total taxes	38.55%	104%	270.1%

(c)   Article III.2, second sentence

8.17.   Mexico notes that the second sentence of Article III.2 of the GATT 1994 stipulates that:

> [n]o contracting party shall otherwise apply internal taxes or other internal charges to imported or domestic products in a manner contrary to the principles set forth in paragraph 1.

In this connection, Mexico also notes that paragraph 1 stipulates that:

> [i]nternal taxes and other internal charges [...] should not be applied to imported or domestic products so as to afford protection to domestic production.

Furthermore, Mexico notes that according to the interpretative note to Article III.2:

> A tax conforming to the requirements of the first sentence of paragraph 2 would be considered to be inconsistent with the provisions of the second sentence only in cases where competition was involved between, on the one hand, the taxed product and, on the other hand, a directly competitive or substitutable product which was not similarly taxed.

8.18.   According to Mexico, the second sentence of Article III.2 must be read in conjunction with the interpretative note. Thus, in order to determine the inconsistency of the adopted measure, the following elements must be examined:

(a)   whether the imported and domestic products are "directly competitive or substitutable" and compete with each other;

(b)   whether the directly competitive or substitutable imported and domestic products are not "similarly taxed"; and

(c)   whether different taxes are levied on imported and domestic directly competitive or substitutable products "so as to afford protection to domestic production."

8.19.   In Mexico's view, spirits of heading 22.08, including tequila and mescal, are "like products", and hence directly competitive or substitutable products with soju.[319] And even assuming, for the sake of argument, that the Panel considers that spirits of HS heading 22.08 are not "like products" to soju, Mexico maintains that they are nevertheless "directly competitive or substitutable products".

---

[319] Appellate Body Report, *Canada - Certain Measures Concerning Periodicals, supra.*

8.20.   Mexico also notes that in *Japan - Taxes on Alcoholic Beverages II*, which presented practically the same characteristics as the case at issue the Appellate Body concluded that:

> "[s]hochu and other distilled spirits and liquors listed in HS 22.08, except for vodka, are 'directly competitive or substitutable products'".[320]

Mexico considers that this conclusion is applicable to the case of Korean soju as well, given the alleged likeness of the Korean and Japanese markets.[321] The Panel in that case accepted the evidence submitted by Japan[322] according to which a shochu-like product is produced in Korea.

8.21.   According to Mexico, Korean soju and the other spirits of HS heading 22.08 are not similarly taxed because as stated in the report of the Appellate Body in *Japan - Taxes on Alcoholic Beverages II*, if a product is not to be considered to have been "similarly taxed," the difference in taxation must be greater than *de minimis*. In the case at issue, the differences in taxes are so great and so evident that there cannot be the slightest doubt that they exceed any *de minimis* requirement that the Panel might set.

8.22.   Mexico argues that the Liquor Tax and the Education Tax introduced by Korea apply to products imported so as to afford protection to domestic production because:

(a)   Both the Liquor Tax Law and the Education Tax Law divide liquors into various categories; however, that division is arbitrary and cannot be justified under Article III of the GATT 1994. Moreover, the difference between the taxes is so great that it is impossible to argue convincingly that the differentials were not introduced with a view to protecting domestic production, as indeed they were.

(b)   Although Korea's arguments are intended to achieve the opposite result it is interesting to examine the relationship between Korea's internal taxes and its tariffs. While the internal taxes favour soju, the tariffs applied by Korea to imports are considerably higher for soju (30 per cent *ad valorem*) than for other spirits of HS heading 22.08 (where they vary between 15 and 20 per cent *ad valorem*). Mexico attributes this particular relationship to a two-stage protection mechanism: First, by levying internal taxes on soju that are considerably lower than for other spirits, Korea is protecting the soju industry in general. However, in Mexico's view, this measure puts Korean soju production in a vulnerable position with respect to other countries

---

[320]   Appellate Body Report, *supra*, Section I, at 123.

[321]   According to Mexico, although Korea, in its first submission (paragraph 91, page 21), ignores the Appellate Body in *Japan - Taxes on Alcoholic Beverages II* and states that the Panel cannot issue a report referring to all products falling under HS22.08 in the abstract, it subsequently recognizes the importance of the tariff classification in determining the likeness of the products.

[322]   Panel Report, *supra*, para. 6.35. Japan also pointed out that Korean law contained a definition similar to Japanese law, dividing *shochu* into two subcategories: "diluted *shochu*" (*shochu* A) and "distilled *shochu*" (*shochu* B).

which also produce soju/shochu,[323] obliging Korea to impose on its soju imports tariffs 50 to 100 per cent higher than those applied to other spirits. As a result, on the one hand soju imports are practically non-existent, while on the other hand, soju accounts for almost the entire Korean production of spirits.

8.23. The Government of Mexico requests that the Panel:

(a) find that Korea has contravened its obligations under the first sentence of Article III.2 of the GATT 1994 in that its internal taxes levied on various spirits of HS heading 22.08 (including tequila and mescal) are higher than those applied to soju;

(b) find that Korea has contravened its obligations under the second sentence of Article III.2 of the GATT 1994 in that its internal taxes afford protection to the domestic production of soju;

(c) find that the provisions applying to the Liquor Tax Law and the Education Tax Law nullify and impair the benefits accruing to Mexico under the GATT 1994;

(d) recommend that Korea amend its measures to bring them into conformity with the provisions of the GATT 1994.

C. *Korea's Response to Third-Party Arguments*

8.24. Korea's response to the Canadian third-party submission is that the submission is limited to the 'so as to afford protection to domestic production' requirement in the second sentence of Article III.2, second sentence. According to Korea, that submission only addresses the situation where this Panel would find a directly competitive and substitutable relationship between a particular product pair of a western-type liquor and a Korean soju.

8.25. Korea notes that Canada has not at all addressed the arguments Korea has made in its first submission in respect of this particular requirement. Korea adds that Canada's submission raises no new viewpoints.

8.26. Korea, however, takes issue with the third party submission of Mexico. According to Korea, Mexico's submission proceeds from the mistaken assumption that Mexico, being a third party, somehow has the rights of a complainant to this dispute. Korea notes that Mexico requests this Panel to find that the Korean Liquor Tax Law and Education Tax Law have nullified or impaired the benefits accruing to Mexico under the GATT 1994. In Korea's view, in order to obtain such a finding, Mexico should have taken recourse to normal dispute settlement procedures itself.324 Mexico has not done so.

8.27. Korea also argues that another misunderstanding of Mexico is that Mexico assumes that it is entitled to introduce products of its own choice into this proceeding, by referring to Tequila and Mescal. Korea does not recall that Mescal has been

---

[323] Mexico noted that Japan mentioned the likeness of its *shochu* with Korean, Chinese and Singapore *soju*.

[324] See Article 10.4 DSU.

mentioned at any point in time by the United States or the European Communities. According to Korea, Tequila was mentioned only in the most perfunctory manner. In Korea's view, if the Panel finds, as Korea has requested, that the only products properly brought into this dispute by the European Communities and the US are certain western-type liquors, notably whisky, brandy, vodka, rum and gin, then that is where the matter ends. Korea concludes that Mexico, being a third party, can only support the conclusions of one of the parties (presumably, the complainants) in this dispute and cannot expand the scope of this dispute.

8.28.   Korea notes that Mexico also argues that Korea's tax system and customs duties are suspect. Mexico refers to, 'a two-stage protection mechanism'. In this connection Mexico draws attention to the fact that Korea maintains somewhat higher tariffs on soju imports than on imports of other distilled liquors. According to Korea, the explanation is much more straightforward than the sinister intentions Mexico believes to have found. No trading partner has asked Korea to reduce its tariffs on soju, and has been willing to bargain for such a reduction.

8.29.   Significantly, according to Korea, Mexico clearly misinterprets the legal standard of Article III.2. In Korea's view, the key issue here is to determine which western-type liquors are in a sufficiently close competitive relationship with Korean sojus on the Korean market. In this connection, Korea has pointed out that standard soju is an inexpensive drink, which Koreans like to drink with their spicy meals. Mexico responds that Tequila and Mescal also go well with spicy food. Korea argues that although it may well be the case that in Mexican consumers like to drink Tequila or Mescal when they eat spicy Mexican food, that is not the issue in this dispute.

8.30.   According to Korea, the issue in this dispute is which liquor Koreans like to drink with their meals; and, more generally, what the position of Tequila and Mescal is on the Korean market (assuming for a moment these products would be concerned by this dispute, which they are not). Korea argues that Mexico has not adduced any evidence to suggest that Korean consumers like to drink Tequila and Mescal with Korea's spicy cuisine; or that Koreans drink Tequila or Mescal straight and not mixed as a cocktail. More generally, according to Korea, Mexico has not shown that Tequila or Mescal directly compete with Korean soju.

8.31.   Korea notes that Mexico makes much of the fact that the tariff classification of Mescal, Tequila and soju are the same. According to Korea, this is not true. The sub-classifications, tariff bindings, and applied rates for tequila and soju are different. Moreover, Mexico goes so far as to say that all products falling under the basic four digit classification HS 22.08 are 'like products'. Even the complainants do not go that far.

8.32.   Korea refers to the Appellate Body in the *Japan - Taxes on Alcoholic Beverages II*, wherein it was said that tariff classifications, when they are sufficiently detailed, can be a helpful indication to decide whether the relationship between products that compete directly with each other is in fact so close that they can be considered 'like'.[325] For this reason, Korea referred to the tariff classification of vodka and

---

[325] Appellate Body Report, *supra*, at 115. See also Panel Report, *supra*, at para. 6.22, stating that 'like' products are a subset of directly competitive and substitutable products.

standard soju, as this is the only product combination which the European Communities and the United States claim to be 'like'. With respect to Tequila and Mescal, the threshold question is not even met: there is no indication to begin with that these products compete directly with the Korean sojus on the Korean market, let alone that they are so competitive on the Korean market that they could conceivably be considered 'like'.

8.33.   Korea reminds Mexico, and the other complainants in this case, once more of the Panel's holding in the *Japan - Taxes on Alcoholic Beverages II*: 'consumers' tastes and habits. change from country to country'.[326] According to Korea, if this case will serve a purpose, it is to show that markets are different. Korea adds that the Japanese market is not, as asserted by Mexico, like the Korean market, the Korean market cannot simply be equated with the Mexican market, etc.

8.34.   According to Korea, therefore, before any conclusions about the possibility of discriminatory taxation within the meaning of Article III.2 are drawn, one has to make a detailed analysis of the market.

IX.   INTERIM REVIEW

9.1.   In letters dated 7 July 1998 the European Communities, the United States and Korea all requested an interim review by the panel of certain aspects of the Interim Report issued to the parties on 26 June 1998. The requests dealt with certain aspects of the descriptive portion of the Interim Report including the summaries of the arguments as well as with the Findings. None of the parties requested a further meeting with the Panel.[327]

9.2.   The major issue of concern of the parties with the descriptive portion (other than some individual and technical points which we have accommodated) was inclusion of the oral statements of the parties. In the initial version of the descriptive portion of the report, little was included from the oral statements. Oral statements generally are intended to be summaries of the written statements, not presentations of new evidence or arguments. Nonetheless, we have accommodated the requests as appropriate. However, we must note a particular difficulty in this regard in accommodating some of the comments of the United States. In part of the comments, the United States did not request specific portions of their oral statements to be included in specific spots in the descriptive portion. Instead, the United States offered a redrafting of its arguments that effectively recast whole portions of their presentation.

9.3.   We have taken note of the implicit approach of the United States that parties to a dispute should submit draft summaries of their arguments for inclusion in the descriptive portion of a panel report. However, this is an approach that should be agreed with all the parties at the outset of a proceeding rather than made by one party at the close of the proceedings. Future panels may wish to adopt such an approach. Unfortunately, no suggestions were made and no discussion of this approach

---

[326]   Panel Report, *supra* at para. 6.21.

[327]   The Interim Report constitutes Section IX of the Final Panel Report. Inclusion of this section makes the Findings portion of the Report Section X. References to paragraph numbers and comments of the parties have been adjusted accordingly.

was held at an early stage of these such proceedings. Therefore, we cannot accept the wholesale changes requested by the United States. Instead, we attempted to include in the descriptive part some of the sections of the U.S. oral statements reflecting the issues identified by the United States.

9.4.   With respect to the Findings, the European Communities requested language changes in several paragraphs. We agree with most of the recommended changes as clarifications of the existing language and have amended paragraphs 10.43, 10.53, 10.100 and 10.101, accordingly.

9.5.   The European Communities disagreed with the finding in paragraph 10.57 that the complainants provided "no evidence whatsoever" with respect to distilled alcoholic beverages not identified during the course of the proceedings. The EC's argument is that they have identified physical characteristics and end-uses common to all distilled alcoholic beverages and, therefore, that all such beverages identified in HS classification 2208 should be included. These general statements included very weak evidence with respect to products not even identified. In addition, these other beverages were not even included in the Dodwell study. Economic studies such as the Dodwell study are not necessary, but they are very useful. In other words, such market surveys are a source of information, not a limitation. Paragraph 10.57 has been amended to clarify this point.

9.6.   The United States made a number of recommended changes in language that we agree provides greater clarity to the existing language. Therefore, we have amended the language in paragraphs 10.1, 10.41, 10.42, 10.43, 10.47, 10.51, 10.74, 10.95, 10.97, 10.100 and 10.101, accordingly.[328]

9.7.   The United States requested changes in paragraphs 10.18 and 10.23 to the effect that the issues covered in those paragraphs should be decided on the basis that the Korean requests were not within the panels terms of reference. We disagree with the US position. Under the US interpretation, many jurisdictional and other issues affirmatively raised by respondents would by definition be outside the terms of reference of a panel because the terms of reference are defined by the substantive issues raised in the complaining party's request for establishment of a panel. We think any panel has the right and obligation to address fundamental jurisdictional questions and issues relating to the proper functioning of the panel raised by any party to the dispute. Accordingly, we declined to change the basis of our decision in this regard.

9.8.   The United States requested we delete paragraph 10.39 relating to discussions during the original negotiating sessions. This paragraph deals with a hypothetical and does not draw any conclusions about the specific products that were discussed in 1947-48. Rather, it was the nature of the discussion and what the discussion itself brought to light about the interpretation of *Ad* Article III:2 which is of relevance. We do not reach a legal or factual conclusion that "such products could not compete 'directly' under Article III." We have amended the language of 10.39 to provide further clarification.

---

[328] The United States made a reference to paragraphs 10.42-10.43 in one comment. We assume they were referring to paragraphs 10.41-10.42.

9.9.   The United States requested that the panel eliminate the two sentences at the end of the footnote in paragraph 10.42. In our view, the first sentence is a useful clarification. The second sentence has been eliminated.

9.10.   The United States recommended changing the fourth sentence of paragraph 10.48. We assume the United States is referring to the fifth sentence. However, it is obvious from the whole paragraph that we are discussing methodology, not the facts of the Korean market. Therefore, we have declined to amend the paragraph.

9.11.   With respect to paragraphs 10.55-10.57, the United States argued that classification under the same tariff heading is in itself evidence that products compete directly. We do not agree with the characterization of the issue proposed by the United States. The products first must be properly identified. As we noted above in regard to the EC's comments, these general statements are very weak evidence at best. The US argument also somewhat begs the question because there is a related issue of what level of detail in the tariff headings is appropriate for such analysis in any given case. The problem in this case is that we were left uninformed about what products constitute the remainder of the category. We declined to make the changes suggested by the United States in this regard beyond the clarification mentioned with respect to the EC comments above.

9.12.   With respect to paragraph 10.81, the United States requested several changes for purposes of clarification. We have eliminated one sentence as redundant, but have otherwise kept the original language.

9.13.   Korea stated that it had great difficulty accepting the outcome of the case. In Korea's view, the complainants failed to prove the necessary elements to establish a violation of Article III:2. In its General Comments, Korea states, among other things, that soju is consumed "primarily" with meals and that whisky and other spirits are consumed "primarily" as cocktails. We note as a general matter that Korea was drawing far too fine a distinction between end-uses for purposes of Article III:2, second sentence. We note that, even in Korea's approach (which we do not accept), it is only a matter of the "primary" use where there are differences. There are overlapping end-uses even within the Korean definition.

9.14.   Korea further states that "Korea finds it difficult to accept that the Panel puts into doubt Korea's description of its own market". Korea implies that any party to a dispute has an exclusive authority to assess the facts relating to its domestic market. We find no support for such a proposition in GATT/WTO jurisprudence. Indeed, that is the very function of a panel in a case such as this, to assess the facts and arguments and make findings based on a weighing of the evidence presented.

9.15.   In its General Comments section Korea also made the specific comment that it did not argue that western-style liquors were found in "expensive restaurants" but soju was not. However, we note that in writing its comments, Korea in fact described the restaurants referred to by the United States that served whisky as well as soju as "expensive" restaurants.[329] This also is how Korea referred to these estab-

---

[329]   Korea referred to the US statements about nine Korean-style restaurants found in the vicinity of the US embassy. However, Korea describes these establishments as "a few *very expensive* Korean restaurants" and "these nine *expensive* restaurants". Korean Comments on the Interim Report at p. 1 (emphasis added).

lishments during the Second Meeting of the Panel. These establishments were not offered as a representative sample and we did not view them that way. Rather, we reviewed all of the arguments of all of the parties and took account of and balanced all of the evidence presented. Arguments here and elsewhere that the Panel "relied" upon any particular piece of evidence or assessment must be evaluated in that light. Korea examines in too isolated a manner the various other factors assessed by us in reaching our conclusions. Ultimately, we relied upon all of the evidence presented, not any single element. In our view, the arguments at that time and in the Korean comments on the Interim Report were not persuasive, in light of all the evidence, in rebutting the case established by the complainants.

9.16.   With respect to paragraph 10.45, Korea emphasized that an analysis of the particular market in question is required. We agree. However, as stated in the Findings, that does not imply that evidence of product relationships from other markets is irrelevant to an assessment of the competitive relationship of the products in the market in question. It is a matter of utilization and weighing of the evidence. Korea then states that it is relevant to look at how Korean manufacturers market shochu and soju in Japan and argues that there are differences. We do not disagree that there are some differences between soju and shochu, but, in our view, the differences are minor and we disagree that such differences contradict our conclusions with respect to the Korean market.[330] We also note that the Korean companies have created products and advertised them in Korean and international markets that emphasize the similarity of soju to western-style beverages which is the question here. We took into account the evidence presented by Korea with respect to soju and shochu. As part of our weighing of the evidence, we also took note of other information from outside of the Korean market for its implications for the situation within the Korean market. We declined to change paragraph 9.45 in this regard.

9.17.   With respect to paragraph 10.52, Korea noted that the figures for premium diluted soju should state that it is five percent of the soju market not the distilled beverages market. We have corrected the reference. Korea also noted that premium soju sales currently have slowed. We do not think this detracts from the conclusions. As complainants noted, sales of imports have also slowed in recent months due to the current financial crisis in Korea.[331] The higher priced products such as premium diluted soju and imports have fallen off and sales of lower priced products have increased. The parties did not present extensive arguments about the relationship of the sales of the products to events occurring during the recent financial crisis[332] and we did not refer to such a period extensively, but, if anything, the similar trends in sales of imports and premium diluted soju (as well as the differential movement of standard diluted soju) in the situation can be taken to support our Findings. We made clarifications to paragraph 10.52 to reflect these comments.

---

[330]   We take note that Japan stated in the panel proceedings of *Japan - Taxes on Alcoholic Beverages II* that soju and shochu were essentially identical products. *Japan - Taxes on Alcoholic Beverages II, supra*, at para. 4.178.

[331]   See EC Answer to Questions, Question 1 from the Panel at 1-2, and accompanying chart.

[332]   We note that the Nielsen study and the Trendscope survey were done in 1998.

9.18.   In comments regarding paragraphs 10.93 and 10.94, Korea took exception to several statements regarding pricing information. Korea stated that "Korea cannot fathom how such huge price differences can lead to a competitive relationship". Our conclusion was that, overall, there was persuasive evidence of a directly competitive relationship in spite of the price differences. We recall our observation that absolute price ratios are not a good basis upon which to assess whether there is a directly competitive relationship between products. Information as to how consumers behave in the face of relative price changes is more persuasive.

9.19.   Korea also stated that it strongly objects to the Panel's alleged approach of narrowing the price differences between the products and argues that the Panel "conveniently" mismatched products because some comparisons were made between imports and premium diluted soju rather than standard diluted soju. However, in the textual discussion of the price differences, the first sentence of the listing stated the price difference between premium diluted soju and standard diluted soju. There followed a listing of the price differences between some imports and premium diluted soju. We included a footnote with further price differences between imports and premium diluted soju and standard diluted soju. We do not understand what Korea apparently thought was concealed by these figures as all information was included. Nonetheless, we will amend the paragraph and footnote to calculate the remaining figures for purposes of clarity. We made the appropriate changes to paragraph 10.94.

9.20.   Also with respect to paragraph 10.94, Korea objected to the Panel's alleged reliance on prices based on alcohol strength to support its conclusions. We made no such reliance. In mentioning price adjusted for alcohol strength in a footnote to the paragraph, we merely observed that this was the manner of the price comparisons used in the case of *Japan - Taxes on Alcoholic Beverages II* and noted that the absolute price ratio differences in the present case were more similar to those in that case than would otherwise appear from a casual reference to the appendices in that case. Or, alternatively, if the prices in the Japanese case were *not* adjusted for alcohol strength, the price ratios between the imported and domestic products in Japan are shown to be more similar to the price ratios of imported and domestic products in Korea than would otherwise appear to be the case. We further clarified the language in the paragraph and footnote to reflect this concern.

9.21.   Korea disagreed with our treatment of distilled and diluted soju. They note that the Korean Fair Trade Commission ("KFTC") statement outlines one difference regarding distillation methods, but that there are others including differences in price. However, the KFTC did not simply state that the method of distillation was a difference; it stated that it was "the *basic* difference".[333] After noting this we went on to discuss the other differences, including price. We declined to change paragraph 10.54 in this regard.

9.22.   With respect to a footnote to paragraph 10.67, Korea argued that the Findings take their statements regarding differences in bottle sizes and types out of context. Korea states that it was emphasizing that the bottles used for exports of soju to Japan were different from shochu and that shochu bottles were meant to be similar

---

[333] Emphasis added.

to imports such as whisky. Presumably, Korea wished us to draw the conclusion that soju is marketed differently from shochu and whisky as a point of product distinction. This, in fact, was the issue we addressed. In any event, we clarified the specific reference to bottle size and shape differences made by Korea.

9.23. Korea requested the panel to amend the Findings in paragraphs 10.63 and 10.64 to "incorporate and consider" Korea's arguments in its Second Oral Statement on whether bottled and tap water are competitive products. We listened to Korea's statements in this regard and considered them. Lack of a specific citation to every single argument made by parties in the Findings does not in any manner imply that such arguments were not considered. We did not find the Korea analogy about tap water and bottled water probative or useful. The analogy is incomplete and refers to different products in different countries and thus no useful inference could be drawn for the inquiry at hand. However, we have added Korea's requested statements to the descriptive portion of the Report but have declined to amend these paragraphs in this regard.

9.24. Korea argued with the statement in paragraph 10.78 that soju and shochu are traditional drinks in their respective countries. Korea argues that sake "is *the* traditional drink of Japan".[334] We did not state that shochu is *the* traditional drink of Japan. We referred to it and soju as traditional drinks without further qualification. We do not agree that there is only one traditional drink per country. Various regions or groups within countries may have traditional drinks We declined to alter this paragraph.

9.25. With respect to paragraph 10.79, Korea noted that references to colourings with respect to premium soju are inaccurate. With respect to mention of the photographic exhibits submitted by complainants, Korea objects to references to pictures of premium diluted soju. We do not agree with the objection; advertisements of premium soju are relevant. Korea also objected to use of advertisements aimed at the Japanese market. Paragraph 10.80 deals with much of the Korea disagreement. However, we take note of their point with respect to some of the photographs. For instance, Exhibit I should not be included in this specific footnote because it is a Japanese product. However, we again note the statement by Japan in *Japan - Taxes on Alcoholic Beverages II* that soju and shochu are essentially identical products.[335] We also take note that Exhibit D is distilled soju rather than diluted soju. However, given our conclusions regarding distilled and diluted soju, no substantive difference results. The paragraph and footnote references were amended as appropriate.

9.26. Korea also objected to references in paragraphs 10.79 and 10.80 to Jinro's website advertisement because, according to Korea, all advertising is essentially local. We do not agree with this argument. As discussed in these and other paragraphs, we consider such evidence relevant. The question is one of evidentiary significance, i.e., how much weight should be given to such evidence. We declined to further amend these paragraphs in this regard.

---

[334] Emphasis added.

[335] *Japan - Taxes on Alcoholic Beverages II, supra*, at para. 4.178.

X.   FINDINGS

A.   *Claims of the Parties*

10.1.   The European Communities and the United States claim that Korea applies its internal tax laws (the Liquor Tax Law and the Education Tax Law) on vodka in excess of taxes applied to soju and is therefore in breach of its obligations under Article III:2, first sentence, of GATT 1994. The complainants also argue that these internal tax laws are applied in a dissimilar manner to other imported distilled alcoholic beverages so as to afford protection to the domestic industry in breach of Korea's obligations under Article III:2, second sentence. The complainants have identified the imported products as all distilled alcoholic beverages described within Harmonized System classification 2208. They have identified specific examples of such beverages as including whiskies, brandies, cognac, liqueurs, vodka, gin, rum, tequila and "ad-mixtures". The complainants have identified soju as the domestically produced distilled alcoholic beverage which they claim receives preferential tax treatment.

10.2.   Korea has responded that its internal tax measures are not inconsistent with its obligations under Article III:2. Korea argues that there are two types of soju, distilled and diluted, and that neither of these products are like the imported products and that the imports and the domestic products also are not directly competitive or substitutable. Korea argues that Article III:2 should be narrowly construed so as not to unduly infringe the sovereign right of Members of the WTO to structure their tax laws as they see fit. Korea claims that the complainants have not proved that with respect to the Korean market the products in question are either like or directly competitive or substitutable.

B.   *Preliminary Issues*

10.3.   Korea raised the following preliminary issues and requested preliminary rulings with respect to:

    (i)   the specificity of the panel requests of the complainants;

    (ii)   the complainants' alleged non-compliance with certain provisions of the DSU relating to the conduct of consultations;

    (iii)   alleged breaches of the confidentiality of the consultation process;

    (iv)   alleged late submission of evidence; and

    (v)   permission to have private counsel attend the Panel meetings and address the Panel.[336]

---

[336]   The question of confidentiality of consultations was first identified in a footnote to Korea's First Submission and further explained by Korea at the first Panel meeting. The issues of specificity of the complaints and adequacy of the consultations were raised for the first time in Korea's Statement at the first Panel meeting. The complainants were given the opportunity to address the issues of confidentiality, specificity and adequacy of consultations in writing in their rebuttal briefs and we delivered our decision on these matters at the beginning of the second Panel meeting. The issue of the alleged late submission of evidence was raised by Korea following the second Panel meeting.

1. Specificity

10.4.   Korea argues that the European Communities, in its request for a panel, has referred to a preferential tax rate on soju vis-a-vis certain alcoholic beverages falling within HS heading 2208. Korea states that the European Communities has not, even in its written submission, clarified its position on the category of alcoholic beverages falling within the scope of this dispute.

10.5.   Korea states that the US request for a panel lacks specificity as well. Korea notes that the United States, in its request for a panel, refers to higher tax rates on "other distilled spirits", while specifically mentioning "whisky, brandy, vodka, rum, gin, and ad mixtures".

10.6.   Korea argues that such vaguely worded complaints violate its rights of defence. According to Korea, HS 2208 is a very broad tariff classification, which covers a wide variety of alcoholic beverages, including non-western liquors such as koryangu, Korean soju, Insam ju, Ogapiju, and Japanese shochu. More precisely, Korea argues that this lack of specificity of the complainants' claims is improper for two reasons:

(i)   it frustrates Korea's right of defense, which Korea argues is a general principle of due process implicit in the DSU;

(ii)   it violates what Korea considers a clear obligation of the DSU, which is that such a request should "identify" the specific measures at issue, and "present the problem clearly", as stipulated in Article 6.

Korea, therefore, requested the panel to issue a preliminary ruling, limiting the products at issue in this dispute.

10.7.   Korea also submits that it is unable to identify which items the United States is referring to by its reference to 'ad-mixtures' in its request for a panel. Korea also claims that the complainants did not clearly distinguish the domestic liquors that are supposed to be more favourably taxed in Korea. Korea states, in particular, that the complainants have not distinguished between Korea's distilled soju, an artisanal product sold at very high prices in tiny quantities, and subject to a 50% tax rate, on the one hand, and, on the other hand, diluted or standard soju, which is an inexpensive drink, consumed in large quantities with meals and taxed at a rate of 35%. Korea argues that in their requests for a panel, both complainants have referred to only one 'soju' product, without acknowledging that there are, in reality, two different products, with two different tax rates.

10.8.   The European Communities notes that its request for a panel refers to ".. certain alcoholic beverages falling within HS 22.08", but rejects Korea's assertion that it has, through its first submission, broadened the scope of its complaint as contained in the request for a panel. The European Communities submits that its first submission refers to "soju and all other distilled spirits and liqueurs falling within HS 22.08". In the EC view, these statements are consistent. According to the European Communities, its panel request is more than sufficiently specific to meet the minimum requirements of Article 6.2 of the DSU.

We address the question here for the first time. The issue of private counsel was raised and addressed prior to the first meeting of the Panel.

10.9.   The United States argues that Article 6.2 of the DSU requires, inter alia, that the request for a panel "identify the specific measures at issue and provide a brief summary of the legal basis of the complaint sufficient to present the problem clearly." According to the United States, its panel request satisfies both these requirements, and it also clearly includes all distilled spirits within HS heading 2208, as maintained in the first US submission. The United States argues that in accordance with Article 6.2, its request for the establishment of a panel defined the Korean measures at issue: the general Liquor Tax Law and the Education Tax; and provided a brief summary of the legal basis of the complaint.

10.10. The United States refers to *European Communities - Regime for the Importation, Sale and Distribution of Bananas (Bananas III)*, where the Appellate Body, according to the United States, noted that this provision concerning the legal basis requires that the request for a panel must be sufficiently specific with respect to the claims being advanced, but need not lay out all the arguments that will subsequently be made in the party's submission.[337] The United States argues that Korea's request that the Panel limit the proceeding to five specific products (whisky, brandy, vodka, rum, and gin) is equally without basis in Article 6.2. According to the United States, the panel request, which defines the terms of reference of the panel, refers to taxation of "other distilled spirits" - i.e., distilled spirits other than soju. By using the term "such as," the United States claims that it sets forth the five products and "ad mixtures" as examples, and not as an exclusive list. According to the United States, the extent to which the United States and the European Communities establish that all such products are "like" or "directly competitive or substitutable" is a matter to be determined through the course of these proceedings, beginning with the first written submission to the Panel.

10.11. As regards the question of defining which soju is referred to, the European Communities states that it regards all the varieties of soju as one product, with the necessary result that 'liqueurs' are more heavily taxed than some soju. According to the European Communities, the question of whether soju is or is not a single product is a substantive issue which cannot be decided by the panel in a preliminary ruling. The United States also argues that with respect to the use of the word "soju," its panel request makes it clear that the tax preference for all soju is covered, giving Korea ample objective notice that the entire category was to be challenged.

10.12. We note that Article 6.2 of the DSU provides in the relevant part that:

> The request for the establishment of a panel shall be made in writing. It shall indicate whether consultations were held, identify the specific measures at issue and provide a summary of the legal basis of the complaint sufficient to present the problem clearly.

10.13. The Appellate Body noted in *Bananas III* that:

> As a panel request is normally not subjected to detailed scrutiny by the DSB, it is incumbent upon a panel to examine the request for the

---

[337] Appellate Body Report on *European Communities - Regime for the Importation, Sale and Distribution of Bananas (Bananas III)*, adopted on 25 September 1997, WT/DS27/AB/R, at para. 141.

establishment of the panel very carefully to ensure its compliance with both the letter and spirit of Article 6.2.[338]

10.14. The question of whether a panel request satisfies the requirements of Article 6.2 is to be determined on a case by case basis with due regard to the wording of Article 6.2. The question for determination before us, therefore, is whether the phrases used by the EC ("certain alcoholic beverages falling within HS heading 2208") and the United States ("other distilled spirits such as whisky, brandy, vodka, gin and ad-mixtures") are specific enough to satisfy the letter and spirit of Article 6.2. In other words, the question is whether Korea is put on sufficient notice as to the parameters of the case it is defending. As the Appellate Body noted in *Bananas III*:

> It is important that a panel request be sufficiently precise for two reasons: first, it often forms the basis for the terms of reference of the panel pursuant to Article 7 of the DSU; and, second, it informs the defending party and the third parties of the legal basis of the complaint.[339]

10.15. Korea argues that each imported product must be specifically identified in order to be within the scope of the panel proceeding. The complainants argue that the appropriate imported product is all distilled beverages. They claim, in fact, that for purposes of Article III, there is only one category in issue. They claim to have identified specific examples of such distilled alcoholic beverages for purposes of illustration, not as limits to the category.

10.16. The issue of the appropriate categories of products to compare is important to this case. In our view, however, it is one that requires a weighing of evidence. As such it is not an issue appropriate for a preliminary ruling in this case. This is particularly so in light of the Appellate Body's opinion in *Japan - Taxes on Alcoholic Beverages II,*[340] that all imported distilled alcoholic beverages were discriminated against. That element of the decision is not controlling on the ultimate resolution of other cases involving other facts; however, it cannot be considered inappropriate for complainants to follow it in framing their request for a panel in a dispute involving distilled alcoholic beverages. While it is possible that in some cases, the complaint could be considered so vague and broad that a respondent would not have adequate notice of the actual nature of the alleged discrimination, it is difficult to argue that such notice was not provided here in light of the identified tariff heading and the Appellate Body decision in the *Japan - Taxes on Alcoholic Beverages II.* Furthermore, we note that the Appellate Body recently found that a panel request based on a broader grouping of products was sufficiently specific for purposes of Article

---

[338] Appellate Body Report on *European Communities - Regime for the Importation, Sale and Distribution of Bananas (Bananas III)*, adopted on 25 September 1997, WT/DS27/AB/R, at para. 142.

[339] *Ibid.*, para. 142.

[340] Appellate Body Report on *Japan - Taxes on Alcoholic Beverages (Japan - Taxes on Alcoholic Beverages II)*, adopted on 1 November 1996, WT/DS8/AB/R, WT/DS10/AB/R, WT/DS11/AB/R, DSR 1996:I, 97, at 123.

6.2.[341] We find therefore, that the complainants' requests for a panel satisfied the requirements of Article 6.2 of the DSU.

2.   *Adequacy of Consultations*

10.17. Korea submits that what it considers to be explicit obligations contained in Articles 3.3, 3.7 and 4.5 of the DSU have been violated. Korea in effect alleges that the complainants did not engage in consultations in good faith with a view to reaching a mutual solution as envisaged by the DSU. According to Korea, there was no meaningful exchange of facts because the complainants treated the consultations as a one-sided question and answer session, and therefore, frustrated any reasonable chance for a settlement. Korea considers this non-observance of specific provisions of the DSU as a "violation of the tenets of the WTO dispute settlement system" and requests the Panel for a ruling .

10.18. Both complainants assert that Korea's claim would appear to be that they have infringed Articles 3.3, 3.7 and 4.5 of the DSU because they did not attempt to reach a mutually acceptable solution to the dispute in the course of the consultations that preceded the establishment of this Panel. The complainants refer to the panel decision in *Bananas III* for the proposition that the conduct of consultations is not the concern of a panel but that the panel need only concern itself with the question whether consultations did in fact take place,[342] and point out that Korea cannot dispute the fact that consultations were in fact held on three separate occasions between itself and both the United States and the EC. The complainants state that, in any event it is not true that they refused to engage in a 'meaningful exchange of facts' during the GATT Article XXII consultations. They allege that it was Korea's attitude during the consultations which prevented such exchange from taking place.

10.19. In our view, the WTO jurisprudence so far has not recognized any concept of "adequacy" of consultations. The only requirement under the DSU is that consultations were in fact held, or were at least requested, and that a period of sixty days has elapsed from the time consultations were requested to the time a request for a panel was made. What takes place in those consultations is not the concern of a panel. The point was put clearly by the Panel in *Bananas III*, where it was stated:

> Consultations are . . . a matter reserved for the parties. The DSB is not involved; no panel is involved; and the consultations are held in the absence of the Secretariat. While a mutually agreed solution is to be preferred, in some cases it is not possible for parties to agree upon one. In those cases, it is our view that the function of a panel is only to ascertain that the consultations, if required, were in fact held. ...[343]

We do not wish to imply that we consider consultations unimportant. Quite the contrary, consultations are a critical and integral part of the DSU. But, we have no man-

---

[341] Appellate Body Report *on European Communities - Customs Classification of Certain Computer Equipment*, adopted on 22 June 1998, (WT/DS62/AB/R, WT/DS67/AB/R), at paras. 58-73.
[342] Panel Report on *Bananas III, supra,* at paras. 7.18-7.19.
[343] Panel Report on *Bananas III, supra,* para. 7.19. The issue was not appealed.

date to investigate the adequacy of the consultation process that took place between the parties and we decline to do so in the present case.

3.   *Confidentiality*

10.20. Korea alleges that both complainants have breached the confidentiality requirement of Article 4.6 of the DSU by making reference, in their submissions, to information supplied by Korea during consultations.

10.21. The European Communities argues that Korea's interpretation of Article 4.6 of the DSU is wrong. According to the European Communities, the confidentiality requirement of Article 4.6 of the DSU concerns parties not involved in the dispute and the public in general. The European Communities stresses that the requirement cannot in any way be read as referring to the panel itself. In the EC view, Article 4.6 cannot be interpreted as a limitation on the rights of parties at the panel stage.

10.22. The United States argues that to the extent Korea is alleging a violation of the DSU, such a claim is not within the terms of reference of the Panel. The United States further argues that Korea's complaints about the alleged inadequacy of the complainants' attempts to settle the dispute or engage in good faith consultations have no bearing on the authority of the Panel or the progress of this proceeding.

10.23. We note that Article 4.6 of the DSU requires confidentiality in the consultations between parties to a dispute. This is essential if the parties are to be free to engage in meaningful consultations. However, it is our view that this confidentiality extends only as far as requiring the parties to the consultations not to disclose any information obtained in the consultations to any parties that were not involved in those consultations. We are mindful of the fact that the panel proceedings between the parties remain confidential, and parties do not thereby breach any confidentiality by disclosing in those proceedings information acquired during the consultations. Indeed, in our view, the very essence of consultations is to enable the parties gather correct and relevant information, for purposes of assisting them in arriving at a mutually agreed solution, or failing which, to assist them in presenting accurate information to the panel. It would seriously hamper the dispute settlement process if the information acquired during consultations could not subsequently be used by any party in the ensuing proceedings. We find therefore, that there has been no breach of confidentiality by the complainants in this case in respect of information that they became aware of during the consultations with Korea on this matter.

4.   *Late Submission of Evidence*

10.24. Korea complains that its rights of defense were violated by the late submission of a market study (the Trendscope survey) by the European Communities. Korea had submitted a study done by the AC Nielsen Company as part of its responses to questions arising from the first substantive meeting of the Panel. The European Communities responded to this with, among other things, the Trendscope survey presented at the Second Meeting of the Panel. The Panel gave Korea a week to respond to this and critique the results, methodology and questions used in the Trendscope survey. Korea argues that this time was insufficient, that it did not have copies in Korean of all the questions -asked, and that it did not have time to provide further questions or comments based upon the answers.

10.25. We do not consider that Korea's rights under the DSU were violated. The European Communities submitted its rebuttal survey at the next available opportunity after receiving Korea's Nielsen survey. Had Korea chosen to submit its survey at the first substantive meeting and the European Communities failed to respond at the next opportunity (in such a case, it would have been in the rebuttal submission), there obviously would have been more merit to the claim because then the European Communities, it could have been argued, delayed submitting their evidence. As it transpired, the European Communities submitted a new piece of evidence at the next available opportunity which Korea then was able to examine for a week in order to provide comments. The survey was not of a particularly complex type and, in our view, Korea had adequate time to respond given the nature of the evidence. The Trendscope survey is not critical evidence to the complainants' case; it serves as a supplement to arguments already made. If we considered that it represented critical evidence, Korea's request for further time for comment would have been given greater weight. While all parties to litigation might prefer open-ended potential for rebutting the other side's submissions, we believe that for practical reasons submissions must be cut-off at some point and such a point was reached in this case. Thus, neither the timing nor the importance of the evidence in question support a finding that Korea's rights have been violated in this instance.

5.   *Private Counsel*

10.26. Korea indicated at the outset of the panel process that it wished to have the right to private counsel at the substantive meetings of the Panel. In Korea's view, in order to fully defend its interests and match the much greater resources of the complaining parties, Korea decided to retain the services of expert counsel with long standing experience in matters of international economic law and international economics.

10.27. Korea refers to the recent opinion of the Appellate Body in *Bananas III*, in which the Appellate Body stated that it found nothing in the WTO Agreement, the DSU, its Working Procedures, in customary international law or the prevailing practice of international tribunals, which prevented a Member from determining its delegation to the Appellate Body's proceedings.[344] Korea adds that the Appellate Body also noted that representation by counsel of a government's own choice in proceedings before it (the Appellate Body) might well be a matter of particular significance to enable WTO Members to participate fully in WTO dispute settlement proceedings. According to Korea, the same holds true with respect to delegations presenting a case before a Panel. Korea further submits that under customary international law, it has the sovereign right to determine the composition of its delegation to panel hearings.[345] Korea also believes its right to counsel of its choice is consistent with what it considers to be basic due process principles implicit in the DSU. Korea indicated that it appreciated that the Panel might have concerns about the confidentiality

---

[344] Appellate Body Report, *supra*, para. 8.

[345] Korea refers to *Korea - Restrictions on Imports of Beef*, adopted on 7 November 1989, BISD 36S/202.

of the proceedings. Korea assured the Panel that it would ensure that any member of its delegation, including private counsel, will fully respect the confidentiality of the proceedings in accordance with applicable rules.

10.28. The European Communities indicates that it has no objection, in principle, to the presence of private counsel as part of Korea's delegation during substantive meetings of the Panel. The European Communities states, however, that they attach great importance to the preservation of confidentiality of panel proceedings. The EC acceptance was, therefore, made conditional upon Korea assuming full responsibility for any breach of confidentiality which may result from the presence at the Panel meetings of non-governmental persons. The European Communities take regard of the assurances given by Korea to the effect that its private counsel, like any other member of its delegation, would fully respect the confidentiality of the proceedings.

10.29. The United States notes that the Members of the WTO have agreed to abide by the rules and procedures in the DSU. They have agreed that dispute practice in the WTO will be guided by, and will adhere to, the established practice applied in disputes under the GATT 1947 system. According to the United States, this practice has excluded the routine presence of private lawyers in panel proceedings. The United States asserts that the GATT and WTO practice reflects the dual nature of the dispute settlement rules in the DSU; namely, reaching mutually agreeable solutions and adjudicating disputes. In the view of the United States, a decision by this panel to permit participation of private lawyers in panel meetings is not a trivial step. The effectiveness of WTO dispute settlement is a major accomplishment of the WTO as an international organization. The balance of elements that created this success has evolved by experience over considerable time. It is also the US view that if the Panel wishes to permit private lawyers or non-lawyer advisors to be in this proceeding, the Panel should consider this decision with great care, and impose appropriate safeguards with respect to the conduct of such persons.

10.30. The United States further argues that Panel must require effective safeguards that ensure that private counsel will not leak confidential business information or other privileged information generated during the panel process, and that if they do, there will be meaningful consequences. According to the United States, there is no excuse for damaging the interests of private parties by leaks of confidential business information; such leaks will in turn damage the reputation of WTO dispute settlement among trading businesses who are the strongest supporters of open trade.

10.31. Having considered the request of Korea for the right to use private counsel at the panel meetings, and the responses the European Communities and the United States, we decided to permit the appearance of private counsel before the Panel and to allow them to address arguments to the Panel in this case. In our view, it is appropriate to grant such a request in order to ensure that Korea has every opportunity to fully defend its interests in this case. However, such permission is granted based on the representations by Korea that the private counsel concerned are official members of the delegation of Korea, that they are retained by and responsible to the Government of Korea, and that they will fully respect the confidentiality of the proceedings and that Korea assumes full responsibility for confidentiality of the proceedings on behalf of all members of its delegation, including non-government employees.

10.32. We note that written submissions of the parties which contain confidential information may, in some cases, be provided to non-government advisors who are not members of an official delegation at a panel meeting. The duty of confidentiality extends to all governments that are parties to a dispute and to all such advisors regardless of whether they are designated as members of delegations and appear at a panel meeting.

10.33. The United States offered several suggestions for new rules and procedures in regard to these questions. However, in our view, the broader question of establishing further rules on confidentiality and possibly rules of conduct specifically directed at the role of non-governmental advisors generally is a matter more appropriate for consideration by the Dispute Settlement Body and is not within the terms of reference of this Panel.

C.   Main Issues

1.   Interpretation of Article III:2

10.34. Article III:2 provides two standards for examining complaints about a Member's internal taxation laws. The first sentence of Article III:2 provides:

> The products of the territory of any Member imported into the territory of any other Member shall not be subject, directly or indirectly, to internal taxes or other internal charges of any kind in excess of those applied, directly or indirectly, to like domestic products.

The second sentence provides:

> Moreover, no Member shall otherwise apply internal taxes or other internal charges to imported or domestic products in a manner contrary to the principles set forth in paragraph 1.

Paragraph 1 of Article III provides:

> The Members recognize that internal taxes and other internal charges, and laws, regulations and requirements affecting the internal sale, offering for sale, purchase, transportation, distribution or use of products, and internal quantitative regulations requiring the mixture, processing or use of products in specified amounts or proportions, should not be applied to imported or domestic products so as to afford protection to domestic production.

The meaning of the second sentence in light of its reference to the first sentence is further clarified in *Ad* Article III as follows:

> A tax conforming to the requirements of the first sentence of paragraph 2 would be considered to be inconsistent with the provisions of the second sentence only in cases where competition was involved between, on the one hand, the taxed product and, on the other hand, a

directly competitive or substitutable product which was not similarly taxed.[346]

10.35. Thus, the first sentence of Article III:2 examines whether products of an exporting country are taxed in excess of the taxes on the "like" domestic product. The second sentence examines whether products of an exporting country are taxed similarly to domestic products which are "directly competitive or substitutable." Both sentences first examine the relationship between the domestic and imported products; however, the second sentence involves additional and different inquiries with respect to two other elements; namely, an examination of the *extent* of the difference in taxation[347] and whether the taxation differences are applied so as to afford protection to the domestic industry.

10.36. The general approach in past Article III:2 cases has been to examine first whether any of the products at issue are "like." However, previous cases have found that the category of like products is a subset of those products which are directly competitive or substitutable.[348] It therefore seems more logical to us to approach the issue by examining the broader category first.

10.37. Before beginning to analyze the evidence presented, we must first decide how the term "directly competitive or substitutable" should be interpreted. Article 31 of the Vienna Convention summarizes the international law rules for the interpretation of treaty language. It provides in paragraph 1 that terms shall be interpreted in good faith in accordance with the ordinary meaning of the terms in their context and in light of the object and purpose of the treaty. According to paragraph 2, the context includes the full text, the preamble, the annexes and any mutually agreed interpretive language. Paragraph 3 provides that account shall also be taken of any subsequent practice or interpretations as well as relevant rules of international law.

10.38. The Appellate Body in *Japan - Taxes on Alcoholic Beverages II* stated that "like product" should be narrowly construed for purposes of Article III:2. It then noted that directly competitive or substitutable is a broader category, saying: "How much broader that category of 'directly competitive or substitutable products' may be in a given case is a matter for the panel to determine based on all the relevant facts in that case."[349] Article 32 of the Vienna Convention provides that it is appropriate to refer to the negotiating history of a treaty provision in order to confirm the meaning of the terms as interpreted pursuant to the application of Article 31. A review of the negotiating history of Article III:2, second sentence and the *Ad* Article III language confirms that the product categories should not be so narrowly construed as to defeat the purpose of the anti-discrimination language informing the interpretation of Article III. The Geneva session of the Preparatory Committee pro-

---

[346] *Ad* Article III has equal stature under international law as the GATT language to which it refers, pursuant to Article XXXIV. See also Appellate Body Report on *Japan - Taxes on Alcoholic Beverages II, supra,* at 116.

[347] If the products are determined to be "like" then *any* taxation of the imported product in excess of the domestic product is prohibited. There is no *de minimis* possibility as there is under the second sentence where *Ad* Article III provides only that they must be "similarly taxed."

[348] Panel Report on *Japan - Taxes on Alcoholic Beverages II, supra,* at 117. This finding was not modified or reversed by the Appellate Body. See, Appellate Body Report, *supra,* at 117.

[349] Appellate Body Report on *Japan - Taxes on Alcoholic Beverages II, supra,* at p. 25.

vided an explanation of the language of the second sentence by noting that apples and oranges could be directly competitive or substitutable.[350] Other examples provided were domestic linseed oil and imported tung oil[351] and domestic synthetic rubber and imported natural rubber.[352] There was discussion of whether such products as tramways and busses or coal and fuel oil could be considered as categories of directly competitive or substitutable products. There was some disagreement with respect to these products.[353]

10.39. This negotiating history illustrates the key question in this regard. It is whether the products are **directly** competitive or substitutable. Tramways and busses, when they are not directly competitive, may still be indirectly competitive as transportation systems. Similarly even if most power generation systems are set up to utilize either coal or fuel oil, but not both, these two products could still compete indirectly as fuels.[354] Thus, the focus should not be exclusively on the quantitative extent of the competitive overlap, but on the methodological basis on which a panel should assess the competitive relationship.

10.40. At some level all products or services are at least indirectly competitive. Because consumers have limited amounts of disposable income, they may have to arbitrate between various needs such as giving up going on a vacation to buy a car or abstaining from eating in restaurants to buy new shoes or a television set. However, an assessment of whether there is a direct competitive relationship between two products or groups of products requires evidence that consumers consider or could consider the two products or groups of products as alternative ways of satisfying a particular need or taste.

10.41. The Panel in *Japan - Taxes on Alcoholic Beverages II* noted that the 1989 Japanese tax reform had eliminated the distinctions between various grades of whisky. The result was that domestic whisky production declined relatively. Its market share fell and both shochu and foreign-produced whisky's market share rose. The Panel stated:

> In the Panel's view, the fact that foreign produced whisky and shochu
> were competing for the same market share [held by domestic whisky]
> is evidence that there was elasticity of substitution between them.[355]

Imported whisky and shochu may each have been competing independently with domestic whisky. We would agree with that panel that showing such indirect competition may provide evidentiary support for a finding of direct competitiveness. However, such a showing is insufficient on its own. To use a hypothetical case for illustration, it is possible that in some markets distilled beverages could be shown to

---

[350] EPCT/A/PV/9, at p. 7.

[351] E/Conf.2/C.3/SR.11, p.1 and Corr. 2.

[352] *Ibid.*, at p. 3.

[353] E/Conf.2/C.3/SR.40, at p. 2.

[354] To follow on from these hypotheticals, it can be noted that some large power generation facilities may be convertible from coal to fuel oil or a series of power stations in a particular market could be set for replacement and alternative fuel sources might be under consideration. In such instances there may be direct competition. Hence the statements of the delegates that a review of the specific market structure is necessary to determine the nature of the competition.

[355] Panel Report on *Japan - Taxes on Alcoholic Beverages II, supra*, at para. 6.30.

compete with wine; beer could also be shown to compete with wine. However, such evidence does not reveal whether the relationship is direct or indirect. More would need to be shown in such a case to establish that distilled beverages and beer are *directly* competitive or substitutable with respect to each other in that market.

10.42. In our view, it is also the case that quantitative analyses, while helpful, should not be considered necessary. In examining the Korean market, a determination of the precise extent of the competitive overlap is complicated by the fact that, as the 1987 and 1996 panels noted in the *Japan - Taxes on Alcoholic Beverages I and II*, the intervention of government policies can cause distortions, including understatement, of the quantitative extent of the competitive relationship. Indeed, there must be some concern that a focus on the quantitative extent of competition instead of the nature of it, could result in a type of trade effects test being written into Article III cases. That is, if a certain *degree* of competition must be shown, it is similar to showing that a certain *amount* of damage was done to that competitive relationship by the tax policies in question. The Appellate Body stated:

> Moreover, it is irrelevant that the "trade effects" of the tax differential between imported and domestic products, as reflected in the volumes of imports, are insignificant or even non-existent, Article III protects expectations not of any particular trade volume but rather of the equal competitive relationship between imported and domestic products.[356]

10.43. The question for us to decide is whether in Korea the domestic and imported products are directly competitive or substitutable. This requires evidence of the direct competitive relationship between the products, including, in this case, comparisons of their physical characteristics, end-uses, channels of distribution and prices.[357]

2. *Evidentiary Issues*

(i) Cross-price elasticity

10.44. The Appellate Body approved the panel's decision in *Japan - Taxes on Alcoholic Beverages II* to look not only at products' physical characteristics, common end-uses, and tariff classifications, but also at the market place. It approved the examination of the economic concept of "substitution" as *one* means of examining the relevant markets. The use of cross-price elasticity of demand was approved but it was specifically noted that it is not the decisive criterion.[358] While a high degree of cross-price elasticity of demand would tend to support the argument that there is a direct competitive relationship, it is only one evidentiary factor. If there is a high quantitative level of competition between products, it is likely that the qualitative nature of the competition is direct. However, the lack of such evidence may be due

---

[356] Appellate Body Report on *Japan - Taxes on Alcoholic Beverages II, supra,* at 110. Obviously, the expectation of competitive conditions must be a reasonable one.

[357] These are the categories of evidence we have examined in this case to determine whether the products in question are directly competitive or substitutable. Obviously, the availability and probative value of categories of evidence may differ from case to case.

[358] Appellate Body Report on *Japan - Taxes on Alcoholic Beverages II, supra,* at 117.

to the governmental measures in question. As noted, both panels in *Japan - Taxes on Alcoholic Beverages I and II* made the observation that government policies can influence consumer preferences to the benefit of the domestic industry. It was stated that:

> a tax system that discriminates against imports has the consequence of creating and even freezing preferences for consumer goods. In the Panel's view, this meant that the consumer surveys in a country with such a tax system would likely understate the degree of potential competitiveness between substitutable products.[359]

This is particularly a problem if the products involved are consumer items that are so-called experience goods which means that consumers tend to purchase what is familiar to them and experiment only reluctantly. This issue will be discussed further below. Thus the question is not of the degree of competitive overlap, but its nature. Is there a competitive relationship and is it *direct*? It is for this reason, among others, that quantitative studies of cross-price elasticity are relevant, but not exclusive or even decisive in nature.

(ii)   Evidence from outside the Korean market

10.45. Other elements of evidence besides cross-price elasticity are relevant to the analysis. In our view, another element of relevant evidence is the nature of competition in other countries. We are mindful of the admonition of the Appellate Body in the case of *Japan - Taxes on Alcoholic Beverages II*, that these disputes must be evaluated on a case-by-case basis taking into account the conditions in the market in question. However, as we are looking at the nature of competition in a market that previously was relatively closed and still has substantial tax differentials, such evidence of competitive relationships in other markets is relevant. Similarly, we consider it relevant as to how Korean manufacturers of soju are marketing their beverages outside Korea. According to Korea, the panel should strictly limit its view to what happens in the Korean market place. Nothing that happens outside Korea can be considered relevant in determining whether the products in question are directly competitive or substitutable within Korea. Also, Korean manufacturer's export marketing efforts are to be given no weight. In our view, this is an overly restrictive approach and does not accord with market realities. It is true that the question to be answered concerns the Korean market, but that in no way implies that what happens in regard to the same products outside of the Korean market is irrelevant to assessing the actual and potential market conditions within Korea.

10.46. In some cases, the only market evidence available may be with respect to non-domestic markets due to the tax, duty and regulatory structure in the country in question. Sometimes, the only reasonable manner of assessing what the market situation would be absent such policy structures is to look at other markets and make a judgement as to whether the same patterns could prevail in the case at hand.

---

[359]   Panel Report on *Japan - Taxes on Alcoholic Beverages II, supra*, at para. 6.28, citing, Panel Report on *Japan - Customs Duties, Taxes and Labelling Practices on Imported Wines and Alcoholic Beverages*, adopted on 10 November 1987, BISD 34S/83, at para. 5.9.

However, we do not need to decide such a stark issue in this case; there is considerable evidence available as to what is taking place within the Korean market. We do not need, in this case, to give substantial weight to conditions in markets outside Korea, but such factors are relevant and should be taken into consideration in determining the nature of the competitive relationships involved here.[360] As noted above, the panels stated in *Japan - Taxes on Alcoholic Beverages I and II* that systems of government tax policies may have the effect of freezing consumer preferences in place in favour of the domestic product. To completely ignore such evidence from other markets would require complete reliance on current market information which may be unreliable, due to its tendency to understate the competitive relationship, because of the very actions being challenged. Indeed, the result could be that the most restrictive and discriminatory government policies would be safe from challenge under Article III due to the lack of domestic market data.

(iii)   Potential competition

10.47. Another question that has arisen is the temporal nature of the assessment of competition. All parties agree that the Panel should look at both actual and potential competition. However, Korea argues that potential competition does not include future competition. They argue that at most, the Panel must make a "but for" decision. That is, but for the taxes would the products be directly competitive or substitutable at the present moment. Korea further argues that if the market changes, then the complainants are within their rights to raise the matter again at some time in the future.

10.48. Korea's arguments in this regard are not persuasive. We, indeed, are not in the business of speculating on future behaviour. However, we do not agree that any assessment of potential competition with a temporal aspect is speculation. It depends on the evidence in a particular case. Panels should look at evidence of trends and changes in consumption patterns and make an assessment as to whether such trends and patterns lead to the conclusion that the products in question are either directly competitive now or can reasonably be expected to become directly competitive in the near future. It is not evident why such an assessment is any more speculative in nature than the "but for" analysis itself. Such an analysis also requires making an assessment about what would happen in the theoretical case of the tax differentials being removed. In our view, the approach suggested by Korea is too static. It would be a profoundly troubling development in GATT/WTO jurisprudence if Members were forced to return to dispute settlement on the same laws over and over only because the market in question had not yet changed enough to justify a finding at a particular moment. Such an interpretation would be contrary to the settled law that competitive expectations and opportunities are protected.[361] As noted above, the Appellate Body in *Japan - Taxes on Alcoholic Beverages II* stated:

---

[360] See, Appellate Body Report on *European Communities - Customs Classification of Certain Computer Equipment, supra*, at para. 93.

[361] We also note that a requirement of substantial current market presence would be a particularly high hurdle for less wealthy exporters.

> Article III protects **expectations** not of any particular trade volume but rather of the equal competitive relationship between imported and domestic products.[362]

According to the 1949 *Working Party Report on Brazil Internal Taxes*:

> [The majority of the working party] argued that the absence of imports from contracting parties during any period of time that might be selected for examination would not necessarily be an indication that they had no interest in exports of the product in affected by the tax, since their **potentialities** as exporters, given national treatment, should be taken into account.[363]

10.49. Similarly, the panel in the 1987 case of United States - Taxes on Petroleum and Certain Imported Substances stated:

> For these reasons Article III:2, first sentence, cannot be interpreted to protect expectations on export volumes; it protects **expectations** on the competitive relationship between imported and domestic products.[364]

The Shorter Oxford English Dictionary defines "potential" as follows:

> *potential* 1. possible as opposed to actual; capable of coming into being; latent.[365]

The same dictionary defines "expectation" as follows:

> *expectation* 1. The action of waiting for someone or something. . . .4. A thing expected or looked forward to.[366]

10.50. The interpretation proposed by Korea is not consistent with the standard meaning of the terms in question both of which clearly have a temporal element to their definitions. We will not attempt to speculate on what could happen in the distant future, but we will consider evidence pertaining to what could reasonably be expected to occur in the near term based on the evidence presented. How much weight to be accorded such evidence must be decided on a case-by-case basis in light of the market structure and other factors including the quality of the evidence and the extent of the inference required. To try to limit the inquiry as to what might happen this instant were the tax laws changed would involve us in making arbitrary distinctions between expectations now and those in the near future. Obviously, evidence as to what would happen now is more probative in nature than what would

---

[362] Appellate Body Report in *Japan Alcoholic Beverages II*, *supra*, at 110 (emphasis added).

[363] *Brazilian Internal Taxes*, BISD II/181 at p. 185, para. 16 (emphasis added).

[364] *United States - Taxes on Petroleum and Certain Imported Substances*, BISD 34S/136, at p. 158, para. 5.1.9 (emphasis added). We do not consider it a meaningful distinction on this issue that this quote refers to the first sentence of Article III:2 rather than the second sentence. To find otherwise would be to imply that one could refer to expectations with respect to determining the market conditions for examining like products but not for examining whether products are directly competitive or substitutable. Given that like products are a subset of directly competitive or substitutable products, this would be illogical.

[365] L. Brown (ed), *The New Shorter Oxford English Dictionary* (Clarendon Press, 1993), Vol. 2 at p. 2310 (emphasis in the original).

[366] *Ibid.*, Vol. 1, at p. 885 (emphasis in original).

happen in the future, but most evidence cannot be so conveniently parsed. If one is dealing with products that are experience based consumer items, then trends are particularly important and it would be unrealistic and, indeed, analytically unhelpful to attempt to separate every piece of evidence and disregard that which discusses implications for market structure in the near future.

3. *Products at Issue*

10.51. In order to determine whether the imported and domestic products are directly competitive or substitutable, it is necessary to properly identify such products. With respect to the domestic product, soju, there are two primary categories identified. There is distilled soju and diluted soju. Distilled soju has been described as soju made from a mix of additives and water blended into an alcohol solution extracted by a method of single-step distillation.[367] It is identified separately in the Korean tax law, although not in Korea's WTO Schedule of tariff bindings. Distilled soju accounts for less than one percent of soju sales in Korea. Distilled soju is taxed at a higher rate than diluted soju.

10.52. The other type of soju is what we have described as diluted soju. There was considerable discussion about the proper appellation for this product. The complainants described it as diluted soju and Korea maintained that it should be referred to as standard soju. We have adopted the name diluted soju for the product for purposes of descriptive clarity only, without any intention of thereby drawing substantive conclusions from the name. Within this category there is standard diluted soju and premium diluted soju.[368] Standard diluted soju is a lower priced product that has been dominant since the 1960's. Premium diluted soju, which generally has additives for flavouring, has been introduced in the past few years. It is higher priced and the advertising for it has cultivated a more "up-market" image. Its market share has grown rapidly and it now represents approximately five percent of soju sales.[369] All parties have agreed that premium and standard diluted soju are variations of one product. Diluted soju is described as:

> soju made from a mix of additives, water and grain solution (or distilled soju solution - the *Liquor Tax Act* classifies soju as being '*diluted*' soju where the ratio of the grain solution or the distilled soju solution amounts to 20% or less of the total volume of alcohol),

---

[367] See Korea First Submission, Attachment 1, Decision of the Fair Trade Commission of the Republic of Korea Case No. 9607, Advertisement 1023, 30 November 1996, at 3.

[368] See discussion at footnote 20, above. To have decided otherwise would have left us discussing "standard soju" and "premium standard soju", terminology which would have been confusing.

[369] The EC argues that it might account for as much as 10 percent of the market. Apparently, it is difficult to judge the market share precisely because there is no legal definition which would assist in compiling statistics. See para. 6.24. Korea states that sales of premium diluted soju have declined recently. We also note that sales of imports have declined at the same time due, presumably, to the current financial crisis in Korea. The lower priced product, standard diluted soju has increased sales. These changes in levels of sales, if anything, can be taken as further support for the relationship of the products. See EC Answers to Questions, Question 1 from the Panel at pp. 1-2, and accompanying chart.

blended into an alcohol solution extracted by a method of "continuous distillation".[370]

10.53. Korea has argued that distilled soju and diluted soju are two separate product categories for purposes of analysis under both sentences of Article III:2. Korea argues that the complainants must prove the imported products are like or directly competitive with or substitutable for each of the two domestic products separately and provide a comparison with each on a product-by-product basis. Complainants, on the other hand, argue that the two types of soju are nearly identical and therefore all soju is a single product for purposes of analysis in this case.

10.54. The distinction between distilled and diluted soju is more relevant to a discussion of like products where the product categories are narrower. The Korean Fair Trade Commission has stated that:

> the basic difference between those two types of soju is whether the alcohol was extracted by means of single-step distillation or continuous distillation.[371]

We are not convinced that this difference is significant. Moreover, in our view, to the extent there are differences between the two types of soju, distilled soju is more similar to the imported products than diluted soju. Distilled soju is higher priced than diluted soju; distilled soju (40-45 percent) has a higher alcohol content than diluted soju (20-25 percent); distilled soju often is used as gifts, an end-use identified by Korea as one also pertaining to imports; distilled soju is aged as is the case with many of the imports. As is discussed further below, we do not think that these types of differences are sufficiently important to meaningfully distinguish between two products. We will proceed with an examination primarily of the competitive relationship of the imported products with diluted soju, including both standard and premium subcategories of diluted soju. If we find that diluted soju is directly competitive with and substitutable for the imported products, it will follow that this is also the case for distilled soju because distilled soju is intermediary between the imported products and diluted soju. Indeed, distilled soju is, on the one hand, more similar to the imported products than diluted soju and is, on the other hand, more similar to diluted soju than are the imported products.

10.55. With respect to the imported products, there is a fundamental and important disagreement between the parties to the dispute. Complainants argue that all distilled beverages are directly competitive or substitutable with each other. They have presented evidence with respect to several categories of such imported products, but not all products within the tariff heading 2208 which constitutes the parameters of the terms of reference. They have argued that they have presented evidence with respect to the primary imported products as examples of the broader category. The EC, in particular, argued that to present information on each and every type of distilled beverage would put too much of a burden on complainants and would overwhelm the Panel with details of little substantive importance. Both complainants have argued that the Appellate Body ruled that all imported distilled beverages were di-

---

[370] Korea First Submission, Attachment 1, *supra*, at 3.
[371] *Ibid.*

rectly competitive with or substitutable for shochu in the case of *Japan - Taxes on Alcoholic Beverages II*. They argue that we should take guidance from the Appellate Body's decision in that case.

10.56. The *Japan - Taxes on Alcoholic Beverages II* case provides unclear guidance for the present case. The panel in that instance made findings with respect to the western-style alcoholic beverages for which specific evidence was provided. However, the panel did not explicitly state that it was not making a determination with respect to the other products within HS 2208. The Appellate Body ruled that, as a matter of law, the panel erred in not making determinations with respect to all of the products within the terms of reference. The Appellate Body went on to find that all imported products identified by HS 2208 were directly competitive with or substitutable for the domestic product, shochu. In that case, the Appellate Body did not further explain its reasoning. We are unaware of the specifics of the *Japan - Taxes on Alcoholic Beverages II* case in this regard. While taking note of the Appellate Body's finding on this issue, we also recall the Appellate Body's statement that findings with respect to Article III:2 are to be made on a case-by-case basis.

10.57. In the present case, we are of the view that we cannot make affirmative findings with respect to products for which the complainants have provided virtually no evidence with respect to their physical characteristics, end-uses, retail outlets or prices.[372] It may be possible that the products identified by the complainants serve as adequate representatives of a broader category, but complainants did not provide such evidence and relied instead on assertions combined with reference to the prior Appellate Body decision regarding Japan. While, as stated, we will make reference to other markets when such markets provide relevant evidence to the determination, the evidence from the Japanese market and the determination of the Appellate Body in that case serves as an inadequate evidentiary basis for us to conclude that all products within HS 2208 are the appropriate category of imported products in the case of Korea. Indeed, to make the determination as requested by the complainants without further evidence could be to, in some circumstances, prejudge the case. If we were to follow their reasoning that the Appellate Body decision in *Japan - Taxes on Alcoholic Beverages II* case had determined the parameters of the imports for all cases, then because soju is within the HS category of 2208, it could be claimed that the whole issue of the case is decided without any evidence relating to the specific case of Korea. To look at it another way, complainants would like us to establish that all products within 2208, including soju, presumptively are covered and then leave it to Korea to prove that soju is not properly included with respect to the Korean market. This could, in some circumstances, have the practical effect of shifting the burden of proof onto the defending party without the complaining parties having first established a *prima facie* case. It may be that such evidence concerning the whole category could be developed with respect to the Korean market or may exist with respect to other markets, as apparently was the case with respect to the Japa-

---

[372] The general statements by the United States and the European Communities regarding the use of the four digit tariff heading and the identified common physical characteristics and end-uses of distilled alcoholic beverages provides very weak evidence for inclusion of all products within HS 2208 given that some of those products were not even identified to the Panel.

nese market, but in this case we can only make determinations with respect to the products specifically discussed by the complainants. These are vodka, whiskies, rum, gin, brandies, cognac, liqueurs, tequila and ad-mixtures.[373] The complainants have not carried their burden of establishing a *prima facie* case with respect to the remainder of the products under HS 2208.[374]

10.58. We include tequila for which evidence was presented. We note that a third party, Mexico, provided arguments with respect to both tequila and mescal. The complainants provided specific evidence for tequila, but not mescal. We consider it appropriate to take into consideration information provided by a third party. In this case, mescal was mentioned without positive evidence of the actual or potential competitive nature of the product in the Korean market. Tequila was included in the Dodwell study where there was evidence of the response of consumers to the relative changes in the prices of soju and tequila. Tequila is a white alcoholic beverage which is also used, among other things, to accompany spicy foods.

10.59. While we have declined to find all products identified by HS 2208 are included in our determination, we also do not accept the Korean argument that we are required to make an item by item comparison between each imported product and both types of soju. Relying on product categories is appropriate in many cases. Indeed, in this case parties generally referred to the category of "whiskies" which included several subcategories of types of whisky such as Scotch (premium and standard), Irish, Bourbon, Rye, Canadian, etc, all of which have some differences. The question becomes where to draw the boundaries between categories, rather than whether it is appropriate to utilize categories for analytical purposes.

10.60. In our view, it is appropriate to group together all of the imported products for which evidence was presented. We note that Korea in its arguments often referred to western-style beverages. The "high-class" restaurants and bars that allegedly did not serve soju, were said to sell western-style beverages. There are some physical differences between the various imported beverages but, as discussed below, we do not find these differences sufficient to make it inappropriate to group them together as imported products. The prices of the imported products show a spread over a certain range, but as with the relationship to soju, we do not think the prices so distinct as to prohibit us from examining the identified imports as a group. The imports appear to be distributed in similar manners for similar purposes. Therefore, based on the evidence, including that discussed more fully in section 4 below,

---

[373] These are contained within portions of Korea's domestic tariff schedule, as follows:

2208.20	Spirits obtained by distilling grape wine or grape marc
2208.30	Whiskeys
2208.40	Rum and tafia
2208.50	Gin and Geneva
2208.60	Vodka
2208.70	Liqueurs and Cordials
2208.90.10	Brandies other than that of heading No. 2208.20
2208.90.40	Soju
2208.90.70	Tequila

[374] See Appellate Body Report *on United States - Measures Affecting the Imports of Woven Shirts and Blouses from India,* adopted 25 April 1997, WT/DS33/AB/R, DSR 1997:I, 323, at 333-338.

we find that, on balance, all of the imported products specifically identified by the complainants have sufficient common characteristics, end-uses and channels of distribution and prices to be considered together.[375]

4.　*Product Comparisons*

10.61. We next will consider the various characteristics of the products to assess whether there is a competitive or substitutable relationship between the imported and domestic products and draw conclusions as to whether the nature of any such relationship is direct. We will review the physical characteristics, end-uses including evidence of advertising activities, channels of distribution, price relationships including cross-price elasticities, and any other characteristics.

(i)　Physical characteristics

10.62. Complainants argue that the defining physical characteristic of both imported and domestic products is the fact that they are distilled beverages. Other differences such as colouring or flavouring have no relevance in an analysis of whether products are directly competitive or substitutable. As summarized by the complainants:

> The basic physical properties of soju and other categories of liquors concerned in this dispute are essentially the same. All distilled liquors are concentrated forms of alcohol produced by the process of distillation. At the point of distillation, all spirits are nearly identical, which means that the raw materials and methods of distillation have almost no impact on the final product. Post-distillation processes such as ageing, dilution with water or addition of flavourings, do not change the basic fact that the product sold is still a concentrated form of alcohol.[376]

10.63. Korea argues that the different physical characteristics are substantial. They argue that distilled liquors can be derived from a variety of sources and that the selection of raw materials can play an important role in determining the ultimate qualities of the finished product. Korea argues that there is a distinction between brown spirits such as whisky and white spirits such as soju and gin. The brown colouring generally comes from aging in barrels whereas white spirits are not aged before bottling. Korea argues that even very minor differences in physical characteristics can be determinative if consumers perceive them as important. To put it another way, in response to a question from the panel, Korea argues that two products which are nearly physically identical can be found not directly competitive or substitutable if consumers perceive them differently. According to Korea the question's reference to nearly physically identical begs the question, because "nearly" must be defined in

---

[375] This decision does not prejudge the substantive discussion; rather we are merely identifying an analytical tool. It is possible that during the course of a dispute, evidence will show that an analytical approach should be revised. In this case, however, we note that the results of the inquiry described in the following sections confirm the appropriateness of grouping the imports together for purposes of analysis.

[376] EC First Submission, at para. 97; US First Submission, at para. 68.

terms of consumer perception rather than comparison of physical characteristics by non-consumers such as chemists.

10.64. We do not agree with Korea's narrow interpretation. The Panel is examining the nature of the competitive relationship and determining whether there is an actual or potential relationship sufficiently direct to come within the strictures of Article III:2, second sentence. The physical characteristics themselves must be reviewed for if two products are physically identical or nearly so, then it obviously means that there is a greater potential for a direct competitive relationship. The United States argued that there can be two products of identical physical properties such as name brand and generic aspirin which are marketed somewhat differently and perceived somewhat differently by consumers. Nonetheless, they would be considered directly competitive or substitutable and the identical or nearly identical physical characteristics would be a significant factor in the analysis. We find this analogy useful.

10.65. The panel on *Japan - Taxes on Alcoholic Beverages II* referred to the usefulness of examining marketing strategies.[377] Marketing strategies that highlight fundamental product distinctions or, alternatively, underlying similarities may be useful tools for analysis. However, marketing strategies sometimes aim to create distinctions that are primarily perceptual between products with very similar physical characteristics. The existence of such perceptions based on marketing strategies rather than physical similarities and potential end uses does not mean that products are not at least potentially competitive. Indeed, it is natural and logical that marketers would recognize the possibility of capitalizing on the tax differentiation to create a marketing advantage.

10.66. As noted above, we have found it most fruitful to first examine whether the imported products are directly competitive or substitutable and only to turn to the question of whether they are like products second. The determination of whether two products are "like" has traditionally turned to a greater extent (although not exclusively), on the physical characteristics of products. It would be an incorrect reading of the law to argue that products' physical similarities were somehow less relevant for the category of directly competitive or substitutable products than for the subcategory of like products. To put it another way, if two products are physically identical or nearly so, it is highly probable that they are "like." They should not then be found to be not directly competitive or substitutable because marketing campaigns (or government tax regimes) have created a distinction in consumer perceptions. Such consumer perception distinctions are relevant but not determinative when the question is the *nature* of an actual or potential competitive relationship rather than merely a quantitative analysis of the current extent of competition. To find otherwise might allow allegedly discriminatory government measures to create self-justifying product distinctions between identical or nearly identical products.

10.67. We note that for purposes of the analysis under Article III:2, second sentence, products do not need to be identical to be directly competitive or substitutable.[378] However, as discussed above, physical similarities are relevant to the in-

---

[377] Report of the Panel on *Japan - Taxes on Alcoholic Beverages II, supra*, at para. 6.28.

[378] Appellate Body Report on *Canada - Certain Measures Concerning Periodicals*, adopted on 30 July 1997, WT/DS31/AB/R, DSR 1997:I, 449, at 473.

quiry, particularly with respect to potential competition. All the products presented to the Panel have the essential feature of being distilled alcoholic beverages. Indeed, Korea imports ethyl alcohol for use as the base ingredient for diluted soju. Such ethyl alcohol is also used in a similar process for vodka and shochu, among other products.[379] All are bottled and labelled in a similar manner.[380] In our view, the differences due to the filtration or aging processes of the beverages described are not so important as to render the products non-substitutable. Aging in barrels will impart some flavour to the product as well as a dark colour, usually amber. But differences in color do not render products non-substitutable. We note that rum also is sold in light and dark versions, albeit not as a result of barrel aging. There have been no arguments that the two types of rums are not competitive due to this physical difference. Some beverages have flavourings added, e.g., juniper berries are added to clear spirits to make gin. However, we find that these differences in flavour or colour are relatively minor. We note that soju may also contain various sweeteners and flavourings. Indeed, the premium soju that has entered the market recently, corresponding to the entry of the imported products, has increased amounts of these additives.[381] While there are some differences in the physical characteristics of the products, weighing the evidence presented, we find that there are fundamental physical similarities between the imported and domestic products that would support a finding that the imported and domestic products in question are directly competitive or substitutable.[382]

(ii)   End-uses

10.68. The issue of end-uses for these products has drawn much attention from the parties in this case. The complainants have argued that all distilled beverages have common end-uses. They have identified these as follows:

1. all of them are drunk with the same purposes: thirst quenching, socialization, relaxation, etc.;

2. all of them may be drunk in similar ways: "straight," diluted with water or other non-alcoholic beverages or mixed with other alcoholic beverages;

3. all of them may be consumed before, after or during meals; and

---

[379] See para. 6.153 and para. 6.161. Korea has argued that this statement takes in too much. It would also imply that certain industrial products might also be like soju or directly competitive or substitutable for it. We agree that this commonality of source material is not, in and of itself, sufficient for our analysis in this case. However, it is a factor which we take into consideration for it does go to show that there is a fundamental similarity in the basic materials used in the manufacturing process.

[380] Korea attempted to place a great deal of emphasis on the differences in bottle sizes and labelling. Korea argued that bottles of soju were very different from bottles of shochu which were, according to Korea, made to look more like whisky. We find these differences relatively minor compared to the similarities in presentation.

[381] See para. 5.55 and para.7.18.

[382] We note that these findings with respect to physical characteristics support our conclusion in section 3, above, that the identified imported products should be considered as a single category.

4.   all of them may be consumed at home or in public places such as restaurants, bars, etc.

10.69. These are very broad categories of end uses. In response to questions from the Panel, the complainants identified "relaxation" from the concentrated alcohol content as perhaps a defining characteristic. They also responded that such beverages as soft drinks could not be included even though they fit some of the end-uses description because they contained no alcohol.

10.70. Korea has structured its defense primarily around two related aspects of the case. First is price, which will be discussed below. Second is differing end-uses. The two are related because Korea argues that the overwhelming end-use for soju, particularly diluted soju, is drinking with meals in Korean-style and other traditional restaurants whereas western-style beverages allegedly are almost never utilized in such a fashion. One of the reasons, allegedly, for this distinction is the great price differences which make western-style beverages too expensive for such frequent use. There are other reasons put forward by Korea for the end-use distinction as well. For instance, soju is said by Korea to be a harsh drink particularly suitable for drinking with spicy Korean food.[383]

10.71. Prior to the second substantive meeting of the Panel, Korea produced a study by the A.C. Nielsen company which Korea argued documented the very distinct end-uses of soju and western-style beverages. The survey concluded that while all Korean restaurants, Chinese restaurants and mobile street vendors deal in standard soju, most cafes/western-style restaurants and bars deal in whisky. The survey also found that 29.3% of the respondents consumed alcoholic beverages at home with meals, while 81% were found to have consumed such beverages with meals at restaurants. The authors of the report claimed that diluted soju was the predominantly consumed alcoholic beverage with meals. Drinking diluted soju with meals was most popular at Korean restaurants (73%), followed by Japanese restaurants (18.7%). Of the 7 beverages offered to the respondents, none of them were consumed with meals at cafes/western style restaurants, bars and hotel bars. Finally, the survey found that soju is predominantly consumed straight (98.6%), while whisky is usually consumed on the rocks (63.8%).

10.72. The complainants responded to this survey by pointing out that there were several categories of overlapping end-uses. For instance, all Japanese restaurants served soju and 40% of them served whisky; a further 6.7% served brandy or cognac. Of the responding Western-style restaurants and cafes, 90% served whisky and a lesser number served other types of western-style beverages. However, 21.7% served soju. Also, the complainants noted that while only 1.7% of the individual respondents drank whisky at home with meals, only 29.3% of all respondents con-

---

[383] We note that Korea elsewhere emphasizes the sweetness of soju for purposes of distinguishing it from shochu. (See para.5.55.) Also, Korea submitted a copy of an advertisement for a standard diluted soju which emphasized its mildness. (Attachment 6 to Korean First Submission) This would seem to imply that Koreans would be willing to substitute allegedly less harsh western-style beverages were they to experience them. Furthermore, it is unclear how Korea's emphasis on the lower alcohol level of diluted soju relative to western-style beverages accords with the assertion of its singular harshness. Finally, it also is unclear why food should be seen as necessary to cushion the effect on the stomach of a *lower* alcohol drink compared to a higher alcohol drink.

sumed any alcoholic beverages at home with meals. Therefore, the proper comparison was of the 1.7% with the 29.3 %, thus leaving 5.8% of all respondents who consumed alcoholic beverages with meals at home as drinkers of whisky as the accompaniment. Complainants have questioned some of the findings of the Nielsen survey, but also have argued that these results are actually indications of overlapping end-uses.

10.73. Complainants have noted that there were almost no western-style beverages in Korea until the last five years following changes in the duty rates on imported distilled beverages. Furthermore, they argue, alcoholic beverages, like many foods and beverages, are experience based products. People tend to purchase what they are familiar with and change their tastes only over a period of time. They will only make minor substitutions for the familiar product at first and higher frequency will tend to occur over a period of time until a fairly stable rate is achieved.[384] The trends shown in the Nielsen survey - as well as the substitutability shown in the EC's market survey, the Dodwell study - constitute, according to complainants, unmistakable evidence of the beginnings of substitutability and common end-uses by imports. Trends are significant with respect to such products. We think there is merit in these arguments and further note that this is another reason why the distinction offered by Korea between potential and future competition is too stark. Reasonable projections of increasing substitutability over a period of time are relevant and valid for determinations made pursuant to Article III:2.

10.74. Korea offers an analogy between the alcoholic beverage market and the automobile market which we do not find particularly useful. Korea argues that the imported products are Ferraris compared to soju's Renault Clio. However, the analogy is inapt. Automobiles are durable goods of great value relative to income that are only purchased periodically, generally only once every several years. It is probable that the purchaser of a Renault Clio has no option to purchase a Ferrari which might cost considerably more than the Clio purchaser's annual salary. Alcoholic beverages, on the other hand, are consumer goods which are purchased frequently, and even the Clio purchaser can afford to purchase a bottle of a more expensive beverage at least occasionally. The ratios between $10 and $100 products may be the same as between $10,000 and $100,000 products, but the purchasing decisions of ordinary consumers in the two situations are quite distinct.

10.75. The EC submitted a market survey conducted by Trendscope during the second substantive meeting of the Panel. It was of the same general type as Korea's Nielsen survey. It examined end-uses but did not go into specific price comparisons as did the earlier submitted Dodwell study. Korea requests that we disregard the Trendscope survey. As discussed above, we decline to disregard the survey; however, we do not, in fact, accord much weight to the submission by the EC. It adds little of probative value to the extensive prior submissions of the parties. What was of more interest was the nature of some of the substantive disagreements of the parties concerning information contained in the Trendscope survey. Among other things there was a disagreement over the correct Korean terms and whether the questioners adequately distinguished between "meals" and "food." Korea apparently

---

[384] See para. 6.120.

puts a great deal of store in this distinction, arguing that one must look exclusively at "meals" where Korean soju predominates rather than at mere "food" which might include snacks where western-style beverages might be consumed.

10.76. We do not consider this a meaningful distinction between end-uses of products, certainly not enough to establish separate and non-competing product categories for purposes of Article III:2, second sentence. Neither this nor other panels should be required to draw such fine distinctions permitting significant differences in the application of the law based upon such differences as saying one beverage is used for snacks and another for meals. In reviewing the evidence of this case, we are not convinced that such a distinction, even assuming Korea's argument that it exists is correct, is sufficient. If a distilled alcoholic beverage is drunk with snacks, the nature of the competitive relationship is that it can be drunk with meals, either as marketing campaigns change or persons become more familiar with products new to the market. Indeed, we are unconvinced in general that the distinction between drinking alcoholic beverages at meals and drinking them either before or after meals was, in the context of this case, sufficient to render the products not directly competitive or substitutable.[385] Furthermore, we do not agree with the whole concept of basing a distinction on preferences for traditional drinks with traditional meals.[386] Korean food may be spicy, but it is not uniquely so in such a manner that soju and only soju is suitable for consumption with meals. It may, in fact, transpire that most Koreans will continue to prefer their traditional drink of soju with traditional food, but based on the information in the surveys and the trends in consumption patterns, it does appear that some Koreans at some times prefer other beverages and that these trends towards substitutability are likely to continue, even with respect to end-use categories we consider overly narrow.

10.77. We also are of the view that the presence of ad-mixtures in the Korean market lends credence to the conclusion of the substitutability of the imported and domestic products. Korea argued that the domestic ad-mixtures are not soju, but as

---

[385] Korea attempts to draw a number of product distinctions based on quite narrow differences. For example, Korea drew distinctions between some products based on whether they were given as gifts. Some of these assertions appeared to be contradictory. For instance, Korea stated that a distinction between diluted soju and brandy was that cognac and brandy were generally used as gifts, unlike diluted soju. However, Korea later stated that distilled soju was distinguishable from cognac and brandy because it was used for gifts while cognac and brandy were sold in "high-brow restaurants." (See para. 5.259 and para. 5.295) When asked to explain, Korea responded with an even finer distinction as to what occasions particular gift beverages are used for. (See para. 7.23) Korea attempts to draw too fine a line between products for purposes of analysis under Article III:2, second sentence.

[386] Korea has argued that the notion that distilled alcoholic beverages are not to be consumed with food is a peculiarly western notion. It is not clear that this assertion concerning "western notions" is necessarily true. Such drinks as vodka and whisky may very well be associated with traditional meals in some of the countries of origin. Furthermore, even if it is true that westerners do not generally drink distilled beverages with meals, it begs the question as to whether Koreans would like to, or sometimes do now, drink western style beverages with their meals. Also, Korea's assertion that "soju is a volume drink; vodka is not" (See para. 5.269) could be questionable based on drinking behaviour in other markets. Again, while our decision is in regard to the Korean market, consumption patterns elsewhere are relevant, at least for purposes of assessing potential competitiveness.

soju is defined in the Liquor Tax Law as essentially diluted ethyl alcohol with some flavorings and additives, it is unclear what point Korea is making with this alleged distinction. If alcoholic beverages can be and often are drunk mixed, either as pre-mixes or mixed after purchase, it shows the potential for substitution between the base drinks and the lack of importance of the distinction which Korea attempts to draw based on alcohol strength.[387]

10.78. End-uses constitute one factor which is particularly relevant to the issue of *potential* competition or substitutability. If there are common end-uses, then two products may very well be competitive, either immediately or in the near and reasonably predictable future. In this regard, we do find it relevant, albeit of less relative evidentiary weight, to consider the nature of the competitive relationship in other markets. If two products compete in a market that is relatively less affected by government tax policies, it might shed light on whether those same two products are potentially competitive in the market in question. Such a comparison is not dispositive by any means; neither should it be ignored. Its relevance consists primarily in whether it tends to corroborate the trends seen in the market in question or whether it reveals inconsistencies with complainants' case which deserve further consideration. In this regard, we note that in Japan there was increasing end-use substitutability between western-style beverages and Japanese shochu as consumers became increasingly familiar with the new product. Both soju and shochu are traditional drinks in their respective countries. Both markets involved small but growing import penetration following partial liberalization. The trends that the panel and Appellate Body observed in Japan appear to be beginning in Korea.

10.79. Article III cases deal with markets[388] and the response of Korean producers to changes in the markets provides significant evidence of at least a competitive relationship between soju and the imports. The trend towards increasingly overlapping end-uses are supported by the marketing strategies of the domestic Korean companies. These companies met the potential threat of imports of western-style beverages by creating and selling premium diluted soju. This beverage had more flavourings and was marketed in a manner more similar to western-style beverages than standard diluted soju. However, it remained within the definition of diluted soju in the Korean tax law. The physical characteristics were changed enough to be more similar to such imports while still enjoying the price advantages provided by lower tax rates. The complainants also produced evidence that these products were

---

[387] The question of mixes highlights another of the inconsistencies that emerge from Korea's narrow product-by-product comparisons. For example, Korea argues that an important distinction between soju and vodka is that soju is almost always drunk straight whereas vodka is a mixing drink. (See paras. 5.268-5.269) If this is an important distinction, it would seem an important similarity then between soju and whisky, for example, that the two are often drunk straight. Or if whisky is mixed, it generally is with ice or water which also would seem to highlight the similarity with diluted soju on the basis of alcohol strength of the consumed product. It is also unclear what the basis is for Korea's assertion that vodka is a mixing drink. While it frequently is served that way, it also is served straight.

[388] Appellate Body report on *Japan - Taxes on Alcoholic Beverages II, supra*, at p. 25.

being advertised as competitive with western-style beverages.[389] Indeed, one advertisement referred to soju as a vodka-like product and also showed a new product called barley soju which clearly is intended to be comparable to imported products such as whiskies.[390] Evidence was also produced from various sources including Korean Air's in-flight magazine showing very similar advertising strategies for distilled soju and western-style beverages.[391]

10.80. Korea argued that advertisements in Korean Air's in-flight magazine should not be considered as aimed at the broad domestic market. Similarly, according to Korea, information from the website of the largest Korean soju producer, Jinro, in English or other advertisements in Japanese would be aimed at the export market not at the Korean domestic market, which is the only relevant one here. We take note of Korea's criticisms of these materials. However, we continue to disagree that the *only* relevant market for collecting data is the Korean domestic market.[392] Rather the Korean market is the one that is the subject of our decision. In assessing the potential for products to be directly competitive with or substitutable for the domestic products it is relevant to look at how the domestic Korean companies produce, advertise and distribute their products in other markets as well as in Korea. Such evidence may be valuable for confirming or challenging trends and identifying important characteristics of the market which is the subject of the determination. In this case, the trends in the Japanese market where shochu and imported western-style beverages became increasingly used for the same purposes and the behaviour of Korean firms that met the challenge of imports with versions of soju increasingly similar to such imported beverages are relevant confirmation of what exists, albeit in a somewhat nascent form, in the Korean market.

10.81. The issue was raised whether the Panel should use the same criteria for defining markets under Article III:2 as under competition law. Korea was generally supportive of utilizing competition law market definitions for purposes of Article III and even went further and queried whether competition law market definitions might be too broad for purposes of Article III. Complainants argued, on the other hand, that Article III has a different purpose from competition law. Article III, they argue, is an anti-discrimination provision aimed at ensuring that government measures do not result in competitive conditions which favor the domestic industry. Therefore, the interpretation should be broad. According to the complainants, antitrust law has a different purpose of addressing the actions of individual firms or persons that threaten competition and such laws generally do not recognize any distinction between foreign or domestic persons. While the specifics of the interaction between trade and competition law are still being developed, we concur that the market definitions need not be the same. Trade law generally, and Article III in particular, focuses on the promotion of economic opportunities for importers through

---

[389] See US Exhibits E and F and EC First Submission, Annex 12. See also the Sofres Report, *supra*, at 117.

[390] US Exhibit Q.

[391] US Exhibit D.

[392] It is not clear that all the advertisements were aimed completely outside the Korean market as Korea claims. The advertisements in U.S. Exhibit D appear to be in Korean as well as English.

the elimination of discriminatory governmental measures which impair fair international trade. Thus, trade law addresses the issue of the potentiality to compete. Antitrust law generally focuses on firms' practices or structural modifications which may prevent or restrain or eliminate competition. It is not illogical that markets be defined more broadly when implementing laws primarily designed to protect competitive opportunities than when implementing laws designed to protect the actual mechanisms of competition. In our view, it can thus be appropriate to utilize a broader concept of markets with respect to Article III:2, second sentence, than is used in antitrust law. We also take note of the developments under European Community law in this regard. For instance, under Article 95 of the Treaty of Rome, which is based on the language of Article III, distilled alcoholic beverages have been considered similar or competitive in a series of rulings by the European Court of Justice ("ECJ").[393] On the other hand, in examining a merger under the European Merger Regulation,[394] the Commission of the European Communities found that whisky constituted a separate market.[395] Similarly, in an Article 95 case, bananas were considered in competition with other fruits.[396] However, under EC competition law, bananas constituted a distinct product market.[397] We are mindful that the Treaty of Rome is different in scope and purpose from the General Agreement, the similarity of Article 95 and Article III, notwithstanding. Nonetheless, we observe that there is relevance in examining how the ECJ has defined markets in similar situations to assist in understanding the relationship between the analysis of non-discrimination provisions and competition law.[398]

10.82. In making our assessment with respect to degree and nature of overlapping end-uses, we wish to make clear that we are not putting a burden of proving the negative on Korea. Rather, we think that the complainants submitted adequate evidence, *inter alia*, in the form of the Dodwell study, anecdotal evidence, and evidence of trends and results in other markets to establish this portion of their case. We also have taken note of the information in the Nielsen and Trendscope studies. All the beverages described are utilized for socialization purposes in situations where the effect of drinks containing relatively high concentrations of alcohol is desired. They may be used in a variety of social settings, including with food, either meals or otherwise. Korea's attempts to rebut this argument ultimately were unpersuasive. The distinctions that Korea would have us draw are too narrow and transitory. We decline to base a decision on whether a particular type of food is a meal or merely a snack. Indeed, as discussed above, we are sceptical of the whole meal-

---

[393] See *Commission v. France*, Case 168/78, 1980 ECR 347; *Commission v. Kingdom of Denmark*, Case 171/78, 1980 ECR 447; *Commission v. Italian Republic*, Case 319/81, 1983 ECR 601; *Commission v Hellenic Republic*, Case 230/89, 1991 ECR 1909.

[394] Council Regulation No. 4064/89 of 21 December 1989 on the control of concentrations between undertakings.

[395] Case No. IV/M 938 - *Guinness/Grand Metropolitan*.

[396] *Commission v. Italy*, Case 184/85, 1987 ECR 2013.

[397] *United Brands v. Commission*, Case 27/76, 1978 ECR 207.

[398] In finding the relationship of the provisions to each other relevant, we do not intend to imply that we have adopted the market definitions defined in these or other ECJ cases for purposes of this decision.

based rationale which is an important part of the Korean case. In balancing the evidence in this regard, we are mindful of the examples offered by the drafters of Article III and *Ad* Article III who considered apples and oranges directly competitive or substitutable products. Thus, we conclude that, on balance, the evidence is that there are current and potential overlapping end-uses sufficient to be supportive of a finding that the domestic and imported products are directly competitive or substitutable.[399]

(iii)   Channels of distribution and points of sale

10.83. There is a considerable degree of overlap between the questions of common end-uses and common channels of distribution. Often, consumer products will be distributed in a manner that reflects their intended end-uses. Channels of distribution tend to reveal present market structure while end-uses deals with both the current overlap, if any, and potential for future overlap. In the present case, it is evident that soju and western-style beverages are currently sold through similar retail outlets in a quite similar manner for off-premise consumption.[400] Korea has argued that when taken from such outlets soju is consumed differently; this argument is addressed in the preceding section. Similarly, the complainants have shown that there are some similarities in other presumably more minor outlets such as duty free sales.

10.84. The primary area of disagreement is with respect to the channels of distribution for on-premise consumption. Korea argues that soju is sold primarily for use with Korean food in Korean-style restaurants. This was broadened and further explained by Korea through the Nielsen survey, which Korea argues provides evidence that most soju for on-premise consumption was sold to traditional Korean-style restaurants, as well as Japanese and Chinese restaurants and mobile vendors. Conversely, western-style beverages were sold for on-premise consumption primarily to cafes/western-style restaurants and bars.

10.85. As discussed above, the complainants have noted that there was overlapping distribution in the Japanese-style restaurants and cafes/western-style restaurants in Korea's Nielsen survey. We also noted from the Nielsen survey that, with respect to sales to cafes/western-style restaurants, while only 13 of the 60 survey respondents said they sold soju compared with 54 of the 60 saying they sold whisky, they sold 22,710 ml per month of soju compared with 11,702 ml of whisky. That is, more soju was sold than whisky in this allegedly western-style beverage channel of distribution. This seems to detract from the Korean claim that this type of on-premise channel of distribution overwhelmingly favoured whisky.

10.86. Korea asserted that western-style beverages are limited for on-premise consumption to "classy" establishments such as "high-class" bars, karaoke bars and

---

[399] We note that the conclusions we reach in this section regarding end-uses supports our conclusion in section 3, above, that the identified imports should be considered a single category.

[400] US Exhibit G; EC First Submission, Annex 11. See also paras. 6.93-6.94 and 6.188-6.189. We note that this evidence also shows that imports are sold in a similar manner to each other and supports our conclusion in section 3, above.

expensive restaurants.[401] In response to these arguments, the United States sent its embassy personnel in Seoul in search of large, traditional Korean-style restaurants to test the hypothesis. They claim to have found nine such establishments in the vicinity of the US Embassy that sold both whisky and soju. This prompted a discussion among the parties as to whether the identified restaurants would be typical or more expensive than normal. The resolution of the question of whether these restaurants were representative or were too expensive to qualify as "traditional Korean-style" is less important than the nature of the discussion itself. We do not think that a product distinction in a dispute under Article III:2, second sentence, can turn on such a thin and changeable distinction as Korea has attempted to make based on whether a restaurant is "high-class" or "expensive" or not. The only meaningful distinction in channels of distribution and points of sale that came to light in this case was the distinction between on-premise and off-premise distribution, but that distinction does not appear to distinguish between the imported and domestic products at issue. We find that, overall, there is considerable evidence of overlap in channels of distribution and points of sale of these products and such evidence is supportive of a finding that the identified imported and domestic products are directly competitive or substitutable.

(iv)   Prices

10.87. Complainants have submitted a study of Korean consumer behaviour (the Dodwell study) related to relative price movements of soju and various western-style beverages, including premium Scotch whisky, standard whisky, cognac, vodka, gin, rum, tequila and liqueurs. The Dodwell study purports to show what happens when either the price of soju increases or the price of western-style beverages decreases, both done in specific increments. The survey also attempted to determine whether there was any evidence of cross-price elasticity. In response to Korea's challenges to the data and methodology, the complainants responded that the study was not attempting to show actual calculations of cross-price elasticity ratios because of difficulties inherent in the situation. Complainants said that the imported products had not been available in sufficient quantities to provide adequate consumer familiarity with the products and, furthermore, the Korean tax measures at issue also skewed the pricing and product availability structure such that it would be difficult to calculate actual cross-price elasticity ratios. As noted above, the complainants argued that alcoholic beverages were experience goods. People tend to consume what they are familiar with. Brand and product loyalty are strong and consumers will change their patterns only slowly over a long period of time following significant marketing activity and dependent upon plentiful product availability. Complainants emphasized the statement in the study that it was intended to "determine whether any evidence exists of cross-price elasticity between different spirits categories" rather than actually calculating such elasticities. Complainants referred to this as a more modest goal that was achievable and all that was possible in the circumstances.

---

[401] Statement of Korea at First Meeting of the Panel, at p. 8; Statement of Korea at Second Meeting of the Panel, at p. 20.

10.88. Complainants stated that the evidence of substitutability was quite strong when the two separate trends of lowering import prices and raising soju prices occurred. The United States summarized this in charts which showed the Dodwell results concluding that the respondents would chose imported brown spirits rather than soju 15.22% of the time under current price conditions, but 28.4% of the time when the price of diluted soju was raised 20% and the price of brown spirits was lowered to its lowest point in the survey. Similarly, with respect to white spirits the choice went from 13.8% for imports at current levels to 23.8% when soju was again increased 20% in price and imports were at their lowest survey levels.[402]

10.89. Korea provided considerable criticism of the Dodwell study. Citing a EC Commission notice on submissions related to EC competition law, Korea argued that any market study done for the purposes of influencing decision makers must be suspect. Korea also noted that surveys based on asking consumers hypothetical questions about opinions rather than direct factual questions are inherently untrustworthy because, among other things, there may be ambiguity in the questions and there was a need to infer factual results from opinions. Korea also noted that the firm retained to do such a survey has an incentive to try to provide answers consistent with the clients desires so that it might be retained again in the future. Specifically, Korea criticized the complexity of the questions and the unrepresentative nature of the respondents. Korea pointed out a number of anomalies in the results such as *increases* in soju consumption when the price increased from 1,100 won to 1,200 won. Korea also complained that premium diluted soju was included in the alternative samples along with imported beverages rather than included along with standard diluted soju as the base for comparison. According to Korea, this skewed the results. Finally, Korea was critical of the formulation of the questions, which Korea argued could be taken by the survey respondents to mean that they were being asked if they would try a bottle of imported beverages as a one-time purchase if offered a special cut rate price.

10.90. The complainants repeated that the Dodwell study had much more modest purposes than calculating cross-price elasticities for alcoholic beverages in the Korean market. Complainants noted that the Korean market had only been even partially deregulated for a few years and cited the findings of both panels examining Japanese alcoholic beverage taxes to the effect that government regulations and taxes often can freeze consumer preferences. In light of this, according to complainants, it stands to reason that the Dodwell study must be based on a selection of persons who have tried western-style beverages in order that they might have a frame of reference. Because of the recent arrival of western-style beverages in the market, they had to be asked a series of hypothetical questions rather than asking merely for factual information about current behaviour. Also, given the nature of alcoholic beverage purchases as on-going decisions on relatively low cost consumables, it was correct to ask whether the respondents to the survey would be willing to purchase some western-style beverages if prices changed rather than asking them if they would change their fundamental drinking habits. Complainants noted that there always will be statistical anomalies in any survey, but that in the case of the Dodwell

---

[402] First Submission of the United States, at paras. 78-85.

study the overall trends were clear even if there was an occasional negative correlation in the data. Finally, complainants have noted that the Dodwell study used the same research methods as the ASI study cited by the panel in *Japan - Taxes on Alcoholic Beverages II.*[403]

10.91. Korea correctly identifies some of the weaknesses and anomalies in the Dodwell study. The responses move in unexpected directions in some instances. However, on balance, we consider that the Dodwell study provided useful information regarding at least the potential competitiveness of the imported and domestic products. We also do not agree that some of the issues highlighted by Korea are detrimental to the results. We do not find it a flaw that the chosen respondents were not an accurate cross-section of all of Korean society. The surveyors selected 500 men between the ages of 20 and 49 from 3 Korean cities who had purchased soju in the past month and whisky in the past 3 months.[404] The age, gender and geographic profiles make sense. It is illogical to ask someone if they would shift to another consumer product - particularly a food or drink item - following a price change if such a person had never sampled such a product, or a similar one, before and the group chosen seems to be the most likely to have done so. We also agree with complainants about the prospective nature of the questions. If one is asking about the response to potential price changes, it is difficult to understand how a question about current behaviour will elicit a useful response. Also, when dealing with a consumable product which has a low price relative to income, it is not necessary that a respondent will permanently change drink preferences. The willingness to occasionally substitute one product for another when there is a relatively high frequency of purchase should be sufficient.

10.92. We must also note a general concern with some of the Korean criticisms of the Dodwell study. Article III serves to protect the expectations of competitive opportunities. Requiring a survey based on current, actual behaviour would prevent a potential market entrant from ever challenging government restrictions.[405] Indeed, it must be recalled that the Appellate Body confirmed that such surveys are not the decisive factor in decision making under Article III:2, second sentence. We do not find the Dodwell study decisive, but it is consistent with other information and is therefore helpful evidence. When dealing with an inquiry in the nature of the competitive relationship between products, quantitative analysis is helpful, but not necessary.

10.93. There was also considerable disagreement between the parties on the level of price differences between soju and imported western-style beverages. Korea used weighted averages and claimed that whisky was nearly 11 times more expensive than soju, making the effect of the taxes negligible. Complainants responded that the price of standard Scotch whisky was only about three times more expensive than premium diluted soju. On the other hand there were even greater variations with

---

[403] See Report of the Panel on *Japan -Taxes on Alcoholic Beverages II, supra*, at para. 6.32.

[404] EC Annex 13 at p. 3.

[405] As noted above in our discussion of potential competition, requiring surveys exclusively on current actual behaviour would make it even more difficult for less wealthy complainants to establish sufficient actual market presence to establish a *prima facie* case of nullification or impairment.

categories such as whisky, for instance between bulk blended-in Korea brands and fine malt Scotches, but Scotch whisky nevertheless was generally considered a single category of beverages. The complainants also argued that because of the high taxes and duties, the imports had tended to be of the higher priced brands thus skewing the numbers used by Korea. Korea further argued that the high priced brand argument was illogical because, unlike the Japanese system of specific duties, the Korean tax system was *ad valorem*. Complainants said that in such a restrictive market, it was not unusual for firms to lead entry into the market with higher priced niche brands to build awareness and sell with an exclusive cachet in segments where premiums could be charged and the consumers had higher incomes and therefore would be relatively less affected by tax levels. Complainants offered some evidence to support their claim by showing consumption patterns of various brands in other selected markets where there was a heavier relative weighting of sales towards lower priced brands than in Korea.[406]

10.94. In examining the evidence before us, we found that, while there currently are significant price differences between the imported and domestic products, overall the differences were not decisive. Korea presented prices as weighted averages which obscured the higher prices for premium diluted soju, which was the small but fast growing category created specifically by Korean manufacturers to be most competitive with imports. The price of premium diluted soju appears to be approximately two times the price of standard diluted soju, while vodka was four times the price and standard whisky four and a half times the price of premium diluted soju.[407] Distilled soju was twice the price of standard whisky.[408] There are greater price differences within some categories, e.g., whisky,[409] which none of the parties argued rendered such subcategories of products not directly competitive or substitutable. Furthermore, we agree with the complainants that absolute price differences are less important than behavioural changes that occur due to relative price movements.[410]

---

[406] See Annex 1 to EC Answers to Questions from the Second meeting of the Panel.

[407] Thus, vodka was approximately eight times the price of standard diluted soju and standard whisky was approximately nine times the price of standard diluted soju.

[408] EC Second Submission to the Panel at Annex 7. Also, from the Dodwell study and other evidence it appears that the following are the relationships between the prices of the other products: Gin is approximately 3.25 times the price of premium diluted soju and 6.5 times the price of standard diluted. Tequila is approximately 5.5 times the price of premium diluted soju and 11 times the price of standard diluted. Liqueur is approximately 5 times the price of premium diluted and 10 times the price of standard diluted. Cognac is approximately 12 times the price of premium diluted soju and 24 times the price of standard diluted soju. We note that Korea offered some lower price comparisons in its Interim Review comments to the effect that vodka was 5.7 times more expensive than diluted soju, while gin was 5 times more expensive and rum 6.2 times more expensive. Korea also stated that cognac/brandy was 19.2 times the price of diluted soju. Korea did not indicate if weighted averaging caused these differences from the figures above.

We note that in the decision in *Japan - Taxes on Alcoholic Beverages II*, adjustments were made for alcohol content. Panel Report in *Japan -Taxes on Alcoholic Beverages II, supra*, Annex VI, Figure 10. When such adjustments are removed, it seems that the absolute price ratio differentials in the present case are more similar to those in Japan than otherwise appears.

[409] See para. 6.105; Dodwell Study.

[410] Indeed, we must reiterate that caution must be exercised in relying on absolute price ratio differences in making product distinctions in a market such as this. Prices can respond to extraneous

When examined as a whole, the price differences are not so large as to refute the other evidence of potential competitiveness and substitutability, and there was evidence that relative price movements are likely to result in changes in consumption patterns. Overall, we found that the data on prices and the potential for changes in consumer behavior based on relative price changes, to be supportive of a finding that the identified imported and domestic products are directly competitive or substitutable.

(v)   Conclusions with respect to "directly competitive or substitutable"

10.95. We are of the view that the weight of the evidence overall supports a finding that the imported and domestic products at issue are directly competitive or substitutable. Complainants have sustained their burden of proof in this case by showing that there is some degree of current competition as well as trends towards relative shifts in consumption from soju to the identified imported distilled beverages. The production and marketing decisions of the Korean beverage companies reflect a realization of this in a very concrete manner by the development and rapid success of premium diluted soju. There clearly is an attempt to develop an image of certain types of soju that shows a direct competitive relationship with imported alcoholic beverages. It is probable that there are different marketing focuses (e.g., whether identifying accompaniment with food as a favored mode of consumption) by the importers compared to standard diluted soju; however, marketing strategies alone should not be the basis for finding products not potentially competitive. Marketing strategies can be changed quickly and if there is substantial other evidence that products are potentially directly competitive, it would be incorrect to find them otherwise based on transitory factors such as marketing strategies especially when such strategies can be shaped by the very government policies in question. On the other hand, when two products which have some present market differentiation begin to be marketed in similar fashions, as is happening in the case of the Korean soju makers, it is strong evidence of potential competition. Again, the purpose of Article III is to protect competitive opportunities, not protect actual market shares. Competitive opportunities should encompass the ability to change marketing strategies without the need for beginning a new dispute settlement case. A mere change in marketing strategy cannot be all that distinguishes success from failure of a complaint pursuant to Article III:2. That clearly would be an overly narrow interpretation of the term directly competitive or substitutable.

10.96. The levels of overlapping end-uses are currently relatively low if end-uses are defined as narrowly as suggested by Korea. However, even within such overly-narrow end-use categories, the evidence must be viewed in light of the relatively recent introduction of the western-style beverages to the market. Furthermore, we do not agree with Korea's argument about the distinctness of current market differentiation. We think Korea has drawn too fine a distinction between products for purposes of Article III:2, second sentence. Again we recall the examples of substitut-

---

factors such as exchange rates or can be affected through product mix or high overhead or distribution costs possibly caused in part by the government policies at issue.

able products offered by the drafters, which included apples and oranges. This also can be seen in the significantly overlapping channels of distribution both for off-premise sales and on-premise sales. In our view, the only meaningful distinction with respect to channels of distribution in this case is the distinction between on-premise and off-premise consumption and both imports and soju are distributed through both channels.

10.97. There is evidence both of some level of current actual competition and significant potential competition. However, complainants do not have to prove that there is a complete overlap in their analysis of substitutability. Moreover, we take guidance from the earlier panel findings that the current market conditions may be skewed by government tax and regulatory policies which tend to freeze consumer preferences in favour of the domestic products. The current price levels are probably the most telling evidence contrary to complainants assertions. In our view, the Dodwell study is a useful piece of evidence showing the potential competitive relationship between the domestic and imported products under various pricing scenarios. It is not perfect evidence, but we do not find the Korean critique conclusive in rebutting its basic premises. Indeed, we find confirmation of some of the basic points about potential competitiveness in both the Korean end-use survey conducted by the AC Nielsen study and the Trendscope survey. Furthermore, we do not accept that the price differences in the present case establish that the products in question are not even potential competitors. Prices are subject to change by extraneous factors such as exchange rates.

10.98. We are of the view that there is sufficient unrebutted evidence in this case to show present direct competition between the products. Furthermore, we are of the view that the complainants also have shown a strong potentially direct competitive relationship Thus, on balance, we find that the evidence concerning physical characteristics, end-uses, channels of distribution and pricing, leads us to conclude that the imported and domestic products are directly competitive or substitutable.

5.   *Not Similarly Taxed*

10.99. The Appellate Body in *Japan - Taxes on Alcoholic Beverages II* summed up its findings with respect to this element of the decision as follows:

> Thus, to be "not similarly taxed", the tax burden on imported products must be heavier than on "directly competitive or substitutable" domestic products, and that burden must be more than *de minimis* in any given case.[411]

10.100. In the present case, the Liquor Taxes on diluted soju are 35 percent and 50 percent on distilled soju. The Education Tax is surtax of 10 percent levied on soju. With respect to imported alcoholic beverages, the Liquor Tax ranges from 50 percent for liqueurs to 100 percent for whisky and brandy. The Education Tax is 30

---

[411]   Appellate Body Report on *Japan - Taxes on Alcoholic Beverages, supra*, at 119. It should be noted that in the case of Japan, the duties were specific and there was an ultimately unsuccessful argument by Japan that the tax/price ratios were not dissimilar. Because Korea's taxes are strictly *ad valorem*, the rates are more easily comparable and there is no such issue.

percent for all imported alcoholic beverages except liqueurs which have a 10 percent rate. Thus the total tax on diluted soju is 38.5 percent; on distilled soju and liqueurs it is 55 percent; on vodka, gin, rum, tequila and ad-mixtures it is 104 percent; on whisky, brandy and cognac it is 130 percent. Thus the tax rate on imported whisky, for example, is more than three times the *ad valorem* rate on diluted soju. These differentials are clearly in excess of *de minimis* levels.[412]

6. So as to Afford Protection

10.101. The Appellate Body in the *Japan Alcoholic Beverages* case stated that the focus of this portion of the inquiry should be on the objective factors underlying the tax measure in question including its design, architecture and the revealing structure.[413] In that case, the Panel and the Appellate Body found that the very magnitude of the dissimilar taxation supported a finding that it was applied so as to afford protection. In the present case, the Korean tax law also has very large differences in levels of taxation, large enough, in our view, also to support such a finding.

10.102. In addition to the very large levels of tax differentials, we also note that the structures of the Liquor Tax Law and the Education Tax Law are consistent with this finding. The structure of the Liquor Tax Law itself is discriminatory. It is based on a very broad generic definition which is defined as soju and then there are specific exceptions corresponding very closely to one or more characteristics of imported beverages that are used to identify products which receive higher tax rates. There is virtually no imported soju so the beneficiaries of this structure are almost exclusively domestic producers.[414] Thus, in our view, the design, architecture and structure of the Korean alcoholic beverages tax laws (including the Education Tax as it is applied in a differential manner to imported and domestic products) afford protection to domestic production. We therefore conclude that there is nullification or impairment of the benefits accruing to the complainants under GATT 1994 within the meaning of Article 3.8 of the DSU.

7. Like Product

10.103. The complainants in this case argued that vodka is like soju.[415] Korea disagreed.[416] We note that there are many similarities between vodka and soju and that these are sufficient to establish that the products are directly competitive or substitutable. However, as the Appellate Body found in *Japan - Taxes on Alcoholic Beverages II*, the concept of "likeness" in Article III:2, first sentence, is to be narrowly

---

[412] The fact that distilled soju and liqueurs are taxed at the same rate does not detract from this finding with respect to the other products and with respect to liqueurs compared to diluted soju.

[413] Appellate Body Report, on *Japan - Taxes on Alcoholic Beverages II, supra,* at 120. See also *Canada - Certain Measures Concerning Periodicals, supra,* at pp. 475.

[414] The only domestic product which falls into a higher category that corresponds to one type of imported beverage is distilled soju which represents less than one percent of Korean production.

[415] See para. 5.100 et. seq.

[416] See para. 5.264 et. seq. and para. 5.296 et. seq.

construed.[417] The question is whether the products are sufficiently close in nature that they fit within this narrow category.

10.104. We find that there is insufficient evidence in this case to make a determination that vodka and soju are like products. We do not find that they are "unlike". Rather we find that there is insufficient evidence in the record of this case to establish that they are like. In making this finding, we recall that the Appellate Body also noted that a determination of whether vodka was like shochu or was instead only directly competitive or substitutable did "not materially affect the outcome of [the] case."[418] We find this conclusion equally valid in the facts of the case at hand. Thus, while we have found that vodka and the other identified imported distilled alcoholic beverages and the domestic products are directly competitive or substitutable, we are unable to conclude that the imported products, or any subcategory of them, are like the domestic products.

XI.   CONCLUSIONS

11.1.   In light of the findings above, we reached the conclusion that soju (diluted and distilled), whiskies, brandies, cognac, rum, gin, vodka, tequila, liqueurs and admixtures are directly competitive or substitutable products. Korea has taxed the imported products in a dissimilar manner and the tax differential is more than *de minimis*. Finally, the dissimilar taxation is applied in a manner so as to afford protection to domestic production.

11.2.   We recommend that the Dispute Settlement Body request Korea to bring the Liquor Tax Law and the Education Tax Law into conformity with its obligations under the General Agreement on Tariffs and Trade 1994.

---

[417]   Appellate Body Report on *Japan - Taxes on Alcoholic Beverages II, supra*, at 112-113.
[418]   *Ibid.*

AUSTRALIA - MEASURES AFFECTING IMPORTATION OF SALMON

Arbitration
under Article 21.3(c) of the
Understanding on Rules and Procedures
Governing the Settlement of Disputes

Award of the Arbitrator
Said El-Naggar
WT/DS18/9

Circulated to Members on 23 February 1999

I.   INTRODUCTION

1.   On 6 November 1998, the Dispute Settlement Body (the "DSB") adopted the Appellate Body Report[1] and the Panel Report[2], as modified by the Appellate Body Report, in *Australia - Measures Affecting Importation of Salmon*. On 25 November 1998, Australia informed the DSB, pursuant to Article 21.3 of the *Understanding on Rules and Procedures Governing the Settlement of Disputes* (the "DSU"), that it would implement the recommendations and rulings of the DSB in this dispute and that, in doing so, it would be "mindful" of the provisions of Article 3.5 of the DSU. Australia indicated that it would require a reasonable period of time to complete the implementation process.

2.   By letter of 27 November 1998, Australia sought Canada's agreement to a 15-month period as the "reasonable period of time" for implementation. In a letter of 14 December 1998, Canada advised Australia that it could not agree to this proposal. Pursuant to Article 21.3 of the DSU, consultations between the parties were held on 30 November, and on 18 and 21 December 1998, but these did not produce agreement on a reasonable period of time for the implementation process.

3.   By communication of 24 December 1998, Canada requested that the reasonable period of time be determined by binding arbitration, pursuant to Article 21.3(c) of the DSU. By joint letter of 11 January 1999, the parties informed the Director-General of the World Trade Organization (the "WTO") that they had agreed that I should act as Arbitrator. The parties were informed, by letter of 13 January 1999, that the Director-General had conveyed their wishes to me and that I had accepted the appointment. Thereafter, by letter of 14 January 1999, the parties intimated to me that they had agreed to extend the time-period for the arbitration process, fixed at 90 days by Article 21.3(c) of the DSU, by a further 19 days, that is until 23 February

---

[1]   *Australia - Measures Affecting Importation of Salmon*, WT/DS18/AB/R, adopted 6 November 1998.

[2]   *Australia - Measures Affecting Importation of Salmon*, WT/DS18/R, adopted 6 November 1998.

1999. Notwithstanding this extension of the time-period for the arbitration process, the parties stated that my award would be deemed to be an award made under Article 21.3(c) of the DSU.

4.   Written submissions were received from Australia and Canada on 22 January 1999 and an oral hearing was held on 2 February 1999.

II.   ARGUMENTS OF THE PARTIES

A.   Australia

5.   Australia argues that it is impracticable to comply immediately with the relevant recommendations and rulings of the DSB, as decisions on implementation require the fulfilment of certain processes in accordance with Australia's legal system. In accordance with those processes, Australia estimates that 15 months from the date of adoption of the Appellate Body and Panel reports represent the shortest period possible for implementation under Australia's legal system.[3]

6.   Australia rejects Canada's suggestion that the DSB's recommendations and rulings can be implemented either by repealing or amending the measure concerned or by granting an import permit under the Quarantine Proclamation 1998 ("QP 1998"), which is the successor to Quarantine Proclamation 86A ("QP86A"). Australia considers that the measure can be brought into conformity with the *Agreement on the Application of Sanitary and Phytosanitary Measures* (the *"SPS Agreement"*) without repeal or amendment since it does not contain an absolute ban. Rather, it allows the Director of Quarantine to permit entry of otherwise prohibited products on the basis of a risk assessment.

7.   As regards Canada's suggestion that a permit be granted to allow imports of Canadian salmon, Australia emphasizes that such a permit must be based on a risk assessment conducted in accordance with procedures determined by Government. Failure to respect those procedures may provide grounds for review under the *Administrative Decisions (Judicial Review) Act 1977* (the *"Judicial Review Act 1977"*).

8.   According to Australia, implementation of the obligation contained in Article 5.5 of the *SPS Agreement* could also not be achieved by the introduction of measures on certain other aquatic products, comparable to those currently applied on salmon, without risk assessments on those other products.

9.   Australia states that decisions on implementation will be taken on the basis of generic risk assessments that have already commenced. These assessments cover: non-viable salmonids, live ornamental finfish and non-viable marine finfish. The measures adopted will be reflective of Australia's obligations under Article 3.5 of the DSU and they may incorporate measures differentiated by country of origin where that is justified by the risk assessments, provided that such measures achieve Australia's appropriate level of protection. It has been estimated that it will be possible to take decisions on the basis of these risk assessment procedures by February 2000.

---

[3]   Australia's written submission, para. 3.

10.   Australia emphasizes that, although it is required to bring its measure into conformity, it is not necessarily required to introduce less trade-restrictive measures. Members are afforded a measure of discretion in the means chosen to implement, provided that the means are consistent with the recommendations and rulings of the DSB, with the covered Agreements, and with the provisions of Article 3.5 of the DSU. Australia's obligation is to ensure that its measures are based on proper risk assessments and that measures applicable to salmon and other relevant aquatic products do not result in discrimination or a disguised restriction on trade.

11.   The mandate of the arbitrator is solely to determine the "reasonable period of time" for implementation. It does not entitle him to suggest or determine ways or means of implementation. The guideline for the arbitrator in determining that period is 15 months from the date of adoption by the DSB of the Appellate Body and Panel Reports. However, this period may be shorter or longer than 15 months, according to the "particular circumstances" of the case. Australia considers that Canada has the burden of proof insofar as it seeks to prove that there are "particular circumstances" justifying a period of time shorter than 15 months. As Australia has not proposed a period longer than 15 months, it is not required to prove "particular circumstances" justifying a 15-month period.

12.   It has been the practice of arbitrators to interpret the reasonable period of time as the shortest period possible, within the legal system of the Member concerned, to effect implementation.[4] But arbitrators are not required to consider the shortest period of time within which the measure can be withdrawn or modified, rather they should consider the shortest period of time for implementation according to the means chosen. In this case, implementation can be effected in a WTO-consistent manner without legislative amendment. Within the framework of Australia's legal system, this means of implementation will require a period of 15 months.

13.   In that respect, Australia states that quarantine decisions are adopted on the basis of delegated legal authority, in accordance with Government decisions on the procedures applicable to the conduct of a risk assessment process. The *Quarantine Act 1908* constitutes the basic framework for the exercise of quarantine authority. The Act provides for the Governor-General to prohibit, by Proclamation, the importation into Australia of, *inter alia*, animals or other articles likely to introduce disease. The Governor-General may also empower the Director of Quarantine to permit the import of otherwise prohibited "things". Proclamations by the Governor-General are subordinate legislation. QP 1998, promulgated by the Governor-General, provides the legal basis for the exercise of the Director of Quarantine's powers to authorize the import of, *inter alia*, the fresh, chilled or frozen salmon from Canada (the "salmon product at issue"). As noted, his decisions are subject to judicial review under the *Judicial Review Act 1977* and must, therefore, be based

---

[4]   Award of the Arbitrator under Article 21.3(c) of the DSU, *EC Measures Concerning Meat and Meat Products (Hormones) ("European Communities - Hormones")*, WT/DS26/15, WT/DS48/13, 29 May 1998, para. 26 and Award of the Arbitrator under Article 21.3(c) of the DSU, *Indonesia - Certain Measures Affecting the Automobile Industry ("Indonesia - Autos")*, WT/DS54/15, WT/DS55/14, WT/DS59/13, WT/DS64/12, 7 December 1998, para. 22.

on the procedures determined by the Government for the conduct of risk assessments.

14.   These procedures are set down in *The AQIS Import Risk Analysis Process Handbook* (the "AQIS Handbook").[5] This Handbook details a series of steps to be taken in the course of an "Import Risk Analysis" procedure. Some of the steps are allocated a specific time-period for completion, but others are not. Those with a specified time-period are generally concerned with public consultation periods and with appeals. A total of 315 days is required for the completion of those steps. Clearly, the remaining steps also require an appropriate time-period for completion. This is estimated on a case-by-case basis by AQIS and the Risk Analysis Panel concerned.

15.   Since the three risk assessment procedures that are relevant to this dispute will be completed by February 2000, Australia requests that the reasonable period of time for implementation be 15 months. Australia is not seeking a 15-month period because that period of time is required to undertake risk assessments, but because risk assessments are a necessary part of the overall decision-making process and that process cannot be completed in less than 15 months. This period does not exceed the "guideline" set down in Article 21.3(c) of the DSU and Canada has the burden of proof in demonstrating that there are "particular circumstances" justifying a shorter period.

B.   Canada

16.   At the core of this arbitration is Australia's contention that the "reasonable period of time" should include the time to conduct new risk assessments. Australia's contention must be rejected, both because it runs directly contrary to the ruling of the arbitrator in *European Communities - Hormones* and because it is manifestly unreasonable for the effective functioning of both the *SPS Agreement* and the dispute settlement system.

17.   Like the present case, the measure at issue in *European Communities - Hormones* was found to be inconsistent with Article 5.1 of the *SPS Agreement* because it was not based on a risk assessment. The European Communities sought to have the time needed to conduct a risk assessment included in the reasonable period of time for implementation. The arbitrator stated that the time needed to conduct scientific studies or to consult with experts had no relevance in determining the appropriate duration of the reasonable period of time.[6] Thus, according to Canada, Australia is seeking allowances for considerations that have been found to be irrelevant to the task confronting the Arbitrator.

18.   Canada considers that Australia wishes to carry out the new risk assessments in order to provide the scientific evidence necessary to demonstrate the consistency of a measure already judged to be inconsistent with the *SPS Agreement*. This ap-

---

[5]   Australia's written submission, Exhibit A. AQIS is an acronym for Australian Quarantine and Inspection Service.

[6]   *European Communities - Hormones, supra,* footnote 4, para. 39.

proach was rejected by the arbitrator in *European Communities - Hormones*.[7] Canada emphasizes that although the measure at issue was adopted 24 years ago and should have been consistent with the *SPS Agreement* as from 1 January 1995, Australia has never been able to provide credible evidence to support it. Indeed, there are several risk assessment studies that conclude that fresh, chilled or frozen salmon from Canada can be imported with negligible risk.[8]

19.   In Canada's view, by seeking to include in the reasonable period the time required to conduct a further risk assessment on salmonids, Australia is, in effect, claiming the benefit of Article 5.7 of the *SPS Agreement* through the guise of implementing the DSB's recommendations and rulings. In addition, by seeking to include the time to do risk assessments on non-salmonid species, Australia is attempting to win through the implementation process that which it was denied by the Panel: a delay in removing or modifying the measure's inconsistency with Article 5.5.

20.   To take account of the time needed to do new risk assessments would invite abuse of Articles 5.1 and 5.5 of the *SPS Agreement*. Findings of inconsistency with either provision would have little or no consequence. A Member could adopt a measure inconsistent with those provisions secure in the knowledge that, even if the measure were found to be inconsistent with the *SPS Agreement*, the Member would then be granted time to conduct risk assessments. Furthermore, the Member might then claim that such risk assessments demonstrated the consistency of the original measure. Such an approach would deprive Articles 5.1 and 5.5 of the *SPS Agreement* of virtually all their effect.

21.   Canada, therefore, submits that it would be manifestly unreasonable to allow Australia to include in the reasonable period of time the time needed to do new risk assessments.

22.   In seeking a 15-month period for implementation, Australia appears to concede that, however else implementation might be accomplished, it can be achieved in 15 months by a decision of the Director of Quarantine. As this 15-month period includes the time to conduct new risk assessments, which in Canada's view are not related to implementation, Australia is implicitly conceding that the Director of Quarantine could make the necessary determinations well within 15 months.

23.   Canada recalls that, in *European Communities - Hormones*, the arbitrator found that:

> Read in context, it is clear that the reasonable period of time,
> as determined under Article 21.3(c), should be the shortest pe-

---

[7]   *European Communities - Hormones, supra,* footnote 4, para. 39.

[8]   New Zealand, *The Risk of Introducing Exotic Diseases of Fish into New Zealand Through the Importation of Ocean-Caught Pacific Salmon from Canada,* prepared by Stuart C. MacDiarmid (September 1994); and M. Stone, S. MacDiarmid and H. Pharo, *Import Health Risk Analysis: Salmonids for Human Consumption* (New Zealand: Ministry of Agriculture Regulatory Authority, 1997); D. Vose, Quantitative analysis of the risk of establishment of *Aeromonas salmonicida and Renibacterium salmoninarum* in Australia as a result of importing Canadian ocean-caught salmon.

riod possible within the legal system of the Member to implement the recommendations and rulings of the DSB.[9]

24.   Furthermore, the arbitrator in *European Communities - Hormones* also stated that where implementation could be accomplished by "administrative means, the reasonable period of time should be considerably shorter than 15 months."[10] In Canada's opinion, the process involved in bringing the impugned measure into conformity with Australia's obligations under the *SPS Agreement* is an administrative, not legislative, process. It can, therefore, be effected in much less than 15 months.

25.   To the best of Canada's knowledge, Australian *law* provides no time limits for administrative determinations by the Director of Quarantine since the procedures set out in the AQIS Handbook are merely policy guidelines and are not legally binding. Canada maintains that AQIS's choice of policy should not adversely affect Canada in terms of what constitutes a reasonable period of time for implementation.

26.   Canada believes that, on the basis of the ample evidence already before Australia and in view of the absence of scientific justification for the measure, there is no reason why Australia should not bring its measure into compliance expeditiously, through the most direct means available: an administrative decision by the Director of Quarantine allowing the importation of fresh, chilled or frozen Canadian salmon.

III.   THE REASONABLE PERIOD OF TIME

27.   My mandate in this arbitration is governed by Article 21.3(c) of the DSU. It provides that when the "reasonable period of time" is determined through arbitration:

> ... a guideline for the arbitrator should be that the reasonable period of time to implement panel or Appellate Body recommendations should not exceed 15 months from the date of adoption of a panel or Appellate Body report. However, that time may be shorter or longer, depending upon the particular circumstances.

28.   The precise meaning of this provision becomes clear when it is read in its context. Paragraph 1 of Article 21 provides:

> Prompt compliance with recommendations or rulings of the DSB is essential in order to ensure effective resolution of disputes to the benefit of all Members.

29.   It should also be noted that the second sentence of paragraph 3 of Article 21 stipulates that the Member concerned shall have a reasonable period of time "[i]f it is impracticable to comply immediately with the recommendations and rulings" of the DSB. Article 3.7 of the DSU explains what is meant by immediate compliance:

---

[9]   *Supra*, footnote 4, para. 26, cited with approval by the Arbitrator in *Indonesia - Autos, supra*, footnote 4, para. 22.

[10]   *Supra*, footnote 4, para. 25.

> A solution mutually acceptable to the parties to a dispute and consistent with the covered agreements is clearly to be preferred. In the absence of a mutually agreed solution, *the first objective of the dispute settlement mechanism is usually to secure the withdrawal of the measures concerned if these are found to be inconsistent with the provisions of any of the covered agreements.* The provision of compensation should be resorted to only if the *immediate withdrawal* of the measure is impracticable and as a temporary measure pending the withdrawal of the measure which is inconsistent with a covered agreement. (emphasis added)

30.   Taken together, these provisions clearly define the rights and obligations of the Member concerned with respect to the implementation of the recommendations and rulings of the DSB. In the absence of a mutually agreed solution, the first objective is usually the *immediate withdrawal* of the measure judged to be inconsistent with any of the covered agreements. Only if it is impracticable to do so, is the Member concerned entitled to a reasonable period of time for implementation. When the reasonable period of time is determined through arbitration, the guideline for the arbitrator is that it should not exceed 15 months from the date of adoption of the panel and/or Appellate Body reports. This does not mean, however, that the arbitrator is obliged to grant 15 months in all cases. The reasonable period of time may be shorter or longer, depending upon the particular circumstances.

31.   A certain difficulty arises in this case because of the divergent views of the parties as to what constitutes implementation. According to Australia, implementation of the recommendations and rulings of the DSB *in casu* involves conducting risk assessments, not only with respect to the salmon product at issue, but also with respect to non-salmonid products. In Australia's opinion, the "reasonable period of time" should be such as to enable it to conduct those risk assessments since they will form the basis of the decisions on implementation. Australia argued, both in its written submission and in its oral statement, that the outcome of the risk assessments currently being conducted cannot be prejudged. Implementation could well result in the continuation of the import prohibition on the salmon product at issue or in the admission, with or without conditions, of that product into the Australian market. It all depends, in the view of Australia, upon the outcome of the risk assessments.

32.   Canada does not share Australia's view on the meaning of implementation of the recommendations and rulings of the DSB. According to Canada, whether or not Australia wishes to carry out studies or risk assessments, the conduct of such studies does not constitute implementation of the recommendations and rulings of the DSB and cannot be included in the calculation of the reasonable period of time. There is no reason, Canada argues, why Australia should not bring its measure into compliance expeditiously through the most direct means available, i.e., an administrative decision by the Director of Quarantine allowing the importation of fresh, chilled or frozen Canadian salmon.

33.   Clearly, what constitutes a "reasonable period of time" depends upon the action which Australia takes under its legal system to implement the recommendations and rulings of the DSB. If implementation is effected by means of an adminis-

trative decision to repeal or modify the measure at issue or by means of a permit granted by the Director of Quarantine, the length of time needed to carry out such a process would be different from what it would be if Australia were to conduct a series of risk assessments.

34.   I believe it is necessary to recall the findings and conclusions of the Appellate Body[11] and of the Panel[12], as modified by the Appellate Body, which are the subject of the recommendations and rulings of the DSB. The relevant aspects may be summarized as follows:

> (a)   the SPS measure at issue in this dispute is the import prohibition on fresh, chilled or frozen salmon set forth in QP 86A (now QP 1998), as confirmed by the 1996 Decision;

> (b)   by maintaining without a proper risk assessment, or without risk assessment, an import prohibition on fresh, chilled or frozen salmon from Canada, Australia has acted inconsistently with Article 5.1 and, by implication, Article 2.2 of the *SPS Agreement*;

> (c)   by maintaining the measure at issue, Australia has acted inconsistently with its obligations under Article 5.5 and, by implication, Article 2.3 of the *SPS Agreement*.

35.   I am mindful of the limits of my mandate in this arbitration. I am particularly aware that suggesting ways and means of implementation is not part of my mandate and that my task is confined to the determination of the "reasonable period of time". Choosing the means of implementation is, and should be, the prerogative of the implementing Member. In the words of the arbitrator in *European Communities - Hormones*:

> ... An implementing Member ... has a measure of discretion in choosing the *means* of implementation, as long as the means chosen are consistent with the recommendations and rulings of the DSB and with the covered agreements.[13] (emphasis in original)

However, he also said:

> ... It would not be in keeping with the requirement of *prompt* compliance to include in the reasonable period of time, time to conduct studies or to consult experts to demonstrate the *consistency* of a measure already judged to be *inconsistent*. That cannot be considered as "particular circumstances" justifying a longer period than the guideline suggested in Article 21.3(c). This is not to say that the commissioning of scientific studies or consultations with experts *cannot* form part of a domestic implementation process in a particular case. How-

---

[11]   *Supra*, footnote 1.

[12]   *Supra*, footnote 2.

[13]   *Supra*, footnote 4, para. 38.

> ever, such considerations are not pertinent to the determina-
> tion of the reasonable period of time.[14] (emphasis in original)

36.   The Appellate Body was unequivocal in its conclusion that the measure in dispute is the import prohibition on Canadian fresh, chilled or frozen salmon, contained in QP 86A and confirmed by the 1996 Decision. It was equally unequivocal in its findings that such an import prohibition is inconsistent with Articles 5.1, 2.2, 5.5 and 2.3 of the *SPS Agreement*. Given these findings and conclusions, it is difficult, indeed, to accept the view that, in the determination of the reasonable period of time, account should be taken of the time needed to conduct risk assessments to demonstrate the consistency of the import prohibition already found to be inconsistent with the provisions of the *SPS Agreement*.

37.   I turn now to the issue of the "reasonable period of time" in the case at hand. As mentioned before, Australia considers 15 months to be the minimum period for implementation in accordance with Australian law. Canada, on the other hand, holds the view that Australia can implement the recommendations and rulings of the DSB in much less than 15 months. Australia maintains that the burden of proof falls on Canada to demonstrate that there are "particular circumstances" justifying a shorter period than the guideline of 15 months. Australia also maintains that, as it has not proposed a period longer than 15 months, it is not required to prove "particular circumstances" justifying a 15-month period.

38.   It has been pointed out that the arbitrator is not obliged to grant 15 months as the reasonable period for implementation in all cases. "Particular circumstances" justifying a longer or shorter period must be taken into account on a case-by-case basis. In the present case, there are certain considerations which persuade me that the reasonable period of time should be significantly less than 15 months. In the first place, Australia's request for 15 months was based on the assumption that a good part, if not most, of that period would be used to conduct a number of risk assessments. In its written submission, Australia points out that the AQIS Handbook details a series of steps to be taken in the course of an Import Risk Analysis procedure under Australian law. Some of the steps are allocated a specific time-period, but others are not. A total of 315 days, i.e., 10½ months, is required for the completion of the time-bound steps for scientific studies under the procedures of the AQIS Handbook.[15] Since I have concluded that conducting risk assessments is not pertinent to the determination of the reasonable period of time, it follows that the reasonable period in this case should be considerably less than 15 months. In the second place, both parties agree with the arbitrator in *European Communities - Hormones* that the reasonable period of time, as determined under Article 21.3(c), should be the shortest period possible within the legal system of the Member to implement the recommendations and rulings of the DSB.[16] Both parties also agree that the process involved in bringing the measure in dispute into conformity with Australia's obligations under the *SPS Agreement* is an administrative, not a legislative, process. As pointed out by the arbitrator in *European Communities - Hormones*,

---

[14]   *Supra*, footnote 4, para. 39.
[15]   Australia's written submission, para. 51.
[16]   *European Communities - Hormones, supra*, footnote 4, para. 26.

when implementation can be effected by administrative means, the reasonable period of time should be "considerably shorter than 15 months."[17]

IV.   THE AWARD

39.   In light of the above considerations, I determine that the reasonable period of time for Australia to implement the recommendations and rulings of the DSB in this case is *eight months* from the date of adoption of the Appellate Body and Panel Reports by the DSB, i.e. eight months from 6 November 1998.

---

[17]   *European Communities - Hormones, supra,* footnote 4, para. 25.

JAPAN - MEASURES AFFECTING AGRICULTURAL PRODUCTS

Report of the Appellate Body
WT/DS76/AB/R

Adopted by the Dispute Settlement Body
on 19 March 1999

Japan, *Appellant/Appellee*

United States, *Appellant/Appellee*

Brazil and the European Communities,
Third Participants

Present:

Beeby, Presiding Member

Lacarte-Muró, Member

Matsushita, Member

TABLE OF CONTENTS

I.   INTRODUCTION

1.   Japan and the United States appeal from certain issues of law and legal interpretations in the Panel Report in *Japan - Measures Affecting Agricultural Products*.[1] The Panel dealt with a complaint by the United States relating to the requirement imposed by Japan to test and confirm the efficacy of the quarantine treatment for each variety of certain agricultural products ("the varietal testing requirement").

2.   Under the Plant Protection Law of 1950[2] and the Plant Protection Law Enforcement Regulation[3] of the same year, Japan prohibits the importation of eight agricultural products originating from, *inter alia*, the United States on the ground that they are potential hosts of codling moth, a pest of quarantine significance to Japan. The prohibited products are apples, cherries, peaches (including nectarines),

---

[1]   WT/DS76/R, 27 October 1998.

[2]   Law No. 151 of 1950, enacted 4 May 1950, most recently amended in 1996.

[3]   Ordinance No. 73 of the Ministry of Agriculture, Forestry and Fisheries, enacted 30 June 1950.

walnuts, apricots, pears, plums and quince. The import prohibition on these products can, however, be lifted if an exporting country proposes an alternative quarantine treatment which achieves a level of protection equivalent to the import prohibition. The exporting country bears the burden of proving that the proposed alternative treatment achieves the required level of protection. In practice, the alternative quarantine treatment proposed is fumigation with methyl bromide, or a combination of methyl bromide fumigation and cold storage. In 1987, Japan's Ministry of Agriculture, Forestry and Fisheries developed two guidelines as model test procedures for the confirmation of the efficacy of this alternative quarantine treatment: the *Experimental Guideline for Lifting Import Ban - Fumigation*, which outlines the testing requirement applicable to initial lifting of the import prohibition on a product, and the *Experimental Guide for Cultivar Comparison Test on Insect Mortality - Fumigation* (the "*Experimental Guide*"), which sets out the testing requirement for approval of additional varieties of that product. The latter requirement is the varietal testing requirement at issue in this dispute.[4] The United States claimed that this varietal testing requirement was inconsistent with the obligations of Japan under the *Agreement on the Application of Sanitary and Phytosanitary Measures* (the "*SPS Agreement*").

3.   The Panel Report was circulated to Members of the World Trade Organization (the "WTO") on 27 October 1998. The Panel found that Japan had acted inconsistently with Articles 2.2, 5.6 and 7 of the *SPS Agreement*. In paragraph 9.1 of its Report, the Panel concluded that Japan:

(i)   by maintaining the varietal testing requirement in dispute with respect to apples, cherries, nectarines and walnuts, acts inconsistently with its obligation under Article 2.2 of the SPS Agreement not to maintain Phytosanitary measures "without sufficient scientific evidence, except as provided for in paragraph 7 of Article 5"; and

(ii)   by maintaining the varietal testing requirement in dispute with respect to apples, cherries, nectarines and walnuts, acts inconsistently with its obligation in Article 5.6 of the SPS Agreement to "ensure that [its phytosanitary] measures are not more trade-restrictive than required to achieve [Japan's] appropriate level of ... phytosanitary protection, taking into account technical and economic feasibility"; and

(iii)   by not having published the varietal testing requirement in dispute with respect to any of the products at issue, acts inconsistently with its obligations under paragraph 1 of Annex B of the SPS Agreement and,

---

[4]   The relevant factual aspects of this dispute are set out in greater detail in the Panel Report in paras. 2.1-2.33, as well as in paras. 6.1-6.119 and 10.1-10.300.

for that reason, with its obligations contained in Article 7 of that Agreement.

In paragraph 9.3 of its Report, the Panel made the following recommendation:

> We *recommend* that the Dispute Settlement Body request Japan to bring its measure in dispute into conformity with its obligations under the SPS Agreement.

4.   On 24 November 1998, Japan notified the Dispute Settlement Body (the "DSB") of its decision to appeal certain issues of law covered in the Panel Report and certain legal interpretations developed by the Panel, pursuant to paragraph 4 of Article 16 of the *Understanding on Rules and Procedures Governing the Settlement of Disputes* (the "DSU"), and filed a notice of appeal with the Appellate Body pursuant to Rule 20 of the Working Procedures for Appellate Review (the "*Working Procedures*").[5] On 4 December 1998, Japan filed an appellant's submission.[6] The United States also filed an appellant's submission on 9 December 1998.[7] The appellee's submissions of both participants were filed on 21 December 1998.[8] On the same day, Brazil and the European Communities filed separate third participant's submissions.[9]

5.   The oral hearing in the appeal was held on 19 January 1999.[10] The participants and third participants presented oral arguments and responded to questions put to them by Members of the Appellate Body Division hearing the appeal.

II.   ARGUMENTS OF THE PARTICIPANTS

A.   *Claims of Error by Japan - Appellant*

1.   *Article 2.2 of the SPS Agreement*

6.   Japan argues that the Panel erred in its interpretation of the term "sufficient scientific evidence" in Article 2.2 of the *SPS Agreement*, and that, accordingly, its conclusion regarding Article 2.2 must be reversed. Specifically, Japan contends that the Panel erred in failing to interpret the term "sufficient scientific evidence" in relation to the SPS measure in question, in accordance with the rule in Article 31 of the *Vienna Convention on the Law of Treaties*[11], which stipulates that a term must be interpreted in its context.

7.   It is Japan's submission that the basic rights and obligations concerning scientific evidence provided in Article 2.2 of the *SPS Agreement* are, in principle, substantiated in Articles 5.1 and 5.2 of the *SPS Agreement*. Japan sees these Articles, therefore, as the key operative provisions prescribing specific requirements of an SPS measure as it relates to scientific principles and scientific evidence of Article

---

[5]   WT/DS76/5.

[6]   Pursuant to Rule 21(1) of the *Working Procedures*.

[7]   Pursuant to Rule 23(1) of the *Working Procedures*.

[8]   Pursuant to Rule 22(1) and Rule 23(3) of the *Working Procedures*.

[9]   Pursuant to Rule 24 of the *Working Procedures*.

[10]   Pursuant to Rule 27 of the *Working Procedures*.

[11]   Done at Vienna, 23 May 1969, 1155 U.N.T.S. 331; 8 International Legal Materials 679.

2.2. According to Japan, the Panel should have dealt with the issues raised in this dispute under Articles 5.1 and 5.2 since the United States has not provided any evidence which indicates that Japan's measure is patently inconsistent with the requirement under Article 2.2.

8.   It is Japan's contention that the measure at issue is an information requirement for approval procedures and that any challenge to an information requirement under Article 2.2 should take into account the unique role of information in the SPS process, and the adequate balance that Article 8 of the *SPS Agreement* seeks to achieve. According to Japan, an information requirement is justifiable when there is some available information suggesting some risk. The fact that a measure is an information requirement should be considered in the discussion of sufficiency.

9.   Japan notes that no language in Article 2.2 suggests that the measure has to be "based on" sufficient scientific evidence. Moreover, in Japan's view, the Panel eventually discarded the requirement of a rational relationship and, instead, based its finding under Article 2.2 on an "actual causal link" between the differences in test results and the presence of varietal differences. Not only does the notion of an "actual causal link" operate as a denial of the precautionary principle, it is also a concept that has no basis in the *SPS Agreement*.

10.   In Japan's view, the Panel failed to give due regard to the precautionary principle, which was recognized in *EC Measures Concerning Meat and Meat Products (Hormones)* ("European Communities - Hormones")[12] and *Australia - Measures Affecting Importation of Salmon* ("Australia - Salmon").[13] Having lawfully established a prohibition on the importation of host plants of codling moth, Japan submits that it is in a position which warrants a precautionary approach and that Japan's varietal testing requirement, therefore, needs to be understood in the context of the precautionary principle, a principle which is echoed by the practice of Member States and reflected in the *Codex Alimentarius*[14] and the *FAO Guidelines for Pest Risk Analysis*.[15]

2.   Article 5.7 of the SPS Agreement

11.   Japan asserts that it has fulfilled the obligation under Article 2.2 to ensure that a measure is not maintained without sufficient scientific evidence, but that even if the Panel's contrary finding is to be upheld, the measure maintained by Japan is, in any case, consistent with Article 5.7 of the *SPS Agreement*. Japan disagrees with the Panel's interpretation according to which Japan has to fulfil the requirements of both the first and second sentences of Article 5.7. According to Japan, the phrase "except as provided for in paragraph 7 of Article 5" in Article 2.2, should be interpreted to refer to the first sentence of Article 5.7, so that a Member should be allowed to claim exemption from the obligation in Article 2.2 when it fulfils the requirements of the first sentence. Japan further asserts that the varietal testing requirement is, in

---

[12]   Adopted 13 February 1998, WT/DS26/AB/R, WT/DS48/AB/R.
[13]   Adopted 6 November 1998, WT/DS18/AB/R.
[14]   *General Principles for the Use of Food Additives*, Codex Alimentarius, Vol. A1, 1995.
[15]   *International Standards for Phytosanitary Measures Part I - Import Regulations, Guidelines for Pest Risk Analysis*, Food and Agriculture Organisation Secretariat, 1996.

any event, maintained in accordance with the requirements of both the first and second sentences of Article 5.7.

12.   With regard to the requirements of the first sentence, Japan rejects the contention of the United States that insufficient scientific evidence within the first sentence of Article 5.7 refers to a situation in which the amount of evidence is insufficient to perform a risk assessment. Japan argues that if this contention is accepted, the concept of "sufficiency" in Article 2.2, and that in Article 5.7, must be interpreted to have different meanings, which, according to Japan, cannot be the case.

13.   With regard to the requirement of the second sentence of Article 5.7, "to seek to obtain additional information", Japan contends that this requirement is met by accumulating information through the experience of successful importation of varieties. In Japan's view, the collection of data through experience meets the express text of the requirement. The second sentence of Article 5.7 obligates Members to "seek" to obtain the information, but does not require actual results.

14.   With regard to the requirement of the second sentence, "to review" the provisional SPS measure "within a reasonable period of time", Japan argues that reasonableness of a time-period should be judged according to the measure in question, and the time needed for the collection of information. The "reasonable period of time" should allow the time needed for the accumulation of knowledge through experience. Japan also submits that as the obligation regarding sufficient scientific evidence was first created by the *SPS Agreement*, the reasonable period of time should, therefore, start counting as of January 1995, the date when the *SPS Agreement* entered into force.

3.   *Article 7 and Paragraph 1 of Annex B, of the SPS Agreement*

15.   Japan contends that the "regulations" referred to in the first paragraph of Annex B are limited to legally enforceable instruments and, therefore, exclude the guidelines for varietal testing. Japan notes that the footnote to the first paragraph of Annex B defining the concept of "regulation" makes reference to laws, decrees or ordinances, all of which are considered to be legally enforceable. Japan submits further that the precedents cited by the Panel in support of its arguments, and in particular the Panel Reports in *Japan - Trade in Semi-conductors*[16] and *Japan - Measures Affecting Consumer Photographic Film and Paper*[17], are inapposite since they do not concern a publication obligation as set out in Article 7 of the *SPS Agreement*.

4.   *Burden of Proof*

16.   Japan contends that the conclusion reached by the Panel under Article 5.6 of the *SPS Agreement*, namely, that the determination of sorption levels is an alternative measure within the meaning of Article 5.6, is based on a factual finding which was neither argued nor proven by the party which bore the burden of proof. While

---

[16]   Adopted 4 May 1988, BISD 35S/116.

[17]   Adopted 22 April 1998, WT/DS44/R.

the United States proposed "testing by product" as their only alternative measure within the meaning of Article 5.6, the Panel went on to find facts that the United States did not even allege to exist. It is Japan's submission that this finding unjustly exempts the United States from discharging the burden of proof. According to Japan, the Panel's finding is inconsistent with the DSU because it is contrary to the principle of burden of proof established in *United States - Measure Affecting Imports of Woven Wool Shirts and Blouses from India* ("*United States - Shirts and Blouses*").[18]

17.   Japan submits that Articles 11 and 13 of the DSU should not be read to authorize panels to establish facts neither contained in the argument of, nor proven by, the parties to the dispute. In Japan's view, Articles 11 and 13 provide for a very conventional role of a judicial organ. If a panel were free to find material facts despite the absence of any argument or proof by the parties, the burden of proof rule would be deprived of any significance. Japan also argues that in a highly technical case, aggressive fact-finding by a non-expert panel can easily harm an objective assessment of the facts.

18.   Japan argues further that if the Panel is allowed to find facts neither argued nor proven by the complainant, the Panel should be obligated in turn to find facts of rebuttal neither argued nor proven by the complainant. Japan, in its written submission, contends that it was not given an opportunity to express its position on whether the determination of sorption levels was a reasonably available measure and significantly less restrictive to trade than the current varietal testing requirement employed by Japan. At the oral hearing, however, Japan said that while it was able to make some comments after having seen the Panel's interim report, it was given very limited time to make comments on the alternative concrete suggestions.

5.   Article 11 of the DSU

19.   Japan argues that the Panel's finding under Article 2.2 disregarded or distorted the evidence before it, and thus violates Article 11 of the DSU. It is Japan's contention that there was lack of proper examination of evidence by the Panel, that the Panel cited the experts' opinions in an arbitrary manner and that its evaluation of evidence was contradictory. Japan submits that this is sufficient to reverse the findings of the Panel as it indicates lack of an objective assessment of the facts, as required by Article 11 of the DSU.

B.   Arguments of the United States - Appellee

1.   Article 2.2 of the SPS Agreement

20.   The United States argues that the Panel correctly found that Japan's varietal testing requirement is maintained without sufficient scientific evidence because there was no "objective and rational relationship" between the SPS measure and the scientific evidence as required by Article 2.2 of the *SPS Agreement*. The United States asserts that Japan's criticism of the Panel's finding ignores the Appellate

---

[18]   Adopted 23 May 1997, WT/DS33/AB/R.

Body's stricture in *European Communities - Hormones*[19] that Articles 2.2 and 5.1 of the *SPS Agreement* should constantly be read together. According to the United States, the Panel did not err in relying on Appellate Body analysis under Article 5.1 when interpreting the obligation not to maintain an SPS measure without sufficient scientific evidence. In any event, the "objective or rational relationship" standard promulgated by the Panel represents no more than a minimal relevancy requirement.

21.   With respect to the precautionary principle, the United States argues that Japan overstates the Appellate Body's conclusions in *European Communities - Hormones*[20], and notes that in that case, the Appellate Body cautioned against using the precautionary principle as a ground for justifying SPS measures that are otherwise inconsistent with the obligations of Members set out in particular provisions of the *SPS Agreement*. The United States notes that even if scientific evidence is insufficient under Article 2.2, a Member may nevertheless adopt a provisional measure if the conditions of Article 5.7 of the *SPS Agreement* have been met.

22.   The United States submits that Japan can only speculate that there may be varietal differences which may affect treatment efficacy. Such speculation gives rise to no more than theoretical uncertainties, and Japan may not justify its measure on this basis.

23.   With regard to the relationship between Articles 2.2 and 5.1, the United States argues that while Article 5.1 may help to interpret Article 2.2, nothing in Article 5.1 supports Japan's conclusion that "the direct application of Article 2.2 should be limited to situations patently inconsistent with the requirement of 'sufficiency' ". The United States observes further that Article 5.1 does not itself specify the quantum of scientific evidence required in a risk assessment. Instead, this requirement is found in Article 2.2.

24.   The United States disagrees with Japan that its varietal testing requirement is an "information requirement" under "approval procedures" within the meaning of paragraph 1(c) of Annex C to the *SPS Agreement*. The United States contends that the varietal testing requirement does not seek to obtain relevant information, since it is not designed to provide information relevant to the question whether there are significant sorption differences among varieties.

2.   *Article 5.7 of the SPS Agreement*

25.   To Japan's assertion that its varietal testing requirement is consistent with Article 5.7 of the *SPS Agreement*, the United States counters that Japan's varietal testing requirement does not meet the requirements of that provision. The United States contends that both sentences of Article 5.7 must be satisfied to qualify for the exemption from Article 2.2 of the *SPS Agreement*. There is, therefore, no basis, according to the United States, for Japan's claim that it may qualify for an exemption from its obligation under Article 2.2 when it meets the requirements of the first sentence of Article 5.7 alone. The reference in Article 2.2 to Article 5.7 is not qualified or limited to only the first sentence of Article 5.7. The second sentence of Arti-

---

[19]   *European Communities - Hormones, supra*, footnote 12.
[20]   *European Communities - Hormones, supra*, footnote 12.

cle 5.7 limits the ability of Members to maintain provisional measures indefinitely. Without this limitation, Article 2.2 would be drained of content.

26.   The United States submits that the information sought and obtained by Japan was not relevant to proving Japan's speculation that varietal sorption differences may exist. In the opinion of the United States, while Article 5.7 may be silent as to specific information collection procedures, it does specifically require Japan to seek the information necessary for a more objective assessment of risk. The obligation to review the measure within a reasonable period of time should not be examined in isolation from the issue of whether a Member is seeking to collect additional information. Japan has not sought to obtain information directly relevant to such a review, and has thereby precluded itself from being in a position to review the varietal testing requirement.

27.   According to the United States, Japan is incorrect in claiming that the references to sufficiency in Articles 2.2 and 5.7 must be coextensive. The reference to sufficiency in Article 5.7 relates to the sufficiency of evidence to conduct a risk assessment. At the time the provisional measure is adopted, the information necessary for an objective assessment of risk is lacking. If there was sufficient information to conduct a risk assessment and that assessment indicated that a measure was not justified, a Member that was unable to adopt a measure under Article 5.1 of the *SPS Agreement* should not then be free to adopt a measure "provisionally" under Article 5.7. Otherwise, the obligation in Article 5.1 would be rendered meaningless.

3.   *Article 7 and Paragraph 1 of Annex B, of the SPS Agreement*

28.   The United States argues that the Panel correctly noted that the definition of sanitary and phytosanitary regulations does not provide a requirement that such measures be legally enforceable. It is the United States' submission that Japan's appeal from the Panel's finding under Article 7 of the *SPS Agreement* rests on an unfounded and unexplained assertion that only prior panel interpretations of Article X of the GATT are relevant to this dispute. Furthermore, the United States asserts that the varietal testing requirement is mandatory, and from the exporter's perspective, this is no different from a measure which is "legally enforceable".

4.   *Burden of Proof*

29.   With regard to the issue of alternative measures under Article 5.6 of the *SPS Agreement*, the United States notes that it emphasized "testing by product" in its Article 5.6 arguments because this alternative meets the requirements of Article 5.6, and because there is no scientific evidence to support even limited sorption testing. This does not change the fact that the claims and proof presented by the United States in this case supported a *prima facie* case under Article 5.6 with respect to sorption testing. It is the United States' submission that the Panel did not independently embark upon the exploration of factual areas not already addressed, either directly or indirectly, by the United States, nor did they consider legal arguments not specifically advanced by the United States.

30.   The United States submits that Japan has not, and cannot, identify any provision in the DSU that supports its contention that panels should be barred from either

exploring the facts presented by the parties or reaching a factual finding that is distinct from one advanced by one of the parties should the factual evidence before a panel so justify. In the opinion of the United States, Article 11 of the DSU clearly authorizes panels to seek clarification of factual and legal arguments from the parties and to seek the facts necessary to permit an "objective assessment of the matter before it ...". Were this not the case, Article 13 of the DSU would not state that "[e]ach panel shall have the right to seek information and technical advice from any individual or body which it deems appropriate." In the United States' view, therefore, Japan argues for a limitation on panel fact-finding that is not justified by the provisions of the DSU.

31. With respect to Japan's contention that it was not given an opportunity to express its position concerning the alternative measure, the United States argues that Japan had more than adequate opportunities to contest the facts found by the Panel on the basis of the statements of the experts, but chose not to do so.

5. *Article 11 of the DSU*

32. The United States submits that a finding of violation of Article 11 of the DSU requires a showing that the Panel demonstrated "deliberate disregard", "refused to consider", "wilfully distort[ed]" or "misrepresent[ed]" the evidence before it. According to the United States, Japan has failed to meet this high standard.

C. *Claims of Error by the United States - Appellant*

1. *Article 5.7 of the SPS Agreement*

33. The United States argues that should the Appellate Body reverse the Panel's finding on Article 5.7 of the *SPS Agreement*, it should still come to the conclusion that Japan failed to meet the requirements of Article 5.7 because: the relevant scientific information is, in fact, sufficient; the varietal testing requirement has not been adopted on the basis of available pertinent information; and the varietal testing requirement is not "provisional".

34. It is the United States' contention that for a measure to be imposed on a provisional basis, there must be an insufficient amount of relevant scientific evidence to be able to perform a risk assessment. With regard to the question of quarantine treatment efficacy, and the need for varietal testing, the United States believes that there is a sufficient amount of evidence, so that this case does not present a situation where there is insufficient relevant scientific evidence within the meaning of Article 5.7 of the *SPS Agreement*. The United States maintains that the varietal testing requirement is anything but provisional. The United States asserts that while Japan's obligation to fulfill the requirements of Article 5.7 may only date from 1 January 1995, this does not change the fact that the measure has been in place for at least 30 years.

2. *Article 5.6 of the SPS Agreement*

35. The United States submits that the Panel erred in law in failing to find that "testing by product" does not achieve Japan's appropriate level of protection. Ac-

cording to the United States, the Panel adopted a "no hypothetical risk" standard, a standard which erects an insurmountable hurdle for parties seeking to demonstrate that an alternative measure achieves a Member's appropriate level of protection, and a standard which was rejected by the Appellate Body in *European Communities - Hormones*.[21] The United States believes, therefore, that the Appellate Body should complete the analysis based on the correct standard and conclude that "testing by product" is an alternative measure within the meaning of Article 5.6 of the *SPS Agreement*.

36.   The United States requests that the Appellate Body modify the Panel's finding under Article 5.6 to clarify that this finding is a finding in the alternative, applicable only if the Appellate Body reverses the Panel's finding under Article 2.2 of the *SPS Agreement*. The United States believes that a clarification of the relationship between the Panel's findings under Articles 2.2 and 5.6 is necessary in order to avoid confusion in the implementation process and to secure a positive solution to the dispute. According to the United States, the alternative measure identified by the Panel, i.e., "determination of sorption levels", is a form of varietal testing and there is insufficient evidence to maintain any varietal testing. The United States is concerned that the Panel's Article 5.6 finding could lead Japan to conclude that it may adopt the "determination of sorption levels" option even though this option is inconsistent with Article 2.2.

3.   Findings on Apricots, Pears, Plums and Quince

37.   With regard to apricots, pears, plums and quince, the United States argues that the Panel erred in failing to extend its findings under Articles 2.2 and 5.6 of the *SPS Agreement* to these four products. According to the United States, the Panel found that the United States failed to establish a *prima facie* case of inconsistency with Articles 2.2 and 5.6 with regard to these products, on the basis of an absence in the record of information or studies specifically relating to them. However, no such information or studies currently exist.

38.   The United States submits that the Panel's finding with respect to apricots, pears, plums and quince is based on contradictory logic and a legally incorrect interpretation of the *prima facie* case required of the United States. According to the United States, the contradiction in the Panel's reasoning is apparent on the face of its decision. The Panel found that because there was insufficient evidence of the existence or relevance of varietal differences, it could not find that the evidence was insufficient. Furthermore, the United States argues that if the Panel's interpretation is to be upheld, complaining parties would be required to prove a negative based on affirmative evidence, namely, to prove that there is no scientific evidence which supports a measure. This interpretation places an impossible burden on complaining parties, rendering the obligation under Article 2.2 unenforceable. It also requires complaining parties to prove the absence of hypothetical risks, an approach which the Appellate Body has already rejected.

---

[21]   *European Communities - Hormones, supra,* footnote 12.

39.   The United States argues that it met the burden of proof for all products, since it established that Japan had failed to provide any scientific evidence to support its measure. The Panel appears to have required the United States to provide evidence for each product, thereby specifically disproving Japan's speculation that variety is significant.

40.   According to the United States, there is nothing in the Panel's analysis of Article 5.6 of the *SPS Agreement* which limits its applicability to any set of products within the Panel's terms of reference. The Panel, therefore, erred in limiting the scope of its Article 5.6 finding because there were no studies on the record specifically relating to apricots, pears, plums and quince. The United States submits that the absence of such studies was irrelevant to the Panel's analysis under Article 5.6.

4.   *Article 5.1 of the SPS Agreement*

41.   It is the United States' submission that if the Appellate Body does not extend the Panel's finding to apricots, pears, plums and quince, or if the Appellate Body reverses the Panel's finding under Article 2.2 in response to Japan's appeal, it should complete the legal analysis under Article 5.1 of the *SPS Agreement* and find that the varietal testing requirement violates that provision. The absence of evidence should have led the Panel to find that the varietal testing requirement is not based on a risk assessment in accordance with Article 5.1, and the Appellate Body should find so now.

42.   In the view of the United States, it is not sufficient that a risk assessment conclude that there is a *possibility* of entry. A proper risk assessment must evaluate the *likelihood*, i.e., the *probability* of entry. In the absence of scientific evidence relating to apricots, pears, plums and quince, any assessment can go no further than conclude that a hypothetical possibility of such a risk exists. According to the United States, Japan's risk assessment is completely silent as to the risk at issue in this case, namely, the risk of entry, establishment or spread of codling moth due to varietal differences which may affect quarantine treatment efficacy.

43.   It is the United States' submission that a risk assessment must evaluate the likelihood of entry, establishment or spread of a pest "according to the SPS measures which might be applied". Japan's risk assessment should have, but did not, discuss the need for, and effectiveness of, varietal testing in reducing risks associated with the entry, establishment or spread of codling moth. Nor did it evaluate or compare the effectiveness of other measures such as product-based testing or integrated pest risk management. Furthermore, the United States asserts that, contrary to what Japan claims, Japan's risk assessment was not conducted in accordance with the *FAO Guidelines for Pest Risk Analysis*.

44.   According to the United States, the above reasoning is applicable to all products; neither Japan's purported risk assessment nor the fact that it fails to address risks associated with varietal differences relates to any specific products.

> 5. *Article 8 and Paragraph 1(c) of Annex C, of the SPS Agreement*

45.   In the event that the Appellate Body accepts Japan's argument that the varietal testing requirement is an information requirement within the meaning of paragraph 1(c) of Annex C of the *SPS Agreement*, and finds it consistent with Article 2.2, the United States argues that the Appellate Body should nevertheless find that the measure is inconsistent with Article 8 and paragraph 1(c) of Annex C, which requires Members to limit information requirements to "what is necessary for appropriate control, inspection and approval procedures". The United States disputes that Japan's varietal testing requirement is consistent with this obligation as it is not limited to what is necessary.

D.   Arguments of Japan - Appellee

1.   Article 5.7 of the SPS Agreement

46.   With regard to Article 5.7 of the *SPS Agreement*, Japan argues that none of the arguments advanced by the United States counter any of the arguments advanced by Japan in its appellant's submission. Japan notes that while the United States attempts to define sufficiency in Article 5.7 to mean an insufficient amount of relevant scientific evidence to be able to perform a risk assessment, the concept of sufficiency should be interpreted to be common in both Article 2.2 and Article 5.7. Japan also notes that the Panel itself acknowledged that there is some scientific evidence to satisfy the requirement of the first sentence of Article 5.7.

2.   Article 5.6 of the SPS Agreement

47.   Japan argues that the United States' claim with respect to the alternative measure is a factual claim that is not subject to appellate review, as it deals exclusively with the evaluation of evidence by the Panel.

48.   According to Japan, the United States makes nine arguments which are mainly an attempt to question Japan's appropriate level of protection, but fails, as a matter of factual proof, to establish a case of inconsistency with Article 5.6 of the *SPS Agreement*. The level of protection by itself cannot be inconsistent with the *SPS Agreement* in the absence of discrimination or a disguised restriction on international trade.

49.   Japan also disputes the United States' claim that the finding under Article 5.6 would necessarily be alternative to the finding under Article 2.2. According to Japan, the United States attempts to equate "appropriate level of protection" which the importing Member may establish with "scientific justification". Japan submits that "sufficiency" of scientific evidence within the meaning of Article 2.2 must be ascertained in relation to the measure in question, which implies that the same scientific evidence may be sufficient for a certain purpose, but not for another. According to Japan, the finding of the Panel on Article 2.2 is limited to the varietal testing requirement as described in paragraphs 2.23 and 2.24 of the Panel Report. There can be other varietal measures which the Panel would find consistent with Article 2.2. Japan asserts, therefore, that the Panel's findings under Article 2.2 and those under Article 5.6 are not mutually inconsistent.

3. *Findings on Apricots, Pears, Plums and Quince*

50.   Japan submits that the claim of error by the United States in respect of apricots, pears, plums and quince is a factual claim not subject to appellate review. Japan states that the United States' claim can be reduced to an argument that the absence of evidence implying presence of varietal difference in apricots, pears, plums and quince would be sufficient to establish a *prima facie* case. As such, this claim challenges factual evaluation of the evidence by the Panel and does not raise any legal issue. Japan argues further that the absence of scientific evidence in regard to these commodities does not constitute any basis for a *prima facie* case. In Japan's opinion, the complaining party should and can establish that such proof or testing is not necessary. Being required to do so does not raise the problem of proving the negative. Japan argues that the case that the United States purports to make is not a *prima facie* case, so that in the absence of an affirmative showing by the United States, Japan should not be required to make an affirmative defence.

51.   With respect to apricots, pears, plums and quince, no finding of inconsistency with Article 5.6 can be made. Since there is no relevant data, it is impossible to find an alternative which would achieve Japan's appropriate level of protection.

4. *Article 5.1 of the SPS Agreement*

52.   Japan submits that it is fully compliant with the requirements of a risk assessment, having evaluated the *likelihood* of entry, establishment or spread of the codling moth in Japan as described in its *1996 Pest Risk Assessment of Codling Moth*. Japan submits that this risk assessment was conducted in accordance with the *FAO Guidelines for Pest Risk Analysis*. According to Japan, its risk assessment considered the likelihood of entry, establishment or spread of the pest due to possible non-efficacy, to the extent that relevant scientific evidence was available.

53.   Japan states further that it is impossible to make any finding under Article 5.1 with regard to apricots, pears, plums and quince because there is neither relevant data nor a treatment.

5. *Article 8 and Paragraph 1(c) of Annex C, of the SPS Agreement*

54.   Japan argues that it did not claim that Article 2.2 of the *SPS Agreement* would not apply to an information requirement. Japan's argument is that the type or characterization of an SPS measure will affect the question of sufficiency of scientific evidence under Article 2.2.

55.   Japan also notes that the United States' claim that Japan's varietal testing requirement is in fact unnecessary was clearly contradicted by the Panel. According to Japan, the Panel indicated, in relation to Article 5.6, that it was not convinced that there was sufficient evidence before it that testing by product would achieve Japan's level of protection for any of the products in issue.

III.   ARGUMENTS OF THE THIRD PARTICIPANTS

A.   *Brazil*

56.   With regard to Article 2.2 of the *SPS Agreement*, Brazil disagrees with Japan's submission that the varietal testing requirement is an information requirement which should be found to be maintained with sufficient scientific evidence within the meaning of Article 2.2. In Brazil's view, the phrase "sufficient scientific evidence" means that there has to be sufficient evidence to support a Member's SPS measure. Brazil also objects to Japan's attempt to compare its varietal testing requirement with the practices of the *Codex Alimentarius* concerning toxicological testing of any new food additive.

57.   On the issue of the requirements of Article 5.7 of the *SPS Agreement*, Brazil submits that Japan is incorrect in stating that it suffices to meet the requirements of the first sentence of Article 5.7. In Brazil's view, the Panel was correct to find that Japan did not fulfill two of the requirements under Article 5.7 and was not, therefore, entitled to the exception provided for in that provision.

58.   With regard to Article 5.6 of the *SPS Agreement*, Brazil submits that the Panel erred in not finding that the "testing by product" alternative would meet Japan's appropriate level of testing, as scientific evidence has demonstrated that this alternative would result in the proper protection of the Japanese fruit culture from codling moth infestation.

59.   With regard to Article 7 of the *SPS Agreement*, Brazil agrees with the Panel that "… a non-mandatory government measure is also subject to WTO provisions, in the event that compliance with this measure is necessary to obtain an advantage from the government or, in other words, if sufficient incentives or disincentives exist for that measure to be abided by."

60.   Brazil argues that the Panel should have concluded that the lack of evidence regarding apricots, pears, plums and quince is in itself the proof that the measure is based on insufficient scientific evidence. According to Brazil, the Panel's finding seems to reward an importing Member for its lack of evidence in support of its contested measure.

B.   *European Communities*

61.   With regard to Article 2.2 of the *SPS Agreement*, the European Communities submits that the empirical evidence submitted by the United States is useful, but not sufficient, to discharge the United States' burden of persuasion nor to overturn the presumption of SPS conformity of the measure at issue. According to the rules on burden of proof, the Panel should have ruled that the United States has not discharged its burden of proof.

62.   The European Communities submits that while the rules on burden of proof under Article 2.2 should have led the Panel to reject the United States' claims, the Panel instead devised a new legal test that in judging the sufficiency of the scientific evidence, the Member maintaining the measure should establish an "actual causal link" between the measure and the scientific evidence on the basis of which it is maintained. It is the European Communities' contention that to require an "actual causal link" is contrary to the text, object, purpose and preparatory history of Article

2.2 of the *SPS Agreement*. Furthermore, the European Communities asserts that the "actual causal link" test is narrower in scope than the rational relationship test adopted by the Appellate Body in *European Communities - Hormones*.[22] In the opinion of the European Communities, a systematic interpretation of Articles 2.2 and 5.1 in context does not reveal that the "sufficiency" threshold under Article 2.2 should be more restrictive than that applied in deciding whether an SPS measure is "based on" a risk assessment.

63.   According to the European Communities, since the concept of risk and risk assessment in the *SPS Agreement* is a qualitative and not a quantitative one, the word "sufficient" cannot be taken to refer to the quantitative, but should be seen as referring to the qualitative aspects of the scientific evidence used by the regulatory authorities of a Member.

64.   With regard to Article 5.7 of the *SPS Agreement*, the European Communities argues that the first sentence of Article 5.7 lays down the requirements that trigger the operation of Article 5.7 and, for that reason, the Panel's refusal to examine whether the measure at issue satisfies all the conditions of Article 5.7 is, in principle, unsatisfactory.

65.   The European Communities submits that, contrary to what the United States claims, an insufficient amount of relevant information can be established not only when the Member having recourse to this provision is not able to perform a risk assessment, but also when the risk assessment shows that the relevant scientific evidence is, for example, insufficient, conflicting, inconclusive or uncertain. The explicit mention made of Article 5.7 in Article 2.2 implies that the conditions for the application of the one provision necessarily affect the application of the other.

66.   The European Communities agrees with Japan that the Panel erred in finding that the obligation "to seek to obtain the additional information" means that the necessary information must be specific enough. The text of Article 5.7 does not lay down any information collection procedures.

67.   The European Communities considers that the Panel erred in implying that the requirement to review the measure within a "reasonable period of time" extends also to the period of time prior to the entry into force of the *SPS Agreement*, or that a period of four years in the application of a measure is not reasonable. According to the European Communities, the obligation to seek to obtain information does not require that actual results be obtained within a specified period of time. The reasonableness of the period of time, as argued by Japan, should be judged according to the risk involved and the nature of the SPS measure which is required to be taken in order to achieve the Member's level of sanitary protection.

68.   With regard to Article 5.6 of the *SPS Agreement*, the European Communities agrees with the Panel that an alternative measure exists, i.e., the "determination of sorption levels", which is reasonably available, significantly less trade-restrictive and achieves Japan's level of phytosanitary protection.

69.   With regard to Article 7 of the *SPS Agreement*, the European Communities agrees with the Panel that the varietal testing requirement imposed by Japan is a

---

[22]   *European Communities - Hormones, supra,* footnote 12.

phytosanitary measure according to the wording of Annex B of the *SPS Agreement*, and consequently, must be published in order to comply with the transparency requirement in Article 7.

70.   With regard to Article 8 of the *SPS Agreement*, the European Communities agrees with the United States that the measure at issue is inconsistent with paragraph 1(c) of Annex C and with Article 8 of the *SPS Agreement*.

IV.   ISSUES RAISED IN THIS APPEAL

71.   This appeal raises the following issues:

(a)   whether the Panel erred in law in finding that the varietal testing requirement is maintained without sufficient scientific evidence within the meaning of Article 2.2 of the *SPS Agreement*;

(b)   whether the Panel erred in law in its application of Article 5.7 of the *SPS Agreement* and in finding that the requirements of the second sentence of Article 5.7 are not fulfilled;

(c)   whether the Panel erred in law by failing to find that "testing by product" achieves Japan's appropriate level of protection as required under Article 5.6 of the *SPS Agreement*;

(d)   whether the Panel erred in law in making a finding under Article 5.6 of the *SPS Agreement* with regard to the "determination of sorption levels" irrespective of whether it had found the varietal testing requirement to be inconsistent with Article 2.2 of the *SPS Agreement*;

(e)   whether the Panel correctly interpreted the scope of application of the publication requirement of paragraph 1 of Annex B of the *SPS Agreement*;

(f)   whether the varietal testing requirement is consistent with Article 5.1 of the *SPS Agreement*;

(g)   whether the varietal testing requirement is consistent with Article 8 and paragraph 1(c) of Annex C, of the *SPS Agreement*;

(h)   whether the Panel's finding under Article 5.6 of the *SPS Agreement* with regard to the "determination of sorption levels" was reached in a manner consistent with the rules on burden of proof;

(i)   whether the Panel erred in law by not extending its findings of inconsistency with Articles 2.2 and 5.6 of the *SPS Agreement* to the varietal testing requirement as it applies to apricots, pears, plums and quince; and

(j)   whether the Panel's finding on Article 2.2 of the *SPS Agreement* is inconsistent with Article 11 of the DSU.

V.   THE SPS AGREEMENT

A.   Article 2.2

72.   Article 2.2 of the *SPS Agreement* stipulates in relevant part:

> Members shall ensure that any sanitary and phytosanitary measure ... is not maintained without sufficient scientific evidence, except as provided for in paragraph 7 of Article 5.

The Panel found that Japan's varietal testing requirement as it applies to apples, cherries, nectarines and walnuts is maintained without sufficient scientific evidence and is, therefore, inconsistent with Article 2.2 of the *SPS Agreement*.[23] Japan appeals this finding. According to Japan, the Panel erred in law in finding that the varietal testing requirement was "maintained without sufficient scientific evidence" within the meaning of Article 2.2.

73.   Japan's appeal raises the issue of the meaning of the phrase "maintained without sufficient scientific evidence" in Article 2.2 and, in particular, the meaning of the word "sufficient". The ordinary meaning of "sufficient" is "of a quantity, extent, or scope adequate to a certain purpose or object".[24] From this, we can conclude that "sufficiency" is a relational concept. "Sufficiency" requires the existence of a sufficient or adequate relationship between two elements, *in casu,* between the SPS measure and the scientific evidence.

74.   The context of the word "sufficient" or, more generally, the phrase "maintained without sufficient scientific evidence" in Article 2.2, includes Article 5.1 as well as Articles 3.3 and 5.7 of the *SPS Agreement*.

75.   Article 5.1 of the *SPS Agreement* requires that an SPS measure be based on a risk assessment. As we stated in our Report in *European Communities - Hormones*:

> ... Articles 2.2 and 5.1 should constantly be read together. Article 2.2 informs Article 5.1: the elements that define the basic obligation set out in Article 2.2 impart meaning to Article 5.1.[25]

76.   In that Report, we found that:

> ... Article 5.1, when contextually read as it should be, in conjunction with and as informed by Article 2.2 of the *SPS Agreement*, requires that the results of the risk assessment must sufficiently warrant - that is to say, reasonably support - the SPS measure at stake. The requirement that an SPS measure be "based on" a risk assessment is a substantive requirement that there be a rational relationship between the measure and the risk assessment.[26]

We agree with the Panel that this statement provides guidance for the interpretation of the obligation under Article 2.2 not to maintain an SPS measure without sufficient scientific evidence.[27]

---

[23]   Panel Report, para. 8.43.
[24]   C.T. Onions (ed.), *The Shorter Oxford English Dictionary*, Third Edition (1983), p. 2180.
[25]   *European Communities - Hormones, supra,* footnote 12, para. 180.
[26]   *European Communities - Hormones, supra,* footnote 12, para. 193.
[27]   Panel Report, para. 8.29.

77.   We also consider it useful in interpreting Article 2.2, and, in particular, the meaning of the word "sufficient", to recall the following statement on Article 5.1 in our Report in *European Communities - Hormones*:

> Article 5.1 does not require that the risk assessment must necessarily embody only the view of a majority of the relevant scientific community. ... In most cases, responsible and representative governments tend to base their legislative and administrative measures on "mainstream" scientific opinion. In other cases, equally responsible and representative governments may act in good faith on the basis of what, at a given time, may be a divergent opinion coming from qualified and respected sources.[28]

78.   Furthermore, in our Report in *Australia - Salmon*, we stated with regard to Article 5.1:

> ... it is not sufficient that a risk assessment conclude that there is a *possibility* of entry, establishment or spread ... . A proper risk assessment ... must evaluate the "likelihood", i.e., the "probability", of entry, establishment or spread ... .[29]

We also made it clear in that Report that *some* evaluation of the likelihood is not enough.[30]

79.   As mentioned above, the context of the phrase "not maintained without sufficient scientific evidence" in Article 2.2 also includes Article 3.3 of the *SPS Agreement*. Pursuant to Article 3.3, Members may introduce or maintain an SPS measure which results in a higher level of protection than would be achieved by a measure based on a relevant international standard, *inter alia*, "if there is a scientific justification" and the measure is not inconsistent with any other provision of the *SPS Agreement*. In *European Communities - Hormones*, we stated:

> ... the footnote to Article 3.3 ... defines "scientific justification" as an "examination and evaluation of available scientific information in conformity with relevant provisions of this Agreement ...".[31]

We also stated:

> [t]his examination and evaluation would appear to partake of the nature of the risk assessment required in Article 5.1 and defined in paragraph 4 of Annex A of the *SPS Agreement*.[32]

In our opinion, there is a "scientific justification" for an SPS measure, within the meaning of Article 3.3, if there is a rational relationship between the SPS measure at issue and the available scientific information.

---

[28]   *European Communities - Hormones, supra,* footnote 12, para. 194.

[29]   *Australia - Salmon, supra,* footnote 13, para. 123.

[30]   *Australia - Salmon, supra,* footnote 13, para. 124.

[31]   *European Communities - Hormones, supra,* footnote 12, para. 175.

[32]   *European Communities - Hormones, supra,* footnote 12, para. 175.

80.   Finally, it is clear that Article 5.7 of the *SPS Agreement*, to which Article 2.2 explicitly refers, is part of the context of the latter provision and should be considered in the interpretation of the obligation not to maintain an SPS measure without sufficient scientific evidence. Article 5.7 allows Members to adopt provisional SPS measures "[i]n cases where relevant scientific evidence is insufficient" and certain other requirements are fulfilled.[33] Article 5.7 operates as a *qualified* exemption from the obligation under Article 2.2 not to maintain SPS measures without sufficient scientific evidence. An overly broad and flexible interpretation of that obligation would render Article 5.7 meaningless.

81.   We note Japan's argument that the requirement in Article 2.2 not to maintain an SPS measure without sufficient scientific evidence should be interpreted in light of the precautionary principle. In our Report in *European Communities - Hormones*[34], we stated that the precautionary principle finds reflection in the preamble, Article 3.3 and Article 5.7 of the *SPS Agreement* and that this principle:

> ... has not been written into the *SPS Agreement* as a ground for justifying SPS measures that are otherwise inconsistent with the obligations of Members set out in particular provisions of that Agreement.

82.   We do not agree with Japan's proposition that direct application of Article 2.2 of the *SPS Agreement* should be limited to situations in which the scientific evidence is "patently" insufficient, and that the issue raised in this dispute should have been dealt with under Article 5.1 of the *SPS Agreement*. There is nothing in the text of either Articles 2.2 or 5.1, or any other provision of the *SPS Agreement*, that requires or sanctions such limitation of the scope of Article 2.2. On the contrary, Article 2.2 sets out, as the title of Article 2 indicates, "Basic Rights and Obligations". In our Report in *European Communities - Hormones*, we agreed with a statement by the panel in that case that Article 5.1 may be viewed as a specific application of the *basic* obligations contained in Article 2.2.[35] This statement can not possibly be interpreted as support for limiting the scope of Article 2.2 "in favour" of Article 5.1. Furthermore, we note that we said the following in our Report in *European Communities - Hormones*:

> We are, of course, surprised by the fact that the Panel did not begin its analysis of this whole case by focusing on Article 2 that is captioned "Basic Rights and Obligations", an approach that appears logically attractive.[36]

83.   We also do not agree with Japan's contention that the Panel "in the end" applied a standard different from its "rational relationship" standard, i.e., the "actual causal link" standard. We understand the Panel to refer, in paragraph 8.42 of its Report, to the absence of an actual causal link between test differences in CxT and LD_{50} values and varietal differences as an illustration or a strong indication of the

---

[33]   See *infra*, para. 89.

[34]   *European Communities - Hormones, supra*, footnote 12, para. 124.

[35]   *European Communities - Hormones, supra*, footnote 12, para. 180.

[36]   *European Communities - Hormones, supra*, footnote 12, para. 250.

absence of a rational relationship between the SPS measure and the scientific evidence.

84.   In the light of the above considerations based on the text and context of Article 2.2 of the *SPS Agreement*, we agree with the Panel that the obligation in Article 2.2 that an SPS measure not be maintained without sufficient scientific evidence requires that there be a rational or objective relationship between the SPS measure and the scientific evidence.[37] Whether there is a rational relationship between an SPS measure and the scientific evidence is to be determined on a case-by-case basis and will depend upon the particular circumstances of the case, including the characteristics of the measure at issue and the quality and quantity of the scientific evidence.

85.   We, therefore, reject Japan's appeal on this issue and uphold the Panel's finding in paragraph 8.43 of the Panel Report that the varietal testing requirement as it applies to apples, cherries, nectarines and walnuts is maintained without sufficient scientific evidence within the meaning of Article 2.2 of the *SPS Agreement.*

B.   Article 5.7

86.   As already discussed above, Article 2.2 of the *SPS Agreement* stipulates that Members shall not maintain SPS measures without sufficient scientific evidence "except as provided for in paragraph 7 of Article 5." In support of its varietal testing requirement, Japan invoked Article 5.7 before the Panel.

Article 5.7 of the *SPS Agreement* reads as follows:

> In cases where relevant scientific evidence is insufficient, a Member may provisionally adopt sanitary or phytosanitary measures on the basis of available pertinent information, including that from the relevant international organizations as well as from sanitary or phytosanitary measures applied by other Members. In such circumstances, Members shall seek to obtain the additional information necessary for a more objective assessment of risk and review the sanitary or phytosanitary measure accordingly within a reasonable period of time.

87.   The Panel found that Japan had not fulfilled the requirements contained in the second sentence of Article 5.7. It did not examine whether Japan's varietal testing requirement met the requirements of the first sentence of Article 5.7. In this connection, the Panel stated:

> ... we thus find that even if the varietal testing requirement were considered as a provisional measure adopted in accordance with the first sentence of Article 5.7, Japan has not fulfilled the requirements contained in the second sentence of Article 5.7.[38]

---

[37]   Panel Report, paras. 8.29 and 8.42.

[38]   Panel Report, para. 8.59.

88.   Japan appeals the Panel's finding under Article 5.7. According to Japan, the Panel erred in its application of Article 5.7 and in its finding that the requirements of the second sentence of Article 5.7 were not fulfilled.

89.   Article 5.7 of the *SPS Agreement* sets out four requirements which must be met in order to adopt and maintain a provisional SPS measure. Pursuant to the first sentence of Article 5.7, a Member may provisionally adopt an SPS measure if this measure is:

> (1)   imposed in respect of a situation where "relevant scientific information is insufficient"; and

> (2)   adopted "on the basis of available pertinent information".

Pursuant to the second sentence of Article 5.7, such a provisional measure may not be maintained unless the Member which adopted the measure:

> (1)   "seek[s] to obtain the additional information necessary for a more objective assessment of risk"; and

> (2)   "review[s] the ... measure accordingly within a reasonable period of time".

These four requirements are clearly cumulative in nature and are equally important for the purpose of determining consistency with this provision. Whenever *one* of these four requirements is not met, the measure at issue is inconsistent with Article 5.7.

90.   Japan's proposition that the wording "except as provided for in paragraph 7 of Article 5" in Article 2.2 refers only to the first sentence of Article 5.7, and that a Member should, therefore, be allowed to claim exemption from the obligation under Article 2.2 when it fulfils the requirements of the first sentence, is without basis in the text of either Article 2.2 or Article 5.7. On the contrary, Article 2.2 refers to Article 5.7 as a whole and Article 5.7 links the first and second sentence with the words "[i]n *such* circumstances" (emphasis added).

91.   We, therefore, conclude that the Panel did not err in its application of Article 5.7 by first examining whether the varietal testing requirement meets the requirements of the second sentence of Article 5.7. Having established that the requirements of the second sentence of Article 5.7 are not met, there was no need for the Panel to examine the requirements of the first sentence.[39]

92.   As to the question whether the Panel erred in finding that Japan has not acted consistently with the requirements of the second sentence of Article 5.7, we note that the first part of the second sentence stipulates that the Member adopting a provisional SPS measure "shall seek to obtain the additional information necessary for a

---

[39]   In *European Communities - Measures Affecting the Importation of Certain Poultry Products*, adopted 23 July 1998, WT/DS69/AB/R, para. 135, we stated that "[j]ust as a panel has the discretion to address only those *claims* which must be addressed in order to dispose of the matter at issue in a dispute, so too does a panel have the discretion to address only those *arguments* it deems necessary to resolve a particular claim. So long as it is clear in a panel report that a panel has reasonably considered a claim, the fact that a particular argument relating to that claim is not specifically addressed in the 'Findings' section of a panel report will not, in and of itself, lead to the conclusion that that panel has failed to make the 'objective assessment of the matter before it' required by Article 11 of the DSU."

more objective assessment of risk". Neither Article 5.7 nor any other provision of the *SPS Agreement* sets out explicit prerequisites regarding the additional information to be collected or a specific collection procedure. Furthermore, Article 5.7 does not specify what actual results must be achieved; the obligation is to "seek to obtain" additional information. However, Article 5.7 states that the additional information is to be sought in order to allow the Member to conduct "a more objective assessment of risk". Therefore, the information sought must be germane to conducting such a risk assessment, i.e., the evaluation of the likelihood of entry, establishment or spread of, *in casu*, a pest, according to the SPS measures which might be applied. We note that the Panel found that the information collected by Japan does not "examine the appropriateness" of the SPS measure at issue and does not address the core issue as to whether "varietal characteristics cause a divergency in quarantine efficacy".[40] In the light of this finding, we agree with the Panel that Japan did not seek to obtain the additional information necessary for a more objective risk assessment.

93.   The second part of the second sentence of Article 5.7 stipulates that the Member adopting a provisional SPS measure shall "review the ... measure accordingly within a reasonable period of time." In our view, what constitutes a "reasonable period of time" has to be established on a case-by-case basis and depends on the specific circumstances of each case, including the difficulty of obtaining the additional information necessary for the review *and* the characteristics of the provisional SPS measure. In the present case, the Panel found that collecting the necessary additional information would be relatively easy.[41] Although the obligation "to review" the varietal testing requirement has only been in existence since 1 January 1995, we agree with the Panel that Japan has not reviewed its varietal testing requirement "within a reasonable period of time".[42]

94.   We, therefore, uphold the Panel's finding that even if the varietal testing requirement were considered to be a provisional measure adopted in accordance with the first sentence of Article 5.7, Japan has not fulfilled the requirements contained in the second sentence of Article 5.7.

C.   *Article 5.6*

95.   Article 5.6 of the *SPS Agreement* prohibits SPS measures that are more trade-restrictive than required to achieve a Member's appropriate level of protection. According to the footnote to Article 5.6, a measure is considered more trade-restrictive than required if there is another SPS measure which:

    (1)   is reasonably available taking into account technical and economic feasibility;

    (2)   achieves the Member's appropriate level of protection; and

---

[40]   Panel Report, para. 8.56.
[41]   Panel Report, para. 8.56.
[42]   Panel Report, para. 8.58.

(3)   is significantly less restrictive to trade than the SPS measure contested.[43]

As we have stated in our Report in *Australia - Salmon*, these three elements are cumulative in nature.[44]

96.   The United States argued before the Panel that the "testing by product" of the efficacy of the quarantine treatment is such an alternative measure within the meaning of Article 5.6. The Panel agreed with the United States that "testing by product" is a measure which is reasonably available, taking into account technical and economic feasibility.[45] It also agreed that "testing by product" is significantly less restrictive to trade than the varietal testing requirement.[46] On the remaining element under Article 5.6, the Panel concluded, however, that:

> ... after having carefully examined all the evidence before us in light of the opinions we received from the experts advising the Panel, we are not convinced that there is sufficient evidence before us to find that testing by product would achieve Japan's appropriate level of protection for any of the products at issue.[47]

97.   The United States appeals this finding. According to the United States, the Panel erred in law by failing to find that "testing by product" achieves Japan's appropriate level of protection. The United States asserts that in concluding that the statement by Dr. Ducom, one of the experts advising the Panel[48], is sufficient to preclude a finding that "testing by product" achieves Japan's appropriate level of protection, the Panel effectively adopted a "no hypothetical risk" standard.[49] According to the United States, we rejected such a standard in our Report in *European*

---

[43] *Australia - Salmon, supra*, footnote 13, para. 194.

[44] *Australia - Salmon, supra*, footnote 13, para. 194.

[45] Panel Report, para. 8.78.

[46] Panel Report, para. 8.79.

[47] Panel Report, para. 8.84.

[48] Paragraph 8.83 of the Panel Report reads in relevant part as follows:

> However, at least one of the experts advising the Panel made equally clear that the US alternative of one treatment for all varieties, including those to be developed in the future, does not, to date, have a scientific basis either. In his answer to Panel question 16, *Dr. Ducom* states:
>
> > "The arguments put forth by Japan for requiring varietal trials are not based on scientific data. They are supported by a few experimental data in which varietal difference exists, in terms of LD_{50}, among a lot of other data in which it does not ...
> >
> > The arguments put forth by the USA are based on a large number of experiments, of which Japan has thoroughly made use.
> >
> > Varietal difference appears several times, but each time, the confirmatory test has revealed sufficient efficacy. *Extrapolation to all available varieties is no more scientific than the Japanese's contrary assertion. This sort of extrapolation is something along the order of intuition. It is unfortunate that there has not been a research program on the subject in order to try to present some scientific proof".*

[49] Appellant's Submission of the United States, para. 38.

Communities - Hormones. Furthermore, the United States contends that a "no hypothetical risk" standard erects an insurmountable hurdle for parties seeking to demonstrate that an alternative measure achieves a Member's appropriate level of protection.[50]

98.   Contrary to what the United States asserts, the Panel did not base its conclusion with regard to "testing by product" under Article 5.6 exclusively on Dr. Ducom's statement. The Panel explicitly stated, in paragraph 8.84 of the Panel Report[51], that it carefully examined *all* the evidence before it in light of the opinions received from its experts and that it subsequently came to the conclusion that it was not convinced that there was sufficient evidence to find that "testing by product" would achieve Japan's appropriate level of protection. It appears to us that the United States' appeal in essence challenges the Panel's consideration and weighing of the evidence before it. As we stated in our Report in *Australia - Salmon*, a panel's consideration and weighing of the evidence before it relates to its assessment of the facts and, therefore, falls outside the scope of appellate review under Article 17.6 of the DSU.[52]

99.   Furthermore, we fail to understand how the Panel would have "effectively" adopted a "no hypothetical risk" standard by concluding that Dr. Ducom's statement[53] is sufficient to preclude a finding that "testing by product" does not achieve Japan's appropriate level of protection.

100.   We, therefore, reject the United States' appeal from the Panel's finding under Article 5.6 with regard to "testing by product".

101.   Apart from appealing the Panel's finding under Article 5.6 with regard to "testing by product", the United States also requests a modification of the Panel's finding under Article 5.6 with regard to the "determination of sorption levels" in order to clarify that this finding is a finding in the alternative, relevant only if the Appellate Body were to reverse the Panel's finding under Article 2.2. In paragraph 131 of this Report, however, we reverse the Panel's finding under Article 5.6 with regard to the "determination of sorption levels". We, therefore, see no further need to address the alternative argument raised here by the United States concerning the relationship between the Panel's finding of inconsistency under Article 2.2 and its finding of inconsistency under Article 5.6.

D.   *Article 7 and Paragraph 1 of Annex B*

102.   Article 7 of the *SPS Agreement*, that is captioned "Transparency", reads:

> Members shall notify changes in their sanitary or phytosanitary measures and shall provide information on their sanitary or phytosanitary measures in accordance with the provisions of Annex B.

Paragraph 1 of Annex B of the *SPS Agreement* stipulates:

---

[50]   Appellant's Submission of the United States, para. 39.

[51]   See *supra*, para. 96.

[52]   *Australia - Salmon, supra*, footnote 13, para. 261.

[53]   See *supra*, footnote 48.

> Members shall ensure that all sanitary and phytosanitary
> regulations which have been adopted are published promptly
> in such a manner as to enable interested Members to become
> acquainted with them.

In a footnote to this paragraph, the sanitary and phytosanitary *regulations* to which this publication requirement applies are defined as:

> Sanitary and phytosanitary measures such as laws, decrees or
> ordinances which are applicable generally.

103.   In paragraph 8.111 of the Panel Report, the Panel found:

> Even though the varietal testing requirement is not mandatory
> - in that exporting countries can demonstrate quarantine effi-
> ciency by other means - in our view, it does constitute a
> "phytosanitary regulation" subject to the publication require-
> ment in Annex B.

In paragraph 8.116 of the Panel Report, the Panel subsequently concluded that:

> ... Japan, by not having published the varietal testing re-
> quirement, acts inconsistently with its obligations under para-
> graph 1 of Annex B of the SPS Agreement and, for that rea-
> son, with its obligations contained in Article 7 of that Agree-
> ment.

104.   Japan appeals this finding. According to Japan, the "regulations" referred to in paragraph 1 of Annex B are limited to legally enforceable instruments. Japan contends that the varietal testing requirement, as set out in the *Experimental Guide*[54], is not a legally enforceable instrument and does, therefore, not fall within the scope of application of the publication requirement of paragraph 1 of Annex B.

105.   We consider that the list of instruments contained in the footnote to paragraph 1 of Annex B is, as is indicated by the words "such as", not exhaustive in nature. The scope of application of the publication requirement is not limited to "laws, decrees or ordinances", but also includes, in our opinion, other instruments which are applicable generally and are similar in character to the instruments explicitly referred to in the illustrative list of the footnote to paragraph 1 of Annex B.

106.   The object and purpose of paragraph 1 of Annex B is "to enable interested Members to become acquainted with" the sanitary and phytosanitary regulations adopted or maintained by other Members and thus to enhance transparency regarding these measures. In our opinion, the scope of application of the publication requirement of paragraph 1 of Annex B should be interpreted in the light of the object and purpose of this provision.

107.   We note that it is undisputed that the varietal testing requirement is applicable generally. Furthermore, we consider in the light of the actual impact of the varietal testing requirement on exporting countries, as discussed by the Panel in paragraphs 8.112 and 8.113 of the Panel Report, that this instrument is of a charac-

---

[54]   See *supra*, para. 2.

ter similar to laws, decrees and ordinances, the instruments explicitly referred to in the footnote to paragraph 1 of Annex B.

108.   For these reasons, we agree with the Panel that the varietal testing requirement, as set out in the *Experimental Guide*, is a phytosanitary regulation within the meaning of paragraph 1 of Annex B, and, therefore, uphold the Panel's finding that Japan has acted inconsistently with this provision and with Article 7 of the *SPS Agreement*.

E.   Article 5.1

109.   The Panel made no finding on the consistency of Japan's varietal testing requirement with Article 5.1 of the *SPS Agreement*. In paragraph 8.63 of the Panel Report, the Panel stated:

> Since we have found earlier that the varietal testing requirement violates Article 2.2, we see no need to further examine whether it also needs to be based on a risk assessment in accordance with Articles 5.1 and 5.2 nor to determine whether in this dispute it is so based.

110.   In its Appellant's Submission, the United States calls upon us to "complete the Article 5.1 analysis and find that the varietal testing requirement violates that provision", in the event that we do not extend the Panel's finding under Article 2.2 to apricots, pears, plums and quince, *or* in the event that we reverse the Panel's finding that the varietal testing requirement as it applies to apples, cherries, nectarines and walnuts is inconsistent with Article 2.2.[55]

111.   We note that there is an error of logic in the Panel's finding in paragraph 8.63. The Panel stated that it had found earlier in its Report that the varietal testing requirement violates Article 2.2, and that there was, therefore, no need to examine whether the measure at issue was based on a risk assessment in accordance with Articles 5.1 and 5.2 of the *SPS Agreement*. We note, however, that the Panel's finding of inconsistency with Article 2.2 only concerned the varietal testing requirement as it applies to apples, cherries, nectarines and walnuts.[56] With regard to the varietal testing requirement as it applies to apricots, pears, plums and quince, the Panel found that there was insufficient evidence before it to conclude that this measure was inconsistent with Article 2.2. The Panel, therefore, made an error of logic when it stated, in general terms, that there was no need to examine whether the varietal testing requirement was consistent with Article 5.1 because this requirement had already been found to be inconsistent with Article 2.2. With regard to the varietal testing requirement as it applies to apricots, pears, plums and quince, there was clearly still a need to examine whether this measure was inconsistent with Article 5.1. By not making a finding under Article 5.1 with regard to the varietal testing requirement as it applies to apricots, pears, plums and quince, the Panel improperly

---

[55]   Appellant's Submission of the United States, para. 62.
[56]   Panel Report, para. 8.43.

applied the principle of judicial economy.[57] We believe that a finding under Article 5.1 with respect to apricots, pears, plums and quince is necessary "in order to ensure effective resolution" of the dispute.[58]

112.   We consider it appropriate for us to complete the legal analysis and examine whether the varietal testing requirement as it applies to apricots, pears, plums and quince is consistent with Article 5.1. As already noted above, Article 5.1 requires that an SPS measure be based on a risk assessment.[59] In our Report in *Australia - Salmon*, we stated with regard to the type of risk assessment required in this case:

> ... a risk assessment within the meaning of Article 5.1 must:
>
> (1)   *identify* the diseases whose entry, establishment or spread a Member wants to prevent within its territory, as well as the potential biological and economic consequences associated with the entry, establishment or spread of these diseases;
>
> (2)   *evaluate the likelihood* of entry, establishment or spread of these diseases, as well as the associated potential biological and economic consequences; and
>
> (3)   evaluate the likelihood of entry, establishment or spread of these diseases *according to the SPS measures which might be applied.*[60]

113.   Japan argued before the Panel that its varietal testing requirement is based on the *1996 Pest Risk Assessment of Codling Moth* (the "*1996 Risk Assessment*").[61] We note, however, that the *1996 Risk Assessment* does not discuss or even refer to the varietal testing requirement or to any other phytosanitary measure that might be taken to reduce the risk. The *1996 Risk Assessment* does not, therefore, "evaluate the likelihood of the entry, establishment or spread" of codling moth "according to the SPS measures which might be applied" within the meaning of Article 5.1.

114.   We, therefore, conclude that the varietal testing requirement as it applies to apricots, pears, plums and quince is inconsistent with Article 5.1 of the *SPS Agreement*.

F.   *Article 8 and Paragraph 1(c) of Annex C*

115.   In paragraph 8.117 of the Panel Report, the Panel stated:

> Given that we have found earlier that the varietal testing requirement is inconsistent with the requirements of Articles 2.2, 5.6 and 7 of the SPS Agreement, we see no need to fur-

---

[57]   We note that the Panel, in paragraph 8.6 of its Report, stated that in light of its terms of reference it was called upon "to examine the [varietal testing requirement] as it applies to all products covered by the contested measure", i.e., apples, cherries, peaches (including nectarines), walnuts, *apricots, pears, plums* and *quince.*

[58]   *Australia - Salmon, supra*, footnote 13, para. 223.

[59]   See *supra*, paras. 75-78.

[60]   *Australia - Salmon, supra*, footnote 13, para. 121.

[61]   Panel Report, para. 4.145 and following.

ther examine whether it is also inconsistent with Article 8, referring to Annex C, of that Agreement.

116.   In the event that we accept Japan's argument that the varietal testing requirement is an information requirement within the meaning of paragraph 1(c) of Annex C, and that Japan's measure is, therefore, consistent with Article 2.2, the United States requests that we find the varietal testing requirement inconsistent with Article 8 and paragraph 1(c) of Annex C, of the *SPS Agreement.*[62]

117.   We note that the United States does not appeal the Panel's failure to make a finding under Article 8 and Annex C of the *SPS Agreement*. It does not challenge the Panel's application of the principle of judicial economy. The United States merely submits to us arguments concerning the consistency of Japan's varietal testing requirement with Article 8 and paragraph 1(c) of Annex C for our consideration should we come the conclusion that the varietal testing requirement is an information requirement, and, therefore, is consistent with Article 2.2. We have not come to this conclusion[63] and we, therefore, do not consider it necessary to address the arguments on Article 8 and paragraph 1(c) of Annex C, submitted by the United States.

VI.   GENERAL ISSUES

A.   *Burden of Proof*

118.   In paragraph 8.103 of the Panel Report, the Panel found:

> ... - on the basis of the evidence before the Panel and the opinions of the experts advising the Panel - it can be presumed that an alternative measure exists (i.e., [the "determination of sorption levels"]) which would meet all of the elements under Article 5.6.

119.   In its reasoning, the Panel explicitly stated that the complaining party, the United States, had "not specifically addressed" the question whether the "determination of sorption levels" is an alternative measure within the meaning of Article 5.6 of the *SPS Agreement*.[64] With regard to the first and third elements under Article 5.6, namely, the economic and technical feasibility of the alternative measure, and the question whether the alternative measure is significantly less trade-restrictive than the SPS measure at issue, the Panel noted, however, that the United States "has given views which are consistent with" the idea that the "determination of sorption levels" meets these two elements.[65] With regard to the second element under Article 5.6, namely, the question whether the alternative measure meets the Member's ap-

---

[62]   Appellant's Submission of the United States, para. 83.

[63]   See *supra*, para. 85.

[64]   Panel Report, footnotes 328, 332 and 333.

[65]   Panel Report, paras. 8.91 and 8.95. The Panel noted, in footnotes 328 and 332, that it had considered all the other arguments of the United States and that none of these arguments went against the idea that the determination of sorption levels would be technically and economically feasible and would be significantly less trade-restrictive than the varietal testing requirement.

propriate level of protection, the Panel stated that "the United States ... suggests that [the "determination of sorption levels"] *would* meet Japan's appropriate level of protection".[66] The Panel noted that the United States submitted that "testing by product" would meet Japan's level of protection and that, since the determination of sorption levels "is more stringent than testing by product, it can thus be presumed that the US view on this alternative would be that it *a fortiori* meets Japan's level of protection".[67]

120.   Japan appeals the Panel's finding under Article 5.6 regarding the "determination of sorption levels", on the basis that it is contrary to the rules on burden of proof, as established by the Appellate Body in *United States - Shirts and Blouses*.[68] In Japan's view, panels cannot find facts neither argued nor proven by the parties.[69] Japan asserts that the Panel "exempts quite unjustly the United States from discharging the distributed burden of proof".[70]

121.   With regard to the rules on burden of proof, we stated in our Report in *United States - Shirts and Blouses*:

> ... various international tribunals, including the International Court of Justice, have generally and consistently accepted and applied the rule that the party who asserts a fact, whether the claimant or the respondent, is responsible for providing proof thereof. Also, it is a generally-accepted canon of evidence in civil law, common law and, in fact, most jurisdictions, that the burden of proof rests upon the party, whether complaining or defending, who asserts the affirmative of a particular claim or defence. If that party adduces evidence sufficient to raise a presumption that what is claimed is true, the burden then shifts to the other party, who will fail unless it adduces sufficient evidence to rebut the presumption.[71]

122.   With regard to the rules on burden of proof in proceedings under the *SPS Agreement*, we noted in our Report in *European Communities - Hormones*, that the panel in that case appropriately described the issue of the burden of proof as one of particular importance, in view of the multiple and complex issues of fact which may arise in disputes under that Agreement.[72] Furthermore, as we noted in *European Communities - Hormones*, the rules on burden of proof are rules "applicable in any adversarial proceedings".[73] We, therefore, agreed with the panel in that case that in proceedings under the *SPS Agreement*:

> The initial burden lies on the complaining party, which must establish a *prima facie* case of inconsistency with a particular

---

[66]   Panel Report, para. 8.98.

[67]   Panel Report, footnote 333.

[68]   Appellant's Submission of Japan, para. 91.

[69]   Appellant's Submission of Japan, para. 90.

[70]   *Ibid.*

[71]   *United States - Shirts and Blouses, supra*, footnote 18, p. 14.

[72]   *European Communities - Hormones, supra*, footnote 12, para. 97.

[73]   *European Communities - Hormones, supra*, footnote 12, para. 98.

provision of the *SPS Agreement* on the part of the defending party, or more precisely, of its SPS measure or measures complained about. When that *prima facie* case is made, the burden of proof moves to the defending party, which must in turn counter or refute the claimed inconsistency.[74]

123.   In this dispute, the United States claimed that the varietal testing requirement is more trade-restrictive than required to achieve Japan's appropriate level of protection and is, therefore, inconsistent with Article 5.6. As already set out above[75], a measure is considered more trade-restrictive than required if there is another SPS measure which:

(1)   is reasonably available taking into account technical and economic feasibility;

(2)   achieves the Member's appropriate level of protection; *and*

(3)   is significantly less restrictive to trade than the SPS measure contested.

124.   As noted above, the United States argued that "testing by product" is an alternative measure which meets the three cumulative elements under Article 5.6. The Panel was not, however, convinced that there was sufficient evidence to find that "testing by product" would achieve Japan's appropriate level of protection.[76]

125.   The Panel then turned its attention to an alternative measure which had been *suggested* by the experts advising the Panel, i.e., the "determination of sorption levels".[77] The Panel explained that it *deduced* this alternative measure from the written answers of the experts to the Panel's questions and from their statements at the Panel's meeting with the experts.[78] We note that the Panel explicitly stated that the United States, as complaining party, did *not specifically argue* that the "determination of sorption levels" met any of the three elements under Article 5.6.[79] On the basis of the evidence before it, including its deductions from the views expressed by the experts[80], the Panel came to the conclusion that it could be presumed that the "determination of sorption levels was an alternative measure which would meet all

---

[74]   *European Communities - Hormones, supra*, footnote 12, para. 98.

[75]   See *supra*, para. 95.

[76]   The United States appeals from this finding, but we have upheld it (*supra*, para. 100).

[77]   Panel Report, para. 8.74.

[78]   *Ibid*.

[79]   Panel Report, footnotes 328, 332 and 333. See *supra*, para. 119.

We note that the United States stated in its Appellee's Submission, para. 79, that it "emphasized [testing by product] in its Article 5.6 arguments because this alternative meets the requirements of Article 5.6, and because *there is no scientific evidence to support even limited sorption testing*." (emphasis added)

We also note that the United States declared before the Panel in its Comments on the Experts' Reponses (p. 3), that "it is not necessary in the context of this dispute for the United States to address the merits of [the "determination of sorption levels"], nor is it within the scope of the Panel's terms of reference to make findings with respect to the comparative efficacy of alternative treatments proposed by technical experts."

[80]   See Panel Report, paras. 8.92 and 8.93 (on the first element) and para. 8.100 (on the second element).

of the elements under Article 5.6".[81] The Panel pointed out that the United States had "given views which were consistent with" the argument that this alternative measure met the first and third elements under Article 5.6 and had "suggest[ed]" that it would meet the second element.[82]

126.   Pursuant to the rules on burden of proof set out above, we consider that it was for the United States to establish a *prima facie* case that there is an alternative measure that meets all three elements under Article 5.6 in order to establish a *prima facie* case of inconsistency with Article 5.6. Since the United States did not even claim before the Panel that the "determination of sorption levels" is an alternative measure which meets the three elements under Article 5.6, we are of the opinion that the United States did not establish a *prima facie* case that the "determination of sorption levels" is an alternative measure within the meaning of Article 5.6.

127.   In paragraph 7.10 of the Panel Report, the Panel stated:

> In deciding whether a fact or claim can ... be accepted, we consider that we are called upon to examine and weigh all the evidence validly submitted to us, including the opinions we received from the experts advising the Panel in accordance with Article 13 of the DSU.

We agree. Article 13 of the DSU allows a panel to seek *information* from any relevant source and to consult individual experts or expert bodies to obtain their *opinion* on certain aspects of the matter before it. In our Report in *United States - Import Prohibition of Certain Shrimp and Shrimp Products* ("*United States - Shrimp*"), we noted the "comprehensive nature" of this authority[83], and stated that this authority is "indispensably necessary" to enable a panel to discharge its duty imposed by Article 11 of the DSU to "make an objective assessment of the matter before it, including an *objective assessment of the facts of the case* and the *applicability of and conformity with the relevant covered agreements* ... .*"[84]

128.   Furthermore, we note that the present dispute is a dispute under the *SPS Agreement*. Article 11.2 of the *SPS Agreement* explicitly *instructs* panels in disputes under this Agreement involving scientific and technical issues to "seek advice from experts".

129.   Article 13 of the DSU and Article 11.2 of the *SPS Agreement* suggest that panels have a significant investigative authority. However, this authority cannot be used by a panel to rule in favour of a complaining party which has not established a *prima facie* case of inconsistency based on specific legal claims asserted by it. A panel is entitled to seek information and advice from experts and from any other relevant source it chooses, pursuant to Article 13 of the DSU and, in an SPS case, Article 11.2 of the *SPS Agreement*, to help it to understand and evaluate the evidence submitted and the arguments made by the parties, but not to make the case for a complaining party.

---

[81]   See Panel Report, para. 8.94 (on the first element), para. 8.97 (on the third element), para. 8.101 (on the second element) and para. 8.103 (on all three elements).

[82]   Panel Report, paras. 8.91, 8.95 and 8.98.

[83]   Adopted 6 November 1998, WT/DS58/AB/R, para. 104.

[84]   *United States - Shrimp, supra*, footnote 83, para. 106.

130.   In the present case, the Panel was correct to seek information and advice from experts to help it to understand and evaluate the evidence submitted and the arguments made by the United States and Japan with regard to the alleged violation of Article 5.6. The Panel erred, however, when it used that expert information and advice as the basis for a finding of inconsistency with Article 5.6, since the United States did not establish a *prima facie* case of inconsistency with Article 5.6 based on claims relating to the "determination of sorption levels". The United States did not even *argue* that the "determination of sorption levels" is an alternative measure which meets the three elements under Article 5.6.

131.   We, therefore, reverse the Panel's finding that it can be presumed that the "determination of sorption levels" is an alternative SPS measure which meets the three elements under Article 5.6, because this finding was reached in a manner inconsistent with the rules on burden of proof.

B.   Findings on Apricots, Pears, Plums and Quince

132.   With regard to the varietal testing requirement as it applies to apricots, pears, plums and quince, the Panel found in paragraph 8.45 of its Report:

> After careful examination we do not consider, therefore, that there is sufficient evidence before us to extend our finding in paragraph 8.43 also to apricots, pears, plums and quince. We only find that Japan maintains the varietal testing requirement without sufficient scientific evidence with respect to apples, cherries, nectarines and walnuts.

In paragraph 8.104 of the Panel Report, the Panel found that, for the same reasons as set out above, it was unable to extend its finding of inconsistency with Article 5.6 of the varietal testing requirement as it applies to apples, cherries, nectarines and walnuts to the varietal testing requirement as it applies to apricots, pears, plums and quince.

133.   The United States appeals these findings. With regard to the Panel's finding under Article 2.2, the United States argues that, under the Panel's interpretation of the burden of proof, complaining parties would be required, based on affirmative evidence, to prove a negative, namely, that there is *no* scientific evidence which supports a measure. According to the United States, this interpretation places an impossible burden on complaining parties and would render Article 2.2 unenforceable.[85] Furthermore, the United States asserts that it did establish a *prima facie* case under Article 2.2 with regard to all products, since it established that Japan failed to provide any specific evidence to support its measure.[86]

134.   We note that the Panel defined, on the basis of the United States' request for the establishment of a panel, the measure in dispute as Japan's varietal testing requirement as it applies to "*US products on which Japan claims that codling moth may occur*".[87] According to Japan, these products are apples, cherries, peaches (in-

---

[85]   Appellant's Submission of the United States, paras. 7 and 22.

[86]   Appellant's Submission of the United States, para. 18.

[87]   Panel Report, para. 8.6.

cluding nectarines), walnuts, apricots, pears, plums and quince. The Panel, thus, considered:

> ... we are called upon to examine the measure before us as it applies to *all* products covered by the contested measure.[88] (emphasis added)

135.   As the parties had only submitted evidence with respect to apples, cherries, nectarines and walnuts, the Panel stated that it would:

> ... therefore, examine the measure at issue on the basis of that evidence and refer to the experts advising the Panel when it comes to evaluating the relevance of that evidence for the other products covered by the measure in dispute.[89]

At its meeting with the experts, the Panel asked them whether their statements about varietal differences concerning apples, cherries, nectarines and walnuts were also valid for apricots, pears, plums and quince. Dr. Heather answered this question with an unqualified "yes" and the two other experts concurred.[90] After having noted that the experts did not further elaborate on their answers and that neither of the parties provided any additional comments or information, the Panel came to the conclusion that there was not sufficient evidence before it to extend its finding of inconsistency with Article 2.2 to apricots, pears, plums and quince.[91]

136.   According to the rules on burden of proof already discussed above[92], the onus was on the United States to make a *prima facie* case that the varietal testing requirement was inconsistent with Article 2.2. In order to do this, the United States was required to adduce evidence sufficient to raise a presumption that the varietal testing requirement was maintained "without sufficient scientific evidence". With regard to the varietal testing requirement as it applies to apples, cherries, nectarines and walnuts, the Panel considered that the United States did adduce sufficient evidence to raise such a presumption.[93] With regard to the varietal testing requirement as it applies to apricots, pears, plums and quince, the Panel considered, after taking into account both the evidence submitted by the United States (or the absence thereof) and the opinions received from the experts[94], that the United States did *not* adduce sufficient evidence to raise such a presumption. As we have already stated in our Report in *Australia - Salmon*[95], the Panel's consideration and weighing of the evidence before it relates to its assessment of the facts and, therefore, falls outside the scope of appellate review under Article 17.6 of the DSU.

---

[88]   Panel Report, para. 8.6.

[89]   *Ibid*.

[90]   Panel Report, para. 8.45.

[91]   We note that the Panel failed to make a finding on peaches which are not nectarines. We consider the Panel's failure to make a finding on peaches other than nectarines, a product at issue in this dispute, to be an error of law (see Appellate Body Report, *Japan - Taxes on Alcoholic Beverages*, adopted 1 November 1996, WT/DS8/AB/R, WT/DS10/AB/R, WT/DS11/AB/R, p. 26). This error on the part of the Panel was not, however, appealed by the United States.

[92]   See *supra*, paras. 121 and 122.

[93]   Panel Report, para. 8.42.

[94]   Panel Report, para. 7.9.

[95]   *Australia - Salmon, supra*, footnote 13, para. 261.

137.   Furthermore, we disagree with the United States that the Panel imposed on the United States an impossible and, therefore, erroneous burden of proof by requiring it to prove a negative, namely, that there are *no* relevant studies and reports which support Japan's varietal testing requirement. In our view, it would have been sufficient for the United States to raise a presumption that there are no relevant studies or reports. Raising a presumption that there are no relevant studies or reports is *not* an impossible burden. The United States could have requested Japan, pursuant to Article 5.8 of the *SPS Agreement*, to provide "an explanation of the reasons" for its varietal testing requirement, in particular, as it applies to apricots, pears, plums and quince. Japan would, in that case, be obliged to provide such explanation. The failure of Japan to bring forward scientific studies or reports in support of its varietal testing requirement as it applies to apricots, pears, plums and quince, would have been a strong indication that there are no such studies or reports. The United States could also have asked the Panel's experts specific questions as to the existence of relevant scientific studies or reports or it could have submitted to the Panel the opinion of experts consulted by it on this issue. The United States, however, did not submit *any* evidence relating to apricots, pears, plums and quince.[96]

138.   We, therefore, conclude that the Panel did not err in law in failing to extend its finding of inconsistency with Article 2.2 to the varietal testing requirement as it applies to apricots, pears, plums and quince.

139.   With regard to the question whether the Panel should have extended its finding of inconsistency with Article 5.6 to the varietal testing requirement as it applies to apricots, pears, plums and quince, we recall that we have reversed the Panel's finding of inconsistency with Article 5.6. This question, therefore, is moot.

C.   *Article 11 of the DSU*

140.   Japan claims that the Panel acted inconsistently with Article 11 of the DSU in making its finding under Article 2.2 on the varietal testing requirement as it applies to apples, cherries, nectarines and walnuts.[97] Article 11 of the DSU reads in relevant part:

> ... a panel should make an objective assessment of the matter before it, including an objective assessment of the facts of the case ...

Japan contends that there was a lack of proper examination of evidence by the Panel, that the Panel cited the views of the experts in an arbitrary manner and that the Panel's evaluation of the evidence was contradictory.

141.   As we stated in our Report in *European Communities - Hormones*[98], not every failure by the Panel in the appreciation of the evidence before it can be characterized as failure to make an objective assessment of the facts as required by Article 11 of the DSU. Only egregious errors constitute a failure to make an objective assessment of the facts as required by Article 11 of the DSU.

---

[96]   Panel Report, para. 8.6.

[97]   Appellant's Submission of Japan, paras. 51-55.

[98]   *European Communities - Hormones, supra*, footnote 12, para. 133.

142.   In our view, Japan has not demonstrated that the Panel, in its examination of the consistency of the varietal testing requirement with Article 2.2, has made errors of the gravity required to find a violation of Article 11 of the DSU. We, therefore, conclude that the Panel did not abuse its discretion contrary to the requirements of Article 11 of the DSU.

VII.   FINDINGS AND CONCLUSIONS

143.   For the reasons set out in this Report, the Appellate Body:

(a)   upholds the Panel's finding that the varietal testing requirement as it applies to apples, cherries, nectarines and walnuts is maintained without sufficient scientific evidence within the meaning of Article 2.2 of the *SPS Agreement*;

(b)   upholds the Panel's finding that even if the varietal testing requirement were considered to be a provisional measure adopted in accordance with the first sentence of Article 5.7, Japan has not fulfilled the requirements contained in the second sentence of Article 5.7 of the *SPS Agreement*;

(c)   concludes that the Panel's consideration and weighing of the evidence in support of the claim of the United States that "testing by product" achieves Japan's appropriate level of protection relates to the Panel's assessment of the facts and, therefore, falls outside the scope of appellate review;

(d)   concludes that, as we have reversed the finding of inconsistency under Article 5.6 of the *SPS Agreement*, there is no need to address the issue of the relationship between the Panel's finding of inconsistency under Article 2.2 of the *SPS Agreement* and its finding of inconsistency under Article 5.6;

(e)   upholds the Panel's finding that the varietal testing requirement, as set out in the *Experimental Guide,* is a phytosanitary regulation within the meaning of paragraph 1 of Annex B of the *SPS Agreement,* and that Japan has acted inconsistently with this provision and Article 7 of the *SPS Agreement*;

(f)   finds that the varietal testing requirement as it applies to apricots, pears, plums and quince is not based on a risk assessment and, therefore, is inconsistent with Article 5.1 of the *SPS Agreement*;

(g)   concludes that there is no need to address the issue of inconsistency with Article 8 and paragraph 1(c) of Annex C, of the *SPS Agreement* as we have upheld the Panel's finding under Article 2.2;

(h)   reverses the Panel's finding that it can be presumed that the "determination of sorption levels" is an alternative SPS measure which meets the three elements under Article 5.6 of the *SPS Agreement,* because this finding was reached in a manner inconsistent with the rules on burden of proof;

(i)   concludes that the Panel did not err in law in failing to extend its finding of inconsistency with Article 2.2 to the varietal testing requirement as it applies to apricots, pears, plums and quince, and concludes that, as we have reversed the Panel's finding of inconsistency with Article 5.6, the issue of extending this finding is moot; and

(j)   concludes that the Panel did not abuse its discretion contrary to the requirements of Article 11 of the DSU.

144.   The Appellate Body *recommends* that the DSB request that Japan bring its varietal testing requirement found in this Report, and in the Panel Report as modified by this Report, to be inconsistent with the *SPS Agreement,* into conformity with its obligations under that Agreement.

JAPAN - MEASURES AFFECTING AGRICULTURAL PRODUCTS

Report of the Panel
WT/DS76/R

Adopted by the Dispute Settlement Body on 19 March 1999
as modified by the Appellate Body Report

TABLE OF CONTENTS

I. INTRODUCTION

1.1.   In a communication dated 7 April 1997, the United States requested consultations with Japan pursuant to Article 4 of the Understanding on Rules and Procedures Governing the Settlement of Disputes ("DSU"), Article 11 of the Agreement on the Application of Sanitary and Phytosanitary Measures ("SPS Agreement"), Article XXIII of the General Agreement on Tariffs and Trade 1994 ("GATT 1994"), and Article 19 of the Agreement on Agriculture regarding the prohibition by Japan of imports of certain agricultural products.[1]

1.2.   The United States specifically alleged that, for each agricultural product for which Japan required quarantine treatment, Japan prohibited the importation of each variety of that product until the quarantine treatment had been tested for that variety, even though the treatment had proven effective with respect to other varieties of the same product. The United States claimed that Japan's prohibition adversely affected exports of US agricultural products, and, furthermore, that Japan's measure appeared to be inconsistent with the obligations of Japan under the SPS Agreement, the GATT 1994 and the Agreement on Agriculture. The provisions of these agreements with which these measure appeared to be inconsistent included, but were not limited to: (i) SPS Agreement, Articles 2, 4, 5 and 8; (ii) GATT 1994, Article XI; and, (iii) the Agreement on Agriculture, Article 4. The measures also appeared to nullify or impair benefits accruing to the United States directly or indirectly under the cited agreements. Consultations were held on 5 June 1997, but failed to settle the dispute.[2]

1.3.   In a communication dated 3 October 1997, the United States requested the Dispute Settlement Body ("DSB") to establish a panel with standard terms of reference as set out in Article 7 of the DSU.[3] The US claims of inconsistency in their Request for the Establishment of a Panel were identical to those set out in their re-

---

[1]   WT/DS76/1 (Request for Consultations by the United States).

[2]   WT/DS76/2 (Request for the Establishment of a Panel by the United States).

[3]   WT/DS76/2 (Request for the Establishment of a Panel by the United States).

quest for consultations, except for an additional claim of inconsistency under Article 7 of the SPS Agreement.

1.4.   On 18 November 1997, the DSB established a panel pursuant to the request of the United States, in accordance with Article 6 of the DSU.[4] In accordance with Article 7.1 of the DSU, the terms of reference of the Panel were:

> "To examine, in the light of the relevant provisions of the covered agreements cited by the United States in document WT/DS76/2, the matter referred to the DSB by the United States in that document and to make such findings as will assist the DSB in making the recommendations or in giving the rulings provided for in those agreements."

1.5.   On 18 December 1997, the Panel was constituted with the following composition:

Chairman:	Mr. Kari Bergholm
Panelists:	Mr. Germain Denis
	Mr. Eiríkur Einarsson

1.6.   The European Communities, Hungary and Brazil reserved their right to participate in the Panel proceedings as third parties.

1.7.   The Panel met with the parties on 2 and 3 April 1998. It met with third parties on 3 April 1998. The Panel consulted scientific and technical experts and met with them on 23 June 1998. The Panel held a second meeting with the parties on 24 June 1998.

1.8.   On 3 July 1998 the Chairman of the Panel informed the DSB that the Panel had not been able to issue its report within six months. The reasons for that delay were stated in document WT/DS76/4.

1.9.   The Panel issued its interim report on 6 August 1998. On 21 September 1998, on request by Japan, an interim review meeting was held with the parties. The Final Report was circulated to the parties on 6 October 1998. The report was circulated to Members in all three languages on [27 October 1998].

II.   FACTUAL ASPECTS

A.   *General*

1.   *Codling Moth*

2.1.   Codling moth (*Cydia pomonella*) is a pest which invades apples, cherries, nectarines and other fruit crops. Newly-hatched larvae of codling moth are known to enter into the fruit. In the United States, the codling moth is a pest of apples and walnuts; it is also known, on occasion, to infest nectarines and cherries. Other hosts of codling moth include apricots, plums, pears and quinces.

2.2.   There are four identifiable life stages of the codling moth: egg, larva, pupa and adult. Mated female adults lay their eggs on a suitable substrate such as leaves, nuts or fruit. All life stages are highly dependent upon temperature for development;

---

[4]   WT/DS76/3 (Constitution of a Panel Established at the Request of the United States).

the higher the temperature, the more rapid the development. After the eggs hatch, newly hatched first stage (instar) larvae find a suitable host to complete their development. They usually burrow into the host. The larvae will molt (shed their skin) four times thereafter inside the fruit, thus producing five larval growth phases called instars. When mature, the fifth instar larvae will exit the host to form a pupae within a silken cocoon. The cocoon is usually formed on the bark of the tree or in the litter at the base of the host plant.

2.3. The next generation of adult moths will exit from the pupae in 1-2 weeks. Depending on temperature, emergence may take longer. Under optimum conditions, developmental time from egg to adult is about 30-40 days. As daylight hours become shorter (10 hours light; 14 hours dark) during the late summer and fall, mature fifth instar larvae will exit the host, but hibernate through the winter as mature larvae within cocoons on bark or litter at the tree base. This larval hibernation (diapause) is a mechanism for survival through the winter. The diapausing larvae will form pupae in the spring when daylight hours and temperature begin to increase toward 14 daylight hours or more. Depending upon temperature, moths will emerge in three to four weeks after the pupae are formed.

2.4. The seasonality of host fruits is important vis-à-vis what life stages of the codling moth might be expected to occur at harvest. In the United States, walnuts are harvested after diapause has been induced in mature larvae. Thus the quarantine treatment for codling moth in walnuts is more severe (using comparatively higher levels of fumigant) than that required for fruits such as cherries and nectarines.

2.5. The fruit development of apples coincides with the time, mid-to-late summer, during which the codling moth is numerous. Severe economic losses can occur if codling moth is not adequately controlled in the field. The quarantine treatment applied to harvested apples is a multiple treatment involving cold temperature and a methyl bromide treatment. The cold treatment destroys most of the codling moth eggs and the fumigation destroys any remaining larvae.

2.6. In contrast to walnuts and apples, cherries are an early spring/early summer crop and only eggs or non-diapausing larvae would be expected to be found. With regard to nectarines, the harvest of nectarines in the United States begins in May and ends in late July to early August, before diapause is induced.

2.7. The Japanese archipelago forms a chain spreading across 3,000 km. from the north to the south between the latitudes 20 to 45 degrees north. Although most of Japan belongs to the temperate monsoon zone, the northern island of Hokkaido lies in a sub-arctic zone and a subtropical climate prevails in the southern edge of the South-western and Ogasawara islands. Ocean currents and prevailing westerly winds contribute to a diversity of climatic conditions. While codling moth is prevalent throughout the temperate zone, the pest has not been discovered in Japan.

2.8. There is no dispute between the parties that Japan is free of codling moth and that it is a pest of quarantine significance to Japan.

2. *Methyl Bromide*

2.9. The Montreal Protocol on Substances that Deplete the Ozone Layer (the "Montreal Protocol") requires developed countries to phase-out the production and importation of methyl bromide beginning in 1999 and ending, with a total phase-out, on 1 January 2005. Developing countries will freeze the production and importation of methyl bromide as of 1 January 2002 and begin a step-down reduction in 2005, with total phase-out by 2015. US law currently calls for a phase-out of methyl bromide production and importation by 1 January 2001.

2.10.   Notwithstanding the above, the use of methyl bromide for quarantine and pre-shipment applications is exempted from the phase-out schedule.[5] The US Administration has expressed willingness to consult with the US Congress on changes to US law if alternatives do not exist for control of key pests as the 2001 phase-out date approaches.

3.   *Technical and Scientific Terms Used in the Parties' Submissions*

CxT value (Concentration times time)

2.11.   The CxT value for a fumigation is an expression of the relationship between fumigant gas concentration and time in the fumigation enclosure or chamber. It is an expression of the active gas dosage to which the pest or test organism is exposed during the time of the treatment. Because the concentration decays during the fumigation time, "concentration" is an average value derived from a number of measurements and requires temperature, load and humidity to be specified for proper definition.

Dose-mortality test (DMT)

2.12.   The dose-mortality test is an experimental procedure in which the response of an organism is estimated for a series of mortality-inducing doses of a specified treatment. Where possible, individual dose-mortality tests target a specific stage of an organism as the susceptibility to a treatment can vary between life stages. The main purposes of dose-mortality testing are to produce data for analysis used for the determination of parameters categorizing the response of an organism, and the comparisons of efficacies of different treatments. In developing quarantine treatments against codling moth for products exported to Japan, dose-mortality testing is used to produce data for analysis for the determination of the least vulnerable stage of the pest and the prediction of a treatment dose to meet a required level of efficacy. The target organism test unit is usually a sub-sample of 20 - 50 insects; the test is typically replicated three times, at each dose level. For a satisfactory result, five or more dose levels are usually required, evenly spaced between 0 and 100 per cent mortality.

Fumigation

2.13.   To kill pathogens or insects by using gas or fumes. A fumigant is a pesticide which acts upon the target pest as a gas. For the purposes of this report, the fumigant is methyl bromide (MB), and "MB treatment" refers to fumigation with methyl bromide.

---

[5]   Article 2H:6 of the Montreal Protocol.

Probit analysis, LD (lethal dose) and probit 9

2.14.   Probit analysis is a biometrical technique for analysis of experimental data in which the quantitative response of an organism, usually expressed as mortality, is subjected to regression analysis with respect to treatment dose. Mathematical transformation of mortality to probability units, termed "probits", assists in conversion of the normal distribution (curve) of the response data to a linear distribution to facilitate analysis. Dose data is frequently, but not invariably, logarithmically transformed for the same purpose of linearity. The outcomes of probit analysis are values such as LD (lethal dose), LC (lethal concentration) or LT (lethal time) for a nominated proportion of the population (for example, 50 per cent or 99.99 per cent), together with nominated confidence or fiducial intervals (for example, 95 per cent).[6] The main purposes of probit analysis are (i) to define susceptibility of a population of target organisms to a treatment in terms of LD, LC or LT values; (ii) subsequent comparisons of susceptibility of populations of target organisms, varying response according to substrates, or treatment; and, (iii) the prediction of the dose required for a specific level of treatment efficacy.

2.15.   Probit 9 is equivalent to a target level of mortality, or level of treatment efficacy, of 99.9968 per cent mortality.

Sorption

2.16.   The sum of adsorption, absorption and chemisorption. Adsorption is a physical surface effect and results from the attraction of molecules to the surface of products[7] and other materials in the fumigation chamber. Absorption is also a physical process whereby the chemical enters into the product and other materials in the fumigation chamber. Chemisorption is an irreversible reaction in which residues are left in the fumigated products and materials. When the pest takes in the fumigant while in a product, or takes in the fumigant while on the surface of the fruit, it may die.

---

[6]   Dr. Heather referred to: Steel, R.G.D. and Torrie, J.H., *Principles and Procedures of Statistics with Special Reference to the Biological Sciences*, McGraw-Hill (1960) p.22.

[7]   In this report the word "product" is used instead of "commodity" or "species".

Variety

2.17.   A category within a species, based on some hereditary difference.[8]

B.   *Japan's Plant Protection Law and the Enforcement Regulation*

1.   *General*

2.18.   The legislation relevant to this dispute is contained in the Japanese Plant Protection Law, enacted on 4 May 1950, as amended (the "Plant Protection Law").[9] The applicable regulation is the Plant Protection Law Enforcement Regulation (the "Enforcement Regulation"), enacted 30 June 1950, as amended.[10]

2.19.   The stated objective of the Plant Protection Law is to ensure the "stabilization and development of agricultural production by inspecting export plants, imported plants and domestic plants, by controlling injurious animals and plants, and by preventing the outbreak or spreading thereof".[11]

2.20.   The Plant Protection Law identifies as "quarantine pests" those pests whose existence has not been confirmed in Japan, or those which exist in part of the Japanese territory and are subject to official control (Article 5.2 of the Plant Protection Law). Subsequent to such identification, the Plant Protection Law establishes an inspection mechanism for imported plants and plant products:

    (a)   all imported plants and plant products have to be accompanied by a phytosanitary certificate, in principle, which states that the plants and plant products are considered free from the quarantine pests (Article 6, paragraph 1 of the Plant Protection Law);

    (b)   in certain cases, a growing-site inspection by the foreign authorities is mandatory (Article 6, paragraph 2). This mechanism was introduced by the 1996 amendment of the Plant Protection Law, and took effect April 1998;

    (c)   upon entering the Japanese territory, plants and plant products have to be inspected by plant quarantine officers at one of the 101 major ports (or airports) of entry designated by the Enforcement Regulation (Article 6, paragraph 3; Article 8, paragraph 1); and,

    (d)   certain plants may be subjected to post-entry inspection at a post-entry quarantine station for viruses and other pests which might not

---

[8]   Webster's Encyclopaedic Unabridged Dictionary of the English Language, 1996 Random House. The International Convention for the Protection of New Varieties of Plants of 2 December 1961, Article 1, (vi) defines "variety" as: "[A] plant grouping within a single botanical taxon of the lowest known rank, which grouping, irrespective of whether the conditions for the grant of a breeder's right are fully met, can be - defined by the expression of the characteristics resulting from a given genotype or combination of genotypes, - distinguished from any other plant grouping by the expression of at least one of the said characteristics and - considered as a unit with regard to its suitability for being propagated unchanged ....".

[9]   Law No. 151 of 1950; most recently amended in 1996. (Japan, Exhibit 6)

[10]   MAFF Ordinance No.73 of 1950. (Japan, Exhibit 7)

[11]   The Plant Protection Law, Article 1.

be detected by the visual inspection at the ports of entry (Article 8, paragraph 7).

2.21. If a plant or a plant product fails to pass the above inspection, it will either be destroyed or disinfected/disinfested under the Plant Protection Law. In order to counter the risk of inadvertent introduction of particularly harmful quarantine pests, the Plant Protection Law delegates to the Ministry of Agriculture, Forestry and Fisheries ("MAFF") the authority to prohibit importation of certain host plants from countries or areas infested by the pests (Article 7, paragraph 1, item 1).[12] This authority is exercised in the form of a list of prohibited products, which is contained in a table annexed to the Enforcement Regulation.[13] This "Annexed Table" identifies the quarantine pest which constitutes the cause of the import prohibition, the countries or areas from which importation is prohibited, and the prohibited host plants and their specific parts.

2.22. In practice, the confirmation process for efficacy of disinfestation treatment consists of two parts: the process applicable to the initial lifting of the import prohibition and the test for the approval of additional varieties. These are contained in two sets of guidelines developed in 1987 and which have, to date, not been published - although they are available to interested parties.[14] The contents of these are summarized below.

2. *Initial Lifting of Prohibition*

2.23. The "Experimental Guideline for Lifting Import Ban - Fumigation" ("Guidelines for initial lifting") outline the procedure applicable to the initial lifting of the prohibition. The procedure includes the following:

Basic Tests (small-scale dose-mortality tests)[15]

(a) Determination of the most resistant stage of insects to fumigation (a comparative test of susceptibility between development stages) estimated through small-scale dose-mortality tests.

(b) Estimation of treatment schedule achieving 100 per cent mortality.

Large-Scale Mortality Test

The efficacy of the chosen treatment is tested using 30,000 insects at the most resistant stage on the variety (the representative variety). Japan accepts the efficacy of the treatment if no insect survives, as an approximation of probit 9.

---

[12] In addition, the Plant Protection Law prohibits the importation of quarantine pests, soil or plants contaminated by soil and packages containing these articles (Article 7, paragraph 1, items 2 to 4).

[13] List of the Plants Subject to Import Prohibition, Plant Protection Law Enforcement Regulation Annexed Table 2. (Japan, Exhibit 8)

[14] Contained in Japan, Exhibit 10.

[15] A glossary of technical and scientific terms is contained in paragraphs 2.11 to 2.17.

On-site confirmatory test

> The results of the test are further confirmed on site by Japanese experts in the on-site test using 10,000 sample insects (on the representative variety).

3.   *Lifting of Prohibition for Additional Varieties*

2.24.   The guidelines for the approval of additional varieties are set out in "Experimental Guide for Cultivar Comparison Test on Insect Mortality - Fumigation". These include:

Basic test (small-scale dose-mortality test)

> As the most resistant development stage of the insect is identified when (part of) the species is approved for the first time, this test targets only the comparative efficacy between the approved varieties and the newly proposed varieties. Response of insects in additional varieties is tested for different levels of treatment (e.g., the amount of fumigant, the length of cold treatment). The results are typically analyzed by comparing LD_{50} by probit analysis. If the new varieties are found to show equivalent or superior effectiveness compared to approved varieties, no large-scale mortality test is necessary. If the result is significantly less effective, however, a new treatment standard has to be developed and tested by a large-scale experiment.

On-site confirmatory test

> This test is performed on one representative variety. Japanese experts are sent to confirm the on-site test.

<table>
<tr><td colspan="5" align="center">TABLE 1
Test Schedule for Initial and Additional Lifting</td></tr>
<tr><td colspan="3">Tests
(purpose)</td><td>Initial lifting of prohibition</td><td>Lifting of prohibition for additional varieties</td></tr>
<tr><td></td><td>Test insects</td><td>Subject varieties</td><td></td><td></td></tr>
<tr><td>Dose-response
(1) identification of the most resistant development stage of the pest; and
(2) identification of the representative variety[16]</td><td>2,000 in total (200 per one dose bracket times five dose brackets in two replicates)</td><td>ALL</td><td>YES (for (1) and (2))</td><td>YES (for (2))</td></tr>
</table>

---

[16]   See paragraph 2.23 (under Large-Scale Mortality Test).

<table>
<tr><td colspan="6" align="center">TABLE 1
Test Schedule for Initial and Additional Lifting</td></tr>
<tr><td rowspan="2">Tests
(purpose)</td><td colspan="2"></td><td rowspan="2">Initial lifting of prohibition</td><td rowspan="2">Lifting of prohibition for additional varieties</td></tr>
<tr><td>Test insects</td><td>Subject varieties</td></tr>
<tr><td>Large-Scale Confirmation of efficacy</td><td>30,000 (10,000 each in three replicates)</td><td>ONE</td><td>YES</td><td>NO*</td></tr>
<tr><td>On-Site Confirmatory Final confirmation</td><td>10,000</td><td>ONE</td><td>YES</td><td>YES</td></tr>
<tr><td colspan="6">* This assumes that the existing treatment would be found by basic tests to be adequate for new varieties. If not, a new treatment would have to be established and confirmed by large-scale tests.</td></tr>
</table>

C.   *Relevant International Standards, Guidelines and recommendations - the IPPC*

1.   General

2.25. The SPS Agreement makes reference, in a number of provisions, to the "relevant international standards, guidelines and recommendations". Annex A:3(c) of the SPS Agreement states that the international standards, guidelines and recommendations relevant for plant health are those developed under the auspices of the Secretariat of the International Plant Protection Convention ("IPPC" or "the Convention") in cooperation with regional organizations operating within the framework of the IPPC.

2.26. The IPPC is an international treaty deposited and administered by the Food and Agriculture Organization of the United Nations (FAO) but implemented through the cooperation of member governments and Regional Plant Protection Organizations. The IPPC currently has 106 contracting parties.

2.27. The purpose of the Convention is to secure common and effective action to prevent the spread and introduction of pests of plants and plant products, and to promote appropriate measures for their control. An important role of the IPPC is that of standard-setting.

2.28. The first text of the international convention was drafted in 1929 and came into force in 1952, adopted by the FAO Conference one year prior to that. Amendments were adopted by the FAO in 1979 and the revised text came into force in 1991. In response to the role of the IPPC in the context of the Uruguay Round and the negotiation of the SPS Agreement, the FAO established a Secretariat for the IPPC in 1992, followed by the formation of the Committee of Experts on Phytosanitary Measures (CEPM) in 1993. Negotiations for amendments to the Convention, in order to reflect contemporary changes, particularly in light of the SPS Agreement, started in 1995 and were finalized in 1997 when the FAO Conference adopted the New Revised Text of the IPPC. The New Revised Text makes provision for the formation of a Commission on Phytosanitary Measures. The amended IPPC will come into force upon ratification by two-thirds of its contracting parties.

2. *Guidelines for Pest Risk Analysis*

2.29.   Generally, IPPC standards have their origin in national or regional initiatives, and/or are drafted by expert groups organized by the IPPC Secretariat. The topics and priorities for draft standards are determined by the Secretariat in consultation with Regional Plant Protection Organizations and their members. IPPC standards fall within two categories: reference standards and other standards.

2.30.   Among the IPPC's completed standards is the Guidelines for Pest Risk Analysis ("PRA Guidelines"), adopted in 1995.[17] The IPPC describes the PRA Guidelines as consisting of three stages. Stage one involves (a) the identification of a pathway, usually an imported product, that may allow the introduction and/or spread of quarantine pests, and (b) the identification of a pest that may qualify as a quarantine pest. Stage two considers the identified pests individually and examines, for each one, whether the criteria for quarantine pest status are satisfied, that is, that the pest is of "potential economic importance to the area endangered thereby and not yet present there, or present but not widely distributed and being officially controlled". Finally, based on the information gathered under Stages one and two, Stage three determines the appropriate phytosanitary measure(s) to be adopted. This pest risk management to protect the endangered areas should be proportional to the risk identified in the pest risk assessment. The three stages are summarized in the PRA Guidelines as: "initiating the process for analyzing risk", "assessing pest risk" and "managing pest risk", respectively.

2.31.   Pest risk management options include[18]:

    (a)   inclusion in list of prohibited pests;

    (b)   phytosanitary inspection and certification prior to export;

    (c)   definition of requirements to be satisfied before export (e.g. treatment, origin from pest-free area, growing season inspection, certification scheme);

    (d)   inspection at entry;

    (e)   treatment at point of entry, inspection station or, if appropriate, at place of destination;

    (f)   detention in post-entry quarantine;

    (g)   post-entry measures (restrictions on use of product, control measures); and,

    (h)   prohibition of entry of specific products from specific origins.

2.32.   Pest risk management options may also concern ways of reducing risk of damage. The PRA Guidelines state that the efficacy and impact of the various options in reducing risk to an acceptable level should be evaluated in terms of the following factors[19]:

    (a)   biological effectiveness;

---

[17]   International Standards for Phytosanitary Measures, Guidelines for Pest Risk Analysis, FAO Publication No.2. (US Exhibit 5)

[18]   PRA Guidelines, p. 20.

[19]   PRA Guidelines, p. 20.

(b)   cost/benefit of implementation;

(c)   impact on existing regulations;

(d)   commercial impact;

(e)   social impact;

(f)   phytosanitary policy considerations;

(g)   time to implement a new regulation;

(h)   efficacy of option against other quarantine pests; and,

(i)   environmental impact.

2.33.   In sum, the PRA Guidelines define a procedure by which a pest risk analysis should be performed, and lay down relevant factors which should be taken into account by the authorities in the process.

III.   CLAIMS OF THE PARTIES

3.1.   The **United States** claimed that Japan's varietal testing requirement as it applied to quarantine treatments for codling moth was an unjustified barrier to trade and was inconsistent with the SPS Agreement. As a result of Japan's measure, maintained ostensibly for plant health ("phytosanitary") reasons, Japan effectively blocked access to its market for US varieties that competed with a number of Japanese produced varieties of the same product. The United States claimed that Japan's varietal testing measure had failed each of the following obligations under the SPS Agreement in that it:

(a)   was maintained without sufficient scientific evidence (Article 2.2);

(b)   was not based on scientific principles (Article 2.2);

(c)   was not based on an assessment, as appropriate to the circumstances, of the risks to human, animal or plant life or health (Article 5.1);

(d)   had not taken into account available scientific evidence; relevant processes and production methods; relevant inspection, sampling and testing methods; prevalence of specific pests; relevant ecological and environmental conditions; and quarantine or other treatment (Article 5.2);

(e)   was more trade-restrictive than required to achieve the appropriate level of sanitary or phytosanitary protection, taking into account technical and economic feasibility (Article 5.6);

(f)   was not transparent in that one Enquiry Point was not responsible for the provision of answers to all reasonable questions from interested Members regarding the measure and there was furthermore no published source for the measure itself (Article 7); and,

(g)   it was reliant upon control and inspection procedures, and applied to a modified product (i.e. a different variety of a product), was not limited in its information requirements to what was necessary for appropriate control and inspection procedures, and was not limited to what was necessary to determine whether adequate confidence existed that the product still met the regulations concerned (Article 8 and Annex C).

3.2.   In its request for consultations, the United States claimed that the fact that Japan's varietal testing requirement was not a legitimate phytosanitary measure meant that it was also inconsistent with Article XI of GATT 1994 and Article 4 of the Agreement on Agriculture. However, the United States did not pursue these claims in its submissions or in its oral statements to the Panel, nor did it request findings with respect to these claims.

3.3.   **Japan** claimed that its policy was fully consistent with the relevant articles of the SPS Agreement, Article XI of GATT 1994 and Article 4 of the Agreement on Agriculture. In particular, Japan emphasized that the measure was entirely based on phytosanitary considerations and that the suggestion by the United States to the contrary was false.

IV.   ARGUMENTS OF THE PARTIES

A.   *The Scope of the Dispute*

4.1.   The **United States** recalled that following the establishment of the Panel, Japan had raised questions concerning the scope of the dispute.[20] The United States reiterated that the scope of the dispute at issue, consistent with the request of the United States for the establishment of the Panel on 18 November 1997[21], was the prohibition by Japan of the importation of any variety of an agricultural product on which Japan claimed that the pest codling moth might occur until such time as the variety had been separately tested with respect to the efficacy of treatment with methyl bromide or treatment with methyl bromide and cold storage.

4.2.   The United States noted that varietal testing applied to potential US fruit exports largely in instances that involved codling moth. The facts submitted by the United States were therefore limited to varietal testing of quarantine treatment efficacy against codling moth on certain products, using the preferred treatment of MB fumigation or a two-component treatment of MB fumigation and cold storage. The scope of the dispute thus concerned the prohibition by Japan on the importation of *any variety of an agricultural product* on which Japan claimed the pest codling moth could occur until such time as the variety had been separately tested with respect to the efficacy of treatment with methyl bromide or methyl bromide and cold storage.

4.3.   In its first submission, **Japan** raised two issues in respect of the scope of the dispute: (1) relevant provisions of the WTO agreements on which the complaining party's claim was based, and (2) the factual scope of the complaint. Japan argued that in its request for bilateral consultations[22], the United States had not clearly identified the relevant provisions and the covered agreements. The United States had stated that relevant provisions "include, but are not limited to" Articles 2, 4, 5 and 8 of the SPS Agreement, Article XI of GATT 1994 and Article 4 of the Agreement on Agriculture. The US request for the establishment of a panel had expanded the legal

---

[20]   This was contained in a letter from Japan to the Chairman of the Panel, dated 13 January 1998.
[21]   WT/DS76/2.
[22]   WT/DS76/1.

basis to "include, but are not limited to" Article 7 of the SPS Agreement.[23] Thereafter, the first written submission of the United States (of 19 February 1998) focused only on Articles 2.2, 5.1, 5.2, 5.6, 7 and 8, on Annex B, paragraph 1, and on Annex C, paragraph 1 (c) and (h). Moreover, Japan noted that although the United States referred to Article XI of GATT 1994 and to Article 4 of the Agreement on Agriculture in a footnote, it did not even attempt to offer a *prima facie* case in that regard.

4.4.   Japan argued that the Panel should find that the phrase "including but not necessarily limited to" did not constitute part of its terms of reference[24] in light of the recent Appellate Body ruling in *India - Patent Protection for Pharmaceutical and Agricultural Chemical Products* ("*India - Pharmaceuticals*"), which held that the phrase failed to comply with the requirement under Article 6.2 of the DSU.[25]

4.5.   Japan argued, furthermore, that the Panel should also eliminate Article 7 of the SPS Agreement from the scope of its investigation, because that article was mentioned by the United States for the first time in its request for establishment of a panel, and no consultation had been held on that particular provision.

4.6.   In regard to the description of the scope of the dispute by the United States, Japan requested that the United States clarify if there was any fruit other than "apples, cherries, nectarines and walnuts" which the United States believed was covered by the complaint. Japan noted that for those four products there was no disagreement between the parties as to the efficacy of the current treatment being applied to the approved varieties. Hence, if the scope of the dispute were limited to those fruits, the matter before the Panel was a highly practical question of how effective the same treatment would be for varieties which had not been approved so far. In addition, Japan requested the United States to clarify if the scope of the examination by the Panel was limited to MB treatment or treatment with methyl bromide and cold storage.

4.7.   The **United States** claimed that Japan had misunderstood the Appellate Body Report on *India - Pharmaceuticals*. In that report, the Appellate Body found that the use of the phrase "including but not necessarily limited to" was "not sufficient to bring a claim relating to Article 63 [of the *TRIPS Agreement*] within the terms of reference of the Panel".[26] Accordingly, the findings of the *India - Pharmaceuticals* Report applied in a situation where a complainant made a claim with respect to a provision of an agreement that was not identified in the request for a panel.[27] The current dispute did not present the Panel with a similar situation. The United States had not made any claim with respect to any provision of an agreement that had not been specifically identified in its request for the Panel at issue. If at some time Japan were to believe that the United States had made such a claim, then Japan could have presented its arguments to the Panel and the United States would have had the opportunity to respond. The United States argued that Japan was seek-

---

[23]   WT/DS76/2.

[24]   WT/DS76/3.

[25]   WT/DS50/AB/R, adopted 19 December 1997, paragraph 90.

[26]   WT/DS50/AB/R, adopted 19 December 1997, paragraph 90.

[27]   The United States noted that it had been described in the Appellate Body Report on *India - Pharmaceuticals* as "there is a failure to identify a specific provision of an agreement that is alleged to have been violated", WT/DS50/AB/R, paragraph 91.

ing a finding in the abstract apparently based on a hypothetical situation, a finding that furthermore would be inconsistent with the practice of judicial economy supported by panels and the Appellate Body.[28]

4.8.   In respect of Article 7 of the SPS Agreement, the United States claimed that Japan was in error in stating that no consultation was held on Article 7 of the SPS Agreement. In fact, Article 7 had been specifically mentioned in the US statement at those consultations.[29] In the course of the US discussions with Japan concerning Japan's measures at issue, and also considering Japan's answers to questions before the consultations, it became clear to the United States that these measures were not transparent and were not clearly set forth anywhere. It was only in the consultations, where Japan provided an oral explanation of the way in which some of its measures operated, that the United States had been able to begin to understand the legal basis and scope of Japan's measures.

4.9.   The United States noted that a consultation request had to provide an "identification of the measures at issue and an indication of the legal basis for the complaint" (DSU Article 4.4). However, nothing in the DSU required that a Member had to ascertain all of the possible legal claims and relevant provisions of the WTO agreements *before* the Member could even request consultations. In this context, the United States noted that the Panel in *European Communities - Regime for the Importation, Sale and Distribution of Bananas* stated:

> "[as to the argument that] consultations must lead to an adequate explanation of the Complainants' case, we cannot agree. Consultations are the first step in the dispute settlement process. While one function of the consultations may be to clarify what the case is about, there is nothing in the DSU that provides that a complainant cannot request a panel unless its case is adequately explained in the consultations. ... Ultimately, the function of providing notice to a respondent of a complainant's claims and arguments is served by the request for establishment of a panel and by the complainant's submissions to that panel."[30]

4.10.   The United States stated that one of the purposes of consultations was to foster a better understanding of the relevant measures and concerns of the various Members in order to promote a satisfactory adjustment of the matter. Consultations were often the first time that the Member maintaining the measure provided a detailed description of the measure and relevant facts and legal documents. Consultations were not a "dress rehearsal" or "moot court" for the panel process requiring Members to have worked out all of their claims and positions in advance and presenting them in the consultations for the other side to practice its prepared responses.

---

[28]   In this respect, the United States recalled the Appellate Body Report in *United States - Measure Affecting Imports of Woven Wool Shirts and Blouses from India*, adopted 23 May 1995, DSR 1997:I, 323, at 332-333.

[29]   The United States referred to US Exhibit 31, p. 5.

[30]   WT/DS27/R/USA, adopted 25 September 1997, paragraph 7.20.

4.11.   The United States noted that the DSU reflected the difference between requests for panels and requests for consultations by using different terms for each. With respect to panels, the DSU required that a request for the establishment of a panel provide a "brief summary of the legal basis of the complaint sufficient to present the problem clearly".[31] However, with respect to consultations, the DSU merely required that requests for consultations give "an indication" of the legal basis for the complaint.[32] Moreover, if a matter had indeed been discussed in consultations, as had been the case with respect to the US claim under Article 7 of the SPS Agreement, the responding party had even less basis to claim unfair surprise. For the above reasons, there was no basis for the Panel to find that the US claim under Article 7 of the SPS Agreement fell outside the scope of the panel proceeding.[33]

4.12.   The United States reiterated that the dispute covered the prohibition by Japan on the importation of *any variety of an agricultural product* on which Japan claimed that the pest codling moth could occur. In this regard, the United States noted that Japan was best positioned to provide a comprehensive list of products to which its measures applied. Due to the lack of transparency of Japan's measures, the United States had had difficulty in ascertaining the full range of agricultural products involved. According to the "List of Plants Subject to Import Prohibition" submitted by Japan in response to US questions in connection with the consultations, the United States understood that Japan's varietal testing requirements, as they pertained to the pest codling moth, also applied to at least the following products: "apricot, cherry, ... plum, pear, quince and peach, ... and apple, ... and fresh fruits and nuts in shell of walnut".[34] The United States requested further clarification from Japan as to whether there were other products that were or could be subject to this import prohibition. For the purposes of the dispute at issue, the relevant treatments were treatment with methyl bromide or treatment with methyl bromide and cold storage.

4.13.   **Japan** explained that the Japanese Government had long since published in the Official Gazette the list of plants subject to import prohibition, namely eight plant products which were host plants of codling moth: apricot, plum, pear, quince, apple, walnut, peach including nectarine and cherry. However, Japan maintained that from a practical point of view, the products to be covered by the current Panel had to be limited to four: apples, cherries, nectarines and walnuts. Japan noted that no data had been provided nor any mention been made of any product other than

---

[31]   Article 6.2 of the DSU.

[32]   Article 4.4 of the DSU.

[33]   In this respect, the United States agreed with the findings of the Panel in *European Communities - Regime for the Importation, Sale and Distribution of Bananas*: "Consultations are, however, a matter reserved for the parties. The DSB is not involved; no panel is involved; and the consultations are held in the absence of the Secretariat. In these circumstances, we are not in a position to evaluate the consultation process in order to determine if it functioned in a particular way. While a mutually agreed solution is to be preferred, in some cases it is not possible for parties to agree upon one. In those cases, it is our view that the function of a panel is only to ascertain that consultations, if required, were in fact held or, at least, requested". (WT/DS27/R/USA, paragraph 7.19)

[34]   Japan clarified that the term "fresh fruits" related solely to walnuts. Furthermore, nectarine was a variety of peach, this was subsequently confirmed by all three experts advising the panel - therefore the term: "peaches, including nectarines" (Section VI of this report deals with the Panel's consultation with scientific experts).

these four products in the US submissions; hence, the other four products should be excluded from the scope the dispute.

4.14.   The **United States** noted that while it had thus far referenced only four products for which it had negotiated entry on some varieties - apples, cherries, walnuts and nectarines - the principles that applied to these products applied equally to the other four products named in the relevant regulation. The United States had an interest in exporting to Japan also plums, pears, quince, peaches and apricots, and had, in fact, requested permission to export to Japan one variety of plums. The omission of the latter products from the debate had only to do with the fact that these had not yet been proposed for export to Japan. Japan's measure was an import prohibition or restriction with respect to these products as well, and the United States had specifically included in its claims all products subject to Japan's measure. Moreover, unlike cherries, nectarines and walnuts, Japan had not pointed to a scientific study regarding any of these other products - presumably because there were no studies that supported its theory of variety affecting efficacy of treatment.

4.15.   The Panel made a preliminary ruling on these matters at its first substantive meeting with the parties on 2 April 1998. The ruling is contained in paragraph 8.4.

B.   The Measure at Issue

4.16.   The **United States** alleged that Japan imposed an absolute ban on all products that Japan asserted were potential hosts to a quarantine pest such as codling moth. The Japanese *legislation* which was applicable imposed an import ban on enumerated "prohibited articles"; this was the Plant Protection Law (described under paragraph 2.18), enacted on 4 May 1950, as amended. The only applicable *regulation* was the Enforcement Regulation, enacted 30 June 1950, as amended. No legislative or regulatory provision specifically described or imposed a requirement of varietal testing to obtain an exemption from such a ban.[35] The *practice* of varietal testing was not formally written in any law or regulation, but stemmed from the implementation of the aforementioned legislation and regulation.

4.17.   The United States noted that Article 7 of the Plant Protection Law specified which products were prohibited for importation; these included "quarantine pests". The annex to Article 9 of the Plant Protection Law Enforcement Regulation specified the pest species that were subject to quarantine, the country(ies) or region(s) from which the pest originated, and the plant species that Japan asserted to be potential hosts to the quarantine pest. The annex listed the plants prohibited from entry, and an appendix to the list also indicated which varieties of products from specified regions were permitted entry into Japan. The United States maintained that the regulation was otherwise unclear on the question of *how* a particular variety might be permitted entry.

---

[35]   According to the United States, Japan had confirmed this under Question 2 of Japan's Response to US Consultation Questions (US Exhibit 3), in which Japan stated: "Lifting of import bans by variety is based on the legislation tabulated below. There is no situation where lifting of import bans by variety is based on legislation other than that given below". The table referred to listed the Plant Protection Law and the Enforcement Regulation.

4.18.   As it had evolved through practice, the ban was lifted only for specific varieties of an identified host product upon satisfaction of "quarantine treatment standards established through a regime of basic testing ... to prove complete mortality of the most resistant stage of the relevant pest in the scale of more than 30,000 test insects being used".[36] "The disinfestation test with a scale of 30,000 test insects is to seek for a disinfestation rate equivalent to probit 9 (99.9968 per cent mortality) which was adopted by the United States in its treatment standard."[37] To satisfy this requirement for permission to export a new variety, Japan required elaborate and repetitive testing procedures, and a public hearing process.[38]

4.19.   The United States acknowledged that the SPS Agreement recognized that countries had a sovereign right to implement legitimate restrictions on trade to protect their plant life and health from the introduction of pests that might cause harm. However, the United States stressed that the SPS Agreement did not permit unjustified import prohibitions that did not address legitimate phytosanitary concerns. The Japanese requirement of varietal testing was exactly the kind of unnecessary and unjustified measure that the SPS Agreement was intended to prohibit.

4.20.   The history of US efforts to export apples, cherries, walnuts, and nectarines illustrated the way in which the Japanese insistence on varietal testing had served as a significant barrier to trade. Since the early 1970s[39], the United States had been engaged in a rigorous research effort to export various fruit products to Japan. An effective quarantine treatment[40] for cherries had first been developed in the United States in 1976; for US walnuts in 1984; for US nectarines in 1986; and an effective treatment for US apples had first been developed in 1986.

<table>
<tr><td colspan="6" align="center">TABLE 2
History of Japanese Approval Process for Varietal Testing on US products</td></tr>
<tr><td>Product</td><td>Date Treatment Developed*</td><td>Testing Process Began</td><td>Confirmatory Test Dates</td><td>Public Hearing Date**</td><td>Approval Date</td></tr>
<tr><td colspan="6">APPLES</td></tr>
<tr><td>Red Delicious</td><td>1986</td><td>Oct. 1969</td><td>17-29 April 1994</td><td>7 and 8 July 1994</td><td>22 August 1994</td></tr>
<tr><td>Golden Delicious</td><td>1986</td><td>Oct. 1969</td><td>17-29 April 1994</td><td>7 and 8 July 1994</td><td>22 August 1994</td></tr>
<tr><td>Gala</td><td>1986</td><td>Oct. 1994</td><td>4 Sept. - 26 Nov. 1997</td><td>Pending</td><td>Pending</td></tr>
<tr><td>Granny Smith</td><td>1986</td><td>Oct. 1994</td><td>4 Sept. - 26 Nov 1997</td><td>Pending</td><td>Pending</td></tr>
</table>

---

[36]   Japan's response to Question 5 of US Consultation Questions. (US Exhibit 3)

[37]   Japan's response to Question 8 of US Consultation Questions. (US Exhibit 3)

[38]   Japan's responses to Questions 5 and 8 of US Consultation Questions. (US Exhibit 3)

[39]   Moffitt, "Methyl Bromide Fumigation Combined with Storage for Control of Codling Moth in Apples," 64(5) J. Econ. Entomol. pp. 1258-1260, 1971. (US Exhibit 21)

[40]   The United States noted that the development of an effective treatment meant that probit 9 security was achieved during large-scale tests of 30,000 codling moths.

TABLE 2
History of Japanese Approval Process for Varietal Testing on US products

Product	Date Treatment Developed*	Testing Process Began	Confirmatory Test Dates	Public Hearing Date**	Approval Date
Jonagold	1986	Oct. 1994	4 Sept. - 26 Nov 1997	Pending	Pending
Fuji	1986	Oct. 1994	4 Sept. - 26 Nov 1997	Pending	Pending
Braeburn	1986	Oct. 1994	4 Sept. - 26 Nov 1997	Pending	Pending
CHERRIES					
Bing	1976	1973	1977		10 January 1978
Van	1976	1973	1977		10 January 1978
Lambert	1976	1973	1977		10 January 1978
Rainier	1976	June 1988	July 1991		12 May 1992
Garnett	1976	June 1993	9 May - 10 June 1994		18 January 1995
Brooks	1976	May 1994	13 May - 14 June 1994		25 October 1996
Tulare	1976	May 1994	13 May - 14 June 1994		25 October 1996
Sweetheart	1976	August 1995	24 July - 18 Aug 1997	Pending	Pending
Lapin	1976	August 1995	24 July - 18 Aug 1997	Pending	Pending
NECTARINES					
Summer Grand	1986	July 1986	July 1986		17 June 1988
Fantasia	1986	July 1986	July 1986		17 June 1988
May Grand	1986	June 1986	June 1986		17 June 1988
Spring Red	1986	June 1986	June 1986		17 June 1988
Fire Brite	1986	June 1986	June 1986		17 June 1988
Red Diamond	1986	June 1986	June 1986		1 March 1995
May Diamond	1986	June 1988	June 1988		December 1990
May Fire	1986	May 1988	May 1988		December 1990
May Glo	1986	May 1988	May 1988		December 1990
Royal Giant	1986	August 1992	August 1992		1 March 1995
WALNUTS					
Hartley	1984	1982	August 1984		1986
Payne	1984	1982	August 1984		1986

<table>
<tr><td colspan="6">TABLE 2
History of Japanese Approval Process for Varietal Testing on US products</td></tr>
<tr>
<td>Product</td>
<td>Date Treatment Developed*</td>
<td>Testing Process Began</td>
<td>Confirmatory Test Dates</td>
<td>Public Hearing Date**</td>
<td>Approval Date</td>
</tr>
<tr><td>Franquette</td><td>1984</td><td>1982</td><td>August 1984</td><td></td><td>1986</td></tr>
<tr><td>Eureka</td><td>1984</td><td>1982</td><td>August 1984</td><td></td><td></td></tr>
<tr><td colspan="6">*   Development of an effective treatment means that probit 9 security was achieved during large-scale tests of 30,000 codling moths.
**   Absence of public hearing date denotes only that the information is not available.
Source: USDA Agricultural Research Service, USDA Animal and Plant Health Inspection Service (US Exhibit 1)</td></tr>
</table>

4.21.   The United States noted that Japan was a major producer and consumer of apples - the twelfth largest producer in the world. In 1995-1996, Japan had produced for commercial use 879,100 metric tons of apples, and consumed 796,883 metric tons of apples. Imports accounted for less than one percent of that consumption (1,089 metric tons).[41]

4.22.   The United States claimed that as a consequence of Japan's unjustified trade restrictions, exports to Japan of cherries, nectarines, apples and walnuts currently represented only a small part of US exports world-wide. In 1996, US apple exports totalled US$409.49 million. Only 0.14 per cent of those exports (US$570,000) went to Japan. Of the total US$78.85 million nectarine (and peach) exports in 1996, only 0.26 per cent (US$185,000) were exported to Japan. In respect of walnuts, 18.91 per cent of US exports went to Japan. While a significant amount of US cherry exports were sent to Japan (61.91 per cent of US exports), this number was not as significant when compared to the number of cherry varieties that were not even considered for export to Japan because the testing of quarantine treatment for each variety would be overly burdensome.

4.23.   It was common practice, according to the United States, to produce new varieties of agricultural products and enhance existing ones to capture a particular preference in the market place, or to modify harvesting time to coincide with demand trends for that fruit. These changes and enhancements could be as benign and subtle as a variation in the color of the product. The modifications of the product represented the sort of variability that did not affect how effective the quarantine treatment would be at killing the plant pests of concern. Yet Japan required *complete testing* and review of each variety, no matter how similar the variety might be to already accepted varieties. The entire testing and approval process for a given variety took anywhere from 2 to 4 years to complete, and was expensive to perform.[42] As a result, the United States claimed that Japan's measures served to restrict or altogether block access to Japan's market for new varieties.

4.24.   The United States claimed that efficacy of MB treatment for apples, cherries, walnuts and nectarines had been conclusively established. Japan was obliged to al-

---

[41]   USDA, Economic Research Service.
[42]   US Exhibit 1.

low importation of all US varieties of these products without delay, subject only to application of the respective protocol of treatment for the product.[43]

4.25.   **Japan** noted that the importance of phytosanitary measures to protect plants against foreign pests had long been recognized under the IPPC (paragraphs 2.25 to 2.33), to which Japan had been a party since 1952. While codling moth was prevalent throughout the temperate zone, the pest had not been discovered in Japan (paragraph 2.6). It was Japan's opinion that, to a considerable extent, this was attributable to Japan's plant quarantine policy. For Japan, (i) the diverse and mild climatic conditions surrounding Japanese agriculture, which allowed for a high risk of the establishment of exotic pests once they were introduced into the country; (ii) the highly concentrated, intensive cultivation, which would be seriously damaged once pests were established; and, (iii) the recent increase in the volume and diversity of plant/agricultural imports, made international plant quarantine essential to Japan. Hence, in order to prevent the entry of quarantine pests, the Plant Protection Law and the Enforcement Regulation identified quarantine pests, and prescribed inspection, disinfestation and other quarantine measures.

4.26.   Japan contended that the exercise of the authority of import prohibition was kept to the minimum necessary on the basis of available scientific evidence. Specifically, the import prohibition applied only to host plants of the quarantine pests which were found to pose a particularly significant risk, as a result of the risk assessment conducted in compliance with the PRA Guidelines of the FAO (paragraph 2.30), and against which no inspection would be effective. Currently these high-risk quarantine pests were 12 species of insects[44], three diseases[45] and pests of rice not found in Japan.

4.27.   Japan stated that prohibited plants, countries or areas of origin and the quarantine pests concerned were subject to continuous review whenever additional information became available in respect of the introduction of a pest into a new area, its eradication, new discoveries on pests and hosts, or development of a risk analysis method. Most recently, Japan had reviewed the regulations in April 1997[46], on the basis of the PRA Guidelines, and, as a result, the sweet potato vine borer had been deleted from - and fire blight had been added to - the quarantine pests whose host plants were subject to import prohibition.[47]

---

[43]   The United States referred to the work plans for cherries, nectarines, and apples. These indicated a thoroughness in testing procedures that would be applied consistently to any product that was subject to quarantine. (US Exhibit 22)

[44]   (i) Codling moth; (ii) Mediterranean fruit fly; (iii) *Bactrocera dorsalis* species complex; (iv) Queensland fruit fly; (v) melon fly; (vi) sweet potato weevil; (vii) West Indian sweet potato weevil; (viii) Colorado potato beetle; (ix) potato cyst nematode; (x) white potato cyst nematode; (xi) citrus burrowing nematode and (xii) Hessian fly.

[45]   Potato wart, tobacco blue mold and fire blight.

[46]   Japan noted at the first substantive meeting that amended regulations were effective as of 1 April 1998.

[47]   Japan noted, in addition, that in light of the latest information on the insect classification, the Oriental fruit fly was reclassified as the *Bactrocera dorsalis* species complex, and the white potato cyst nematode was separated from the potato cyst nematode.

4.28.   Japan recalled that the MAFF had the authority to lift the import prohibition. This was done by the de-listing of the product from the Annexed Table to the Enforcement Regulation (an amendment of the Enforcement Regulation). This was, according to Japan, the subject matter at issue in the current dispute (characterized by the United States as "varietal testing"). Japan claimed that contrary to the arguments of the United States, the import prohibition was not absolute (paragraph 4.16). The Japanese Government had accommodated foreign governments' requests for lifting of the prohibition. The number of products de-listed from the ban was evidence of this. The criteria established through past practice for de-listing were the following:

(a)   lifting was subject to a proposal of an alternative measure by the foreign government;

(b)   the level of protection required of the measure was that equivalent to import prohibition; and,

(c)   the exporting government bore the burden of proving that the proposed measure achieved the required level of protection.

4.29.   In respect of the first criteria, Japan claimed that an active measure was necessary to counter the quarantine pest, because inspection did not work effectively against the pest. Such a measure could be: complete eradication of the pest from the territory, establishment of a pest-free area, or disinfection/disinfestation treatment prior to shipment. The purpose of involvement of the foreign government was to ensure implementation of the measure in the foreign jurisdiction. In respect of the second criteria, the requirement of equivalency was self-explanatory; Japan noted that the parties to the dispute at issue were not in conflict over the level of protection. Third, for practical reasons, the importing country was at a disadvantage in respect of the gathering of sufficient information on exotic pests (which did not exist domestically), for varieties that often were not produced in Japan, hence, the exporting government had the burden of proving that the proposed measure achieved the required level of protection.

4.30.   Japan claimed that these criteria had been designed as part of the policy for the implementation of domestic law through *past practice*. They represented fundamental policy orientation and were not published as a document. However, for the key process of demonstration of efficacy of quarantine treatment, MAFF had developed test guidelines in order to enhance transparency and these were made available for exporting countries.

4.31.   The description of the Japanese practice by the United States was misleading (paragraphs 2.18 to 2.24). Japan did not demand "complete testing and review of each variety" (paragraph 4.23), the requirement depended on the US export strategy. If the United States proposed to export more than one variety, complete testing including a large-scale test (30,000 test insects in three replicates) would be required on only one *representative variety*. That is, if the United States were to apply for approval of 100 varieties of the same product, complete testing would be required only of the one variety which demonstrated the lowest degree of sensitivity to the proposed treatment in dose-mortality tests and a probit analysis. The concept of a representative variety applied equally to approval of additional varieties. As long as efficacy of the treatment in use was confirmed with respect to additional varieties by dose-mortality tests, what was required was an on-site confirmatory test (10,000 test insects) for one representative variety alone. Even if the results of dose-mortality tests were unsatisfactory, a large-scale test was necessary for only one representative variety of the additional varieties.

4.32.   Japan maintained that the essence of the requirement was a demonstration that a proposed treatment would be effective on all varieties which the exporting government proposed to ship to Japan. The exporting government was free to propose any method for the purpose of this demonstration.

4.33.   Japan pointed out that what the United States had referred to as the testing procedure (in paragraph 4.18) were the contents of the "Experimental Guidelines for the Lifting Import Ban" and the "Experimental Guide for Cultivar Comparison Test on Insect Mortality"[48] which the MAFF had provided as a model confirmation process for a proposed disinfestation treatment of insects. Japan stressed that these were *model* guidelines, they did not have the force of law, and were not imposed by the MAFF. Exporting governments were free to propose their own confirmation method.

4.34.   Japan stated that the US data cited in paragraph 4.22 showed that Japan was the largest importer of American cherries, and was a major (the largest, if members of the European Communities were treated separately) importer of US walnuts.

4.35.   According to the **United States**, to have the ban lifted on a new variety, the testing procedure included: (i) an initial test to estimate the basic dose-response of the pest in question, in or on the variety in question; (ii) data review by a MAFF official; and, (iii) a large-scale test consisting of a total of 30,000 insects at 10,000 insects in each of three successive individual trials. If successful, only then was an on-site confirmatory test conducted in the presence of MAFF staff. Resulting data was again reviewed by a MAFF official, and following confirmation of efficacy, a public hearing in Japan was required on lifting the ban for the particular variety. The United States noted that where there was an accepted quarantine treatment for another variety of the same product, Japan allowed for a comparison dose-mortality test. The same treatment was tested simultaneously on the new and old variety and the results were compared to ascertain whether there were differences in response of the insects. The results of this test were reviewed by Japanese officials. If there were no differences, then an on-site confirmatory test was required with 10,000 insects generally divided into three replications, in the presence of a MAFF official. This process was rarely employed, however, because it was possible that the old variety was no longer cultivated or the harvest time for one variety did not coincide with another.

4.36.   In respect of the concept of representative variety, the United States noted that as a matter of practical application of these tests, there were occasions where the United States would seek to introduce more than one variety at the same time. Japan was correct in asserting that in some circumstances, because of the varietal testing requirement, a representative variety could be chosen to perform the confirmatory tests. But that did not mean that significant time and resources had not already been devoted to dose-mortality testing on all of the proposed varieties. Dose-mortality testing could take as long as a month or more to perform on a given set of

---

[48]   Contained in Japan, Exhibit 10.

varieties. It was also important to bear in mind that the benefit of allowing for a representative variety was not always realized. This was because it was difficult to test certain varieties simultaneously due to the fact that they were harvested at different times. Moreover, with some fruit products, new varieties were developed so rapidly and there were so many varieties that it was not practical to conduct this type of intensive varietal testing. Thus, while not all of the varieties that had been tested by the United States had undergone confirmatory testing, a large proportion of the varieties had; and more importantly, *all* varieties had been subjected to some form of detailed testing.

4.37.　In this respect, the United States noted that it had tested seven varieties of apples, nine varieties of cherries, four varieties of walnuts and ten varieties of nectarines. There had never been a difference in results from one variety to another. Every confirmatory test had uniformly achieved Japan's level of quarantine protection against the codling moth at the same exact treatment level for a product.[49] Moreover, Japan was not able to point to a single example in which any agricultural exporting country in the world had had to modify a treatment for killing codling moth among varieties of the same product. Japan had *approved* the treatments for ten varieties of nectarines, two varieties of apples, seven varieties of cherries and three varieties of walnuts. This was despite differences in dose-mortality tests and despite differing CxT values. Japan had approved these varieties because of the ability of the United States to demonstrate that the quarantine treatment provided the desired level of mortality. Every article published on the efficacy of MB and/or MB and cold storage for disinfestation of codling moth had demonstrated that there were no differences among varieties that affected efficacy of a quarantine treatment.

4.38.　**Japan** countered that large-scale demonstration (i.e., the large-scale confirmatory test or the on-site confirmatory test) applied to *one* representative variety which was found, in dose-mortality testing and the probit analysis, to be the most resistant to a treatment. Thus, contrary to what had been suggested by the United States, the number of varieties which had been subject to either form of large-scale demonstration had been: **two** varieties of apples (as opposed to seven as the United States had claimed), **seven** varieties of cherries (as opposed to nine), **one** variety of walnuts (as opposed to four) and **three** varieties of nectarines (as opposed to ten) (Table 3). Japan's policy was not such that would require unnecessary testing on *all* varieties.

---

[49]　US Exhibit 2.

TABLE 3
History of Lifting and Large-Scale Demonstration of US Fruits
(i.e. either large-scale confirmatory test or on-site confirmatory test)

	Approved Year	Varieties	Large-Scale Test	On-site Confirmatory Test
Apples	1994	Red Delicious Golden Delicious	Red Delicious	Red Delicious
	(under way)	Gala Braeburn Jonagold Fuji Granny Smith		Fuji
Cherries	1978*	Bing Van Lambert	Bing Van Lambert	Bing Van Lambert
	1992	Rainier		Rainier
	1995	Garnet		Garnet
	1996	Brooks Tulare		Tulare
	(under way)	Sweetheart Lapin		Sweetheart
Nectarines	1988	Summer Grand May Grand Fantasia Spring Red Firebrite Red Diamond	May Grand	May Grand
	1993	May Diamond Mayfire May Glo		May Diamond
	1995**	Royal Giant	Royal Giant	Royal Giant
Walnuts	1986***	Franquette Payne Hartley	Hartley	Hartley

*   At that time, each of the varieties was subjected to large-scale demonstration.
** The large-scale test was necessary because the element of the treatment was modified (fruit containers were changed from wooden bins to export carton boxes).
*** The representative variety was selected by the CxT value.

4.39.   Conversely, five varieties of apples (out of seven), seven varieties of nectarines (out of ten), two varieties of cherries (out of nine) and two varieties of walnuts (out of three) had been, or were being, approved by the small-scale laboratory experiment alone. It was therefore not correct to state that "all varieties have been subjected to some form of detailed testing". On the contrary, the present confirmation mechanism used the dose-mortality test to screen so that not all varieties needed to be subjected to large-scale demonstration, either by the large-scale confirmatory test or the on-site confirmatory test.

C. *Application of the SPS Agreement*

4.40.   The **United States** argued that the SPS Agreement applied to "all sanitary and phytosanitary measures which might, directly or indirectly, affect international trade" (Article 1.1). In this sense, Japan's measures were phytosanitary measures[50], as defined by the SPS Agreement in Annex A, and directly or indirectly affected international trade.

4.41.   According to the United States, the definition demonstrated that whether a measure was a sanitary or phytosanitary measure depended on the *purpose* of the measure. Japan had stated that the purpose of varietal testing was to protect plant life or health within Japan from the establishment and spread of certain pests that could cause harm to its agriculture.[51] In order to export varieties to Japan, the exporting country had to obtain certification that it had met Japanese requirements.

4.42.   As the definition of a "sanitary or phytosanitary measure" in Annex A of the SPS Agreement specifically listed "testing procedures" as being included in sanitary and phytosanitary measures, Japan's measure at issue was a phytosanitary measure. The United States further argued that Japan's measure was a "procedure to check and ensure the fulfilment of sanitary or phytosanitary measures" (chapeau to Annex C of the SPS Agreement). In addition, the United States was of the view that as a phytosanitary measure, it was subject to all of the requirements of Articles 2, 5, and 7 of the SPS Agreement. As an Annex C measure, it was also subject to all of the requirements of Article 8 and Annex C of the SPS Agreement.

4.43.   Japan's measure applied to imports of certain agricultural products such as apples, cherries, walnuts, and nectarines. It prohibited the importation of any agricultural product that had been identified by Japan as a host to a quarantine pest. The ban was only lifted upon a showing that a quarantine treatment for a pest achieved Japan's level of protection for each variety of the agricultural product, irrespective of the fact that an effective quarantine treatment had been accepted for another variety of the same product. Therefore, the Japanese requirement of varietal testing adversely affected international trade.

4.44.   **Japan** did not dispute that the measure at issue was covered by the SPS Agreement. Japan argued that the requirement of demonstration of efficacy was consistent with international practice. There was nothing in the SPS Agreement which prevented enforcement of that requirement.

D. *Burden of Proof*

4.45.   The **United States** claimed that Japan had failed to present "minimally sufficient evidence" as to why variety mattered in regard to MB quarantine treatment. Instead, Japan insisted that the exporting country had to provide evidence as to why variety did not matter. This was clearly contrary to the obligations of the SPS Agreement.

---

[50]   Relating to the protection of the life or health of plants.

[51]   In the Government of Japan's response to Question 2 of US Consultation Questions, Japan had stated that "GOJ designates pests and diseases, which do not exist in Japan but which could conceivably cause serious damage to agriculture if outbreak were to occur, and prohibits imports of their host plants". (US Exhibit 3)

The United States accepted that it had the burden to establish a *prima facie* case that the measure of varietal testing was inconsistent with the SPS Agreement In this dispute, the United States maintained that it had shown that Japan's measure was not based on scientific evidence and a risk assessment, that all available scientific and empirical evidence indicated that differences among varieties did not affect efficacy of treatment against codling moth; that the testing of efficacy of quarantine treatment by product alone achieved Japan's level of protection against the risk of entry, establishment and spread of codling moth; and that testing and treatment by product was a significantly less trade restrictive measure available to Japan. The United States had met its burden of proof. As the Appellate Body in *EC Measures Concerning Meat and Meat Products ("EC - Hormones")* stated, "when the prima facie case is made, the burden of proof moves to the defending party, which must in turn counter or refute the claimed inconsistency".[52]

4.46.   **Japan** contended that the United States had not submitted any demonstration that the proposed product-by-product approach would be effective for all varieties. The requirement of demonstration, which was the exercise of domestic authority under the Plant Protection Law, was not only reasonable in light of the disparity of information but was consistent with established international practice. Furthermore, Japan noted that there was no disagreement between the parties in this respect; the United States had accepted this principle in that it had stated that it was reasonable for the importing country to require the exporting country to propose and substantiate the efficacy of an approach that achieved the importing country's level of phytosanitary protection (paragraph 4.50). There was nothing in the SPS Agreement which prevented enforcement of the requirement of demonstration as such; it was not per se inconsistent with the SPS Agreement. It was the responsibility of an applicant to prove safety (or absence of harm) of a medicinal product, for example; it was not the obligation of Member governments under the SPS Agreement to disprove safety. No Member government of the WTO allowed the applicant the luxury of obtaining governmental approval of a drug, food additive or phytosanitary treatment simply because inefficacy and/or danger thereof had not been proven. Nor was it Japan's obligation to scientifically demonstrate that varieties resulted in different degrees of efficacy of a treatment by, for example, conducting large-scale tests at Japan's expense. Such interpretation of the provisions of the SPS Agreement was tantamount to denial of the requirement of demonstration by the exporting government. The issue was rather whether or not the importing authorities had acted in conformity with the Agreement in perceiving the risk presented by the eventual importation of a different variety. Japan claimed that there *was* data which suggested the possible presence of varietal difference in efficacy of a treatment which gave rise to the concern. Hence, the requirement under the SPS Agreement of scientific evidence or a risk assessment was fully met. Insofar as the requirement of demonstration was thus consistent with the SPS Agreement, the exporting government had to show, with scientific evidence, that a given treatment would be effective for the proposed varieties.

---

[52]   WT/DS/26/AB/R, adopted 13 February 1998, paragraph 98.

4.47.   Japan noted that it did not impose a particular measure, as long as a proposed alternative method demonstrated efficacy equivalent to the import prohibition.[53] For instance, for lemons, grapefruits and ponkan oranges, Japan had approved importation on a product-by-product basis (although the relevant pest, fruit fly, and the relevant treatment, cold treatment, were not covered by the terms of reference of the current dispute). This was because most of these citrus varieties had been developed by somatic mutation, such as bud mutation, and their varietal differences were not known to be significant.

4.48.   Japan argued that the United States had not submitted any relevant evidence in this regard. Nor had any convincing argument to support the absence of varietal differences been made. In order for the United States position to prevail under Articles 2.2 and 5.1, it had to prove that the varietal risk was either non-existent or insignificant in light of scientific evidence and/or a risk assessment. It was not sufficient for the United States to prove that there were risks other than those resulting from varietal differences including "natural variation". The United States had repeated arguments that (i) laboratory test results were unreliable and that (ii) the existing treatment had been effective so far. In doing so, the United States had failed to show that Japan was not abiding by the requirement of scientific basis or evidence. Hence, Japan urged the Panel to apply the burden of proof principle which was stated in the *EC - Hormones* case correctly. The United States had failed to make a *prima facie* case.

4.49.   The **United States** stressed that it was important not to confuse the fact that the exporter would typically assume the burden of meeting the importing country's concerns with the question of the burden of proof for dispute settlement purposes. The United States had always accepted that in the current proceeding it bore the burden of presenting facts and arguments sufficient to establish a presumption that Japan's measure was inconsistent with the cited WTO Agreements. However, this did not alter the fact that *Japan* was required to have sufficient scientific evidence to *maintain* its measure and to base its measure on a risk assessment. The United States had proven that Japan did not have sufficient scientific evidence or a risk assessment to justify its *assumption* that variety mattered. The United States did *not need to prove* that there were no varietal differences that mattered for purposes of treatment efficacy. This was a fundamental issue of burden of proof under the SPS Agreement; in *EC - Hormones,* the European Communities claimed that it could ban meat because it was not proven that there was no risk. This approach had not been accepted by the Appellate Body.

4.50.   The United States noted that as a general proposition, assuming that a product proposed for export was indeed a potential host for a pest appropriately determined to be a pest of quarantine significance, it was reasonable for the importing country to require the exporting country to propose and substantiate the efficacy of an approach that achieved the importing country's level of phytosanitary protection. As Japan acknowledged, such a proposal could involve eradication of the pest from the territory, establishment of a pest-free area, or a disinfestation treatment (paragraph 4.29). The

---

[53]   MB fumigation, cold treatment, vapor heat treatment, dry heat treatment, phosphine fumigation and a combination of these alternatives were an example of specific disinfestation measures which Japan had already approved.

United States maintained, however, that such an approach could also involve integrated pest-management practices and a systems approach, which did not necessarily involve a disinfestation treatment. Indeed, the United States had long proposed integrated pest-management practices for codling moth in conjunction with MB fumigation and, in the case of apples, cold treatment. The United States believed it had established the efficacy of this approach for apples, cherries, nectarines, and walnuts.

4.51.   In the absence of a recognized pest-free area, it was the experience of the United States that Japan did not permit importation of any varieties of the relevant products without demonstration of the efficacy of the applicable MB quarantine treatment for codling moth on each and every variety. This rigid criterion for demonstration of efficacy was not a reasonable procedural requirement.

4.52.   The United States noted that in connection with Japan's claims regarding lemons, grapefruits and ponkan oranges, Dr. Ducom (an expert advising the Panel[54]) had stated that there was no scientific basis for distinguishing these products from the products at issue in considering whether product-based testing was feasible. Further, the United States pointed out that the treatments developed for each product had been uniformly effective for the entire commodity.

4.53.   **Japan** noted in respect of integrated pest management or other techniques, that while they were effective to reduce the level of infestation, they did not eliminate the risk of the pest to the level equivalent to an import prohibition. Disinfestation had been chosen in the light of these considerations, and not because pre- or post-harvest techniques were irrelevant.

E.   *Articles 2.2, 5.1 and 5.2*

1.   *General*

4.54.   The **United States** argued that the Japanese varietal testing requirement was maintained without sufficient evidence in contravention of Article 2.2. Furthermore, it was not based on an assessment of risk in contravention of Articles 5.1 and 5.2. The SPS Agreement indicated in Article 2.2 that a Member was not allowed to maintain a phytosanitary measure "without sufficient scientific evidence" and a measure had to be "based on scientific principles". Article 5.1 stated that a Member had to ensure that its phytosanitary measure was based on an assessment, "as appropriate to the circumstances, of the risks to ... plant life or health".

4.55.   In relation to risk assessment, the United States recalled that the Appellate Body Report on *EC - Hormones* had made it clear that Article 5.1 could "be viewed as a specific application of the basic obligations contained in Article 2.2 of the SPS Agreement".[55] Thus, the United States argued, Article 2.2 and Article 5.1 of the SPS Agreement were necessarily linked together. Under Articles 5.1 and 5.2 of the SPS Agreement, Japan was required to base its SPS measure, in this instance variety-by-variety testing for quarantine efficacy, on a risk assessment. Such an assessment was

---

[54]   See Section VI of this report in respect of the Panel's consultation with scientific experts. The experts advising the Panel are listed under paragraph 6.4.

[55]   *Op. cit.*, p.72, paragraph 180.

important in establishing whether the measure was "based on scientific principles", and was not "maintained without scientific evidence" (Article 2.2).

4.56. The United States stressed its request that the Panel make findings with respect to both Article 2.2 and Article 5.1 of the SPS Agreement. In the view of the United States, the heart of the dispute was the fact that Japan's measure did not merely lack an assessment of risk, it lacked sufficient scientific evidence to support the measure. This had also been stressed by the Appellate Body's statement in *EC - Hormones* that "Articles 2.2 and 5.1 should constantly be read together. Article 2.2 informs Article 5.1: the elements that define the basic obligation set out in Article 2.2 impart meaning to Article 5.1".[56] Furthermore, in that dispute, where the Panel made a finding under Article 5.1 but not Article 2.2, the Appellate Body expressed that it was "surprised by the fact that the Panel had not begun its analysis of this whole case by focusing on Article 2 that is captioned 'Basic Rights and Obligations,' an approach that appears logically attractive".[57]

4.57. The United States stressed that a failure to make a finding with respect to Article 2.2 could lead to confusion rather than furthering the objective of "providing security and predictability to the multilateral trading system".[58] If the Panel were to make a finding on all of the elements necessary to make a determination with respect to Article 2.2 (which in this dispute would be inherent in a finding with respect to Article 5.1), and yet not actually make that determination, it could be perceived by some as implying that Japan's ban was *not* maintained without sufficient scientific evidence. This negative implication would be inaccurate. Japan's measure did not merely lack a risk assessment, it was not supported by scientific evidence. In that regard, the lack of sufficient scientific evidence was a more fundamental and fatal flaw than the lack of a risk assessment, and thus was a more important finding than a finding under Article 5.1.

2.   Article 2.2

(a)   General

4.58. The **United States** recalled that Article 2.2 of the SPS Agreement required a Member to base its phytosanitary measures on scientific principles and prohibited a Member from maintaining sanitary and phytosanitary measures "without sufficient scientific evidence". The SPS Agreement did not define "based on scientific principles". However, at a minimum, to base a measure on scientific principles required that a WTO Member had *identified a particular risk* that the measure was designed to protect against, and conducted some review of scientific evidence or other relevant scientific information to demonstrate that the measure in fact protected against that risk. The risk that had to be addressed was whether there was a possibility of the inadvertent entry of codling moth from US products, on a variety-by-variety basis, in light of pre- and post-harvest practices and quarantine treatment. In other words, the risk of introduction of codling moth *in the absence* of the varietal testing requirement. The United States noted that the strongest wording Japan had been able to

---

[56]   *Op. cit.*, p.72, paragraph 180.
[57]   *Ibid.*, paragraph 250.
[58]   Article 3.2 of the DSU.

employ was that "it is *possible* there *may* be variation in the efficacy of disinfestation even if the same quarantine treatment is applied to different varieties" [emphasis added].[59] Yet the Appellate Body Report on *EC - Hormones* had noted that a theoretical risk would always remain because "science can *never* provide *absolute* certainty that a given substance will not ever have adverse health effects. We agree with the Panel that this theoretical uncertainty is not the kind of risk which, under Article 5.1, is to be assessed".[60]

4.59.   The United States claimed that Japan had never been able to provide an explanation as to why it was necessary to test each variety of a product. There was no scientific reason why the types of differences that distinguished one apple, nectarine, walnut or cherry from another would be relevant to the effectiveness of the quarantine treatment. Empirical evidence supported the fact that with quarantine treatment for codling moth using the preferred treatment of MB and/or a two component treatment of MB and cold storage, the particular *variety* of the product did not matter for purposes of the quarantine treatment needed.[61] In other words, the quarantine treatment had always been equally effective irrespective of variety. The additional and redundant testing required by Japan had never been proven necessary.

4.60.   **Japan** noted that the main thrust of the US argument appeared to be that there was no scientific basis for varietal testing. Japan maintained that its position was based on a sufficient amount of available literature and scientific data which indicated the possible presence of a statistically significant difference in the efficacy of known disinfestation measures across varieties of the same products, differences which could require application of a different treatment.

4.61.   Japan claimed that the import prohibition fully met the criteria, developed by the Appellate Body in *EC - Hormones*, of being "based on" scientific evidence, or a risk assessment:

> "... Article 5.1, when contextually read as it should be, in conjunction with and as informed by Article 2.2 of the SPS Agreement, requires that the results of the risk assessment must sufficiently warrant - that is to say, reasonably support - the SPS measure."[62]

4.62.   Japan had relied on the following available evidence which had led to the conclusion that the import prohibition was warranted against codling moth:

    (a)   Honma, K. (1976) *Plant Protection* 30: 237-244. (in Japanese)

    (b)   Proverbs, M.D. *et al.*, (1982) *Can. Entomol.* 114: 363-376.

    (c)   Moffitt, H.R. *et al.*, (1988) *J. Econ. Entomol.* 81: 1511-1515.

    (d)   Beers, E.H. *et al.*, (1988) In *Orchard Pest Management*, pp. 63-68.

    (e)   MAFF (1995) In *Handbook of Agricultural Statistics*, pp. 225-238. (in Japanese)

    (f)   IIE (1995) *Distribution Maps of Pests,* Series A. No. 9, CAB International.

---

[59]   Japan's response to Question 4 of US Consultation Questions (US Exhibit 3).

[60]   *Op. cit.,* paragraph 186 (italics in original).

[61]   US Exhibit 2.

[62]   *Op. cit.,* paragraph 193.

(g)   Tokyo Astronomical Observatory (1995) In *Chronological Scientific Tables*, pp.198-199. (in Japanese)

(h)   Yamaguchi, A. & A. Otake eds. (1986) In *Disease and Invertebrate Pests of Fruits Trees,* pp. 226-230. (in Japanese)

(i)   Japan Tariff Association (1993, 1994, 1995) In *Japan Exports & Imports* No. 12, p. 94. (1993), p. 93. (1994), p. 93. (1995).

4.63.   These pieces of literature contained or lead to the following findings:

(a)   Codling moth could survive in areas where the effective cumulative temperature (the yearly sum of the daily temperature figures which are 10 degrees or above) was 600 day-degrees and the lowest monthly temperature of the coldest month fell below 10 degrees centigrade. Most Japanese regions met this criteria.

(b)   The insect was able to establish itself in Japan in light of the amount of host plants.

(c)   When codling moth larvae diapaused through the winter in cocoons, and, after the pupal stage in early spring, the moth emerged during the blooming season of apples.

(d)   In contrast to a sedentary pest such as scale, codling moth was able to spread by flight. There was a report that the moth could move within a range of 300 to 500 feet, and records that they had flown 1,000 to 2,000 feet. Moreover, a Canadian study on control by sterile insect releases found that male moths released from a point were recaptured in traps 3.5 kilometres to 7.2 kilometres away.

(e)   The larvae entered into the apple fruits at every growing stage, and it severely damaged commercial value.

(f)   In an area not subject to pest control, the infestation rate in pears was 57.3 per cent to 100 per cent.

(g)   Newly hatched larvae entered into the fruits from the calyx end or from cracks, and were very difficult to detect.

(h)   Export markets could be lost.

(i)   Control costs could increase.

4.64.   From the above findings, Japan drew the following conclusions and decided that import prohibition was the appropriate phytosanitary measure:

(a)   codling moth had a high potential (grade a) of entry and establishment, while its spread potential was medium (grade b);

(b)   the pest was highly likely to cause grave damage (grade a) to agricultural production once it was introduced into the country; and,

(c)   there was no practical, effective inspection method to detect the presence of the moth inside fruits, and the level of management difficulty was the highest (A1).

4.65.   The **United States** claimed that Japan was mischaracterizing the dispute. The issue was not whether codling moth was of quarantine significance. That was not in dispute. What was in dispute was whether there was any scientific basis for Japan's assumption that variety affected efficacy of treatment against codling moth. Japan had asserted that variety presented a risk in relation to quarantine treatments with methyl bromide, and yet it could not support this theoretical uncertainty with scientific evidence. In fact, Japan had instituted this requirement *before* any of the scientific studies on which it claimed to rely had been conducted.[63] Japan had yet to explain why varieties needed to be tested separately. If each variety needed to be tested separately because varietal differences "could" matter, then why not separately test by a whole series of other arbitrary factors, such as by color, by ripeness, or by length of time in shipment? In essence, Japan had *assumed* variety mattered, and then challenged exporting countries to prove it did not. According to the United States, this was not the way the SPS Agreement was structured.

4.66.   The United States noted that addressing the risk at issue came down to an exporting Member's ability to kill the pest in question, codling moth, in each variety of a product. This was the fundamental question that had to be analyzed under Articles 2.2 and 5.1 of the SPS Agreement. Japan had established a particular level of mortality that it wanted any quarantine treatment to achieve. This was, however, not the same as an appropriate level of protection. There was no dispute over that mortality level. The United States wished to clarify the mortality level did not relate to: sorptive patterns, CxT findings, preliminary dose-mortality testing or the other information and procedures that scientists used to identify a treatment that would kill codling moth on a given product. The significance of those data and techniques was in the contributions that they made to scientists' conclusions about the fumigant dosage needed to *achieve the required level of pest mortality.*

4.67.   Japan had suggested that the existence of risks could be inferred from the studies it had submitted. Yet none of the these studies were structured in such a way that they answered the basic questions of fact which might serve as scientific evidence for the risk at issue. Even if Japan had been accurate with respect to the significance of every piece of data it had cited, and the conclusions of each and every study, the question would remain whether Japan's varietal testing requirement was supported by sufficient scientific evidence, and whether the risk at issue was more than hypothetical. The United States maintained that responses by the experts advising the Panel had been very helpful in clarifying that it was not possible to attribute the data variations cited in these studies to varietal differences, let alone to differences of a magnitude that could affect treatment efficacy. The United States stressed that all of the experts had confirmed that the existence of varietal differences affecting treatment efficacy could *not be determined on the basis of the evidence before the Panel.*

4.68.   **Japan** claimed that the risk it faced was not the "theoretical uncertainty" the Appellate Body had referred to in *EC - Hormones*. The present case was substantially different from *EC - Hormones*; while the safety of the substances was internationally established in the *EC - Hormones* case, no one doubted the risk posed by codling moth to Japan. While the European Communities only asserted that safety of hormones was not proven beyond doubt, Japan's concern was based on available

---

[63]   The United States noted that the earliest reference wherein Japan identified any basis for its assumption that variety affects efficacy of quarantine treatment was in the Wearing *et al.*,1980 Study on New Zealand Cherries (contained in Japan, Exhibit 13).

data. This data was the basis for Japan's scientific concern over the efficacy of the treatment across varieties.

4.69.   Hence, Japan disagreed with the US argument that Japan referred only to theoretical uncertainty as the basis for "varietal testing" for MB fumigation, and, therefore, that Japanese policy was not based on a risk assessment. First, Japan recalled that there was *no* requirement of "complete testing and review of each variety" under the Japanese policy (paragraph 4.23). All that was required of *each* variety was the demonstration of efficacy in small-scale laboratory experiments to compare dose-response with other varieties (at the time of initial lifting), or with the approved treatment level (at the time of additional lifting). Large-scale demonstration was only required of a representative variety. Second, Japan noted that there was nothing inherently wrong about Japan's concern in respect of varietal differences. Japan claimed that the United States had itself established different treatment standards for different varieties of mangoes (paragraph 4.136 and following paragraphs).

4.70.   Japan noted that in the case of MB fumigation to counter codling moth, data was available in the form of varietal dose-response results which suggested the possible presence of differences in efficacy of fumigation treatment between varieties. Japan's hypothesis was that characteristics of a particular variety could affect fumigation efficacy, possibly by their impact on the CxT value (explained in further detail in paragraph 4.109 and after). In light of available data and present knowledge of the fumigation process, this was a reasonable argument. Japan's policy was thus based on a scientific hypothesis which was in turn supported by empirical data, in full conformity with the obligations contained in Article 2.2 and Article 5.1.

4.71.   Japan noted that the United States apparently found rationale for the product-by-product testing in the fact that the efficacy of the treatment applied for one variety of a product had never varied from that of the treatment applied to another variety of the same product. The United States repeatedly emphasized the fact that an MB fumigation standard had not been modified in the past. Japan acknowledged that it was true that existing treatment levels of host plants of codling moth had been found effective for additional varieties. However, as a matter of science, all this proved was the efficacy of the treatment on the *tested* varieties; it fell short of showing absence of varietal difference within a product altogether. Possibly, the US argument could be founded on an intuitive judgement, based on past experience. However, out of 100 varieties of nectarines in commercial production, only three varieties had been tested by a large-scale (10,000 to 30,000 insects) test. Similarly, out of 44 varieties of apples, only two had been tested by the large-scale test.

4.72.   Japan further noted that, according to the US argument, if there were 100 varieties in one product category, a treatment based on a selective test of any variety would have to be presumed to be effective for the other 99 varieties. Far more scientific evidence than provided by the United States in the current proceedings was needed before Japan could reach such a conclusion. The implications of the US arguments were: (i) that the present quarantine treatment would be effective for unapproved varieties (including varieties yet to be developed) of apples, cherries, nectarines and walnuts; and, (ii) for other products which the United States claimed to be within the terms of reference, they would seek to apply a single treatment for all varieties (including varieties yet to be developed).

4.73.   The United States had not provided any information on disinfestation of unapproved varieties or unapproved products. Obviously, there was no information on products yet to be developed, possibly through rapidly advancing biotechnology. Nor had the United States presented a theoretical argument regarding the absence of varietal difference in the disinfestation effects of these products. Japan had to conclude that the United States had not performed the required demonstration of efficacy of treatment across varieties.

4.74.   The **United States** stated that it found unremarkable Japan's conclusion that the United States had not proven, with scientific certainty, the absence of varietal differences. This conclusion did not more than state, as the Appellate Body Report in *EC - Hormones* recognized, that science could never, with absolute certainty, prove the negative. This did not excuse Japan from its obligations to base its requirement on a risk assessment and sufficient evidence, obligations which Japan had failed to fulfill.

(b)   Probit 9, Dose-Mortality Tests and Confirmatory Tests

4.75.   The **United States** noted that dose-mortality tests were a critical tool to determine what commercial treatment might be effective. The dose-mortality test result established a range of treatments for varieties from which scientists could compare and estimate a final treatment for the product as a whole. The highest minimum dose observed in the dose-mortality tests that scientists believe would achieve the level of protection required by Japan (probit 9) was supplemented by 10-20 per cent in the second stage of testing, the confirmatory tests, to account for all sources of variation in the dose-mortality tests. Thus it was the confirmatory test that was the relevant indicator of efficacy of treatment.

4.76.   The primary reason for the 10-20 per cent (buffer) increase of dose in confirmatory tests, as well as the reason why scientists did not rely on dose-response results to establish a commercial quarantine treatment, was that not every replicate of a dose-mortality test would exactly mirror another. Such factors as experimental error, physical condition of the fruit, sorption of the fumigant by packing material, and load of fruit in the chamber could account for differences in results. Phytotoxic[64] effects and effects on residue levels would ordinarily establish the upper bound for a proposed buffer.

4.77.   The United States noted that dose-response data could vary from test to test with the same species of insect in the same variety. It was well established that insect susceptibility to insecticidal treatment differed greatly among individual insects, and that the response of insect populations varied. Since each test necessarily required new insects, the response of test insects would differ naturally among tests and that accounted in part for the observed variability in dose-mortality test results.[65]

---

[64]   Toxic or injurious to plants.

[65]   Finney, D.J., (1964) "Statistical Methods in Biological Assay," Griffin, London, pp. 91-92, *Cited in* Robertson, Preisler, Hickle and Gelernter, "Natural Variation: A Complicating Factor in Bioassays with Chemical and Microbial Pesticides", 88(1) J. Econ. Entomol. 1-10, 4-6. (1995). Finney states, "In general the assumption that a response curve once determined can be used in

With small scale dose-mortality tests, using limited numbers of pests, it was unlikely that variability of insects relative to susceptibility to the fumigant would be fully represented. Confirmatory tests, however, contained sufficient numbers of insects (10,000 to 30,000) to ensure representation of insects at all levels of MB susceptibility.

4.78.   Thus, because of natural variation of the test insect population, as well as other factors that ensured that no *one* dose-mortality test would be exactly the same as another, it was impossible to conclude that differences in variety were the explanation for variations in dose-response results. The United States argued that Japan's own acceptance of varieties that exhibited differences in dose-response results established that Japan recognized effective quarantine treatment always accommodated some differences in dose-mortality testing.

4.79.   Confirmatory tests established the efficacy of treatment for a product because they took into consideration *all of the sources of variation that could be attributed to the smaller scale tests* - most notably the variation in a pest population, and the experimental error that was bound to occur from one small-scale test to the next. A confirmatory test would show if a treatment were too low because there would be an unacceptable rate of survival of the pest. However, confirmatory tests would not indicate if a treatment were too high.

4.80.   The United States noted that although confirmatory tests were necessary in the initial development of a quarantine treatment, they were unnecessary for every new variety of the same product. The confirmatory test administered to the initial variety, with a target pest population of 30,000 insects, was of such a design and order of magnitude to include a "real world" range of the pest population (and therefore relative levels of tolerance to methyl bromide) to detect an inadequate treatment; in other words, such a large-scale test would capture the range of susceptibility of insect population. The United States noted that 30,000 codling moths was a substantially larger number of insects than had ever been encountered in either dose-mortality tests or the actual conditions of US products proposed as candidates for export to Japan.[66] The United States noted that the experts advising the Panel had affirmed that the incidence of codling moth on commercially marketable US products was low. Pest population levels for US products were measured, at most, in extremely low numbers, not hundreds per fruit, as encountered in the confirmatory test. Any treatment that could kill 30,000 codling moths in one application would not have difficulty killing the rare individual codling moth that might appear in a particular commercial shipment. Dr.

---

future assays is inadmissible. Because of natural variation, responses of a group of insects tested at any one time will therefore never be exactly the same as responses of another group tested at either the same time or at a different time, regardless of the extent to which bioassay techniques are standardized". In examining responses of Colorado potato beetle, diamondback moth, and western spruce budworm to three chemical and one microbial pesticides, Robertson *et al.,* concluded that , "Studies of resistance, control of product quality, and tests of treatment efficacy are complicated by variation in response to a pesticide (whether chemical or microbial) that occurs within generations of a particular strain or within cohorts of a population: such variation is a natural phenomenon when any bioassay is repeated". (US Exhibit 11)

[66]   The United States referred, in general, to US Exhibits 7, 8, 9, 10, 16 and 30 as well as US Exhibit 22: Work Plans already in place for the export to Japan of certain varieties of US products.

Heather had further emphasized the robustness of methyl bromide treatment. The United States further claimed that no literature or scientific data supported an inherent variability in the products to indicate that a successful confirmatory test on 30,000 insects would not be uniformly successful for all varieties of the host product. The buffer of treatment used by scientists accounted for the natural variability of the pest and the experimental variability seen in small scale dose-mortality tests. Due to these factors, a confirmatory test would account for the variability in small scale tests and establish a treatment that was appropriate for all varieties of a product.

4.81.   **Japan** claimed that empirical dose-response results confirmed the proposition that varietal differences could affect the mortality effect of MB fumigation. Data which indicated the presence of such statistically significant differences was contained in:

(a)   a 1987 study on American nectarines, in which Summer Grand was found significantly more susceptible to MB fumigation[67],

TABLE 4
Susceptibility of Codling Moth Eggs to MB Fumigation
(2 hours, 21 °C) in 6 Nectarine Varieties (American Nectarines)

Variety	No. of Sample Insects	LD_{50}(95%CL) (g/m^3)
Summer Grand	**2,210**	**6.3 (2.2 - 9.1)**
May Grand	2,458	14.2 (11.1 - 17.0)
Firebrite	1,880	18.8 (14.7 - 22.8)
Spring Red	1,019	17.7 (14.0 - 20.9)
Fantasia	1,548	17.6 (14.0 - 20.0)
Red Diamond	1,445	18.4 (17.1 - 19.8)

---

[67]   Yokoyama, Miller and Hartsell, "Methyl Bromide Fumigation for Quarantine Control of Codling Moth (Lepidoptera: Tortricidae) on Nectarines,"80 J. Econ. Entomol. 840-842, 1987. (US Exhibit 14)

(b) a 1987/88 test on New Zealand cherries in which LD_{50} showed a significantly lower value for Bing than for Rainer and Sam[68], and

<table>
<tr><td colspan="3" align="center">TABLE 5
Susceptibility of 1-day-old Codling Moth Eggs to MB Fumigation
(2 hours, 12°C) in 5 Cherry Varieties (New Zealand Cherries)</td></tr>
<tr><td align="center">Variety</td><td align="center">LD_{50} (95%FL)
(g/m^3)</td><td align="center">LD_{99} (95%FL)
(g/m^3)</td></tr>
<tr><td>Dawson</td><td align="center">33.6 (31.8 - 35.1)</td><td align="center">61.1 (55.9 - 69.8)</td></tr>
<tr><td>Bing</td><td align="center">30.0 (28.9 - 30.9)</td><td align="center">46.8 (44.7 - 49.6)</td></tr>
<tr><td>Rainier</td><td align="center">33.8 (32.1 - 35.3)</td><td align="center">62.2 (57.2 - 70.3)</td></tr>
<tr><td>Sam</td><td align="center">35.4 (33.8 - 36.6)</td><td align="center">52.9 (49.6 - 58.6)</td></tr>
<tr><td>Lambert</td><td align="center">32.3 (29.9 - 34.0)</td><td align="center">52.9 (48.4 - 61.7)</td></tr>
</table>

(c) a 1983/84 study on disinfestation of New Zealand nectarines in which Fantasia showed a significantly lower LD_{50} than Redgold.[69]

<table>
<tr><td colspan="3" align="center">TABLE 6
Susceptibility of 1-day-old Codling Moth Larvae to MB Fumigation
(2 hours at 12°C) (New Zealand Nectarines)</td></tr>
<tr><td align="center">Variety</td><td align="center">LD_{50} (95%FL) (g/m^3)</td><td align="center">LD_{99} (95%FL) (g/m^3)</td></tr>
<tr><td>Fantasia</td><td align="center">10.96 (10.56 - 11.33)</td><td align="center">21.15 (19.82 - 22.93)</td></tr>
<tr><td>Redgold</td><td align="center">12.09 (11.54 - 12.59)</td><td align="center">32.86 (29.83 - 37.12)</td></tr>
</table>

4.82. Japan reaffirmed that it used the results of the dose-mortality test (which was part of the "basic test" paragraph 2.23) in the screening process to select a representative variety.[70]

4.83. Probit analysis[71] typically estimated LD_{50} by measurement of the mortality rate in different doses and regression analysis of the statistically processed data (e.g., probit-conversion). The use of LD_{50} value was justified on the basis of relative accuracy of estimation; the confidence level diminished as the value departed from the 50 per cent. A leading textbook of the analysis stated:

---

[68] Waddell, Birtlex, Dentener and Wearing, "Disinfestation of New Zealand Cherries Cultivar Comparison Test 1987/88", New Zealand. Department of Scientific and Industrial Research, Entomology Division, 1988. (Japan, Exhibit 17)

[69] Batchelor, Wearing, O'Donnel, "Disinfestation of New Zealand Nectarines 1983/1984", 1984. (Japan, Exhibit 18)

[70] Japan claimed that the estimation of LD_{50} by probit analysis was commonly used for evaluation of toxicity of agricultural chemicals or for comparison of tolerance of pests to disinfestation treatment. Japan referred to e.g., OECD Guidelines for Testing of Chemicals, adopted 17 July 1992 (Japan, Exhibit 19) for the use of LD_{50} value to assess toxicity of industrial chemicals; Knowles, C. (1988) J. Econ. Entomol.81;1586-1591 for comparison of LD_{50} values between different insect groups. (Japan, Exhibit 20).

[71] Definition in paragraph 2.14.

> "As will become apparent in later chapters, by experiment with a fixed total number of subjects effective doses in the neighbourhood of ED_{50} [effective dose 50%] can usually be estimated more precisely than those for more extreme percentage levels, and this is characteristic of the stimulus; its chief disadvantage is that, especially in toxicological work, much greater interest may attach to doses producing nearly 100% responses than to those producing only 50%, in spite of the difficulty of estimating the former."[72]

4.84.   The use of the LD_{50} value (estimated on the basis of the dose-mortality test results) in comparing efficacy of insecticide agents was a generally accepted scientific method of analysis. While the United States claimed that the dose-mortality test was effective only for estimating the ultimate quarantine treatment, it was typically utilized for the comparison of susceptibility of developmental stages of the treatment, in developing treatment schedules.[73]

4.85.   Japan noted that the United States had pointed to "experimental error, physical condition of the fruit, sorption of the fumigant by packing material, and load of fruit in the chamber", as well as "natural variation of the test insect population", and claimed that "[t]he condition of any particular fruit could affect dose-response results". The conclusion drawn was that small scale dose-mortality tests were unable to correct for these variations. Of these other exogenous variables, "experimental error, physical condition of the fruit, sorption of the fumigant by packing material, and load of fruit in the chamber" were the factors which scientists who conducted these tests were responsible for controlling and consciously made equal.[74] Indeed Japan noted that scientists endeavoured to set conditions that resembled each other as closely as possible and test insects were taken from artificially reared groups. For example, Yokoyama and other authors of the 1987 experiment on nectarines described in detail conditions of the fumigation chamber, wrapping of fruits, the load factor, time of fumigation, conditions of the codling moth and their rearing, and, from these descriptions, one could recognize that the scientists exerted efforts to ensure as much similarity between test samples. What would *not* be acceptable - if these factors affected the results - was the *data* they generated, and not Japan's hypothesis. In Japan's view, any responsible scientist would have to ensure that such exogenous factors did not falsify the results. It was not scientifically correct to reject a statistical conclusion on the grounds of experimental errors. If there were such exogenous factors as the United States claimed, their presence would mean that it was dangerous to draw any kind of conclusion from the results of such an experiment. None of the experts advising the Panel had concluded that experimental errors explained all of observed differences in the LD_{50} values across varieties.

---

[72]   Probit Analysis (3rd ed.) Finney, D.J. (1971).

[73]   Japan referred to a letter of 9 May 1997 from Robert G. Spade, Assistant Deputy Administrator, PPQ, which stated that: "During the development of quarantine treatment schedules, does-response data is used only to identify the least susceptible life stage of a target insect and to estimate effective treatment dosages". (Japan, Exhibit 34).

[74]   Japan noted that statistical analysis, significance testing in particular, was precisely the tool to correct for experiment error.

4.86.   Japan claimed that another possible explanation for these factors was that they resulted from inevitable sampling error. If this was the case, the US position that confirmatory tests were the relevant indicator would be justifiable. However, Japan noted again that finding ways to alleviate, if not eliminate, problems of this kind belonged to the scientists of the government of exporting countries. Japan claimed that while there were always variables other than varietal differences, this was a statement of truth for any natural phenomenon. It was the responsibility of the exporting government to identify the variables and establish a treatment which would satisfactorily incorporate them so that Japan's level of protection would be achieved despite natural variation. The reason Japan chose to address the issue of varietal difference was because one could reasonably assume the presence of a route by which fruit characteristics of a particular variety might affect the outcome of a disinfestation treatment through their impact on CxT values. On the other hand, it was an established practice to ignore crop-to-crop or other natural variations in fruits or insects. The issue was the level of protection which an importing Member had the authority to choose.

4.87.   In respect of the issue of the "buffer", Japan noted that while the United States claimed that the buffer was likely to cover conceivable varietal differences, the experts advising the Panel had not made any definitive arguments in this regard, nor had the United States explained the scientific grounds for their conviction. The United States seemed to rely intuitively on the past record of the efficacy of the treatment for additional varieties. However, as Dr. Heather had pointed out, this was a question of "risk management". In other words, the risk of inefficacy existed, and the rest was to be determined by the policy of the importing country.

4.88.   Further, in regard to the buffer dose, Japan could not share the view of Dr. Heather and Mr. Taylor who had stated that the 10-20 per cent additional buffer dose might possibly cover the presupposed varietal differences. Japan argued that the buffer dose proposed by the United States had been established on the basis of *laboratory scale* dose-mortality tests. However, conditions for *large-scale commercial application* were different and the effect of gas sorption far from negligible. The amount of gas equivalent to the buffer dose would be sorbed to warehouses and containers. This coupled with inevitable gas leakage could mean the CxT values might be lowered to risky levels. Japan maintained that according to US data, as much as 20 per cent of the methyl bromide dose could be sorbed by picking bins, warehouses and possible leakage. On that basis, Japan could hardly assume that the 10-20 per cent buffer dose would cover possible differences of the magnitude of varietal variations.

(i)   Nectarines

4.89.   According to the **United States**, in the consultations Japan had suggested that a scientific basis for requiring testing for each variety arose from USDA data for the development of an MB quarantine treatment for codling moth in nectarines for export to Japan. The research alluded to by Japan was presented in two articles by American scientists, one in 1987 and the second in 1990. In the first study (1987), dose-mortality tests were conducted on six early- to mid-season varieties of nectarines: May Grand, Fire Brite, Red Diamond, Spring Red, Summer Grand and Fantasia. The test results had shown that the level of methyl bromide estimated to produce

50 per cent mortality in codling moth on Summer Grand was significantly lower than for the remaining five varieties.[75] In 1990, three additional varieties of nectarines were tested (May Diamond, Mayfire and May Glo). The dose-response of these suggested that a lower amount of methyl bromide was necessary to achieve 100 per cent mortality.[76] Nevertheless, the higher dose established in 1987 was used for the confirmatory tests. The United States argued that the principal reason a higher dose had been established in 1987, was because the Summer Grand variety that had "stuck out" in dose-mortality tests in 1987, had also required the highest minimum dose to achieve 100 per cent mortality.

4.90.   In the 1990 study on nectarines, the authors had looked at different insect and fruit interactions to evaluate the necessity for varietal testing. Dose-response data had been obtained for eggs fumigated on different fruit substrates (i.e., different species: nectarines, plums, peaches, apples) as well as eggs on waxed paper inserted into the fumigation chamber with a load of fruit. The authors compared LD_{50} and LD_{95} for codling moth eggs. The scientists found that while there might have been slight apparent numerical differences in codling moth susceptibility to methyl bromide (dose-response) on various substrates, this *did not affect the efficacy* of the quarantine treatment, nor had these differences been anything but natural variations in the response of the test insects. The highest minimum doses tested that caused 100 per cent mortality of codling moth on nectarines, peaches, plums and apples, and waxed paper during dose-mortality tests were well below the 48 g/m^3 methyl bromide that was used in the ultimate quarantine treatment for nectarines established through confirmatory tests. Based on these results, the authors of the study had concluded that testing for efficacy of methyl bromide against codling moth eggs on *every* nectarine cultivar proposed for export to Japan was unnecessary to show the efficacy of the quarantine treatment.[77]

4.91.   The United States claimed that, in consultations, Japan had pointed to the relative susceptibility to methyl bromide of codling moth eggs on Summer Grand and noted differences in the physical characteristics of the fruit as an indicator of significant differences among varieties of the same agricultural product which warranted varietal testing. Yet the United States was of the view that the authors' comment regarding flaws in Summer Grand did not state or imply that these flaws were characteristic of the variety. Because varieties ripen at different times, scientists had only a small window of opportunity to test the quarantine treatment simultaneously on several varieties. Thus idiosyncratic aspects of the physical condition of the specific fruit due to harvest practices, weather conditions, the amount of time one variety may have been stored while waiting for other varieties to be harvested for testing, and other external factors were reflected in the dose-mortality tests. The condition of any particular fruit could affect dose-response results.

---

[75]   *Op. cit.*, pp. 840-842. (US Exhibit 14)

[76]   Yokoyama, Miller and Hartsell, "Evaluation of a Methyl Bromide Quarantine Treatment to Codling Moth (Lepidoptera: Tortricidae) on Nectarine Cultivars Proposed for Export to Japan," 83 J. Econ. Entomol. 466-471, 1990. (US Exhibit 12)

[77]   Yokoyama, Miller and Hartsell, "Evaluation of a Methyl Bromide Quarantine Treatment to Codling Moth (Lepidoptera: Tortricidae) on Nectarine Cultivars Proposed for Export to Japan," 83 J. Econ. Entomol. Pp. 466, 468, 470. (US Exhibit 12).

4.92.   Moreover, although Summer Grand required less methyl bromide than the other varieties to achieve 50 per cent mortality of the test insects, it required more methyl bromide to achieve 100 per cent mortality of the test insects than the other five varieties tested. This apparently contradictory information indicated that the natural variation of the insect, and factors such as experimental error, fruit condition, and factors that could affect the amount of fumigant to which insects are exposed, such as sorption by the packing material and load in the chamber, all played a role in differing dose-response results.[78]

4.93.   It was also significant to note that over the summer of 1997, Vail and Yokoyama had re-tested two varieties of nectarines - May Grand and Summer Grand. In the dose-mortality tests, the level of methyl bromide required to achieve a lethal dose for 50 per cent and 95 per cent of codling moth eggs *did not* differ significantly.[79] This was in contrast to the initial 1987 nectarine study results. The United States argued that these 1997 results confirmed that the differences noted in 1987 were due to natural variation of the insects and other experimental variables. The authors of the 1997 study had stated the "extremely high numbers of insects killed in large-scale confirmatory tests and the virtual non-host status of nectarines attest to the high level of security afforded to this treatment to prevent introduction of codling moth to Japan via nectarine cultivars". In re-testing this variety in 1997, however, results of dose-mortality testing had indicated that the highest minimum dose for Summer Grand was now a dose closer to the six varieties tested in 1990. This indicated that a dose closer to that seen with dose-mortality tests for the 1990 batch might be the more appropriate level of treatment for nectarines.

4.94.   More significantly, the confirmatory test applied in 1987 had established the efficacy of the treatment on *all* nectarines tested. A dose that was 20 per cent greater than the highest minimum dose required for 100 per cent mortality during the dose-mortality testing had been proposed as a quarantine dose for these six varieties.[80] This treatment had proven successful to achieve Japan's level of protection and had been accepted by Japan for all six varieties. As it was the large-scale confirmatory tests at a lower dose had not been done in 1990, because the 1987 results indicated that a higher dose was necessary. Thus confirmatory tests at 48 g/m^3 were completed (which was the dose established in 1987 that was derived from the highest minimum dose believed to achieve Japan's level of protection in the dose-mortality tests with 10-20 per cent added) and showed that this dose was effective for all nectarine varieties. Hence, the United States reaffirmed that confirmatory tests were the only relevant indicator of efficacy of a quarantine treatment. The United States main-

---

[78]   The United States noted that probit model of analysis looked only at the linear relationship between dose and mortality (as stated in US Exhibit 28). There were other, more sophisticated statistical models which included consideration of natural variation of the test insect population. Such a model had been used to re-analyze all varieties in the 1987 and 1990 studies by Yokoyama *et al.*, Taking natural variation into consideration, it had been shown that the LD$_{50}$s among varieties were not significantly different (in Robertson and Yokoyama, "Effect of Nectarine Cultivar on Response of Codling Moth (Lepidoptera: Tortricidae) to Methyl Bromide Fumigation," Unpublished, 1998. (US Exhibit 15))

[79]   Vail and Yokoyama, "Nectarines: The Issue of Varietal Testing", unpublished. (US Exhibit 16)

[80]   MB fumigation at 48 g/m^3 for 2 hours at 21° C or above and 50 per cent or less load.

tained that Japan's claim that variations in dose-mortality tests obtained from two groups of varieties tested three years apart were the result of inherent varietal differences was scientifically invalid. Such a position ignored natural variation in responses of insects, and lack of a common control among tests (i.e., no one variety was tested in both years). Dose-mortality testing would inevitably show natural variability among dose-response results. This did not justify re-establishment of confirmed quarantine treatments for codling moth on a given product.

4.95.   The United States noted that similar findings on different host fruit species and other insect species had been published in Japan; Misumi had investigated quarantine control through MB fumigation of the Japanese mealybug and the citrus mealybug naturally infesting Satsuma mandarins.[81] All stages of the two species of pests were reared on fresh pumpkins as an alternative to Satsuma mandarins because of difficulty in rearing mealybugs on the Satsuma mandarin. The physical and chemical differences between Satsuma mandarins and pumpkin were considerable. Yet despite the use of different host plants, the authors concluded this was of no significance to the efficacy of the fumigation process. Hence, Japanese scientists were willing to accept efficacy of quarantine treatment for a pest as it related to two radically different *products*, pumpkins and mandarins. This experiment supported the position of the United States that requiring exhaustive data on individual varieties of a product was not necessary. The study demonstrated that methyl bromide, when applied at specified concentrations over specified periods of time, killed codling moth in the same way, regardless of variety, and even regardless of substrate.

4.96.   **Japan** recalled that at the time of the *additional* lifting of the ban for the 1990 varieties, even though a dose of 20 g/m^3 had been proven effective to ensure 100 per cent mortality, the United States had chosen to propose 48 g/m^3 as the treatment level.[82] The United States did have the option to propose 20 g/m^3 or 24 g/m^3, adding a "buffer", as the treatment for the additional three varieties. Japan accepted the application of the existing treatment[83] as the on-site confirmatory test had demonstrated its efficacy. This did, however, raise a practical question as to what level of treatment the United States would have proposed had the six varieties (tested in 1987) not been approved initially. It was reasonable to assume that they would *not* have proposed 48 g/m^3, but would have chosen a level around 24 g/m^3 instead. The United States could not argue that "confirmatory tests … showed that this dose (of 48 g/m^3) was effective for all nectarine varieties" (paragraph 4.94). At the most, the United States could argue that this dose was effective for the six varieties tested in 1987, and might be effective for the same varieties in the future.[84] A

---

[81]   Misumi, Kawakami, Mizobuchi and Tao. No. 30 Res. Bull. PL. Prot. Japan 30: 57-68, 1994. (US Exhibit 13, in Japanese)

[82]   Japan noted that the scientists had determined the treatment level of 48 g/m^3 by multiplying the complete mortality dose of 40 g/m^3 by 1.2 times (buffer).

[83]   Paragraph 4.94.

[84]   Japan noted that Robertson (*Op. cit.*, US Exhibit 15) re-analyzed the data on American nectarines (1987 and 1990) by a statistical method developed by the author and concluded that no statistical difference was observed. However, the analysis failed to reject even a 190-times difference of confidence level. Such a wide degree of ambiguity was not acceptable to Japan.

similar problem arose with respect to New Zealand cherries of the Bing variety (from paragraph 4.103).

TABLE 7
Doses which Achieved 100 per cent Mortality of One-day-old Eggs

Year	Varieties	Dose (g/m^3)
1987	**Summer Grand**	40
	May Grand	35
	Firebrite	35
	Spring Red	35
	Fantasia	30
	Red Diamond	30
1990	May Diamond	15.0
	Mayfire	17.5
	May Glo	20.0

4.97.   Japan acknowledged that the issues of natural variation within the same insect group or year-to-year variation of the fruits were scientifically genuine. There would always be variables *other* than varietal differences. The existence of various exogenous variables did not by itself prove that observed differences were *not* attributable to varieties. The task of a scientific demonstration began, not ended, with the discovery of variables. Therefore, Japan had no reason to doubt the 1997 data on two cultivars of nectarines (May Grand and Summer Grand) which indicated, contrary to the 1987 test data, absence of a statistically significant difference between LD values. Explanatory variables other than varietal differences could include natural variation in insects or crops. However, Japan pointed out, once it was assumed that populations were different year-to-year, or case-by-case, any increase in the sample number was pointless, and large-scale confirmatory tests could not predict efficacy of a treatment either, because the confidence in the tests would end at the termination of that particular crop year (for the particular crop population), or with the last individual of that particular group of codling moth (for the particular insect population). This also belied the US claim that "the confirmatory test applied in 1987 established the efficacy of the treatment of *all* nectarines tested" (paragraph 4.94) The United States should have argued that the test did not confirm efficacy of the treatment for any variety in any year except 1987. Alternatively, the United States meant to say that there were unknown exogenous variables which *significantly* affected the results of these studies. However, from a practical point of view, this argument was equally empty; efficacy of a treatment could never be established.
4.98.   Japan noted, in respect of the US reference to the 1987 nectarine study (paragraph 4.89), that the authors had stated that "no differences in egg susceptibility to MB were found among five infested cultivars". Hence, the conclusion had applied only with respect to the *five* varieties out of total of *six* varieties tested. In fact, a difference in efficacy had been found between the last variety (Summer Grand) and the others tested. The authors acknowledged that "[a] comparison of the

LD$_{50}$'s showed that eggs on Summer Grand were significantly (non-overlap of 95 per cent CL) more susceptible to MB fumigation than eggs on other cultivars".[85]

4.99.   In respect of the US reference to the 1990 nectarine study (paragraph 4.90), Japan noted that the authors had stated, "[w]e propose that a c x t product of 68.0±3.0 gh/m^3 methyl bromide ... would be a useful measurement to help maintain treatment security for control of codling moth on all nectarine cultivars".[86] The proposed measurement of the CxT product was the basis for the cited conclusion. However, the present treatment of nectarines did not control the CxT value during the fumigation process. Consequently, its efficacy across all cultivars could not be assumed from the authors' statement.

4.100. In respect of the US reference to the Vail *et al.*, 1997 re-test of Summer Grand and May Grand nectarines (paragraph 4.93), Japan pointed out that the authors had not demonstrated that a "high level of security" was equivalent of Japan's level of protection. Furthermore, the authors had not denied contribution of varietal differences; they had stated "the source of variation cannot be attributed *solely* to cultivar differences". (emphasis added).

4.101. The **United States** refuted Japan's claim that the order in which dose-mortality tests were conducted could result in the establishment of a treatment for one variety that would fail on additional varieties. As it had not been shown that variations in dose-mortality test data reflected underlying varietal differences affecting treatment efficacy, there was no evidence to support this assertion. The 1997 retest of the 1987 Summer Grand nectarine data indicated that the 1987 test results were anomalous. Had the results been in reverse order, there would have been no reason to believe that a treatment based on the lower dosage levels would not have been effective. And had the anomalous 1987 data been too low rather than too high, this would not have resulted in an ineffective quarantine treatment since the confirmatory test on the same variety would have failed. The United States stressed that an ineffective treatment would not be established in the first place, let alone be permitted to remain in place for future varieties. In addition, the United States noted that a confirmatory test could never indicate whether a dose was too high, only if was too low.

4.102. **Japan** noted, in this respect, that the results which the United States now described as "anomalous" were the United States' own test results which had formed the basis for lifting the ban on the importation of the products at issue.

(ii)   Cherries

4.103. **Japan** recalled the conclusion of the authors of a 1987/1988 New Zealand study on cherries:

> "For the range of mortalities that we considered, the relationship between the c x t sum and the injected dose is close to linear, with a non zero constant term that varies between cultivars and between season. Thus, the injected dose that is required to achieve a given mortality

---

[85]   *Supra* note 67, p.841. (US Exhibit 14)
[86]   *Supra* note 76, p.470. (US Exhibit 12)

will vary between cultivars. Factors that may affect the sorption pattern of any one cultivar require further investigation."[87]

4.104. In the case of New Zealand cherries, Japan noted that the same treatment level had been initially established for the Dawson and Bing varieties. When Rainier, Sam and Lambert varieties were additionally approved, test results showed a significantly higher level of efficacy for the Bing variety in comparison to Dawson, Rainier and Sam in terms of non-overlap of 95 per cent confidence intervals of LD_{50} and LD_{99}. As it was, since the treatment level had been set at a level which would ensure effective treatment of Dawson, the less susceptible variety, its efficacy was confirmed for the additional three varieties as well. Similar to the case of nectarines, the data implied a possibility, however, that, had Bing alone been approved initially, the treatment could have been established at a level which would have been found ineffective for Dawson, Rainier or Sam (Table 5, above).

4.105. Hence, Japan argued there were cases where, while the actual treatment levels were not modified, variations did exist to such a degree that different treatment levels could have been proposed depending on the sequence in which the varieties were tested. By no means did this imply that varietal difference did not exist because the same treatment of the pest had been found effective for all approved varieties of the respective products.

4.106. The **United States** pointed out that the authors of the New Zealand study on cherries had concluded that "although the results indicated a higher injected dose when 'Rainier' had been fumigated compared to 'Bing', the large change between seasons in the results for 'Sam' indicated that seasonal differences (perhaps associated with differences in maturity) may have been more important than cultivar"[88] Many factors could have contributed to a variation in Bing in 1987. The authors had noted that "sources of variation that may affect results include the insect material, cherry sorption, and measurement and circulation of methyl bromide within the chambers".[89] For example, Sam cherries had different sorption patterns between 1987 and 1989. Again, the Japanese overlooked the existence of natural variation of the test insects, whether it occurred in the United States or another exporting nation.

4.107. Most significantly, the United States claimed that Japan had also ignored the stated conclusion of the authors that the developed quarantine treatment for cherries was applicable to all cherry varieties. "Where complete kill is the objective, the commercial rate used by cherry exporters is 64 g/m^3, 12° C, 2 hours, and 40% load. *This treatment controls codling moth eggs potentially infesting any of the cultivars considered"*.[90] [emphasis added]. For all season-cultivar combinations, in both

---

[87] Maindonald, Waddell and Birtles, "Response to Methyl Bromide Fumigation of Codling Moth (Lipidoptera: Tortricidae) Eggs on Cherries", New Zealand. J. Econ. Entomol. 85(4): 1220-1230, 1992. (Japan, Exhibit 21 and US Exhibit 4)

[88] Maindonald, Waddell and Birtles, "Response to Methyl Bromide Fumigation of Codling Moth (Lipidoptera: Tortricidae) Eggs on Cherries", New Zealand. J. Econ. Entomol. 85(4): p.1227. (Japan, Exhibit 21 and US Exhibit 4)

[89] Maindonald, Waddell and Birtles, "Response to Methyl Bromide Fumigation of Codling Moth (Lipidoptera: Tortricidae) Eggs on Cherries", New Zealand. J. Econ. Entomol. 85(4): p.1227. (Japan, Exhibit 21 and US Exhibit 4), p.1224.

[90] *Ibid.*, p.1229. (Japan, Exhibit 21 and US Exhibit 4)

years, the highest lethal dose levels of methyl bromide at the LD_{95} had still been at least 10 g/m^3 below the "complete kill" commercial dose used to do the confirmatory test. As the authors further noted in the article abstract: "The commercial treatment thus affords a high level of security". Japan had incorrectly interpreted the significance of these studies and erroneously concluded that the efficacy of treatment could vary within a product.

4.108. The United States argued that there was always a degree of variability in any dose-mortality test from variety to variety and even *within the same fruit variety*. Such variations were the inevitable result of differences in natural conditions and testing environments, from crop to crop and year to year. Japan had already accepted a certain dose-response variability in allowing imports of the varieties that it had already approved. This normal variability in testing results could not constitute a legitimate basis for denying approval for other varieties of the same products. **Japan** maintained that the existence of various exogenous variables did not in itself prove that the observed differences were *not* attributable to varieties.

(c)　CxT Values

4.109. **Japan** claimed that in the specific case of MB fumigation, the link between varietal differences and divergent efficacy of the fumigation treatment could manifest itself by way of the difference in the CxT value.[91] The process could take the following sequence: When MB gas was injected into the fumigation chamber, it would be absorbed by the surface or the pulp of the fruits. If the sorption varied depending on the variety of the fruits, the amount of fumigant remaining in the chamber air would vary in an inverse relationship to the sorption. Then the CxT value, a known indicator to control the degree of efficacy of the treatment[92], would vary as well depending on the variety of the fruit. Japan claimed that it could reasonably be assumed, by ways of the CxT values, that there was a route by which the characteristics of a fruit of particular variety could affect the outcome of disinfestation efficacy.

4.110. Japan claimed that there were three empirical cases which demonstrated a statistically significant difference in the CxT value between tested variety samples, including the case of three cultivars of walnuts the United States referred to in their submission[93]:

---

[91]　Japan noted that in fact, the mode of action of MB treatment on insects was not fully known, and there could be other mechanisms by which varietal differences could affect the efficacy and referred to by Bell *et al.*, (Price and Chakrabarti, "The Methyl Bromide Issue", 1996. (Japan, Exhibit 11))

[92]　Japan noted that E. J. Bond had stated that "[t]he use of integrated c x t products is particularly useful in routine fumigations when the reaction of a particular species or groups of species has been carefully worked out under the range of conditions likely to be encountered. It has been used successfully in large-scale eradication campaign" (Bond, E.J., "Manual of Fumigation for Insect Control", 1984. (Japan, Exhibit 12)).

[93]　Japan noted that in addition, in a test on New Zealand cherries, it had been found that "[g]as chromatograph readings during the fumigations suggested that 'Bing' cherries absorbed less methyl bromide than 'Dawson' cherries", Wearing, Batcholor, Maindonald, "Disinfestation of New Zealand Cherries", Department of Scientific and Industrial Research, 1981. (Japan, Exhibit 13)

(a)   1985 tests on three varieties (Hartley, Payne and Franquett) of American walnuts (1985 Walnut Test Report): CxT values had been significantly different between Franquett (75.7 gh/m^3 at the first replicate; 71.5 gh/ m^3 at the second replicate) and Payne (109.4 gh/m^3, and 99.9 gh/m^3, respectively). [94]

<table>
<tr><td colspan="5" align="center">TABLE 8
Fumigant Concentration and CxT Values for 3 Varieties of
American Walnuts</td></tr>
<tr><td align="center">Variety</td><td align="center">Replicates</td><td colspan="2" align="center">Fumigant Concentration (g/m^3)</td><td align="center">CxT Value
(gh/m^3)</td></tr>
<tr><td></td><td></td><td align="center">Immediately after
Injection of Fumigant</td><td align="center">4 hours after
Injection</td><td></td></tr>
<tr><td>Hartley</td><td align="center">1</td><td align="center">54.0</td><td align="center">16.2</td><td align="center">101.0</td></tr>
<tr><td></td><td align="center">2</td><td align="center">54.1</td><td align="center">15.0</td><td align="center">87.4</td></tr>
<tr><td>Payne</td><td align="center">1</td><td align="center">51.2</td><td align="center">18.9</td><td align="center">109.4</td></tr>
<tr><td></td><td align="center">2</td><td align="center">50.8</td><td align="center">17.5</td><td align="center">99.9</td></tr>
<tr><td>Franquett</td><td align="center">1</td><td align="center">51.3</td><td align="center">12.7</td><td align="center">75.7</td></tr>
<tr><td></td><td align="center">2</td><td align="center">33.7</td><td align="center">12.9</td><td align="center">71.5</td></tr>
</table>

(b)   1988 tests on three varieties (May Glo, Mayfire and May Diamond) of American nectarines: CxT values of May Diamond had showed a statistically significant difference with the other two cultivars for most of the doses. [95]

<table>
<tr><td colspan="5" align="center">TABLE 9
CxT Values of American Nectarine Varieties and Doses
(2 hours, 21°C, 50% Load Factor)</td></tr>
<tr><td align="center">Variety</td><td colspan="4" align="center">CxT Values (gh/m^3±SD) for Fumigant Doses</td></tr>
<tr><td></td><td align="center">48 g/m^3</td><td align="center">64 g/m^3</td><td align="center">96 g/m^3</td><td align="center">128 g/m^3</td></tr>
<tr><td>May Glo</td><td align="center">64.8±0.8</td><td align="center">86.6±1.8</td><td align="center">132.7±5.1</td><td align="center">173.8±7.3</td></tr>
<tr><td>Mayfire</td><td align="center">63.8±1.2</td><td align="center">86.4±3.4</td><td align="center">135.0±4.9</td><td align="center">182.4±10.2</td></tr>
<tr><td>May Diamond</td><td align="center">72.4±4.4</td><td align="center">98.2±8.4</td><td align="center">158.2±7.5</td><td align="center">208.2±9.7</td></tr>
</table>

---

[94]   Vail, Hartsell and Tebbets, "Walnut On-Site Operational (Demonstration) Test Report to Japanese Ministry of Agriculture, Forestry and Fisheries", USDA/ARS, 1985. (Japan, Exhibit 14)
[95]   Vail, "Efficacy of Methyl Bromide for Codling Moth on Nectarines - Consideration of Nectarines as a Product Group", USDA, 1988. (Japan, Exhibit 15)

(c) 1997 tests on three varieties (Fantasia, Flavortop and Shuhou) of Japanese nectarines: There had been a statistically significant difference in CxT values between Shuhou and Fantasia. [96]

TABLE 10

Residual Gas Rate of Fumigant, CxT Value and Fumigant Sorption of Fantasia, Shuhou and Flavortop Nectarine Varieties in MB Fumigation

($48g/m^3$, $20°C$, 2 hours, $0.143t/m^3$ Load Factor)

Variety	Replicates	Weight (kg)	No. of Fruits (Unit)	Residual Gas Rate (%)	CxT values		Sorption (mg/kg)
					gh/m^3	Mean ± SD	
Fantasia	1	4.218	32	68.2	71.1	71.0	133.1
	2	4.213	32	67.1	69.9	±1.1	139.8
	3	4.218	32	68.4	72.0		134.2
Shuhou	**1**	**4.217**	**30**	**69.7**	**66.1**	**66.0**	**146.7**
	2	**4.212**	**30**	**70.3**	**65.9**	**±0.2**	**144.9**
Flavortop	1	4.213	26	69.7	69.8	68.8	136.2
	2	4.216	26	68.4	67.8	±1.4	141.9

4.111. Japan noted that these significant differences were attributable to varieties as the CxT value was affected by physical and chemical properties of the fruits, which were attributable to varietal characteristics. For example, in the case of walnuts, Japan suspected that the differences in the oil content of the walnuts, a qualitative feature of the particular variety, affected the sorption of fumigant and the resulting CxT values. Similarly, the CxT value variation in the 1997 nectarine experiment (third table under paragraph 4.110) was considered attributable to Shuhou's rougher surface, another feature characteristic of the variety, compared to other varieties.

4.112. Japan noted that despite test-to-test variation, statistical analysis using Tukey's multiple range test had found a *statistically significant* difference in the CxT values between Payne and Franquett varieties of walnuts. Statistically speaking, Franquette's CxT value was lower than that of Payne at the confidence level of 95 per cent. Similarly, the same statistical tool had found a significant difference among the nectarine varieties in the second and third experiments set out in paragraph 4.110 above.

4.113. Japan claimed that the study on Satsuma mandarins and pumpkins which the United States had cited (paragraph 4.95) was in fact fully consistent with the present Japanese practice. Japan recalled that the hypothesis underlying the Japanese policy was that varietal differences could be such as would affect sorption of fumigant by the fruits, resulting in different CxT values and hence efficacy of MB fumigation treatment. In the cited experiment, faced with the difficulty of rearing and placing

---

[96] Research Division, Yokoyama Plant Protection Station, "Methyl Bromide Sorption in Nectarine Varieties", unpublished, 1997. (Japan, Exhibit 16)

mealybugs on Satsuma mandarins[97], scientists had chosen to use pumpkins as a proxy for Satsuma mandarins because the CxT values between the two plants were remarkably close. It was incorrect to state that "Japanese scientists were willing to accept efficacy of quarantine treatment for a pest as it related to two radically different products". Quite the contrary, these products were almost identical as far as the crucial factor - the CxT value - was concerned. This experiment by no means undermined the hypothesis relating to the varietal differences.

TABLE 11			
CxT Values for Satsuma Mandarins and Pumpkins[98]			
Subject	**Replicates**	**Load (kg)**	**CxT Value (mgh/l)**
Satsuma	1	1.45	92
Mandarins	2	1.50	92
	3	4.10	98
Pumpkins	1	1.45	94
	2	1.50	93
	3	4.10	95

4.114. The **United States** claimed that minor differences in CxT values between varieties did not indicate differences in varieties of a single product. While CxT values could assist in developing a commercial treatment to kill codling moth, they did not in and of themselves indicate differences in varieties. The difference in CxT could be just as pronounced within the same variety. The experts advising the Panel had not accepted the notion that these differences could be attributed to varietal differences and had furthermore pointed out that, whatever the cause of CxT variation between varieties, these differences had not been observed to affect treatment efficacy.

4.115. Reasons for CxT value variations included (i) minor differences in leakiness of fumigation chambers; (ii) the amount of toxicant taken up by the product or the packaging material; (iii) the amount of product being fumigated (the load); (iv) the accuracy of the various measurements used to calculate the CxT; and, (v) the times at which the concentrations in the chambers were sampled. The United States stressed that CxT values were used by researchers only as a control mechanism for fumigation trials. They were not useful for concluding that there were differences in varieties. In addition, the United States pointed out that the experts advising the Panel had confirmed that test-to-test variation was inevitable in small-scale tests because of natural variations in pest populations, testing equipment and conditions, and product samples. Also, variations within a product were likewise inevitable from season to season, tree to tree and fruit-to-fruit within a variety. The experts

---

[97] Japan noted that it was difficult to rear mealybugs on Satsuma mandarins because, under conditions suitable to the insects, the fruits easily decayed and/or the peel hardened. If one tried to place mealybugs on Satsuma mandarins after rearing them on other fruits, on the other hand, their natural mortality would be very high because of possible damage the insects would suffer upon such placement.

[98] *Supra* note 81, pp.57-68. (US Exhibit 13)

had, according to the United States, in this regard noted that fruit-to-fruit variation could greatly exceed variety-to-variety variation, if any. Variation could also occur because of the difficulty of having different varieties in the same physiological state because of ripening times.

4.116. Importantly, the United States stressed that the experts advising the Panel had made very clear that it was not possible to conclude that that test-to-test variation in CxT values were attributable to varietal differences rather than any of the other sources of variation described.

4.117. In the 1992 New Zealand study on cherries, the CxT values for the Sam variety of cherry varied from one season to the next (paragraph 4.106). Moreover, from the Summer Grand and May Grand varieties of nectarines tested in the Vail *et al.,* 1997 nectarine re-test (paragraph 4.93), it was possible to see that CxT values differed within the same varieties compared to the 1987 nectarine study results. In large-scale US tests of nectarines, it was again evident that there could be as much difference in CxT values within a single variety as among varieties. The difference in CxT value ranges within May Grand nectarines, in 1991, was comparable to the difference between May Grand and Royal Giant nectarines in 1989 and 1991[99] (Table 12 below). The United States noted that in respect of walnuts, the Hartley variety referred to by Japan exhibited a difference in CxT values from one test to the next; this difference was greater than the difference in CxT values between the varieties Hartley and Payne.[100] Hence, in the view of the United States, these results illustrated that there could be any number of reasons why CxT values varied and their variations were not indicative of any varietal characteristics.

<table>
<tr><td colspan="4">TABLE 12
CxT Values From Large-scale Tests on
U.S. Nectarine Varieties in Carton Containers</td></tr>
<tr><td></td><td>1989</td><td>1991</td><td>1992</td></tr>
<tr><td>Royal Giant</td><td>69.6
72.1</td><td></td><td>67.8</td></tr>
<tr><td>May Grand</td><td></td><td>70.8
79.4</td><td></td></tr>
<tr><td>Fantasia</td><td></td><td>73</td><td></td></tr>
</table>

4.118. In respect of walnuts, the United States noted that Japan had pointed to the results of the 1985 Walnut Research Report[101] to assert that a difference in CxT values in dose-mortality tests applied to varieties of fruits supported the need for varietal testing. Again, the United States claimed that test-to-test variation of *one*

---

[99] Yokoyama, Miller, and Hartsell, "Methyl bromide efficacy and residues in large-scale quarantine tests to control Codling moth (Lepidoptera: Tortricidae) on nectarines in field bins and shipping containers for export to Japan". 87 J. Econ. Entomol. 730-735, 1994. (US Exhibit 36)

[100] US Exhibit 31.

[101] Vail, Nelson, Hartsell and Tebbetts. "Development of a Quarantine Treatment for the Codling Moth in Walnuts for Export to Japan. (Not published in a scientific journal). Walnut Research Report 1985. Walnut Marketing Board, Sacramento, CA., pp.149-154. (US Exhibit 17)

variety had been as great as that found among all three tested varieties of walnuts.[102] CxT values were an indication of how much toxicant was available to the target insect. Regardless of the observed differences in the CxT values, there was no difference in the efficacy of the quarantine treatment for the three varieties of walnuts. Japan approved the methods and data generated during these studies and had not requested different quarantine schedules for the three varieties.[103] In this respect, the United States noted that in bilateral talks in March 1997, the parties had discussed the Japanese decision not to allow import of the walnut variety Eureka due to perceived differences in sorption of methyl bromide. In fact, Japan had refused importation because, although its de-sorption rate had not been significantly different, Eureka had consistently higher residues, likely attributable to higher natural oil content (that would retain the methyl bromide), as compared with other varieties of walnuts.[104] Concerns over methyl bromide residues were exclusively related to food safety and had nothing to do with the efficacy of the quarantine treatment. The United States insisted that perceived differences in de-sorption rates (rate at which fumigant leaves a product) did not indicate varietal differences with respect to quarantine protection. Although Eureka had consistently higher residues than the other three varieties tested, these differences had not been statistically significant and had not affected treatment efficacy. In fact, preliminary tests showed that there was no survival of test larvae in any of the varieties treated. The authors of the 1991 report on the 1985 tests on walnuts, had stated that "no significant differences were found in mortality of larvae among the four walnut cultivars tested, nor was variation in the size of walnuts of each cultivar a significant factor".[105] At the second substantive meeting of the Panel, the United States submitted an article which clarified that oil content in walnuts did not vary by variety.[106] Hence, even if sorption was affected by oil content, there was no basis for concluding that this varied by variety.

4.119. The United States pointed at the Japanese admission that for apples, cherries, nectarines and walnuts, there was no disagreement as to the efficacy of the treatment as applied to the approved varieties (paragraph 4.6). The United States claimed that implicit in this acknowledgement was a recognition that there would be variations in the preliminary dose-mortality testing and these differences did not alter the final quarantine treatment. These variations were evident in the test results of these ap-

---

[102]   Vail, Nelson, Hartsell and Tebbetts. "Development of a Quarantine Treatment for the Codling Moth in Walnuts for Export to Japan. (Not published in a scientific journal). Walnut Research Report 1985. Walnut Marketing Board, Sacramento, CA., p.150. (US Exhibit 17)

[103]   The United States recalled that the uniform treatment for walnuts was $56g/m^3$ methyl bromide fumigation for 4 hours at 15.6° C at 100mm HG, and a load factor of less than 50 per cent.

[104]   Hartsell, Tebbets, and Vail, "Methyl Bromide Residues and Desorption Rates from Unshelled Walnuts Fumigated with a Quarantine Treatment for Codling Moth (Lepidoptera: Tortricidae)" 84 J. Econ. Entomol. pp. 1294-1297, 1991. (US Exhibit 18)

[105]   Hartsell, Vail, Tebbets and Nelson. "Methyl Bromide Quarantine Treatment for Codling Moth (Lepidoptera: Tortricidae) in Unshelled Walnuts", 84 J. Econ. Entomol. pp. 1289-1293, 1991. (US Exhibit 19)

[106]   Greve, McGranahan, Hasey, Soder, Kelly, Glodhammer and Labavitch, "Variation in Polyunsaturated Fatty Acids Composition of Persian Walnut", Department of Pomology, University of California, USA , J. Amer. Soc. Hort. Sci 117(3):518-522, 1992. (US Exhibit 40)

proved varieties. Japan's recognition acknowledged that CxT values could vary, but that they were not relevant in reaching efficacy (in killing the required amount of codling moth). To suggest that the variations of data in dose-mortality testing on its own represented differences in varieties was inconsistent with this concession on the part of Japan.

4.120. Moreover, the United States claimed that CxT was not an indicator of *likeness* among varieties or products. In reference to Satsuma mandarins and pumpkins Japan had asserted that it was within reason to accept treatment for a pest on two different products so long as the two products had identical CxT values (paragraph 4.113). This ignored all other physical aspects of the product such as size, as well as what biological stage of the pest would interact with a product. The United States recalled that the CxT value measured the amount of fumigant outside of a product in a fumigant chamber. Yet codling moth was not only on the outside of nectarines. The pest actually burrowed into apples, cherries and walnuts. CxT was silent on the way the fumigant interacted with the pest *inside* the product. If CxT were the standard of efficacy, then treatments would be developed that were ineffective in addressing the stage of pest, where the pest was located on the product, and the obvious differences among products that necessitate different treatments. Irrespective of what accounted for differences in CxT values, it had to be remembered that these values were merely tools in estimating and establishing a treatment level that resulted in mortality. Treatment efficacy did not rely on CxT values. It relied on the ability to kill the required level of pests.

4.121. Finally, the United States claimed that Japan had, in attempting to justify its theory, mischaracterized the meaning of the article by E.J. Bond that it cited (footnote 92 to paragraph 4.109). While Japan seemed to be suggesting that Bond linked CxT values to variety of the product and differences among those varieties, he was in fact discussing CxT values as they related to the pest, and specifically the role of CxT values as a tool to observe the interaction of the fumigant and the pest. The Bond article did not suggest that differences in CxT indicated differences in variety.[107]

4.122. In addition, the United States noted that Japan had stated that the method it used to test the statistical significance of walnut data was "Tukey's multiple range test". However, tests such as Tukey's were based on an analysis of variance. In order to be used correctly, several assumptions had to be met, among them the requirement that samples used in replicates had to be randomly and independently selected and the requirement that the variances of the different samples were homogeneous. Tukey's test was not relevant to an analysis of the walnut data Japan examined[108] because this data failed to meet both assumptions. For each of the varieties listed in Table 8 (page 364), the walnuts used in each "replicate" were taken from the same batch of walnuts. The samples were thus not independently selected, and it was inaccurate to describe the test on each variety as "replicates". Second, the variances of the data for each variety were not homogeneous.[109] Finally, the United States pointed to the observation of the experts advising the panel that even if Japan had demonstrated "statistically significant"

---

[107] Bond 1994, p.25. (Japan, Exhibit 12)
[108] In paragraph 81 of Japan's first submission.
[109] US Exhibit 39.

differences in CxT, such differences would not necessarily have been a reflection of significant biological differences which could affect efficacy.

4.123. In sum, CxT values did not indicate differences among varieties. Those differences were just as pronounced *within* varieties. The United States claimed that Japan implicitly had to have understood this conclusion since it did not require different quarantine treatments or testing for the same variety despite differences in CxT values within varieties.

4.124. **Japan** contended that among the exogenous factors to which the United States attributed the differences in varieties (as set out in paragraph 4.115), the load factor had been controlled in the second and third of the three empirical cases described in paragraph 4.110 above. Other factors, such as leakiness of fumigation chambers or the measurement error, called for further empirical confirmation. They by no means vindicated the US position that varietal differences were irrelevant to the statistically significant differences in CxT values. In addition, the factor of "the amount of toxicant taken up by the product", which the United States admitted affected the variation in CxT values, was exactly what Japan believed was a key determinant of the values which could be attributable to varietal differences. Japan contended that even though codling moth larvae burrowed into the pulp from the exterior of the fruit, it respired the surrounding, fumigated air. It was therefore reasonable to assume that that CxT was indicative of some interaction with the fumigant.

4.125. In respect of the US argument in paragraph 4.117, regarding the 1992 New Zealand study on cherries, Japan noted that the cited results indicated possible interaction of variables, and by no means proved the absence of a link between a significant difference of CxT values and varietal differences. Japan reiterated that it was the scientists' responsibility to identify variables, account for them and devise ways to alleviate statistical problems, unless one were to discard the CxT value in phytosanitary experiments.[110] After all the efforts to discredit the statistical significance of variation of the CxT values, the United States had nevertheless admitted that they had value as "tools in estimating and establishing a treatment level that results in mortality" (paragraph 4.120). If the values could vary for "any number of reasons", and if scientists were incapable of controlling these reasons, Japan failed to understand how the values could "estimate" or "establish" any parameter.

4.126. Furthermore, in respect of the same study, Japan noted that the authors' conclusion applied only to the *five* varieties tested for efficacy confirmation: "[b]ecause the five cultivars of cherry that we considered have different sorption patterns, different injected doses are required to achieve a given level of mortality. ... Where complete kill is the objective, the commercial rate used by cherry exporters is 64 g/m^3, 12 C, 2 hours, and 40 per cent load. This treatment controls codling moth eggs potentially infesting any of the cultivars considered".[111] Japan stressed that the authors had, in fact, acknowledged the presence of varietal difference; for they had stated: "We found differences in sorption of methyl bromide between cultivars and

---

[110] In this respect, Japan noted that it was puzzled by the small number of samples in the 1997 retest (30 individuals compared to 160 in 1987).

[111] *Op. cit.*, p.1229. (Japan, Exhibit 21 and US Exhibit 4)

between seasons"[112] and, "For the range of mortalities that we considered, the relationship between the c x t sum and the injected dose is close to linear, with a non zero constant term that varies between cultivars and between season. Factors that may affect the sorption pattern of any one cultivar require further investigation." [113] Japan reiterated that with regard to nectarines, the same authors had suggested that the CxT value "would be a useful measurement to help maintain treatment security for control of codling moth on all nectarine cultivars".[114]

4.127. With regard to walnuts, the reason why Japan did not request different quarantine schedules for the three varieties was because, under the concept of a representative variety discussed before, Japan had accepted the large-scale efficacy data on Hartley and found that the proposed treatment would disinfest codling moth to the satisfactory level. It was not because varietal differences were irrelevant.

4.128. Japan noted, in respect of the US citation of the Hartsell *et al.*, 1991 walnut study on MB treatment (paragraph 4.118), that the study did not include comparative tests of varieties and the cited conclusion was drawn from the result of 100 per cent mortality which was achieved for all varieties stored in the same fumigation chamber at the same time. Absence of varietal differences could not be proved under such conditions. In fact, in a preliminary study it was stated the "[t]here were no significant differences due to cultivar except Eureka, which had higher residue at all three temperatures tested and is indicative of the higher oil content found in this cultivar", and that "[a]ll cultivars desorb MB at about the same rate with the exception of Eureka which due to its higher oil content has a slightly longer retention time".[115] Japan had concluded from these results that the Eureka variety tended to retain MB at a higher level due to its oil content and could show differences in efficacy, and that further comparative tests would be needed on the variety. In the end, the United States had dropped the Eureka variety from the request for approval, and import prohibition was lifted for the other three varieties in 1986. Japan stressed that the issue of MB residue in Eureka was not related to concern over food safety.

4.129. With regard to Bond's study (paragraph 4.121), Japan had cited an authoritative view on the utility of the CxT value as an indicator of efficacy of fumigation. The Japanese argument was simply that if CxT value varied depending on the variety, efficacy of a treatment might vary according to varieties.

4.130. The **United States** maintained that Japan had misinterpreted the scientific data. Japan was alleging that the primary basis for its assumption (that variety mattered) was that differences in CxT values meant that there were differences in sorption between varieties that affected efficacy of treatment. The fact that CxT values had been observed to be different in tests involving different varieties appeared to be the sole basis of Japan's theory that variety mattered. Yet the experts advising the Panel had stated that there was no evidence to support Japan's suggestion that sorption differences had been shown to be large enough to affect treatment efficacy. Such differences, would, in their expert opinion, have to be "significant" or "large" in order to create sorption dif-

---

[112] *Op. cit.*, p.1222. (Japan, Exhibit 21 and US Exhibit 4)
[113] *Ibid.*, Discussion, p.1228. (Japan, Exhibit 21 and US Exhibit 4)
[114] *Supra* note 76, p.470. (US Exhibit 12)
[115] *Supra* note 101, p.107. (US Exhibit 17)

ferences of sufficient magnitude to affect treatment efficacy. Furthermore, Dr. Ducom had emphasized that there was a lack of precise studies on factors contributing to differences in sorption levels and that the "notion of CxT has not been studied enough". In respect of sorption and apples, the United States pointed out that Dr. Heather had explained that while sorption might have an impact on MB treatment, it would have no impact on cold treatment. Thus, there were no grounds to even speculate that sorption differences among apples could affect treatment efficacy.

4.131. Moreover, the United States noted that, according to Dr. Ducom, if Japan were serious about developing sufficient scientific evidence to support its theory that CxT variations might be related to varietal differences affecting treatment efficacy, Japan could conduct specific studies on the matter. Yet no effort had been undertaken in this respect. In fact, Japan had not put its own theory into practice. In regard to those products that Japan indicated exhibited differences in CxT values (nectarines and walnuts), the fact remained that Japan had never attempted to confirm its hypothesis, to explore *why* CxT values varied, or to link differences in CxT values with differences in products. In regard to other products subject to this measure (apples, apricots, cherries, pears, peaches, plums and quince) Japan had not made any such observations or assertions regarding variations in CxT. Therefore, presumably there was no basis for applying its measure *a priori* to these products.

4.132. The United States reiterated that the measure of efficacy was not CxT values, but whether the exporting country could eliminate the pest of concern at a sufficient rate to achieve Japan's level of phytosanitary protection. Differences in CxT values were the result of "real world" variables typically seen in testing procedures and did not indicate that varietal differences affected the efficacy of quarantine treatment. Under the SPS Agreement, Japan was required to have a scientific basis for its assumption that variety did matter, but its embrace of CxT values as the basis of such a theory fell short of that responsibility.

4.133. The United States claimed that if Japan truly believed that CxT values were the indicator of efficacy, there would be no need to show that the dose of fumigant resulted in a particular level of mortality of the pest. Yet the ability of the United States to gain access for a variety of fruit into Japan depended upon its ability to show that the requisite amount of codling moth had been killed. CxT values could vary from Payne walnuts to Franquette walnuts, but the MB treatment was the same because that treatment killed codling moth uniformly in both varieties. There could be differences in CxT values between May Glo and May Diamond nectarines, but the MB treatment was identical for these two varieties because that treatment killed the codling moth uniformly. It was evident that CxT was not a direct indicator of efficacy of treatment. The indicator of efficacy of quarantine treatment was the ability to uniformly achieve the required level of mortality of codling moth. In every instance, regardless of CxT values, and regardless of variety, the level of phytosanitary protection required by Japan had been achieved with a treatment that was uniform for all varieties of a product.

4.134. The United States also noted that the arbitrary manner in which the measure was applied further called into question its scientific basis. As Japan had explained it, if an exporting country had ten varieties of a commodity available for export, a so-called representative variety could be used in a confirmatory test. Yet if those same ten varieties were proposed in sets of five over two different years, a confirmatory test that previously would have sufficed for all ten varieties had now to be applied twice. There was no logic to this application. Moreover, the United States noted that Dr. Heather had pointed out that if one were to accept that dose-response tests could be used to establish varietal differences, why then would it be necessary to follow-up these tests on newly tested varieties with a confirmatory test?

4.135. **Japan** noted that it had never claimed that varietal differences *always* resulted in differences in CxT values. What was argued was that there existed studies which detected a statistically significant difference of CxT values between varieties. Furthermore, replication-to-replication variation was in itself irrelevant; testing in replicates was exactly for the purpose of eliminating experimental bias. Presence of replication-to-replication variation by no means impaired the utility of the CxT value as an indicator of varietal difference. Japan pointed out that Dr. Ducom had endorsed the presence of the link between varietal differences and differences in the CxT value. In any event, it was the United States' responsibility to identify relevant variables which they claimed existed and establish a treatment which would satisfactorily incorporate them so that Japan's level of protection would be achieved despite such variations.

(d)   Comparison with Other Products

4.136. **Japan** noted that while the main focus of the dispute at issue related to fumigation, there were cases where certain differences in efficacy of thermal treatment between different varieties were observed. Japan recalled that the United States had established standards which treated mango varieties differently for hot water treatments.[116] The immersion time was set differently according to varieties with physical differences (the size and shape) of the mango. The treatment time was shorter for fruits with a flat and long shape, or for smaller fruits.

4.137. Japan did not doubt that the United States had a genuine reason to differentiate the varieties as they related to physical characteristics of the fruits, in light of their impact on the efficacy of the treatment. Under the same logic, Japan's policy of differentiating varieties was justifiable as they related to physical/chemical characteristics of the fruits, which might impact on efficacy of treatment. Moreover, in 1993, when additional varieties of Thai mangoes (Nam Dokmai, Rad and Pimsen Daeng) were investigated, Japan had found by a mortality comparison that the existing vapor heat treatment (46.5° Celsius for 10 minutes, developed for the Nang Klamguan variety) was not sufficient. This resulted in a new vapour heat treatment (the temperature to be raised by a fixed rate to 43 degrees Celsius and held at over 47 degrees for 20 minutes).[117]

4.138. Japan noted that other countries also considered varietal differences in their design of quarantine treatment. According to a Japanese survey, in addition to the Republic of Korea, both Canada and Australia considered relevant issues surrounding varietal differences. Japan noted that Australia had indicated in a communication to Japan that when new varieties were proposed for approval into Australia, their "likely procedure would involve re-evaluation of the relevant pest risk analysis (PRA)," and that "[t]he PRA process would consider any relevant technical infor-

---

[116]   PPQ Treatment Manual. (Japan, Exhibit 22)

[117]   Unahawutti, U. *et al.*, Unpublished, 1991. (Japan, Exhibit 23)

mation on varietal differences". Hence, contrary to the United States' assertion, Australia would perceive the risk of varietal differences and act accordingly.[118] In the case of New Zealand, the authorities' manual for development of fruit fly disinfestation treatment stated:

> "A disinfestation treatment may need to be developed for each variety of fruit separately. While a variety may be described formally in the procurement of proprietary rights, where a variety is not formally described or where varieties can be shown to be morphologically and physiologically similar, definition of the distinctive fruit types must be provided (for example, ovoid eggplant as opposed to oblong eggplant, or long green chili as opposed to small yellow chili)."[119]

4.139. The **United States** noted that Japan, in referring to thermal treatments as used on mangoes from Thailand, was attempting to infer that the US practice of treatment for mangoes made distinctions based on variety; this was distorting the scope of the dispute by introducing alternative treatments which were not within its scope. It was clear to the United States that the scope of the dispute related to products that could be host to codling moth and for which the quarantine treatment of methyl bromide or methyl bromide and cold storage was used.

4.140. Nevertheless, the United States was compelled to rebut the assertion made by Japan that the United States differentiated quarantine treatment for pests on a variety-by-variety basis. US scientists were aware that such objective morphological characteristics as fruit size and shape, irrespective of variety, were important parameters in determining the schedule for heat treatments. The treatment schedule for mangoes in the United States was not by variety but by size and shape, which could vary within the same variety. As Dr. Heather had noted, size and shape of the fruit "are a varietal characteristic but not exclusively so". The larger or rounder the fruit, the longer it took to heat the fruit to the centre. Thus the heating rate for fruit that was small or flat was much faster than for fruit that was large or round. This was evident from the heat treatment schedules for mangoes found in the APHIS Plant Protection and Quarantine Treatment Manual.[120] Moreover, the United States did not require testing of new mango varieties, but assigned a treatment based on the size and shape of the proposed import variety. Furthermore, the United States noted that the experts advising the Panel had stated that reactions of different products to different treatments "have nothing to do with each other" and that fumigation bore little relationship to other treatments.[121] It was therefore not relevant to compare thermal treatment on mangoes with fumigation on the products at issue.

4.141. The United States also noted that Japan had indicated that Canada, Australia and New Zealand all took into account varietal differences in quarantine treatments. Recent communications with these countries clearly refuted this assertion:

---

[118] Japan, Exhibit 38.

[119] MAF, Regulatory Authority Standard., paragraph 3.2.1. (Japan, Exhibit 24)

[120] United States Department of Agriculture, Animal and Plant Inspection Service, Treatment Manual, V.2, pp. 5.45 - 5.58. (US Exhibit 32)

[121] See Section VI of this report, Question 15.

(a)   Australia had indicated in a communication with the United States, that it did not require assessments by variety for fumigation quarantine treatments.[122] In respect of the letter from Australia referred to in paragraph 4.138 above[123], the United States emphasized that Australia did not require varietal testing nor did Australia apply different quarantine treatments based on variety. The letter in fact indicated that Australia had not prejudged the need for a varietal testing requirement, that it would examine "any relevant scientific or technical information on varietal differences" in deciding whether to extend existing treatments to additional varieties. The United States maintained that the experts had confirmed that there was no scientific evidence that varietal differences affected efficacy.

(b)   The Government of New Zealand had similarly confirmed that it did not differentiate between varieties of a product[124]; moreover, the "MAF Regulatory Authority Standard 155.02.03 Specification for the Determination of Fruit Fly Disinfestation Treatment Efficacy" addressed the possibility of a statement of varieties for dimethoate dip treatments for fruit fly in tomatoes.[125] All other fruit fly treatments were determined on a species basis.

(c)   The Government of Canada, in a communication dated 17 April 1998, had confirmed that it did not require testing by variety for quarantine treatments.[126]

Hence, in sum, none of these countries required varietal testing for quarantine treatments.

4.142. In respect of Australia ((a) above), **Japan** restated that contrary to the United States' assertion, Australia also considered varietal differences in their design of quarantine treatment and would act accordingly (paragraph 4.138). Japan refuted the US statement that the treatment schedule for mangoes was not by variety. Clearly the US schedule referred to varieties. If, as the United States implied, a "flat, elongated" variety such as Frances was sometimes treated as a "rounded" variety, an almost insurmountable administrative problem would arise. It appeared impractical to implement the schedule without a predetermination of the treatment on a varietal basis. Although this schedule was for hot water treatment and not MB fumigation, it did show that concern over varietal difference was quite common.

3.   Article 5.1

4.143. The **United States** recalled that Article 5.1 of the SPS Agreement required WTO Members to "ensure that their sanitary or phytosanitary measures were based

---

[122]   Letter to Ms. Audrae Erickson from Mr. Paul Morris, dated 20 April 1998. (US Exhibit 33)
[123]   Letter to Mr. Takeo Kocha from Mr. Christopher W. Wood, dated 18 June 1998. (Japan, Exhibit 38)
[124]   Letter to Ms. Audrae Erickson from Mr. Tony Pautua, dated 9 April 1998. (US Exhibit 34)
[125]   Dated 22 November 1994. (Japan, Exhibit 24)
[126]   Letter to Ms. Audrae Erickson from Dr. J.E. Hollebone, dated 17 April 1998. (US Exhibit 35)

on an assessment, as appropriate to the circumstances, of the risks to human, animal or plant life or health, taking into account risk assessment techniques developed by the relevant international organizations".

4.144. The United States noted that in bilateral consultations, Japan had asserted that it had conducted a risk assessment according to the procedures set out in the FAO PRA Guidelines (these procedures are described in paragraphs 2.29 and below).[127] The document provided to the United States subsequent to the consultations, however, did not support this assertion. In the view of the United States, Japan had not followed the FAO guidelines.[128] The document which Japan described as a "risk assessment" merely asserted that codling moth was a pest of quarantine significance.[129] This was not in dispute. What was in dispute was whether *the measure* taken by Japan to ensure its level of protection was based on scientific principles, maintained with sufficient scientific evidence, and *based on an assessment of risk*. On this point, the Japanese document was silent. In other words, Japan's consideration of factors such as the ability of the pest to survive in Japan's climate, the biology of the moth as it related to crop seasons in Japan, the ability of the pest, once it had entered Japan, to infest and harm crops, or, the costs of such harm - were *only* relevant to the determination that codling moth was a quarantine pest. It was the practice of lifting the import ban only upon a showing that the same quarantine treatment was effective for every variety of a product that was the phytosanitary measure at issue. The United States had seen no assessment of that measure.

4.145. **Japan** argued that it had conducted a full-scale risk assessment in 1996 to ensure that current plant quarantine measures, and import prohibition in particular, were scientifically justified. This risk assessment was fully consistent with the PRA Guidelines established by the FAO. In this process, Japan had evaluated the "likelihood or entry, establishment or spread of a pest ... within the territory ... according to the ... phytosanitary measures which might be applied, and of the associated potential biological and economic consequences..." (SPS Agreement, Annex A, paragraph 4) Furthermore, Japan stressed that an individual risk assessment of a particular plant was performed whenever an exporting government requested the lifting of an import prohibition of the product, or other modification of quarantine measures.

4.146. The immediate impetus for the full-scale risk assessment had come in 1995, when the FAO adopted the PRA Guidelines. In this risk analysis, Japan's objective had been to identify particularly dangerous pests which might not be countered by the normal screening process and which were likely to cause serious damage, and to effectively prevent their introduction by means of import prohibition or otherwise. In order to ensure objectivity of the analysis, Japan had sought advice on the selection of relevant factors and the pest risk assessment procedure from 28 researchers belonging to various national laboratories. Further professional input to the draft

---

[127] Japan's response to Question 3 of US Consultation Questions. (US Exhibit 3)

[128] The United States noted that reference to the FAO Guidelines was not intended to establish a particular risk assessment framework, nor did it imply that failure to comply with the FAO guidelines necessarily constituted a violation of the SPS Agreement.

[129] Japan, Exhibit 9.

procedure was given by an Expert Committee in June and September 1996. The committee advised on the standards by which phytosanitary measures were chosen according to the level of the risk. This advice and internal review resulted in a numerical evaluation standard. The 12 members of the expert committee were those recommended by the Japanese Society of Applied Entomology[130] and Zoology and the Phytopathological Society of Japan (six experts in entomology and nematology and six experts in plant pathology).

4.147. Following the procedure developed with academic input, Japan identified 117 species of agricultural/forestry pests on the basis of documentary evidence as those which could cause a serious damage once they were introduced into the Japanese territory, and analyzed the risk of each of them. Through this process, the 15 quarantine pests, including codling moth, were found not to be adequately detectable by the normal inspection procedure. Japan therefore decided to maintain an import prohibition on host plants of these pests. Furthermore, Japan concluded that ten quarantine pests were detectable by growing-site inspection of the government by the exporting country.[131] While their risk of introduction and damage was comparable to that of the 15 species, as from April 1998, host plants of these pests were allowed to be imported into Japan subject to completion of the growing-site inspection.

4.148. With regard to codling moth, Japan described the 3-stage process as follows: **Stage 1** of the analysis consisted of the re-evaluation of 117 specific pests, initiated in 1996. In terms of the PRA Guidelines, the initiation was justified as the result of "[a] policy decision ... to revise phytosanitary regulations or requirements concerning specific pests".[132]

4.149. In **Stage 2**, Japan developed a relative, numerical evaluation standard which graded pests from "a" (high) to "c" (low), and assessed each factor of the analysis according to the standard. Valuation was objectively based on Japanese and foreign literature.

4.150. First, the guidelines required an assessment of the pest's establishment potential in light of biological suitability of the PRA area and a pest's survival capability. In light of the Japanese environmental conditions and the abundance of host plants, as well as known characteristics of the codling moth, Japan's analysis found that codling moth had a grade "a" establishment potential.

4.151. Second, in respect of the spread potential, the Guidelines required an assessment of possible spread in light of biological factors such as suitability of the natural and/or managed environment for natural spread of the pest, movement with products or conveyances, or potential natural enemies of the pest in the PRA. In the present case, codling moth showed a relatively low reproductive capacity and was graded "b" in terms of spread potential.

---

[130] Entomology: the study of insects.

[131] (i) Sugar beet nematode; (ii) false root-knot nematode; (iii) banana burrowing nematode; (iv) Fusarium wilt of pea; (v) bacterial wilt of beans; (vi) watermelon bacterial fruit blotch; (vii) Stewart's wilt; (viii) Goss's bacterial wilt and blight; (ix) broad bean stain virus and (x) broad bean true mosaic virus.

[132] PRA Guidelines, Item 8, paragraph 1.2.

4.152. Third, the PRA Guidelines required consideration of factors affecting economic consequences of the pest introduction and spread. In this analysis, type of damage, crop losses, loss of export markets, increases in control costs, environmental damage, or perceived social costs such as unemployment were incorporated in the Japanese analysis of pests. Host plants (apples, cherries and other fruits) of the insect were produced in great quantity in Japan. The potential substantial damages led Japan to conclude that the insect was graded "a" in terms of economic importance.

4.153. Factors which affected the introduction potential were enumerated in the "partial checklist" in paragraph 2.3 of the PRA Guidelines.[133] Codling moth was capable of surviving the transportation stage, hidden inside the fruits which would be imported in large quantities. Factors affecting establishment (e.g., number and frequency of consignments of the product, intended use of the product) had to also be considered.[134] In respect of these factors, codling moth ranked high, and grade "a" was given to the insect.

<table>
<tr><td colspan="2" align="center">TABLE 13
Overall Risk Grading of Pests Based on the Score of Grades</td></tr>
<tr><td align="center">Score of Grades in Stage 2 Analysis</td><td align="center">Overall Risk Grading</td></tr>
<tr><td>a for "potential economic importance" and at least two a's for the other potentials</td><td>A (very high risk)</td></tr>
<tr><td>At least one a</td><td>B (high risk)</td></tr>
<tr><td>No a</td><td>C (low risk)</td></tr>
<tr><td>All c's</td><td>D (very low risk)</td></tr>
</table>

4.154. In summary, as outlined above in respect of the Stage 2 analysis, codling moth was graded "b" in terms of spread potential after establishment, but was given grade "a" in the rest of the Stage 2 analysis. Subsequently, Japan performed overall grading of the risk the pest posed and found that the insect's overall risk was grade "A" (very high risk). It thus met the requirement of a quarantine pest under this stage of the analysis, and Japan decided to proceed to Stage 3.

4.155. Under **Stage 3** of the PRA Guidelines, pest risk management entailed the task of choosing appropriate phytosanitary measures against quarantine pests identified through the Stage 2 analysis. Possible phytosanitary measures were enumerated in paragraph 3.1 of the Guidelines. Notably, the Japanese inspection process, disinfection/disinfestation or import prohibition defined under the Plant Protection Law all appeared in the menu of options under the PRA Guidelines (paragraph 2.30).

---

[133] The factors are: (i) opportunity for contamination of products or conveyances by the pest; (ii) survival of the pest under the environmental conditions of transport; (iii) ease or difficulty of detecting the pest at entry inspection; (iv) frequency and quantity of pest movement into the PRA area by natural means, and (v) frequency and number of persons entering from another country at any given port of entry.

[134] The checklist further enumerated: (i) number of individuals of a given pest associated with the means of conveyance; (ii) intended use of the product and (iii) environmental conditions and availability of hosts at the destination and during transport in the PRA area.

4.156. The choice of an appropriate phytosanitary measure (or measures) was based on efficacy and impact of these options, and, for this purpose, paragraph 3.2 of the PRA Guidelines identified 9 factors which were relevant to the efficacy and impact, and required that these be considered in the policy choice (paragraph 2.32). In order to incorporate these factors in an operational model, Japan first developed a standard decision tree of five questions to evaluate the degree of difficulty (or ease) in managing the risk of the pest, with the results expressed in five levels from A1 to C.

4.157. These assigned levels reflecting the degree of difficulty (or ease) in managing the risk of the pest were then combined with the grades of overall risk (A to D) determined by Stage 2. Resulting combinations, which appeared in the left two columns of the Table 14 below were linked to specific risk management measures in the right column, in order to prevent the pest's introduction into the Japanese territory.

4.158. In the case of codling moth, Japan recalled that newly hatched larvae were known to enter into fruits, and it was virtually impossible to detect these larvae by normal visual means. Growing-site inspection was equally ineffective because the insect penetrated the products in the post-harvest stage. Finally, post-entry inspection was impractical because it would destroy the product's commercial value. Thus the insect was classified in "LEVEL A1" according to the decision tree.

4.159. Under the PRA (Stage 2) and the study of management options (Stage 3), the overall risk of the codling moth was evaluated to be A (very high risk), and the level of difficulty of management was in the highest bracket, A1. Japan found it to be impossible to properly manage the risk of the pest by means other than import prohibition, and decided to maintain the measure.

TABLE 14
Choice of Appropriate Phytosanitary Measures Based on Overall
Risk Grading and Levels of Management Difficulty

Overall Risk Grading	Levels of Management Difficulty	Quarantine Measures
A	A1	Import prohibition of host plants
	A2	Growing site inspection
	B1	Post-entry quarantine inspection
	B2	Import inspection by specific techniques
B	B1	Post-entry quarantine inspection
	B2	Import inspection by specific techniques
	C	Normal import inspection
C	B2	Import inspection by specific techniques
	C	Normal import inspection
D	-	(Non-quarantine pests)

Note: Even though other combinations of risk evaluation and difficulty may exist theoretically, Japan noted that there were no known examples. Therefore, the above combinations exhausted all practical possibilities.

4.160. The **United States** restated that the document which Japan asserted was its assessment of risk under Article 5.1 of the SPS Agreement, merely addressed whether the codling moth was a pest of quarantine significance. That was not in dispute. However, the Appellate Body Report in *EC - Hormones* made it clear that Article 5.1, relating to assessment of risk, "may be viewed as a specific application of the basic obligations contained in Article 2.2 of the SPS Agreement". Japan had been unable to provide a risk assessment relating to the varietal testing measure because there was no scientific basis warranting the measure.

4.161. In other words, Japan had been unable to provide a risk assessment because there was no scientific evidence that warranted testing by variety to achieve effective quarantine treatment against codling moth. In particular, there was no scientific evidence supporting the necessity of varietal testing (as opposed to testing by product) for quarantine treatment efficacy against codling moth with MB and/or MB fumigation and cold storage. Japan contended that it was *possible* that varietal differences within the same agricultural product *might* affect the efficacy of the treatment.[135] Faced with the uniformly lethal efficacy of the quarantine treatment in all confirmatory tests and the dearth of scientific evidence in support of varietal testing, Japan had offered descriptions of dose-response variation in support of the measure. However, these descriptions ignored the conclusions of the scientific studies done on quarantine treatments for codling moth, and abundant US empirical evidence that there were no differences among varieties that affected efficacy of quarantine treatment. The uniform success of treatments accepted by Japan also belied this notion.[136] The United States noted that none of the small-scale dose-mortality studies and studies relating to CxT cited by Japan constituted a risk assessment. Japan had never claimed otherwise. At most, these studies were designed to provide data relevant to a risk assessment.

4.162. The United States noted that in its submission Japan had indicated that it performed an individual risk assessment each time a country requested that the import ban be lifted for the product (paragraph 4.145). Yet, for years the United States had sought the lifting of the ban for certain products only to be thwarted by the varietal testing requirements of Japan. While Japan had indicated that it was open to proposals other than varietal testing, experience had shown that there was little flexibility to accept an equally effective alternative. The United States was unaware of any individual risk assessment that had been done for apples, cherries, nectarines, or walnuts.

4.163. **Japan** maintained that an *overall* risk assessment relating to varietal testing had been conducted. Japan held that the efficacy of any proposed *alternative* disinfestation treatment of host plants had to be demonstrated by the exporting country. In fact, Japan stressed that the element which needed to be based on a risk assessment was the substantive requirement that efficacy of disinfestation treatment be demonstrated. The United States had not challenged the necessity of confirmation. Falling short of such proof, Japan assumed that the initial risk assessment continued to govern in respect of the pest and its host plants, and varietal testing would con-

---

[135] In response to US Question 4 in consultations, Japan had stated: "It is *possible* there *may* be variation in the efficacy of disinfestation even if the same quarantine treatment is applied to different varieties. For that reason GOJ requires that the efficacy of quarantine standards be confirmed". [emphasis added]. (US Exhibit 3)

[136] US Exhibit 2.

tinue to apply. In other words, the "risk assessment" relating to varietal testing was performed as part of the overall risk assessment of the pest.

4.164. In terms of the PRA Guidelines, lifting of import prohibition could be understood as an alteration of the quarantine measure (which constituted part of the "risk management" to be performed in Stage 3 under the terminology of the PRA Guidelines, see paragraph 4.155).[137] It was the element of "biological effectiveness" (paragraph 4.156) of the proposed treatment that Japan considered in requiring demonstration of the absence of varietal difference of treatment efficacy.

4.165. Moreover, the "risk assessment" relating to varietal testing was made each time Japan determined if a proposed treatment would ensure the required level of protection against the risk of codling moth:

(a)   when an exporting government sought approval of additional varieties (of apples, for example), Japan investigated what alternative measure would achieve the required level of protection;

(b)   it was the responsibility of the exporting government to demonstrate that a treatment (e.g., the existing treatment for other varieties) would achieve the level of protection;

(c)   available data suggested that efficacy of a treatment could vary depending on the varieties;

(d)   other factors listed in Article 5.2 were also considered to verify if any new information was available; and,

(e)   unless new discoveries in the above process had lead to a different conclusion, the exporting government had to positively demonstrate either that varietal differences would not affect the efficacy of a treatment, or that the treatment they proposed would achieve the level of protection for other varieties by tests ("varietal testing").

4.166. Japan further argued that the Appellate Body in *EC - Hormones*, had discarded the notion of a "minimum procedural requirement" from Article 5.1. Accordingly, all that was required was that an SPS measure be based on a risk assessment which might be carried out by anyone. The fact that the risk assessment had taken into account all relevant scientific factors and was consistent with FAO PRA guidelines had been affirmed by Mr. Taylor.

4.167. The **United States** noted that Dr. Heather had explained that an assessment of the risk associated with varietal differences, if any, would focus on two elements: (i) the interaction between the physical and physiological characteristics of the product and the fumigant which resulted in higher sorption in one variety than another; and, (ii) higher susceptibility of the product to pest which resulted in consistently higher levels of infestation risk on one variety than another. There was no indication in the document submitted by Japan (Japan, Exhibit 9) that either of these factors had been considered. Furthermore, the United States recalled that Mr. Taylor had stated that the risk assessment was sufficient to justify a measure to ensure that

---

[137]   Japan noted that a conditional lifting of the import prohibition corresponded to an alteration of the measure from "prohibition of entry of specific commodities from specific origins" to "definition of requirements to be satisfied before export".

the *pest* was kept out of Japan, and not the *product*. In other words, if an efficacious treatment had been established, Japan would not be justified to continue to ban the product.

4.168. The United States also noted that, while compliance with the FAO Guidelines was not dispositive in the case at issue, Japan itself had admitted in its submission that the risk assessment it submitted related only to Stage 2 of the FAO Guidelines. Consideration of the need for quarantine requirements such as Japan's varietal testing requirement would fall under Stage 3. The United States noted that section 3.3 of the FAO Guidelines emphasized that "it is not justified to complete only Stages 1 and 2 and then take phytosanitary measures without [completion of Phase 3]." However, Japan had done precisely this.

4.169. The United States concluded that no risk assessment existed with respect to the question of whether differences in varietal characteristics could affect treatment efficacy. The varietal testing requirement was thus not based on a risk assessment as required by Article 5.1. This was valid even if Japan's Exhibit 9 was considered a risk assessment as that exhibit was not rationally related to the varietal testing measure and did not reasonably support it since it contained no assessment of risks attributable to varietal differences affecting treatment efficacy. Hence, as Japan had not assessed the risk, consistent with Articles 5.1 and 5.2 of the SPS Agreement, it had no basis to make a scientific determination about the potential for entry and establishment of codling moth in Japan. Because the varietal testing requirement was not based on a risk assessment under Article 5.1, it necessarily was not based on sufficient scientific evidence under Article 2.2 and was inconsistent with that obligation as well.

4. *Article 5.2*

4.170. Serving as a guideline for evaluation of risk, the **United States** pointed out that Article 5.2 suggested that Members take into consideration "available scientific evidence; relevant processes and production methods; relevant inspection, sampling and testing methods; prevalence of specific diseases and pests; existence of pest- or disease-free areas; relevant ecological and environmental conditions; and quarantine or other treatment". There was no evidence that Japan had complied with this obligation. Japan had not taken into consideration the relevant risk factors for contamination by the pest, which would necessarily include: an understanding of the growth patterns of the pest[138], which products were considered to be preferred host of the pest, and what pre- and post-harvest techniques were implemented to reduce levels of infestation.[139] Although there was a significant body of published information on these topics, the United States maintained that Japan had not factored any of these considerations into their pest risk analysis. Neither had Japan given consideration to the intended use of the product - which in the case of exported fruit was for consumption and not for propagation.

---

[138] US Exhibit 29.
[139] US Exhibit 30.

4.171. Furthermore, contrary to Article 5.2, Japan had not examined relevant process and production methods; prevalence of codling moth; or relevant environmental and ecological conditions as these factors related to US apples, cherries, walnuts, and nectarines.[140] Had Japan engaged in such an assessment of risk of introduction of codling moth to Japan, it might have examined the biology of the codling moth to discern what stage was most tolerant to MB fumigation, what stage of tolerance of the pest would be expected at harvest, and when if at all the codling moth would be most abundant on a particular fruit product. Such technical issues were of value in developing the appropriate quarantine treatment.[141]

4.172. An assessment of risk might also have examined, as required under Article 5.2, the prevalence of codling moth on US products. Codling moth was rarely found in exported US fruit mainly due to the combination of integrated pest management (IPM) and production and post-harvest practices. IPM practices included monitoring of moth activity to determine when generations appeared and in order to predict when egg laying would occur. Use of moth-trap catch data, combined with historical and environmental data, permitted relatively accurate predictions of moth activity. These predictions, plus field observations, dictated when and what type of control was necessary.[142] There were studies that demonstrated that the presence of codling moth on US apples[143] and on walnuts[144] was relatively limited; and that US cherries[145] and nectarines[146] were not preferred hosts of the codling moth.[147] Moreover, Japan had not taken into consideration the existence of uniform and effective US quarantine treatments for the pest in the relevant fruit product.[148]

4.173. The United States claimed, thus, that the document which Japan had asserted was its risk assessment did not take into account the factors listed in Article 5.2. It did not, and could not, demonstrate any objective or rational relationship between Japan's varietal testing requirement, on the one hand, and scientific evidence of a phytosanitary risk on the other.

---

[140] Article 5.2 of the SPS Agreement indicated that when carrying out a risk assessment, "Members shall take into account available scientific evidence; relevant processes and production methods; relevant inspection, sampling and testing methods; prevalence of specific diseases or pests; existence of pest- or disease-free areas; relevant ecological and environmental conditions; and quarantine or other treatment".

[141] US Exhibit 29.

[142] Jang and Moffitt, "Systems Approaches to Achieving Quarantine Security" in Sharp and Hallman, Quarantine Treatments for Pests of Food Plants, West View Press, Boulder, San Francisco, Oxford, 1994, pp.225-237. (US Exhibit 7)

[143] Moffitt, "A Systems Approach to Meeting Quarantine Requirements for Insect Pests of Deciduous Fruits," 85 Proceedings, Washington State Hortic. Association, 1989. pp.223-225. (US Exhibit 8)

[144] Vail, Tebbets, Mackey and Curtis, "Quarantine Treatments: A Biological Approach to Decision-Making for Selected Hosts of Codling Moth (Lepidoptera: Tortricidae)", 86(1) J. Econ. Entomol, 1993, pp.70-75, 72. (US Exhibit 9)

[145] Ibid. (US Exhibit 9)

[146] Curtis, Clark and Tebbets, "Incidence of Codling Moth (Lepidoptera: Torticidae) in Packed Nectarines," 84(6) J. Econ. Entomol., 1991, pp.1686-1690. (US Exhibit 10)

[147] US Exhibit 30.

[148] US Exhibit 2.

4.174. **Japan** noted that on this question of law, the United States seemed to argue that Japan's entire pest risk analysis had not taken into account the factors listed in Article 5.2. In respect of available scientific evidence, Japan claimed that the 1996 pest risk analysis had relied on the data set out under Article 2.2, as they were available in 1996. In respect of relevant process and production methods, Japan claimed that there were no known processes or methods of cultivation which could avoid codling moth completely. In respect of relevant inspection, sampling and testing methods, Japan noted that there were no known inspection, sampling and testing methods, either by exporting countries or by Japan, which would effectively detect and prevent introduction of the insect into Japan. Japan had taken into account that the host fruits were for consumption. In respect of the prevalence of specific diseases or pests, Japan had identified areas infested by pests, including the United States, by available literature and other surveys. In respect of existence of pest- or disease-free areas, Japan had not been able to obtain information regarding the presence of a pest-free area within a country or area infested by the moth. Furthermore, relevant ecological and environmental conditions - the biological characteristics of codling moth and the Japanese environmental conditions had been examined, and it had been found that the insect could be successfully introduced and established in Japan. Finally, in respect of quarantine treatment or other treatment, Japan recalled that codling moth eggs or young larvae which entered into the fruits at the calyx were very difficult to detect. Although no comprehensive quarantine treatment of host plants had been developed so far, effective treatments had been established for certain varieties of American cherries, nectarines, in-shell walnuts and apples, Canadian cherries, New Zealand cherries, nectarines and apples.

4.175. Japan further rebutted the US claims set out in paragraph 4.171: (i) Japan had considered the biology of the codling moth in order to discern what stage was the most tolerant to MB fumigation - this factor constituted the core of the "basic test"; (ii) in respect of the stage of tolerance of the pest that could be expected at harvest, Japan noted that the test guidelines required exporting governments to investigate development stages of the insect which could be encountered at harvest, and that the most resistant of possible development stages found on harvested fruits be tested for a treatment; (iii) in respect of when the codling moth would be most abundant on a particular fruit product, Japan noted that as the harvest season would not vary for a variety, variation in the number of individuals would not affect the kinds of tests required.

4.176. In respect of the US claim that Japan had not taken into account the fact that codling moth was rarely found in exported US fruit (paragraph 4.172), Japan noted that the concept of IPM was to manage the insect population so that harmful populations be diminished and maintained at a level lower than an economic injury level. By definition, it did not achieve the level of protection equivalent to import prohibition. This risk would not be eliminated by import procedures alone, for there was no inspection technique which would effectively discover the pest. Disinfestation had been chosen in light of these considerations, and not because pre- and post-harvest techniques were irrelevant. Furthermore, although the United States had pointed out that there were studies that demonstrated that the presence of codling moth on US apples and walnuts was relatively low; and that US cherries and nectarines were not preferred hosts to the codling moth (also in paragraph 4.172), Japan noted that available literature confirmed the presence of codling moth in apples, walnuts, cherries and nectarines.[149] In a previous case, dead larvae because of fumigation were found upon inspection of exported cherries.[150]

4.177. The **United States** noted that the approach taken by Japan was to evaluate each factor on its own to achieve Japan's level of protection was a peculiar approach to risk assessment. The United States claimed factors such as the biology of the codling moth, the prevalence of codling moth on various US products, the scientific evidence and the empirical data, had to be viewed as complementary factors and cumulative in effect to assess the risk of codling moth from US products for export to Japan. This differed significantly from the position of Japan, which examined each aspect of risk as a "zero sum" matter. In other words, if, as they had asserted, there was no inspection process that completely accounted for the presence (or lack) of codling moth on exported products then there was risk irrespective of the fact that the United States engaged in rigorous pre- and post-harvest techniques to reduce the prevalence of codling moth in the first place.

F.   Article 5.6

4.178. The **United States** argued that the Japanese varietal testing requirement was inconsistent with Article 5.6 in that it was significantly more trade-restrictive than required to achieve the appropriate level of phytosanitary protection. Article 5.6 required that:

> "Without prejudice to paragraph 2 of Article 3, when establishing or maintaining sanitary or phytosanitary measures to achieve the appropriate level of sanitary or phytosanitary protection, Members shall ensure that such measures are not more trade-restrictive than required to achieve their appropriate level of sanitary or phytosanitary protection, taking into account technical and economic feasibility."[151]

4.179. The United States noted that the "appropriate level of sanitary or phytosanitary protection" was defined in paragraph 5 of Annex A of the SPS Agreement as: "The level of protection deemed appropriate by the Member establishing a sanitary or phytosanitary measure to protect human, animal or plant life or health within its territory." For the purpose of the dispute at issue, the level of protection could be achieved by a certain rate of mortality of the pest (probit 9 level of mortality).

4.180. The United States noted that in order to fulfil the requirements of Japan, the United States had conducted the testing procedure on seven varieties of apples, nine varieties of cherries, ten varieties of nectarines, and four varieties of walnuts. The efficacy of the quarantine treatment had always been shown in the confirmatory

---

[149]   Chapman, P.J. & S.E. Lienk, 1971. (Japan, Exhibit 25)

[150]   Japan noted that during the export inspection of 1997 cherries, four dead larvae had been found. Because the sampling was conducted only on 1 per cent and it was difficult to fully discover the pest by inspection, Japan had assumed that a fair number of fruits were infested.

[151]   The footnote to Article 5.6 of the SPS Agreement reads: "For purposes of paragraph 6 of Article 5, a measure is not more trade-restrictive than required unless there is another measure, reasonably available taking into account technical and economic feasibility, that achieves the appropriate level of sanitary or phytosanitary protection and is significantly less restrictive to trade".

tests, in which the exact same treatment for the product uniformly achieved Japan's level of quarantine protection irrespective of variety. The United States had never had to modify a quarantine treatment for codling moth for varieties of the same product. Hence, according to the United States, these results conclusively demonstrated that Japan's varietal testing requirements had no value in providing additional quarantine protection.

4.181. The United States further claimed that the uniform experience of efficacy of treatment for varieties against codling moth was not limited to the United States. Japan had yet to identify any instance where a quarantine treatment developed by any country (New Zealand, Australia, Chile, South Africa, Spain, Israel, and others) for codling moth on fruit to be imported into Japan had been changed for subsequent varieties. The United States maintained that no other country had ever had to modify a treatment among varieties to achieve Japan's level of protection for codling moth. Additionally, the accepted international practice in the area of pest quarantine treatment by virtually every other country in the world was to require testing by product, not by variety. In this respect, the United States noted that as an example, with respect to quarantine practices for all arthropods (pests), the United States had for decades cleared fruit by pest and plant species, not by variety. In the operation of these quarantine approvals by species, there had never been any indication of varietal differences that required modification of the established treatment for the product. Therefore, it was evident that testing by product (in which a treatment was established with one variety, or group of varieties, and then applied to all other varieties of that product subsequently sought for export), provided an equal level of quarantine protection and was significantly less trade restrictive.

4.182. Article 5.6 was violated if there was a reasonably available alternative, taking into account technical and economic feasibility, which achieved Japan's level of quarantine protection and was significantly less trade restrictive. Because there were no varietal differences that affected the efficacy of quarantine treatment, the same established treatment would achieve the appropriate level of protection for all varieties of a product. The United States noted that testing by variety took a minimum of 2-4 years to complete per variety, was resource intensive and costly to perform, and, furthermore, seriously delayed market access of US products. On the other hand, testing by product was significantly less trade restrictive. The Japanese requirement of varietal testing was significantly more trade-restrictive than required, and testing by product was a reasonably available alternative which achieved Japan's level of phytosanitary protection.

4.183. **Japan** stated that its lifting of import prohibition was indeed a result of the discharge of its obligation under Article 5.6. Whenever Japan found a measure which achieved the appropriate level of protection and was significantly less restrictive, the import prohibition was replaced with such a measure. In this particular case, however, Japan had found data which suggested presence of varietal differences in efficacy of MB fumigation, and a hypothesis which explained such a variation.

4.184. The United States had challenged Japan under the assumption that "[b]ecause there are no varietal differences that affect the efficacy of quarantine treatment, the same established treatment will achieve for all varieties of a product the appropriate level of protection". However, the US evidence did not support their position; the United States had simply submitted a hypothesis which not only cast doubt on laboratory results but on large-scale tests as well. Japan claimed that prior to the lifting of the import prohibition on certain products subject to implementation of an alternative measure, efficacy of the measure had to be demonstrated by the exporting government, and this was a reasonable requirement in light of the asymmetric presence of information on exotic pests and goods. As the United States had not proven species-wide efficacy, Japan was not obliged to accept their alternative at this stage.

4.185. Japan pointed out that it had nevertheless made efforts to alleviate the burden of exporting governments. Japan had accepted the concept of a representative variety. This was why there was no requirement of a full-scale testing of each variety. In additions, for approval of additional varieties, the size of samples in large-scale demonstrations had been reduced from 30,000 to 10,000 insects.

4.186. The **United States** noted that other than recognition of pest-free zones or eradication of a pest from a region or country, Japan had never accepted an alternative to its varietal testing regime with respect to codling moth or other pests of similar significance to Japan. The United States stressed that it considered testing by product as the *only acceptable quarantine measure in the context of the dispute at issue*. It was acceptable that the first variety of a particular product from any source should be subject to the full range of testing. Japan's required procedures for the development of a quarantine treatment included a large-scale test with sufficient numbers of insects to validate that treatment for the product. After such validation, *no further testing was necessary for additional varieties*. The United States claimed that to be required to treat 10,000 insects and to use the necessary quantity of fruit for each additional variety would be virtually as time-consuming and burdensome as the current requirement to do dose-mortality tests for each variety and confirmatory testing on representative varieties. Hence, to accept the requirement of confirmatory tests on each subsequent variety would be tantamount to acknowledging that varieties made a difference in the ultimate efficacy of MB quarantine treatment for codling moth, a notion unsupported by scientific evidence, data, or principle.

G.   Article 5.7

4.187. **Japan** claimed that varietal testing could be considered a provisional measure. The rationale of the present policy to require efficacy confirmation on a variety basis was that available evidence suggested a possible presence of varietal differences in the efficacy of disinfestation treatment. This policy was based on a scientific hypothesis, it did not presume, *a priori*, varietal differences in all circumstances. Import prohibition could be lifted on a product basis subject to sufficient demonstration. As an example, in respect of fruits whose varietal difference was attributed to bud mutation (e.g., lemons), and no major differences were anticipated, a single treatment would ensure an appropriate level of protection for all varieties of the product.

4.188. Once the import prohibition had been lifted on a particular variety subject to a disinfestation treatment, new data would be accumulated on the effects of a treatment or on the characteristics of prohibited items, and it would then be possible to reach a level of confidence on broader applicability of the existing treatment. This was a reasonable assumption; however, until that had been achieved, Japan insisted on its right to maintain the prohibition, on a provisional basis, on importation of the other varieties. Japan based its measure on available pertinent information as set out in its risk assessment and recognized that the importing government was required to "seek to obtain the additional information necessary for a more objective assessment of risk and review the ... phytosanitary measure accordingly within a reasonable period of time" (Article 5.7).

4.189. The **United States** noted that it had been engaged in detailed negotiations with Japan for over two decades. Although Japan had chosen to present a risk assessment on an undisputed matter, Japan was intimately aware of the evidence that had been discussed in the US submissions and what the evidence signified. That evidence was relevant and sufficient, and specifically addressed the specific mortality level of codling moth required by Japan. The United States had firmly established that efficacy of treatment by product achieved Japan's required level of mortality. The varietal testing requirement could not be characterized as a provisional measure - invocation of Article 5.7 was not a supportable claim.

4.190. The United States pointed out that although Japan claimed it believed it had presented sufficient scientific evidence to meet the obligations of Articles 2.2 and 5.1, Japan also claimed that the measure nonetheless was a provisional measure. These two positions were diametrically opposed. Indeed, Article 2.2 listed Article 5.7 as an *exception* to its requirements, because it was considered that Article 5.7 would permit a measure to be applied even where the "sufficient scientific evidence" requirement of Article 2.2 was not met. Similarly, Article 5.7 applied *only* where the relevant scientific evidence was insufficient to permit a risk assessment. Consequently, the United States argued that Japan's claim that it had enough evidence to satisfy the requirements of Articles 2.2 and 5.1 with respect to its ban meant that Japan's ban failed to meet the threshold requirement of Article 5.7. Moreover, the United States claimed that this was not a situation in which there was insufficient scientific evidence, because there was no evidence supporting Japan's claim that variety mattered, and because all evidence in the case at issue, including the success of uniform treatments of different varieties exported to Japan and the absence of failures by product-based testing regimes in other countries, indicated that varietal differences did not affect treatment efficacy.

4.191. The United States noted that the measure had gone into effect 48 years ago. Therefore, the measure could hardly be called "provisional". Moreover, there was no evidence that Japan had undertaken a process to yield "within a reasonable period of time" a more objective assessment of risk so that it could review whether the "provisional measure" should be continued. Japan had therefore failed to meet the requirement of Article 5.7 that an objective risk assessment be done within a reasonable time.

H. Article 7 (Annex B)

4.192. The **United States** argued that the Japanese measure lacked transparency, and was thus inconsistent with Article 7. Article 7 and Annex B set out a number of requirements that Members had to follow in regard to transparency of an SPS measure. Specifically, Annex B, paragraph 1 required that "Members shall ensure that all sanitary and phytosanitary regulations which have been adopted are published promptly in such a manner as to enable interested Members to become acquainted with them". The United States had made a specific request to the Enquiry Point for Japan which had admitted that there was no published source for varietal testing.[152] The measure had been developed over time through a series of protocols and practice.

4.193. The United States noted that the lack of transparency was made more evident by the lack of a risk assessment on the varietal testing measure. Had the measure been based on scientific principles, maintained with sufficient scientific evidence, based on an assessment of the risks, and not significantly more trade-restrictive than required to achieve the appropriate level of protection, it would have been possible to justify in a transparent fashion the legitimacy of the measure. As the requirement of varietal testing could not fulfil any of these WTO requirements, it was not surprising to find that the measure lacked transparency.

4.194. **Japan** noted that the claim of the United States related to the guidelines developed by the MAFF concerning confirmation of efficacy of disinfestation treatment.[153] These had been distributed to foreign plant quarantine authorities for the purpose of transparency. The contents of the guidelines were not mandatory and exporting governments could choose to demonstrate efficacy of treatment by other means. Consequently, these guidelines did not fall under the concept of "regulations" under paragraph 1 of Annex B. In other words, they did not constitute enforceable regulations covered by Article 7. Nevertheless, these guidelines were available to any interested foreign government through Japan's Enquiry Point, consistent with paragraph 3(b) of Annex B.

4.195. The Annexed Table to the Enforcement Regulation identified the quarantine pest which constituted the cause of the import prohibition, the countries or areas from which importation was prohibited, and the prohibited host plants and their specific parts. Japan pointed out that this allowed any exporter of agricultural products to know in advance which items were prohibited, as well as the quarantine pests concerned. In contrast, other countries, including the United States, generally prohibited importation of all plants and chose a quarantine measure on the basis of a risk analysis only after the filing of an import permit. Under such a mechanism, a foreign exporter was not able to know in advance whether or not the products were exportable, and which quarantine pests had to be guarded against. In this sense, Japan claimed that its regulations were characterized by a greater degree of transparency.

4.196. The **United States** claimed that the assertion by Japan that these were simply "guidelines" and not "regulations" was a novel claim, and one that departed from the issue at hand. In consultations Japan had indicated that while the varietal testing requirement was not published, the lifting of an import ban was based on *specific legislation*. Irrespective of the informal process by which US scientists, in consultation with Japan, had devised procedures to test by variety[154] the fact remained that

---

[152] Japan's response to Question 2 of US Consultation Questions. (US Exhibit 3)

[153] Contained in Japan, Exhibit 10.

[154] The United States noted that these had been printed for the first time in a hand-out in Japan's Exhibit 10.

the requirement itself - that which linked the import prohibition with the requirement that it could only be lifted by variety - had to be published.

4.197. The United States argued that the issue of transparency was indicative of a much larger problem. The requirement at issue arose from specific legislation and regulations and yet there was no published source that explained what procedures were necessary to have a product removed from the import prohibition list. The United States, the European Community and numerous other exporting countries had no access to phytosanitary protocols in which Japan had already negotiated and approved treatment for a particular product.[155] In short, without publication of this information, an exporter had no way to discern what was necessary to move a product from the prohibited list to a list approved by Japan for entry. The purpose of transparency was to ensure that Members were carrying out their obligations under the SPS Agreement. An absence of transparency contributed to the overall impression that this measure was far from being consistent with those obligations.

4.198. In respect of transparency, **Japan** noted that anyone who wished to be informed about approved phytosanitary protocols for approved items could refer to MAFF notifications, published in the Government Gazette. If these were difficult to locate, the MAFF could be contacted directly.

I.   *Article 8 (Annex C)*

4.199. The **United States** claimed that as a matter of control and inspection procedures, the Japanese measure was inconsistent with Article 8. The United States noted that sub-paragraphs (a) through (i) of paragraph 1 of Annex C did not replace any of the requirements of Articles 2, 5, and 7, but complemented them by imposing additional, more specific disciplines on Annex C measures. An Annex C measure therefore could be in breach of Articles 2, 5, 7, and 8. However, if an Annex C measure was inconsistent with Articles 2 and 5, as was the case with the Japanese measure at issue, then it was not a legitimate sanitary or phytosanitary measure. To a certain extent, then, the requirements of Annex C.1(a)-(i) would be secondary with respect to such an illegitimate measure since, under the SPS Agreement, the measure could not be maintained in the first place.

4.200. Article 8 and Annex C set out several standards that Members had to observe in the operation of control and inspection. The varietal testing requirement was such a procedure because Japan required control and inspection of the quarantine treatment of a variety of a product before it could be approved for export into its country. The exporting country had to provide certification that the quarantine treatment applied to the variety in question achieved the appropriate phytosanitary level of protection of Japan.

4.201. Annex C, paragraph 1(c) required that Members limit information requirements to "what is necessary for appropriate control, inspection and approval procedures". Yet, because the varietal testing requirement was not based on scientific principles, was maintained without sufficient scientific evidence, was not based on

---

[155] Third Party Oral Statement by the European Community, paragraph 8.

an assessment of the risks, and was more trade-restrictive than required to achieve the appropriate level of protection, Japan's measure was inappropriate.

4.202. **Japan** noted, in respect of paragraph 1(c), that the information required was what was necessary to demonstrate the efficacy of a treatment. Japan recalled that it did not necessarily demand complete testing of each variety (paragraph 4.31). The requirement under paragraph 1(c) was consequently fully met. Nevertheless, Japan remained willing to consider more appropriate ways to fulfil the informational requirements of exporting governments.

4.203. The **United States** further argued that Japan had, contrary to Article 8 and Annex C, paragraph 1(h), not limited the required procedures for a "modified product" to what was "necessary to determine whether adequate confidence exists that the product still meets the regulations concerned". The United States claimed that a requirement that allowed for uniform treatment for a product without testing by variety would be an appropriate limitation. To require the United States to provide information on the efficacy of treatment for every variety when there was already an existing and efficacious treatment for the product was not *limiting* Japan's information requirements to what was necessary.

4.204. While there were no differences among varieties of a product that affected efficacy of quarantine treatment, there were any number of varieties that were developed for the purpose of improving marketability. The difference could be as benign as improving the color or inducing ripeness more quickly. A variety of nectarine could be modified so it ripened one week faster than another variety. A variety of cherry could be modified so that it had a more vibrant color. A variety of apple could be modified so that it tasted sweeter than another variety. While these were modifications, they did not represent a difference in variety such that it affected efficacy of treatment. These modification were therefore not a change in the specifications of the product for purposes of efficacy treatment for codling moth. The United States had demonstrated that variety did not affect efficacy of MB quarantine treatment. Accordingly, no "further procedure" was "necessary" within the meaning of paragraph 1(h) of Annex C for new varieties. Thus, Japan's measure at issue, which did require further procedures for new varieties, was inconsistent with paragraph 1(h) because it went far beyond what was "necessary".

4.205. In respect of consistency with paragraph 1(h), **Japan** pointed out that the issue of whether different varieties fell within the concept of 'modified products' had to be addressed. Japan claimed that such changes typically referred to alterations of additives or ingredients in processed foods and did not cover varietal differences. Even if the provision were to apply to varietal differences, under the Japanese system, required information was limited to what was "necessary to determine if it is able to obtain sufficient confidence of conformity" of additional new varieties to those approved subject to the quarantine treatment. Japan did not require varietal testing on "modifications of the product" as long as it was demonstrated, based on scientific evidence, that they "represent the sort of variability that in no way affects how effective the quarantine treatment will be at killing the plant pests of concern", as set out by the United States in paragraph 4.23. Even if varieties were "modified products", Japan considered that different varieties had to be tested to "determine whether adequate confidence exists" and that the "modified products" still met the regulations concerned. Moreover, Japan noted that the requirements of confirmation at the time of approval of additional varieties were far less rigorous than the requirements which applied to the initial lifting of the import prohibition. In this sense, the Japanese policy was fully consistent with paragraph 1(h). Japan noted that if there were "no differences among varieties of a product that affect efficacy of quarantine treatment" no demonstration would be required, by tests or otherwise. Japan was therefore in full conformity with paragraph 1(h) of the Annex C.

4.206. Regarding the definition of "modified products", the **United States** noted that, contrary to Japan's assertion, Annex C nowhere circumscribed or narrowed the scope of the phrase "modified products" to mean "alterations of additives or ingredients in processed foods". The text of paragraph 1(h) provided no basis for exclusion of the products at issue.

V.   SUMMARY OF THIRD PARTY SUBMISSIONS

A.   *Brazil*

5.1.   Brazil noted that its interest in the dispute derived from its own experience in dealing with Japanese import prohibition and quarantine requirements for fruits under the Plant Protection Law and the Enforcement Regulation. Japan constituted an important potential market for Brazilian products. Since 1986, Brazilian authorities had been in consultations with Japan with a view to initiating exports of Brazilian mangoes to Japan, which were currently prohibited under the cited legislation.

5.2.   In order to eradicate an insect that was of concern to Japanese authorities (the Mediterranean fruit fly, or *ceratitis capitata*), Brazil had undertaken the necessary research and had developed a treatment of immersion in hot water for the Tommy Atkins variety of mangoes. The test results had, in Brazil's view, met Japan's requirement eliminating 30,000 individuals of the pest. Yet Brazil had still not received authorization to initiate exports. Japanese authorities had requested that Brazil use a treatment of hot *vapour*, which was ten times more expensive than the treatment based on immersion in hot water. Brazil had not understood the reasoning behind this request, since the treatment that had been tested and adopted had been proven to be successful and was currently being utilized by another exporter of mangoes to Japan (Mexico) for treatment against the same insect. Brazil believed that the case of the mango could prove to be useful to the Panel, since the import prohibition was based on the same legislation that was used by Japan to establish quarantine treatments and import prohibitions for the fruit varieties that were of direct interest to the United States. Brazil was still pursuing a bilateral solution to the problem, in accordance with the principles set out in Article 3.7 of the DSU.

5.3.   On the core issue of varietal testing requirements, Brazil shared the views expressed by the United States that testing by product (commodity-by-commodity) was an alternative measure that was reasonably available and was significantly less trade restrictive. In more general terms, Brazil noted the long history of bilateral negotiations that were necessary to permit the importation of different varieties of fruits into Japan. In the case of a developing country like Brazil, which was still negotiating the lifting of an import prohibition on a *single* variety of a fruit, this was a precedent that certainly did not reflect the balance of rights and obligations under the SPS Agreement, and specifically the operation of the Articles cited by the United States in its complaint.

5.4.   In the case before the Panel, there were clearly differences of view concerning such key issues as "risk assessment", "sufficient scientific evidence", "scientific justification" and "appropriate level of protection". There was also an important discussion, from Brazil's point of view, concerning the recourse to alternative measures and the need to avoid discriminating or trade restrictive SPS measures.

5.5.   In respect of Articles 2 and 5 of the SPS Agreement, Brazil attached special importance to the issue of necessity and to guaranteeing that measures were based on scientific principles and not maintained without sufficient scientific evidence. These guidelines, alongside the obligation not to discriminate, were important guarantees to avoid SPS measures that resulted in a "disguised restriction on international trade". Article 5 of the SPS Agreement spelled out, in detail, the elements that had to be taken into consideration in analyzing the necessity for a measure and in deciding on the nature of the measure.

5.6.   The treatment advocated by Brazil to combat the Mediterranean fruit fly was used by another WTO Member for the same product for export to the Japanese market. Nevertheless, Brazil had been called upon to use another treatment, which was more expensive. While Brazil remained ready to cooperate with Japanese authorities, it noted that it had not yet received adequate explanations - of scientific or other nature - as to the reason for not being accorded the right to use a quarantine treatment that had been proven to be effective in tests conducted by Brazil and which were accepted by Japan for exports of another Member affected by the same pest. It was Brazil's belief that Japanese authorities had to take into consideration the concepts of a reasonable (and cost-effective) available alternative and of non-discrimination.[156] Brazil also questioned whether the minimization of negative trade effects was being taken into consideration by Japan.

5.7.   Since the provisions of Articles 2 and 5 of the SPS Agreement spelled out a series of guidelines that had to be followed both individually by Members and in cooperation between Members concerned, one of Brazil's major concerns was the issue of threshold in the application and interpretation of these provisions. This was more so due to the fact that in the operation of the Plant Protection Law and of the Enforcement Regulation, Japan insisted that the burden of proof, relating to the acceptability of a substitute disinfestation measure (equivalent to an import prohibition), rested on the exporting Member.

5.8.   The issue of burden of proof - scientific evidence or scientific justification - and of different interpretations of results recorded in scientific tests constituted an important part both of the US and of the Japanese submissions concerning the need for varietal testing. While Brazil did not wish to comment on the specific discussion of the significance of the statistical differences recorded in the laboratory tests referred to by both parties, it was concerned with the extent to which an exporting country had to go in order to confirm the validity of a specific measure, especially in light of its current experience in the consultations related to tests to prove the efficacy of treatment for the Mediterranean fruit fly in Brazilian mangoes. Since Japan

---

[156]   Brazil noted that the United States had referred to discrimination in relation to Japanese domestic production of fruits. However, Brazil's present concern was related to discrimination in relation to other WTO Members that exported to Japan.

itself recognized that most information was received from the exporting Member, Brazil believed that the concept of equivalence, which was contained in Article 4, should also be taken into consideration in the examination of information provided concerning the pest and the proposed method of treatment. [157]

5.9.   The correct implementation of the provisions of Articles 7 and 8 of the SPS Agreement concerning transparency and standards for control and inspection were a further guarantee against unnecessary burdens imposed on exporting Members. Brazil noted the reservations of the United States in relation to the implementation by Japan of these two provisions, especially the problem of lack of sufficient transparency of the SPS measure which Brazil had also experienced. Since Brazil did not yet export mangoes to Japan, it was not in a position to provide its experience with Article 8 requirements, but, since its future exports would be affected by the same procedures, it was concerned with what seemed to amount to unnecessary information requirements.

5.10.   Brazil did not question Japan's right to implement sanitary and phytosanitary measures. Brazil was also aware of its rights under Article 5.8 of the SPS Agreement. The objective of Brazil's participation as a third party in the Panel proceedings was to express its concern with the possibility that measures designed to protect plant health were being implemented without the necessary justification and in such a way as to create negative trade effects or even as to constitute disguised barriers to trade.

B.   European Communities

The factual and scientific aspects of the case

5.11.   The European Communities noted that it would comment on the factual and scientific aspects of the case on the basis of its experience in its attempts to export fresh fruits and vegetables to Japan. The task was particularly difficult as the first written submissions of the parties contained several conflicting statements on a number of crucial scientific issues. The following aspects of the dispute would be addressed:

(a)   the issue of varietal testing of quarantine treatment efficacy against codling moth;

(b)   the questions raised by the practice of Japan to require varietal testing for certain types of fruits and pests;

(c)   the complexity and lack of transparency of the Japanese system of procedures for granting import authorization for fruits and vegetables; and,

(d)   the hindrance to trade which could be a consequence of such repeated varietal testing as applied by Japan.

5.12.   The European Communities noted that it had experienced a number of difficulties in its attempts to export fruits and vegetables to Japan and that many of these

---

[157]   Brazil noted that although Article 4 was included in the terms of reference of the Panel, it had not been cited by either of the parties to the dispute in their first submissions.

difficulties arose from a variety of causes linked to the system of phytosanitary measures enacted by the Japanese authorities. The European Communities was directly affected by the measures which the Panel was being asked to consider: for example, authorization was granted in August 1997, after several years of testing and discussion, to allow France to export Golden Delicious apples to Japan. However, if France wished to export any other variety of apple in light of consumer reaction to its Golden Delicious already shipped, the whole approval procedure would have to start anew.

5.13.   The European Communities wished to underline that it did not contest the right of Japan, or of any other Member, to protect plants within its territory from the introduction of harmful pests. Indeed, the European Communities operated its own system of measures to protect plant health in full accord with the terms of the SPS Agreement.

5.14.   At issue was the conformity with the SPS Agreement of the requirement for varietal testing to prove the efficiency of disinfestation for quarantine pests. In this regard, the European Communities questioned the scientific basis of Japan's application of varietal testing for these purposes. While the application of particular treatments could vary a little for different varieties of the same fruit or vegetable, for example, due to the inherently different physical characteristics of the varieties (as in the example of mangoes pointed out by Japan), the European Communities questioned the need of requiring a completely new series of tests for a different variety of the same fruit or vegetable. Varietal testing could be justified if the characteristics and other properties of the varieties in question were such that differences could be expected which were relevant for the objective to be achieved. However, it appeared to the European Communities that the measure in question was applied to an extent beyond that which was necessary to protect plant life and health.

5.15.   The European Communities second concern with regard to varietal testing was the apparent lack of consistency in its application by the Japanese authorities. The attention of the Panel had been drawn by the United States to the requirement of varietal testing in relation to apples, cherries, nectarines and walnuts. However, for other varieties of pests and fruits and vegetables import authorization seemed to have been granted without reference to full varietal testing. In the experience of the European Communities, import prohibition in certain instances was lifted for all varieties at once, while it was evident from the facts of the dispute at issue that this was not the case for other products. The European Communities was unaware of any explanation on the part of Japan of such a differentiated application.

5.16.   A third issue that the European Communities raised concerned the low degree of transparency and high degree of complexity of the particular part of the Japanese phytosanitary regulatory system at issue. The European Communities had asked, in recent deregulation requests, for a flow chart of approval procedures for import authorization of plants and plant products. Japan had also been asked to simplify and provide greater transparency of approval procedures for fresh fruit and vegetables. To date, these requests had not been fulfilled. In fact, the import authorization procedure was not clearly defined from beginning to end and normally proceeded on a step-by-step basis, with Japan defining the successive steps; as soon as one hurdle was overcome another appeared on the list. The whole process usually took several years, even before a trial shipment was allowed. Moreover, it involved extensive series of tests, numerous visits to Tokyo for discussions with Japanese experts, public hearings and extended on-site inspections by Japanese experts in the country wishing to export. It was likely that the chances of exporting agricultural products to Japan would be improved if Japan were willing to make available the phytosanitary protocols which it had negotiated with one country to any other interested Member of the WTO.

5.17.   The system of varietal testing as applied by Japan appeared to impede trade. The heavy procedural requirements of Japan imposed a considerable burden on the exporting country, both in terms of manpower, time and money. Under the system of varietal testing, exporters had to take the risk of selecting a particular variety and endure a lengthy and complex procedure to gain approval. Yet, if the initial assessment of Japanese consumer reaction were proven wrong, then the investment of time, money and manpower would be wasted and the procedure had to be started all over again for another variety. This appeared to be further compounded by the fact that Japan did not seem to allow for testing and approval procedures to take place for several varieties at the same time. All this represented a serious deterrent to those exporters wishing to gain a foothold in the Japanese market for particular types of fruits and vegetables which had not been previously exported to that market.

Comments on the legal aspects of the case

Burden of proof

5.18.   The European Communities considered that the dispute raised the issue of burden of proof. This was a particularly complex problem in cases where science and law interacted. The allocation of the burden of proof was an important legal question which could directly affect the outcome of a dispute settlement procedure. It was recalled that the Appellate Body had pointed out that the initial burden rested on the complaining party, which had to establish a *prima facie* case of inconsistency with a particular provision of the SPS Agreement. When the *prima facie* case was made, the burden of proof moved to the defending party, which had to counter or refute the claimed inconsistency.[158]

5.19.   "Burden of proof" was an ambiguous term. It was important to distinguish between: (1) burden of producing evidence, (2) burden of persuasion, and (3) minimally sufficient evidence. These concepts applied to very different aspects of fact-finding and responded to very different situations.

5.20.   First, with respect to any factual issue, there could be various *burdens of producing evidence* placed on parties. Under the DSU structure, a panel was not an investigative institution with the capacity to generate its own evidence. There had to be rules concerning which party had to produce evidence before the Panel and how much evidence had to be produced in order for the party not to suffer adverse findings by default. Initially, a complaining party had to "*present evidence and argument sufficient to establish a presumption*" (*prima facie* case) that a Member had acted

---

[158]   *EC - Hormones*, paragraphs 98, 108-109.

inconsistently with its obligations under the SPS Agreement.[159] That is, the complaining party had to produce sufficient evidence on any factual issue essential to its claim that a violation was occurring.[160] Evidence had to be produced: (i) that was sufficient to support its requested finding, *and* (ii) that would be sufficient to persuade the Panel that what was claimed was true, *if no* counter-evidence were to be produced. A *prima facie* case had, therefore, to be of sufficient weight to persuade the Panel and of sufficient quality to pass appellate review for reasonableness.

5.21.   Second, the Panel would have to assess *all* the evidence for and against any factual proposition and should adopt the proposition as a finding only if the evidence supported the proposition. What was required was a determination by the Panel that the proposition at issue was more likely to be true than false. On any factual issue there had to be a "default rule" for making a finding when the weight of evidence was in "equipoise" - that is, when it appeared to the Panel that the evidence for a proposition seemed equal in weight to the evidence for its negation. The party with the *burden of persuasion* was the party who had to suffer an adverse finding unless it persuaded the Panel to its view by a preponderance of the evidence. It did not seem correct, however, to speak (despite the practice and conventional wisdom) of any definitive or permanent "shift" in the burden of proof in such a case, because the proof obligations of both parties continued ("back and forth") throughout the entire litigation process.

5.22.   Third, a panel was not authorized to make a finding if there was not, in the record before it, minimal evidence that any reasonable person would consider necessary to support such a finding.

5.23.   In the present case, the United States argued effectively that the confirmatory tests were the relevant indicator of efficacy of quarantine treatment. Japan contested this by arguing that its policy of requiring confirmation on a varietal basis was supported by available evidence that suggested a possible presence of varietal difference in the efficacy of disinfestation treatment (MB fumigation). This was a scientific question and it was not clear whether the Panel would be able to resolve it, even with the assistance of scientific experts.

5.24.   Japan also contested the US argument that it required complete testing and review of each variety. Yet, Japan did not deny that large-scale testing was required for initial lifting of the import prohibition as well as for additional approval, if the results of the dose-mortality tests were unsatisfactory. Japan did not deny that on-site confirmatory tests for one representative variety was required for additional varieties, even if dose-mortality tests were confirmed. Japan also admitted that dose-mortality tests were required in all cases for all varieties for initial and additional lifting of the import prohibition. Nevertheless, Japan had not provided, in the view of the European Communities, any reasonable response to the US argument that it (or any other country that applied a quarantine treatment for codling moth on fruit to be exported to Japan) had never had to modify a quarantine treatment for codling moth for varieties of the same commodity. The reply of Japan that they had accepted

---

[159]   *The United States - Measures Affecting Imports of Woven Wool Shirts and Blouses from India,* WT/DS33/AB/R, adopted on 23 May 1997.
[160]   Appellate Body Reports on *EC - Hormones and Indian Woven Wool Shirts and Blouses.*

that the proposed treatment (on Hartley walnuts) would disinfest codling moth to the satisfactory level (not because varietal differences were irrelevant) was not convincing. Japan needed to bring forward *minimally sufficient evidence* to convince the Panel that varietal differences did affect, for each product in question, the fumigation efficacy. It did not seem enough to argue that this was a reasonable hypothesis or argument, as posited by Japan.

5.25.   Moreover, the European Communities pointed out that it did not share the interpretation made by Japan of the *EC - Hormones* case. Contrary to what Japan appeared to argue, the European Communities had not "only asserted that safety of hormones was not proven beyond doubt".[161] The Appellate Body Report on *EC - Hormones* clarified that the European Communities did "indeed show the existence of a general risk of cancer" and that its studies were "relevant but do not appear to be sufficiently specific to the case at hand".[162] It was clear also from other parts of the Appellate Body Report on *EC - Hormones* that the issue there concerned the incorrect interpretation made by the United States and the panel of the concept of risk under Article 5.1 of the SPS Agreement, as requiring a certain magnitude or threshold level of risk to be demonstrated in the risk assessment.[163]

5.26.   The European Communities considered that what Japan needed to prove in this particular case, in light of the evidence brought by the United States, was that its risk assessment sufficiently warranted or reasonably supported the SPS measure at stake.[164] It was necessary for Japan to establish the rational link between the measure and its risk assessment.

The Panel's role in reviewing the scientific judgments made by WTO Members

5.27.   Under the DSU rules, the Panel had to decide whether the Japanese measures were based on a risk assessment as appropriate to the circumstances (Article 5.1). The Panel should also judge whether these measures were based on scientific principles and were maintained with sufficient scientific evidence (Article 2.2). In this regard none of the parties to the dispute had attempted to shed any light on the interpretation to be given to the concept of "sufficient scientific evidence" in Article 2.2 of the SPS Agreement.

5.28.   In respect of the *standard of review* the European Communities noted that the Appellate Body had clarified in *EC - Hormones* that the Panel should make "an objective assessment of the facts".[165] A panel could not conduct its own risk assessment. With respect to any of the many scientific issues involved in the risk assessment conducted by a WTO Member, a panel could not substitute its own scientific judgment for that of the WTO Member applying an SPS measure. It appeared also that panels should not substitute the scientific judgment of individual scientists or

---

[161]   This was, according to the European Communities, the wrong interpretation of EC arguments made by the panel.

[162]   *Op. cit.*, paragraph 200.

[163]   *Op. cit.*, paragraphs 184-186. The European Communities noted that this discussion was linked to the concept of "zero risk" policy, which was not summarized at all in the Appellate Body Report on *EC - Hormones.*

[164]   *Op. cit.*, paragraph 193.

[165]   *Ibid.*, paragraph 117.

experts, which might be chosen by it in accordance with Article 11 of the SPS Agreement, with that of the WTO Member that carried out the risk assessment. A panel's mandate in considering the evidence invoked by a WTO Member maintaining an SPS measure was *not* to determine whether it agreed that such evidence constituted the "best evidence" available, but merely to determine whether that Member's risk assessment sufficiently warranted or reasonably supported the measure at hand.

Arbitrary, unjustifiable or disguised restriction on international trade

5.29.   In accordance with Articles 2.3 and 5.6 of the SPS Agreement, the European Communities believed that the United States bore the burden of showing that the Japanese measures were arbitrary, unjustifiable or constituted a disguised restriction on international trade. In particular, the United States had to show that there was another reasonably available measure which was less restrictive on trade and which could achieve the level of protection chosen by Japan.

5.30.   In this respect the European Communities observed that, with regard to the varieties of apples, cherries, nectarines and walnuts of US origin which had already been approved for export to Japan, the same varieties coming from another WTO Member should also be allowed to be imported into Japan on the same conditions. As Article 2.3 of the SPS Agreement provided, Members should not arbitrarily or unjustifiably discriminate between Members *where identical or similar conditions prevail*. Therefore, another WTO Member wishing to export the same varieties of products to Japan should be given the opportunity to show that indeed identical or similar conditions prevailed in respect of the varieties in question.

Conclusion

5.31.   The European Communities was of the view that the varietal testing system of Japan was too cumbersome and appeared to be applied in a manner which was more restrictive than necessary to achieve its stated objective. The Japanese system was also characterized by lack of transparency which could further impede trade in such products.

C.   Hungary

5.32.   Hungary noted that Article 2.1 of the SPS Agreement clearly stipulated the right of Members to take phytosanitary measures which were necessary for the protection of plant life or health. Nevertheless this right was conditional upon the fulfilment of all relevant provisions of the Agreement. Pursuant to Article 2.2, Members were obliged to "...ensure that any ...phytosanitary measure is applied only to the extent necessary to protect ... plant life or health, is based on scientific principles and is not maintained without sufficient scientific evidence...". An exception to the latter provision was provided for in Article 5.7.

5.33.   According to its submission, Japan had conducted a full-scale risk assessment concerning the plant quarantine measures in operation, including with respect to codling moth. However there was no indication as to whether, in accordance with Article 5.1, any risk assessment of the varietal testing of codling moth had been performed. Indeed, Japan's main argument with regard to the scientific rationale of varietal testing seemed to relate to the variation of the CxT values between varieties (in MB fumigation test on codling moth). Japan apparently interpreted this variation as an indicator of the degree of efficacy of the fumigation treatment.

5.34.   It was Hungary's view that Japan had neither been able to show unequivocally that variation of CxT values was a direct function of varietal differences nor had Japan established unambiguously that differences in CxT values necessarily affected the efficacy of the fumigation treatment at issue. At the very least this had been partly acknowledged by Japan when it argued the possibility of a "presence of varietal difference in the efficacy of disinfestation treatment".[166] Also, Japan had stated that its policy was based only "on a scientific hypothesis".[167] On the basis of available scientific knowledge, Hungary agreed with US arguments which questioned the scientific justification of varietal testing, in that: (i) minor differences in CxT values between varieties did not indicate differences in varieties of a single commodity; (ii) test-to-test variation of one variety was as great as that found between varieties; and, (iii) studies had indicated that the same variety of a commodity could show variations in dose-mortality tests from crop year to crop year, or even according to the stage of ripening of the particular variety. Hungary believed that the fact that there had not, to date, been any instance where the complaining party had had to modify a quarantine treatment for codling moth for varieties of the same commodity was of particular relevance to the dispute as it appeared to constitute strong evidence of the effectiveness of the established fumigation treatment across the different varieties of fruits. On the basis of the Japanese line of reasoning, it would be just as natural to expect numerous cases where modifications of treatment would have been required.

5.35.   Hungary maintained that the evidence put forward by the United States clearly demonstrated that the varietal testing requirement was inconsistent with the obligations set out in Article 2.2 of the SPS Agreement. As an alternative justification of the measure, Japan briefly invoked Article 5.7 of the Agreement, but failed to meet the criteria set out therein as the relevant scientific evidence was not "insufficient" but simply did not exist. The lack of a specific risk assessment appeared to support the impression that there had been no "objective assessment of risk" specifically in regard to varietal testing. Moreover, the long period since the requirement of varietal testing had been applied should have allowed Japan either to scientifically underpin or eliminate this testing requirement "within a reasonable period of time".

5.36.   In summary, on the basis of the two first submissions by the parties as well as Hungary's own knowledge of the matter, it was Hungary's view that the Japanese authorities *a priori* assumed the existence of "varietal differences" with regard to basic and processed agricultural products which then supposedly justified the requirement of separate testing of products not considered to be the "same". Hungary was not aware of any scientific basis for the "same-product" concept which seemed to be contrary to Article 2.2. Furthermore, there was, in Hungary's view, no provision in the Agreement, not even Article 5.7, that would allow WTO Members to introduce or maintain phytosanitary measures on the basis of hypotheses, assump-

---

[166]   Japan's first submission, paragraph 154.
[167]   *Ibid.*

tions or assertions. Neither could any support for this position be found in the report of the Appellate Body in *EC - Hormones*. Such interpretation would prevent the SPS Agreement from fulfilling its basic role, that of ensuring that SPS measures were not applied for reasons unrelated to the protection of sanitary and phytosanitary health. A contrary interpretation would open the door for effectively misusing SPS measures as disguised restrictions on trade.

5.37.   Finally, Hungary noted in respect of control, inspection and approval procedures that although there was no specific time period established in the SPS Agreement, Annex C paragraph 1(a) required that "such procedures are undertaken and completed without undue delay". As had been stated by the complaining party and borne out by Hungary's own experience, the testing and approval process for a given variety took anywhere from 2 to 4 years to complete. This could hardly be qualified as being a reasonable delay. The extremely long time involved in such procedures added up to the unusually heavy burden countries wishing to export agricultural products had to shoulder when trying to comply with SPS requirements applied by Japan. Hungary believed that the procedural aspects of an SPS measure also deserved a high degree of attention when judging their conformity with the SPS Agreement, as they themselves could act as a disguised restriction of trade which was prohibited under the Agreement.

VI.   PANEL'S CONSULTATION WITH SCIENTIFIC EXPERTS

A.   *Panel's Procedures*

6.1.   The Panel recalled that paragraph 2 of Article 11 of the SPS Agreement provided that:

> "In a dispute under this Agreement involving scientific or technical issues, a panel should seek advice from experts chosen by the panel in consultation with the parties to the dispute. To this end, the panel may, when it deems it appropriate, establish an advisory technical experts group, or consult the relevant international organizations, at the request of either party to the dispute or on its own initiative."

6.2.   Noting that this Panel involved scientific or technical issues, the Panel consulted with parties regarding the need for expert advice. Neither party objected to the Panel's intention to seek advice from individual experts. On 27 February 1998, the Panel informed the parties of its decision to seek scientific and technical advice as foreseen in paragraphs 1 and 2, first sentence, of Article 13 of the DSU, and pursuant to paragraph 2, first sentence, of Article 11 of the SPS Agreement. The following is an excerpt from the Panel's decision in that regard[168]:

---

[168]   The full decision (which also includes the timetable for the proceedings) is contained in a fax dated 27 February 1998, sent to both parties from the Panel.

Nature of advice

On the basis of the first submissions from both parties, the Panel will determine the areas in which it intends to seek expert advice.

Selection of experts and questions to experts

(a)   The Panel will seek expert advice from individual experts.

(b)   The number of experts the Panel will select will be determined in light of the number of issues on which advice will be sought, as well as by how many of the different issues each expert can provide expertise on.

(c)   The Panel will solicit suggestions of possible experts from the Secretariat of the International Plant Protection Convention (IPPC), and, subsequently, from the parties. The parties should not contact the individuals suggested.

(d)   The Panel does not intend to appoint experts who are nationals of any of the parties involved in the dispute unless the parties agree with such appointment or in the event the Panel considers that otherwise the need for specialized scientific expertise cannot be fulfilled. Parties are, however, free to include in their delegations scientific experts of their own nationality and may, of course, submit scientific evidence produced by their own nationals.

(e)   The Secretariat will seek brief CVs from the individuals suggested. To the extent possible, these will be provided to the parties.

(f)   The Panel will prepare specific questions for the experts. These will be provided to the parties.

(g)   The parties will have the opportunity to comment on and to make known any compelling objections to any particular expert under consideration. At the same time, the parties will have the opportunity to comment on the proposed questions, or suggest additional ones, before the questions are sent to the experts.

(h)   The Panel will inform the parties of the experts it has selected, and submit the questions to the experts.

(i)   The experts will be provided with all relevant parts of the parties' submissions on a confidential basis.

(j)   The experts will be requested to provide responses in writing; copies of these responses will be provided to the parties. The parties will have the opportunity to comment in writing on the responses from the experts.

Meeting with Experts

(a)   Should the Panel decide it opportune, or should a party so request, a meeting with experts, immediately prior to the second substantive meeting, may be held. Prior to such a meeting, the Panel would ensure that: (i) the parties' comments on the experts' responses would be provided to the experts; (ii) the experts would individually be provided with their colleagues' (the other experts) responses to the Panel's questions.

6.3.   The experts were invited to meet with the Panel and the parties to discuss their written responses to the questions and to provide further information. A summary of the written responses provided by the experts is presented below. The transcript of the meeting with the experts, held on 23 June 1998, is contained in Annex A of this report (Section 10).

6.4.   The experts advising the Panel were:

(a)   Dr. Neil Heather, Entomologist, University of Queensland, Corinda, Australia;

(b)   Dr. Patrick Ducom, Fumigation Expert, Lormont, France; and,

(c)   Mr. Robert Taylor, Fumigation Specialist, Natural Resources Institute, Chatham, United Kingdom.

B.   Questions to the Experts   and their Compiled Responses (Summarized)

Question 1: In relation to the concepts: probit analysis, dose-mortality test, and confirmatory test, could you: (i) state your understanding of these concepts; (ii) indicate the purpose of the tests; (iii) comment on the validity of using dose mortality tests for comparing the efficacy of quarantine treatment between varieties of the same commodity by calculating LD50 for each variety; (iv) comment on the confidence in predicting the level of mortality between varieties and the relative efficacy of quarantine treatment when using, for the approval of an additional variety, (1) only the procedure outlined in (iii); (2) the procedure outlined in (iii) and confirmatory tests; and (3) only confirmatory tests (to confirm the efficacy of the treatment already imposed for a variety of the same commodity); and, (v) indicate, in respect of the testing options outlined in (iv), how the type and quantity of the information derived from the tests on different varieties of the same commodity may vary, and what the causes for such variations may be.

6.5.   In respect of the understanding of the concepts and the purpose of the tests, **Dr. Ducom** noted that the dose-mortality test, analyzed by the probit method, was the key to all trials concerning a living organism's response to a toxic. The test was widely used by scientists in efficacy studies on pests. It was informative in respect to the *sensitivity* of a species to a toxic. According to Dr. Ducom, the utilization of LD_{50} in dose-mortality test to compare the efficacy of quarantine treatment posed two problems:

(a)   Japan had demanded that variety X be compared to a reference variety. However, it was sometimes impossible to have two varieties at the same time in the same physiological conditions if these had different ripening dates. This could lead to abnormal differences in the behavior of gas;

(b)   the tests did not render a reliable statistical analysis given the fact that the number of insects and fruit in question was low and that the causes of variation, of whatever nature, had a great influence on the results. The following were two examples based on the Yokoyama nectarine trials, 1987.[169]

- The "Summer Grand" variety had a LD_{50} of $6.3g/m^3$ compared to 15 - 18 for the other varieties tested, but the dose that killed 100 per cent of the insects was $40g/m^3$, compared to 30 - 35 for the others.

- Yokoyama and Vail, 1997, re-tested the "Summer Grand" and another variety tested in 1987 and found equivalent results in contradiction with those from 1987.[170]

6.6.   Dr. Ducom noted that in practice, the LD_{50} test constituted a fairly unreliable method to compare the *efficacy* of quarantine. Furthermore, Japan imposed a subsequent confirmatory test which was long and costly.

6.7.   The confirmatory tests, by using a sufficient number of insects, gave the statistical confidence which permitted achieving the desired threshold of 99.9968 per cent mortality (probit 9). This test obtained a sufficient degree of confidence, but it was also costly.

6.8.   Dr. Ducom noted that while the dose-mortality test (LD_{50}) did not give any confidence in respect of the varietal factor, it did give an indication of the relative sensitivity of the products tested. However, these indications undoubtedly did not allow for the determination of the part played by the variety itself in relation to the other factors which could have an influence on the test results, such as fruit ripeness, annual climatic differences, etc. In this respect, the confirmatory test gave absolutely no indication of varietal differences, it either worked or it did not.

6.9.   **Dr. Heather** noted that probit analysis was a biometrical technique for analysis of experimental data in which the quantitative response of an organism, usually as mortality, was subjected to regression analysis with respect to treatment dose, i.e., "dose-response" data. Mathematical transformation of mortality to probability units termed "probits" assisted in conversion of the normal distribution (curve) of the response data to a linear distribution to facilitate analysis. Dose data was frequently, but not invariably, logarithmically transformed for the same purpose of linearity. The outcomes of probit analysis were values such as LD (lethal dose), LC (lethal concentration) or LT (lethal time) for a nominated proportion of the population i.e., 50 per cent or 99.99 per cent, together with nominated confidence or fiducial intervals i.e., 95 per cent.[171]

6.10.   The main purposes of probit analysis were:

(a)   to define susceptibility of a population of target organisms to a treatment in terms of LD, LC or LT values;

(b)   subsequent comparisons of susceptibility of populations of target organisms;

---

[169]   *Supra* note 67. (US Exhibit 14)
[170]   *Supra* note 79. (US Exhibit 16)
[171]   Dr. Heather referred to Steel, R.G.D. and Torrie, J.H., *Principles and Procedures of Statistics with Special Reference to the Biological Sciences*, McGraw-Hill (1960) p.22.

    (c)   subsequent comparisons of varying response according to substrates, such as commodities;

    (d)   subsequent comparisons of treatments; and,

    (e)   prediction of the dose required for a specific level of treatment efficacy.

Comparisons were the most appropriate use of probit analysis.

6.11. *Dose-mortality (dose-response) testing* was an experimental procedure in which the response of an organism was estimated for a series of mortality-inducing doses of a specified treatment. It pertained to a group of tests known generally as bioassays. Dr. Heather noted that individual dose-mortality tests had to target a specific stage of an organism wherever possible as the susceptibility to a treatment could vary between life stages. The more direct the effect of the treatment or toxin on the target organism, in general, the more precise and reliable were the results.

6.12. The main purposes of dose-mortality testing were to produce data for analysis, possibly, but not exclusively by probit analysis, for:

    (a)   determination of above-mentioned parameters categorizing the response of an organism;

    (b)   comparisons of efficacies of different treatments, organisms or substrates; and,

    (c)   prediction of a treatment dose to meet a required level of efficacy.

6.13. The target organism test unit was usually a sub-sample of 20 to 50 individuals typically replicated 3 times, at each dose level. For a satisfactory result, 5 or more dose levels were usually required, evenly spaced between 0 and 100 per cent mortality. The dose variable could be concentration or duration.

6.14. *Confirmatory test* was a term that had restricted usage in a quarantine sense. By contrast, *probit analysis* and *dose-mortality testing* were widely used in pesticide science. A confirmatory test as used by US researchers equated to a *large-scale test* as used by Japanese researchers. The concept applied to a single dose response test on sufficient numbers of the target organism to ensure that a required efficacy had been attained at a nominated statistical confidence level. Countries such as Japan and New Zealand had customized this test by requiring a number of sub-samples of minimum size. This had the practical advantage that it could then be used in an iterative way to establish the minimum dose required to achieve a desired efficacy.

6.15. *Validity:* In principle, dose-mortality bioassays were a valid method to characterize the responses of test organism populations for comparison of the efficacies of quarantine treatments between varieties of the same commodity, if adequate precision could be achieved. Use of LD_{50} values for this purpose would be acceptable where the more desirable whole response line comparison was not valid. Since the LD_{50} was effectively the mean response of the bioassay test population and where confidence belts were narrowest, it was arguably the most robust point of comparison. Nevertheless it had to be supported by other point-wise comparisons such as at the LD_{95}, making the slopes of the lines more readily apparent. These LD (LC or LT) values would give more precise definition of response if the population of the bioassay organism was relatively homogeneous in its response to the treatment.

6.16.   In respect of *confidence*, Dr. Heather noted that in practice, large-scale confirmatory testing was usually the most practicable and reliable assurance that a treatment was effective.

6.17.   *Variance*: Dr. Heather noted that in phytosanitary experimentation variance was intrinsic to both commodity[172] and organism. If variance was *not* evident it would be cause for concern. The dose-responses of an organism to a quarantine treatment could be expected to be influenced by unavoidable variation within each commodity sample whether it was based varietally or otherwise. A test organism on the surface of a commodity would be relatively unaffected by interaction with the commodity and hence less variable in response than one present internally. As the stage for most codling moth tests was the egg, an external stage, it could be expected that its intrinsic susceptibility to the fumigant would be the same or closely similar for each commodity, given that all other conditions were the same.

6.18.   For a fumigation, variance originating from a commodity would be expected to be mainly the result of *sorption* although other causes were possible. The resultant decay of the concentration affected the dose received by the target organism and warranted monitoring during the course of the fumigation, which was normal practice.

6.19.   Dr. Heather noted in addition that other causes of commodity variation included interaction of the parent scion with rootstock and interstock, production locality, weather, site orientation, water management, nutrition, pests and diseases and their treatments, fruit initiation including pollination, orientation of fruit on trees, ripeness and maturity. This meant that where differences between varieties were small, fruit to fruit variation could greatly exceed variety to variety variation. Such variation was an inherent characteristic and was usually overcome by ensuring adequate robustness of the treatment.

6.20.   **Mr. Taylor** noted that probit analysis was the application of a statistical programme to data obtained from dose-mortality tests. It permitted a straight line to be drawn between dosage and mortality and from this critical dosages and mortality levels to be determined.

6.21.   Dose-mortality tests were tests conducted at laboratory level in order to determine the quantity of a toxicant, such as methyl bromide, required to cause a particular level of mortality of an examined insect (i.e., 50 or 90 per cent of the population).

6.22.   Confirmatory tests were conducted on a large-scale to confirm that the dose and exposure period derived from smaller tests would provide the level of quarantine treatment required in the field. The principal purpose of a confirmatory test was that by using large numbers of insects, account was taken of any natural variations that might occur within insect populations. This would include the testing of individuals that were more tolerant to methyl bromide than the general population, and which might not be present where much smaller numbers of insects were tested.

---

[172] Dr. Heather referred to Beverly, R.B., Latimer, J.K., and Smittle, D.A. *in:* "Postharvest Handling: a Systems Approach" Shewfelt, R.L. and Prussia S.E. , eds. Academic Press Ch 4, pp.74-98. *and* Hoffman, P.J., and Smith, L.G., *in:"* Postharvest Handling of Tropical Fruits" , eds Champ, B.R., Highley, E. and Johnson, G.I., ACIAR Proceedings No. 50, pp261-268.

6.23.   According to Mr. Taylor, LD_{50} values were extremely useful in comparing the toxicity of different chemicals and in the measurement of resistance. However, these values were less useful in investigations of much higher levels of toxic response such as were necessary in relation to quarantine treatments, where LD values of 99 or 99.9 were sought.

Question 2: In Japan's first submission[173], it is stated that "experimental error, physical condition of the fruit, sorption of the fumigant by packing material, and load of fruit in the chamber are the factors which scientists should be responsible for controlling in dose-mortality tests. Indeed, scientists who conducted these tests describe that test conditions were consciously made equal". To what extent is it feasible, technically and scientifically, to control such factors? Does the Japanese statement mean that differences in dose mortality tests for different varieties cannot be attributed to any of these factors?

6.24.   **Dr. Ducom** noted that although there were controllable factors such as the load of fruit in the chamber, the temperature, the packing material, the geographic and annual climatic differences[174], there were other factors that were impossible to control: the physical and physiological conditions of the fruit, ripeness, the precise stage of the insects at the time of treatment, small experimental errors, unexpected leaks in the chamber, etc. Those who carried out experiments were aware that the results of tests varied from one to another without the researchers necessarily understanding why. Nevertheless, if, hypothetically, all the factors mentioned above were identical, then the difference, if one existed, could be attributed to variety.

6.25.   **Dr. Heather** pointed out that "experimental error" in this context would be expected to include small errors in measurement, equipment imperfections, ambient conditions and biological response variation in test organism populations. It could be minimized and standardized from test to test but would always be present to some degree.

6.26.   Variation in "physical condition of the fruit" from test to test could be minimized but not eliminated. Handling injury, range of ripeness and maturity, and the need to have fruit in a condition susceptible to infestation at levels required for experimentation all contributed to unavoidable variation in the physical condition of the fruit. This could have some effect on sorption levels despite best efforts to standardize it.

6.27.   "Sorption of the fumigant by packaging material" and the walls of the chamber could be standardized by researchers but some variability would always remain.

6.28.   "Load in the test chamber" could be standardized by the control of fruit size, weight and number, but again small levels of variation would be unavoidable.

6.29.   Any experimental result would have background variation. It was usual to standardize procedures ("consciously made equal") as far as possible but always, some variation would remain. Its presence could be taken as evidence of the integrity of the experimenters. Statistical analyses were used to minimize the effects but it

---

[173]   Japan's first submission, paragraph 93.
[174]   Dr. Ducom referred to Exhibit 1 attached to his answers to the Panel's questions "PD Exhibit 1".

would not be possible to eliminate them totally. Dose-mortality was a bioassay and as such was relatively imprecise compared to a physical measurement, even when measuring the direct effect on an organism.

6.30.   **Mr. Taylor** noted that the Japanese position appeared to be that all tests should be conducted under such standardized conditions that any physical differences arising between tests, including those of the fruit, should be accounted for in the experimental procedure. Whilst it might be expected that conditions such as temperature, atmospheric pressure, loading, and even the type and condition of packing material could be controlled very accurately in test programmes, it was difficult to state with exact and absolute confidence that none of these factors could ever affect the results of tests. For this reason it would appear to be too dogmatic to state that differences in dose-mortality could not be attributed to any of the physical factors.

Question 3: Some of the results derived from dose-mortality tests seem to indicate differences for different varieties of the same commodity tested. The parties indicated that a number of factors may explain these differences[175]. Is it possible scientifically or technically to determine, by statistical or other methods, the relevant impact of each of these specific factors? If so, with what degree of scientific and/or statistical certainty for each factor? In your expert view, can one determine that varietal difference is one of these factors? On the basis of the results of the dose-mortality tests presented by the parties to the Panel (if appropriate, for each of the commodities tested), as an expert, is it possible to make such a determination?

6.31.   **Dr. Ducom** claimed that it was impossible by a simple dose-mortality test to determine the relevant impact of the factors playing a role in varietal differences, mainly because varieties ripened at different times. This had been adequately explained by the United States.[176] The dose-mortality test presented by the parties were designed to give information on insect *sensitivity*. The search for possible causes of varietal variations could not be determined with precision by them, but only with a specific research program.

6.32.   **Dr. Heather** noted that variability of the test organism, the test equipment, the test conditions and the test sample of fruit would all influence differences in LD_{50} values from one variety to another. However, it was probable that in most of the experiments under discussion, the major source of variability would be differential *sorption* by the commodity. Although statistical differences were evident between some varietally based experiments, this did not provide an assurance that the origin of the difference lay predominantly in varietal characteristics.

6.33.   Whether it would be possible to statistically identify the magnitude of the varietally based components required expert biometrical comment.

Question 4: In the US first submission[177], it is stated that "the accepted international practice in the area of pest quarantine treatment by virtually every other country in the world is to require testing by commodity, not by variety". To

---

[175]   See, e.g., the US first submission, paragraphs 33, 41, 42, 50 and Japan's first submission, paragraphs 92-94.
[176]   Dr. Ducom referred to the US first submission, paragraph 41.
[177]   US first submission, paragraph 96.

your knowledge, is it common practice for governments to require variety-by-variety testing for high-risk quarantine pests?[178] **How common is the variety-by-variety testing requirement compared to, for example, testing by commodity?**

6.34.   **Dr. Ducom** stated that he had no knowledge of any variety-by-variety testing requirement for quarantine except the Japanese requirements.

6.35.   **Dr. Heather** noted that although the United States submission contended that international practice was to test by commodity and not by variety, at least two countries, Japan and New Zealand had, in the past, adopted the practice of limiting acceptance to varieties tested although their prohibitions might be listed by commodity.[179] That the United States had maintained the general policy of accepting the variety used for testing as fully representative of the commodity was evidenced by their own proclaimed schedules.[180]

6.36.   Although the term "international practice" was used, many countries that imported fruit did not actively enforce phytosanitary barriers. It was thus difficult to generalize on the basis of past policy. Before the SPS Agreement came into force, decisions made by countries importing commodities subject to quarantine considerations would have been more influenced by government policies, procedures and precedents.

6.37.   **Mr. Taylor** noted that as far as he was aware, it was not common practice for governments to require variety-by-variety testing, and it was more usual for testing to be undertaken on a commodity basis.

Question 5: Considering the current Japanese varietal testing guidelines, how long would it technically take (1) to conduct these tests and (2) once these tests are conducted, to come to an administrative decision on acceptability of a new variety of an already tested commodity?

6.38.   **Dr. Ducom** noted that a varietal test according to the Japanese guidelines was a time-consuming procedure. The exact amount of time it would take would differ greatly depending on whether there was already any active research on the insect at issue. If a test site was permanently set up for mass rearing, the preparation of the insect stages for the specific harvest date was not a major problem. It would, however, demand a sufficient number of insects to take into account unavoidable incidents. There were two series of tests to conduct that would necessitate a one-year interval because there was only one harvest per year:

(a)   the dose-mortality test which required two to three months (the treatment itself having to be carried out during the harvest); and,

(b)   the confirmatory test which was best conducted the following year (this test would entail three more months of work).

---

[178]   The footnotes to paragraph 27 of Japan's first submission identify pests considered by Japan to fall within this category.

[179]   Dr. Heather referred to Japan, Exhibit 24: New Zealand MAF *Regulatory Authority Standard 155.02.03* (1994).

[180]   Dr. Heather referred to USDA APHIS *Treatment Manual* Section 2.15 and T101. (1992 or subsequent).

6.39.   In a case were no mass rearing had been previously set up, it would have to be established. It would take at least 1 to 2 years to domesticate the codling moth.

6.40.   In respect of the administrative decision, in theory, the results of the confirmatory test were immediate and authorization could be given soon thereafter. However, an additional year would be reasonable. The whole process could take at least 3 to 4 years.

6.41.   **Dr. Heather** noted that the answer to the question depended on whether a *new* pest and commodity were involved, whether a research infrastructure already existed and whether the same or a similar pest and commodity had been the subject of comparable research elsewhere.

6.42.   A reasonable expectation for research and preparation of a submission where there was an established rearing method for the pest would be between 2 to 3 seasons. After that, consideration by Japanese experts could take up to 1 year or longer depending on their backlog of submissions. Questions from the Japanese experts to be answered, possibility involving further research, could take a further season or longer. After acceptance of a proposal, there would be a need for a (Japanese) confirmatory trial which, depending on the availability of the commodity, might not be possible before the next production season. Further time would be required for Japanese authorities to prepare for a Public Hearing and subsequent regulatory amendment. Dr. Heather noted that for Australia, the time for the above procedure would usually span over 3 to 7 years.

6.43.   **Mr. Taylor** noted that the test would need to be conducted over more than one season and also with fruit of varying maturity, so that a period of two years would be necessary. He maintained that it ought to be possible to reach an administrative decision regarding acceptance of tests on a new variety of a commodity already tested within a period of twelve months.

Question 6: In the submissions before the Panel, which documents do you consider to contain the fullest statement of the scientific *rationale* - if any such rationale exists - behind Japan's current varietal testing requirements in respect of apples, cherries, nectarines and walnuts? Is such scientific rationale (if any) linked to the commodity which is examined, or does it apply equally across the commodities?

6.44.   **Dr. Ducom** noted that Japan's concern was reflected in the statement that, in a few cases, the sensitivity of a given insect stage apparently differed according to the variety that it was on. Turning this into a general principle amounted to a precautionary principle more than any scientific rationale. Japan based its precautionary principle on the fact that too high sorption risked resulting in an insufficient CxT value. According to Dr. Ducom, this argument was not without merit, but he questioned why Japan did not then demand as a criterion for approval the obtainment of a defined CxT value, rather than the setting of initial fumigation conditions.

6.45.   **Dr. Heather** noted that the *rationale* advanced by Japan for "varietal testing" was given in section III.E of the first written submission of Japan and defended in II.A of their second written submission. Japan therein identified sorption of the fumigant gas as the major reason for differences in LD_{50} and CxT parameters between varietal samples and attributed these to "physical and chemical properties of the fruits, which are then attributable to varietal characters" (paragraph 4.111). In Dr.

Heather's view, neither parameter was ideal for showing that there were consistent realistic differences in efficacy of a treatment between varieties of a commodity, yet no alternatives appeared more practicable. The CxT product was an average of the fumigant concentrations measured over the fumigation time and the true LD_{50} was modified by MB sorption by the commodity. Also, individual LD value comparisons did not take into account the slope of the response line and hence did not measure the overall or direct response of the insect population.

6.46.   Essentially, the Japanese argument hinged on whether the differences in test samples that affected these parameters were predominantly varietal characteristics and whether they were of sufficient magnitude to realistically affect treatment efficacy. It was the Japanese view that they did both and this was believed to be the basis of their *rationale*.

6.47.   The Japanese preferred model first required dose-mortality testing of the pest stage and commodity variety(s) to ensure that differences did not influence treatment efficacy. By using the stage/variety combination, if any, for which the pest was most difficult to kill for the remainder of testing, the greatest risk was deemed to be covered. On this basis subsequent testing of additional varieties should only need to be comparative unless greater difficulty of kill of the pest was demonstrated. The Japanese model acknowledged this but required a further confirmatory test, the reason for which was not readily apparent.

6.48.   It was theoretically correct that results of an experiment were only proven for that exact set of conditions, but this overlooked the purpose of experiments, which was to provide guidance for wider use. The major problem was to determine the extent to which differences were varietal in origin.

6.49.   **Mr. Taylor** noted that the documents contained within the second written submission of Japan contained the fullest statement of the scientific evidence behind Japan's contention that testing by variety was necessary to establish the efficacy of quarantine treatments. The submission contained references and data to show that differences in sorption and CxT value had been shown between different varieties of cherries, nectarines and walnuts. No data were presented with reference to apple varieties.

Question 7: In respect of the risk of entry, establishment or spread of codling moth due to differences in varieties that could affect the efficacy of the quarantine treatment, what are the technical/scientific factors relevant in an assessment of risk? To what extent has Japan taken these factors into account?

6.50.   **Dr. Ducom** stated that he did not know risk assessment techniques adequately enough to respond to this question.

6.51.   **Dr. Heather** noted that risk of entry, establishment or spread of codling moth due to differences in varieties that could affect the efficacy of the quarantine treatment would relate predominantly to:

(a)   interaction between physical or physiological characteristics of the commodity and the fumigant resulting in higher sorption (fumigant inactivation) in one variety than another, and

(b)   higher susceptibility of the commodity to the pest for a range of reasons resulting in consistently higher levels of infestation risk in one variety than another.

Japan had concentrated on the first, paying close attention to LD_{50} and CxT values.

6.52.   The practice of quarantine was one of *risk management*. A key criterion adopted by Japan for quarantine treatments for otherwise prohibited commodities was that the treatment had to provide a measure of protection equivalent to import prohibition. While import prohibition could effectively exclude commercially traded commodities, it still had to deal with traveller-carried contraband, so in a sense, exclusion of a pest was always less than absolute. Quality requirements normally ensured that commercially traded fruit was essentially free of codling moth infestation even where a quarantine disinfestation treatment was not obligatory.

6.53.   A important factor was the low pre-treatment incidence of codling moth in commercially marketable host commodities from the United States compared to near 100 per cent artificially infested experimental material, i.e., walnuts less than 0.03 per cent; nectarines, less than 0.0003 per cent; cherries, less than 0.00007 per cent; and apples less than 0.00008 per cent as shown in exhibits (these estimates needed to be considered in conjunction with their variance).

6.54.   **Mr. Taylor** noted that in 1995, the FAO adopted new guidelines on pest risk assessment (PRA), the purpose of which was to ensure that pests were defined as quarantine pests on the basis of scientific principles in order to prevent unfair restrictions on trade. In the case of codling moth, Japan, in its first submission to the Panel (pages 9-15) reported on the PRA conducted in 1996, the assessment being conducted together with that for other pests. The Japanese assessment concluded the following:

(a)   Codling moth was not present in the country.

(b)   Environmental conditions in Japan were such as to give a grade 'a' for the potential for establishment of codling moth within Japan.

(c)   In relation to the potential for the pest to spread within Japan, this was graded as 'b' taking into account the insect's relatively low reproductive capacity.

(d)   Economic consequences to Japan of the establishment of codling moth were assessed to be of particular significance because host plants such as apples and cherries were produced in great quantity. As a consequence, the PRA analysis resulted in an 'a' grading.

6.55.   In summarizing the assessment, Japan concluded that codling moth presented a very high risk and an overall grade 'A' was given. It was noted that the analysis with respect to codling moth incorporated all the guidelines for PRA (recommended and adopted by FAO).

6.56.   It would appear that Japan did take into account all of the technical and scientific factors necessary in making a proper risk assessment for the entry of codling moth.

Question 8: In the US first submission[181] it is stated that "[e]very article published on the efficacy of methyl bromide and/or methyl bromide and cold storage for disinfection of codling moth has demonstrated that there are no differences among varieties that affects efficacy of a quarantine treatment". Could you comment on this? On the basis of the scientific evidence before the Panel, to what degree does the mortality of codling moth differ between varieties of

---

[181]   US first submission, paragraph 83.

the same commodity, of either apples, cherries, nectarines or walnuts, when treated with methyl bromide (MB) or MB and cold storage?

6.57.   **Dr. Ducom** noted that the conclusions of authors who had published articles on the efficacy of methyl bromide had always been that the differences in sensitivity that might exist among different varieties was insignificant. The major argument was that the 20 per cent buffer was sufficient to exceed the limit of a possible difference in varietal sensitivity.[182] Dr. Ducom noted that there was a need for research on the factors which influenced sorption. Reported differences between varieties were significant with traditional probit statistical methods (the LD_{50} values were different). However, it was very difficult from that to derive any practical conclusions. A great part of the present problem lay therein.

6.58.   **Dr. Heather** noted that the US view, that there were no published differences among varieties that affected efficacy, was true if the criterion used was large-scale test results. If the criterion used was statistically significant differences between experimental samples of different varieties there were differences as identified by Japan, but there was no certainty that they were attributable to unique varietal characteristics. In subsequent research on additional varietal samples these differences were too small to cause the efficacy of a treatment, based on varieties used in initial trials, to fail in further testing. This was equally true for commodity-specific treatments with methyl bromide or methyl bromide and cold storage, for apples, nectarines, cherries or walnuts. For each of these, the Japanese minimum efficacy test requirement of no survivors from tests on more than 30,000 insects had been met (3 x >10,000).

6.59.   The treatments for apples, cherries, nectarines and walnuts differed, in part because the fumigations had to be done at different handling temperatures and this affected the toxicity of methyl bromide to the insects. Also, for apples that were cold tolerant in storage, fumigation was supplemented with cold storage treatment. The actual tolerance of codling moth eggs to methyl bromide was unlikely to differ between these commodities. If all were fumigated at the same temperature, the treatments could be expected to be much closer.

6.60.   Japanese concerns were valid, that a low treatment based on dose-mortality testing followed by large-scale trials on a single varietal batch could have resulted in a treatment that would fail on other varieties. It would largely depend on the amount of the "buffer" increase in relation to the difference between varietal samples. Each instance of a very low threshold of susceptibility in a variety in one season's experiments[183] was shown to be anomalous as testing progressed, but some varieties were lower than others in both LD and CxT parameters.

Question 9: Can a difference in the "sorption" level of MB during MB fumigation between different varieties of the same commodity affect the efficacy of the

---

[182]   Dr. Ducom noted that the amelioration of statistical methods allowed for a reworking of the first results and invalidated the hypothesis of a statistical difference despite the large difference interpreted as significant with traditional methods. (US Exhibit 15)

[183]   *Supra* note 67 (US Exhibit 14); 1992 New Zealand study on cherries for Sam cherries (US, Exhibit 4 and Japan, Exhibit 21).

quarantine treatment? If so, do such differences indicate differences in varietal characteristics or are they partly/mostly/completely due to other variables? Could you list the factors which you consider contribute to differences in sorption levels.

6.61. **Dr. Ducom** stated that sorption on cereal grains had been covered by Banks 1992, showing its importance in the success or failure of fumigation[184], but there was little understanding of the sorption of methyl bromide on fresh fruits.

6.62. Sorption levels had a direct influence on the efficacy of a treatment, but this influence was not usually measured directly. It was measured using the CxT value. If the sorption was too high, then the resulting CxT value would be too low, and there was a risk of insufficient efficacy.

6.63. It was, however, possible to find several cases where the influence of sorption on the CxT value was nonexistent: for example in Yokoyama 1994[185], the set of sorption values (sorption having diverse origins: variety, annual climatic differences, packing material, but with the same concentration of 48 g/m^3) was organized in ascending order[186]; the corresponding CxT values were distributed at random but within narrow limits. Generally, the inverse was found, this was the case related in Question 3 by the Research Division of Yokohama Plant Protection Station, where the sorption - CxT value relationship was linear.[187]

6.64. Dr. Ducom stated that to his knowledge, no complete study specific to fresh fruit had been conducted in the United States on the variety-sorption relationship. This would have been a good way to respond to the question in a precise manner or to model possible interactions. Intuitively, it was conceivable that variety could be an intrinsic factor in sorption variation, as was the case, for example, in a study of sorption in raisins.[188] This study was based on the partition coefficient of methyl bromide between the gaseous phase (the only part of gas that is active on the insect) and the solid phase, i.e. the fruit (the part of sorbed gas that is not utilizable by the insect.) This coefficient was directly linked to sorption and allowed it to be modeled. The study showed that this coefficient could vary considerably between varieties and thus influenced the efficacy of a given general "raisin" dose. The varietal aspect could be the result of interactions like the physiological state of the fruit, its ripeness, etc.

6.65. Dr. Ducom noted that there was a lack of precise studies on this subject. *A priori*, one could cite almost anything, the size of the fruit, the nature of the epidermis, the average sugar content, the ripeness of the fruit, its physiological condition, the time between harvest and fumigation, etc. However, in respect of the issue at hand, there was a case which merited study.

6.66. **Dr. Heather** noted that differences in sorption levels attributable to varietal characteristics, together with differences in sorption levels attributable to other causes between batches of a commodity, would cause gas concentrations to decay

---

[184] Dr. Ducom referred to PD Exhibit 2.
[185] Dr. Ducom referred to US Exhibit 36.
[186] Dr. Ducom referred to PD Exhibit 3.
[187] Dr. Ducom referred to US Exhibit 13.
[188] Dr. Ducom referred to PD Exhibit 4.

differentially and hence affect the efficacy of fumigation against the pest. Sorption was an inherent characteristic of fumigation as a treatment method. Factors contributing to differences in sorption levels justified detailed comment by an expert in fumigation chemistry.

6.67. **Mr. Taylor** noted that difference in the level of sorption of methyl bromide between different varieties of the same commodity could affect the efficacy of quarantine treatment if the level of sorption of a particular variety was of sufficient magnitude to reduce the concentration of methyl bromide gas below the level required to cause insect mortality. However, this would require significant differences between varieties to cause this difference in the level of sorption. Three types of sorption of a fumigant could occur: adsorption, absorption and chemisorption.

(a)   Adsorption of a gas such as methyl bromide was a physical surface effect and resulted from the attraction of molecules to the surface of a commodity being treated. The larger the surface area the larger may be the adsorption effect. An example would be the case where a commodity had a very rough and therefore greater surface area compared to another with a much smoother surface. Adsorption would be expected to be less in the latter, but the differences in the magnitude of adsorption would probably be small and likely to be insufficient to affect the efficacy of quarantine treatment.

(b)   Absorption of methyl bromide was also a physical process, but here the chemical entered into the commodity and was held in either solids or liquids. Methyl bromide was absorbed particularly by oils and fats in which it dissolved and, in commodities with a high oil or fat content such as nuts, application rates of methyl bromide were very much affected by this factor. It had been shown that the level of absorption could be affected by the commodity moisture content; the higher the moisture level the higher the sorption.

(c)   Chemisorption was a third type of sorption and, being chemical in nature, was an irreversible reaction in which residues were left in the fumigated commodity. Methyl bromide reacted in particular with proteins and amino acid groups in a reaction known as methylation, which led to a splitting of the methyl bromide molecule and resulted in inorganic bromide residues. The rate of chemical reactions increased with increasing temperature and for this reason chemisorption took place more readily the higher the temperature.

6.68.   Mr. Taylor noted that both adsorption and absorption were reversible reactions and were affected by the temperature, sorption being greater at lower temperatures. For this reason, methyl bromide application rates had to be greater at lower temperatures.

6.69.   Sorption of methyl bromide was of particular importance for durable commodities because different types of commodities, depending on their chemical constituents, required more or less fumigant to achieve the level of treatment required. Durable commodities could be conveniently placed in groups according to the dosage rates required. These commodity groups were very much connected with oil and fat content, although other facts such as fineness of the commodity which could affect the rate of gas penetration were important and could even affect the length of exposure necessary for effective treatment.

Question 10: The US states in its submissions to the Panel that "minor differences in CxT values between varieties do not indicate differences in varieties of a single commodity"[189]. They also state that "CxT values differ for tests on the same variety as well as for tests of different varieties"[190]. In respect of walnuts, the US stated in its first submission that "test to test variation of one variety was as great as that found among all three tested varieties"[191]. The US arguments are further expanded in paragraphs 20-32 of their rebuttal submission. Japan states that the "link between varietal differences and divergent efficacy of the fumigation treatment may manifest itself by way of the difference in the 'CxT' value"[192]. Japan uses three empirical cases in its first submission to support its point that there were *statistically significant differences* in the CxT values between the tested variety samples (see paragraphs 80-87, first submission). Japan further elaborates its arguments in paragraphs 35-42 of its rebuttal submission. In light of the above, (i) could you define CxT values and explain what they are an indication of; (ii) could you explain "Tukey's multiple range test" and its relevance to this issue[193]; (iii) have the results of the referenced reports (in the context of CxT values) been accurately assessed in the parties' submissions?; (iv) could you list those factors which might be the cause of variations of CxT values between varieties; and, (v) to the extent that varietal differences is among the listed factors, what kind of varietal differences are you referring to? could such differences affect the efficacy of MB fumigation?

6.70.   **Dr. Ducom** noted that the notion of the concentration times product, or here the CxT value, was fundamental in fumigation. What killed the insect was not only the dose of gas introduced, but the quantity of gas inhaled during the entire gas exposure period. The measurement of gas concentrations throughout fumigation permitted the monitoring of the efficacy from the initial condition over the evolution time. The CxT value depended on the gas concentration in the chamber, which varied depending on the following factors:

(a)   initial dose introduced into the chamber;

(b)   the load, which could increase or decrease the free concentration of gas according to the sorption of the commodity;

(c)   the sorption of the commodity and of everything present in the chamber; and

(d)   possible leaks.

6.71.   The CxT value was universal once the target stage and the treatment temperature were defined. All the other factors mattered little, even the nature of the commodity, since they were accounted for by the measurement of gas concentration. Dr. Ducom stated that in his opinion, this notion had been criticized wrongly by the

---

[189]   US first submission, paragraph 50.

[190]   US rebuttal submission, title 1. on p.8.

[191]   US first submission, paragraph 50; reference is made to US Exhibit 17, pp. 149-154.

[192]   Japan's first submission, paragraph 78.

[193]   Japan's first submission, paragraph 84.

United States[194]; it had been stated that the CxT value varied according to the ripeness of the fruit, the geographic conditions, etc. In fact, the CxT value was simply used backwards, because the trials were conducted according to the doses and not the CxT value. If a study using CxT values was undertaken, it was possible to say that to obtain a given CxT value, the initial necessary dose would vary according to the ripeness of the fruit, the geographic conditions, etc. It had also been stated that the "CxT certainly is not indicative of any varietal characteristics"; but this was, according to Dr. Ducom, not true.[195]

6.72.   Dr. Ducom reiterated that the CxT value could be specifically set and the parameters could subsequently be manipulated. Contrary to this, present conditions to impose a recognized effective treatment consisted in fixing initial intangible conditions (temperature, treatment length, gas tightness of the chamber, nature of the packing material and load) that would make any variation impossible.

6.73.   Dr. Ducom agreed that the confirmatory test constituted a necessary condition to define the quarantine level for a given species of pest. It was furthermore possible to associate the test to a CxT value, which was then acquired once and for all. This was the case, for example, proposed by Yokoyama for nectarines $(68\pm3\text{gh/m}^3)$.[196] This objective CxT value could thus become the sole criterion for success in quarantine treatment.

6.74.   In respect of Tukey's multiple range test, Dr. Ducom noted that as he was not a statistician, he could not give any precise opinion on the statistic quality of that test. However, as he understood it, it was not relevant to the resolution of the problem. In the precise case of walnuts, the oil content, for example was a factor of varietal selection. It was clear that under that case, there would be varietal differences in sorption, and thus in the CxT values, because methyl bromide was very soluble in oils.

6.75.   In respect of the referenced reports (in the context of CxT values in the parties' submissions), Dr. Ducom noted that it seemed, in general, that the notion of CxT had not been studied enough and that that was apparent in the submissions. Indeed, for the Japanese, this notion seemed primordial.[197] But even so, they did not make use of any American data with the notion of CxT and they continued to demand the dose-mortality tests and confirmatory tests without any reference to CxT values. The Americans had also shown to be illogical in the same way.[198] Contrary to the Japanese, the American officials minimized their interest in CxT values, whereas researchers made concrete propositions for confirmatory tests.[199] Dr. Ducom noted that he completely accepted the references presented by Japan in response to Question 9 as set out in US Exhibit 3.[200]

---

[194]   Dr. Ducom referred to the US Oral statement of 2 April 1998, paragraph 38, third point.

[195]   Dr. Ducom referred to PD Exhibit 4, Table A3, p.248.

[196]   Dr. Ducom referred to US Exhibit 12 (*supra* note 76).

[197]   Dr. Ducom referred to Japans first submission, paragraph 79-86, 104 and 128.

[198]   Dr. Ducom referred to the second US submission, paragraph 28.

[199]   Yokoyama proposed a CxT of 68 gh/m^3 for the quarantine treatment of nectarines (Dr. Ducom referred to US Exhibit 12; see also *supra* note 76).

[200]   Dr. Ducom referred to Japan's references to: Bell 1996; FAO 1983 and Bond 1984 in response to Question 9 as set out in US Exhibit 3.

6.76.   In respect of whether varietal difference could affect treatment efficacy, Dr. Ducom noted that it was rarely possible to foresee the influence of a varietal factor on sorption, and thus on the CxT value. Only experimentation and modeling using numerous examples could respond to this question. However, *a priori*, it was difficult to see what significant influence a color or a different ripeness could have on the behavior of gas. On the other hand, one could easily see that a different oil content from one walnut variety to another would lead to a pronounced difference in the behavior of gas, though not necessarily in the efficacy of treatment.

6.77.   According to **Dr. Heather**, the CxT value for a fumigation was an expression of the relationship between fumigant gas concentration and time in the fumigation enclosure or chamber. It was generally expressed as CT= k but was more properly expressed as $C^nT=k$ where n was a toxicity index.[201] As such, it was an expression of the active gas dosage to which the pest or test organism was exposed during the time of the treatment. Because the concentration decayed during the fumigation time from the causes already discussed, "concentration" was an average value derived from a number of measurements and required temperature, load and humidity to be specified for proper definition. It could be inferred from Bond that it would be more usual to manipulate fumigant concentration and time to arrive at a required CxT value than to use CxT as a record of dose.[202] The CxT relationship could be very complex. It was a field of expertise related to physical chemistry of gases and should only be commented upon in detail by an expert in that discipline.

6.78.   Dr. Heather stated that Tukey's multiple range test was best explained by an expert in biometry.[203] It compared results between experiments, in contrast to other commonly used tests of significance which compared treatments within an experiment. As such it was said to be less sensitive in the identification of significant differences.

6.79.   Dr. Heather claimed that no inaccuracies were apparent in the assessment of referenced reports with respect to CxT values by either Japan or the United States, which, understandably, used specific findings to support their submissions.

6.80.   The main factors in experimental variance would be expected to be:

    (a)   unavoidable experimental variation including those resulting from measurement, equipment function, small temperature fluctuations and chamber load; and,

    (b)   sorption differences in commodity samples, including variety-linked differences if any.

6.81.   Dr. Heather noted that varietal differences of importance would be expected to be mainly sorption related. Further clarification would lie in the spheres of expertise of fumigation chemistry and plant physiology. Such differences would need to

---

[201]   Dr. Heather referred to Winks, R.G., The Biological Efficacy of Fumigants: Time/Dose Response Phenomena, in *Pesticides and Humid Tropical Grain Storage Systems* (eds B. R. Champ and E. Highley) ACIAR Proceedings No. 14 pp211-221 1986.

[202]   Dr. Heather referred to Bond, E.J., *Manual of Fumigation for Insect Control*. FAO Plant Production and Protection Paper 54 (1984), pp.20-27. (Japan, Exhibit 12)

[203]   Dr. Heather referred to Steel, R.G.D. and Torrie, J.H., *Principles and Procedures of Statistics with Special Reference to the Biological Sciences* Mc Graw-Hill Book Company (1960), p. 109.

be large to affect the efficacy of fumigation and should be apparent to experienced researchers and risk analysts. The consistent success of the large-scale confirmatory tests under discussion indicated that no overall differences of this magnitude occurred.

Question 11: Japan states that varietal differences accounted for at least some of the observed differences in CxT values between dose-mortality tests (and that CxT values are indicative of treatment efficacy). Technically and scientifically, if additional varieties were tested only for CxT values, and those values were within the range already observed for other varieties, to what extent would any further efficacy testing of the variety be necessary?

6.82. **Dr. Ducom** stated that if varieties were tested to find the CxT value, then no further testing was necessary. The success of the system required:

   (a)   that the trials be conducted according to precise guidelines approved by both parties (in particular, the number of fruits should be quite large in each replicate to minimize the effects of sampling); and,

   (b)   that the treatment standard clarify the CxT value necessary to obtain the desired efficacy. This value was the one found in the confirmatory test, for example for nectarines, 68 gh/m3. [204]

6.83. Dr. Ducom stressed that the results of these tests were sufficient in themselves to give confidence in the conformity of the candidate variety without having to include the reference variety and insects for efficacy confirmation. This would not bring any supplementary information. Furthermore, research on the CxT value per variety was an operation which could be rapidly conducted, since only the variety of fruit to be tested was used. Fumigation only lasted two hours and the result was known immediately.

6.84. **Dr. Heather** stated that if the CxT value for a required efficacy against a pest was known then a fumigation treatment that met or exceeded that specification could be expected to achieve the quarantine security level required. This would hold true for all batches of a commodity, including those of differing varieties, provided that temperature, load and any other relevant requirements were met.

6.85. Fumigation of agricultural commodities could be specified according to CxT requirements of the pest or pest group with consideration given to levels of concentration which might be phytotoxic to the host commodity. The requirement by the United States in its own gazetted treatments, that specified concentration levels be met part way through the MB fumigations for some commodities, appeared to be an example of this approach. [205]

6.86. **Mr. Taylor** stated that CxT values were used to indicate the fumigant concentration and exposure period required to achieve a 99 per cent mortality of all development stages of an insect, at a particular temperature and humidity, under practical conditions. If these values were obtained for additional varieties and were found to fall

---

[204] Dr. Ducom referred to US Exhibit 12 (*supra* note 76).
[205] Dr. Heather referred to USDA APHIS PPQ *Treatment Manual* Section 2.15 and T101. (1992 or subsequent)

within the range already observed for other varieties, it would be difficult to justify why further testing would be necessary.

Question 12: To the extent, if any, that there are varietal differences in apples, cherries, nectarines or walnuts, which could affect the efficacy of MB treatment, can these differences be so high that they are not covered by the 10-20 % "buffer" normally added to the highest minimum dose (minimum dose for 100% mortality) derived from dose-mortality tests for one variety of a given commodity? Is the "highest minimum dose" (to which this "buffer" is added) calculated for each variety separately or, in case an application is made for several varieties, for all these varieties taken together? Could you elaborate on any differences there might be between the general practice and the procedures followed by Japan.

6.87.   **Dr. Ducom** noted in respect of the calculation of the highest minimum dose that it was always measured on one variety, never, to his knowledge, on a mixture of several varieties. This was linked to the fact that generally a single variety was studied and not a mixture of several varieties, to avoid the introduction of systematic heterogeneity.

6.88.   The research procedure for quarantine treatment imposed by Japan corresponded to the general guidelines accepted by all countries (research on the least sensitive stage that could be present in fruit, confirmatory test), except concerning the varietal difference aspect. There were no variety-by-variety trials elsewhere.

6.89.   **Dr. Heather** noted that there was no evidence apparent from the experiments which formed the basis for treatments for apples, cherries, nectarines and walnuts that the 10-20 per cent buffer added to the experimental dose would be inadequate to cover differences of the magnitude shown between varietal samples.

6.90.   If only one variety had been represented in the initial testing, the possibility that other varieties which might be proposed subsequently could have higher predicted minimum dose requirements would be greater. Even so, the likelihood of this exceeding the 10-20 per cent "buffer" appeared low. Also, it would almost certainly have been a matter of scientific rigour on the part of researchers to ensure that the initial test fruit were as representative of commercial exports as possible.

6.91.   At the levels of efficacy concerned, the incidence of survivors due to varietal differences would be very low. For a minimum efficacy of 99.99 per cent there would be less than 1 survivor from 10,000 *on average overall,* so the actual effect of varietal differences on quarantine risk was extremely small and difficult to evaluate.

6.92.   Normally, the dose to which the 10-20 per cent buffer was added would have been estimated from the varietal trial in which the LD values had been highest hence, "the highest minimum dose". How this dose was chosen was a matter of subjective judgment, but if the minimum efficacy required was 99.99 per cent the $LD_{99.99}$ could be computed together with fiducial limits and either the LD value or its higher fiducial limit used as the dose to which the 10-20 per cent was added. This tended to over-estimate the dose required. Alternatively, the lowest experimental dose for which there were no survivors (100 per cent mortality) in the varietal trial with the highest levels of survival could be used as the minimum effective dose and the "buffer" of 10-20 per cent added.

6.93.   The Japanese large-scale confirmatory test differed in size and procedure from some other countries, including the United States, but these were matters of detail. It was in its varietal and country-oriented procedural approach to conditional lifting of import prohibition that Japan differed most from the United States and other countries.

6.94.   **Mr. Taylor** noted that any varietal differences affecting the efficacy of MB treatment were unlikely to be so great that the buffer of 10-20 per cent failed to account for these differences. Effective quarantine treatment was therefore to be expected. It was not clear from the documentation submitted whether the highest minimum dose to which the "buffer" was added was calculated for each variety or separately for several varieties taken together.

Question 13: In the US first submission[206] it is stated that "confirmatory tests are the relevant indicator of efficacy of quarantine treatment. Therefore this normal variability in testing results [derived from dose-mortality tests] cannot constitute a legitimate basis for denying approval for other varieties of the same commodities". Could you comment on this in relation to codling moth treated with MB fumigation? Are confirmatory tests (using the treatment found to be effective for an original variety) sufficient to demonstrate efficacy of quarantine treatment for additional varieties (e.g., to achieve a probit 9 mortality level)?

6.95.   **Dr. Ducom** noted that a dose-mortality test did not replace a confirmatory test. But if one accepted the postulate that whatever the dose-mortality test result was, it would not question the standard already accepted, then what was the purpose of these dose-mortality tests?

6.96.   **Dr. Heather** noted that the broader applicability of a confirmatory test done on samples of one variety of a commodity depended on the extent of variation of mortality attributable to varietal characteristics. For quarantine purposes, it was the effect of the treatment on the pest that was of principal importance. A decision on whether to extend acceptance to all varieties of a commodity from a country could be based on factors that included:

    (a)   past experience with other pests or other treatments on the commodity;

    (b)   legislative or procedural requirements of the importing country;

    (c)   the performance of the same or similar treatments in use by other countries for the same or other varieties;

    (d)   the extent of differences between varieties; and,

    (e)   small or large-scale tests on a representative range of varieties.

6.97.   A large-scale confirmatory test against a pest on a commodity was highly effective in providing assurance that the treatment as tested would meet an efficacy requirement. It provided good assurance for the extension of an existing successful treatment to additional varieties of a commodity, provided that the initial varietal sample was representative of the commodity. The target efficacy had to be ade-

---

[206]   US first submission, paragraph 56.

quately specified. Probit 9 as a target efficacy level needed to have a specified confidence level that enabled the required test sample size to be determined. It was better understood when expressed as the percentage mortality to be achieved (99.9968%) and confidence level required.

Question 14: Considering the scientific evidence before the Panel, would the MB treatment approved by Japan for some varieties of apples, cherries, nectarines or walnuts mentioned in US Exhibit 1, meet probit 9 protection for the varieties of each or any of these commodities mentioned in US Exhibit 1 which have not yet been allowed for import into Japan?

6.98.   **Dr. Ducom** answered that "yes", a positive confirmatory test constituted the best proof of efficacy. All the species and varieties having passed this test positively would then satisfy all the quarantine requirements.

6.99.   **Dr. Heather** noted that where additional varieties of apples, nectarines, cherries and walnuts had been subjected to a successful confirmatory test to meet probit 9 as defined by Japan, there would not appear to be any technical quarantine reason why they would not be acceptable to Japan, subject to their approval procedures. Some of the varieties of apples in question were being accepted by Japan from New Zealand and would necessarily require a codling moth disinfestation treatment the same as, or equivalent to, that developed by the United States for varieties already approved.[207]

6.100. In the absence of a large-scale confirmatory test, it was not possible to be absolutely certain that additional varietal samples would meet the standard required. Where it could reasonably be expected that they would, this had to be the basis of the risk management decision.

Question 15: Is it relevant to compare the varietal treatment of apples, nectarines, cherries and walnuts to the differential treatment of other agricultural commodities? (e.g., thermal treatment of mangoes where characteristics such as size and shape influence the treatment of the fruit)[208]. In respect of other agricultural commodities, can you give examples of actual cases where concern over varietal differences has given rise to diverging phytosanitary requirements between varieties of the same commodity?

6.101. **Dr. Ducom** stated that the reactions of a vegetable product to a gas compared to a physical phenomenon such as temperature had, *a priori*, nothing to do with each other. In the first case, one had to deal with the problems of sorption of a chemical or physico-chemical nature. In the second case, it was a question of thermal conductivity. Dr. Ducom was not aware of cases where concern over varietal differences had given rise to diverging phytosanitary requirements between varieties of the same commodity.

6.102. **Dr. Heather** stated that the main relevance of the comparison of the US approach to hot water treatment of mangoes and the Japanese approach to MB fumi-

---

[207]   Dr. Heather referred to Japan, Exhibit 8, attached table 24.

[208]   Japan's first submission, paragraphs 108-113; US rebuttal submission 13-16; and, Japan's rebuttal submission paragraph 25.

gation was the possible modification of the treatment by the commodity before it acted on the pest. For mangoes, it was the time taken for the centre of fruit to reach a temperature lethal to any internally feeding fruit fly larvae. Because it was not practicable to use electronic temperature probes in hot water dips, a total time of treatment needed to be specified according to size and shape of fruit, which was a varietal characteristic but not exclusively so. Mangoes from Thailand for export to Japan were "vapour heat" treated using differing schedules according to variety. Part of the reason for this related to perceived varietal susceptibility to treatment injury.

6.103. **Mr. Taylor** stated that fumigation was a very special method of quarantine treatment and bore little relationship to any other method of treatment. Of the factors affecting the efficacy of fumigation, sorption could be considered to be particularly important, but size and shape of fruit were not factors that could affect treatment efficacy such as by influencing the movement of the fumigant. Size and shape of fruit could not be compared to the differences found between some durable commodities, wheat flour for example being very different to whole wheat grains, the former greatly restricting the movement of methyl bromide because of the particle size. Mr. Taylor was not aware of other commodities where concern over varietal differences had caused the need for diverging phytosanitary requirements.

Question 16: Japan states in its second submission[209] that "it is true that existing treatment levels of host plants of codling moth have been found effective for additional varieties. However, as a matter of science, all this proves is the efficacy of the treatment on the *tested* varieties. It falls short of showing absence of varietal difference within a commodity altogether" [emphasis added][210]. Japan also states that the United States cannot possibly provide any information of products yet to be developed which "may utilize rapidly advancing biotechnology"[211]. Yet, the United States considers that "testing by commodity is the only acceptable quarantine measure in the context of this dispute" and that after the first variety of a particular commodity has been tested according to current Japanese procedures, "no further testing is necessary for additional varieties"[212]. Is there a scientific basis for either of the parties views set out above?

6.104. **Dr. Ducom** stated that the arguments put forth by Japan for requiring varietal trials were not based on scientific data. They were supported by a few experimental data in which varietal difference existed, in terms of LD_{50}, among plenty of other data in which they did not. These observations had led Japan to suspect all existing varieties, as well as those of the future (where, in Japan's view, genetic engineering and biotechnology could create even greater differences). This was not based on any scientific data.

6.105. The arguments put forth by the United States were based on a large number of experiments, of which Japan had thoroughly made use. Varietal difference appeared several times, but each time the confirmatory test had revealed sufficient

---

[209] Japan's second submission, paragraphs 45-48.
[210] Japan's second submission, paragraph 45.
[211] Japan's second submission, paragraph 48.
[212] US answer to the Panel's Question No. 4 (addressed to the United States), 21 April 1998.

efficacy. Extrapolation to all available varieties was no more scientific than Japan's contrary assertion. This sort of extrapolation was something along the order of intuition. It was unfortunate that there had not been a research program on the subject in order to try to present some scientific proof.

6.106. **Dr. Heather** stated that the Japanese view on applicability of experimental results was technically correct but, in practice, the purpose of experimentation was to provide guidance for decisions on a broader basis. There was a strong case for flow-on where varietal differences were unlikely to impinge on fumigation efficacy. However, most countries would reserve their right to make exceptions if they foresaw a risk that efficacy might be compromised by varietal or other differences. The problem was more one of risk management as the scientifically definable differences would normally be small and difficult to determine due to variability.

6.107. Specification of a treatment as a CxT value for the pest instead of an initial fumigant amount and time could overcome this problem, but would require a level of monitoring which would need to be practicable. The United States used this approach to varying degrees in its methyl bromide quarantine treatments as mentioned in paragraph 6.85 above.

Question 17: Could you describe the nature of the varietal differences between the varieties of the commodities listed in US Exhibit 1 (e.g., colour, taste, shape). Could the nature of these differences affect the efficacy of MB treatment?

6.108. **Dr. Heather** noted "Granny Smith" and "Delicious" apples differed in colour, shape, flavour and time of maturity. Dr. Heather was not aware of any major differences in susceptibility to codling moth other than those possibly phenology based. As confirmed by US large-scale trials, the required efficacy had been achieved for both of these varieties and, given the combined lethal potential and broad applicability of methyl bromide and cold treatment, it was highly unlikely that there would be any differences in efficacy between any common commercial apple varieties. One problem that might occur was susceptibility of some varieties to treatment injury.

Question 18: Is it scientifically correct to say that "peach" includes "nectarines"?

6.109. **Dr. Ducom** affirmed that "peach" indeed was the general term that referred to the species Prunus persica. The notion of species was well clarified; two individuals belonged to the same species if they were able to exchange genes to produce viable offspring. The peach species had undergone natural mutations. Some mutations concerned the shape; the flat peach variety, platicarpa. Another, of relevance to the question, caused the peach to shed its epidermal fuzz: this was the variety nucipersica, the nectarine.

6.110. **Dr. Heather** noted that Willis gave the systematic botanical (species) classification of peach as *Prunus persica* and categorized nectarine as a variety of peach.[213] The US submission gave sub-species status to nectarine as *P. p. nuciper-sica.*[214] Taxonomic status at this level tended to be subjective. Classification as a sub-species implied stable characteristics which could be recognized for descriptive purposes. If the species defined the commodity, nectarine would be a variety of peach.

6.111. **Mr. Taylor** affirmed that it was scientifically correct to say that "peach" included "nectarines" because a nectarine was a smooth-skinned mutant of peach. It was botanically classified as a variety of peach *Prunus persica, nucipersica.*

C. Additional Written Questions Sent to the Experts Advising the Panel

1. Additional Question on Walnuts

6.112. On 25 June 1998, the Panel sent the following additional question to the experts advising the Panel:

"At the second substantive meeting of the Panel, on 24 June 1998, the United States submitted the attached publication (US Exhibit 40[215]) with a cover letter by its author. The Panel would kindly ask for your views on the following:

On the basis of this publication, could you express your view on:

(a)   whether and to what extent the oil or fat content differs between varieties of walnuts *because of varietal characteristics*; and.

(b)   whether any such differences are significant enough to affect quarantine efficacy."

6.113. Dr. Heather noted that his interpretation of the paper by L. Carl Greve *et al.,* was that it examined the genotype - environment relationships affecting the percentage of polyunsaturated fatty acids in oil of walnuts. Dr. Heather did not find any information on total oil content as a varietal characteristic. Therefore, the paper, in his view, did not provide any further clarification on the extent to which the oil content of walnuts could affect quarantine treatment efficacy and, consequently, quarantine security. The paper did, however, provide additional insight into the complexity of the relationship between inherent varietal characteristics and the environment.

6.114. Dr. Ducom noted that differences between varieties in walnut commodities, if any, could easily be shown by way of the oil content. Methyl Bromide was soluble in oil or fat and the decrease in gas concentration in the fumigation chamber resulting from this sorption was measurable in sorption trials. If one variety had a difference in oil content large enough to modify the sorption pattern and consequently the CxT value, then the efficacy of the quarantine treatment could be affected. On the

---

[213] Dr. Heather referred to Willis, *A Dictionary of the Flowering Plants and Ferns,* Cambridge University Press, (1960).

[214] Dr. Heather referred to US Exhibit 15, p.2.

[215] Variation in Polyunsaturated Fatty Acids Composition of Persian Walnut, L. Carl Greve, et. al., J. Amer. Soc. Hort. Sci. 117 (3), pp. 518-522, 1992.

basis of the publication in question (US Exhibit 40), variety was one of the different factors which could affect the oil content of the fruits. However, the authors had shown that its influence was less important than the environmental conditions (location, light, irrigation, etc.). In Dr. Ducom's view, differences such as those presented in the publication appeared not to be large enough to have any noticeable influence on the sorption and thus the CxT value and efficacy. Only trials designed for the purpose of answering that specific question could give an adequate response.

6.115. Mr. Taylor noted that he agreed with the conclusions of L Carl Greve that environment, genotype, nut maturity and interaction of these factors appeared to be the most important parameters determining the fatty acid content in walnuts. The greater differences in fatty acid content composition found from year to year within the same variety than between varieties in a single year was also very important evidence demonstrating that varietal differences were unlikely to be the most important factor affecting sorption of methyl bromide and, therefore, the efficacy of methyl bromide fumigations.

2. *Confirmation of the Panel's Understanding of Scientific Evidence and Opinions*

6.116. On 28 July 1998, the Panel sent 10 pages of its draft findings (in this report: paragraphs 8.73 to 8.101) to the experts advising the Panel to confirm that the scientific evidence referred to therein had been correctly reflected and, in particular, to ascertain that the references to the experts' opinions had - from a technical and scientific point of view - been accurately reflected. The answers by the experts (summarized in the following three paragraphs), together with the Panel's draft findings as sent to the experts, were provided to the Parties at the time the Panel submitted its interim report to the Parties.

6.117. Dr. Heather stated that the Panel's interpretation of his submissions had been correct with one exception. This exception was with respect to the use of the term probit 9. In the view of Dr. Heather, if the term probit 9 - or any other probit value, or their equivalent mortality percentages - were used in a definitive sense, it was important to give them in conjunction with a confidence (or precision) level. Thus, in order to avoid the need to specify the precision of the probit 9 level of protection, Dr Heather suggested that that level of protection was better stated as "no survivors from tests on a minimum of 30,000 individuals", instead of stating that Japan's level of protection was "probit 9", or "99.9969 per cent mortality".

6.118. Dr. Ducom noted, in general, that the Panel had understood what had been explained and that the text was logical. In particular, Dr. Ducom drew the Panel's attention to the fact that the two treatments for apples (cold treatment and MB fumigation) were independent from one another. While the cold treatment killed the egg stage of codling moth, the MB fumigation killed the fifth larval stage (5th instar).[216] In his view, the sorption problems were the same for apples as for other fruits but did not affect the efficacy of cold treatment.

---

[216] See paragraph 2.2 for the codling moth larval stages.

6.119. Mr. Taylor stated that the draft findings accurately reflected his scientific and technical opinion.

VII.   INTERIM REVIEW[217]

7.1.   On 1 September 1998, the United States and Japan requested the Panel to review, in accordance with Article 15.2 of the DSU, precise aspects of the interim report that had been issued to them on 6 August 1998. Japan also requested the Panel to hold a further meeting with the parties on the issues identified in its comments on the interim report. We met, accordingly, with the parties on 21 September 1998.

A.   *Comments by the United States*

7.2.   Following comments from the United States we redrafted paragraphs 8.77, 8.93 and 8.96 in order to clarify that, according to the experts advising the Panel, varietal differences - and the resulting difference in sorption levels between varieties - need to be *significant* to affect the efficacy of the already approved MB treatment.

7.3.   With respect to paragraphs 8.82 and 8.99, the United States reiterated its view that - although no disagreement exists as to the level of *mortality* Japan requires - Japan never defined its appropriate level of *protection*. We redrafted these paragraphs to take account of this point of view. We also noted Japan's view that its level of protection is that achieved by the import prohibition and that the level of mortality it requires for lifting the import prohibition is one of the technical requirements to ensure efficacy of an alternative measure.

7.4.   As a result of a US comment, we added paragraph 8.102 in order to make clear that our findings under Article 5.6 would stand even if the measure in dispute were not in violation of Article 2.2. Doing so, we agree with Japan that our finding under Article 5.6 is not an alternative finding *stricto sensu,* in the sense that it only stands if we would have decided that Article 2.2 is *not* violated. What we wanted to clarify is that our Article 5.6 finding stands irrespective of our finding under Article 2.2.

7.5.   As a result of other comments from the United States, we also slightly redrafted certain other paragraphs of the findings section of our report.

B.   *Comments by Japan*

7.6.   Japan, in turn, provided editorial suggestions to the descriptive part. Where the additions requested had been referred to earlier during the proceedings, we incorporated them in the final report.

7.7.   As a result of comments by Japan, a question arose as to the product scope of our finding in paragraph 8.42. Japan submitted that nowhere in the report did it find a *prima facie* case of an Article 2.2 violation established by the United States for the

---

[217]   According to Article 15.3 of the DSU, "the findings of the final report shall include a discussion of the arguments made at the interim review stage". The following section entitled "Interim Review" is therefore part of the findings of our report.

products other than apples, cherries, nectarines and walnuts. Japan argued that the United States did not submit any evidence in respect of these other products and that the Panel made an error in substituting the absent evidence, which parties must submit, with the experts' answer to a Panel question. On that ground, Japan requested us to exclude products other than apples, cherries, nectarines and walnuts from the scope of our Article 2.2 finding in paragraph 8.42. The United States responded that for the other four products in dispute (apricots, pears, plums and quince), the presumption of an Article 2.2 violation was established as a result of the fact that Japan did not submit any scientific evidence for these products. According to the United States, the SPS Agreement makes it clear that the burden has never been on it to present scientific evidence that varietal testing is *not* required. Instead, the United States argued, Japan has an obligation under Article 2.2 to base its varietal testing requirement for all products covered by this case on sufficient scientific evidence.

7.8.   In paragraphs 8.44 and 8.45 we specify that the scope of our finding that Japan maintains the varietal testing requirement without sufficient scientific evidence extends to four of the eight products at issue (apples, cherries, nectarines and walnuts). When addressing the product coverage of our report, we have distinguished two issues. First, the product coverage of our *terms of reference*. In paragraph 8.6 we find that the Panel was given the task to examine the measure in dispute as it applies to eight products. This is not what Japan contested in its comments on the interim report. Second, the product coverage of our *finding that Japan maintains the varietal testing requirement without sufficient scientific evidence*. This is the issue raised by Japan in its comments on the interim report and dealt with in paragraphs 8.44 and 8.45.

7.9.   In our view, Japan is correct when it states that it is for the United States to establish a presumption that there is not sufficient scientific evidence in support of the measure in dispute. It is also true, in our opinion, that the United States has to do so for each of the eight products which fall within our terms of reference. However, we do not agree that, in assessing whether such presumption was established, we cannot take into account both the evidence submitted by the United States and the opinions we received from the experts in accordance with Article 13 of the DSU.[218]

7.10.   In our view, the *prima facie* case to be established in a WTO dispute settlement proceeding relates to the substantive issue of what a party invoking a fact or claim needs to prove for that fact or claim to be accepted by a panel; that is, evidence (1) which is sufficient to raise a presumption that the alleged fact or claim is correct and (2) that has not been sufficiently rebutted by the opposing party. In deciding whether a fact or claim can thus be accepted, we consider that we are called upon to examine and weigh all the evidence validly submitted to us, including the opinions we received from the experts advising the Panel in accordance with Article 13 of the DSU.

---

[218] Article 13 of the DSU provides, in its first paragraph: "Each panel shall have the right to seek information and technical advice from any individual or body which it deems appropriate"; and, in its second paragraph: "Panels may seek information from any relevant source and may consult experts to obtain their opinion on certain aspects of the matter".

7.11.   With respect to paragraphs 8.38 and 8.39, Japan submitted that the only evidence in support of the Panel's reasoning is a quote from *Dr. Heather* with respect to only one study before the Panel. We recall, however, that a whole series of other evidence is referred to in paragraph 8.40 and footnotes 273 to 276.

7.12.   In response to Japan's comment that there is no support for the statement in paragraph 8.42 that "not a single instance has occurred ... where the treatment approved for one variety of a product has had to be modified to ensure an effective treatment for another variety of the same product", we clarified and expanded this paragraph. In so doing, we also addressed Japan's claim that the United States did not submit a *prima facie* case.

7.13.   Following a comment by Japan on paragraph 8.46, relating to the quarantine efficacy of the treatment required for apples, we also redrafted that paragraph. We further modified paragraph 8.84 to avoid the possible US misunderstanding that our finding in paragraph 8.84 does not apply to apples.

7.14.   With respect to paragraph 8.84, Japan requested the Panel to find that the United States did not establish a *prima facie* case that testing by product would meet Japan's level of protection. In reply we specify in that paragraph that the finding we make is arrived at after a careful examination and weighing of all the evidence before us.

7.15.   Japan's comments on other parts of our findings also prompted us to slightly redraft certain other paragraphs of our findings.

VIII.   FINDINGS

A.   *Claims of the Parties*

8.1.   The United States challenges the way Japan lifts its import ban on products that may carry the pest known as codling moth. Japan requires testing and demonstration of quarantine efficacy for each variety of a product that may carry codling moth. Only once this is done will the import ban be lifted and this only for the particular variety or varieties tested. Hereafter we refer to the contested measure as Japan's "varietal testing requirement". The United States claims that this measure is inconsistent with Articles 2, 5, 7 and 8 of the SPS Agreement. Japan requests the Panel to find that its measure is fully consistent with the SPS Agreement.

B.   *Japan's Plant Protection Regime*

8.2.   On 4 May 1950, Japan enacted the Plant Protection Law. Article 7 (paragraph 1, item 1) of that Law provides that plants designated by Ministerial Ordinance, which have been shipped from or passed through districts designated by that Ordinance, are prohibited for import into Japan. By Ministerial Ordinance of 30 June 1950 (Plant Protection Law Enforcement Regulations) eight products originating from, *inter alia*, the United States (excluding the Hawaiian Islands) were listed as prohibited plants. These products are: apricot, cherry, plum, pear, quince, peach, apple and walnuts, imported as fresh fruit.[219] They are prohibited for impor-

---

[219]   With respect to walnuts, the ban also applies to walnuts in the shell.

tation on the ground that they are potential hosts of codling moth. The Ministerial Ordinance of 30 June 1950 also lists other products as prohibited for import because they are hosts of other pests. However, there is a possibility to obtain exemptions from the import ban. Such exemptions are granted on a variety-by-variety basis. Since 1969 a series of varieties of certain products, originating from specific areas, have been exempted from the import ban. Moreover, since 1978 the import ban has been lifted for certain varieties of the US products at issue.

8.3.   In order to obtain an exemption from the import prohibition, Japan imposes the following procedure. The exporting country has to propose an alternative measure which would achieve a level of protection which is equivalent to that met by the import prohibition. The exporting country bears the burden of proving that the proposed alternative would reach the appropriate level of protection. Japan submits that this procedure is a "fundamental policy orientation". It has not been published as a document. In practice, the alternative measure proposed is disinfestation. With respect to hosts of codling moth, disinfestation consists of fumigation with methyl bromide ("MB") or a combination of MB fumigation and cold storage (as required in the treatment approved by Japan for apples). As a model test procedure for confirmation of the efficacy of this quarantine treatment, the Ministry of Agriculture, Forestry and Fisheries of Japan ("MAFF") developed two guidelines: (1) the "Experimental Guideline for Lifting Import Ban - Fumigation" and (2) the "Experimental Guide for Cultivar Comparison Test on Insect Mortality - Fumigation". These guidelines were introduced in 1987 and have, according to Japan, not "generally been published". They are summarized in paragraphs 2.23 - 2.24 of this report.

C.   The Panel's Preliminary Ruling of 2 April 1998

8.4.   At our first substantive meeting we made the following preliminary ruling at the request of Japan:

> "Having carefully reviewed the written submissions made by the parties on the preliminary issues before us and having heard the oral arguments made by Japan in this respect, we rule as follows.
>
> (i)   We first examine Japan's request to exclude Article 7 of the SPS Agreement from our examination on the grounds that it was only mentioned for the first time in the US panel request (document WT/DS76/2) and that no consultations were held on it. We note that our terms of reference (set out in document WT/DS76/3) direct us to examine the matter before us "in the light of the relevant provisions of the covered agreements cited by the United States in document WT/DS76/2". This document, the US panel request, specifically cites Article 7 of the SPS Agreement. We thus consider that claims under that provision fall within our terms of reference.
>
> (ii)   We next address Japan's request for a finding that the phrase "including but not limited to", mentioned in the US panel request, does not constitute part of our terms of reference. We note that the United States, in its first submission, did not make any claim with respect to a provision not specifically

mentioned in the US request for this Panel. Japan did not contest this. Consequently, there is no claim before us (other than the one under Article 7 of the SPS Agreement we just dealt with) on which to make a ruling of whether or not it falls within our terms of reference.

(iii)   Thirdly, as to the Japanese measures in dispute, we note that the United States, in its first submission at paragraph 74, limited these to "the prohibition by Japan on the importation of any variety of an agricultural product on which Japan claims that the pest codling moth may occur until such time as the variety has been separately tested with respect to the efficacy of treatment with methyl bromide or treatment with methyl bromide and cold storage". We regard this statement as setting the factual parameters of this case. It limits the scope of this dispute to (1) agricultural products on which Japan claims that the pest codling moth may occur (in its oral statement Japan stated that there are eight such products: apricot, plum, pear, quince, apple, walnut, peach including nectarine, and cherry; in its first submission, the United States only addressed four products: apples, cherries, nectarines and walnuts) and (2) varietal testing with respect to the efficacy of treatment with methyl bromide or treatment with methyl bromide and cold storage".

D.   *The Scope of the Measure in Dispute*

8.5.   The measure at issue in this dispute is only one element of Japan's plant protection regime. The scope of this measure is limited in several respects.[220]

8.6.   Firstly, only the varietal testing requirement imposed by Japan for lifting the import prohibition on *US products on which Japan claims that codling moth may occur* is in dispute. The request for this Panel, which sets out the scope of our mandate[221], does not further limit the product coverage of the Japanese measure challenged to certain specific products only. At our first substantive meeting, Japan stated that it considers the following US products to be hosts of codling moth: apricots, cherries, plums, pears, quinces, peaches (including nectarines[222]), apples and walnuts. We consider, therefore, that we are called upon to examine the measure before us as it applies to all products covered by the contested measure. However, as we already noted in our preliminary ruling[223], the parties only submitted evidence with respect to apples, cherries, nectarines and walnuts. We shall, therefore, exam-

---

[220]   See our preliminary ruling at point (iii), quoted in paragraph 8.4.

[221]   Our terms of reference are, in accordance with Article 7.1 of the DSU, defined in document WT/DS76/3 and specify that the matter we need to examine is the one referred to in document WT/DS76/2, i.e., the request for the establishment of this Panel.

[222]   According to the experts advising the Panel, it is scientifically correct to say that peach includes nectarine (see their answers to Panel question 18, paragraphs 6.109 - 6.111).

[223]   See our preliminary ruling at point (iii), quoted in paragraph 8.4.

ine the measure at issue on the basis of that evidence and refer to the experts advising the Panel when it comes to evaluating the relevance of that evidence for the other products covered by the measure in dispute.

8.7.   Secondly, we only need to examine Japan's varietal testing requirement to the extent it applies to the demonstration of efficacy of *MB treatment or of MB treatment combined with cold storage* as a treatment against codling moth. We are not called upon to address the varietal testing requirement as it applies to any other treatment or any other pest.

E.   Matters not in Dispute

8.8.   It is important to note what this dispute is *not* about. The United States does not contest that codling moth is a serious pest of quarantine significance. Nor is it in dispute that codling moth is exotic to Japan (i.e., is not found in Japan); that it does occur in the United States; and that the importation of US fruit infected with codling moth could result in the introduction of codling moth in Japan which, in turn, would have serious consequences for Japan's agricultural and forestry production. The legitimacy and need for Japan to protect its plants against codling moth is not at issue.[224]

8.9.   Moreover, the United States does not challenge the original import prohibition imposed on US host plants of codling moth. The United States acknowledges that Japan conducted a risk assessment to determine that codling moth is a pest of quarantine significance for which an original import prohibition *might* be justified.[225] The United States refers rather to the possibility of obtaining exemptions from this import prohibition and contests the conditions imposed for lifting this prohibition, in particular the fact that it is lifted variety-by-variety.

8.10.   Even with respect to the conditions for lifting the ban, the United States agrees that, as a general proposition, it is reasonable for Japan to require that the exporting country propose and substantiate the efficacy of an alternative approach or a treatment that achieves Japan's level of phytosanitary protection. Following that line of reasoning, the United States does not contest the testing requirements imposed by Japan for approval of imports of the initial variety of a particular product, i.e., those contained in the "Experimental Guideline for Lifting Import Ban - Fumigation". The United States contends, however, that after such validation no further testing is necessary for additional varieties. It, therefore, challenges not only the content but the very existence of any guidelines imposed for approval of additional varieties, *in casu*, those contained in the "Experimental Guide for Cultivar Comparison Test on Insect Mortality - Fumigation".

---

[224]   See, for example, the expert opinions of *Dr. Heather and Mr. Taylor*, Transcript, paragraphs 10.204 - 10.210.

[225]   However, in so acknowledging, the United States did not take a position as to whether this risk assessment complies with the requirements in the SPS Agreement, arguing that this risk assessment does not relate to the matter in dispute. Nor did the United States state that this risk assessment *does* justify the import ban in accordance with the SPS Agreement. See also the expert opinions referred to in footnote 224 and *Dr. Heather and Mr. Taylor*'s answers to question 7 of the Panel, summarized at paragraphs 6.51 to 6.56.

8.11.   We further note that there is no disagreement as to the efficacy of the treatment applied to the specific varieties of US apples, cherries, nectarines and walnuts which have so far been exempted from the import prohibition. The United States does not dispute the level of mortality, established by Japan, that any quarantine treatment has to achieve (i.e., complete mortality in large-scale tests on a minimum of 30,000 codling moths[226]), nor does the United States, or Japan, contest that this level of mortality is reached for the varieties already approved for import after they have been treated as required.

8.12.   Japan does not contest that the measure at issue is a phytosanitary measure covered by the SPS Agreement, invoked by the United States. Referring to Article 1.1 and paragraph 1 of Annex A of the SPS Agreement[227], we agree with the parties that the SPS Agreement applies to the measure at issue.

8.13.   Finally, with respect to the question of burden of proof under the SPS Agreement, we note that both parties refer to the Appellate Body Report on *EC - Measures Affecting Meat and Meat Products (Hormones)* (hereafter referred to as "*EC - Hormones*").[228] Reviewing this report, we agree with the parties that, in this dispute, it is for the United States to establish a *prima facie* case of inconsistency of the Japanese measure at issue with each of the provisions of the SPS Agreement the United States invokes. Once this is done, it is for Japan to counter or refute the claimed inconsistency. In other words, if "[the United States] adduces sufficient evidence to raise a presumption that what is claimed is true, the burden then shifts to [Japan], who will fail unless it adduces sufficient evidence to rebut the presumption".[229] In response to a Japanese comment on the interim report, we stress that the issue of burden of proof in a WTO dispute settlement proceeding set out above is different and should be distinguished from what a Member requires from an exporting country before it will approve the import of that country's products. The latter issue is dealt with in paragraphs 8.10 and 8.30.

---

[226]   See paragraph 2.23 under "Large-Scale mortality test". See also answer by *Dr. Heather* summarized in paragraph 6.117.

[227]   Article 1.1 of the SPS Agreement provides that the Agreement applies to "all ... phytosanitary measures which may, directly or indirectly, affect international trade". Paragraph 1 of Annex A to the SPS Agreement clarifies, *inter alia*, that "[a]ny measure applied: (a) to protect ... plant life or health within the territory of the Member from risks arising from the entry, establishment or spread of pests" is a phytosanitary measure for purposes of the SPS Agreement.

[228]   Adopted 13 February 1998, WT/DS26/AB/R, stating as follows in paragraph 98: "The initial burden lies on the complaining party, which must establish a *prima facie* case of inconsistency with a particular provision of the *SPS Agreement* on the part of the defending party, or more precisely, of its SPS measure or measures complained about. When that *prima facie* case is made, the burden of proof moves to the defending party, which must in turn counter or refute the claimed inconsistency". See also the Panel Reports on *EC - Hormones*, op. cit., respectively, at paragraphs 8.51 and 8.54.

[229]   Appellate Body Report on *United States - Measure Affecting Imports of Woven Wool Shirts and Blouses from India*, adopted 23 May 1997, WT/DS33/AB/R, DSR 1997:I, 323, at 334.

> F.   *Scientific Basis and Risk Assessment (Articles 2.2, 5.1, 5.2 and 5.7)*
>
> 1.   *The SPS Provisions Invoked and their Relationship*

8.14.   We first examine the US claims under Articles 2.2, 5.1 and 5.2. In this respect, Japan also invokes Article 5.7. These Articles provide in relevant parts as follows:

Article 2.2:

"Members shall ensure that any ... phytosanitary measure is applied only to the extent necessary to protect ... plant life or health, is based on scientific principles and is not maintained without sufficient scientific evidence, except as provided for in paragraph 7 of Article 5".

Article 5.1:

"Members shall ensure that their ... phytosanitary measures are based on an assessment, as appropriate to the circumstances, of the risks to ... plant life or health, taking into account risk assessment techniques developed by the relevant international organizations".

Article 5.2:

"In the assessment of risks, Members shall take into account available scientific evidence; relevant processes and production methods; relevant inspection, sampling and testing methods; prevalence of specific diseases or pests; existence of pest- or disease-free areas; relevant ecological and environmental conditions; and quarantine or other treatment".

Article 5.7:

"In cases where relevant scientific evidence is insufficient, a Member may provisionally adopt ... phytosanitary measures on the basis of available pertinent information, including that from the relevant international organizations as well as from ... phytosanitary measures applied by other Members. In such circumstances, Members shall seek to obtain the additional information necessary for a more objective assessment of risk and review the ... phytosanitary measure accordingly within a reasonable period of time".

8.15.   We examine these provisions together, in light of the following statement by the Appellate Body in its report on *EC - Hormones*:

"... Articles 2.2 and 5.1 should constantly be read together. Article 2.2 informs Article 5.1: the elements that define the basic obligation set out in Article 2.2 impart meaning to Article 5.1".[230]

---

[230] Adopted on 13 February 1998, WT/DS26/AB/R, paragraph 180. See also panel report on *Australia - Measures Affecting Importation of Salmon*, currently on appeal, WT/DS18/R, paragraph

8.16.   The United States submits that Article 2.2 does not allow Japan to maintain a phytosanitary measure, in this instance the varietal testing requirement, "without sufficient scientific evidence" and that Article 2.2 requires such measure to be "based on scientific principles". According to the United States, Articles 5.1 and 5.2 require Japan to base the varietal testing requirement on a risk assessment. We first examine the US claims under Article 2.2, taking due account of the more specific obligations imposed under Articles 5.1 and 5.2.

2.   *Scientific Basis*

(a)   Claims and Arguments by the Parties[231]

(i)   The United States

8.17.   The United States submits that, at a minimum, to base a measure on scientific principles a WTO Member has to identify a particular risk that the measure is designed to protect against, and to conduct some review of scientific evidence or other relevant scientific information to demonstrate that the measure in fact protects against that risk. According to the United States, the risk to be addressed in this case is the risk of introduction of codling moth *in the absence* of the varietal testing requirement.

8.18.   The United States notes that the strongest wording Japan has been able to employ is that it is *possible* there *may* be variation in the efficacy of disinfestation if the same quarantine treatment is applied to different varieties. Referring to the descriptions of variations in dose-mortality tests[232] between varieties, offered by Japan in support of the measure[233], the United States submits that these descriptions ignore the conclusions of the scientific studies carried out on quarantine treatments for codling moth. In this respect, the United States recalls that to date the quarantine treatment approved for one variety of a product has always proven to be effective for all other tested varieties of the same product. The United States submits that it tested seven varieties of apples, nine varieties of cherries, four varieties of walnuts and ten varieties of nectarines and that in every instance the treatment applied for one variety of a product has never varied from that applied to another variety of the same product.

8.19.   With respect to the six specific studies submitted by Japan[234], the United States points out that all of the tests reported therein are dose-mortality tests which are small-scale tests. The United States argues that the differences in dose-mortality tests for different varieties in these studies cannot constitute a valid scientific basis for the varietal testing requirement because it is in the nature of dose-mortality tests to vary among varieties and even within the same variety from year to year. The

---

8.51: "We recall that Articles 5.1 and 5.2 may be viewed as one of the specific applications of the basic obligations contained in Article 2.2".

[231]   The parties' arguments with respect to Article 5.7, to which Article 2.2 explicitly refers, are outlined later in paragraphs 8.50 and following.

[232]   The meaning of a "dose mortality test" is explained in paragraph 2.12.

[233]   Set out in paragraphs 8.21 and 8.23.

[234]   Set out in paragraphs 8.21 and 8.23.

United States points to leakage of the fumigation chamber, fruit load, experimental errors, sorption by packaging material, natural variation of pest population and fruit-to-fruit variation such as different ripening times, seasonal variations and physical condition of the fruit as factors explaining the differential. According to the United States, confirmatory tests (which are conducted on a larger scale) are a better indicator of efficacy of a treatment: since confirmatory tests take account of the variability in (small-scale) dose-mortality tests, they establish a treatment that is appropriate for all varieties of a product. The United States further submits that the highest minimum dose observed in the dose-mortality tests that scientists believe would achieve the level of protection required by Japan, is supplemented by a 10-20 per cent buffer in the second stage of testing (the confirmatory tests). According to the United States, this buffer will offset all sources of variation in the dose-mortality tests, including any possible varietal differences.

(ii)   Japan

8.20.   Japan responds that there is a sufficient amount of literature and scientific data which indicates the possible presence of a statistically significant difference in the efficacy of known disinfestation measures across varieties of the same product, and that such a difference could require application of a different treatment.

8.21.   First, Japan submits that in the specific case of MB fumigation the link between varietal differences and the divergent efficacy of a fumigation treatment may manifest itself by way of a difference in the CxT value for different varieties, i.e., a difference in the relationship between the fumigant gas concentration in the fumigation chamber and the time-period of fumigation.[235] Japan specifically refers to three studies which allegedly demonstrate a statistically significant difference in CxT values between tested variety samples:[236] (1) 1985 tests on three varieties of American walnuts where, according to Japan, CxT values were significantly different between the Franquett variety and the Payne variety[237]; (2) 1988 tests on three varieties of American nectarines where, according to Japan, CxT values of the May Diamond variety showed a statistically significant difference from the other two cultivars for most of the doses[238]; and (3) 1997 tests on three varieties of Japanese nectarines where there was, according to Japan, a statistically significant difference in CxT values between the Shuhou variety and the Fantasia variety.[239]

8.22.   According to Japan, differences in CxT values between varieties could be an indicator of differences in the efficacy of a fumigation treatment. Japan argues as follows: When MB gas is injected into the fumigation chamber to disinfest a particular load of fruit, it is absorbed by the surface or the pulp of the fruit. If the de-

---

[235]   The concept of a CxT value is further explained in paragraph 2.11.

[236]   These studies are described in more detail in the descriptive part of our report, paragraphs 4.109 - 4.135.

[237]   Vail, P. V. et al., Walnut On-Site Operational (Demonstration) Test Report to Japanese MAFF, USDA/ARS, Horticultural Crops Research Laboratory, Fresno, California, 2-14 December 1985.

[238]   Vail, P. V. et al., Report on Efficacy of Methyl Bromide for Codling Moth on Nectarines: Consideration of Nectarines as a Product Group, Prepared for Approval by the Japanese MAFF, Horticultural Crops Research Laboratory, Fresno, California, December 1988.

[239]   Research Division, Yokohama Plant Protection Station, MAFF, 1997, Unpublished.

gree of sorption varied depending on the variety of the fruit, the amount of fumigant remaining in the chamber air will vary in an inverse relationship to the sorption. Then the CxT value, which is determined by the gas concentration remaining in the chamber and which is a known indicator to control the degree of efficacy of the treatment, will vary as well depending on the variety of the fruit. According to Japan, the physical and chemical properties of fruits are factors affecting sorption (e.g., differences in oil content or a rougher surface) and can be attributable to varietal characteristics. Therefore, Japan concludes, the reported differences in CxT value are due to varietal differences and are an indicator of differences in the efficacy of a fumigation treatment.

8.23.   Second, Japan submits three studies, derived from dose-mortality tests[240], which indicate a difference in LD 50 values (i.e., the level of dose required in the tests to kill 50 per cent of all codling moths[241]) between tested variety samples:[242] (1) 1987 tests on six varieties of American nectarines where, according to Japan, one of the varieties tested, namely Summer Grand, was found significantly more susceptible to MB fumigation (i.e., had a lower LD_{50} value) than the others[243]; (2) 1987/1988 tests on five varieties of New Zealand cherries where, according to Japan, the LD_{50} value for the Bing variety was significantly lower than that for two of the other varieties tested, namely Rainer and Sam[244]; and (3) 1983/1984 tests on two varieties of New Zealand nectarines where, according to Japan, the Fantasia variety showed a significantly lower LD_{50} value than the Redgold variety.[245]

8.24.   Japan agrees with the United States that there may be a range of exogenous factors (e.g., differences in leakage of the fumigation chamber, fruit load, experimental errors, sorption by packaging material, natural variation of pest population and fruit-to-fruit variation such as different ripening times, seasonal variations and physical condition of the fruit) which may also account for the differential in CxT and LD_{50} values reflected in the studies it refers to. However, Japan claims that most of these other variables can be controlled in such a manner as to minimize their effects and that such control is a normal practice for scientists. The Japanese hypothesis is that characteristics of a particular variety may affect fumigation efficacy and that there is not sufficient evidence to disprove this possibility. This is, according to Japan, a reasonable argument. For Japan, its policy of variety-by-variety testing is therefore based on a scientific hypothesis which, in turn, is supported by empirical data, in full conformity with the obligations contained in Article 2.2.

8.25.   Japan acknowledges that existing treatment levels of host plants of codling moth have been found effective for additional varieties. However, for Japan, all this proves is the efficacy of the treatment on the *tested* varieties. According to Japan,

---

[240]   The meaning of a "dose mortality test" is explained in paragraph 2.12.

[241]   The notion of LD values is further explained in paragraph 2.14.

[242]   These studies are dealt with in more detail in paragraphs 4.81 - 4.108.

[243]   Yokoyama V.Y. et al., Methyl Bromide Fumigation for Quarantine Control of Codling Moth (Lepidoptera: Tortricidae) on Nectarines, Journal of Economic Entomology 80, 1987, pp. 840-842.

[244]   Waddel, B.C. et al., Disinfestation of New Zealand Cherries, Cultivar Comparison Test 1987/1988, Department of Scientific and Industrial Research, Auckland, June 1988.

[245]   Batchelor, T.A. et al., Disinfestation of New Zealand Nectarines 1983/1984, Department of Scientific and Industrial Research, July 1984.

this falls short of showing absence of varietal difference within a product altogether. Japan notes that only a limited number of varieties have been tested in full-scale trials. On the question of a buffer, Japan claims that in large-scale trials the buffer is not always added to the "highest minimum dose", as the United States argues. Japan submits that in some instances the amount of fumigant absorbed by, *inter alia*, bins or the interior of warehouses may exceed the 10 to 20 per cent buffer. Japan further refers to *Dr. Ducom*'s response to Panel question 12 relating to the buffer[246] and highlights the uncertainty of the effect of the buffer. On these grounds, Japan concludes that the United States has not performed the required demonstration of efficacy of a treatment across all varieties.

> (b) Is the Varietal Testing Requirement Maintained Without "Sufficient Scientific Evidence" in the Sense of Article 2.2?

8.26. We first examine that part of Article 2.2 requiring Japan to "ensure that [the varietal testing requirement] ... is not maintained without sufficient scientific evidence".

8.27. We recall that Article 2.2 provides for an alternative to the requirement not to maintain phytosanitary measures without sufficient scientific evidence, namely to adopt provisional measures in accordance with Article 5.7.[247] Whether Japan can validly invoke Article 5.7 in this dispute, is addressed below in paragraphs 8.48 and following.

> (i) The Meaning of a Measure "Maintained Without Sufficient Scientific Evidence"

8.28. As referred to above[248], the general obligations in Article 2.2 have to be read together with the more specific obligation imposed on Japan in Article 5.1, namely the obligation to ensure that the varietal testing requirement is "based on" a risk assessment. The Appellate Body, in its report on *EC - Hormones,* elaborated on the meaning of the term "based on" as used in Article 5.1 as follows:

> "We believe that "based on" is appropriately taken to refer to a certain *objective relationship* between two elements, that is to say, to an *objective situation* that persists and is observable *between an SPS measure and a risk assessment*".[249]

> "We believe that Article 5.1, when contextually read as it should be, in conjunction with and as informed by Article 2.2 of the SPS Agreement, requires that *the results of the risk assessment must sufficiently warrant - that is to say, reasonably support - the SPS measure at stake*. The requirement that an SPS measure be "based on" a risk assessment is a

---

[246] See paragraphs 6.87 and following.

[247] Article 2.2 provides that "Members shall ensure that any ... phytosanitary measure ... is not maintained without sufficient scientific evidence, *except as provided for in paragraph 7 of Article 5*" (emphasis added).

[248] See paragraph 8.15.

[249] Op. cit., paragraph 189, pp. 76-77, italics in original, underlining added.

substantive requirement that there be a *rational relationship between the measure and the risk assessment*".[250]

8.29.   We consider this statement (with respect to Article 5.1) to provide guidance also for our examination as to whether the varietal testing requirement is "maintained without" sufficient scientific evidence (in the sense of Article 2.2). In our view, for a phytosanitary measure to be "maintained without" sufficient scientific evidence, there needs to be a lack of an objective or rational relationship between, on the one hand, the phytosanitary measure at stake (*in casu*, the varietal testing requirement) and, on the other hand, the scientific evidence submitted before the Panel (*in casu*, in particular the six studies referred to by Japan[251]).

8.30.   When conducting this examination, we consider it to be important to make a clear distinction between (1) the Japanese requirement that it is for the exporting country (*in casu*, the United States) to demonstrate the efficacy of the quarantine treatment it proposes in order to gain access to the Japanese market for certain products and (2) the Japanese requirement that the exporting country (*in casu*, the United States) needs to make such demonstration *for each variety* of a given product. The United States does not contest the first requirement.[252] It accepts that it needs to demonstrate quarantine efficacy. Only the fact that it needs to do so for each variety, i.e., only the second requirement (the varietal testing requirement), is at issue in this dispute. Under Article 2.2, Japan has the obligation not to maintain this requirement without sufficient scientific evidence.[253]

8.31.   Our task in this dispute is to determine whether or not Japan, *to date*, is in breach of this obligation[254]; not whether *in the future* scientific evidence could be produced which would allow Japan to comply with its obligation.[255] If to date there were not sufficient scientific evidence in support of the varietal testing requirement, Japan would be in breach of its obligations under the SPS Agreement.[256]

(ii)   The Opinions of the Scientific Experts Advising the Panel

8.32.   To determine whether or not the varietal testing requirement is maintained without sufficient scientific evidence (i.e., whether there is a lack of an objective or rational relationship between the measure at issue and the scientific evidence before the Panel), we need to refer to the opinions we received from the experts advising

---

[250]   Op. cit., paragraph 193, underlining added.

[251]   See paragraphs 8.21 and 8.23.

[252]   See paragraph 8.10.

[253]   Unless the Japanese measure is imposed in accordance with Article 5.7, a provision to which Article 2.2 explicitly refers. As noted earlier, this question is dealt with in paragraphs 8.48 and following.

[254]   In this respect, we recall the rules on burden of proof we set out earlier in paragraph 8.13.

[255]   Article 11 of the DSU directs us to "make an objective assessment of the matter before [the Panel], including an objective assessment of the facts of the case".

[256]   Assuming the measure cannot be considered to be a provisional measure in accordance with Article 5.7, an issue we examine below in paragraphs 8.48 and following.

the Panel.[257] We recall that these expert opinions are opinions on the evidence submitted by the parties. We are not empowered, nor are the experts advising the Panel, to conduct our own risk assessment.[258]

8.33.   At the end of our meeting with the experts advising the Panel, we requested them to confirm a number of understandings we had drawn from their answers and statements. The experts unanimously confirmed the following understandings:

- First, referring to the evidence before the Panel, there *may* be differences between varieties of the products in dispute which *may*, in turn, be relevant for quarantine purposes, i.e., which *may* affect the efficacy of an MB treatment approved for one variety of a product if applied to another variety of the same product.[259]

- Second, the question whether varietal differences, if any, are significant for quarantine purposes *cannot be determined on the basis of the evidence before the Panel.*[260]

- Third, if, and to the extent that, differences between varieties are significant for quarantine purposes, they are mainly or even exclusively related to different levels of sorption of the fruit.[261]

---

[257]   For the procedures we followed to appoint these experts and to obtain their views, see paragraphs 6.1 and following.

[258]   See also panel report on *Australia - Salmon*, op. cit., paragraphs 8.41, 8.126 and 8.172.

[259]   See Transcript, paragraphs 10.268 - 10.273. *Dr. Heather* stated the following (confirmed by the other two experts):

> "My understanding, *my belief is not that there are differences but there may be differences*. I don't believe that the occurrence of the differences has been proven and that they may be relevant for quarantine purposes. So there are two sets of uncertainties in my mind in this statement. There's no certainty that even if differences exist that they are relevant for quarantine purposes between varieties of the products in dispute" (Transcript paragraph 10.270, italic added).

[260]   See Transcript, paragraphs 10.274 - 10.279. As noted in the previous footnote, *Dr. Heather* stated unambiguously:

> "*I don't believe that the occurrence of the differences has been proven and that they may be relevant for quarantine purposes*".

See also the introductory statement by *Dr. Ducom*:

> "the questions of the Panel are relevant but often there is no clear response to give because *we miss data on the exact subject on variety by variety testing*" (Transcript, paragraph 10.39, italic added).

See also *Mr. Taylor*:

> "one of the things that has come out from this meeting which I have found extremely interesting is that *we do need more information before we can say categorically that variety in fruit is a major factor affecting the efficacy of treatment*" (Transcript, paragraph 10.266, italic added).

[261]   Transcript, paragraphs 10.280 - 10.285. See also, for example, the introductory statement by *Mr. Taylor*:

> "So I would just say then that sorption seems to me to be something that we need to know more about. If it can be shown that the levels of sorption are such that they are significant enough to remove the fumigant to an extent that it is going to raise some doubt as to the efficacy of the treatment, then of course we could say that varietal testing was necessary. *But unless we can show that it seems to me*

As noted earlier[262], the scientific evidence before the Panel (i.e., the evidence evaluated by the experts advising the Panel) relates to either apples, cherries, nectarines or walnuts. However, in the view of the experts advising the Panel the understandings referred to above equally apply to the other products at issue (apricot, pear, plum and quince).[263]

8.34.   Replying to a US question (posed at the meeting with the experts) as to whether the experts are aware of any situation where differences in variety have resulted in a different treatment level for the products at issue in this case, *Mr. Taylor* stated: "No, I have no information or have seen any published data so the answer I have to give is no"; *Dr. Heather* replied: "In my experience there have been no differences of this kind. In fact it's been to the contrary. Most of my experience has been with insecticide dips with the material dimethoate and here we find that the same treatment not only goes across varieties but across commodities but I can see that this sorption problem with methyl bromide is something very special and that's why I wish to defer to my colleagues with experience as fumigation experts".[264]

8.35.   When we asked the experts advising the Panel whether, in their expert opinion, there is an objective or rational relationship between, on the one hand, the varietal testing requirement imposed by Japan for MB treatment and, on the other hand, any of the evidence submitted by the parties, they stated unanimously that - even though in theory there may be relevant varietal differences - to date there is not sufficient evidence in support of the varietal testing requirement.[265]

> that the need to test by variety does still need to be established. (Transcript, paragraph 10.48, italic added).

See also *Mr. Taylor*, Transcript, paragraph 10.140:

> "*I don't think any of us are in dispute that sorption would be a major factor affecting the efficacy of* treatment, and if it can be demonstrated that sorption is of sufficient magnitude between different varieties, this would affect the efficacy of treatment, but I think that this has still to be shown and to be demonstrated" (italic added).

[262]   See paragraph 8.6.

[263]   Transcript, paragraphs 10.223 - 10.225.

[264]   Transcript, paragraphs 10.155 - 10.158. The question was not directed at *Dr. Ducom* who did not answer it.

[265]   Transcript, paragraphs 10.167 - 10.174:

Dr. Ducom: "... the arguments are not statistically good. Scientifically, they may be good, but in practice they may be too narrow. But the answer is really difficult".

Mr. Taylor: "I have to agree with Dr. Ducom. The answer is very difficult otherwise perhaps we would not be here. Again I think in theory there may be some differences which perhaps exist, but in practice it is difficult to show these and it seems very difficult in fact to say that at this time the differences that might make the difference between treatments efficacious and non-efficacious have not yet been reached and therefore I think at this moment in time that the evidence is not sufficiently strong although in theory it does have some possible validity. But at this stage, as Dr. Ducom has said, and in practical terms, it's very difficult to say yes there is something which is sufficiently demonstrated to show that there is a real problem which has to be addressed in terms of maybe variety-by-variety testing, and which could lead to differences in the treatment techniques that are used".

Dr. Heather: "More to agree with both of my colleagues. I'd say yes there is a relationship but it is an incomplete one but this is a real world and to totally complete the relationship of these and decide on how important it is, I think would probably be beyond the resources even of the United

8.36.   In his written answer to Panel question 16, *Dr. Ducom* states the following: *"The arguments put forth by Japan for requiring varietal trials are not based on scientific data.* They are supported by a few experimental data in which varietal difference exists, in terms of LD_{50}, among a lot of other data in which it does not. These observations lead them to suspect all existing varieties and even more so those of the future, in which, in their eyes, genetic engineering and biotechnology might well create even greater differences. *This is not based on any scientific data".*[266]

8.37.   According to the experts advising the Panel, there is scientific evidence before us - in the form of small-scale dose-mortality tests[267] carried out on different varieties of the same product - which indicate different test results (either a different CxT value[268] or a different LD_{50} value[269]) for different varieties.[270] This cannot be disputed. The statistical and biological relevance of the differences in these test results and, especially, the factors causing them are less clear.

8.38.   First, the experts advising the Panel question the value to be attached to the test results for purposes of checking quarantine efficacy.[271] They express doubts as to whether LD_{50} values derived from dose-mortality tests can be used to compare the efficacy of quarantine treatment between varieties.[272] They also note that even

---

States and Japan in the time available, and I'm not sure that it would really add anything of great value to the argument".

[266]   See paragraphs 6.104 - 6.105.

[267]   The concept of a dose-mortality test is explained in paragraph 2.12.

[268]   The concept of a CxT value is explained in paragraphs 2.11 and 8.21.

[269]   The concept of an LD50 value is explained in paragraphs 2.14 and 8.23.

[270]   See paragraphs 8.21 - 8.23.

[271]   In this respect, it should, from the outset, be recalled that all the studies referred to by Japan were designed and carried out in order to *comply* with the varietal testing requirement. None of the studies before us specifically examines the appropriateness of the requirement itself.

[272]   See answers to Panel question 1 by *Dr. Ducom*: "In practice, the LD50 test constitutes a fairly unreliable method to compare the efficacy of quarantine" and *Mr. Taylor*: "LD50 values are extremely useful in comparing the toxicity of different chemicals and in the measurement of resistance. However, these values are less useful in investigations of much higher levels of toxic response such as are necessary in relation to quarantine treatments, where LD values of 99 or 99.9 are more appropriate and useful". In his answer to Panel question 12, at para.6.8, however, *Dr. Ducom* noted that "while the dose-mortality test (LD_{50}) did not give any confidence in respect of the varietal factor, it did give an indication of the relative sensitivity of the products tested". See also *Dr. Heather's* statement at the meeting with the experts:

> "[The LD50 value] is not a precise numerical measure and of necessity it has had to be used in a rather less precise way than it would otherwise be. It is not a direct measurement on the insect, it is a measurement on the insect where it is influenced by the fruit in the chambers so it is not a precise measurement. In fact, if you look at an LD value it's easy to take one figure but realistically you should be looking at what we call the confidence limits or the fiducial limits and these are ranges within which that value falls and perhaps would lead to a better understanding if we thought of it in that way. As you recall, because the quarantine treatments are not measured at the median dose or the LD50 dose but at the extreme dose, these limits become very wide and it is not wise to take arithmetic cognizance" (Transcript, paragraph 10.41).

though the test results - both with respect to CxT and LD_{50} values - show statistical differences between varieties, biologically speaking these differences are not pronounced.[273]

8.39.   Second, and more importantly, the experts advising the Panel are of the view that even if confidence is given to these differences in the test results there is no evidence before the Panel that these differences - both in CxT and LD_{50} values - are due to varietal differences.

8.40.   In the studies referred to by Japan, the same tests were carried out on different varieties and in some instances the results differed. However, according to the experts advising the Panel, these differences could have been caused by a series of factors which are *not* related to varietal differences, such as differences in leakage of the fumigation chamber, fruit load, experimental errors, sorption by packaging material, natural variation of the pest population and fruit-to-fruit variation such as different ripening times, seasonal variations and physical condition of the fruit. Japan contends that experimental factors can be and were controlled to the extent possible. However, Japan does not contest that other factors (not related to varietal differences) could also explain the differences in the test results. The differences *might* also be linked to varietal differences. However, on this *Dr. Ducom* states the following (confirmed by the other two experts advising the Panel[274]):

---

[273]   At the meeting with the experts *Dr. Ducom* stated:

> "... the scientific facts given by Japan are may be too narrow. I mean, for example, when they give some differences between varieties the confidence limit is not a biological fact, it is a statistical fact. I mean, biologically speaking, the difference does not matter ... just one per cent makes, statistically speaking, there is a significant difference while biologically speaking there is no difference" (Transcript, paragraph 10.39. See also *Dr. Ducom* at Transcript, paragraph 10.186).

See also the statement by *Dr. Heather* at the meeting with the experts:

> "... statistically demonstrated differences ... must always be viewed against the background of the biological conditions which give rise to them. What is biologically unlikely, but statistically shown, must be viewed with some reserve. Biological creditability is just as important as statistical demonstration of differences." (Transcript, paragraph 10.43).

[274]   Addressing, for example, a study conducted on three varieties of nectarines and 13 apple varieties (Kawakami, F., et. al., Methyl Bromide Sorption in Fruit Varieties, Research Division, Yokohama Plant Protection Station, Japan Exhibit 36), *Dr. Heather*, speaking on behalf of all three experts, stated:

> "... the authors obviously attributed the differences to varietal characteristics. We are of the opinion that it is not possible to attribute them solely to varietal characteristics on the evidence that's present in this paper. It may well be true but it requires, it would require... to reach that firm conclusion would require more information." (Transcript, paragraph 10.218).

With respect to the same study, *Dr. Ducom* noted the following:

> "This study was very interesting but the problem is that it was made on apples, which were not at the same stage of storage because some were one month in storage and others had three month's storage - so the variety is not the only factor which can change the value we can read. So in practice that means that varieties may be a factor but maybe not very important and maybe some other factors influence that data. *The problem of all these studies is that they are just descriptive studies. We take some apples, or peaches, or nectarines, and we look at the con-*

> "It is impossible by a simple DMT [dose-mortality test] to find out the relevant impact of the factors playing a role in the varietal differences ... mainly because varieties ripen at different times ... The DMT presented by the parties are designed to give information on insect sensitivity. The search for possible causes of varietal variations cannot be determined with precision by them, but only with a specific research program".[275]

> "There is a lack of precise studies on this subject. *A priori*, one could cite almost anything, the size of the fruit, the nature of the epidermis, the average sugar content, the ripeness of the fruit, its physiological condition, the time between harvest and fumigation, etc. However, in this, there are hypotheses that merit studying".[276]

8.41. The experts advising the Panel point out that so far no attempt has been made to determine whether varietal differences actually constitute a factor which causes the differences in the test results.[277] And this even though, according to the experts advising the Panel, technically speaking such determination can relatively easily be made, for example, by conducting sorption tests on different varieties of a product.[278] Japan did not further test or try to confirm its so-called hypothesis ac-

---

> *centration but the reason why it differs, we don't know. There is no fundamental*
> *work on that and we can just say this works, or it does not work and so on"*
> (Transcript, paragraph 10.259, italic added).

See also *Dr. Heather*'s answers to Panel question 1: "... where differences between varieties are small, fruit to fruit variation could greatly exceed variety to variety variation. Such variation is an inherent characteristic and is usually overcome by ensuring adequate robustness of the treatment"; to Panel question 3: "Although statistical differences are evident between some varietally based experiments, this does not provide an assurance that the origin of the difference lies predominantly in varietal characteristics"; and to Panel question 8: "If the criterion used is statistically significant differences between experimental samples of different varieties there are differences as identified by Japan, but there is no certainty that they are attributable to unique varietal characteristics. In subsequent research on additional varietal samples these differences were too small to cause the efficacy of a treatment based on varieties used in initial trials, to fail in further testing".

[275] *Dr. Ducom*'s answer to Panel question 3.

[276] *Dr. Ducom*'s answer to Panel question 9. Answering a US question at the meeting with the experts - as to whether varietal differences are widely known to result in significant differences in efficacy of treatment as opposed to a number of sources of fruit variation which include temperature, moisture, daylight, rainfall, cultivation conditions and other natural conditions of the harvest year, which according to Japan are not widely known to result in significant differences in efficacy of treatment - *Dr. Ducom* stated as follows:

> "It's the same. My opinion is that differences are of the same [nature], maybe, of the same amount [importance]. I mean, I do not understand what Japan says. I mean why temperature, moisture and so on? Since they are not known they are counted for nothing. That I cannot understand. The same thing for variety. If we use the same argument varieties [aren't more significant than other variables] are just nothing because [we have little data for varieties] we don't know the answer for varieties. Or, if we take into account variety we should take into account daylight, moisture, rainfall and so on" (Transcript. paragraph 10.162).

[277] See footnote 260.

[278] Since, according to the experts advising the Panel, varietal differences, if and to the extent they exist, would mainly or exclusively be due to differences in sorption, tests could, for example, be

cording to which varietal differences affect quarantine efficacy. However, as Japan itself notes: "The task of scientific demonstration begins, not ends, with a discovery of variables".[279]

(iii)   Evaluation by the Panel

8.42.   We carefully reviewed all the evidence before the Panel in accordance with the rules on burden of proof we set out earlier.[280] After this review and referring, in particular, to the expert opinions quoted above[281], we consider that, to date, it has not been sufficiently demonstrated that there is a rational or objective relationship between the varietal testing requirement and the scientific evidence submitted to the Panel. In our view, the United States established - on the basis of scientific reports and with the support of the opinions of the experts advising the Panel[282] - that so far not a single instance has occurred in Japan or any other country, where the treatment approved for one variety of a product has had to be modified to ensure an effective treatment for another variety of the same product. We acknowledge that this part of the evidence before us, of course, only relates to those products and varieties for which to date an application for approval to import was made. The United States further provided evidence, supported by the opinions received from the experts advising the Panel, which suggests that varietal differences do not matter for quarantine efficacy, at least not to the extent reflected in the current Japanese varietal testing requirement.[283] Moreover, even though Japan may have some data - taken from several individual studies - possibly hinting at relevant varietal differences, no evidence before this Panel makes the actual causal link between the differences in the test results and the presence of varietal differences. On these grounds and after having carefully weighed the evidence and opinions of the experts advising the Panel submitted to us, we thus consider that the United States has raised a presump-

---

conducted on different varieties of a product to check whether there are any such differences in sorption. See *Dr. Ducom*'s statement at the meeting with experts:

> "I just advise something about sorption. Levels are important for varieties but that means no insects, no LD50 trials to show that sorption is different. I mean we don't need any insects and any dose mortality tests to show that sorption is different and it makes very different, it's very easy, it's easier to run a sorption test than the dose mortality test. That's an important point in practice" (Transcript, paragraph 10.142).

See also the following statement of *Mr. Taylor* at the meeting with the experts:

> "I think we're all agreed that sorption is one of the major factors involved and, I think that, as Dr. Ducom said earlier, one of the things that should be done is the testing of samples just with methyl bromide [no insects to be involved] to see if we can determine the extent to which these varieties do absorb methyl bromide. Also it would be nice to try and relate any differences we find to chemical or physical characteristics more definitely" (Transcript, paragraph 10.266).

See also statements by *Dr. Ducom and Mr. Taylor*, Transcript, paragraphs 10.187 - 10.196.

[279]   Second submission of Japan, p. 15.

[280]   See paragraph 8.13.

[281]   See paragraphs 8.32 - 8.41.

[282]   See paragraph 8.34.

[283]   See, for example, paragraphs 8.35, 8.39 and 8.40.

tion that Japan's varietal testing requirement is maintained without sufficient scientific evidence and that this presumption has not been sufficiently rebutted by Japan.

8.43.　We thus find that Japan maintains the varietal testing requirement without sufficient scientific evidence in the sense of Article 2.2.

8.44.　According to the scientific experts advising the Panel, the statements they provided on varietal differences are - to the best of their knowledge - equally valid for all US products here at issue.[284] At the meeting with the experts, we asked them the following:

> "You know that the scope of this dispute does not cover only the four products, apples, cherries, nectarines and walnuts, but also apricots, plums, pears and quince, even if we have not received any material from either party concerning those four other products. So now the Panel wants to ask you the following question: To the best of your knowledge is what you have stated about varietal differences concerning apples, cherries, nectarines and walnuts, would that also be valid for apricots, plums, pears and quince?".[285]

We put this question before the experts since the scope of our mandate covers all eight products[286] and taking into account the Appellate Body's view that a panel needs to make findings with respect to all products falling within its terms of reference.[287]

8.45.　*Dr. Heather* answered "yes" to this question and the other two experts concurred. However, the experts did not further elaborate on their answer. Nor did any of the parties provide any additional comments or information which could enlighten us as to the existence or relevance of varietal differences for the four products for which no specific studies are before us. After careful examination we do not consider, therefore, that there is sufficient evidence before us to extend our finding in paragraph 8.43 also to apricots, pears, plums and quince. We only find that Japan maintains the varietal testing requirement without sufficient scientific evidence with respect to apples, cherries, nectarines and walnuts.

8.46.　With respect to two of the four products to which our finding in paragraph 8.43 does apply (apples and walnuts), the experts advising the Panel made certain additional remarks. First, with respect to apples and the cold treatment they undergo before entering Japan (in addition to fumigation), the experts advising the Panel were even more categorical in their opinion that no evidence before the Panel provides a causal link between varietal differences and a divergent efficacy of the required treatment. Since, according to the experts advising the Panel, the efficacy of cold treatment is not linked to the sorption characteristics of the fruit - the allegedly most important factor which could explain possible varietal differences, if any exist[288] - most (if not all) varietal differences which might exist would be offset by the

---

[284]　See paragraph 8.33 *in fine* and footnote 263.

[285]　Transcript, paragraphs 10.223 - 10.225.

[286]　See paragraph 8.6.

[287]　See Appellate Body report on *Japan - Taxes on Alcoholic Beverages*, adopted on 1 November 1996, WT/DS8/AB/R, DSR 1996:I, 97 at 117.

[288]　See paragraph 8.33 and footnote 261.

cold treatment.[289] One expert advising the Panel noted, however, that cold treatment kills the codling moth eggs whereas MB fumigation kills the larvae.[290] The quarantine efficacy across varieties of apples due to the cold treatment would thus only seem to apply to the killing of codling moth eggs.

8.47.   Second, with respect to walnuts, the experts advising the Panel pointed at a specific factor which may influence the sorption level of walnuts, namely their oil or fat content. This could also explain the different test results referred to by Japan.[291] However, according to the experts advising the Panel, so far no information is available which shows that the total oil content is a varietal characteristic which could - by means of a different sorption level - affect the quarantine efficacy of an MB treatment.[292] Therefore, the fact that no evidence before this Panel makes the causal

---

[289]   In reply to the Panel's question whether "anything in the apples study submitted by Japan [Kawakami, F., et. al., Methyl Bromide Sorption in Fruit Varieties, Research Division, Yokohama Plant Protection Station, Japan Exhibit 36]... change any of your earlier opinions as to the relevance of varietal differences for quarantine efficacy", *Dr. Heather* replied:

> "I don't think there is anything in the apple study which impinges on this. Apples are unique in that they have a combined treatment of cold and of methyl bromide and both of these are quite efficacious in their own way. Perhaps I should say at this stage there was a question also from Japan as to why I believe that apples would not differ very much amongst themselves varietally. The reason for this is that cold treatment as a contributing treatment to the codling moth control does not have a sorption problem so there should not be the same degree of variation between varieties of apples because of this cold treatment factor that you would find in a treatment which relied only on methyl bromide" (Transcript, paragraph 10.257).

See also *Dr. Heather*'s reply to Panel question 17:

> "... given the combined lethal potential and broad applicability of MB and cold, it is highly unlikely that there would be any differences in efficacy between any common commercial apple varieties".

[290]   In his comments on the Panel's draft findings now contained in paragraphs 8.73 - 8.101 (received according to the procedure outlined in paragraph 6.116), *Dr. Ducom* clarified that the combined treatments for apples (MB fumigation and cold treatment) affect two different stages of the codling moth: the cold treatment kills the codling moth eggs, the MB fumigation the larvae (see summary in paragraph 6.114). Dr. Ducom noted the following: "There are indeed two treatments for apples, but they apply to two different and separate stages. The cold kills the eggstage and the gas the fifth larval stage" (translation from French)".

[291]   See paragraph 8.21.

[292]   As outlined in paragraphs 6.112 - 6.115, after the Panel's second substantive meeting, we addressed an additional question to the experts dealing with walnuts (with reference to a study submitted by the United States, Variation in Polyunsaturated Fatty Acids Composition of Persian Walnut, L. Carl Greve, et. al., J. Amer. Soc. Hort. Sci. 117 (3), pp. 518-522, 1992, US Exhibit 40) namely "whether and to what extent the oil or fat content differs between varieties of walnuts *because of varietal characteristics*" and "whether any such differences are significant enough to affect quarantine efficacy" (emphasis in original). *Dr. Heather* answered, *inter alia*:

> "I did not find any information on total oil content as a varietal characteristic ...
> Therefore, [the US study] does not provide any further clarification of the extent to which oil content of walnuts might affect quarantine treatment efficacy and consequently, quarantine security".

Dr. Ducom stated, *inter alia*:

> "... the differences between varieties in walnut commodities could be, if any, easily showed since we have a very good tool with the oil content ... variety is one of

link between the differences in the test results and the presence of varietal differences, also applies to walnuts.

(c)   Is the Varietal Testing Requirement a Provisional Measure under Article 5.7?

8.48.   At this juncture - and before we can find, following our considerations and finding in paragraphs 8.42 and 8.43, whether or not Article 2.2 is violated in this dispute - we recall that Article 2.2 provides that "Members shall ensure that any … phytosanitary measure … is not maintained without sufficient scientific evidence, *except as provided for in paragraph 7 of Article 5*" (emphasis added). We note that Japan invokes Article 5.7 in support of its varietal testing requirement. We therefore need to examine next whether the varietal testing requirement is a measure meeting the requirements in Article 5.7. If the varietal testing requirement meets these requirements, we cannot find that it violates Article 2.2.

8.49.   Article 5.7, in relevant parts, provides as follows:

> "In cases where *relevant scientific evidence is insufficient*, a Member may *provisionally* adopt … phytosanitary measures *on the basis of available pertinent information*, including that from the relevant international organizations as well as from … phytosanitary measures applied by other Members. In such circumstances, *Members shall seek to obtain the additional information necessary for a more objective assessment of risk and review the … phytosanitary measure accordingly within a reasonable period of time*" (italic added).

(i)   Arguments by the Parties

8.50.   Under Article 5.7, Japan argues that the *rationale* for its varietal testing requirement is that "available pertinent information" suggests a possible presence of varietal differences in the efficacy of a disinfestation treatment. Once the import prohibition is lifted for a particular variety, Japan expects that new data will be accumulated on the effects of the treatment approved for that variety in order to reach a sufficient level of confidence as to the broader applicability of that treatment to other varieties. Until such level of confidence is achieved, Japan claims to have the right to maintain, on a provisional basis, the import prohibition for all other varieties

---

> the different factors which may affect the oil content of the fruit. But the authors have shown that it's influence is less important than the environmental conditions … Differences like presented in the publications seem to be not large enough to have a noticed influence on the sorption and thus on CT and efficacy. But only trials designed for that purpose could definitively give the good answer".

Mr. Taylor stated, *inter alia*:

> "The greater differences in fatty acid content composition found from year to year within the same variety than between varieties in a single year is also very important evidence demonstrating that varietal differences are unlikely to be the most important factor affecting sorption of methyl bromide and, therefore, the efficacy of methyl bromide fumigations".

See also the statements by *Mr. Taylor*, Transcript, paragraph 10.140 and by *Drs. Heather and Ducom*, Transcript, paragraphs 10.290 - 10.292.

of the same product. In this respect, Japan further submits that it has not been demonstrated that the present treatment for any of the US products allowed for import will control the risk at the required level with respect to all other varieties.

8.51.   Japan recognizes, however, that under Article 5.7 it is required to "seek to obtain the additional information necessary for a more objective assessment of risk and review the ... phytosanitary measure accordingly within a reasonable period of time". In this respect, Japan submits that its obligation to collect information is discharged by Japan's practice of requiring the exporting countries to submit data each time approval of additional varieties is sought, as well as by MAFF at the Yokohama Plant Protection Station (Research Division) which is seeking to collect information and continues to study the effectiveness of the existing treatments for new varieties.

8.52.   In response, the United States submits that Japan's construction of Article 5.7 is patently incorrect. For the United States, Article 5.7 has a threshold requirement that in order for a measure to be provisional, there must be an insufficient amount of relevant scientific evidence to be able to perform a risk assessment. According to the United States, in this case there is a sufficient amount of evidence. For the United States, all evidence in this case, including the success of uniform treatments on different varieties exported to Japan and the absence of failures by commodity-based testing regimes in other countries, indicates that varietal differences do not affect treatment efficacy.

8.53.   The United States further submits that it strains credulity to describe a 50-year old measure as "provisional". The United States argues that, contrary to what is required in Article 5.7, there is no evidence that Japan has undertaken a process to produce a more objective assessment of risk "within a reasonable period of time" so that it can review whether the "provisional measure" should be continued.

(ii)   Evaluation by the Panel

8.54.   In our view, the first sentence of Article 5.7 allows Members to provisionally adopt phytosanitary measures if two elements, cumulative in nature, are met:

- the measure is imposed in respect of a situation where "relevant scientific information is insufficient"; and

- the measure is adopted "on the basis of available pertinent information".

However, even if a measure meets both of these elements, the second sentence of Article 5.7 imposes additional obligations on the Member provisionally adopting the measure, namely the obligation to

- "seek to obtain the additional information necessary for a more objective assessment of risk"; and

- "review the ... phytosanitary measure accordingly within a reasonable period of time".

8.55.   Therefore, even if we were to assume that the varietal testing requirement is a phytosanitary measure provisionally adopted in accordance with the first sentence of Article 5.7, i.e., even if we were to assume that in this case "relevant scientific information is insufficient" *and* there is "available pertinent information" before the Panel on which Japan can base the varietal testing requirement, the second sentence of Article 5.7 obliges Japan to "seek to obtain the additional information necessary for a more objective assessment of risk" *and* to "review the ... phytosanitary measure accordingly within a reasonable period of time".

8.56.   As to the obligation imposed on Japan to "*seek to obtain the additional information necessary for a more objective assessment of risk*", Japan refers to the fact that exporting countries provide additional information when they apply for access. We note, however, that the studies these countries provide are designed and carried out to *comply* with the varietal testing requirement. They do not examine the appropriateness of the requirement itself. This is also the case for the two reports before the Panel which were carried out by MAFF's Research Division.[293] No further information or evidence was submitted to us. As pointed out earlier[294], not a single study before the Panel actually addresses the specific issue as to whether varietal characteristics cause a divergency in quarantine efficacy. The requirement that the information necessary to review an SPS measure must be specific enough, was referred to by the Appellate Body in *EC - Hormones*.[295] In this respect, we further recall that the experts advising the Panel stated that a study or research project to determine whether varietal differences do matter for quarantine efficacy - which would mainly involve sorption tests - could be carried out relatively easily.[296]

8.57.   Moreover, with respect to the obligation imposed on Japan to "*review the ... phytosanitary measure accordingly within a reasonable period of time*", we note that, according to Japan, testing variety-by-variety for lifting the import ban imposed in the Plant Protection Law, was first applied in 1969 when the ban was lifted for Hawaiian papayas of the Solo variety, i.e., on a variety basis. For the US products at issue, hosts of codling moth, the import ban was first lifted in 1978. The issue of varietal testing, and the question as to whether it can be scientifically justified, has thus been around for almost 30 years and, with respect to the specific products and pest at issue, for 20 years. During this period of time Japan has been in a position to obtain further information on varietal differences and their relevance to quarantine efficacy. Moreover, since the entry into force of the SPS Agreement on 1 January 1995, Japan has been under an explicit obligation to collect additional information to enable it to more objectively review the appropriateness of the varietal testing requirement.

8.58.   On these grounds, we consider that there is no evidence before us which indicates that Japan sought to "obtain the information necessary for a more objective assessment of risk" and reviewed the varietal testing requirement accordingly "within a reasonable period of time". We consider, therefore, that the United States has established a presumption that Japan did not comply with the requirements in the second sentence of Article 5.7. We also consider that Japan has not been able to rebut this presumption.

---

[293]   All but two of the studies before the Panel were conducted on behalf of exporting countries. The two exceptions are two studies carried out by MAFF's Research Division (1997 tests on three varieties of Japanese nectarines, Research Division, Yokohama Plant Protection Station, MAFF, 1997, Unpublished, Japan Exhibit 16 and Kawakami, F., et. al., Methyl Bromide Sorption in Fruit Varieties, Research Division, Yokohama Plant Protection Station, Japan Exhibit 36).

[294]   See paragraph 8.42: no evidence before this Panel makes the causal link between the differential in the test results and the presence of varietal differences.

[295]   Op. cit., paragraph 200.

[296]   See footnote 278.

8.59.   Following the rules on burden of proof we set out earlier[297], we thus find that even if the varietal testing requirement were considered as a provisional measure adopted in accordance with the first sentence of Article 5.7[298], Japan has not fulfilled the requirements contained in the second sentence of Article 5.7.

8.60.   In its comments on the interim report, Japan noted that the information gathered through successive demonstrations by exporting countries constitutes experience and that experience is a legitimate means to gather information under Article 5.7. We agree with this point of view. Of course, Japan can take into account the evidence submitted so far by exporting countries. However, in our view, this method of collecting information has, to date, not provided the information "necessary for a more objective assessment of risk" and an appropriate review of the varietal testing requirement "within a reasonable period of time".

(d)   The Panel's Conclusion under Article 2.2

8.61.   We have found above that the varietal testing requirement - in so far as it applies to imports of apples, cherries, nectarines and walnuts - is neither (1) maintained with sufficient scientific evidence in the sense of Article 2.2[299] nor (2), in the event it were a provisional measure in accordance with the first sentence of Article 5.7, a measure maintained in conformity with the second sentence of Article 5.7.[300] We recall, however, that Article 2.2 requires Japan to ensure that the varietal testing requirement is "not maintained without sufficient scientific evidence, except as provided for in paragraph 7 of Article 5". Consequently, we come to the conclusion that Japan, by maintaining the varietal testing requirement with respect to apples, cherries, nectarines and walnuts, acts inconsistently with its obligations under Article 2.2.

8.62.   Given this conclusion under Article 2.2, we see no need to further examine what is required for a phytosanitary measure to be "based on scientific principles" in the sense of Article 2.2, nor to determine whether in this dispute the varietal testing requirement is so based.

3.   *Risk Assessment*

8.63.   Since we have found earlier[301] that the varietal testing requirement violates Article 2.2, we see no need to further examine whether it also needs to be based on a risk assessment in accordance with Articles 5.1 and 5.2 nor to determine whether in this dispute it is so based.

---

[297]   See paragraph 8.13.
[298]   See paragraph 8.54.
[299]   See paragraph 8.42.
[300]   See paragraph 8.58.
[301]   See paragraph 8.61.

G.   Measures not More Trade-Restrictive than Required (Article 5.6)

1.   Arguments by the Parties

8.64.   The United States further claims that the Japanese varietal testing requirement is inconsistent with Article 5.6 in that it is significantly more trade-restrictive than required to achieve Japan's appropriate level of phytosanitary protection. The United States submits that because there are no varietal differences that affect the efficacy of a quarantine treatment, the same established treatment will achieve for all varieties of a product the appropriate level of protection. The United States argues that neither it, nor any other country exporting to Japan, has ever had to modify a quarantine treatment for codling moth for additional varieties of the same product. According to the United States, these results conclusively demonstrate that Japan's varietal testing requirement has no value in providing additional quarantine protection.

8.65.   The United States posits testing by product as a reasonable alternative under Article 5.6. The United States accepts that the first variety of a particular product from any source should be subject to the full gamut of testing. However, it is the US view that after such validation, no further testing at all for additional varieties is necessary. Because testing by variety takes a minimum of 2-4 years to complete per variety, is resource intensive and costly to perform, and seriously delays market access of US products, the United States argues that testing by product is also less trade-restrictive.

8.66.   The United States submits that to be required to only conduct confirmatory tests for each additional variety (as referred to in a question by the Panel to the United States), would be virtually as time-consuming and burdensome as the current requirement to do dose-mortality tests for each variety and confirmatory testing on representative varieties.

8.67.   Although the United States pointed out, in its rebuttal submissions, that it considers testing by product to be the only acceptable quarantine measure in the context of this dispute, in its oral statement at the second substantive meeting it also referred to an alternative measure posited by the experts advising the Panel[302] as a confirmation of the fact that Japan's varietal testing requirement is more trade-restrictive than required.[303] The alternatives submitted by the experts advising the Panel are outlined below.[304]

8.68.   Japan responds that its lifting of the import prohibition for specific varieties is a result of the discharge of its obligation under Article 5.6. According to Japan, whenever it finds a measure which achieves its appropriate level of protection and is significantly less restrictive, the import prohibition is replaced with such a measure.

---

[302]   An approach to treatment based on a fixed CxT value to be met by monitoring the MB dose in the fumigation chamber. See additional Panel question 9, posed at the meeting with experts (Transcript, paragraph 10.197), and below paragraph 8.76.

[303]   In its answer to an additional Panel question at the second substantive meeting, the United States no longer seemed to consider testing by product as the only alternative, stating that "it remains the *preferred* quarantine measure" (US answers of 24 June 1998, question 1, p.1, emphasis added).

[304]   See paragraphs 8.76 and 8.77.

In this particular case, however, Japan submits that it found data which suggests the presence of varietal differences in efficacy of MB fumigation, and a hypothesis which explains such a variation. On that basis Japan requires testing by variety. As the United States has not proven product-wide efficacy, Japan concludes that it should not be obliged to accept the US alternative at this stage.

8.69.   Japan points out that it already made efforts to alleviate the burden put on exporting countries. First, Japan accepts the concept of a representative variety. This means, for example, that for an application for access of five varieties of a product, a large-scale confirmatory test will only need to be carried out for one of the five varieties, i.e., the variety which is shown to be the least sensitive to the treatment in dose-mortality tests. This is why, Japan submits, there is no requirement of full-scale testing of each variety. Second, for approval of additional varieties, the number of codling moth insects required in large-scale demonstrations has been reduced from 30,000 to 10,000.

2.   Elements under Article 5.6

8.70.   We note that Article 5.6 provides in relevant part:

> "... when establishing or maintaining ... phytosanitary measures to achieve the appropriate level of ... phytosanitary protection, Members shall ensure that such *measures are not more trade-restrictive than required to achieve their appropriate level of ... phytosanitary protection, taking into account technical and economic feasibility*" (italic added).

A footnote to Article 5.6 states the following:

> "For purposes of paragraph 6 of Article 5, a measure is not more trade-restrictive than required unless there is another measure, reasonably available taking into account technical and economic feasibility, that achieves the appropriate level of ... phytosanitary protection and is significantly less restrictive to trade".

8.71.   Article 5.6 must be read in context. We consider, in particular, that the more specific language of Article 5.6 should be read in light of the more general language in Article 2.2 providing that:

> "Members shall ensure that any ... phytosanitary measure is applied *only to the extent necessary to protect* ... plant life or health" (italic added).

8.72.   In this dispute, Article 5.6 provides that the varietal testing requirement not be "more trade-restrictive than required to achieve [Japan's] appropriate level of ... phytosanitary protection, taking into account technical and economic feasibility". According to the footnote to Article 5.6, the varietal testing requirement shall be considered to be "more trade-restrictive than required" if there is another phytosanitary measure which:

- is "reasonably available taking into account technical and economic feasibility";

- "achieves [Japan's] appropriate level of ... phytosanitary protection"; and

- is "significantly less restrictive to trade" than the varietal testing requirement.

These three elements are cumulative in nature. Only when the United States has raised a presumption, not sufficiently rebutted by Japan, that all three elements are present, can the varietal testing requirement be found to be inconsistent with Article 5.6.

3. *Alternative Measures before the Panel*

(a) Testing by Product

8.73.   The first alternative before the Panel is the one posited by the United States. It involves testing product-by-product (instead of variety-by-variety).[305] Once a variety of a product has been approved, no further testing at all would be required for any other varieties of that product.

(b) Alternatives Derived from the Testing of Possible Differences in Sorption

8.74.   The scientific experts advising the Panel suggest other alternatives based on the testing of possible differences in sorption. We deduced these alternatives from their written answers to our questions and, more particularly, from their statements at the expert meeting. Subsequently, at our second substantive meeting with the parties, both parties have expressed their views on these alternatives. Moreover, before issuing our interim report we sent a draft of those parts addressing these alternatives to the experts for their comments.[306] We shall, therefore, also examine whether any of these alternatives meet the three elements under Article 5.6.

8.75.   We recall that one of the basic understandings confirmed by the experts advising the Panel is that if, and to the extent, there are differences between varieties, these would be mainly or even exclusively related to different levels of sorption of the fruit.[307] Therefore, to control any possible varietal differences, the experts advising the Panel note that, as an alternative to the varietal testing requirement, one could either monitor or test the sorption characteristics of the different varieties of the products at issue.

(i) Monitoring a Predetermined CxT Value During Commercial Treatment

8.76.   According to the experts advising the Panel, quarantine efficacy against codling moth could be achieved by determining a fixed CxT value, i.e., a certain concentration of the fumigant in the chamber during a certain period of time, to be obtained during quarantine treatment. This CxT value would be so determined that if a codling moth were fumigated with this concentration during this time, it would die, irrespective of the host product or variety on which it occurs. To obtain this CxT value during commercial treatment, the MB concentration in the chamber would need to be monitored. If the concentration drops below that required by the CxT value, an additional dose

---

[305]   See paragraph 8.65.
[306]   See paragraphs 6.116 and following.
[307]   See paragraph 8.33 and the references in footnote 261.

would need to be injected in the chamber. As long as the CxT value were met, varietal differences (if there are any, such as sorption) would not affect quarantine efficacy nor would any other factors.[308]

---

[308] See *Dr. Ducom*'s answer to Panel question 10:

"The notion of the concentration-time product, or here the CT value, is fundamental in fumigation. What kills the insect is not only the dose of gas introduced, but the quantity of gas inhaled during the entire gas exposure period. The measurement of gas concentrations throughout fumigation permits one to correlate the efficacy observed not only at the initial concentration introduced, but also during its evolution over time, that is to say, the CT value. This quantity depends on the gas concentration in the chamber whose variation factors are:

- an initial dose introduced into the chamber,
- the load which could increase or decrease the free concentration of gas according to the sorption of the commodity,
- the sorption of the commodity and of everything present in the chamber,
- eventual leaks.

A CT value is universal once the target stage and the treatment temperature are defined. All the other factors matter little, even the nature of the commodity, since they are accounted for by the measurement of gas concentration ... The difference [with the current Japanese testing requirements] is that the CT is definitively acquired and that one could then vary the different initial parameters. On the contrary, the present conditions to impose a recognized effective treatment consists in fixing initial intangible draconian conditions (temperature, treatment length, gas tightness of the chamber, nature of the packing material and load) that would make any variation impossible. ... Finally, I completely agree to admit that the confirmatory test constitutes a necessary condition to define the quarantine level for a given species of pest. One can also associate the test to a CT value which is then acquired once and for all ... This objective CT value could become the sole criterion for success in quarantine treatment" (See also *Dr. Ducom*'s written answers to the Panel's questions, p. 11).

See also *Dr. Heather*'s answer to Panel question 11:

"If the CxT value for a required efficacy against a pest is known then a fumigation treatment that meets or exceeds that specification can be expected to achieve the quarantine security level required. This should hold true for all batches of a commodity, including those of differing varieties, provided that temperature, load and any other relevant requirements are met".

See also the experts' answers to additional Panel question 9 at the meeting with the experts, Transcript, paragraph 10.198 - 10.202. See also *Mr. Taylor*'s closing statement at the meeting with experts, Transcript, paragraph 10.267:

"I would like to say in conclusion that I found one of the most interesting parts of the meeting came in question 9 when the Panel asked us if in that statement rather, whether their understanding of what we were talking about was in fact the case and I think it is clear we are saying here that if you have the right amount of gas for the right amount of time it will kill the pest because basically that's what fumigation's all about. It doesn't matter which gas you're using. If you have the lethal concentration for the required time this will kill the pest and that's really what we want to try and achieve, so this long and somewhat complicated discussion about CxT products is in fact very relevant because if we do achieve the desired CxT product in a commercial treatment we should end up with an efficacious treatment which should satisfy the requirements for quarantine".

(ii)   Determine Whether the Sorption Level of Additional Varieties Differs from that of the Already Approved Variety

8.77.   For the approval of additional varieties of a product for which a treatment for one or more varieties has already been accepted, Japan currently imposes dose-mortality tests for all varieties and an on-site confirmatory test - preceded, if required[309], by a large-scale confirmatory test - for one representative variety.[310] Instead, the experts advising the Panel suggest that Japan could simply determine the sorption level of each of the additional varieties when treated as required for the already approved varieties.[311] For those additional varieties which do not exceed the sorption level of the already approved varieties, there would be no need for further testing or confirmation. The commercial treatment (i.e., a fixed dose-temperature-time relationship, as is the case today) for the initial variety could then also be approved for the additional variety. For those additional varieties which do have a higher sorption level, it could then be determined - if need be by means of additional tests - whether the level of sorption is of sufficient magnitude to reduce the concentration of MB gas below the level of insect mortality required by Japan.[312] If this were to be the case, a different commercial treatment for the additional variety could then be imposed.

---

[309] *In casu*, in the event any of the additional varieties demonstrate, in the dose-mortality tests, significantly lower disinfestation effects than the already approved varieties.

[310] See paragraph 2.24.

[311] See answer by *Dr. Ducom* to Panel question 11:

> "If varieties are tested to find the CT value, then no further testing is necessary. The success of the system implies: (1) that the trials be conducted according to precise guidelines approved by both parties. In particular, the number of fruits should be quite large in each replicate to minimize the effects of sampling; (2) that the treatment standard clarify the CT value necessary to obtain the desired efficacy. This value is the one found in the confirmatory test, for example for nectarines, 68 gh/m^3 (Yokoyama, 1990.) The results of these tests are sufficient in themselves to give confidence in the conformity of the varietal candidate without having to include the reference variety and insects for efficacy confirmation. This would not bring any supplementary information".

See also answer by *Mr. Taylor* to Panel question 11:

> "CxT values are used to indicate the fumigant concentration and exposure period required to achieve a 99% mortality of all development stages of an insect at a particular temperature and humidity under practical conditions. If these values were obtained for additional varieties and were found to fall within the range already observed for other varieties it would be difficult to justify why further testing would be necessary".

See further the answers to additional Panel question 9 at the meeting with the experts, Transcript, paragraph 10.198 - 10.202. See also the experts' answers to questions by Japan dealing with this alternative approach, Transcript, paragraphs 10.233 - 10.253.

[312] The experts advising the Panel noted that the differences in sorption would need to be significant in order to affect treatment efficacy. See *Mr. Taylor*'s answer to Panel question 9, at paragraph 6.67 and his statement at the meeting with the experts, Transcript, paragraph 10.82; *Dr. Heather*'s answer to Panel question 10, at paragraph 6.81.

> 4. *Does any Alternative Meet all of the Elements in Article 5.6?*

> (a)   Testing by Product[313]

8.78.   Japan does not contest that testing by product is "reasonably available taking into account technical and economic feasibility" (i.e., it meets the first element under Article 5.6). We agree. Technically and economically speaking it is easier to implement testing by product, both for Japan and the exporting country, than the various tests and procedural steps currently imposed to obtain approval for additional varieties. Indeed, under the testing by product alternative no further testing at all of additional varieties would be required.

8.79.   Japan does not contest either that testing by product is "significantly less restrictive to trade" than the varietal testing requirement (i.e., it meets the third element under Article 5.6). We agree. Under the testing by product alternative, market access for additional varieties would be automatic. No additional testing would be required.

8.80.   Japan only contests the remaining element under Article 5.6, namely whether testing by product would "achieve [Japan's] appropriate level of ... phytosanitary protection".

8.81.   Both parties agree that it is up to Japan to determine its appropriate level of phytosanitary protection with respect to codling moth. We agree since the SPS Agreement (in paragraph 5 of Annex A) defines the "appropriate level of ... phytosanitary protection" as "[t]he level of protection *deemed appropriate by the Member* establishing a ... phytosanitary measure to protect ... plant life or health within its territory"[314], *in casu*, the level deemed appropriate by Japan.

8.82.   Both parties also agree on the level of mortality that Japan is seeking with respect to coddling moth.[315] We consider that, for present purposes, this level of mortality can be regarded as Japan's appropriate level of protection. Japan will lift the import prohibition if it can be replaced by a measure which achieves the same level of protection as that reached by the import prohibition. With respect to measures imposing disinfestation, this level is complete mortality in large-scale tests on a minimum of 30,000 codling moths.[316] For the testing by product alternative, the question thus becomes *whether the treatment approved for the first variety of a product would meet the same level of protection, i.e., complete mortality in large-scale tests on a minimum of 30,000 codling moths, with respect to all other varieties of that product.*

8.83.   Referring to the opinions we received from the experts advising the Panel, we consider that - to date and on the basis of the evidence before the Panel - it is not possible to state with an appropriate degree of certainty that one and the same treatment would be effective for all varieties of a product. In the view of the experts advising the Panel, there is no evidence before us which establishes a causal link between divergent quarantine efficacy and the presence of varietal differences (i.e., evidence which

---

[313]   See paragraph 8.65.
[314]   Emphasis added.
[315]   See paragraph 8.11.
[316]   See paragraph 2.23 under "Large-Scale mortality test" and paragraph 8.11. See also answer by *Dr. Heather* summarized in paragraph 6.117.

could justify Japan's varietal testing requirement).[317] However, at least one of the experts advising the Panel made equally clear that the US alternative of one treatment for all varieties, including those to be developed in the future, does not, to date, have a scientific basis either. In his answer to Panel question 16, *Dr. Ducom* states:

> "The arguments put forth by Japan for requiring varietal trials are not based on scientific data. They are supported by a few experimental data in which varietal difference exists, in terms of LD_{50}, among a lot of other data in which it does not ...
>
> The arguments put forth by the USA are based on a large number of experiments, of which Japan has thoroughly made use.
>
> Varietal difference appears several times, but each time, the confirmatory test has revealed sufficient efficacy. *Extrapolation to all available varieties is no more scientific than the Japanese's contrary assertion. This sort of extrapolation is something along the order of intuition. It is unfortunate that there has not been a research program on the subject in order to try to present some scientific proof*".[318]

8.84.   Therefore, after having carefully examined all the evidence before us in light of the opinions we received from the experts advising the Panel, we are not convinced that there is sufficient evidence before us to find that testing by product would achieve Japan's appropriate level of protection for any of the products at issue.

> (b)   Alternatives Derived from the Testing of Possible Differences in Sorption
>
> (i)   Monitoring a Predetermined CxT Value During Commercial Treatment[319]

8.85.   The United States recognizes that the process of monitoring a predetermined CxT value could be less trade-restrictive than the current regime of testing by variety. For the United States, this would depend on a number of assumptions, including (1) the new treatment methodology would not apply for varieties already approved for entry to Japan nor for those varieties for which an application is currently pending; (2) with respect to new commodities, the initial variety on the basis of which the fixed CxT value would be determined, would not be subject to an on-site confirmatory test; and (3) since the treatment of apples also involves cold treatment, which is not affected

---

[317]   See paragraph 8.42.

[318]   *Dr. Ducom's* written answers, pp. 10-11, underlining added. At the meeting with the experts, Japan referred to this statement, noting that *Dr. Ducom* seems to concur "that there is no valid scientific ground to conclude that a treatment established for a particular variety by confirmatory tests would be efficacious for any additional variety" (Transcript, paragraph 10.92). *Dr. Ducom* replied as follows: " Yes that is correct. I mean I cannot see any more scientific basis on the Japanese side than on the USA's side to say [that each] variety must be carefully treated ... or for one we can have all varieties. I hope you understand. In my opinion it is not scientific to say that one variety is equal to all others ..." (Transcript, paragraph 10.93).

[319]   This alternative is outlined in paragraph 8.76.

by sorption, the approved treatment for some varieties of apples should be extended to all varieties of apples without further testing.

8.86.   The United States submits that the question of technical and economic feasibility requires more extensive research and examination. The United States notes that increasing the time and/or dose of an MB treatment to achieve a particular CxT value could result in residues unacceptable for reasons of human health and/or conflict with applicable US environmental laws and regulations.[320] The United States also points out that in order to conduct precise measurements of CxT values, gas chromatographs would be required. However, for commercial applications of MB a fumiscope (which is less precise) is much more commonly available. Fumiscopes are also significantly less expensive and simpler to operate than gas chromatographs. The United States further argues that since monitoring of each treatment would be required, treatments would become more labour intensive than current applications of accepted treatments.

8.87.   Japan submits that it does not have information on whether the process of monitoring a predetermined CxT value would be technically or economically feasible for exporting countries. Consequently, Japan is not certain if the process would be less trade-restrictive than the present regime.

8.88.   When we asked the experts advising the Panel whether in their expert opinion the process would be technically and economically feasible, *Dr. Ducom* answered "yes".[321] *Mr. Taylor* stated that it is technically feasible, but reserved his judgment on the economic feasibility, adding that it is probably economically feasible.[322] *Dr. Heather* deferred to the other two experts.[323]

---

[320] In answering an additional Panel question, the parties referred to the Montreal Protocol on Substances that Deplete the Ozone Layer which mandates the phasing-out of MB in developed countries by 2005 (Article 2H). However, they also noted that the use of MB for quarantine and preshipment application is exempted from this phasing-out schedule (Article 2H:6). According to the United States, the production and importation of MB is to be phased-out in the United States by 1 January 2001. The United States noted that its administration has expressed a willingness to consult with the US Congress on changes to US law if alternatives do not exist for control of key pests as the 2001 phase-out date approaches.

[321] See Transcript, paragraph 10.198.

[322] *Mr. Taylor* stated:

"Yes I have to agree with Dr. Ducom. In many cases of course of fumigation of other situations, such as the treatment of flour mills, there is regular monitoring, as we call it, of the fumigant level. It may be necessary to increase the fumigant concentration by adding more fumigant for example, because of some factor, maybe leakage, etc., so I mean this is certainly something that can be done, and is done, and if this type of technology was employed whereby the concentration is monitored regularly and it is found to reach the required level, in other words, you will end up with the CxT product value that you have said is necessary, then this will be an effective treatment and I mean so this is technically feasible. I will reserve judgment on the economic feasibility to those that know more about the topic than myself. But probably it is. I would think it to be probably technically and economically feasible." (Transcript, paragraph 10.200).

[323] *Dr. Heather* stated:

"I'd have to defer to my colleagues who know more, who have more practical experience of fumigation, but I am aware that grain in my home State is controlled by the use of a CxT approach rather than an outright dose" (Transcript, paragraph 10.202).

8.89.   Referring to the arguments made by the parties[324], the evidence before us and the opinions of the experts advising the Panel, we are of the view that, to date, there is not enough evidence before the Panel to enable us to find that the process of monitoring a predetermined CxT value would be technically and economically feasible and significantly less restrictive to trade than the current regime (i.e., fulfils the first and third element under Article 5.6).

8.90.   We note, however, that according to the opinions of the experts advising the Panel[325], this alternative would not only guarantee, to a high probability, quarantine efficacy irrespective of possible varietal differences, but also irrespective of any other variables such as crop-to-crop and year-to-year differences within the same variety, i.e., differences which are not taken into account under the current regime.[326]

(ii)   Determine Whether the Sorption Level of Additional Varieties Differs from that of the Already Approved Variety[327]

8.91.   Japan does not contest that determining the sorption level of additional varieties, and comparing it with the sorption level of an approved variety, is "reasonably available taking into account technical and economic feasibility". The United States has given views which are consistent with this.[328]

8.92.   Under this alternative, the initial variety of a product would be subject to the existing testing requirements; a certain treatment (including a fixed exposure time, dose and temperature) would then be determined. For additional varieties there would only be a need to determine to what extent, if any, the sorption characteristics of the additional varieties differ from those already approved. Such determination would only require a one-time test for each additional variety. According to the experts advising the Panel, this test would be a relatively easy one; at least easier to conduct than the currently required dose-mortality test since it involves neither codling moths nor LD trials. In this respect, *Dr. Ducom* notes the following:

> "I just advise something about sorption. Levels are important for varieties but that means no insects, no LD_{50} trials to show that sorption is different. I mean we don't need any insects and any dose mortality tests to show that sorption is different and it makes very different, it's

---

[324]   See paragraphs 8.85-8.87.

[325]   See paragraph 8.76 and footnote 308.

[326]   See, for example, the statement by *Dr. Ducom* that

> "[a] CT value is universal once the target stage and the treatment temperature are defined. All the other factors matter little, even the nature of the commodity, since they are accounted for by the measurement of gas concentration" (*Dr. Ducom's* answer to Panel question 10).

[327]   This alternative is outlined in paragraph 8.77.

[328]   The United States did not specifically address the technical and economic feasibility of this third alternative. However, the Panel considered all other US arguments in this respect. None of these arguments go against the idea that this third alternative would be technically and economically feasible.

very easy, it's easier to run a sorption test than the dose mortality test. That's an important point in practice".[329]

Mr. Taylor, in turn, states:

"... there are quite well known methods by which accurate levels of sorption can be tested ... certainly techniques such as these have been conducted over many years so there should be no problem in actually conducting these trials. As Dr. Ducom said, to determine the sorption of fumigant would not involve insects in these test, just the gas and the commodity, and from these tests to see to what extent there is a difference between varieties as between commodities, and to determine just to what extent this is an important factor and whether the level of sorption is very high or very little difference exists between the two".[330]

8.93.   If, as a result of sorption tests, the sorption level of the additional variety is *not* higher than the sorption level of the initial variety, the same treatment can be applied for both varieties, without further testing or confirmation. If the sorption level of the additional variety *is* higher than that of the initial variety, it could then be determined - if need be by means of additional tests - whether the level of sorption is of sufficient magnitude to reduce the concentration of MB gas below the level of insect mortality required by Japan.[331] If this were to be the case, a different commercial treatment for the additional variety could then be imposed.

8.94.   On these grounds, we consider that the process of determining the sorption level of additional varieties can be presumed to be "reasonably available taking into account technical and economic feasibility" (i.e., to meet the first element under Article 5.6).

8.95.   Japan does not contest that the process of determining the sorption level of additional varieties is "significantly less restrictive to trade" than the varietal testing requirement. The United States has given views which are consistent with this.[332]

8.96.   Under this alternative, testing for most (if not all) additional varieties would be limited to a sorption test. If the sorption level is *not* higher than that of already approved varieties, no further testing or confirmation would be required. In that event, market access would be obtained significantly more easily than under the current regime. If the sorption level *is* higher than that of already approved varieties,

---

[329]   Transcript, paragraph 10.142. See also *Dr. Ducom*'s statement, Transcript, paragraph 10.188.

[330]   Transcript, paragraph 10.192. See also *Dr. Ducom*'s written answers, p. 8 ("Research on the CT per variety is an operation which could be rapidly conducted, since only the variety of fruit to be tested is used. Fumigation only lasts two hours and the result is known immediately") and p. 11 ("For the USA, this system is quick and low-cost").

[331]   The experts advising the Panel noted that the differences in sorption would need to be significant in order to affect treatment efficacy. See *Mr. Taylor*'s answer to Panel question 9, at paragraph 6.67 and his statement at the meeting with the experts, Transcript, paragraph 10.82; *Dr. Heather*'s answer to Panel question 10, at paragraph 6.81.

[332]   The United States did not specifically address whether this third alternative is significantly less trade-restrictive. However, the Panel considered all other US arguments in this respect. None of these arguments go against the idea that this third alternative would be significantly less trade-restrictive.

further examination and, if need be, additional testing could then be required. In that case, market access would be obtained in circumstances no more difficult than under the current regime.

8.97.   On these grounds, we consider that the process of determining the sorption level of additional varieties can be presumed to be "significantly less restrictive to trade" than the varietal testing requirement (i.e., to meet the third element under Article 5.6).

8.98.   Japan has *not* accepted that the process of determining the sorption level of additional varieties would achieve its appropriate level of protection. The United States, on the other hand, suggests that this process *would* meet Japan's appropriate level of protection".[333]

8.99.   We recall that it is for Japan to determine its level of phytosanitary protection and that, in this case, the level of mortality sought by Japan for codling moth is not in dispute.[334] Japan's level of mortality is complete mortality in large-scale tests on a minimum of 30,000 codling moths.[335] For the alternative of determining the sorption level of additional varieties, the question thus becomes *whether the treatment approved for the initial variety of a product would meet the same level of protection, i.e., complete mortality in large-scale tests on a minimum of 30,000 codling moths, with respect to all other varieties of that product which have the same (or lower) sorption levels as the initial variety.*

8.100.   According to the experts advising the Panel, this would be the case.[336] *Dr. Ducom* notes, for example:

> "If varieties are tested to find the CT value [an indication of the amount of fumigant sorbed], then *no further testing is necessary ...* The results of these tests are sufficient in themselves to give confidence in the conformity of the varietal candidate without having to include the reference variety and insects for efficacy confirmation".[337]

Mr. Taylor, in turn, states:

> "CxT values are used to indicate the fumigant concentration and exposure period required to achieve a 99% mortality of all development stages of an insect at a particular temperature and humidity under practical conditions. If these values were obtained for additional va-

---

[333]   The United States did not specifically address whether this third alternative would meet Japan's appropriate level of protection. However, the United States submits that testing by product would meet Japan's level of protection. Since this third alternative is more stringent than testing by product, it can thus be presumed that the US view on this alternative would be that it *a fortiori* meets Japan's level of protection.

[334]   See paragraphs 8.81-8.82.

[335]   See paragraph 2.23 under "Large-Scale mortality test" and paragraph 8.11. See also answer by *Dr. Heather* summarized in paragraph 6.117.

[336]   See the expert opinions referred to in footnote 311.

[337]   *Dr. Ducom*'s written answer to Panel question 11, underlining added. See also *Dr. Ducom*'s written answers to the Panel's question, p. 11: "For Japan, [the alternative] is acceptable in terms of efficacy". Dr. Ducom then refers to a statement by Japan itself according to which "the CT value, a known indicator to control the degree of efficacy of the treatment, will vary as well depending on the variety of the fruit" (First submission of Japan, paragraph 78).

rieties and were found to fall within the range already observed for other varieties *it would be difficult to justify why further testing would be necessary*".[338]

8.101. On the basis of the evidence before the Panel and the views we received from the experts advising the Panel, we thus consider that it can be presumed that the process of determining the sorption levels of additional varieties - so as to ensure that these levels do not differ in a way which would affect the efficacy of MB treatment - "achieves [Japan's] appropriate level of ... phytosanitary protection" (i.e., meets the second element under Article 5.6). We also consider that Japan has not been able to rebut this presumption.

(c)   The Panel's Conclusion under Article 5.6

8.102. Irrespective of whether Article 2.2 is violated in this case, we offer the following conclusion with respect to Article 5.6. Indeed, even if we were to have found that Japan's measure is maintained with sufficient scientific evidence in accordance with Article 2.2, we would then be called upon to examine whether the measure is consistent with Article 5.6.

8.103. We have considered above that - on the basis of the evidence before the Panel and the opinions of the experts advising the Panel - it can be presumed that an alternative measure exists (i.e., determining the sorption level of additional varieties as described in paragraphs 8.76 and 8.91 and following) which would meet all of the elements under Article 5.6.[339] In so doing, we are not endorsing this or any other specific alternative measure as the measure to be put in place by Japan.

8.104. We thus conclude that the varietal testing requirement maintained by Japan is more trade-restrictive than required within the meaning of Article 5.6. For the same reasons as those outlined in paragraphs 8.44 and 8.45, on the basis of the evidence before us, we only make this finding with respect to apples, cherries, nectarines and walnuts.

H.   *Transparency of Phytosanitary Measures (Article 7 and Annex B of the SPS Agreement)*

1.   *Arguments by the Parties*

8.105. The United States also claims that the varietal testing requirement has not been published, making it inconsistent with Article 7 of the SPS Agreement.

8.106. Japan does not contest that the varietal testing requirement is in effect and applied. Japan acknowledges, moreover, that it has not been published. Japan argues, however, that the guidelines developed by the MAFF concerning confirmation of efficacy of a disinfestation treatment have been distributed to foreign plant quarantine authorities for the purpose of transparency. Japan stresses, moreover, that these guidelines are available to any interested foreign government through Japan's Enquiry Point in accordance with paragraph 3 (b) of Annex B to the SPS Agreement

---

[338] *Mr. Taylor's* written answer to Panel question 11, underlining added.
[339] See paragraphs 8.94, 8.97 and 8.101.

and that anyone who wants to know more about approved products can refer to the MAFF notifications published in the Official Gazette or contact MAFF itself. Japan further contends that the guidelines do not constitute enforceable phytosanitary "regulations" under paragraph 1 of Annex B. According to Japan, they are only a model and are not mandatory since exporting countries may choose to demonstrate efficacy of treatment by other means. Finally, according to Japan, these guidelines are not generally published because they are a highly technical document addressed to foreign plant quarantine authorities.

8.107. In response, the United States submits that irrespective of the informal process by which US scientists, in consultation with Japan, have devised procedures to test by variety, the fact remains that the varietal testing requirement itself should be published. According to the United States, the net result is that absent such publication, an exporter has no way to discern what is necessary to move a product from the prohibited list to a list approved by Japan for entry.

2.   *Evaluation by the Panel*

8.108. We note that Article 7 provides in relevant part:

> "Members ... shall provide information on their ... phytosanitary measures in accordance with the provisions of Annex B".

Paragraph 1 of Annex B, in turn, states that:

> "Members shall ensure that all ... phytosanitary regulations which have been adopted are published promptly in such a manner as to enable interested Members to become acquainted with them".

A footnote to this paragraph specifies that the "phytosanitary regulations" referred to are:

> "phytosanitary measures such as laws, decrees or ordinances which are applicable generally".

8.109. Therefore, in our view, for a measure to be subject to the publication requirement in Annex B, three conditions apply: (1) the measure "[has] been adopted"[340]; (2) the measure is a "phytosanitary regulation"[341], namely a phytosanitary measure such as a law, decree or ordinance[342], which is (3) "applicable generally".[343]

8.110. The fact that the varietal testing requirement challenged by the United States "[has] been adopted" and is "applicable generally" is not in dispute. We only need to examine whether this requirement is a "phytosanitary regulation" in the sense of paragraph 1 of Annex B.

8.111. Even though the varietal testing requirement is not mandatory - in that exporting countries can demonstrate quarantine efficiency by other means - in our view, it does constitute a "phytosanitary regulation" subject to the publication requirement in Annex B. The footnote to paragraph 1 of Annex B refers in general

---

[340] See paragraph 1 of Annex B of the SPS Agreement.
[341] See paragraph 1 of Annex B of the SPS Agreement.
[342] See footnote to paragraph 1 of Annex B.
[343] *Ibid.*

terms to "phytosanitary measures such as laws, decrees or ordinances".[344] Nowhere does the wording of this paragraph require such measures to be mandatory or legally enforceable. Moreover, Paragraph 1 of Annex A to the SPS Agreement makes clear that "phytosanitary measures include all relevant laws, decrees, regulations, requirements and procedures". It does not, in turn, require that such measures be mandatory or legally enforceable. The interpretation that measures need not be mandatory to be subject to WTO disciplines is confirmed by the context of the relevant SPS provisions, a context which includes provisions of other WTO agreements and the way these provisions define "measure", "requirement" or "restriction"[345], as interpreted in GATT and WTO jurisprudence.[346] This context indicates that a non-mandatory government measure is also subject to WTO provisions in the event compliance with this measure is necessary to obtain an advantage from the government or, in other words, if sufficient incentives or disincentives exist for that measure to be abided by.

8.112. We consider that in this case the varietal testing requirement, as set out in the "Experimental Guide for Cultivar Comparison Test on Insect Mortality - Fumigation" (hereafter referred to as "the guidelines"), does provide sufficient incentives for it to take effect. Indeed, if an exporting country abides by the guidelines, its request for entry of a certain variety of a product will be granted. If an exporting country accepts

---

[344] In accordance with Article 3.2 of the DSU and established WTO jurisprudence, we shall interpret these terms in paragraph 1 of Annex A in accordance with the interpretative rules of the 1969 Vienna Convention on the Law of Treaties ("Vienna Convention"), in particular Article 31 thereof which provides in relevant part as follows: "1. A treaty shall be interpreted in good faith in accordance with the ordinary meaning to be given to the terms of the treaty in their context and in light of its object and purpose".

[345] For example, the Illustrative List of Trade-Related Investment Measures ("TRIMs") contained in the Annex to the Agreement on TRIMs indicates that TRIMs inconsistent with Articles III:4 and XI:1 of the GATT include those which are "mandatory or enforceable under domestic law or under administrative rulings, *or compliance with which is necessary to obtain an advantage*" (emphasis added).

[346] Recently, for example, the panel on *Japan - Measures Affecting Consumer Photographic Film and Paper* (adopted on 22 April 1998, WT/DS44/R), addressing a claim of non-violation nullification and impairment under Article XXIII:1(b) of the GATT, stated the following (at paragraph 10.49):

> "a government policy or action need not necessarily have a substantially binding or compulsory nature for it to entail a likelihood of compliance by private actors in a way so as to nullify or impair legitimately expected benefits within the purview of Article XXIII:1(b). Indeed, it is clear that non-binding actions, which include sufficient incentives or disincentives for private parties to act in a particular manner, can potentially have adverse effects on competitive conditions of market access".

See also the panel report on *Japan - Trade in Semi-Conductors* (adopted on 4 May 1988, BISD 35 S/116), where the panel found (at paragraph 109) that although measures are not mandatory, they could be considered as "restrictions" subject to Article XI:1 of the GATT in the event "sufficient incentives or disincentives existed for non-mandatory measures to take effect". Similarly, the panel on *EEC - Regulation on Imports of Parts and Components* (adopted on 16 May 1990, BISD 37S/132) considered (at paragraph 5.21) that the term "laws, regulations or requirements" contained in Article III:4 of the GATT included requirements "which an enterprise voluntarily accepts in order to obtain an advantage from the government".

the varietal testing requirement and follows the guidelines, it will do so in order to obtain an advantage from the government. We thus consider that the varietal testing requirement is a phytosanitary regulation in the sense of paragraph 1 of Annex B.

8.113. We note, moreover, that even though Japan submits that the guidelines are only a test model and that exporting governments may choose to demonstrate efficacy of treatment by other means, Japan asserts that so far no exporting government ever proposed such other means[347] and that Japan, accordingly, never accepted any alternative means.

8.114. We thus find that the varietal testing requirement meets all three conditions for a measure to be subject to the publication requirement in paragraph 1 of Annex B. The requirement thus needs to be "published promptly in such a manner as to enable interested Members to become acquainted with them".

8.115. Japan acknowledges that it has not published the varietal testing requirement. The fact that Japan distributed the guidelines to foreign plant quarantine authorities does not mitigate the lack of publication. In our view, distribution to a limited number of addressees and MAFF's general availability to answer any queries, does not equal prompt publication which enables interested Members to become acquainted with the varietal testing requirement. The publication by MAFF of the protocols relating to approved products does not ensure publication of the varietal testing requirement itself. It only informs Members of products which have met this requirement. Moreover, we do not consider that the highly technical nature of the varietal testing requirement can excuse Japan from publishing it.

3.   The Panel's Conclusion under Article 7

8.116. On these grounds[348] we conclude that Japan, by not having published the varietal testing requirement, acts inconsistently with its obligations under paragraph 1 of Annex B of the SPS Agreement and, for that reason, with its obligations contained in Article 7 of that Agreement. Since Japan has not published the measure at issue with respect to any of the products falling within our mandate, our finding applies to all of these products.

I.   Obligations with Respect to Control, Inspection and Approval Procedures (Article 8 and Annex C of the SPS Agreement)

8.117. Given that we have found earlier that the varietal testing requirement is inconsistent with the requirements of Articles 2.2[349], 5.6[350] and 7[351] of the SPS

---

[347] The United States, however, asserts that it did propose alternatives, including 100 per cent inspection of certain apples and inspection for certification of cherries (in both instances without fumigation) and the use of a systems approach for nectarines, but that Japan rejected these alternatives.

[348] See paragraphs 8.108 - 8.115.

[349] See paragraph 8.61.

[350] See paragraph 8.104.

[351] See paragraph 8.116.

Agreement, we see no need to further examine whether it is also inconsistent with Article 8, referring to Annex C, of that Agreement.

J.   Concluding Remark

8.118. In footnote 320, we noted that the parties to this dispute referred to the fact that the substance methyl bromide - used in the quarantine treatments at issue here - needs to be phased-out in accordance with the Montreal Protocol on Substances that Deplete the Ozone Layer ("Montreal Protocol"). However, the parties to this dispute also noted that Article 2H:6 of the Montreal Protocol exempts the use of Methyl Bromide for quarantine and preshipment application from this phasing-out schedule.

8.119. Without embarking on an examination of the Montreal Protocol, we do want to stress that nothing in this report should be read in a way which would affect the rights and obligations of WTO Members party to the Montreal Protocol.

IX.   CONCLUSIONS

9.1.   In light of the findings above, we reach the conclusion that Japan

(i)   by maintaining the varietal testing requirement in dispute with respect to apples, cherries, nectarines and walnuts, acts inconsistently with its obligation under Article 2.2 of the SPS Agreement not to maintain phytosanitary measures "without sufficient scientific evidence, except as provided for in paragraph 7 of Article 5"; and

(ii)   by maintaining the varietal testing requirement in dispute with respect to apples, cherries, nectarines and walnuts, acts inconsistently with its obligation in Article 5.6 of the SPS Agreement to "ensure that [its phytosanitary] measures are not more trade-restrictive than required to achieve [Japan's] appropriate level of ... phytosanitary protection, taking into account technical and economic feasibility"; and

(iii)   by not having published the varietal testing requirement in dispute with respect to any of the products at issue, acts inconsistently with its obligations under paragraph 1 of Annex B of the SPS Agreement and, for that reason, with its obligations contained in Article 7 of that Agreement.

9.2.   Since Article 3.8 of the DSU provides that "[i]n cases where there is an infringement of the obligations assumed under a covered agreement [including the SPS Agreement], the action is considered *prima facie* to constitute a case of nullification or impairment", we conclude that to the extent Japan has acted inconsistently with the SPS Agreement it has nullified or impaired the benefits accruing to the United States under the SPS Agreement.

9.3.   We *recommend* that the Dispute Settlement Body request Japan to bring its measure in dispute into conformity with its obligations under the SPS Agreement.

X. ANNEX A - TRANSCRIPT OF THE JOINT MEETING WITH EXPERTS

Chairman

10.1. [*introductory statement by the Chairman*] ... with that introduction I would first invite all the participants to introduce themselves and then I would suggest that we start with the opening comments of the experts. Dr. Ducom, Dr. Heather and Mr. Taylor in that order. May I first ask that the experts present themselves?

Dr. Ducom

10.2. Mr. Chairman, thank you. First of all I am French and my mother-tongue is French, is not English, that's why my brief statement will be short. Officially I belong to the French Ministry of Agriculture, but in this session I am not mandated by my Ministry. I am just a private expert here. Some highlights - First of all, pardon? [*Chairman interrupts*]

Chairman

10.3. Thank you. If there is need for translation we have here bilingual persons which can assist you if necessary.

Dr. Ducom

10.4. My problem is that I can understand but to express myself is much more difficult.

Chairman

10.5. And of course you are very correct, all the experts are in their personal capacity and do not represent an institution or country. Ok, Dr. Heather?

Dr. Heather

10.6. I am Neil Heather. I come from Brisbane, Australia where prior to ceasing duty with the Queensland State Department of Primary Industries, I was research leader of what we call the Market Access Quarantine Group, responsible for developing fruit-fly treatments for access to export markets from Australia, i.e., quarantine disinfestation treatments. I am currently affiliated with the University of Queensland at Gatton College where I am termed an Honorary Research Consultant so I have no organizational responsibilities of any kind.

Chairman

10.7. Thank you. And Mr. Taylor?

Mr. Taylor

10.8. Thank you Mr. Chairman. Good morning Ladies and Gentlemen. I am very happy to be here and pleased to have been invited to this Panel and to visit Geneva again. I am employed at the Natural Resources Institute in the United Kingdom which until 1996 was a government agency but since that time we've been sold off and we are now part of the University of Greenwich. Much of our work continues in the same manner and we are largely funded by the UK government although I am *here* representing myself, as I do, on the methyl bromide technical options committee. So I stand as an individual. I spend most of my time working overseas in developing countries on pest control activities, particularly with fumigation. Thank you.

Chairman

10.9.   Thank you Mr. Taylor. I now turn to the United States delegation.

Mr. Brinza

10.10. Thank you Mr. Chairman. My name is Dan Brinza from the United States. I will ask other members of the US delegation to take the mike very briefly to introduce themselves, starting with the head of delegation.

United States (Mr. Hirsh)

10.11. Good morning Mr. Chairman. My name is Bruce Hirsh and I am an Assistant General Counsel with the Office of the United States Trade Representative.

Mr. Bonner

10.12. Good morning. Peter Bonner, US Department of Agriculture.

Mr. Vick

10.13. My name is Ken Vick, United States Department of Agriculture.

Mr. Thaw

10.14. I'm John Thaw with Plant Protection and Quarantine, Department of Agriculture.

Mr. Leesch

10.15. I'm Jim Leesch. I'm with the US Department of Agriculture, Agricultural Research Service.

Mr. Fedchock

10.16. Craig Fedchock with US Department of Agriculture, APHIS.

Ms. Roberts

10.17. I'm Donna Roberts with the US Department of Agriculture here at the Mission in Geneva.

Ms. Erickson

10.18. Audrae Erickson, US Trade Representatives Office, Washington DC.

Chairman

10.19. Thank you. I now return to the Japanese delegation please.

Mr. Yokota

10.20. Thank you Mr. Chairman. My name is Jun Yokota. I'm the Deputy Director-General of the Economic Affairs Bureau, the Ministry of Foreign Affairs. I would like to turn to my colleagues to present themselves.

Mr. Kato

10.21. My name is Takashi Kato. I'm from the Ministry of Agriculture, Forestry and Fisheries and Deputy Director-General in the Agricultural Production Bureau. Thank you.

Mr. Nakakita

10.22. My name is Hiroshi Nakakita from National Food Research Institute, studying about how to control stored product insect.

Mr. Kawakami

10.23. My name is Fusao Kawakami. I work in the Research Division of Yokohama Plant Quarantine Station. For many years I engage in the development of the disinfestation methods for quarantine so I [was involved in] research data submitted from foreign countries.

Mr. Sato

10.24. My name is Kimihiko Sato, Tokyo University of Agriculture and Technology.

Mr. Sakai

10.25. My name is Masaki Sakai, Agriculture Counsellor, Embassy of Japan, Washington DC.

Mr. Saito

10.26. My name is Noboru Saito. I am working for Plant Production Division, Ministry of Agriculture, Forestry and Fisheries. Thank you.

Mr. Sanatani

10.27. My name is Sanatani. I am from Ministry of Agriculture in Tokyo.

Ms. Hirota

10.28. My name is Mitue Hirota. I come from the Ministry of Foreign Affairs.

Mr. Yokoi

10.29. My name is Yukio Yokoi, Plant Protection Division, Ministry of Agriculture, Forestry and Fisheries.

Mr. Shiragaki

10.30. My name is Tatsunori Shiragaki from the Ministry of Agriculture.

Mr. Motai

10.31. My name is Futao Motai from the Ministry of Foreign Affairs, Japan.

Mr. Yamashita

10.32. My name is Masayuki Yamashita. I'm with the Japanese Mission here in Geneva.

Mr. Nirei

10.33. I am Hideo Nirei from the Authority Bureau of Ministry of Foreign Affairs.

Mr. Chujo

10.34. Kazuo Chujo, Ministry of Foreign Affairs.

Mr. Ito

10.35. My name is Koichi Ito, Japanese Mission in Geneva. Thank you.

Chairman

10.36. Thank you for these introductions. I think that we now can start our discussion according to the procedures I proposed, and that means that I will start by giving the floor one by one to our experts for any general introductory remarks they believe are appropriate.

10.37. So first, in alphabetical order, Dr. Ducom, you have the floor.

Dr. Ducom

10.38. Thank you Mr. Chairman. I have just five remarks on the question and my answers, mainly on the questions.

10.39. First of all, the questions of the Panel are relevant but often there is no clear response to give because we miss data on the exact subject on variety by variety testing. Second point, it seems that both sides want to keep their habits; the arguments can be seen as black or white and each party has found, for example in their answers to the questions, arguments against each other in the same paper. The third point is that the scientific facts given by Japan are maybe too narrow. I mean, for example, when they give some differences between varieties the confidence limit is not a biological fact, it is a statistical fact. I mean, biologically speaking, the difference does not matter ... just one per cent makes, statistically speaking, there is a significant difference while biologically speaking there is no difference. We have examples of that. The fourth point. For the USA position one variety for all is maybe uncomfortable because biology or physiology is sometimes surprising. That may be the problem. And the last point is that maybe that the concept of CxT product is not used enough in this dispute, or in this matter.

Chairman

10.40. Thank you Dr. Ducom. Then I turn to Dr. Heather.

Dr. Heather

10.41. Thank you. As with Dr. Ducom I have had some difficulty through not seeing all of the working data but had I seen it, there would not have been sufficient time to perhaps look at it in the detail that's required. Just to perhaps go through your original questions, if I may. The concepts: I think in my view, the most important part here is the interpretation put on the LD values, the LD_{50} value for example. This is not a precise numerical measure and of necessity it has had to be used in a rather less precise way than it would otherwise be. It is not a direct measurement on the insect, it is a measurement on the insect where it is influenced by the fruit in the chambers so it is not a precise measurement. In fact, if you look at an LD value it's easy to take one figure but realistically you should be looking at what we call the confidence limits or the fiducial limits and these are ranges within which that value falls and perhaps would lead to a better understanding if we thought of it in that way. As you recall, because the quarantine treatments are not measured at the median dose or the LD_{50} dose but at the extreme dose, these limits become very wide and it is not wise to take arithmetic cognizance. You must take into account the truest statistical interpretation of these figures. Sorry I have talked too much on that but I think it is a very important thing; that precision is easily misplaced.

10.42. The confirmatory tests, I have every confidence in and I think that's fairly well accepted throughout [by all parties]. There's been some consideration about the higher susceptibility of (a question asked by Japan) on the higher susceptibility of a commodity for a range of reasons which are outside of the direct interaction between the fruit and the treatment. But here we can have such instances as a late variety of fruit compared to an early variety of fruit; there will be many more insects in the place of origin of the late maturing variety than there were in the beginning. This is the type of background that I wish that comment to be interpreted against.

10.43. The sorption I would like to leave to my colleagues who are rather more wise in the theory of the behaviour of gases and fumigants than I, although I have used them to an extent where I've some understanding of them. The statistical analysis, or the CxT product value, by the way, is a much more precise measure than a LD value, much more precise, because it is a physical measurement rather than a biological one. There's been some misunderstanding perhaps about Tukey's multiple range test. It is simply a less sensitive type of analysis which means that it should be more reliable, but could I say that for statistically demonstrated differences, these must always be viewed against the background of the biological conditions which give rise to them. What is biologically unlikely, but statistically shown, must be viewed with some reserve. Biological creditability is just as important as statistical demonstration of differences. I think that they were the main points that would arise. Could I ask Mr. Chairman do you wish us to address the additional questions? Thank you.

Chairman

10.44. Yes, as you know the Panel has distributed yesterday evening some additional questions. My intention is to raise them after we have discussed the questions raised by the United States and the Japan, and of course I will raise only those of them which have not already been covered by the questions of United States or Japan. So the order will be the questions by the United States, the questions by Japan, the questions by Panel. Ok. Then Mr. Taylor?

Mr. Taylor

10.45. Thank you Mr. Chairman. I don't have too much to say at this particular time. I think one of the things that we must accept is that temperature is very, very important in fumigation and also particularly in the case of methyl bromide sorption is of overwhelming interest and knowledge of what is happening is terribly important.

10.46. If I might just digress very, very briefly - there is another fumigant, phosphine, which is used for durable commodities. There is little or no sorption of phosphine and, therefore, the dosage rates really don't vary much at all for different commodities. It may be rather an over simplification but it could be said that, compared do methyl bromide, there is just one dosage rate for phosphine. Coming back of course to the subject matter of methyl bromide, we do have an overwhelming difference in as much as there is a lot of sorption by commodities, and in fact, in durable commodities which I have to refer to because they are my main area of experience, certainly in the original schedules drawn up for commodity fumigation a commodity dosage was specified. So in fact great importance was taken of the particular commodity in deciding what the application rate should be because there was such a large difference between commodities that you had to define the commodity and then decide what the dose should be based on that commodity, let alone on what insect you were controlling. So in brief, the fact that there may be a high fat or oil content in which the methyl bromide would dissolve meant that a lot of the gas was lost, so certainly the sorption factor is very important and so important that this created differences in terms of dosage rates used. Now whether or not these differences exist in fruit is something which I am certainly not confident to comment on, but the differences certainly, if they were there, would be sufficient to cause different dosage rates to be required and therefore testing programmes to be necessary. But if the differences between varieties are so small that there is little or no sorption, then it seems to me that varietal testing is perhaps not something which needs to be taken into consideration, particularly if tests have shown, for example, that the chemical composition of the fruit varieties do not vary very much. Because again, going back to what I said about the durable commodities, certainly the differences there are very significant and are so significant that dosage rates are specified for different commodities but not of course for different varieties, for example, of wheat.

10.47. One other point, I would just like to reiterate what Dr. Heather said. LD_{50} values are very useful if you are comparing insects, for example, for levels of resistance. But I don't think in this case we're looking to define dosage rates even for - shall we say, non-quarantine treatments, we would want to use LD_{50} - we'd want to use higher levels of control such as, well, certainly the LD_{99} or $LD_{99.9}$. And therefore the LD_{50} I don't think is at all relevant in this situation.

10.48. So I would just say then that sorption seems to me to be something that we need to know more about. If it can be shown that the levels of sorption are such that they are significant enough to remove the fumigant to an extent that it is going to raise some doubt as to the efficacy of the treatment, then of course we could say that varietal testing was necessary. But unless we can show that it seems to me that the need to test by variety does still need to be established. Thank you Mr. Chairman.

Chairman

10.49. Thank you Mr. Taylor. I now turn to the United States delegation and you have the floor.

United States (Mr. Hirsh)

10.50. Thank you very much Mr. Chairman. First of all, on behalf of the US delegation I would like to thank the experts for agreeing to serve and for their very helpful comments today and their responses. We very much appreciate your taking the time to be with us today. With your permission, Mr. Chairman, I would like to take about five minutes just to consult with the delegation to consider in light of the initial comments by the experts whether we want to ask certain questions, if that's permissible?

[break]

United States (Mr. Hirsh)

10.51. Thank you Mr. Chairman. We just have a few brief questions. All of the questions - for all the questions, any of the experts are welcome to respond. We've noted in some instances that one or more of the experts have focused on the particular question we directed initially to them.

10.52. The first question we have is a request for clarification from Mr. Taylor on his introductory comments. With respect to the differences in sorption that you have noted for durable commodities we want to just clarify that those differences have been observed on a commodity by commodity basis.

Mr. Taylor

10.53. Yes, certainly, on a commodity by commodity basis, yes, the differences are there although some commodities are so similar that certainly for practical purposes commodities are often grouped together. As I say, for practical purposes certain cereals may be grouped together and then other different types of commodities - so that there may be five or six different groups, yes.

United States (Mr. Hirsh)

10.54. But the observed differences have not been on a variety basis but on a commodity basis?

Mr. Taylor

10.55. You're exactly right, yes. And in fact, I've never even heard anybody raise the subject of varieties of rice or wheat or maize requiring to be examined in as much as there might be some differences. So, no, it is merely on a commodity by commodity basis.

United States (Mr. Hirsh)

10.56. Thank you. Also, one or two enquires with regard to the differences in sorption that you have noticed between commodities, durable commodities. Have the magnitude of those differences been obvious?

Mr. Taylor

10.57. Oh yes, yes certainly. The work that was done probably many, many years ago, perhaps even I think before I became involved in this topic, I think maybe even in the 1950s, a lot of work was done and certainly the differences were very obvious to the extent that fumigations carried out at a particular dosage would certainly not control insects to the level required if those same dosage rates were used on perhaps the next group of commodities where the level of sorption was considerably higher. So, yes I think this has been well documented and, as I say, there's a lot of evidence in the literature going back to the 1950s and '60s to substantiate this.

United States (Mr. Hirsh)

10.58. Thank you. The next question we'd like to direct initially at Dr. Heather. Because of the presence of other uncontrollable sources of variation in small scale tests, we don't think that it's possible to conclude that the differences in CxT values referred to by Japan are attributable or can be attributed to varietal differences affecting efficacy of treatment. However, regardless of the source of these variations, were the variations in CxT large enough to affect the efficacy of the fumigation treatments for the commodities that have been raised in this proceeding?

Dr. Heather

10.59. I find it difficult to give a precise, clear answer on that. The problem, ... I think I just better leave it at that please.

United States (Mr. Hirsh)

10.60. The next question we note is similar to one that the Panel will shortly be asking but we would like to come at the issue from a slightly different perspective. And that is with regard to the Panel's additional Question 3, Japan refers to various sources of fruit variation including temperature, moisture, daylight, rainfall, cultivation conditions and other natural conditions of the harvest year and Japan states that these sources of variation, quote, are not widely known to result in significant differences in efficacy of treatment, and this question is for Dr. Ducom initially. Are varietal differences, quote, widely known to result in differences in efficacy of treatment?

Dr. Ducom

Could you repeat please?

United States (Mr. Hirsh)

10.61. We note that Japan has referred to a number of sources of fruit variation which include temperature, moisture, daylight, rainfall, cultivation conditions and other natural conditions of the harvest year, and Japan states that it has not considered these sources of variation because, quote, they are not widely known to result in significant differences in efficacy of treatment. And my question is are varietal differences widely known to result in significant differences in efficacy of treatment?

Dr. Ducom

10.62. It's the same. My opinion is that differences are of the same [nature], maybe, of the same amount [importance]. I mean, I do not understand what Japan says. I mean why temperature, moisture and so on? Since they are not known they are counted for nothing. That I cannot understand. The same thing for variety. If we use the same argument varieties [aren't more significant than other variables] are just nothing because [we have little data for varieties] we don't know the answer for varieties. Or, if we take into account variety we should take into account daylight, moisture, rainfall and so on.

United States (Mr. Hirsh)

10.63. Thank you. I would like to first ask whether any of the experts have had a chance to review the study on apples which Japan recently submitted in Exhibit 36. This only came in last Friday so I'm not sure whether you have had a chance, but before asking my question I want to find out whether any of you have had an opportunity to review that study?

Dr. Ducom

10.64. Which one?

Chairman

10.65. Could you repeat the number of the exhibit?

United States (Mr. Hirsh)

10.66. Sure. It's Exhibit 36. It was submitted, I believe, last Friday together with Japan's comments on Mr. Taylor's responses.

Chairman

10.67. So may I ask the experts, have you received the parties' comments to Mr. Taylor's responses? Ok, they have them, yes.

United States (Mr. Hirsh)

10.68. In that study, with respect to apples, the author states on the final page of the study that the factors affecting different CxT products were not specified in the test. For example, it appears that there were no controls for length of time and storage, maturity of the fruit and fruit size. In addition, we reviewed the CxT product data in Table 3 and in Table 5. In particular, the data for the Mutsu and the Fuji in each table and that data appears to indicate that the two are not statistically different in Table 5, but they are statistically different in Table 3. In light of the uncontrolled factors in this experiment and the inconsistent data, is Japan's conclusion warranted that the differences in CxT values noted in Table 5, quote, were obviously attributed to varietal differences?

Chairman

10.69. Ok, I want to give some explanation now. The experts received that document when they arrived in Geneva and they also had other documents which they received yesterday so I think they have not been able to study these documents in detail. So could we agree that we give some time to the experts so that they could answer your question later?

United States (Mr. Hirsh)

10.70. Certainly. Thank you very much.

Chairman

10.71. Ok, so we postpone answer to this question to a later stage, ok.

United States (Mr. Hirsh)

10.72. Those are the only questions which we have right now, Mr. Chairman. We do reserve the right later following Japan's questions to follow up further.

Chairman

10.73. Ok, thank you. Does Japan have any follow-up questions to those questions United States raised?

Japan (Mr. Yokota)

10.74. Mr. Chairman, may we confer within ourselves for a few minutes?

Chairman

10.75. Ok.

[break]

Japan

10.76. Mr. Chairman?

Chairman

10.77. Japan you have the floor.

Japan

10.78. Yes, we have one immediate follow-up question.

Chairman

10.79. Ok.

Japan (Mr. Saito)

10.80. I'd like to have one question but in Japanese so I ask to interpret my question.

Japan (Mr. Saito - interpreted)

10.81. I have a question to Mr. Taylor. Within the response to the US question ... [can you hear, can you hear? Can you hear Ok? Let me start again...] I have a question to Mr. Taylor. In the first question from the United States, Mr. Taylor responded saying that the sorption difference among the cereals are commodity wise and varietal differences insignificant. But we would like to ask what is Mr. Taylor's view with regard to the fruits which are the issue here in this Panel?

Mr. Taylor

10.82. Thank you for the question. I am not a specialist in the fumigation of perishables, I regret to say. Therefore I find it very difficult to respond in any firm way to give you a definite reply to this. All I could say is that the differences I would think would have to be very significant in order to make it necessary to, for example, adjust dosage rates and/or time periods for the fumigation. If these differences were so significant that the amount of methyl bromide available for the fumigation process was significantly reduced by different varieties, then, in theory, this would be a significant factor, but I think this has still to be demonstrated. Now you could say well why are there no differences between different varieties of cereals? Again, the answer to that I cannot give you. In fact, I think that in practicable fumigation the application rates always have such a margin [excess over and above the minimum dosage] that any small differences would be accounted for by this margin, or excess that is used. I would imagine that where the United States uses a 10-20% buffer, as I think is the term used, this again would account for it [any small differences]. So in practical terms, as I say, I think we would need to find that there is a significant difference between the varieties and that this needs to be demonstrated. I feel that I cannot say any more on this subject from my own personal point of view. Thank you.

Chairman

10.83. I'd like to ask do the other experts like to add something to this? I don't see. Ok. Then I give the floor to Japan to present your, so to say, own questions.

Japan (Mr. Yokota)

10.84. Thank you Mr. Chairman. May I first of all, and on behalf of the Government of Japan, specially thank Dr. Ducom, Dr. Heather and Mr. Taylor for agreeing to serve as experts on this Panel and to give us their very valuable opinions on this matter. We have prepared a series of questions and I would like to ask Dr. Kawakami to present them.

Japan (Mr. Kawakami - interpreted)

10.85. I would like to speak regarding those questions raised by the Panel and I consider there are five points of importance so I would like to raise them one by one. First of all we should like to express our heartfelt appreciation to the Panel for giving us the opportunity to present our views on the pending issues of today. Also we should like to give our highest respect to the three respectable experts, Dr. Heather, Dr. Ducom and Mr. Taylor for rendering valuable comments from the technical point of view on the methyl bromide situation of perishable products which we think is a highly complicated aspect of treatment technology and in which much more research and investigation are needed for the situation of the issue in question. The Panel sought for expert comments from technical point of view on as many as 18 questions. Of all these questions we consider that the following five issues of argument are particularly important.

10.86. First issue: Whether or not to be the use of dose response ... [*interruption*]

Chairman

10.87. Excuse me, excuse me Japan's delegation that I interrupt. But I think that this submission is better suited for tomorrow, because today we are expected to use the expertise of the experts that are present. Your presentation is welcomed, most welcomed to the Panel but I think it is more appropriate to present it tomorrow when we meet between the parties and the Panel, and today we should devote our time and effort to use the expertise of the experts to the greatest extent. So if you could agree with that, I would like to ask you to postpone this presentation for tomorrow. Thank you. But if you have specific questions to the experts you are welcome of course.

Japan (Mr. Sanatani)

10.88. Ok. Thank you Mr. Chairman. We have prepared five questions to put to the experts. Maybe we can deliver the written questions to the members in this room? The first question is to Dr. Heather and Mr. Taylor. I will read. Dr. Heather states in response to Question 12, quote: if only one variety has been presented in the initial testing the possibility that other varieties which might be proposed subsequently could have higher predicted minimum dose requirements would be greater. Even so, the likelihood of this exceeding 10-20% buffer appears low, end of quote. Similarly, Mr. Taylor states, quote: any varietal differences affecting the efficacy of MB treatment are unlikely to be so great that the buffer of 10-20% fails to account for these differences. Effective quarantine treatment is therefore to be expected, end of quote. Japan wishes to know the grounds for these assumptions that possible varietal differences in most cases could be covered by the buffer 10-20% surrounding the buffer. So, shall I stop here or continue to finish it?

Chairman

10.89. I think it's better to take the questions one by one. So, Mr. Taylor and other experts who..?

Dr. Heather

10.90. Perhaps if I could give the first response on this, please. The grounds for my conclusion were that each of the varieties which had been tested in each of the commodities always met the large confirmatory dose test. There was never any suggestion of failure. Therefore, had the dose been pitched too low in the first place, this would have shown up as survivors from the large scale test. The basis of this problem is partly that we are judging differences at points where they are quite discrete but the effectiveness of the treatment becomes apparent at very, very high efficacies when there are very, very few survivors and this has the effect of bringing together the differences so that they are no longer apparent.

Chairman

10.91. Mr. Taylor, do you want to respond also? Ok. May I ask Japan to proceed to the next question?

Japan (Mr. Sanatani)

10.92. Thank you Mr. Chairman. The second question is posed to all the experts. I read, Dr. Heather states in response to Question 13: The broader applicability of a confirmatory test done on samples of one variety over commodity depends on the extent of variation of mortality attributable to varietal characteristics and a large scale test provides assurance for the extension of an existing successful treatment to additional varieties of a commodity, provided that the initial varietal sample is representative of the commodity. In response to Question 16, Dr. Ducom states: Extrapolation to all available varieties is no more scientific than the Japanese's contrary assertion. They seem to concur that there is no valid scientific ground to conclude that a treatment established for a particular variety by confirmatory tests would be efficacious for any additional variety. Is this correct?

Dr. Ducom

10.93. Yes that is correct. I mean I cannot see any more scientific basis on the Japanese side than on the USA's side to say [that each] variety must be carefully treated ... or for one we can have all varieties. I hope you understand. In my opinion it is not scientific to say that one variety is equal to all others, ... but [choosing one variety as representative of all is the same sort of argument for me] to say maybe one variety, it's the same for me. Ok.

Chairman

10.94. Thank you. Other experts, do you want to add?

Dr. Heather

10.95. Just responding to the first part of the question. The broader applicability of the context of that statement was to start with the basic facts and say yes, technically, if you develop a treatment on one and seek to apply to others. And then I went on to say that there were no real grounds to be concerned, I think you'll find.

Chairman

10.96. Thank you. Could you now proceed to your third question Japan?

Japan (Mr. Sanatani)

10.97. Mr. Chairman. Before we proceed, can we take some time to reflect on the answers ...?

Chairman

10.98. Of course.

Japan (Mr. Sanatani)

10.99. Mr. Chairman, if you permit us to go back to the question number one, we have some comments to put on our answers to number 1.

Chairman

10.100. I think the place of the comments are tomorrow, but if you have follow-up questions, if your follow-up questions, if you want to seek further clarification from the experts, you are welcome.

Japan (Mr. Saito)

10.101. OK. Thank you Mr. Chairman. So let us go back to question number one and this time in Japanese.

Japan

10.102. (*Interpreted*) Concerning the question one in the replies from experts Dr. Heather stated as follows... we asked in our question whether this buffer of 10-20% could cover all these differences in the varieties, among the varieties, are based on scientific grounds and if this buffer has the scientific grounds and in response to our question we, as far as we can understand, after the various confirmatory test, the efficacy did not show a significant difference and that this is the data of empirical of nature. What we are questioning here is that in all cases whether the buffer 10-20% could absorb all this varietal difference and if that buffer would have the scientific grounds in this manner. And if possible I would like to invite the comments from, or replies from all the experts. Thank you.

Chairman

10.103. OK. I give the floor to the experts.

Dr. Heather

10.104. I am a little anxious if I understood the question clearly enough, but as far as I understand, Japan is questioning where the 10 per cent or 20 per cent buffer came from. It is difficult to project with certainty, by regression analysis, the [dose required for] efficiency and effectiveness of a certain fumigant. By analyzing the data, examining a certain range of doses of the fumigant (if the fumigant has 100 per cent effectiveness, or effectiveness of killing insects), by adding to the fumigant some amount, which one actually does in practice, in the actual research, we have examined all varieties under a series of trials. Then we obtain the data from there. A normal procedure then is to confirm the data by a larger-scale confirmation test. However, one can attain this objective by somewhat different means; one is by taking a "single replicate", which Japan is demanding currently. Another would be by setting "confirmatory loss" to as low a level as possible, based on research among them. If there are surviving insects, we conduct such trials repeatedly. We call this the "repeated iterative approach". In other words, it is the idea to seek for, to the extent possible, the lowest value to attain confirmation of effect on a certain target. I think, therefore, that this can be regarded as a somewhat different approach. Both, I think, are means to meet the very difficult problems we have to solve. To be practical does not mean it is unscientific.

Chairman

10.105. I would like to give the floor to Dr. Ducom.

Dr. Ducom

10.106. I would like to add a question: why is the buffer 10 or 20 per cent? This may be accidental and so why not 5 per cent? It is difficult to say these are enough for the variety, because we cannot recognize them as a *fait accompli* [what is needed]. It implies to hypothesize, to some extent, how much the sorption level is for each variety.

Chairman

10.107. OK. Thank you. Japan.

Japan

10.108. [Microphone not on. Probably Japan asking Dr. Taylor to respond as well]

Mr. Taylor

10.109. I agree with the opinion of the two experts, in particular, with Dr. Ducom's. In other words, we have no data on sorption. There are no data indicating the difference of sorption between varieties. So, the 10 to 20 per cent buffer was set arbitrarily (at random); it was not based on scientific examination. However, such numerical difference [is the one which could absorb the difference enough]. A 20 per cent [buffer] would be a substantial increase in volume. I cannot add anything more, but I agree with the opinions so far expressed by my colleagues, the two specialists. We have no data as to what constitutes the rate of sorption of each variety. If we do, we could possibly decide whether this 10 or 20 per cent is too high or too low, and a 5 per cent buffer may well be enough. But we can present no scientific evidence other than that.

Chairman

10.110. Thank you Mr. Taylor. Japan?

Japan

10.111. Thank you, Mr. Chairman. Since we have finished questions number one and two, we would like to move on to question number three, which is a question for Dr. Heather and Mr. Taylor.

Japan (Mr. Sanatani)

10.112. ..... Dose-response testing is a tool commonly used for the purpose of comparing reactive resistance to a treatment such as between development stages of insects. Results of the tests are statistically analyzed using probit analysis, normally by way of comparison of LD50 values. This is supported by Exhibits 19 and 20 of the Japanese submission. There is no disagreement among on this point; in particular, Dr. Heather and Mr. Taylor explicitly acknowledges the effectiveness of dose-response testing and probit analysis. Japan solicits the experts' opinion as to possible application of dose-response data and probit analysis to a comparative inquiry into differential effects of fruit on mortality. Thank you.

Dr. Heather

10.113. It would be a very interesting study, but in such study, from my experience, variation will [originate from both the] fruits and their harmful insects, and it will depend, I think, on how such a treatment is indirectly given. Therefore, it would be difficult to obtain practically useful data from such a study.

Chairman

10.114. Mr. Taylor.

Mr. Taylor

10.115. I agree with the opinion of Dr. Heather. It would be very interesting to know how useful the data will be that comes out as a result. Of course, if Japan is really thinking of doing this, it would be useful. If Japan could make public the result, it will shed light on the issues for which the answer is unknown, or there is no data. Thank you.

Chairman

10.116. Japan.

Japan (Dr. Nakakita)

10.117. I am not good at English and would like to intervene in Japanese. Dr. Ducom, I believe you mentioned that LD_{50} cannot be used for these kind of purposes and as a basis of your saying that, the Journal of Economic Entomology submitted by the United States, the 1987, and which refers to six varieties of nectarines, they are indicating the comparative tests and ... codling moth eggs ... 6.3 grammes per cubic metres. This is the LD_{50} and this was the lowest value obtained among those six varieties. However, with regard to the efficacy at the higher concentration level Summer Grand, is the variety that indicated the highest resistance. So Dr. Ducom seems to be saying that the LD_{50} does not really have the validity, I believe that's what you said. But looking at this report this does indicate the difference between the varieties. And I believe that in this regard this is a report that should command lots of attention. So I believe that this report should attract attention in that regard. But in 1997, in the United States, another report published in the United States which refers to the Summer Grand's test results of 1987 and it came up with a newer data that replaces the old data of '87 and in this new report the value of LD_{50} was not that small. And LD_{95} also indicated the value that is not that much different from the LD_{95} of other varieties. So, the data obtained in the testing done in '87 with regards to the Summer Grand's resistance was in a way negated. And also, May Grand, the variety called the May Grand, the LD_{50} and the LD_{95} are listed next to each other and when you look at those in May Grand LD_{50} and also LD_{95} both indicate a higher resistance than that of Summer Grand but the 100% mortality values is lower by 25% than that of the Summer Grand, so I am somewhat dubious with regards to the reliability of this report. What is your observation on this report Dr. Ducom?

Dr. Ducom

10.118. It is very difficult to answer, to know what happened. For myself we have carried out a lot of trials like that and sometimes we have found black and sometimes white. I don't know why, although I should. I would appreciate it if I could know what happened. But, no, I have no answer. I don't know why. That's the only thing. It's when you do trials like this one with LD_{50} or Probit 9 analysis. Like Dr. Ito says, it depends, sometimes it works. When we say it works, it is logical with what we want to get, but if the results are not what we want, then we say it doesn't work. I don't know what the truth is. I have no more comment about that. I am sorry Kawakami-san.

Chairman

10.119. OK. Thank you.

Japan (Dr. Nakakita)

10.120. Thank you. I would like to ask Mr. Taylor, do you regard this as a scientifically reliable data?

Mr. Taylor

10.121. Could you just refresh my memory as to which, are we comparing the 1987 report with the more recent one? Is this what you are asking me to report on, or to give my opinion on? Please could you just, when you say you would like me to give opinion on to...

Mr. Nakakita

10.122. The report. 1997, sorry. That's the year the Americans submitted report. And '87 which was on general insect product research.

Mr. Taylor

10.123. Thank you Dr. Nakakita. I find it difficult to make any firm statement. I mean I have read these two papers but it's very difficult to know why there is this difference and to actually give with any affirmity which of the two is correct and why there is a difference. I mean Dr. Ducom has already stated that sometimes you get one set of results and sometimes you get another set of results when you may be expecting similar results. I'm sorry, I cannot with any confidence give you any other answer than to say that unless there are any differences that have not been accounted for in these two experimental programmes which we might have to re-examine to see whether there was anything about the two experiments which leads to that conclusion. I don't know whether Dr. Ducom would like to make any comment as whether he thinks there might have been some possible experimental difference which has not been taken into account?

Chairman

10.124. OK. I think you cannot extract more from our experts.

Japan (Mr. Nakakita)

10.125. Thank you very much Mr. Taylor and Dr. Ducom.

Chairman

10.126. OK. Can we move now to your fourth question?

Japan (Mr. Sanatani)

10.127. Thank you Mr. Chairman. I read: In the course of dose-response testing and tests on CxT values, fruit and insects are inserted into a small and highly airtight fumigation chamber. The material of this chamber shows a low level of sorption. Moreover, packages and other factors which might affect the result are consciously eliminated. Japan considers, in light of these experimental conditions, that, should there be any significant differences between test subjects, it is reasonably to estimate a link between fruit and the results. Japan wishes to ask experts about their thinking on this issue. And if it's possible we like to deliver pictures of the dose mortality tests and with your permission I would like to invite my colleagues to put some explanation on it.

Japan cont'd (Dr. Kawakami)

10.128. In these photographs these are the pictures of the dose-response tests. This is testing of the sorption. This is a very small scale gas tight chamber. The chamber itself doesn't really have any gas sorption and we place two different varieties and we examine the rate of sorption for those responses. And of course we have to look at the factors such as the packing materials' existence or chamber's air tightness but those factors are eliminated. Within this chamber only the fumigants and fruits and possibly the pests that are staying when the fruits are inside of the chamber. The Panel seems to share a view that the data is somewhat varied but we feel that the data obtained from this kind of an experiment is highly reliable so I believe this kind of a test does indicate the different responses or susceptibility of different varieties of fruits to a given measures. So if we could have your comments on this we would appreciate it.

Mr. Taylor

10.129. Could I please ask [the Japanese side if] this chamber is dosed with fumigant when it is completely empty. If this is repeated what level of variation would there be doing a test on the chamber before any fruit is put into it? In other words, what variation would they expect between tests prior to using the chamber actually for experimental work? So an empty chamber of this particular type, would they have any indication of what is a variation if, say, four or five tests were carried out on an empty chamber? What might be the variation it might expect using obviously exactly the same dosage technique and measuring technique?

Japan (Dr. Kawakami)

10.130. Of course before we carry out our test the emptiness and absorption characteristics of gas are studied, but in this regard there is no variation. As for in terms of percentage it would be in the magnitude of under one percent of variation and of course that is based on the empty chamber.

Chairman

10.131. Dr. Ducom?

Japan (Dr. Kawakami)

10.132. In addition these tests using these kind of facilities, are quite generally conducted worldwide. In the United States probably Dr. Ducom would use the same technique and in the United States and New Zealand I note instances where these facilities are used and these kind of tests are conducted and they are all of quite a similar nature.

Chairman

10.133. OK. Who wants to take the floor, Dr. Ducom or Mr. Taylor? Dr. Ducom.

Dr. Ducom

10.134. Yes, we do use something like that but my problem, my concern is the number of fruits used. For example, for stored product sorption trials we use, for example, 200 millilitre glass jars [tape change] ... that means about 100 grammes of wheat, which means 2,000 [cereal grain] kernels. If you take six apples, or something like that, variation must be very high. I mean, if we could use something like 1,000 or 2,000 apples each time it could be very more much precise and confidence limits could be very good. We do [it using the same small amount of apples as you because that is what you ask of us] like you because you ask just that, but I would prefer to know that each variety is tested using a lot of fruits to be able to smooth the differences.

Chairman

10.135. Mr. Taylor, do you want to add?

Dr. Heather

10.136. Perhaps I could just have a word. I would compliment the Japanese researchers on the quality of their laboratory equipment. Speaking from my own view point I had no doubt whatever about the results coming from such an experimental set up. Where I have reserved my judgment is on the application of those findings or to attribute those findings entirely to varietal differences. It has been my experience with a number of fruits that they vary greatly from year to year, from the locality where they are grown even though they are the same variety, and even in a batch of fruit there will be fruit to fruit variation. Now, I am not certain, I am not convinced that sufficient of the variation is unique to the variety to justify the conclusion that the data, the differences in the data, prove that the cause of this difference is varietal, predominantly varietal, it could never be totally. And this is the reservation I have.

Chairman

10.137. Ok, thank you. Can we now proceed to your next question Japan?

Japan (Mr. Sanatani)

10.138. Thank you Mr. Chairman. Now I move on to question number five. Dr. Heather clearly acknowledges that differential sorption levels due to varieties and other causes could affect efficacy of fumigation. While he refers the question of causes of sorption levels to other experts in fumigation chemistry, Dr. Ducom and Mr. Taylor acknowledge that sorption of methyl bromide takes place in oil contents, surface or protein and variation of these factors result in different sorption levels. Differences in variety often mean differential content levels, such as the oil content in in-shell walnuts. Japan believes from these statements of experts that they recognize possible varietal differences which affect sorption levels and hence efficacy of a treatment, and wishes to ask the experts to confirm this. Thank you Mr. Chairman.

Chairman

10.139. Mr. Taylor?

Mr. Taylor

10.140. Thank you Mr. Chairman. I don't think any of us would fail to agree that sorption and, as I mentioned earlier, temperature are the most important factors affecting the efficacy of fumigation assuming that we're not losing gas due to leakage. And certainly the mention of in-shell walnuts is very applicable. Differences in variety of course, where there is sufficient difference of sorption could well, therefore, affect the efficacy of the treatment. Surface area is again a particular property which, if it was sufficiently great, would affect the treatment. But the oil content, and of course anything else such as the protein which would remove a certain quantity of the gas from the free space, are all important factors that we agree on, and have been researched over many years. So I don't think any of us are in dispute that sorption would be a major factor affecting the efficacy of treatment, and if it can be demonstrated that sorption is of sufficient magnitude between different varieties, this would affect the efficacy of treatment, but I think that this has still to be shown and to be demonstrated. We go back to the obvious difference between durable commodities where some commodities virtually absorb no methyl bromide, rice, for example, compared to in-shell walnuts. I mean the dosage rates would be dramatically different and if we use the dosage rates that we recommend for rice, for high oil content commodity such as walnuts or any of these similar commodities, such as peanuts, then the efficacy of the treatment would not be in doubt, it would not be effective. So I just have to summarize what is your question and what it is that we confirm. I certainly would confirm that if the difference in sorption between varieties was of a sufficient magnitude, then there would be need to consider whether or not the treatment would be efficacious using rates which had been recommended for a variety where there was little or no sorption. Thank you.

Chairman

10.141. Dr. Ducom?

Dr. Ducom

10.142. Just a comment. Yes, I agree totally with Bob's statement. I just advise something about sorption. Levels are important for varieties but that means no insects, no LD_{50} trials to show that sorption is different. I mean we don't need any insects and any dose mortality tests to show that sorption is different and it makes very different, it's very easy, it's easier to run a sorption test than the dose mortality test. That's an important point in practice.

Chairman

10.143. OK, thank you. Have you now concluded your questions Japan?

Japan (Mr. Sanatani)

10.144. Yes, Mr. Chairman.

Chairman

10.145. Thank you. I now turn to the United States. If you have any follow-up questions to the experts on the basis of the questions presented by Japan.

United States (Mr. Hirsh)

10.146. Thank you Mr. Chairman. May we have a few minutes to consult?

Chairman

10.147. Of course.

[break]

Chairman

10.148. Ok. United States, are you ready to proceed?

The United States (Mr. Hirsh)

10.149. We are Mr. Chairman. Just one follow-up question for Dr. Ducom. In connection with the question regarding whether it is possible for the United States to prove the negative, that is to say that United States understands that it is not possible to prove a negative and that it's not possible to state with scientific certainty that at no time in the future will there possibly be a varietal difference that might, as a hypothetical matter, affect treatment of efficacy. But, Dr. Ducom, are you aware of any circumstances in which a difference in variety has in practice required a difference in a treatment level among the products at issue?

Dr. Ducom

10.150. I am not a [fortune teller] definition man, or something like that. I cannot answer that. That's why there is a variety problem. We don't know, you don't know.

Intuitively I can imagine that there is no difference between varieties. When you see one nectarine next to another it seems the same. It seems to be obvious that they are the same, but sometimes, we cannot [prove it], it's not a proof and to be able to have proof we need some tools.

United States (Mr. Hirsh)

10.151. I understand, but let me rephrase the question. Are you aware of any circumstances in which variety has made a different, not for the purposes of establishing with scientific certainty that there will never be a difference but just simply are you aware of any situation which variety has made a difference in a treatment level and we'll take an answer from any of the experts on this.

Dr. Ducom

10.152. Not as far as I am used to study anything like that. Not in perishables. Yes for stored products like nuts, which are in fact stored products.... There are differences in varieties in walnuts because of oil contents. Maybe we can have the same for raisins, but maybe you do not agree with that, but for perishables, no. I can imagine it like Japan says, but have never seen something like that.

United States (Mr. Hirsh)

10.153. If I might ask one more follow-up question? With regard to walnuts, if in fact the oil content among varieties did not differ, would you then state that there would not be a difference among the varieties?

Dr. Ducom

10.154. Probably yes [not], but I have never done any trials on that. But I can imagine that there is no difference in the [varieties as far as methyl bromide is concerned] because the oil content is the main factor of sorption for walnuts.

United States (Mr. Hirsh)

10.155. Thank you, and if any of the, if either Mr. Taylor or Dr. Heather would like to answer the question regarding whether they're aware of any situations where differences in variety have resulted in a different treatment level for the products at issue in this case.

Mr. Taylor

10.156. No, I have no information or have seen any published data so the answer I have to give is no.

Chairman

10.157. I think that, Ok Dr. Heather?

Dr. Heather

10.158. In my experience there have been no differences of this kind. In fact it's been to the contrary. Most of my experience has been with insecticide dips with the material dimethoate and here we find that the same treatment not only goes across varieties but across commodities but I can see that this sorption problem with methyl bromide is something very special and that's why I wish to defer to my colleagues with experience as fumigation experts.

United States (Mr. Hirsh)

10.159. Thank you very much. That's our only follow-up question.

Chairman

10.160. Ok, thank you. Now I ask your patience for the Panel to have an internal consultation. So this is the same privilege as we have given to the parties.

[break]

Chairman

10.161. And thank you for your patience for waiting us.

United States (Mr. Hirsh)

10.162. Mr. Chairman, if I may be recognized? Before proceeding to the Panel's questions would it be possible to ask the experts whether they've had a chance to consider our final question?

Chairman

10.163. I forgot that. Any volunteers? Ok, perhaps we could have a coffee break or a lunch break and we go to that question after that but we will see because now we can anyway proceed with the questions by the Panel. During our recent break we considered whether we could delete some of our questions because they have already been covered and yes indeed that is the case but we have tried to compensate that by elaborating some new questions in addition.

10.164. So, I first note that we will not present the questions one, two and three because we consider that we have already received adequate answers to the questions which are there. So I will straightaway proceed with our question number four and I will read it: In its answer to US question eight Japan states there is a precedent in which Japan has approved importation of all varieties in a commodity, namely lemons, grapefruits and ponkan oranges are approved subject to a cold treatment against fruit flies. This is because varietal differences of these commodities are minor for reasons of their history of development by somatic mutation such as bud mutation, and they are not known to lead to a significant difference in the efficacy of a treatment. Are apples, nectarines, walnuts and cherries different in this respect? Is the

Japanese position quoted above scientifically reconcilable with its position on MB treatment for apples, nectarines, walnuts and cherries? Dr. Ducom.

Dr. Ducom

10.165. Thank you. The question is difficult. There is an affirmation. I mean genetically speaking what is the difference between a mutation and crossing to get a new variety? I mean, for example, you can have small differences or big differences. The difference between peach and nectarine is a mutation. We have a big difference and though somatic mutation must lead to big differences, I cannot agree with that argument. But not scientifically speaking.

Dr. Heather

10.166. I would find it difficult to answer directly without seeing the genetic origins of each of the varieties involved but I would have thought that lemons would not have fitted the bud mutant definition but I would like to reserve that decision. It's something that I would have to research.

Chairman

10.167. OK, thank you. I now move to our question number five. In your expert opinion is there an objective or rational relationship between the varietal testing requirement imposed by Japan for MB treatment and any of the evidence submitted by the parties?

Dr. Ducom

10.168. I've a quick answer. In the absolute yes, in practice no.

Chairman

10.169. Could you repeat that?

Dr. Ducom

10.170. In absolute, maybe yes, but in practice no. I mean the arguments are not statistically good. Scientifically, they may be good, but in practice they may be too narrow. But the answer is really difficult.

Chairman

10.171. Ok, Mr. Taylor?

Mr. Taylor

10.172. I have to agree with Dr. Ducom. The answer is very difficult otherwise perhaps we would not be here. Again I think in theory there may be some differences which perhaps exist, but in practice it is difficult to show these and it seems very difficult in fact to say that at this time the differences that might make the difference between treatments efficacious and non-efficacious have not yet been reached and therefore I think at this moment in time that the evidence is not sufficiently strong although in theory it does have some possible validity. But at this stage, as Dr. Ducom has said, and in practical terms, it's very difficult to say yes there is something which is sufficiently demonstrated to show that there is a real problem which has to be addressed in terms of maybe variety-by-variety testing, and which could lead to differences in the treatment techniques that are used.

Chairman

10.173. Thank you. Do you want to add something?

Dr. Heather

10.174. More to agree with both of my colleagues. I'd say yes there is a relationship but it is an incomplete one but this is a real world and to totally complete the relationship of these and decide on how important it is, I think would probably be beyond the resources even of the United States and Japan in the time available, and I'm not sure that it would really add anything of great value to the argument.

Chairman

10.175. OK, thank you. I only want to state already now that we in the Panel also appreciate when you answer that you don't know. Then we move to our question number six. Here perhaps some words of explanation why we are asking this question. It is because the SPS agreement uses these expressions like "specifications of a product" and "modified product". Those are quotations from the SPS Agreement and now that's why we are presenting this question. The question is: From a technical or scientific point of view, first, can the development of new varieties of a product be considered as changes in the specifications of the product, and secondly, can a new variety of a product be regarded as a modified product?

Dr. Ducom

10.176. It is always difficult to answer your questions. It's about the relationship between the product and methyl bromide, you are talking about. I mean that a specification of a product means sorption model with methyl bromide. We are not talking about generally speaking, the colour we don't care about. We just want to know if the change in the new varieties has a different [reaction to] version against methyl bromide. I mean we should have tools to know that. You know, a fruit can be the same, appear in the same shape, the same as a colour and so on and may have another reaction to methyl bromide. Why not? We don't know. If we have no tools we cannot say if a new variety is a new variety of it or .... [*interrupted*]

Chairman

10.177. Excuse me. Now I think I should have explained more in detail what we are asking. Here we are not asking of methyl bromide or the efficacy, anything. This is just a biological question I would say. Whether new varieties can be regarded as that. You see, in our [SPS] agreement we have provisions that if a product for instance has already been approved then if the specification has been changed or the product has been modified then a new approval should concentrate only on those changes which have happened. So that is why we are asking this question. It is not related directly to methyl bromide or any efficacy questions but just how you could, would interpret this or could you interpret these words in our Agreement?

Dr. Ducom

10.178. That's the kind of question we are not experts to answer but I should say, yes, there are some changes in specifications, but it's just in my own opinion.

Chairman

10.179. Do you want to ask something?

Dr. Heather

10.180. Only to say that the judgment becomes a subjective one and it really depends on the breadth of the definition of the product in the first place and the size of the changes in relation to that.

Chairman

10.181. Ok, thank you. We now move to our question number seven. In Dr. Ducom's answer to Panel question three it is stated that the dose mortality tests presented by the parties are designed to give information on insect sensitivity. The search for possible causes of varietal variations cannot be determined with precision by them but only with a specific research program. Is it technically possible by such a research program to determine the degree to which variety matters for quarantine efficacy of MB treatment?

Dr. Ducom

10.182. I am sure that either the US or Japan can imagine the design for a research program on that. I mean as far as I know, never, there has never been a study on that because may be no need had appeared before. Now we are at the point where perhaps that kind of research could be carried out. I'm sure we can find something to approach [evaluate] the varietal differences.

Chairman

10.183. So your answer is yes?

Dr. Ducom

10.184. Yes.

Chairman

10.185. OK, thank you. I then move to question number eight but here we have added something, for Dr. Ducom's delight! Namely we would like Dr. Ducom to elaborate not only on the amelioration of statistical methods which invalidated the hypotheses of a statistical difference mentioned in his answer to Panel question eight, and also if you could elaborate on what you said today on the difference between biologically relevant difference and a statistically relevant difference between varieties of a product, as it relates to the studies before the Panel, because we must admit that we didn't fully understand these two notes of you.

Dr. Ducom

10.186. First of all about amelioration of statistical method, it appears with Yokoyama and Robertson presented in US Exhibit 15. It's about the re-analysis of data from the experiment on nectarines from 1987 and with probit analysis ... [found that] there are very big differences between Summer Grand and other varieties of nectarine. And with the new software like Polo and new methods created by Jacqueline Robertson, they found that the difference is not significant, even if the probit lines of the LD_{50} or $_{95}$, are very, very different. With a new statistical approach we [suddenly no longer have] can have no more differences. For people who don't know statistical, it means like poor arrangements but in fact in statistics you can choose the best tool because all are relevant. ... For the same experiment you have bad tools and good tools, statistical good tools, statistical bad tools, and times also helps - I mean now we have better tools than before. That's for the first point [change of tape] biological and statistical answer and significance. I mean when you have two differences between, for example, LD_{50} for Fantasia and, or, OK, two varieties of nectarine which is 10 milligram by cubic metres and the overlap, the confidence limits, is maybe 11.36 and the other one is 11.45, you say statistically it's different, but biologically speaking it's not different. But the problem is that statistically we can make the difference biologically we cannot make the difference. We can imagine that there is no difference, but we cannot prove without any further trials. That's the problem.

Chairman

10.187. We now have an additional question to whomever wants to answer it. We have discussed quite with some length already the impact of sorption. Now the Panel would like to know a little bit more about this. First, how is the sorption test conducted and how feasible would it be to test sorption values for each variety? And has this been done in any of the studies before the Panel? Dr. Ducom?

Dr. Ducom

10.188. Sorption tests may be carried out very easily, I guess, for the people who are used to make trials on perishables or stored products. I mean, the interest is that it could be made without insects and just after the crop, the time exactly when fumigation has to take place. That means, for example, for the apples - the paper we have not time to read exactly from Kawakami-san - when you carry out experiments on apples some are cropped maybe in August or September, others in October. We put all them in the [cold chamber] fridge, in the, ok in the fridge, and the reaction may be different. If you do trials at the August for the August harvest, [or wait until] October and November, each one in his ripeness time or in the time where fumigation has to take place, maybe two months later, for each one, but not three months for one [may lead to different results]. And with enough fruit I guess we could have some good answers on sorption and maybe also try to know what the factors which make a high sorption are; maybe it's due to proteins, I don't know, of the nature of the skin, I don't know. That's the research program could that could be allowed to find the factors which can influence the sorption.

Chairman

10.189. Ok, and the last part of our question was has this been done in any of studies before the Panel?

Dr. Ducom

10.190. No I don't think so, not by itself. But maybe in Kawakami-san ['s paper] I don't know.

Chairman

10.191. Ok, Mr. Taylor?

Mr. Taylor

10.192. Thank you Mr. Chairman. One or two comments. You mention how a sorption test was carried out. Well by exposing the commodity in question to a known concentration and the concentration of the methyl bromide is measured very accurately over a period of time to see to what extent the gas concentration falls. Another way of course, an additional way, is to measure to see if there are reaction products and to see whether there are bromide residues within a commodity treated. So there are several ways to actually test to what degree a particular commodity will absorb the gas. There are quite well known methods by which accurate levels of sorption can be tested. I mean, we have to appreciate that some of the sorption is permanent where the actual gas reacts with a commodity, a sort of chemical reaction which leads to the bromide residues. On the other hand, some of the sorption is reversible and the gas will be eventually released again from the product. But certainly techniques such as these have been conducted over many years so there should be no problem in actually conducting these trials. As Dr. Ducom said, to determine the sorption of fumigant would not involve insects in these test, just the gas and the commodity, and from these tests to see to what extent there is a difference between varieties as between commodities, and to determine just to what extent this is an important factor and whether the level of sorption is very high or very little difference exists between the two. Thank you.

Chairman

10.193. Thank you very much so, and also, to Mr. Taylor the last part of our question, has this been done in any of the studies before the Panel?

Mr. Taylor

10.194. I don't recall having seen this having been done, just on a variety by variety basis in which we could actually say this variety absorbs this much and another variety absorbs a different value or the same value. I don't recall having seen this being done specifically on a sorption test basis for different varieties.

Chairman

10.195. Ok, but do I understand correctly then your answer is that there exist methods, established methods to do such tests and that the results are rather reliable?

Mr. Taylor

10.196. Yes, I think that's correct, yes. This work could certainly be conducted I'm sure either in Japan or the US and their research programs could conduct this technique if they were minded to do so.

Chairman

10.197. OK. Thank you very much. Now I turn to our question number nine which is rather lengthy. We have been made aware of a so-called CxT value and now we try to test whether we have understood anything. And so the question reads as follows: It is the Panel's understanding that quarantine efficacy for a certain pest at a certain stage can be obtained by determining the concentration of the fumigation in the chamber and the time the pest is exposed to it by determining a fixed CxT value, that is to say that if a codling moth is fumigated for a certain amount of time at a certain concentration the test will die. If the fumigation process can be monitored so that the concentration of the gas is maintained at the required level during the required period time varietal differences, such as sorption, as well as any other factors would not affect quarantine efficacy and probit 9 mortality would be ensured. Is this understanding correct? Would such process be technically and economically feasible?

Dr. Ducom

10.198. Yes and yes. Ok.

Chairman

10.199. Yes, I would also ask the other experts. Mr. Taylor?

Mr. Taylor

10.200. Thank you, Chairman. Yes I have to agree with Dr. Ducom. In many cases of course of fumigation of other situations, such as the treatment of flour mills, there is regular monitoring, as we call it, of the fumigant level. It may be necessary to increase the fumigant concentration by adding more fumigant for example, because of some factor, maybe leakage, etc., so I mean this is certainly something that can be done, and is done, and if this type of technology was employed whereby the concentration is monitored regularly and it is found to reach the required level, in other words, you will end up with the CxT product value that you have said is necessary, then this will be an effective treatment and I mean so this is technically feasible. I will reserve judgment on the economic feasibility to those that know more about the topic than myself. But probably it is. I would think it to be probably technically and economically feasible.

Chairman

10.201. Thank you. Dr. Heather?

Dr. Heather

10.202. To the first part of the question, yes, I believe so. To the second part, I'd have to defer to my colleagues who know more, who have more practical experience of fumigation, but I am aware that grain in my home State is controlled by the use of a CxT approach rather than an outright dose.

Chairman

10.203. Ok, thank you. That was most helpful so I conclude that more or less the Panel has understood what you have said. Ok, then I have one last question at this stage and this is of another character and it reads as follows: Does the risk assessment conducted by Japan for preventing the introduction of codling moth provide scientific basis to ban the import of the products in dispute? I repeat, does the risk assessment conducted by Japan for preventing the introduction of codling moth provide scientific basis to ban the import of the products in dispute?

Dr. Heather

10.204. I would agree that codling moth is of sufficient importance as a pest and the risk to Japan, which does not have this insect, is major and, yes, on that basis they are entirely [justified]. Their conclusion that it's a pest which requires an initial ban on importations [I would agree] to be quite appropriate.

Chairman

10.205. Ok, Dr. Ducom and Mr. Taylor, do you want to add?

Dr. Ducom

10.206. I am not an expert on pest risk analysis and therefore I cannot answer.

Chairman

10.207. Ok. Mr. Taylor?

Mr. Taylor

10.208. I would agree with Dr. Heather that certainly it does seem as if there is sufficient risk from the pest to ensure that measures are taken to keep it out but I would not like to go so far as to say that it's a ban on the import of the commodities. I wouldn't like it to be recorded that I would say that. I would certainly say that the risk analysis seems to be sufficient to make sure that the pest is kept out but I would repeat that I would not like it to be taken down in perpetuity that I had said that the products therefore ought not to be allowed in. But I would say that obviously the Japanese government obviously wants to make sure that the measures that they take to keep the pest out are as good as can be possibly effected.

Chairman

10.209. Ok. Dr. Heather?

Dr. Heather

10.210. If I could add to my comment. The initial reaction is prohibition. This is a normal quarantine regulatory approach and then there is conditional admission which usually depends on a treatment. I think conditional was the word Japan uses, it's quite appropriate. So this was my intent to say that initially prohibition and then some measures are required.

Chairman

10.211. Ok. Thank you very much. That was most helpful.

10.212. Now I want to inform you that it is the intention of the Panel to still ask some, I would say, short, and I hope, simple questions which are of a confirmatory nature. That means that we have tried to understand the scientific and technical background for this dispute and now we want to get confirmation or not confirmation by the experts, but before I present those, I would say, confirmatory questions, we need some time. So I announce a coffee break of, say, 15 minutes and I hope that the experts could use those 15 minutes in preparing their answer to the question by United States which is still outstanding. Ok, could we agree so? So, 15 minutes.

[break]

Chairman

10.213. ... for the delegations, United States and Japan, whether you still have some additional questions you want to present to the experts? This is the last, ok, last opportunity for that. And after that I will give the floor to the experts one by one for any concluding remarks they want to make. After that I will announce lunch break. After the luncheon we will reconvene again and then, as I announced at the beginning of the meeting, the Panel has the intention to present some, I would say, confirmatory questions to the experts, whether we have understood some of the scientific and technical facts in a correct way. Can we follow this procedure? Ok.

10.214. Ok, so first we take the United States' question. Perhaps you could repeat the question because at least I have not, I cannot quite recollect what it was!

United States (Mr. Hirsh)

10.215. Give me one more chance at it. We refer you to the recent study by Japan included in Japan's Exhibit 36. With respect to apples the author states on the final page of the study, quote, the factors affecting the different CxT products were not specified in the test. For example, it appears that there were no controls for length of time in storage maturity of fruit and fruit size. In addition, we reviewed the CxT product data in Table 3 and Table 5, in particular the data for the Mutsu and Fuji in each table which indicates that the two are not statistically different in Table 5 but they are statistically different in Table 3. In light of the uncontrolled factors in this study and the inconsistent data, is Japan's conclusion warranted that the differences in CxT values noted in Table 5 were, quote, obviously attributed to varietal differences?

Chairman

10.216. Ok, now I give the floor to the experts. Dr. Heather?

Dr. Heather

10.217. It was a little difficult to decide who should answer this. Taking the statistical differences first we've noted that the method used is a Tukey's multiple range test which is a statistical test I believe appropriate to comparing results of trials rather than treatments within trials and statistics are better explained by a biometrician but I would not be surprised to see a difference proven or shown, not proven, shown, in one case and absent in another. This is just one of those aberrations that is possible when you analyze data so that's part of it.

10.218. The second part, if I'm right, was where the author obviously attributed the differences to varietal characteristics. We are of the opinion that it is not possible to attribute them solely to varietal characteristics on the evidence that's present in this paper. It may well be true but it requires, it would require… to reach that firm conclusion would require more information. The age of the fruit which was involved, it would be normal to treat fruit which was freshly harvested but then again it would also be possible to have involved fruit which had been harvested for some time and which was subsequently determined to export it so that it is not an unreasonable, it's not unreasonable to store fruit for a while before fumigating it but it would have been nice to have a small scale test to show the difference between freshly harvested and stored fruit so it's more the scope of the experiment. Do I have one more other question to answer?

United States (Mr. Hirsh)

10.219. I think that was it.

Dr. Heather

10.220. Thank you very much. I would like to congratulate the authors of this paper. Really, it's a very comprehensive piece of work and our only, the only exception we take to it is that some of the conclusions have gone perhaps a little further than we believe the data supported.

United States (Mr. Hirsh)
10.221. Thank you very much.

Chairman
10.222. Thank you. Taking into account the time I had to change the procedure I proposed. So before the lunch-break I will present one additional question by the Panel to the experts. And after that we will break and that will give the parties also the opportunity to consider any additional questions you wanted to present and also gives opportunity to the experts to consider what kind of concluding remarks you want to present.
10.223. Ok. So I will now present one question by the Panel and after that we have heard the reply we will break for lunch. This question here again I think I need some, I need to give some explanation to the experts. You know that the scope of this dispute does not cover only the four products, apples, cherries, nectarines and walnuts, but also apricots, plums, pears and quince, even if we have not received any material from either party concerning those four other products. So now the Panel wants to ask you the following question: To the best of your knowledge is what you have stated about varietal differences concerning apples, cherries, nectarines and walnuts, would that also be valid for apricots, plums, pears and quince?

Dr. Heather
10.224. Yes.

Chairman
10.225. All? All answered yes. Ok, that was clear and short. And now we can break for lunch and we will continue at three o'clock, thank you.

[lunch break]

Chairman
10.226. .... outlined before the lunch-break the procedures would now be that I first give the floor to the United States if they have any additional questions still to the experts, then to Japan for the same purpose, then the Panel still has one small question to present to the experts. After that I will give the floor to the experts in alphabetical order for any concluding remarks, and after as a grand finale I will present some so-called confirmatory questions to the experts from the Panel. Ok. So, I now give the floor to the United States.

United States (Mr. Hirsh)
10.227. Thank you Mr. Chairman. We have no additional questions.

Chairman
10.228. Thank you. Japan?

Japan (Mr. Yokota)

10.229. Thank you Mr. Chairman. We have three additional questions related, all of them related to questions from Panel number nine, so I'll pass the floor to Mr. Sanatani to ...

Chairman

10.230. Ok. You're welcome. Could you take them one by one?

Japan (Mr. Sanatani)

10.231. Allow me to speak in Japanese. This is our follow-up questions, or rather confirmation to the additional question number nine from the Panel. There are three points.

10.232. The first point: Regarding the method described in the point nine, or question nine, when the pest is directly exposed to the fumigant, we understand that model dosage may be constant. Assuming there is a difference of sorption amongst the varieties in order to maintain a certain CxT value and therefore to kill the codling moth we would probably need to change the dosage or the duration of the time of the exposure depending on the varieties. And this is our understanding but was this the understanding on the part of the experts when they answered or commented on this point?

Dr. Heather

10.233. Yes, it's my understanding that either dose or time could be varied but in my reading on this topic and my experience, my contacts with colleagues who have worked in detail on it, I understand it's most unwise to work towards the end of the spectrum on either time or dose.

Mr. Taylor

10.234. Yes, I agree certainly with Dr. Heather's comments. I would have thought that there might be such a situation, if I could just mention a rather similar situation. In some countries cut flowers are fumigated with methyl bromide and the dosage is metered in and I think there are situations where the time would be fixed, but it may also be possible to monitor the concentration and a small amount of gas is injected automatically, if necessary, in order to keep the concentration at the level required. And I also mentioned earlier that this is certainly the sort of situation existing in flour mills, so as to maintain the concentration that has been predetermined while keeping a fixed time. This was the way I assumed that fumigation would probably be done but of course the time or the concentration could be the variable factor. It would seem to me that fixing the time would be better, particularly if it's a perishable commodity where time is relatively important and therefore, if possible, to have the concentration as a variable and, as I've said, situations exist where automatic injection can take place to maintain the concentration which has been calculated to be necessary.

Chairman

10.235. Dr. Ducom?

Mr. Ducom

10.236. I want to just add something. It may be not necessary to add some methyl bromide or to increase the time. If by habit we know exactly for that variety or that commodity and that load, or that packaging and so, we can maybe have the same kind of things we have now, I mean dosage at the departure, but this dosage may be one time 48, for example, and one time - because it's another variety or another boxes - it's 52 and so on without any change after but with checking CxT. Just what I mean, it's not necessarily obliged to add some methyl bromide or time. We can adjust if you know exactly the product and where we are working.

Chairman

10.237. Ok, thank you. The next question from Japan?

Japan (interpreted Mr. Sanatani)

10.238. The second question relates to the method described in question number nine. Is this relating to the laboratory level or is this also including the commercial scale level or it refers to both situations?

Dr. Heather

10.239. My expectation is that it would refer to the commercial operation, the operational situation rather than laboratory although it may well be necessary to look at it first at the laboratory level, but it would be an operational procedure.

Chairman

10.240. I understand that the question is does there exist commercial applications already now or only on the laboratory level?

Dr. Heather

10.241. My knowledge is only with grain where I know the grain bulks are being fumigated by monitoring the CxT product but I don't know of any fruit but that does not mean that that's not being done because methyl bromide is not widely used for fruit in my country.

Chairman

10.242. Ducom?

Dr. Ducom

10.243. In fact, it's necessary to have a confirmatory test with CxT for one variety, exactly like with insects. But for all other varieties at laboratory but maybe not six or seven or 14 apples, maybe much more, but at the laboratory level could be done on all other varieties.

Chairman

10.244. Thank you. Now I turn back to Japan.

Japan (interpreted Mr. Sanatani)

10.245. What we are discussing here, if including the commercial scale level, then various conditions are different such as the air tightness or methyl bromide dispersion speed and homogeneity. All these conditions may differ between the laboratory vis-à-vis the commercial scale level. What's your comment on these points?

Mr. Taylor

10.246. Yes, thank you for your question. I agree that they're may well be a number of variables, certainly at the commercial level. Temperature may be a variable so it is something we should certainly calculate into our design of dosing and I think one of the reasons why it might be necessary to have some sort of monitoring coupled to an injection system is that, on a commercial scale, in order to achieve the predetermined CxT product we would need to be able to take account of these differences and, as I say, I know certainly in flour mills there are systems where automatic monitoring and automatic dosing can take place. It would be possible to programme into the system such a design that would take account of these differences such as you quite rightly mention, for example leakage, which could account for losses which may vary from time to time, depending on the degree of sealing attained in a chamber. One would hope that these losses would not be too great. But certainly I think at the level of quarantine efficacy we might certainly need, if we were working on CxT values, to be able to take account of these differences and an automatic system I hope would take care of these variables. Thank you.

Chairman

10.247. Thank you Mr. Taylor. Any other comments to this? Dr. Ducom?

Dr. Ducom

10.248. Just one comment. Temperature is normally given. You have to work at a given temperature but for gas-tightness of the chamber we can check before. The Japanese know that and USA too. And for homogeneity we know that we can do that with fans adapted to the size of the chamber. We can do that.

Chairman

10.249. Thank you, Dr. Ducom. Japan you have still the floor.

Japan (interpreted Mr. Sanatani)

10.250. This would be our last question. If the CxT value is one of the useful indicator of the efficacy of fumigation I think Japan agrees to this in the argument so far. However, when it comes to the mode of action of methyl bromide it is not completely clarified yet, so besides the atmospheric concentration of the fumigants which is described in the CxT value, there are other factors that would affect the efficacy such as the structure of the surface and the contents. There are many unknown factors. So we wonder if the CxT value alone could really guarantee the efficacy of the pest control. This may attach upon very much of the expert matters so I would like to call on our expert to expand on this.

Japan (interpreted Mr. Kawakami)

10.251. In case of the grain I understand the fumigation time duration is very long, or relatively long, so that would take care of most of the problems and that's our understanding. But in case of fruits we have to do the fumigation in a relatively short period of time and so that could produce some problems and with regards to the pest insects inside of the fruits, besides the sorption we have to look at the penetration factor as well. As mentioned earlier the surface structure and mode of action, how they would interact or how those pests residing within inside of the fruit meat, how that and the methyl bromide interact, so I would like the experts to share with us your knowledge on these matters.

Chairman

10.252. Thank you. Dr. Ducom?

Dr. Ducom

10.253. I cannot understand this mode of action problem. I don't know of any data on the problem created by something you call mode of penetration. When we are working on CxT value, we are working for efficacy. For example if we work the fifth instar larvae of codling moths, we can run that with just one dose at the beginning or with the CxT value, and then we can do a confirmatory test with that. It doesn't matter if the insect is inside and if the CxT inside the apple is different than the CxT outside, the correlation between both is always the same. It's the same, for example, for wood to kill an insect inside the gallery in the wood. It's always about, for example, for methyl bromide like 20°, it's 200 [grams per cubit meter] or something like that, but the CxT above, the ambient CxT must be something like 1,000 to kill at 200 inside the gallery. It's the same for apples. I mean nevertheless it doesn't matter if the insect is in the apple or outside, the CxT in the confirmatory tests will take into account. And the problem of surface in context I cannot understand. I cannot understand the question. It was a question I would like to have asked before. I cannot understand the arguments and I don't see any scientific data on that.

Chairman

10.254. Any other experts want to expand to this, or not? Ok, if that concludes the questions from the Japanese delegation I now turn to the United States delegation. Do you have any follow-up questions to this?

United States (Mr. Hirsh)

10.255. We've no follow-up questions.

Chairman

10.256. Thank you. Then I will take up one small question which the Panel still wants to present to the experts and it is simply does anything in the apples study submitted by Japan, which was discussed earlier during this day, change any of your earlier opinions as to the relevance of varietal differences for quarantine efficacy? Dr. Heather?

Dr. Heather

10.257. I don't think there is anything in the apple study which impinges on this. Apples are unique in that they have a combined treatment of cold and of methyl bromide and both of these are quite efficacious in their own way. Perhaps I should say at this stage there was a question also from Japan as to why I believe that apples would not differ very much amongst themselves varietally. The reason for this is that cold treatment as a contributing treatment to the codling moth control does not have a sorption problem so there should not be the same degree of variation between varieties of apples because of this cold treatment factor that you would find in a treatment which relied only on methyl bromide.

Chairman

10.258. Thank you very much. That was very useful for the Panel also. Dr. Ducom?

Dr. Ducom

10.259. Just one comment. This study was very interesting but the problem is that it was made on apples, which were not at the same stage of storage because some were one month in storage and others had three month's storage - so the variety is not the only factor which can change the value we can read. So in practice that means that varieties may be a factor but maybe not very important and maybe some other factors influence that data. The problem of all these studies is that they are just descriptive studies. We take some apples, or peaches, or nectarines, and we look at the concentration but the reason why it differs, we don't know. There is no fundamental work on that and we can just say this works, or it does not work and so on.

Chairman

10.260. Ok, thank you. I now think that we can move to the concluding remarks by the experts and as I promised I will give the floor alphabetical order, that means first to Dr. Ducom.

Dr. Ducom

10.261. Thank you Mr. Chairman. The work was very intensive, mainly for me because it's in English. But I don't know if our work will be taken into account by both parties because the fact that variety can or cannot be an important factor could be clarified just by studies and not only by talking between people of good civility or something. And that's why it was important to talk about it, but my feeling is that some study are to be made by US, I guess, or people who want to [export to] go in Japan on each variety, something easy to do, and maybe Japan has to accept some rules. And the last point, I am very, my concern is for example the last question they [Japan] ask for, if structure and context makes a difference insects mode of action, that is new and for me it makes no sense and is a problem for me.

Chairman

10.262. Thank you Dr. Ducom. Dr. Heather please?

Dr. Heather

10.263. Thank you Mr. Chairman. We are very fortunate, Mr. Taylor and myself, that Dr. Ducom's name starts with a "D" so he has set the scene for us very well. The only comment that I would like to add to that is one that methyl bromide is what I would like to call a very robust treatment. It has the capacity, the reserve capacity, to overcome many small variations which will occur in operation. Some of these may be fruit variations, others will be operational processes. This is why it has been such a successful treatment over the years so in terms of the confidence which countries have in using methyl bromide, it is a very good treatment. I think this needs to be taken into account and we should not be too distracted, I think is the word I should use, about apparent differences in measurement of some of the parameters that were involved because it is the overall efficacy that works and this has been, I think, very well demonstrated in the large scale trials under discussion here and also on the many other commodities that both Japan and the United States have worked on over the years. Thank you.

Chairman

10.264. Thank you Dr. Heather. Mr. Taylor?

Mr. Taylor

10.265. Perhaps not for the record or for the minutes or whatever we're saying of this meeting, I find it interesting that here I am talking about effectiveness of methyl bromide, etc. when in the last three countries I've been to in the last few weeks I've been talking about nothing but alternatives to methyl bromide and trying to find alternatives which will allow us to phase out methyl bromide quickly and easily, but this of course is not proving an easy task, and for the quarantine and pre-shipment use this is going to be a very difficult task.

10.266. But coming back more to the situation at hand I think one of the things that has come out from this meeting which I have found extremely interesting is that we do need more information before we can say categorically that variety in fruit is a major factor affecting the efficacy of treatment. I think we're all agreed that sorption is one of the major factors involved and, I think that, as Dr. Ducom said earlier, one of the things that should be done is the testing of samples just with methyl bromide [no insects to be involved] to see if we can determine the extent to which these varieties do absorb methyl bromide. Also it would be nice to try and relate any differences we find to chemical or physical characteristics more definitely.

10.267. And the other thing that I would like to say in conclusion that I found one of the most interesting parts of the meeting came in question nine when the Panel asked us if, in that statement, whether their understanding of what we were talking about was in fact the case. I think it is clear we are saying here that if you have the right amount of gas for the right amount of time it will kill the pest because basically that's what fumigation's all about. It doesn't matter which gas you're using. If you have the lethal concentration for the required time this will kill the pest and that's really what we want to try and achieve, so this long and somewhat complicated discussion about CxT products is in fact very relevant because if we do achieve the desired CxT product in a commercial treatment we should end up with an efficacious treatment which should satisfy the requirements for quarantine. I would conclude there Mr. Chairman. Thank you.

Chairman

10.268. Thank you very much Mr. Taylor. I now proceed to the final set of questions by the Panel. I would call this a confirmatory testing of the understanding of the Panel. However this is not a large scale confirmatory test but just a small scale confirmatory test, and because these questions are all phrased, yes, and I ask that this to be distributed to the experts so that you can look on them and also to the parties, because these are phrased in a way that we ask for your confirmation of our understanding, of course we would be most happy if you could answer just "yes" but if our understanding is not correct then of course you have to elaborate in which respect our understanding has not been correct. And because these five questions are inter-linked we decided to distribute them in writing for you because otherwise if we had presented them one by one the questions could have been misunderstood. So I hope you take these five questions in combination, as linked together. And I now give you some time to consider this. And you may of course discuss with each other if you can reach a consensus reply.

[break]

Chairman

10.269. Ok, and I will read the questions one by one and ask your responses. And as to the parties you will have the opportunity to comment on these questions and the answers tomorrow. Ok, first, considering your responses to the Panel's questions it is the Panel's understanding that there are differences which may be relevant for quarantine purposes between varieties of the products in dispute, is this understanding correct? Dr. Heather?

Dr. Heather

10.270. My understanding, my belief is not that there are differences but there may be differences. I don't believe that the occurrence of the differences has been proven and that they may be relevant for quarantine purposes. So there are two sets of uncertainties in my mind in this statement. There's no certainty that even if differences exist that they are relevant for quarantine purposes between varieties of the products in dispute.

Chairman

10.271. Thank you. Dr. Ducom?

Dr. Ducom

10.272. Maybe, yes.

Chairman

10.273. Ok, Mr. Taylor?

Mr. Taylor

[Mr. Taylor gestured his confirmation of the other experts' answers]

Chairman

10.274. Ok, thank you. The second question is: It is also the Panel's understanding that the question whether these differences are significant for quarantine purposes cannot be determined on the basis of the evidence before the Panel. Do you agree?

Mr. Taylor

10.275. Yes.

Chairman

10.276. Dr. Heather?

Dr. Heather

10.277. Essentially yes, with the proviso of those double uncertainties that I referred to in the first one.

Chairman

10.278. Ok, Dr. Ducom?

Dr. Ducom

10.279. Yes.

Chairman

10.280. Yes? Ok. Then the third question: To the extent that differences between varieties are significant for quarantine purposes, is the Panel's understanding correct that they are mainly or even exclusively related to different levels of sorption of the fruit? Dr. Heather?

Dr. Heather

10.281. Could I defer to the fumigation specialist on this one please?

Chairman

10.282. Ok. Of course. No need that everyone answers to every question, only within the limit of your competence of course. Dr. Ducom?

Dr. Ducom

10.283. Yes. Just two points. The first, we don't need any insects and the second one, we can, we must, we have to do that, at the time when the fumigation has to be made.

Chairman

10.284. Ok, thank you. Mr. Taylor?

Mr. Taylor

10.285. I agree.

Chairman

10.286. You agree. Thank you.

10.287. Now, the most lengthy question no. 4. In respect of the products at issue it is the Panel's understanding that the degree of varietal differences which have an effect on quarantine efficacy may vary between products. For instance, we have stated that methyl bromide is absorbed particularly by oils and fats and that the oil content of walnuts which is a varietal factor has a significant effect over sorption of methyl bromide. Hence it is the Panel's understanding that in the specific case of walnuts varietal differences in respect of oil content may affect quarantine treatment to a greater extent than varietal differences for the other products in dispute. Is this understanding correct? Dr. Heather?

Dr. Heather

10.288. Again on the effect of the oils I would like to defer to Mr. Taylor and Dr. Ducom. But could I please raise the point that walnuts are unique amongst all the commodities which we have been considering at this meeting. They have this oil problem which to my knowledge is not shared by any of the fruits and so they are a commodity which needs to be differentiated against, rather than the varietal problem.

Chairman

10.289. Thank you. Mr. Taylor?

Mr. Taylor

10.290. Thank you Mr. Chairman. Obviously the points that Dr. Heather just mentioned are very relevant. And the distinct differences between the fruit and the walnuts, so in my view I would have thought that the Panel's understanding of this situation is correct.

Chairman

10.291. Thank you. Dr. Ducom, do you want to add?

Dr. Ducom

10.292. Just to add that we have at least for walnuts the reason why the sorption exists and if we had something like that for apples and nectarines we should be in a good way.

Chairman

10.293. Ok, thank you Dr. Ducom. And now the last question, it is also the Panel's understanding that an added buffer of 10-20% will with a high probability cover any varietal differences of apples, cherries and nectarines but that this may not be the case for walnuts. Is this understanding correct? Dr. Heather?

Dr. Heather

10.294. Again, even for walnuts, the work was not done on a single variety, it was done on a number of varieties so it's not just the 10-20%, it's also the fact that you had a spread of samples or representation of walnuts as a commodity. Apart from that, yes.

Chairman

10.295. Ok. Dr. Ducom?

Dr. Ducom

10.296. Why not 30, 40, 5% like I said before? I mean,..

Chairman

10.297. ... No, 10-20 because that is what......

Dr. Ducom

10.298. Ok, but why not 10-20, why not? But the question, the answer is that when question is answered the question of 10-20 will be answered too? I mean we don't know if 10-20% [is high enough], we can imagine it's large enough but there is no scientific proof of that. The only proof could be to have some sorption data on other varieties to say, oh it's must too high and so on. In practice 10-20 may work, but it may not work. It seems to work because all the data of the confirmatory tests made by the USA work but we don't know for the rest.

Mr. Taylor

10.299. I have nothing to add to that.

Chairman

10.300. Thank you, Mr. Taylor. That concludes our session for today. I will once more thank very much the three experts. Your contribution has been most helpful. I think that the Panel now can work on a much more solid basis as to the scientific and technical facts which we have to take into account. Of course now we have to go further and take into account the legal aspects. And that's our job, but anyway, it is impossible to tackle the legal aspects without having a correct understanding of the underlying scientific and technical issues. So once more very much thanks for your excellent contribution, and I also want to thank the parties for their questions which have also facilitated the understanding of the Panel of the relevant issues in this case and I invite the parties to the second substantive meeting tomorrow morning at 10 o'clock and this will be in Room F. So Room F tomorrow morning at 10 o'clock. Ok, thank you very much and the meeting is adjourned.

Cumulative Index of Published Disputes

DSR 1996:I

United States – Standards for Reformulated and Conventional Gasoline, complaints by Venezuela (WT/DS2) and Brazil (WT/DS4)

Report of the Appellate Body
Report of the Panel

European Communities – Trade Description of Scallops, requests by Canada (WT/DS7), Peru (WT/DS12) and Chile (WT/DS14)

Report of the Panel (Request by Canada)
Report of the Panel (Request by Peru and Chile)

Japan – Taxes on Alcoholic Beverages, complaints by the European Communities (WT/DS8), Canada (WT/DS10) and the United States (WT/DS11)

Report of the Appellate Body
Report of the Panel

0 521 78095 0 Hardback   0 521 78581 2 Paperback

DSR 1997:I

Japan – Taxes on Alcoholic Beverages, complaints by the European Communities (WT/DS8), Canada (WT/DS10) and the United States (WT/DS11)

Award of the Arbitrator under Article 21.3(c) of the DSU

United States - Restrictions on Imports of Cotton and Man-made Fibre Underwear, complaint by Costa Rica (WT/DS24)

Report of the Appellate Body
Report of the Panel

Brazil - Measures Affecting Desiccated Coconut, complaint by the Philippines (WT/DS22)

Report of the Appellate Body
Report of the Panel

United States - Measure Affecting Imports of Woven Wool Shirts and Blouses from India, complaint by India (WT/DS33)

Report of the Appellate Body
Report of the Panel

Canada - Certain Measures Concerning Periodicals, complaint by the United States (WT/DS31)

Report of the Appellate Body
Report of the Panel

0 521 78096 9 Hardback   0 521 78582 0 Paperback

DSR 1997:II

European Communities - Regime for the Importation, Sale and Distribution of Bananas, complaints by Ecuador, Guatemala, Honduras, Mexico and the United States (WT/DS27)

Report of the Appellate Body
Report of the Panel (Complaint by Guatemala and Honduras)
Report of the Panel (Complaint by Mexico)
Report of the Panel (Complaint by the United States)

0 521 78325 9 Hardback   0 521 78892 7 Paperback

DSR 1997:III

European Communities - Regime for the Importation, Sale and Distribution of Bananas, complaints by Ecuador, Guatemala, Honduras, Mexico and the United States (WT/DS27)

Report of the Panel (Complaint by Ecuador)

0 521 80101 X Hardback   0 521 80506 6 Paperback

DSR 1998:I

European Communities - Regime for the Importation, Sale and Distribution of Bananas, complaints by Ecuador, Guatemala, Honduras, Mexico and the United States (WT/DS27)

Award of the Arbitrator under Article 21.3(c) of the DSU

India - Patent Protection for Pharmaceutical and Agricultural Chemical Products, complaint by the United States (WT/DS50)

Report of the Appellate Body
Report of the Panel

European Communities - Measures Concerning Meat and Meat Products (Hormones), complaints by the United States (WT/DS26) and Canada (WT/DS48)

Report of the Appellate Body

0 521 78326 7 Hardback   0 521 78893 5 Paperback

DSR 1998:II

European Communities - Measures Concerning Meat and Meat Products (Hormones), complaint by Canada (WT/DS48)

Report of the Panel

0 521 78327 5 Hardback   0 521 78894 3 Paperback

DSR 1998:III

European Communities - Measures Concerning Meat and Meat Products (Hormones), complaint by the United States (WT/DS26)

Report of the Panel

Argentina - Measures Affecting Imports of Footwear, Textiles, Apparel and Other Items (WT/DS56)

Report of the Appellate Body
Report of the Panel

0 521 78328 3 Hardback   0 521 78895 1 Paperback

DSR 1998:IV

Japan - Measures Affecting Consumer Photographic Film and Paper, complaint by the United States (WT/DS44/R)

Report of the Panel

0 521 78329 1 Hardback   0 521 78896 X Paperback

DSR 1998:V

European Communities - Measures Concerning Meat and Meat Products (Hormones) (WT/DS26/15, WT/DS48/13)

Award of the Arbitrator under Article 21.3(c) of the DSU

European Communities - Customs Classification of Certain Computer Equipment (WT/DS62/AB/R, WT/DS67/AB/R, WT/DS68/AB/R) (WT/DS62/R, WT/DS67/R, WT/DS68/R)

Report of the Appellate Body
Report of the Panel

European Communities - Measures Affecting the Importation of Certain Poultry Products (WT/DS69/AB/R), (WT/DS69/R)

Report of the Appellate Body
Report of the Panel

0 521 80096 X Hardback   0 521 80501 5 Paperback

DSR 1998:VI

Indonesia - Certain Measures Affecting the Automobile Industry (WT/DS54/R, WT/DS55/R, WT/DS59/R, WT/DS64/R)

Report of the Panel

India - Patent Protection for Pharmaceutical and Agricultural Chemical Products (WT/DS79/R)

Report of the Panel

0 521 80097 8 Hardback   0 521 80502 3 Paperback

DSR 1998:VII

United States - Import Prohibition of Certain Shrimp and Shrimp Products (WT/DS58)

Report of the Appellate Body

Report of the Panel

0 521 80098 6 Hardback   0 521 80503 1 Paperback

DSR 1998:VIII

Australia - Measures Affecting Importation of Salmon (WT/DS18)

Report of the Appellate Body

Report of the Panel (Request by Canada)

0 521 80099 4 Hardback   0 521 80504 X Paperback

DSR1998:IX

Guatemala – Anti-Dumping Investigation Regarding Portland Cement From Mexico (WT/DS60)

Report of the Appellate Body

Report of the Panel

Indonesia – Certain Measures Affecting the Automobile Industry (WT/DS54/15, WT/DS55/14, WT/DS59/13, WT/DS64/12)

Award of the Arbitrator (under Article 21.3(c) DSU)

0 521 80100 1 Hardback   0 521 80505 8 Paperback